The Papers of
George Washington

The Papers of
George Washington

Dorothy Twohig, *Editor*

Philander D. Chase, *Senior Associate Editor*

Beverly H. Runge, *Associate Editor*

Frank E. Grizzard, Jr., Edward G. Lengel, Mark A. Mastromarino,
and Jack D. Warren, *Assistant Editors*

W. W. Abbot, *Editor Emeritus*

Retirement Series
3

September 1798–April 1799

W. W. Abbot and Edward G. Lengel, *Editors*

UNIVERSITY PRESS OF VIRGINIA

CHARLOTTESVILLE AND LONDON

This edition has been prepared by the staff of
The Papers of George Washington
sponsored by
The Mount Vernon Ladies' Association of the Union
and the University of Virginia
with the support of
the National Endowment for the Humanities,
and the National Historical Publications and
Records Commission.
The preparation of this volume has been made possible by a grant from the
Norman and Lyn Lear Foundation and the National Trust for the Humanities.
The publication of this volume has been supported by a grant from
the National Historical Publications and Records Commission.

THE UNIVERSITY PRESS OF VIRGINIA

First published 1999

∞ The paper used in this publication meets the minimum requirements of the
American National Standard for Information Sciences—Permanence
of Paper for Printed Library Materials, ANSI Z39.48–1984.

Library of Congress Cataloging-in-Publication Data
Washington, George 1732–1799.
  The papers of George Washington. Retirement series / Dorothy
Twohig, editor ; Philander D. Chase, senior associate editor ;
Beverly H. Runge, associate editor ; Frank E. Grizzard, Jr. . . . [et
al.], assistant editors.
    p.   cm.
  Includes index.
  Contents: 1. March–December 1797. . . . 3. September 1798–April 1799.
  1. Washington, George, 1732–1799—Archives.   2. Presidents—United
States—Archives.   3. United States—Politics and
government—1797–1801—Sources.   I. Twohig, Dorothy.   II. Title.
E312.72 1998
973.3′092—dc21
ISBN 0-8139-1737-9 (v. 1 : alk. paper)   97-6770
ISBN 0-8139-1838-3 (v. 3 : alk. paper)   CIP

Contents

NOTE: Volume numbers refer to the *Retirement Series*.

Editorial Apparatus	xix
Symbols Designating Documents	xx
Repository Symbols and Abbreviations	xx
Short Title List	xxii

1798

To James Anderson, 16 September	1
To John Francis, 16 September *see* 2:617	
To John McDowell, 16 September *see* 2:579	
To James McHenry, 16 September	4
From Alexander Spotswood, 16 September	6
From Benjamin Stoddert, 16 September	10
From William Jones, 17 September *see* 2:600	
From John McDowell, 17 September *see* 2:579–80	
From Timothy Pickering, 18 September	11
From John Trumbull, 18 September	13
From Daniel McCarty, 19 September *see* 2:607–8	
From James McHenry, 19 September	14
From Andrew Belknap, 20 September *see* 3:86	
From John C. Ogden, 20 September	27
From James McHenry, 21 September	29
From Bushrod Washington, 21 September	31
From Thomas Law, 22 September	32
From Alexander Spotswood, 23 September	33
To Alexander Hamilton, 24 September	34
To Alexander Spotswood, 24 September	35
To John Adams, 25 September	36
From Marmaduke Leigh, 25 September	44
To G. W. Snyder, 25 September *see* 2:555	
To James McHenry, 26 September	44
To Benjamin Stoddert, 26 September	45
From Charles Carter, 27 September	48
From the District of Columbia Commissioners, 27 September	49
From Alexander Spotswood, 27 September	50

To William Washington, 27 September   51
To the District of Columbia Commissioners,
     28 September   52
From Henry Lee, Jr., 28 September   55
To Zechariah Lewis, 28 September   55
To William Russell, 28 September   56
To Henry Lee, Jr., 29 September   57
Document regarding Colvill Estate,
     30 September   *see* 1:123
From Alexander Hamilton, 30 September   58
To James McHenry, 30 September   59
To the Bank of Pennsylvania, 1 October   *see* 3:67
From Landon Carter, 1 October   60
To James McHenry, 1 October   63
To James McHenry, 1 October   65
To Timothy Pickering, 1 October   66
To James Ross, 1 October   66
To Israel Shreve, 1 October   67
From G. W. Snyder, 1 October   *see* 2:555–56
From Joel Barlow, 2 October   68
From James McHenry, 2 October   72
From the District of Columbia Commissioners,
     3 October   73
From Timothy Pickering, 3 October   74
To William Augustine Washington, 3 October   76
To the District of Columbia Commissioners, 4 October   77
To William Herbert, 4 October   78
To Landon Carter, 5 October   79
From William Herbert, 5 October   80
From Henry Lee, Jr., 5 October   80
To John McDowell, 5 October   *see* 3:79
From James McHenry, 5 October   81
From James McHenry, 5 October   82
To William Augustine Washington, 5 October   83
Address from the Virginia Militia, 6 October   83
From Rawleigh Colston, 6 October   85
To Andrew E. Belknap, 8 October   86
To William Herbert, 8 October   86
To Samuel Hodgdon, 8 October   87
From John Adams, 9 October   87
To Benjamin Stoddert, 9 October   88

From Bartholomew Dandridge, 10 October 89
From Samuel Knox, 10 October 90
To G. W. Snyder, 10 October   *see* 2:556
Memorandum of Agreement with James Welch,
   11 October 92
From the Charles Town Academy Trustees,
   13 October 93
From Timothy Pickering, 13 October 94
To Samuel Knox, 14 October   *see* 3:92
To James McHenry, 15 October 97
   Enclosure: Troop Quotas, 15 October 100
To Timothy Pickering, 15 October 102
From Timothy Pickering, 15 October 103
From James McHenry, 16 October 103
From James McHenry, 16 October 104
To the District of Columbia Commissioners,
   17 October 105
From G. W. Snyder, 17 October   *see* 2:556–57
From George Blagdin, 18 October 106
From the District of Columbia Commissioners,
   18 October   *see* 3:106
From Richard Bland Lee, 18 October 106
From James McHenry, 18 October 108
To Timothy Pickering, 18 October 108
To Charles Cotesworth Pinckney, 18 October 110
To William Thornton, 18 October 110
To Mildred Thornton Washington, 18 October 111
From Bushrod Washington, 19 October 113
From James Washington, 19 October 114
From William Washington, 19 October 116
From James McHenry, 20 October 117
From Timothy Pickering, 20 October 117
To the South Carolina Society of the Cincinnati,
   20 October 119
To John Adams, 21 October 120
To Rawleigh Colston, 21 October 121
To Alexander Hamilton, 21 October 121
To Henry Knox, 21 October 122
To James McHenry, 21 October 124
To James McHenry, 21 October 126
To Edward Carrington, 22 October 128

To the District of Columbia Commissioners,
  22 October   130
To Thomas Marshall, Jr., 22 October   131
To Henry Knox, 23 October   *see* 3:120
To James McHenry, 23 October   132
From Thomas Pinckney, 23 October   133
To William Richardson Davie, 24 October   134
From John Lambert, 24 October   136
To Thomas Law, 24 October   136
To G. W. Snyder, 24 October   *see* 2:557
From Isaiah and Alexander Thomas, 24 October   137
To the Virginia Militia, 24 October   *see* 3:85
To Bushrod Washington, 24 October   138
To Charles Carter, 25 October   *see* 3:49
From the District of Columbia Commissioners,
  25 October   138
From William Thornton, 25 October   139
To James McHenry, 26 October   141
From James McHenry, 26 October   142
To Timothy Pickering, 26 October   143
From James Ross, 26 October   144
To the District of Columbia Commissioners, 27 October   144
To Richard Bland Lee, 27 October   *see* 3:108
From Timothy Pickering, 27 October   150
To William Thornton, 28 October   152
From John Quincy Adams, 29 October   154
From Alexander Hamilton, 29 October   155
From Israel Shreve, 29 October   156
From James McHenry, 30 October   157
From William Thornton, 30 October   159
From William Washington, 30 October   159
From John Frederick Ramnitz, 31 October   161
To James Anderson, 1 November   164
From James McHenry, 1 November   168
From John C. Ogden, 1 November   169
From Peyton Short, 1 November   171
From Charles Cotesworth Pinckney, 2 November   172
From John Frederick Ramnitz, 2 November   *see* 3:163
To James Anderson, 3 November   173
To William B. Harrison, 4 November   175
From Benjamin Hawkins, 4 November   177

From Henry Knox, 4 November   178
To Henry Lee, Jr., 4 November   178
To James McHenry, 4 November   180
To Alexander Spotswood, 4 November   181
Agreement with George Blagdin, 5 November   *see* 3 : 149–50
To John Greenwood, 5 November   182
From Samuel Hodgdon, 6 November   182
From Anna Young, 6 November   183
From James Anderson, 7 November   185
From Maryland Masons, 7 November   *see* 3 : 189
From Samuel Washington, 7 November   186
To Maryland Masons, 8 November   188
From James McHenry, 9 November   189
To Alexander Hamilton and Charles Cotesworth
      Pinckney, 10 November   191
From James McHenry, 10 November   193
To Alexander Hamilton, 12 November   197
From Alexander Hamilton, 13 November   *see* 3 : 199
To James McHenry, 13 November   198
Notes on an Interview with George Logan and
      Robert Blackwell, 13 November   200
From Angelica Church, 14 November   *see* 3 : 213
From John B. Church, 14 November   *see* 3 : 213
From William Richardson Davie, 14 November   202
To James McHenry, 14 November   204
From James McHenry, 14 November   204
From Andrew Moore and Samuel Legrand Campbell,
      14 November   207
From James McHenry, 16 November   209
From James McHenry, 16 November   209
From Philip Rootes, 16 November   210
To Elizabeth Willing Powel, 17 November   211
From James McHenry, 19 November   211
From Philip Schuyler, 20 November   212
To Isaiah and Alexander Thomas, 20 November   *see* 3 : 137–38
To Anna Young, 20 November   *see* 3 : 185
From Lawrence Lewis, 21 November   214
To Alexander Spotswood, Jr., 22 November   216
From Alexander Spotswood, 24 November   218
From John Gerard William De Brahm, 26 November   220
From James McHenry, 26 November   *see* 3 : 249

From James McHenry, 29 November   221
Candidates for Army Appointments from Virginia,
    November   225
To Elizabeth Willing Powel, 1 December   240
To Lawrence Lewis, 2 December   241
From Elizabeth Willing Powel, 3 December   242
From Elias Boudinot, 4 December   242
To Angelica Church, 4 December   *see* 3:213
To John B. Church, 4 December   *see* 3:213
To Philip Church, 4 December   *see* 3:213
To Elizabeth Willing Powel, 4 December   243
To Philip Schuyler, 4 December   *see* 3:213–14
From James McHenry, 5 December   244
To Alexander Addison, 6 December   244
To John Greenwood, 7 December   245
From Sally B. Haynie, 7 December   *see* 2:84
Indenture with Washington Academy, 7 December   *see* 3:208
From Elizabeth Willing Powel, 7 December   246
To Elizabeth Willing Powel, 7 December   246
From Clement Biddle to Tobias Lear, 8 December   247
To Elizabeth Willing Powel, 9 December   247
From Alexander Spotswood, Jr., 9 December   *see* 3:217–18
To James Anderson (of Scotland), 10 December   *see* 2:453
From Adam Hoops, 10 December   *see* 2:546
To John Sinclair, 10 December   *see* 2:395
From James McHenry, 11 December   248
To John Greenwood, 12 December   *see* 3:245–46
To Charles Carroll, Jr., 13 December   248
To James McHenry, 13 December   250
To James McHenry, 13 December   *see* 3:251–58
To James McHenry, 13 December   *see* 3:258–65
To James McHenry, 13 December   265
From James McHenry, 13 December   267
To James McHenry, 14 December   267
To James McHenry, 16 December   268
From Jacob Reed, 19 December   270
From Rawleigh Colston, 20 December   271
From Bernard Hubley, Jr., 20 December   272
From William Russell, 20 December   273
To William Thornton, 20 December   274
From Israel Shreve, 21 December   275

From William Thornton, 21 December   276
From Charles Carroll, Jr., 23 December   *see* 3:249–50
From David Shepherd Garland, 24 December   277
From Alexander Spotswood, 24 December   278
To George Washington Motier Lafayette, 25 December   279
To Lafayette, 25 December   280
From John Sevier, 25 December   285
To William Vans Murray, 26 December   286
From David Stuart, 27 December   288
To William Richardson Davie, 28 December   288
From John Greenwood, 28 December   289
To Richard Raynal Keene, 28 December   291
From James McHenry, 28 December   291
To William Washington, 28 December   293
From William Richardson Davie, 30 December   294
    Enclosure: List of North Carolinians
        Wanting Army Commissions, c.30 December   295
To John Marshall, 30 December   297
To Charles Cotesworth Pinckney, 30 December   *see* 3:298
To David Stuart, 30 December   298
To William Thornton, 30 December   299
To Henry Lee, 31 December   *see* 3:180
From John Augustine Spotswood, 31 December   301
To Bushrod Washington, 31 December   302
From John Augustine Spotswood, 1798   *see* 3:301–2
From John Bard, Sr., 1798   *see* From Charles Buxton,
    27 April 1799

1799
From Mrs. E. Gravatt, 4 January   *see* To Mrs. E. Gravatt,
    29 July 1799
To Timothy Pickering, 4 January   304
To David Stuart, 4 January   304
From James McHenry, 5 January   305
To Philip Rootes, 5 January   *see* 3:210–11
To John Greenwood, 6 January   *see* 3:290–91
To James McHenry, 6 January   306
To William Russell, 6 January   *see* 3:274
From John Marshall, 8 January   308
From Daniel Call, 10 January   311
To William Richardson Davie, 10 January   *see* 3:295

From Lawrence Lewis, 10 January 311
From Samuel Lewis, Sr., 10 January   *see* 3:313
From James McHenry, 10 January 312
From John Jacob Ulrich Rivardi, 10 January   *see* 3:396–97
To Israel Shreve, 10 January 314
From John Greenwood, 11 January   *see* 3:291
From William Heth, 12 January 315
From George Turner, 14 January 316
To Patrick Henry, 15 January 317
To Timothy Pickering, 15 January   *see* 3:337
To Samuel Lewis, Sr., 16 January   *see* 3:313
To John Quincy Adams, 20 January 320
To Clement Biddle, 20 January 321
To Bryan Fairfax, 20 January 322
To William Heth, 20 January   *see* 3:316
To John Sinclair, 20 January 326
To James Washington, 20 January 327
From James McHenry, 21 January 328
From James McHenry, 22 January   *see* 3:328
To Clement Biddle, 23 January   *see* 3:321–22
From Elijah Brainerd, 23 January 328
To Lawrence Lewis, 23 January 332
To Robert Lewis, 23 January 333
To John Tayloe, 23 January 334
From William B. Harrison, 24 January 336
From Timothy Pickering, 24 January 337
To Bartholomew Dandridge, 25 January 338
To Francis Deakins, 25 January 340
To James McAlpin, 27 January 340
To James McHenry, 27 January 342
From John Francis Hamtramck, 28 January   *see* 3:437
From James Lloyd, 28 January 344
To James McHenry, 28 January 344
To Clement Biddle, 29 January   *see* 3:322
From Henry Lee, Jr., 29 January 346
To William Thornton, 30 January 347
From Alexander Addison, 31 January   *see* 3:407
To John Sevier, 31 January 348
To Samuel Washington, 31 January 349
To John Adams, 1 February 350
To Clement Biddle, 1 February 351

To James McHenry, 1 February *see* 3:354
From James McHenry, 1 February 352
From Jedediah Morse, 1 February *see* 3:402
From Thomas Peter, 1–2 February 353
From Timothy Pickering, 2 February 355
To James McHenry, 4 February 356
From Clement Biddle, 5 February 357
To Uvedale Price, 5 February *see* 2:166
To William B. Harrison, 6 February 358
To James McHenry, 6 February 360
To Jonathan Trumbull, Jr., 6 February 361
From Timothy Pickering, 8 February 362
To James McAlpin, 10 February 363
To James McHenry, 10 February 364
To Timothy Pickering, 10 February 365
From John Tayloe, 10 February 366
From William Heath, 11 February 368
To James Lloyd, 11 February 369
From Patrick Henry, 12 February 370
From James McHenry, 12 February 372
From John C. Ogden, 12 February 373
To John Tayloe, 12 February 374
From William Taylor, 12 February 375
From William Thornton, 12 February 376
From Robert Lewis, 13 February 377
From William Thornton, 14 February 378
To William Augustine Washington, 14 February 379
From Alexander Hamilton, 15 February 380
From James McAlpin, 15 February *see* 3:364
To Timothy Pickering, 15 February 381
To William Thornton, 15 February 382
To James Welch, 15 February 383
From Alexander Hamilton, 16 February 383
To James McHenry, 16 February 384
To James Anderson, 17 February 384
To Thomas Law, 17 February 385
To Clement Biddle, 18 February 386
From Alexander Hamilton, 18 February 386
From John Adams, 19 February 387
To George Deneale, 19 February 389
From Timothy Pickering, 21 February 389

From Ezekiel L. Bascom, 22 February   391
From Jonathan Trumbull, Jr., 22 February   392
To Jane Dennison Fairfax, 23 February   394
From John Moody, 23 February   *see* 3:408–9
To Andrew, Catherine, and William Ramsay, 23 February   394
From James Anderson, 25 February   395
To Alexander Hamilton, 25 February   395
To Alexander Hamilton, 25 February   398
To James McHenry, 25 February   *see* 3:353
To James Ewing, 26 February   399
To Alexander Hamilton, 26 February   *see* 3:387
From Henry Lee, Jr., 28 February–3 March   399
To Jedediah Morse, 28 February   402
From Timothy Pickering, 28 February   402
To William Heath, 1 March   *see* 3:369
To Elijah Brainerd, 2 March   *see* 3:331
To John Jacob Ulrich Rivardi, 2 March   *see* 3:397
To John Adams, 3 March   403
To William Booker, 3 March   404
To Timothy Pickering, 3 March   405
To Alexander Addison, 4 March   407
To James McHenry, 4 March   408
To John Moody, 4 March   408
To William B. Harrison, 5 March   409
From Charles Cotesworth Pinckney, 8 March   411
From James Welch, 10 March   413
From Timothy Pickering, 11 March   413
From Bartholomew Dandridge, 12 March   415
List of Houses at Mount Vernon, 13 March   417
From Alexander Hamilton, 14 March   418
To William Thornton, 14 March   419
From Alexander Spotswood, 15 March   420
From Macleod & Lumsden, 16 March   *see* 3:382
To Joseph Anthony, 17 March   421
To George Ball, 17 March   422
To Clement Biddle, 17 March   423
To Benjamin Lincoln, 17 March   424
To John Page, 17 March   *see* 3:422–23
To Tobias Lear, 18 March   425
To James McAlpin, 18 March   *see* 3:364
To William Thompson, 18 March   425

Contents

From William Thornton, 18 March 426
To Timothy Pickering, 20 March 427
To John Frederick Ramnitz, 20 March 428
From Clement Biddle, 21 March 429
From William Thompson, 23 March   *see* 3:426
To William Thornton, 24 March 430
From John Trumbull, 24 March 430
From John Churchman, 25 March 434
To Julius Burbidge Dandridge, 25 March 436
To Alexander Hamilton, 25 March 436
To John Francis Hamtramck, 25 March   *see* 3:437
To James McHenry, 25 March 438
To Alexander Spotswood, 25 March 444
From Joseph Anthony, 26 March   *see* 3:421
To Tobias Lear, 26 March 445
From John Tayloe, 26 March 446
From Mason Locke Weems, 26 March 447
From Alexander Hamilton, 27 March 447
From William B. Harrison, 28 March 448
From Samuel Washington, 28 March 451
From James McHenry, 30 March 451
To Tobias Lear, 31 March 452
From James McHenry, 31 March 453
To Charles Cotesworth Pinckney, 31 March 458
To Charles Cotesworth Pinckney, 31 March 459
To Benjamin Stoddart, 31 March 461
To John Tayloe, 31 March 461
To William Washington, 31 March 462
To Mason Locke Weems, 31 March 463
From Nicholas Fitzhugh, 1 April 464
To Samuel Washington, 2 April 464
From Elijah Brainerd, 3 April   *see* 3:332
From Alexander Hamilton, 3 April 466
From Benjamin Lincoln, 3 April 467
From John Page, 5 April   *see* 3:423
To William Booker, 7 April 468
To James McHenry, 7 April 468
To James McHenry, 7 April 469
To James Welch, 7 April 470
From Thomas Law, 9 April 472
To Edward Carrington, 10 April   *see* 3:474

To Alexander Hamilton, 10 April   473
To William B. Harrison, 10 April   474
To James McHenry, 10 April   476
From James McHenry, 10 April   *see* From James McHenry,
     2 May 1799
To Daniel Morgan, 10 April   477
From John Sevier, 10 April   *see* 3:349
From Bushrod Washington, 10 April   479
From Clement Biddle, 11 April   480
From William Hambly, 13 April   481
From James Anderson (of Scotland), 15 April   482
From Alexander Hamilton, 17 April   *see* 3:474
To Henry Lee, Jr., 18 April   484
From John Searson, 18 April   485
From Lafayette, 19 April   *see* From Lafayette, 9 May 1799
From William Thornton, 19 April   487

Index   489

Illustrations

Washington's plan for his Capitol Hill houses   53

Editorial Apparatus

Transcription of the documents in the volumes of *The Papers of George Washington* has remained as close to a literal reproduction of the manuscript as possible. Punctuation, capitalization, paragraphing, and spelling of all words are retained as they appear in the original document. Dashes used as punctuation have been retained except when a period and a dash appear together at the end of a sentence. The appropriate marks of punctuation have always been added at the end of a paragraph. Errors in spelling of proper names and geographic locations have been corrected in brackets or in annotation only if the spelling in the text makes the word incomprehensible. When a tilde is used in the manuscript to indicate a double letter, the letter has been silently doubled. Washington and some of his correspondents occasionally used a tilde above an incorrectly spelled word to indicate an error in orthography. When this device is used the editors have silently corrected the word. In cases where a tilde has been inserted above an abbreviation or contraction, usually in letter-book copies, the word has been expanded. Otherwise, contractions and abbreviations have been retained as written and a period has been inserted after an abbreviation. When an apostrophe has been used in a contraction it is retained. Superscripts have been lowered and if the word is an abbreviation a period has been added. If the meaning of an abbreviation or contraction is not obvious, it has been expanded in square brackets: "H[is] M[ajest]y." Editorial insertions or corrections in the text also appear in square brackets. Angle brackets ⟨ ⟩ are used to indicate illegible or mutilated material. A space left blank in a manuscript by the writer is indicated by a square-bracketed gap in the text [ ]. Deletions from manuscripts are not indicated. If a deletion contains substantive material, it appears in a footnote. If the intended location of marginal notations is clear from the text, they are inserted without comment; otherwise they are recorded in the footnotes. The ampersand has been retained and the thorn transcribed as "th." The symbol for per (⅊) is used when it appears in the manuscript. The dateline has been placed at the head of a document regardless of where it occurred in the manuscript.

Since GW read no language other than English, incoming letters written to him in foreign languages were generally translated for his information. Where this contemporary translation has survived, it has been used as the text of the document, and the original version has been included in the CD-ROM edition of the Washington Papers. If there is no contemporary translation, the document in its original language has been used as the text. All of the documents printed in this volume, as well as the routine documents omitted from it and various ancillary materials, may be found in the CD-ROM edition of the papers.

Symbols Designating Documents

AD   Autograph Document
ADS   Autograph Document Signed
ADf   Autograph Draft
ADfS   Autograph Draft Signed
AL   Autograph Letter
ALS   Autograph Letter Signed
D   Document
DS   Document Signed
Df   Draft
DfS   Draft Signed
L   Letter
LS   Letter Signed
LB   Letter-Book Copy
[S]   Used with other symbols to indicate that the signature on the document has been cropped or clipped.

Repository Symbols and Abbreviations

CD-ROM:GW   *see* Editorial Apparatus
CSmH   Henry E. Huntington Library, San Marino, Calif.
CtHi   Connecticut Historical Society, Hartford
CtY   Yale University, New Haven
DGW   George Washington University, Washington, D.C.
DLC   Library of Congress
DLC:GW   George Washington Papers, Library of Congress
ICHi   Chicago Historical Society, Chicago
ICU   University of Chicago
IEN-D   Northwestern University, Dental School, Chicago
LNHT   Tulane University, New Orleans
MB   Boston Public Library
MBOS   Old South Association, Boston
MdAA   Maryland State Archives, Annapolis
MdHi   Maryland Historical Society, Baltimore

MGG	Groton School, Groton, Mass.
MH	Harvard University, Cambridge, Mass.
MHi	Massachusetts Historical Society, Boston
MHi-A	Adams Papers, Massachusetts Historical Society, Boston
MiDbGr	Greenfield Village and the Henry Ford Museum, Dearborn, Mich.
MiU-C	William L. Clements Library, University of Michigan, Ann Arbor
MoSW	Washington University, St. Louis
MWalJFK	John F. Kennedy Library, Waltham, Mass.
MWiW	Williams College Library, Williamstown, Mass.
NbO	Omaha Public Library, Omaha
Nc-Ar	North Carolina Department of Archives and History, Raleigh
NcU	University of North Carolina, Chapel Hill
NGenoW	Wadsworth Library, Geneseo, N.Y.
NhD	Dartmouth College, Hanover, N.H.
NHi	New-York Historical Society, New York
NIC	Cornell University, Ithaca, N.Y.
NjMoNP	Washington Headquarters Library, Morristown, N.J.
NjP	Princeton University, Princeton, N.J.
NjR	Rutgers University, New Brunswick, N.J.
NN	New York Public Library, New York
NNMM	Metropolitan Museum of Art, New York
NNPM	Pierpont Morgan Library, New York
OCHP	Cincinnati Historical Society, Cincinnati
OTM	Toledo Museum of Art, Toledo, Ohio
PHC	Haverford College, Haverford, Pa.
PHi	Historical Society of Pennsylvania, Philadelphia
PPIn	Independence National Historical Park, Philadelphia
PPRF	Rosenbach Foundation, Philadelphia
PU	University of Pennsylvania, Philadelphia
PWacD	David Library of the American Revolution, Washington Crossing, Pa.
ScC	Charleston Library Society, Charleston, S.C.
Vi	Library of Virginia, Richmond
ViA	Association for the Preservation of Virginia Antiquities, Richmond
ViHi	Virginia Historical Society, Richmond
ViMtV	Mount Vernon Ladies' Association of the Union
ViU	University of Virginia, Charlottesville
ViW	College of William and Mary, Williamsburg, Va.

Short Title List

Annals of Congress.   Joseph Gales, Sr., comp. *The Debates and Proceedings in the Congress of the United States; with an Appendix, Containing Important State Papers and Public Documents, and All the Laws of a Public Nature.* 42 vols. Washington, D.C., 1834–56.

ASP.   Walter Lowrie et al., eds. *American State Papers: Documents, Legislative and Executive, of the Congress of the United States.* 38 vols. Washington, D.C., 1832–61.

Bailey, *Manual of Cultivated Plants.*   L. H. Bailey. *Manual of Cultivated Plants Most Commonly Grown in the Continental United States and Canada.* New York, 1951.

Betts, *Jefferson's Garden Book.*   Edwin Morris Betts, ed. *Thomas Jefferson's Garden Book, 1766–1824, with Relevant Extracts from His Other Writings.* Philadelphia, 1944.

Black's Law Dictionary.   Henry Campbell Black. *Black's Law Dictionary.* St. Paul, Minn., 1968.

Burgess, *Virginia Soldiers of 1776.*   Louis A. Burgess, ed. *Virginia Soldiers of 1776.* 3 vols. 1929. Reprint. Spartanburg, S.C., 1973.

Columbia Hist. Soc. Recs.   *Records of the Columbia Historical Society.*

Crozier, *Virginia County Records.*   William Armstrong Crozier, ed. *Virginia County Records: Spotsylvania County, 1721–1800.* Vol. 1. New York, 1905.

Custis, *Recollections.*   George Washington Parke Custis. *Recollections and Private Memoirs of Washington.* New York, 1860.

Day Book.   Manuscript Cash Memorandum Book, 1 Sept. 1797–20 Feb. 1799, in John Carter Brown Library, Providence, R.I.

De Vorsey, *De Brahm's Report.*   Louis De Vorsey, ed. John Gerard William De Brahm. *Report of the General Survey in the Southern District of North America.* Columbia, S.C., 1971.

Diaries.   Donald Jackson and Dorothy Twohig, eds. *The Diaries of George Washington.* 6 vols. Charlottesville, Va., 1976–79.

Executive Journal.   *Journal of the Executive Proceedings of the Senate of the United States of America.* Vol. 1. Washington, D.C., 1828.

Fitzpatrick, *Writings of Washington.*   John C. Fitzpatrick, ed. *The Writings of George Washington from the Original Manuscript Sources, 1745–1799.* 39 vols. Washington, D.C., 1931–44.

Griffin, *Boston Athenæum Washington Collection.* Appleton P. C. Griffin, comp. *A Catalogue of the Washington Collection in the Boston Athenæum.* Cambridge, Mass., 1897.

Harris, *Thornton Papers.*   C. M. Harris, ed. *Papers of William Thornton.* 1 vol. to date. Charlottesville, Va., 1995—.

Harrison, *Princetonians, 1769–1775.* Richard A. Harrison. *Princetonians, 1769–1775, A Biographical Dictionary.* Princeton, N.J., 1980.

JCC. Worthington C. Ford et al., eds. *Journals of the Continental Congress.* 34 vols. Washington, D.C., 1904–37.

King, *Life and Correspondence of King.* Charles R. King, ed. *The Life and Correspondence of Rufus King.* 6 vols. New York, 1894–1900.

Lear, *Letters and Recollections.* Tobias Lear. *Letters and Recollections of George Washington.* New York, 1906.

Ledger C. Manuscript ledger in Morristown National Historical Park, Morristown, N.J.

Life of Pickering. Octavius Pickering and Charles W. Upham. *The Life of Timothy Pickering.* 4 vols. Boston, 1867–73.

Mattern, *Madison Papers.* David B. Mattern et al., eds. *The Papers of James Madison.* Vol. 17. Charlottesville and London, 1991.

Mount Vernon Ledger, 1797–98. Manuscript ledger owned by Morristown National Historical Park, Morristown, N.J.

Munson, *Alexandria Hustings Court Deeds, 1783–97.* James D. Munson, comp. *Alexandria, Virginia: Alexandria Hustings Court Deeds, 1783–1797.* Bowie, Md., 1990.

Munson, *Alexandria Hustings Court Deeds, 1797–1801.* James D. Munson, comp. *Alexandria, Virginia: Alexandria Hustings Court Deeds, 1797–1801.* Bowie, Md., 1991.

Palmer, *Stoddert's War.* Michael A. Palmer. *Stoddert's War: Naval Operations during the Quasi-War with France, 1798–1801.* Columbia, S.C., 1987.

Pa. Mag. *Pennsylvania Magazine of History and Biography.*

Papers, Colonial Series. W. W. Abbot et al., eds. *The Papers of George Washington, Colonial Series.* 10 vols. Charlottesville, Va., 1983–95.

Risjord, *Chesapeake Politics.* Norman K. Risjord. *Chesapeake Politics, 1781–1800.* New York, 1978.

Rutland, *Mason Papers.* Robert A. Rutland, ed. *The Papers of George Mason, 1725–1792.* 3 vols. Chapel Hill, N.C., 1970.

1 *Stat.* Richard Peters, ed. *The Public Statutes at Large of the United States of America.* Vol. 1. Boston, 1845.

Stinchcombe and Cullen, *Marshall Papers.* William C. Stinchcombe, Charles T. Cullen et al., eds. *The Papers of John Marshall.* Vol. 3. Chapel Hill, N.C., 1979.

Syrett, *Hamilton Papers.* Harold C. Syrett et al., eds. *The Papers of Alexander Hamilton.* 27 vols. New York, 1961–87.

Todd, *Life and Letters of Barlow.* Charles Burr Todd. *Life and Letters of Joel Barlow, LL.D.: Poet, Statesman, Philosopher.* New York and London, 1886.

Trumbull, *Autobiography*.   John Trumbull. *The Autobiography of Colonel John Trumbull*. Theodore Sizer, ed. New Haven, 1953. Reprint. New York, 1970.

U.S. Army Insignia and Uniforms.   William K. Emerson. *Encyclopedia of United States Army Insignia and Uniforms*. Norman, Okla., 1996.

Va. Report of 1799–1800.   *The Virginia Report of 1799–1800, Touching the Alien and Sedition Laws; Together with the Virginia Resolutions of December 21, 1798, Including the Debate and Proceedings Thereon in the House of Delegates of Virginia and Other Documents Illustrative of the Report and Resolutions*. New York, 1970.

Weems, *Life of Washington*.   Mason L. Weems. *The Life of Washington*. Marcus Cunliffe, ed. Cambridge, Mass., 1962.

The Papers of George Washington
Retirement Series
Volume 3
September 1798–April 1799

sensibility is affected. This, & not being able to open my lips upon subjects very interesting to my pecuniary concerns by way of explaining my situation in ⟨*illegible*⟩ too feeling a manner, without receiving a long letter by way of repremand for *Scolding*, & constant intimations, if I am not satisfied with your services you are ready to quit my employ upon due notice, is carrying sensibility too far, to an unreasonable and improper length. I certainly may see things, which in my judgment, may require a change, and speak of them without meaning to wound your feelings; or that could be construed into a disapprobation of your ⟨*illegible*⟩ conduct; or ⟨*illegible*⟩ desire of parting with you.

It must be obvious to yourself, that it is by my Rents, and the Sales of my lands that I have been enabled to get along; & to support the expence of this house. The Farms do little more than support themselves, and those who overlook them. It is not to be wondered at then (especially after being often told that money would be coming in) that I now and then express myself strongly ⟨when⟩ I am called upon for the payment ⟨of⟩ almost every article ⟨that is⟩ bought, of magnitude. Yet, seeing that you struggle hard to put these farms in a more profitable ⟨*illegible*⟩, I believe I have said as little relative to the calls upon me for money, as most men in my situation would have done.

I will, once for all, Mr Anderson, say (and I never profess what I do not feel) that I have an esteem, regard & friendship for you; but I shall re⟨peat⟩ that this will never prevent me from expressing my mind fully and freely in all matters relative to my business. I never have, to your face or behind your back, insinuated any thing that could, by the most forced construction, imp⟨ugn⟩ your honesty, integrity, industry, sobriety or zeal; but the contrary: I see no cause therefore for such a display of sensibility when at any time I may speak feelingly to you on matters relative to my own concerns, when none of these are ⟨arraigned⟩.

Your Sons intention to leave my employ is as unexpected *by* me as the determination seems sudden ⟨by him⟩; and I am sorry for it: but as I have had no other concern with the distillery than to provide what was asked, all I can say concerning it, is, that you must, against the ⟨*illegible*⟩ concern, supply his place in the best manner you can.[3] With esteem & regard I am Your friend &ca

Go: Washington

ALS (letterpress copy), ViMtV.

1. Anderson's long letter of "complaint & remonstrances" has not been found, but this was not the first time that GW had responded to such a letter. See for example his letters to Anderson of 22 May and 11 June 1798.

2. The cash account in Anderson's Mount Vernon Ledger, 1797–98, p. 187, indicates that Archibald Morton, a neighbor, received from the mill at Mount Vernon 21 bushels of wheat on 29 Oct. 1798.

3. The distillery built by Anderson at Mount Vernon in 1797 had been under the management of Anderson and his son John since it began its operation early in 1798. See James Anderson to GW, 21 June 1797, n.4, and GW to Anderson, 22 May 1798, n.2. See also GW to Robert Lewis, 26 Jan. 1798, n.2. The Andersons continued to operate the distillery for GW, but in the fall of 1799 GW decided to rent the distillery along with the mill and Dogue Run farm to Lawrence Lewis (see GW to Anderson, 10 Sept. 1799, n.2).

To James McHenry

Private & confidential
My dear Sir,   Mount Vernon 16th Sepr 1798.

Your confidential letter—dated Trenton the 10th Instant, with its enclosures, have been duly received.

The latter are returned. The contents of them have filled my mind with much disquietude & embarrassment; but it is impossible for me to make any move, in consequence, at this time, from the want of *Official* ground; without betraying your confidential communication.[1]

I can perceive pretty clearly however, that the matter is, or very soon will be brought, to the alternative of submitting to the Presidents forgetfulness of what *I* considered a compact, or condition of acceptance of the Appointment with which he was pleased to honor me, or, to return him my Commission. And as that compact was ultimately, and at the time, declared to him *through you*, in your letter written from this place, and the strong part of it inserted *after* it was first drawn, at my request to avoid mis-conception, I conceive I have a right, and accordingly ask, to be furnished with a copy of it.[2]

You will recollect too, that my acceptance being conditional, I requested you to take the Commission back, that it might be restored—or annulled—according to the Presidents determination to accept, or reject, the terms on which I had offered to serve; and that, but for your assuring me, that it would make no difference whether I retained or returned it and conceiving that the latter might be considered as an evidence of distrust it would have been done. Subsequent events, evince that, it would have been a measure of utility for though the case *in principle* is the same—yet such a memento of the fact could not so easily have been forgotten or got over.

After the declaration in the Presidents letter to you, of Augt the 29th (which is also accompanied with other sentiments of an alarming nature) and his avowed readiness to take the responsibility of the measure upon himself, it is not probable that there will be any departure from the resolution he has adopted; but I should be glad, notwithstanding to know the result of the Representation made by the Secretaries, as soon as it comes to hand. And, if there is no impropriety in the request, to be gratified with a sight of the Memorial also.[3] I am always, with much sincerity, Your Affectionate Servant

Go: Washington

P.S. If you see no impropriety in the measure, & do not object to it, it would be satisfactory to me to receive a copy of the Powers, or Instructions from the President under which you acted when here.[4]

ALS, LNHT: George and Katherine Davis Collection; ALS (letterpress copy), DLC:GW.

1. For the enclosures, see notes 1 and 2 to McHenry's letter of 10 September.

2. McHenry arrived at Mount Vernon on 11 July to solicit GW's acceptance of the commission of lieutenant general and commander in chief of the army. McHenry wrote to John Adams the next day: "I arrived here yesterday evening and delivered your letter [of 7 July] to the General. I have had much conversation with him, and have now the pleasure to inform you, that I expect to bring you his acceptance of the appointment with the proviso that he is not to be called into activity till such time as in your opinion circumstances may render his presence with the army indispensible. He appears to me to have maturely studied the vast consequence of the steps that have been taken, and the importance of maintaining at every hazard the ground we have assumed. This I can perceive has had its full share of influence in determining him to give up the happiness he enjoys in these charming shades." Later in the letter McHenry wrote that he would "obtain from him the names of the persons he considers the best qualified for his confidential officers and without whom I think he would not serve" (MHi-A). McHenry enclosed a copy of this letter in his letter to GW of 26 October.

3. John Adams in his letter to McHenry of 29 Aug. declared his firm intention to rank Knox first and Hamilton last among the major generals. See GW to Hamilton 14 July, n.5, for a quotation from and description of Adams's letter.

McHenry wrote GW on 10 Sept. enclosing Adams's letter and informing GW that members of the cabinet were drafting a memorial to the president protesting the demotion of Hamilton. On 19 Sept. he wrote GW that it had been decided that Wolcott alone should sign the memorial. The memorial, dated 17 Sept., is in MHi-A and is printed in part in Syrett, *Hamilton Papers*, 22:10–14.

4. McHenry on 26 Oct. supplied GW with a copy of Adams's instructions, contained in the president's letter to McHenry of 6 July 1798: "It is my desire that you embrace the first opportunity to sett out on your Journey to Mount Vernon, and wait on general Washington with the Commission of Lt General and Commander in Chief of the armies of the United states, which by the advice and consent of the Senate has been signed by me. The reasons and motives which prevailed with me, to Venture on such a Step as the nomination of this great and illustrious character whose Voluntary resignation alone occasioned my introduction to the office I now hold were too numerous to be detailed in this Letter, and are too obvious and important to escape the observation of any part of America or Europe; but as it is a movement of great delicacy, it will require all your address to communicate the Subject in a manner, that Shall be unoffensive to his feelings, and consistent with all the respect that is due from me to him. If the General Should decline the appointment all the world will be Silent, and respectfully acquiesce—If he Should accept all the world except the Enemies of this Country will rejoice—If he should come to no decisive determination, but take the Subject into consideration I Shall not appoint any other General untill his conclusion is known. His advice in the formation of a List of officers would be extremely desireable to me—The names of Lincoln, Morgan, Knox, Hamilton, Gates Pinckney, Lee, Carrington, Hand Mughlenburgh Dayton Burr, Brooks, Cobb, Smith, may be mentioned to him and any others that occur to you; particularly I wish to have his opinion of the Man, most suitable for Inspector General & Adjutant General & Quarter Master General—his opinion on all subjects must have great Weight, and I wish you to obtain from him, as much of his reflections upon the times and service as you can" (MHi-A).

From Alexander Spotswood

Dear Sir   Sunday Newpost Septr 16. 1798
    your favour of the 14th was forwarded to me last evening by Mr Park—and which I now proceed to answer—tho not so Fully as you or myself wish.[1]
    My overseer Roger Farril accepts your Terms—and will be with you Soon after christmas—but Says, should Richard Rhodes decline your Bussiness—he shall give the preference to the Farm at £45 pr year &c.
    From Rhodes I have received no Answer to my letters; I shall write again to day—and on Monday week will write you again—I shall also write this day to Mr Richards—and desire him to Send

the young man who engages as a Joiner to my house to receive a letter from me; and proceed on immediately to Mount Vernon—Mr Richards is much to be depended on—and from the appearance, & deportment of this Young man who is Single I Flatter myself he will please you.[2]

I Feel much Flattered, by your confidence; in a repetition of your request—that I would put on Paper Such officers, with there grades that served in the Revolutionary war with Celebrity—I recollect Speaking to you much in the praise of a gentleman who Served in my Regiment. but at that time I could say nothing of his political Sentiments—Since, I have Seen a peice published in the papers with his Signature—which denote him no Freind to goverment—therefore, Valluable as I look on him as an officer. I shall pass him over—& begin with Colonels Edwd Carrington & Wm Heth—these are Sensible, genteel men—and who acted in there Stations last war with great Credit—and would be in my opinion an ornament, as well as a great acquisition to the Army—these gentlemen have famylies—and held very lucrative posts under goverment—the former Superviser, the latter Collector at Bermuda Hundred—and as I have reason to beleive, there other property is not great—particularly that of the latter—it is doubtful whether they would Relinquish there present profitable Situations, for a post in the Army.

Mr Hoard—this gentleman left the army at the close of the war with the Rank of Captain—he was in Bufords defeat—and I have understood that many of the officers should Say had he commanded; the Tables would have been turned on Tarlton—who contrary to all good faith—so soon as the men had laid down there arms on certain stipulated Conditions, he let his horse loose on them; & began his usual masacre—when this gentleman with his Company alone, flew to there arms—and fought most gallantly—until overpowered, he Taken prissoner, and covered with wounds the marks of which he carries now in his face.

This gentleman lived near me for three years—he is a man of good Sense, very independant in His property, possesses a fine Temper—and I think a respectable man—and altho I cannot Say any thing within my Knowledge, of his millitary Talents—yet certain I am—from his Activity, & Industry—and being well acquainted with Bussiness—that he would be a valluable acquisition in the Staff department—he holds I think the rank of majr in the

80,000 Malitia, that has been drafted as the first requisitiond and he assures me his determination is, to end his days in the Army. if he can get an appointment—and to render his country every Service in his power.[3]

Mr Francis Thornton the Son of Mr F. Thornton of the fall Hill—he possesses a clear & independant Fortune—a gentleman of good Sense & pleasing manners—and fine moral character—he wishes a company—& assures me, as I believe he can raise it very quick.[4]

These four gentlemen I am well acquainted with—I Know they are all much attached to you—and have been uniformly from the begining warm Freinds to Goverment & good order—Mr Green The Younger Son of Colo. John green, now 23 years of age—and in a pretty line of Bussiness in Fredericksburg—he wishes much to get into the army—I can say nothing of this gentleman of my own Knowledge—Farther, than he has a most wining Countenance—appears to be a Sensible Active man, and possesses genteel & easy manners—The gentlemen of Respectability here that I know to be frds to goverment Speak of him in the Highest Terms—not only as a Moral man, but one who has been a uniform and Steady freind to goverment—which he himself has assured me is the case—and with his life he will ever Support—the measures of goverment—If What I have here Said should incline you to promote this gentleman—certain I am—was you to see him—you would recommend—or appt him to a Company without hesitation.[5]

The other Valluable feild officrs that I remember—are all removed to the western Country—those that remain; I can Say nothing for—and certain I am—that if appointments are confined to those alone who Served dureing the war—that the regiment to be raised in this State, will never be officered to your wishes.

If you desire, I will look about & with the assistance of some of my freinds, who are as warm freinds to goverment as myself—endeavour to make out a list of young gentlemen from 17 to 23 years of age who are of genteel & respectable famylies—and of good moral characters, and send you a list of the Same, Speaking of Such as I know myself—and of others agreable to Such information as I get from my freinds—The times are really perrilous—and I well know the Utmost Caution ought & will be observed, in the Military appointments.

for the Jaccobins I am assured, & beleive, are playing Another game—more Serious than any of there past acts.

All of a Sudden they have in these parts become calm—not a Sentance of pollitics—& I am assured; & beleive that vast Numbers of them through the country are new applicants for commissions—and will leave no Stone unturned to get into the army and there make there last effort to sow & rear the Seeds of Sedition.

with my family you are congratulated on yr return of health— which we most devoutly wish, may be of long duration.

Mrs Spotswood &c. unite in there best regards to you Mr[s] Washington, Miss Custis & Washington as well as Sir Yr Sincerely & affect. Hb. st

Alexr Spotwood

P.S. My Son John arrived the last of August at Baltimore from Jamaica—and is now comeing up our river—he has been very fortunate to Steer so often as he has done—clear of a Fraternal Hug.[6]

The only service mr Thornton ever Saw was at the head of his Company agt the insurgents.

ALS, DLC:GW.

1. Andrew Parks of Fredericksburg was at Mount Vernon on 4 Sept. with his wife, GW's niece Harriot Washington Parks (*Diaries*, 6:314–15).

2. Spotswood first wrote GW on 30 Aug. about the possibility of hiring Richard Rhodes as an overseer at Mount Vernon. For other correspondence regarding the unsuccessful attempt to hire Rhodes, see Spotswood to GW, 11 Sept., and GW to Spotswood, 24 September. Mr. Richards has not been identified.

3. See James McHenry to GW, 11 May 1799, and note 1 to that document. "Bufords defeat" took place in South Carolina on 29 May 1780, when a mixed body of Continental soldiers and horse under Colonel Abraham Buford was defeated by Lt. Col. Banastre Tarleton's force of Loyalists and British.

4. Francis Thornton (b. 1760) of Fall Hill, Spotsylvania County, was the nephew of Mildred Thornton Washington, who was married to GW's brother Charles. Francis Thornton appears among the applicants for a captain's commission on the list of Candidates for Army Appointments from Virginia, November 1798, printed below.

5. Thomas Green, seventh child of Col. John Green of Culpeper County, later settled in Kentucky. He is misnamed John Greene on the list of Candidates for Army Appointments from Virginia, November 1798, printed below. See also Spotswood to GW, 24 Nov., and GW to McHenry, 28 Jan., 4 Feb. 1799.

6. After Capt. John Augustine Spotswood came to Mount Vernon on 4 Oct., GW supplied him with a letter of introduction to Secretary of the Navy Benjamin Stoddert to whom Spotswood wished to apply for a commission in the navy. See GW to Stoddert, 9 Oct. 1798, and *Diaries*, 6:318–19. Captain Spotswood returned to Mount Vernon on Christmas Day 1798, by which time he seems to have

abandoned the idea of entering the U.S. Navy. He was, however, given a navy command in 1800 (see John Augustine Spotswood to GW, 31 Dec. 1798, n.1, and *Executive Journal*, 1:338).

From Benjamin Stoddert

Sir   Trenton [N.J.] 16. Septr 1798.

You will I know, pardon me for trespassing on your time, my object being the Public good.

If we are to create such a navy, as will make our Commerce respected, and this I cannot doubt, will be the policy of our Country, one Navy yard at least must be established for building Ships. This subject will probably engage the attention of Congress at the ensuing Session, and it will be my Duty, to lay before them the best information in my power to obtain.

The place marked out on the plan of the City of Washington, for the Marine Hospital, has always appeared to me, to be among the most eligible situations in the United States for a Navy yard. The result of all the enquiries I have been able to make, since I have been in office, serves but to confirm me more strongly in this opinion. No place further south, will admit of the same degree of Security against an Enemy—no place to the Northward or Eastward will afford Timber so good, so cheap, or in such abundance. I might add, all other materials for Building & arming of Ships. The Springs in the Neighbourhood, at least 40 feet higher than the Surface of the River water—or Goose Creek or Rock Creek, any of them would afford water to fill locks, to prevent the difficult & sometimes dangerous operation of launching—and Ships by means of such locks, could be repaired without the tedious operations of discharging & heaving down. It is perhaps desireable that the principal navy yard should be under the Eye of Government. It is certainly Just that it should be in the centre of the Union, if it can be so placed with equal advantages to the whole Community.[1]

Nothing of consequence to the Welfare of the Country escapes your penetration. Will you Sir permit me the liberty of soliciting your opinion on this very important subject? The depth of Water in every part of the Channel of the River is a consideration of great magnitude. It has been suggested that about Maryland point the Water is too shallow to admit the passage of Ships of the line—drawing, fully armed, & provisioned, 24 feet.[2]

Joining in the universal prayer for the preservation of a life of inestimable value to the Country—I have the honor to be with the highest respect & esteem sir Yr most Obed. Servt

Ben. Stoddert

ALS, DLC:GW; copy, CtHi: Oliver Wolcott, Jr., Papers.

Benjamin Stoddert (1751–1831), a successful merchant in Georgetown, became the first secretary of the navy in May 1798.

1. See GW's reply of 26 September. On 25 Feb. 1799 Congress appropriated one million dollars for the construction of ships for the navy (1 *Stat.*, 621-22). Stoddert spent $135,000 of this money on the purchase of sites for six navy yards, including that of the Washington navy yard (Palmer, *Stoddert's War*, 127). See also William Thornton to GW, 1 Sept. 1799.

2. Maryland Point is in western Charles County, Md., where the Potomac River bends its course from south to east, about fifteen miles below Port Tobacco.

From Timothy Pickering

(confidential)

Sir,   Trenton [N.J.] Sept. 18 1798.

I wrote you a hasty letter on the 13th—Upon further consideration, we have judged it most advisable that a letter should be written by Mr Wolcott alone; in order that the strong point of view in which the facts and arguments in the case may be placed, may be presented by *Reason* only, to which the mind yields more willingly than to *formal advice*, in the *semblance* of official authority. This is particularly the more eligible, seeing Mr Wolcott cannot be suspected of *intermeddling* in the primary arrangements; having been absent in Connecticut from a day or two after your own nomination, until the Senate had adjourned; and may therefore be well supposed to step forward with an unbiassed mind. Accordingly Mr Wolcott has written to the President, & the letter was dispatched by yesterday's mail.[1] To-day the Secretary of War transmits to the President the commissions for Generals Hamilton, Pinckney & Knox, to be arranged as he shall finally think proper. However, the arguments in support of the orignal arrangement (Hamilton, Pinckney, Knox) are irrefragable, and I trust will prove irresistable.[2]

In a former letter I mentioned that Genl Knox appealed to a rule adopted for the regulation of rank in the army of our revolution.[3] This rule, I suppose (for I can find no other to which he can refer) is the resolve of Congress of the 24th of November 1778 in the printed journals⟨.⟩ But an examination of it will show that it does not support his pretensions; being made to apply to the *army* and *state of things then existing.* Besides, it cannot *now* have any binding force; all those old resolves of Congress being at this time but the *records* of the *temporary* laws or regulations for conducting the revolutionary war: except only as to transactions begun at that period and remaining unfinished. If, however, we admit them as *legally* obligatory at this moment, then we appeal to another Resolve—that of the 4th of January 1776, in these words—"In all elections of officers by Congress, where more than one are elected on the same day, to commands of the same rank, they shall take rank of each other according to their election, and the entry of their names in the minutes, and their commissions shall be numbered to shew their priority." This is a resolution of *general* and *universal* application, to all elections of officers *by Congress,* under the former government, and in its *principle* precisely to the case in question: whereas the Resolve to which General Knox appeals is *confined,* expressly, *to officers appointed under the authority of Congress, by virtue of their resolution of the 16th of September 1776, or of any subsequent resolution prior to the 5th of January 1777.*[4] This is a complete refutation of Genl Knox's claim under *former rules.* If we lay them aside, and recur to simple principles, his claim will likewise be without support. We must then consider the comparative merits of the competitors—your opinion of them (who have had the best opportunities of knowing them, as well in military as civil life)— that opinion, *after it was requested,* announced to the President— the President's nomination of the candidates to the Senate, and their approbation, in the order of nomination founded on your recommendation. To these considerations may be added, the *public voice,* concurring with yours, in designating Mr Hamilton for the *second place* in the armies of the United States. But between the President and yourself, the force of your opinion does not rest merely on the order in which you arranged the names of the three gentlemen: your private letter of July 9th (I think that was the date) to Colo. Hamilton, which you left open, and permitted the Secy of War to take a copy, but of which the original was submitted to the President's perusal, explicitly declares, that "as to your friend General Knox, whom you love and esteem, you have ranked him below both the others, Hamilton & Pinckney."[5] This, in Mr Wolcott's letter, is presented to the President's recollection, and the wound it must give your feelings, if your opinion formally requested & so explicitly and forcibly given, should be disregarded; and when too you had in the same private letter, and otherwise, said you had consented to take the field with the reservation of having officers about you, in the most important stations, in whom you could confide: and consequently that the persons whom you specially recommended for such confidential and important posts, should be arranged in the order you judged would insure to you their assistance, and prove most advantageous to the public service.

The letter contains many other strong and persuasive arguments and motives for adhering to your arrangement: and I shall be astonished beyond measure, if that arrangement does not finally prevail. I have the honour to be with great respect, sir, your most obt servt

Timothy Pickering

ALS, DLC:GW; copy, MHi: Pickering Papers; copy, DLC: Hamilton Papers.

1. For Oliver Wolcott's letter to John Adams, see GW to James McHenry, 16 Sept., n.3.

2. For a summary of the dispute over the ranking of the three major generals, see GW to Hamilton, 14 July, n.5. See also James McHenry to GW, 19 September.

3. See Pickering to GW, 1 September (second letter).

4. For the texts of these resolutions, see *JCC*, 12 : 1154–56, 4 : 29.

5. This is GW's letter to Alexander Hamilton of 14 July.

From John Trumbull

Sir   London Septr 18th 1798

By the Ship Nancy, Captain Davidson bound to Alexandria, I have sent a small Box, addressed to you, and containing the Four Pair of Prints for which you did me the honour to subscribe so long since, and two Volumes which I was requested by my friend Mr West to forward to you with his best Respects: the prints are the finest impressions and, for security are rolled, and enclosed in a Tin Case. I hope they will come safely to your hands, and meet your approbation.

I hope also that the pair which I had the Honour to send to you by the Suffolk, Capt. Lovell to Alexandria, in March last, came safe.[1]

In common with my Countrymen and the World, I am happy to see you again the Defender and Guardian of our Country; and I earnestly hope that the result of the Task which you now assume will prove as beneficial to mankind, and as glorious to yourself as was your former Command. I beg my best Respects to Mrs Washington, and Am, with the highest Respect, sir Your most obedient and Obliged Servant

Jno. Trumbull

ALS, DLC:GW.

1. Trumbull sent to GW in March 1798 proofs of his first engravings of his paintings *The Death of Gen. Warren at the Battle of Bunker's Hill* and *The Death of Gen. Montgomery in the Attack on Quebec*. At that time Trumbull promised to send later the four copies of each engraving for which GW had subscribed and paid in part in 1790. See Trumbull to GW, 6 Mar. 1798. GW wrote John Trumbull's brother, Jonathan, on 6 Feb. 1799 saying "four copies of the Prints of the Deaths of Montgomery & Warren" had "just arrived." For GW's payment for the engravings, see GW to Joseph Anthony, 17 Mar. 1799, n.1. In his letter to John Trumbull, 25 June 1799, GW indicates that the two volumes that Benjamin West had Trumbull forward were Uvedale Price's volumes on the picturesque. See also Price to GW, 31 Mar. 1798, and note 1 to that document.

From James McHenry

(Confidential)

My dear General.   Trenton [N.J.] 19 Sepr 1798

I received your letter of the 14th instant yesterday evening.

Be assured I regret and lament from the bottom of my soul the delays, and heart distressing obstructions which have prevented the nomination of the field and other officers for the 12 additional regiments and cavalry. It is not however (whatever the public opinion may be) to me that any of them can be ascribed; for whatever depended upon me, to propose, or to do, has been proposed or done.[1]

It is best, I beleive, to give you a brief statement of facts, and the circumstances that have embarrassed and delayed the public service. I reckon among these. 1st The rejection of the Presidents nomination of Colo. Smith as adjutant General. 2 His considering General Knox intitled to priority of rank to either Generals Hamilton or Pinckney, and 3d His present distance from the seat of government. I shall say a few words respecting each of these causes.

Immediately upon my return to Philadelp⟨hia⟩ from Mount Vernon, I made the President acquainted with the result of my mission, with which he appeared very well pleased, particularly with your letter. He was then at breakfast, and I had not seen my own family. After having visited them, I laid before him the paper signed by yourself, containing the names of the persons you had selected for the General officers and General Staff; and informed him, that the three first in particular, vz. Hamilton Pinckney & Knox, were expected, by you to rank in the order they were arranged in your list.[2]

As the Congress had adjourned before my return, and the Senate were detained by the President, to receive his nominations, in consequence of my mission, it was his intention to have offered them the day on which I arrived. He accordingly wrote a message, in which he inserted the names of Generals Hamilton Pinckney & Knox in the order in which they were arranged by you, and also General Dayton for adjutant general and Col. Smith for one of the three Brigadiers. Previously to his thus writing their names down, he observed that in his opinion, Col. Hamilton, former rank considered, was not intitled to stand so high, and that he did not know, what were the merits which gave General Pinckney preference to Knox. I mentioned to him your opinions, and to prevent any misunderstanding of what you desired, or the motives by which you had been actuated to the arrangement you had proposed, I thought it adviseable and proper to communicate to him, immediately, the private letter you had written to Col. Hamilton on the subject, and given to me open with permission to take a copy of it.[3] It appeared to me, at the time, that it settled the arrangement, as he made no further observations, and was only prevented from sending in the nominations as arranged in his message and your list, by Mr Pickerings coming in and informing him that the senate had adjourned 'till next day.

I waited upon the President the day following and found that something or other, of which I was ignorant, had caused a very great change in his mind. He now said he could not think of placing Hamilton before Knox, that Knox for various reasons, (among others his former rank in the army) was clearly intitled to rank next to General Washington: he finally however agreed to follow your arrangement upon my admitting that any of the parties, if dissatisfied with the order of arrangement might have their claim discussed and settled by a board of officers or the commander in chief.

I thought the business now finally arranged. He was writing down in a fresh message (the first being blotted) the names of the Generals, when Mr Pickering came in. Some conversation ensued, when Mr Pickering made an observation which seemed to place General Dayton's military talents above Col. Smiths. This gave offence to the President⟨;⟩ he grew warm in Col. Smiths praise; Mr Pickering was silent, and no more was said on the subject, except by the President, who added, I will nominate him for adjutant General and Dayton for Brigadier. Till then I had expected he would have nominated General Dayton for Adjutant General, as had been fixed upon the day before, and I still think he would, but for the observations made by Mr Pickering whose objections to Smith I was not apprised of at that time.[4]

Mr Pickering now mentioned Governor Sevier for a Provisional army Brigadier. I considered him an unprincipled man; but as it was only an appointment which might always remain nominal, and as giving it to him, might have a good effect in Tenessee, I waved my objections and it was acceded to. White had been pressed upon the President by strong and influential characters, was expected to command the Cavalry, and assigned to the Provisional list, on their account, and to preserve the cavalry for a better officer.[5]

But wherefore was any of the General officers or staff for the Provisional army appointed? The act for raising a provisional army makes the concurrence of the Senate indispensable to the appointment of the Major and Brigadier Generals. As these then, could not be appointed in the recess, and as it was possible the service of some of them might be wanted before the next meeting of Congress in course, the President considered it to be his duty to appoint them It was besides holding out to the world a determination to prepare our whole military force for action; at least, that we were in earnest to raise the Provisional troops, by omitting no arrangement necessary thereto.[6]

It was not till these points had been decided upon, that it was mentioned to me, that Smiths nomination would not be concurred in; that he was a swindler in fact, and a disorganizer—that he had betrayed a moneyed trust, and that the Eastern States could have no confidence in government, was such a person to be appointed adjutant general of the army. This information was

given to me by Mr Pickering. I told him he ought to have mentioned it sooner; that he had said to the President in my presence,
before my going down to Mount Vernon, that Smith would be
proper to take command of a regiment; that neither General
Washington nor I had any knowledge or information that suspicions of fraud attached to Smiths character. It may be proper also
to remark that I spoke with Hamilton about an appointment for
Smith before seeing you and that he concurred in its propriety.
The fact was Mr Pickering being persuaded of the truth of those
suspicions, thought it to be his duty to take an active part with
the Senators to defeat his appointment, and most of the Senators
entertaining the same opinions, Smith was rejected nearly by an
unanimous vote. The President who judged more favourably of
Smith, and it may be more justly, from a more intimate knowledge
of facts, was exceedingly irritated by the rejection and felt much
anger, especially against Mr Pickering. He said he was certain
there had been intriguing to produce it, that it could not have
been accomplished otherwise; for if his son in law was in debt and
embarrassed, so were Lee and Knox who therefore ought to have
met the same fate—That his son in law had called his creditors
together to submit to them a full view of his affairs, and he beleived would be able to procure from them proofs of their being
satisfied of his intergrity and that he was no disorganizer. His
anger which was very great seemed to be directed chiefly against
Mr Pickering whom he considered as the chief instrument in his
rejection.[7]

I advocated Mr Pickering as a man of the strictest integrity, who
would not I was persuaded do any act which was the least contrary
to his duty. I then proposed that Mr Dayton might be nominated.
No: he would give them an adjutant general; he would immediately nominate Col. North. I said I questioned whether North
would serve, and that others could be found better qualified. He
might refuse if he pleased, that was none of his affair; he would
nominate no other.

The nomination of North was instantly made and concurred in,
and he has accepted of his appointment.[8]

A few days after these transactions the President suddenly left
Philadelphia for Quincy, without apprising either Mr Pickering or
me with the day of his intended departure. Mr Wolcott was absent
in Connecticut.

You will perceive that I consider the impression made upon the

Presidents mind by his disappointment respecting Smith as having influenced it upon other subjects.

With respect to the 2d cause. viz. his considering General Knox intitled to priority of rank to Generals Hamilton or Pinckney.

This has operated very powerfully as an obstructor to all the army arrangement.

Upon contemplating the details for organizing the 12 regiments of Infantry, I found I could not execute them, with a dispatch proportioned to the emergency and to the public expectation, while the President remained at Quincy, unless I adopted a course arising out of that situation. It appeared to me that if I was first to concenter information in this department from all quarters of the United States, there to digest an arrangement to communicate it to the President for his determination, to receive back that determination, and then to transmit the result to the parties, a great and incalculable portion of time must be consumed.

I therefore submitted in a letter to the President under date of the 4th of August ulto what may be resolved into the following propositions.[9]

1st. That the arrangement for the four Eastern States and Vermont should be made out under his immediate direction, commanding the aid if necessary of Major General Knox and Brigadier General Brooks, who reside within these States.

2. That the arrangement for New York, Pennsylvania, New Jersey, Delaware & Maryland should be prepared by myself with the aid of the general officers within these States for his final determination.

3. That the arrangement for the Southern States (including the cavalry) should be made by General Washington, with the like aid of the general officers in that Quarter, subject in like manner to his determination.

4. That four of the 12 regiments should be raised within the States of New Hampshire, Massachusetts, Rhode Island Connecticut and Vermont & Four within the States of New York, New Jersey, Pennsylvania Delaware & Maryland: and four within the States of Virginia, N. Carolina, Tenessee, South Carolina & Georgia.

5. That to facilitate the arrangement I inclosed him a list of all the officers of the late army, in the lines of the five States first mentioned, and also of all the applications for military appointments, by persons within those States which had come to this office.

6. That I submitted as the result of conferences with the Commander in chief and Inspector General, united with my personal knowledge of some of the characters, the following gentlemen of the late army as worthy of consideration for the command of regiments vz. Lemuel Trescot, David Cobb, & William Hall of Massachusetts: Jeremiah Olney, Henry Sherburne & Wm Peck of Rhode Island: Henry Dearborne and Nicholas Gilman of New Hamphire: also Col. Talmadge for adjutant General in the event of the non acceptance of Col. North & Elijah Waldsworth of Litchfield for Major.[10]

7. That he should permit me to call to my aid, the Inspector General, and likewise General Knox, and to charge them with the management of particular branches of the service.

8 That General Washington should be permitted to appoint a Secretary.

The President acknowledges the receipt of this letter of the 4th of August on the 14th of same month.[11]

He signified that its contents are of much importance. Desires that General Washington may consider himself in the public service and authorised to appoint aids and secretaries. Thinks that calling any other general officers into service at the present, will be attended with difficulty unless their rank were first settled. That in his opinion General Knox, is legally intitled to rank next to General Washington, and that no other arrangement will give Satisfaction. That if general Washington is of this opinion, and will consent to it, I may call General Knox and Hamilton into service; and that I might depend upon it the five New England States will not patiently submit to the humiliation that has been meditated for them.

To this I immediately answered on the 22d Augt.[12]

"That after what has passed with, and the conceptions of General Washington respecting the relative grades of Generals Hamilton Pinckney and Knox; the order observed by the President in presenting their names to the Senate and by the Senate in advising to their appointments, I could not help apprehending some disagreeable consequences to the public service should a different relative grade be now known to be *decisively* contemplated. That in submitting this suggestion to his judgement, it was indispensable I should observe, that as well the choice of these gentlemen, as their relative military rank, proceeded originally & exclusively from General Washington, and that I had had no agency direct or indirect, before or while at Mount Vernon, in deciding his mind, either to the choice or the arrangement of the rank of those he had selected. That I had informed him, General Washington made the right to name the general officers and general Staff a condition of his acceptance, and had presented accordingly the Generals list to him on my return. That when the General communicated his choice to me I was aware it might be objected to; but having had difficulties to encounter, and certain impressions to remove, resulting from his not being consulted previously to his nomination, I did not think it prudent to loose the ground he had conceded, or indeed, that I should gain any thing by any effort of mine to persuade him out of his opinions. That I only therefore mentioned to him, what I afterwards found incorporated in his letter to Col. Hamilton vz. that I concurred in his selection of officers; but whatever respected the persons named by him, and their relative rank must finally rest with the President. That the circumstances detailed seemed to require that I should submit to his serious deliberation, whether it was proper or expedient to attempt an alteration in the rank of the gentlemen in question, and if so, whether it would not be better to transfer the decision to others than undertake to determine it himself."

The President on the 29th of August replied.[13] "That my proposition for settling the relative rank of the gentlemen in question was not approved of. That his opinion was, and always had been, that as the law now stands, the order of the nomination or of recording has no weight or effect; but that officers appointed on the same day, in whatever order, have a right to rank according to antecedent services. That he made the nomination according to the list presented to him by me, from General Washington, in hopes that rank might be settled among them by agreement, or acquiescence, beleiving at the same time and expressing to you that belief, that the nomination and appointment would give Hamilton no command at all, nor any rank before any Major General. That this was still his opinion. That he was willing to settle all decisively at present by dating the commissions: Knox on the 1st day, Pinckney on the 2d, and Hamilton on the 3d.["]

"You speak to me, he adds, of the expediency of attempting an alteration of the rank of the gentlemen in question. You know, Sir, that no rank has ever been settled by me. You know my opinion has always been as it is now, that the order of the names in the nomination and record was of no consequence."

"General Washington has through the whole conducted [himself] with perfect honour and consistency. I said and I say now, if I could resign him the office of President I would do it immediately, and with the highest pleasure; but I never said I would hold the office, and be responsible for its exercise, while he should execute it. He has always said in all his letters, that these points must ultimately depend upon the President."

"The power and authority is in the President. I am willing to exert this authority at this moment & to be responsable for the exercise of it. All difficulties will in this way be avoided. But if it is to be refered to General Washington, or to mutual and amicable accommodation among the gentlemen themselves I foresee it will come to me at last, after much altercation and exasperation of passions, and I shall then determine it exactly as I should now, Knox Pinckney & Hamilton."

"There has been too much intrigue in this business both with General Washington and me. If I shall ultimately be the dupe of it I am much mistaken in myself."

To this letter (a part of which being personal, and unmerited, not a little wounded my feelings) I replied on the same day I received it vz. the 6th of Sepr inst.[14]

"I had the honour to receive by this mornings mail your letter dated Quincy Augt 29th ulto. [”]

"In making out the commissions for generals Knox, Pinckney & Hamilton I shall follow the order you prescribe and date General Knox's on the first day, General Pinckney's on the 2d & General Hamiltons on the 3d."

"You observe to me 'There has been too much intrigue in this business, both with General Washington and me. If I shall ultimately be the dupe of it I am much mistaken in myself.[’]"

"Will you excuse the liberty I take in expressing how much I feel affected at this observation, lest you should attach in your mind, any portion of the intrigues, if any have been employed, to me. It will, Sir, be a relief to me, to be ascertained of your opinion in this particular, because I flatter myself I can convince you, that abhorring indirect practices, I never even contemplated any; or should you not be convinced, I can immediately retire from a situation which demands a perfect and mutual confidence, between the President and the person filling it."

I received yesterday the following answer to this letter dated Quincy 13th inst.[15]

"I have received your favour of the sixth and approve of your determination to make out the commissions in the order of Knox on the first day, Pinckney on the second, and Hamilton on the third. This being done you may call Generals Knox & Hamilton into service as soon as you please.["]

"Your request to be informed, whether I attach any portion of the intrigues, which I alluded to, if any have been employed, to you, is reasonable: and I have no scruple to acknowledge, that your conduct through the whole, towards me, has been candid: I have suspected however, that extraordinary pains were taken with you, to impress upon your mind, that the public opinion, and the unanimous wish of the federalists, was that General Hamilton might be first and even commander in chief: that you might express this opinion to General Washington more forcibly than I should have done, and that this determined him to make the arrangement as he did. If this suspicion was well founded I doubt not you made the representation with integrity. I am not and never was of the opinion, that the public opinion demanded General Hamilton for the first, and I am now clear that it never expected or demanded any such thing.["]

"The question being now settled, the responsability for which I take upon myself I have no hard thoughts concerning your conduct in this business, and hope you will make your mind easy concerning it."

["]I have the honour &c.["]

Conceiving the whole of this business of a very serious nature, and intimately connected with the public interest, I communicated the letters from the President to me, as they were received, to Mr Wolcott Mr Pickering & Mr Stoddert, as also my answers to him. The services of General Hamilton being considered too important and consequential to be easily parted with, it was proposed, that they should join in a respectful representation to the President. After however a good deal of deliberation the idea of a joint address was relinquished for a representation from Mr Wolcott alone, who did not appear to be implicated in his suspicions of intrigue. This has been accordingly drawn up and forwarded. It contains the grounds upon which you were induced to expect your arrangement would be adopted, and reasons resulting from the relative talents of the Generals and public opinion.[16]

Thus have the arrangements, for officering the army been delayed and my public duties and private hours embittered and perplexed.

It may be that the President has conceived certain prejudices unfavourable to General Hamilton that has influenced him in the present case; and yet I cannot doubt of his beleiving the public opinion to be what he states it, altho' I have the strongest reasons and proofs to think of it other wise than he does.

Respecting the third cause of delay⟨,⟩ vz. the distance of the President from the seat of Government I need make few or no observations. It has paralized every matter measure and thing appertaining to the new army. It is embarrassing to me and my operations beyond description.

You will perceive that of all the propositions made to the President in my letter of the 4th of Augt ulto he has only signified his concurrence in the one which enabled you to appoint a Secretary, and to my calling in the aid of Generals Hamilton & Knox upon the condition of general Knox being placed first and general Hamilton last in the order of rank; consequently that I am left to conclude, my propositions relative to the mode of ascertaining the fittest characters to be drawn into the army from the different divisions I have described and the proportion of troops to be raised in each division is still under consideration; or from his silence that it is meant I should pursue the accustomed course, and select and forward for his correction & approbation a list for the whole, with all the recommendations for examination.

I do not imagine the latter to be intended, and expect, as soon as the question relative to Hamilton & Knox is finally settled, that I shall receive his orders to proceed agreeable to my first propositions. I may be disappointed. Be this however as it may, I should think it proper, that you should prepare the list of officers for the 4 regiments for the Southern division, and for the 6 additional companies of cavalry, that no time may be lost when his determination is manifested, to obtain his consent to their being commissioned, and to commence the recruiting business.

The annexed copy of a letter to Samuel Hodgdon superintendent of military Stores dated the 25th of Augt will shew you that I have early attended to your request to learn the state of our magazines.[17]

It will also be perceived from the inclosed copy of a letter from the Secry of the treasury to Rufus King what articles we may expect from abroad in all this year. vz. muskets with Bayonets complete to the amount of 35,686£ Stg. From cannon for the naval service to the amount of 6,000£ Stg & even cannon for the land service equal to 4,000£ Stg.[18]

Besides this provision Mr Wolcott has power to contract for the fabrication within the United States of 40,000 stands of arms, and has already closed for about half the number.

In addition, I expect the two arsenals of Springfield and Shanondoah will turn out in the course of next year near 7,000 stands of good muskets.

It is now necessary I should mention to you a difficulty I have to overcome, in which you may assist me, by a strong question to Mr Pickering expressive of your surprise that no steps appear to have been taken to obtain so indispensable an article as clothing for the new army.

Mr Wolcott is of opinion, that the first thing that requires to be attended to, is to fill our magazines with whatever will be necessary and indispensable to the prosecution of a vigorous war. In this I fully agree with him. He thinks also that to raise the army, or any part of it at this time will be to incur an expence without any adequate advantage. That the enemy knowing our magazines to be filled with every thing necessary to carry on war, will produce upon them, for a time at least the same effect, as if we were to add to our stores an army ready disciplined for military operations. Further that the appointment of the officers, and putting them in a situation to commence inlistments upon as it were a given signal, will be all that the present situation of things absolutely requires. That by following this course we shall husband our means and keep them up for emergencies.

I consider all this, except what respects filling our magazines with munitions of war as idle theory. I have before observed that I hold it proper we should exert ourselves to fill our magazines with the most essential military articles to the extent of our means: but as neither officers nor soldiers can be created in a day, I hold it to be no less necessary, threatened as we are, to prepare an army, by discipline, to meet such an enemy as we are likely to have to encounter. I should have no confidence in troops suddenly assembled, and cannot think it good policy to depend upon a militia to meet the first operations of an enemy enured to war, and having no better support than such raw troops. We ought not, I beleive, in case of an invasion to the Southward, calculate upon drawing militia from the Eastern States to assist in subduing it; but we may avail ourselves of the regular troops raised there, for that service. If therefore our army is not to be inlisted, until the approach of an enemy, or that we received certain information from Europe of preparations for the embarkation of one, the defence of the Southern States may be left intirely to its own militia, and half the Country be overrun and plundered before any thing like a regular force can be collected and disciplined for action. But it is needles to mention such reasons to you. These and many others are too much impressed on your mind by past experience to require any commentary.

Mr Wolcott, I suspect, is somewhat alarmed about the means, and may think it safe to trust a good deal to the chapter of chances than hazard any serious draughts upon the latter to pay and support an army that may never be wanted. In order to give him a distinct view of the extent of the calls of my department, I made out at his instance the inclosed table which I communicated to him. I beleive it contains a tolerably correct exhibit of the sums I may want besides shewing the objects for, and the periods at which, the money will be wanted. I add also to this table a copy of my letter which accompanied it. What impression will result I know not.[19]

These things my dear and revered Sir, are mentioned, to satisfy your solemn and affecting inquiries. You will now see, (altho' I may not have apprised you of all my proceedings) the reasons, in the very nature of the transactions just detailed, which have prevented me from making to you certain communications until they became unavoidable and necessary as well for your information as my justification. You will also be sensible, that I have not been idle nor inattentive to the importance of the objects which interest our country, and has drawn you into your present situation. with the most ardent and affectionate regards I am my dear General ever yours

James McHenry

ALS, DLC:GW; ADf, MdAA. McHenry had not completed this letter when he wrote to GW on 21 Sept., and GW did not receive it until 28 September (GW to McHenry, 1 Oct.).

1. Congress had provided for the formation of the twelve additional regiments of the New Army in an act of 16 July 1798 (1 *Stat.*, 604–5). For McHenry's ideas concerning the arrangement of these forces, see notes 1 and 2 to his letter to GW of 8 August. For descriptions of the New Army and the proposed Provisional Army, see McHenry to GW, 3 July 1798, n.1.

2. GW's letter to John Adams accepting conditionally the commission as lieutenant general and commander in chief of the army is dated 13 July 1798. The "paper signed" by GW is printed above as Suggestions for Military Appointments, 14 July.

3. See GW to Alexander Hamilton, 14 July. McHenry may have secured a copy of this letter while at Mount Vernon.

4. See James McHenry to GW, 18 July, and note 4 of that document. Jonathan Dayton (1760–1824) of Elizabethtown, N.J., served in the Revolutionary War, rising to the rank of captain in the Continental army. He was a delegate from New Jersey to the Federal Constitutional Convention in 1787. A prominent Federalist, from 1791 to 1799 he was a member of the House of Representatives, in which he served two terms as speaker. Although he was never brought to trial, his political career came to an end after he was charged in 1807 with conspiring with Aaron Burr to commit treason.

5. John Sevier (1745–1815) of Tennessee contributed to the victory of King's Mountain in 1780 and had since gained notoriety as an Indian fighter. He was the first governor of Tennessee, serving from 1796 to 1801 and 1803 to 1809. Anthony Walton White (1750–1803) of New Jersey served as a lieutenant colonel of Continental Dragoons in the Revolutionary War, an appointment he had obtained with GW's assistance. In 1797 he became surveyor of the port and inspector of revenue for New Brunswick, New Jersey. For GW's involvement in the dispute regarding Sevier and White, see McHenry to GW, 18 July, n.3, and 14 Sept., GW to McHenry, 22 July, n.3, GW to Timothy Pickering, 9 Sept., n.2, and Sevier to GW, 25 Dec. 1798.

6. In an act of 28 May 1798 (1 *Stat.* 558–61), amended 22 June (1 *Stat.* 569–70), Congress provided for a Provisional Army of 10,000 men to be raised only in the event of a declaration of war against the United States or an actual or imminent invasion. See also McHenry to GW, 3 July, n.1.

7. See McHenry to GW, 18 July, n.4. In a letter to McHenry of 15 October, GW expressed his high opinion of William Stephens Smith's military abilities and mentioned him as a possible candidate for command of one of the twelve additional regiments authorized by the act of 16 July. Smith's financial affairs came up for renewed discussion in GW's meetings with Alexander Hamilton and Charles Cotesworth Pinckney in Philadelphia in November and December, however, creating doubts in GW's mind as to Smith's integrity (see GW to McHenry, 13 Dec. [second letter], and note 2 of that document). McHenry explained John Adams's views of Smith's affairs in a letter to GW of 28 Dec. and wrote again on 5 Jan. 1799 that Smith's nomination had been "concurred in."

8. Timothy Pickering expressed his opinion of the relative abilities of William North (1755–1836) of New York and Jonathan Dayton in his second letter to GW of 1 Sept., to which GW replied on 9 September. See also John Adams to GW, 9 October.

9. This letter is in MHi-A.

10. See GW's Suggestions for Military Appointments of 14 July, where all of these names appear except for William Hall, Henry Dearborne (1751–1829), Nicholas Gilman (1755–1814), and Elijah Wadsworth (1746/7–1817).

11. This letter is in DLC: McHenry Papers.

12. This letter, misdated 20 Aug., is in MHi-A.

13. This letter is in MHi-A.

14. This letter is in MHi-A.

15. This letter is in DLC: McHenry Papers.

16. See GW to McHenry, 16 Sept., n.3.

17. An extract from this letter is in DLC:GW. It reads: "I have written this day to Lieutenant General Washington as follows, 'In order that you may understand the state of our military stores I have directed the Superintendant to furnish you with a detailed account of the same, our Brass and Field Artillery Muskets Gun powder &c.' It will therefore be necessary that you make out with accuracy such an account as I have promised and as promptly as possible." See McHenry to GW, 16 November (second letter).

18. A copy of the letter from Oliver Wolcott, Jr., to Rufus King, dated 3 July, is in DLC:GW.

19. A copy of McHenry's letter to Wolcott, dated 3 Sept., is in DLC:GW. The table that accompanied this letter has not been found.

From John C. Ogden

Sir   Septr 20th 1798

More than ten years have elapsed, since from time to time, I have most respectfully and circumstantially, stated the doings of Calvinists in The United States, in their concerted endeavors to defeat that liberty, toleration and protection in religion, which our laws establish, and upon which our national honor, happiness and safety depend.[1]

The moderation, caution, prudence, polite & respectful attention paid by you, and other leaders of every faith (except the Calvinists) to our religious rights, have been abused and perverted by this party, to the purposes of sacrilege, infidelity and sedition.

These assertions are serious and true. The Church in every part of The States, has been pillaged. Laws exist in the northern and eastern States, which subvert universal toleration and safety.

Colleges endowed, founded, and supported by all denominations and from public money, are seized upon, for the private purposes of ambitious men.

Prejudices are circulated from Colleges and pulpits, which constantly excite feuds, and perpetuate usurpations.

Concerts of prayer, missions, and projects to urge on the millenium, are improved and abused, by ecclesiastical tyrants.

To obtain this system, the Calvinists opposed Great Britain, thirty years ago. To secure it since our establishing of independence, the late peace, and a new government, all the artillery of prejudice, misrepresentation—pulpits, colleges and confederations of Calvinists have been directed.

The world will look to all conscientious christians and churchmen to decide whether these things are proper. Printed statements have been circulated, which may be confirmed by public records.

As a professor of christianity, and a churchman, Your Excellency can decide, whether you embarked in the revolution to give undue power to any body of men, over the consciences of your self or others. Whether you expected or can justify the plunderings of the church, the usurpations of the colleges and the injuries done from thence, to the community to which you belong, or the families of these whose fathers, brothers, & sons fell in the late war.

During life, and after death, your contemporaries and our posterity will seek for General Washingtons opinions and procedure, after these wrongs. In them are contained perpetual sources for feuds and confusions.

It is not decent for us to solicit your opinion. It would however gratify the church and your countrymen to have it. In civil office, your influence and safety would have been in danger. But at the head of a new army, or as a private man, the opportunity now presents for you to speak.

Death and the world where justice reigns are fast approaching. No duty can be more worthy of your attention than this, while heaven lengthens out your valuable life. Copies of this letter will be forwarded without delay to Presidents Adams & Jefferson, to the Governors of the States, and heads of literary, ecclesiastical and other departments.

Those who have been honored by you in war and in civil stations, with proofs of distinguished politeness, confidence, and partiality, have been the chief agents in these nefarious procedures. These usurpations and their abettors are too publicly known to be forgotten, and too many in every part of the States, are selecting every ⟨occurence⟩ for the records of historians, for us to expect that such transactions will pass into oblivion, or such practices be viewed as harmless and inoffensive. With the highest veneration for my country's guardian and friend I have the honor to be your devoted servant

John C. Ogden

ALS, DLC:GW.

John Cosens Ogden (1751–1800) was an Episcopal clergyman in Portsmouth, N.H., from 1786 until his retirement in 1797, after his mind had become "deranged" (Harrison, *Princetonians, 1769–1775,* 93–97).

1. Between 30 Oct. 1789 and 26 Nov. 1796 Ogden wrote to GW nine times. He resumed writing to GW on 4 Sept. 1798 and continued writing to him until June 1799. Tobias Lear's acknowledgment on 4 Feb. 1790 of Ogden's letter of 20 Jan. 1790 is the only response to any of Ogden's letters that has been found. Ogden's letter to GW of 4 Sept. 1798 begins: "How far you ever condescend to second such requests as the following to Governor Jay, I cannot tell. If it is consistent with your line of proceeding I know that I have only to hint at the favor." Ogden followed this with a copy of his letter of the same date to Gov. John Jay of New York. Ogden asked Jay to help him secure the post of collector of the customs at New Haven, Conn., upon the fast approaching death of the present collector. For good measure, Ogden enclosed in his letter to GW of 4 Sept. copies of two other letters that he had written to Jay, one dated 17 Aug. and the other 29 Aug. 1798. On 1 Nov. Ogden wrote GW about the recent struggle of the Episcopalians in New Hampshire and Vermont with the "Calvinists," and then on 12 Feb. 1799 he wrote from "Prison" in Litchfield, Connecticut. It was Oliver Wolcott, Jr., he wrote, who had "cast" him into prison "for a small sum due honestly to him." Wolcott had done this, Ogden explained, because he wished to have the post of New Haven collector of the customs, to which Ogden aspired, for a relative and also because Wolcott had "joined with the church plunderers in Portsmouth to destroy" him. In his final two letters to GW, dated 13 May and 17 June 1799, Ogden wrote about his continued persecution and the continuing misdeeds of the Calvinists. Ogden's letters to GW are in DLC:GW.

From James McHenry

(Confidential)

My dear Sir   Trenton [N.J.] 21 Sepr 1798

I received your letter of the 16 inst. yesterday evening. I thought it of consequence to make another effort, and acquaint the President with a part of its contents, in aid of the representation signed by Mr Wolcott, and to lose no time in conveying it to him. Inclosed is the copy of what I have which you will be pleased to return. I rejected on consideration that part which is crossed. 1st because it was only a repetition and elucidation of my proposition before submitted to him and rejected and 2d because I am of opinion he ought decisively to support your arrangement against General Knox's pretensions.[1]

I began yesterday a long letter which I do not believe I shall be able to finish to day.[2] It will explain the causes which have delayed the public service, and contain the particulars required by your letter of the 14th inst.

I shall also send you with this detail a copy of the letter written by me to the President from Mount Vernon, and copy of his instruction⟨s⟩ to me.[3]

With respect to the representation to the President. It was concluded, as the President had expressed suspicions which might affect either Mr Pickering or myself or both, that it would have a better effect, coming from Mr Wolcott alone, who had been absent from the seat of government part of the time to which the suspicion of intrigue could apply. It was accordingly signed by him.

Will it be amiss to send me in a distinct letter that part of yours of the 16th inst. which I have quoted?[4]

I still count upon the Presidents acting wisely and yielding. He has shewn great obstinacy but I think he cannot resist the display of facts which have been laid before him in the representation aided as they will be by your letter. Mr Pickering I beleive intends to transmit to you its substance. If he does not I shall obtain a copy and forward it. Yours ever and affectionately

James McHenry

ALS, DLC:GW; ADf, MdAA; copy, DLC: Hamilton Papers.

1. McHenry's letter to Adams, dated 21 Sept., quotes the third (beginning with the words "I can perceive") and fourth paragraphs of GW's letter to McHenry of 16 September (MHi-A). See GW to McHenry, 16 Sept., n.3.

2. McHenry dated his "long letter" 19 September. See the source note to that letter.

3. See GW to McHenry, 16 Sept., nn.2 and 4.

4. Instead of doing this, GW chose to write himself to John Adams. See GW to Adams, 25 September.

From Bushrod Washington

My dear Uncle   Richmond Septr 21 1798

I have lately recieved a letter from Mr Thomas Turner of King George, in which he expresses an ardent desire to enter into the service of his Country in the military line, and requests that I would mention him to you. This I do with much pleasure, because a long and intimate acquaintance with him assures me that there are few candidates who can possess more worth than he does. Warmly and I believe sincerely attached to the Government, he feels all that indignation which an American ought to feel against the unjust & unprovoked aggressions of our enemy. He possesses an extremely good understanding, and in point of bravery, I believe few, if any exceed him. He was one of those who marched to the westward against the insurgents; upon the termination of that service, he recieved a commission from the Commander in chief, and annexed himself to the fœderal army where he did duty for twelve months. Since that time, he has recieved a Commission from the Governor of this state. In the different stations in which he has been placed, I have always understood that his conduct has been unexceptionable. His wish is to be appointed a Captain in the Cavalry, or major in the infantry, of the 10.000 establishment. I am informed, that he will be highly recommended to you by others.[1]

Permit me now my dear Uncle, to remind you of Capt. Black-burne's application about which something was said when I was at Mount Vernon. At his request I had taken the liberty of mentioning his wishes to Mr Chs Lee, who was kind enough to communicate them to the Secretary at War. His motive for desiring an appointment in the infantry is, that he may have it in his power to render more essentiel services to his Country than he could do in the artillery, and where he might at the same time have an opportunity of discharging his duty with more credit to himself. In his present station, a Scientific knowledge of engineering is essentiel; in the service he solicits, he supposes himself competent to the discharge of the duties annexed to it. Another thing is, that a bilious habit which he unfortunately possesses is badly suited to the unhealthy air of Norfolk. Intimately acquainted with the many good qualities which he possesses believing that he will make a valuable officer, I shall be very happy if you should deem it proper to grant his request.[2]

I am happy to inform you that Genl Marshall has declared himself for this district and that his prospects at this time are as flattering as we would wish; I mean as to the principal County about which any apprehensions were entertained. So far as we have heard from the more distant Counties, we have no reason to fear for his success.[3] I am my dear Uncle Yr Affect. Nephew

Bushrod Washington

ALS, PPRF.

1. Thomas Turner (1772–1839) was justice of King George County in 1798 and a member of the House of Delegates from that county from 1798 to 1799. He appears on the list of Candidates for Army Appointments from Virginia, November 1798, printed below. Although he was eventually offered a commission as captain in the 7th Infantry Regiment, Turner's preference for the cavalry led him to decline the offer. His continuing attempts, with the help of GW and Bushrod Washington, to secure an appointment in the cavalry proved to be of no avail. See Bushrod Washington to GW, 10 April 1799, GW to Bushrod Washington, 5 May 1799, and source note, and GW to James McHenry, 6 June 1799, and note 8 of that document.

2. See GW's reply of 31 December. Richard Scott Blackburn (c.1760–1805) of Prince William County served in the Corps of Artillerists and Engineers during the Revolutionary War. He was a member of the Virginia legislature from 1790 to 1791 and was commissioned a captain of artillery in 1794. See his entry in the List of Candidates for Army Appointments from Virginia, November 1798, printed below.

3. See John Marshall to GW, 8 Jan. 1799, n.3, 1 May 1799, and GW to Marshall, 5 May 1799.

From Thomas Law

Dear Sir—   [22 September 1798]

Unless you are irrevocably fix'd, as the Lots are so nearly equal in respect to prospect & nature of the ground permit me to observe that a House in the South Lot will rent better & promote the object you have in view more [1]—Vizt the encouragemt of accomodations for Congress, as it will be forming an Avenue by cooperating in building & all the digging will be for public improvement— If you purchase Mr Carrolls Lot[2] of 52 by 100 at 8 Cents it will amt to $ 416
and the Commsrs at 10 to   520
                        Dollars $ 936

now the rent of mine will be 30$ Dollars ℔ annum you being liable for taxes &ca.[3]

Pardon this intrusion which I make that by Houses being together Society may be promoted & others encouraged to join—If *upon my honor* I was not *convinc'd* that the S[ou]th is more valuable than the other & that your House would rent better there— I would not write this altho' my desires are strongly in favor of your fixing in the ⟨N.⟩J. Avenue. Persons doing business on the E. Branch may Lodge in the House on the S[ou]th Lot but not on the N[or]th Lot—a neighborhood raises the value of property, & it is an object to build where a neighborhood will soonest be & pavement lights &ca & to fill up between the Harbor & Capitol. With every apology I remain with sincere esteem & affec. yr mo. obt

T. Law

ALS, DLC:GW.

1. The "South Lot" to which Law is referring probably is the one on Pennsylvania Avenue which Alexander White recommended to GW in his letter of 8 September. Thomas Law may well have accompanied GW when he viewed the available lots near the Capitol on 21 September. See White to GW, 8 Sept., n.1

2. For GW's purchase of Daniel Carroll's lot, see District of Columbia Commissioners to GW, 27 September.

3. See GW's references to the house that Law was building for rental on Capitol Hill in GW to District of Columbia Commissioners, 4 October.

From Alexander Spotswood

dear Sir   Newpost Setpr 23d 1798.

My last—dated I think on the 16—informed you, that my overseer had accepted your Terms—but that he Should Take the farm in preference to the home house—should Rhodes decline Takeing yr bussiness—From Whoom I have recd no answer to my Several letters, the first of which I am certain was lodged at his house—Consequently you had better look out—but should Rhodes come to my house, or write me after to day; and incline to go into your employ—I will then engage him Conditionally, provided you are not Supplied—and write you—Thomas Brooks the Joiner was with me yesterday—I gave him a letter—and you may expect him at Mt Vernon, on the 3d of October.[1]

Since my last—I have recollected a Mr Stith who Served in the revolutionary war—at the end of which I beleive he retired with the Rank of Majr. However, yr list will tell his grade—I know Nothing of his Military Talents—but have heard him Spoken of well as an officer—I am equally a Stranger to his political Sentiments—but Mr Lawrance Washington of choptank, who I know is, and has been a steady goverment man—assures me that Mr Stith has been uniformly, a constant & Steady frd to goverment—he is now I think about 42 yrs of age—& a Sensible genteel Man.[2] My family are all in Orange & well—I hope your health Continues. Present me Sr Respectfully to Mrs Washington Miss Custis &c. and belive me very devotedly yr sincere & afft. obt st

A. Spotswood

ALS, DLC:GW.

1. See Spotswood to GW, 30 Aug., n.3, and 11, 16 September.

2. John Stith (1755–1808) of Brunswick County served as a captain during the Revolutionary War and was brevetted major in 1783. He appears on the List of Candidates for Army Appointments from Virginia, November 1798, printed below.

To Alexander Hamilton

Private

My dear Sir,   Mount Vernon 24th Sep. 1798.

I have seen the correspondence between the President of the United States & Secretary of War, on the subject of the relative rank of the three Major Generals first appointed. But as it was given in confidence, unaccompanied with an Official letter, I had no ground on which I could proceed, without betraying that confidence.[1] I have therefore written for an official account of the President's determination, as the foundation of the representation I propose to offer him, on this occasion.[2]

Until the result of this is known, I hope you will suspend a final decision, and let matters remain in Statu quo till you hear again from Your Affectionate

Go: Washington

ALS, DLC: Hamilton Papers; ALS (letterpress copy), DLC:GW.

1. James McHenry sent the correspondence to GW on 10 September. See notes 1 and 2 to that document; see also McHenry to GW, 19 September.

2. See GW to McHenry, 26 September.

To Alexander Spotswood

Dear Sir   Mount Vernon 24th Sep. 1798.

As the Season is far advanced for *good* Overseers to be disengaged, and as you had heard nothing from Richard Rhodes at the date of your last—Septr the 16th—and a Man in your neighbourhood one —— Garrett Overseer for a Mr Fontain Murray at a ⟨place⟩ called White Plains near Fredericksburgh, has been strongly recommended to me by Mr Betton & others, & who *was* willing to come to me, but informed I was supplied. Now, to avoid further delay I have desired Mr Anderson to write to Garrett, which letter is enclosed, and left open for your perusal; to be sent to him or not, according to the advice you may have received from Rhodes. If the latter declines coming, or requires higher Wages than I mentioned in my last, in that case, you will oblige me by sending Anderson's letter to Garrett—On the other hand, if Rhodes positively accepts, on the terms mentioned, Mr Andersons letter may be destroyed, or returned to me: My object you will readily perceive is to be placed upon a certainty; and as soon as it can be done.[1]

I shall depend upon your Overseer, Roger Farril, for my Mansion house concern; and Brookes the Joiner, to overlook my Carpenters—If you have heard from the latter, since my acceding to his terms, be so good as to let me know at what time I may expect him to be here; as his services, as a Joiner, are immediately necessary. What age do you take him to be?[2]

I thank you for the information you have been so kind as to give me respecting the characters of the Officers in the revolutionary Army; and shall do the same for your characters of the young Gentlemen who have never been in Service & are desirous of it; as it is my wish to see Corps formed of the best materials, but it wd be useless to begin with Gentlemen under age, as I believe it is a rule at the War Office, to Commission none below that—knowingly.

Believing, as I firmly do, that the opposers of Government will stick at nothing to injure it; I can readily conceive the probability of the Plan you have suggested; but I hope, & trust, they will be disappointed in that as they have been in all their other nefarious schemes.

I thank you, and the rest of the family at New Post, for your kind congratulations on my perfect recovery; and we offer ours on the safe arrival of yr Son John, who has so often escaped the fraternal *squeezes* of our *magnanimous friends*—Our best regards are presented to you all—and I am Dear Sir Your Obedt & affecte and obedeient Servt

Go: Washington

P.S. Since writing the aforegoing letter, I have received your favour of the 23d Instt from the Post Office: but the contents thereof rendering no alteration necessary, I send it as it is, with a request, that as you have not heard from Rhodes, that you would be so good, instead of sending the letter of Mr Anderson to Garrett, that you wd send for the latter to come to you, and deliver it yourself—this will enable you to know Garretts determination; without which you would be ignorant, and consequently more at a loss for an answer to Rhodes, if he should come to you *after* Andersons letter goes to Garrett. Whereas, if the latter accepts the offer made him by the former, the matter is finished as it respects Rhodes. On the contrary a conditional agreement with Rhodes & speedy advice thereof to me will bring the affair at once to a point with him. Yours as before. Go: W.

ALS, NIC.

1. For GW's search for an overseer, see Spotswood to GW, 30 Aug., n.3. Fontaine Maury, who lived in Fredericksburg, was a planter in Spotsylvania County. Solomon Betton of Loudoun County, who was married to Lucinda Mercer, the daughter of the late James Mercer of Fredericksburg, owned a farm in Spotsylvania County (Crozier, *Virginia County Records*, 1:473). Anderson's enclosed letter has not been found.

2. See Spotswood to GW, 23 September.

To John Adams

Sir,   Mount Vernon 25th Septr 1798.

    With all the respect which is due to your public station, and with the regard I entertain for your private character, the following representation is presented to your consideration. If in the course of it, any expression should escape me which may appear to be incompatible with either, let the purity of my intentions; the candour of my declarations; and a due respect for my own character, be received as an apology.

The subject on which I am about to address you, is not less delicate in its nature, than it is interesting to my feelings. It is the change which you have directed to be made in the relative rank of the Major Generals, which I had the honor of presenting to you, by the Secretary of War; the appointment of an Adjutant General *after* the first nomination was rejected; and the *prepared* state you are in to appoint a third, if the second should decline, without the least intimation of the matter to me.[1]

It would have been unavailing, *after* the nomination and appointment of me to the Chief command of the Armies of the United States, (without any previous consultation of my sentiments) to have observed to you the delicate situation in which I was placed by that act. It was still less expedient, to have dwelt more than I did, on my sorrow at being drawn from my retirement; where I had fondly hoped to have spent the few remaining years which might be dispensed to me, if not in profound tranquillity, at least without public responsibility. But if you had been pleased, previously to the nomination, to have enquired into the train of my thoughts upon the occasion, I would have told you with the frankness & candour which I hope will ever mark my character, on what terms I would have consented to the nomination; you would then have been enabled to decide whether they were admissible, or not.

This opportunity was not afforded *before* I was brought to public view. To declare them *afterwards*, was all I could do; and this I did, in explicit language, to the Secretary of War, when he honoured me with your letter of the 7th of July; shewed me his powers; and presented the Commission. They were, that the General Officers, and General staff of the Army should not be appointed without my concurrence. I extended my stipulations no farther, but offered to give every information, and render every service in my power in selecting good officers for the Regiments.[2]

It would be tedious to go into all the details which led to this determination; but before I conclude my letter, I shall take the liberty of troubling you with some of them. Previously to the doing of which, however, let me declare, and I do declare, in the most unequivocal manner, that I had nothing more in view in making this stipulation, than to insure the most eligable characters for these highly responsible offices; conceiving that my opportunities, both in the Civil & Military administration of the Affairs of this

Country, had enabled me to form as correct an opinion of them as any other could do.

Neither the Secretary of War, nor myself, entertained any doubt, from your letters to me, and Instructions to him, that this was the meaning and object of his Mission. Unwilling, however, to let a matter of such serious importance to myself remain upon uncertain ground, I requested *that* Gentleman to declare this in *his official letter* to you (supposing, as was the case, that the one I should have the honor of writing to you, might be laid before the Public, and that to incumber it with stipulations of that sort, would be improper). Nay more, as the acceptance was conditional, & you might, or might not be disposed to accede to the terms, I requested him to take the Commission back, to be annulled, or restored, according to your conception of the propriety, or impropriety of them. His remark upon this occasion was, that it was unnecessary, inasmuch as, if you did not incline to accept my services upon the conditions they were offered, you would be under the necessity of declaring it; whilst, on the other hand, silence must be construed into acquiescence. This consideration, and believing that the latter mode would be most respectful, as the other might imply distrust of your intentions, arrested that measure.

This, Sir, is a true, candid & impartial statement of facts. It was the ground on which I *accepted* and *retained* the Commission; and was the authority on which I proceeded to the arrangement that was presented to you by the Secretary of War.

Having *no idea* that the General Officers for the Provisional army would be nominated at that time they were, I had not even contemplated characters for those appointments.[3]

I will now, respectfully ask, in what manner these stipulations on my part, have been complied with?

In the arrangement made by me, with the Secretary of War, the three Major Generals stood—Hamilton, Pinckney, Knox. and in this order I expected their Commissions would have been dated. This, I conceive, must have been the understanding of the Senate. And certainly was the expectation of all those with whom I have conversed. But you have been pleased to order the last to be first, and the first to be last. Of four Brigadiers for the Provisional army, one I never heard of as a Military character, has been nominated and appointed; and another is so well known to all those who served with him, in the Revolution, as (for the appointment) to have given the greatest disgust, and will be the means of preventing many valuable Officers of that army from coming forward.[4] One Adjutant General has been, & another is ready to be appointed in case of the non-acceptance of Mr North, not only without any consultation with me, but without the least intimation of the intention;[5] although in the letter I had the honor to write you on the 4th of July in acknowledgment of your favour of the 22d of June preceeding, and still more strongly in one of the same date to the Secretary of War, which (while here) his Clerk was, I know, directed to lay before you, I endeavoured to shew, in a strong point of view, how all important it was that this officer (besides his other qualifications) should be agreeable to the Commander in Chief, and possess his *entire* confidence. To increase the Powers of the Commander in Chief—or to lessen those of the President of the United States, I pray you to be persuaded, was most foreign from my heart. To secure able Coadjutors in the arduous task I was about to enter upon, was my *sole* aim. This the public good demanded—and this must have been equally the wish of us both. But to accomplish it, required an intimate knowledge of the *componant* parts of the characters among us, in the higher grades of the late army. and I hope (without incurring the charge of presumption) I may add, that the opportunities I have had to judge of these, are second to none. It was too interesting to me, who had staked every thing which was dear & valuable upon the issue, to trust more to chance than could be avoided. It could not be supposed that I was insensible to the risk I was about to run—knowing that the chances of losing, was at least equal to those of encreasing, that reputation which the partiality of the world had been pleased to bestow on me. No one then, acquainted with these circumstances; the sacrafices I was about to make; and the impartiality of my conduct in the various walks of life, could suppose that I had any other object in view than to obtain the best aids the country afforded, & my judgment could dictate.

If an Army had been in actual existence, and you had been pleased to offer the command of it to me, my course would have been plain: I should have examined the Constitution of it; looked into its organization; and enquired into the character of its Officers &ca—As the Army was to be raised, & the Officers to be appointed, could it be expected (as I was no Candidate for the Office) that I would be less cautious, or less attentive to secure these advantages?

It was not difficult for me to perceive that if we entered into a

Serious contest with France, that the character of the War would differ materially from the last we were engaged in. In the latter, time, caution, and worrying the enemy until we could be better provided with arms, & other means, and had better disciplined Troops to carry it on, was the plan for us. But if we should be engaged with the former, they ought to be attacked at every step, and, if possible, not suffered to make an establishment in the Country—acquiring thereby strength from the disaffected and the Slaves, whom I have no doubt they will arm—and for that purpose will commence their operations South of the Potomack.

Taking all these circumstances into view, you will not be surprised at my sollicitude to intrench myself as I did; nor is it to be supposed that I made the arrangement of the three Major Generals without an eye to possible consequences. I wished for time, it is true, to have effected it, hoping that an amicable adjustment might have taken place, & offered, at a very short summons, (inconvenient as it would have been) to proceed to Philadelphia for that purpose; but as no subsequent notice was taken thereof, I presumed there were operative reasons against the measure, and did not repeat it.

It is proper too I should add, that, from the information which I received from various quarters, & through different channels, I had no doubt in my mind that the current sentiment among the members of Congress, and particularly among those from New England, was in favor of Colonel Hamilton's being second in command—and this impression has been since confirmed in the most unequivocal manner by some respectable members of that body, whom I have myself seen & conversed with, on the subject.[6]

But if no regard was intended to be had to the *order* of my arrangement, why was it not altered before it was submitted to the Senate? This would have placed matters upon Simple ground. It would then have been understood as it is at present, namely—that the Gentlemen would rank in the order they were named: but the change will contravene this, and excite much conversation, & unpleasant consequences.

I cannot lay my hand readily upon the resolves of the old Congress, relative to the settlement of Rank between Officers of the same grade, who had been in service & were disbanded, while a part of the Army remained in existance; but if I have a tolerable recollection of the matter, they are totally irrevelent to the present case. Those resolves passed, if I am not mistaken, at a time when the proportion of Officers to men was so unequal as to require a reduction of the former: or when the Army was about to undergo a reduction in part, and the officers might be called upon again.[7] But will a case of this sort apply to Officers of an army which has ceased to exist for more than fourteen years? I give it frankly as my opinion (if I have not entirely forgotten the principle on which the Resolves took place) that they will not: and I as frankly declare, that the only motive I had for examining a list of the Officers of that army, was to be reminded of names. If the rule contended for was to obtain, what would be the consequences, & where would the evil end? In all probability resort will be had to the field Officers of the Revolutionary army to fill similar grades in the augmented, and Provisional Corps which are to be raised. What then is to be done with General Dayton, who never ranked higher than Captain? The principle will apply with equal force in that case as in the case of Hamilton and Knox. The injury (if it is one) of putting a junr over the head of a Senr Officer of the last war, is not ameliorated by the nominations or appointments of them on different days. It is the act itself, not the manner of doing it, that affects.

I have dwelt longer on this point than perhaps was necessary, in order to shew, that in my opinion, former rank in the Revolutionary Army ought to have no influence in the present case, farther than may be derived from superior experience, brilliant exploits, or general celebrity of character. And that, as the Armies about to be raised are commencing de novo, the President has the right to make Officers of Citizens, or Soldiers, at his pleasure; and to arrange them in any manner he shall deem most conducive to the public weal.

It is an invidious task, at all times, to draw comparisons; and I shall avoid it as much as possible; but I have no hesitation in declaring, that if the Public is to be deprived of the Services of Coll Hamilton in the Military line, that the Post he was destined to fill will not be easily supplied; and that this is the sentiment of the Public, I think I can venture to pronounce. Although Colo. Hamilton has never acted in the character of a General Officer, yet his opportunities, as the principal & most confidential aid of the Commander in chief, afforded him the means of viewing every thing on a larger scale than those whose attentions were confined to Divisions or Brigades; who knew nothing of the correspondences of the Commander in Chief, or of the various orders to, or transactions with, the General Staff of the Army. These advantages, and his having served with usefulness in the Old Congress; in the General Convention; and having filled one of the most important departments of Government with acknowledged abilities and integrity, has placed him on high ground; and made him a conspicuous character in the United States, and even in Europe. To these, as a matter of no small consideration may be added, that as a lucrative practice in the line of his Profession is his *most certain* dependence, the inducement to relinquish it, must, in some degree, be commensurate. By some he is considered as an ambitious man, and therefore a dangerous one. That he is ambitious I shall readily grant, but it is of that laudable kind which prompts a man to excel in whatever he takes in hand. He is enterprising, quick in his perceptions, and his judgment intuitively great: qualities essential to a great military character, and therefore I repeat, that his loss will be irrepairable.

With respect to General Knox, I can say with truth, there is no man in the United States with whom I have been in habits of greater intimacy; no one whom I have loved more sincerely; nor any for whom I have had a greater friendship. But, esteem, love & friendship, can have no influence on my mind when I conceive that the subjugation of our Government and Independence, are the objects aimed at by the enemies of our Peace; and when, possibly, our all is at stake.

In the first moments of leisure, after the Secretary of War had left this place I wrote a friendly letter to Genl Knox, stating my firm belief that if the French should invade this country, with a view to conquest, or to the division of it, that their operations would commence to the Southward, and endeavoured to shew him, in that case, how all important it was to engage General Pinckney, his numerous family, friends & influential acquaintance, *heartily* in the cause. Sending him, at the same time, a copy of the arrangement, which I supposed *to be final*; and in a subsequent letter, I gave him my opinion fully with respect to the relative situation of himself & Colo. Hamilton; not expecting, I confess, the difficulties which have occurred.[8]

I will say but little, relatively to the appointment of the Brigadiers before alluded to; but I must not conceal, that after what had passed, and my understanding of the compact, that my feelings were not a little wounded by the appointment of any, much more such characters, with out my knowledge.

In giving these details, I have far exceeded the limits of a letter, but hope to be excused for the prolixity of it. My object has been, to give you a clear and distinct view of my understanding of the terms on which I received the Commission with which you were pleased to honor me.

Lengthy as this letter is, there is another subject, not less interesting to the Commander in Chief of the Armies (be him whom he may) than it is important to the United States, which I beg leave to bring respectfully to your view. We are now, near the end of September, and not a man recruited, nor a Battalion Officer appointed, that has come to my knowledge. The consequence is, that the spirit and enthusiasm which prevailed a month or two ago, and would have produced the *best* men in a short time, is evaporating *fast*, and a month or two hence, may induce but few, and those perhaps of the *worst* sort, to Inlist. Instead therefore of having the augmented force in a state of preparation, and under a course of discipline, it is now to be *raised*; and possibly may not be in existence when the Enemy is in the field: we shall then have to meet veteran Troops, inured to conquest, with Militia, or raw recruits; the consequence of which is not difficult to conceive, or to foretell.

I have addressed you, Sir, with openness & candour—and I hope with respect; requesting to be informed whether your determination to reverse the order of the three Major Generals is final—and whether you mean to appoint another Adjutant General without my concurrence. With the greatest respect & consideration I have the honor to be Sir, Your Most Obedient and Most Humble Servant

Go: Washington

ALS, MHi-A; ALS (letterpress copy), DLC:GW; ADfS, DLC:GW; extract, DLC: Hamilton Papers. GW sent his draft of the letter, which he characterizes as a "rough draught," to James McHenry on 26 September. McHenry returned the draft to GW on 2 Oct. and urged GW to send the letter to Adams, which he did. Adams received the letter in Quincy on 8 Oct. and replied the next day. The draft has many strike-outs and interlineations, all in GW's hand. GW's emendations seem to have been made for the sake of clarity, precision, or nicety of style. Hamilton's clerk, Philip Church, in 1818 wrote below the extract: "copied from the original by myself, at the desire of General Hamilton."

1. For a summary of the controversy over the ranking of the three major generals under GW, see GW to Alexander Hamilton, 14 July, n.5.

2. See GW to Adams, 13 July.

3. For the terms of the acts to create twelve additional regiments for the regular army and to provide for the possible creation of a Provisional Army, see McHenry to GW, 3 July, n.1.

4. GW is referring to John Sevier and Anthony Walton White. See James McHenry to GW, 19 Sept., and note 5 of that document.

5. See McHenry to GW, 19 Sept., and notes 7 and 8 of that document.

6. GW struck out most of his first version of this paragraph.

7. See Timothy Pickering to GW, 18 Sept., and note 4 of that document.

8. GW's letters to Henry Knox are dated 16 July and 9 August.

From Marmaduke Leigh

Sir   Alexandria Sept. 25th 1798

I am told you wish to dispose of your Lands on the ohio river in the State of Virginia, I would willingly become a purchaser of a tract of your Land, particularly that tract below the Little Kenhawa river.

Should the price and terms of payment suit me, As I am acquainted with the quality of your Lands on the ohio river, If you will Let me know your price and the terms of payment I will Let you know if it will Suit me to become a purchaser.[1] I have the honour to be Sir your most obedient Servant

Marmaduke Leigh

ALS, DLC:GW.

1. Marmaduke Leigh has not been identified, and no response to this letter has been found.

To James McHenry

Private

My dear Sir,   Mount Vernon 26th Sepr 1798.

Your confidential letter of the 21st instant is before me; but the long letter which is promised therein, has not got to hand. Probably the messenger who carries this, and other letters to the Post Office this afternoon, may return with it.[1]

As you have given extracts of my letter of the 16th to the President, & informed him, that you thought it necessary to apprise me of his seeming determination, relatively to the rank of Major

Generals Hamilton & Knox, I conceived I had sufficient ground to proceed upon; and have, accordingly, in a letter of yesterday's date, given him my ideas in a lengthy detail, on the *whole* of that *business*; that I may know at *once*, & *precisely*, what I have to expect.[2]

The rough draught of it I send for your perusal,[3] but with express desire that the contents may not be devulged, unless the result should make it necessary for me to proceed to the final step. You will readily perceive, that even the *rumour* of a misunderstanding between the President & me, while the breach can be repaired, would be attended with unpleasant consequences. If there is no disposition on his part to do this, the Public must decide which of us is right, and which wrong.

I thought it best to communicate my ideas to the President on this subject as soon as I had ground to act upon; it being easier, at all times, to prevent an evil, than to provide a remedy for it.

The draught of my letter to the President you will please to return. I shall say nothing more, until I receive the letter you have promised; except that I am always Your affecte Servant

Go: Washington

ALS, LNHT: George and Katherine Davis Collection; ALS (letterpress copy), DLC:GW; copy, DLC: Hamilton Papers.

1. This is McHenry's letter of 19 September.
2. GW's letter to John Adams is dated 25 September.
3. See the source note to GW to Adams, 25 September.

To Benjamin Stoddert

Sir,   Mount Vernon, Septr 26th 1798.

It will afford me pleasure to give you any information in my power, and any opinion, so far as I am able to form one, on the subject of your letter of the 16th instant; which did not come to my hands till the 24th.

I cannot entertain a doubt, but it will be the policy of this Country to create such a navy as will protect our commerce from the insults and depredations to which it has been subjected of late, and to make it duly respected. To effect this, there must be, as you observe, at least one navy Yard established for building Ships. That this should be under the Eye of the Government, and as near the Centre of the United States as it can be fixed, with equal advantages to the whole of the Community, I think no one will deny.

Whether or not the States to the northward of the Potomac are able to supply timber for Ship-building in such quantities—of such quality, and upon such terms as may be desireable, is more than I can tell. But I will venture to say, that no place, either north or south of this, can be more effectually secured against the attack of an Enemy; and that the Banks and vicinity of this River, both above and below tide water, abound with the best of Ship timber, is well known. Whenever the Navigation above tide water shall be completed (which I trust will be at no very distant period) there will be opened, not only an inexhaustible store of timber for building; but an abundant supply of the largest and best white pine trees for masts of any dimensions, as there are extensive forests of them about the head of the Potomac. Besides which, no part of the United States affords better Cedar & Locust than the Lands about this River. You know that Iron of the best quality can be furnished from the works on the River, and as cheap as from any part of the United States; and the establishment of a public foundery and Armory at the junction of the Potomac and Shanandoah, will afford no small advantage in arming the Ships.

The articles of Tar, Pitch, live Oak &c. can be brought here *at least* upon as good terms as to any place north of this: And if hemp, cordage &c. are to be imported, they can certainly come here as readily as to any other part of the United States. But, should hemp be furnished from our own lands, (which is very desireable) this River is the Market to which it would be most likely to be brought in the greatest abundance; for, to say nothing of the rich bottoms on this River and its branches, which are exceedingly well calculated for raising hemp, it is so valuable an article that it will bear transportation across the Allegany from the rich lands of the Ohio, where it can, and undoubtedly will be produced in large quantities.

With respect to security against the attacks of an Enemy, no place can have advantages superior to the Federal City and Alexandria. Should proper works be erected on Diggs' point (which you well know) at the junction of the Potomac and Piscatiqua Creek,[1] it would not be in the power of all the navies in Europe to pass that place, and be afterwards in a situation to do mischief above; for every vessel, in passing up the River, must, from the course of the channel, (and the Channel is so narrow as to admit but of one Vessel's going abreast) present her bows to that point long before she comes within gun-shot of it, and continue in that direction until she comes directly under the point, from whence shot may be thrown upon her deck almost in a perpendicular direction. Should she be so fortunate as to pass the works, she must expose her stern to the fire from them, as far as a shot can reach. Thus exposed to be raked fore and aft, for such a distance, without once being able to bring her broad side to bear upon the Fort, you can readily see how almost impossible it will be for a vessel to pass this place; provided it be properly fortified and well supplied. And what makes it the more important, is, that it cannot be attacked by land with any prospect of success; for it has the River on one side—Piscataqua Creek on another side (each nearly a mile wide) and the opposite Banks very low—a very deep Ravine (level with the Creek) on the third side from whence the height is almost, if not altogether inaccessable—and a very narrow approach on the fourth side. In a word, the works might be insulated—and one range of batteries over another constructed sufficient for an hundred or more pieces of Cannon.

Another advantage which this River affords is, that altho' the distance, in the course of the River, from its mouth to the Federal City, is between 150 and 200 miles; yet, from the heights about Cedar point (say Laidler's Ferry)² no vessel can enter the River undiscovered—and by means of Signals established on the prominent Eminencies, between that place and the site just mentioned, and the Federal City, notice thereof, and of the number & description of the Vessels, may be conveyed to those places in a few minutes. Besides, there are not many winds, I beleive, that will serve Vessels the whole distance.

How far the place marked out in the plan of the Federal City, for a Marine Hospital, may be eligible for a Navy Yard, either from its situation or extent, I am unable to say. From your Knowledge and information on this subject you are better able to judge than I am. But that Locks or dry Docks, for building or repairing Ships, are essential to a Navy Yard, is certain; and there is no doubt but abundance of Water, to supply such, may be had from the Streams which you mention: and I think it is by no means chimerical to say, that the water of the Potomac may, and will be brought from above the Great Falls into the Federal City, which would, in future, afford an ample supply for this Object.

But, after enumerating all the superior advantages which this

River offers for the establishment of a Navy-Yard, every thing will depend upon the depth of water; and this is so important a point, that an accurate examination of it should be made, and no reliance placed on vague information.

Should it not be found sufficient for Ships of the Line fully armed & provisioned, might not some measures be taken to deepen the Channel over the bar at Maryland point, the only place, I am told, that requires it? Or, might not a Naval Arsenal, or a depôt for provisions, be established, with security, below the shallow parts of the River, where the Ships might arm or take in their provisions? These, however, are mere suggestions, which may, or may not be worth attending to.

I thank you, Sir, for the good wishes you express for my health, which I most sincerely reciprocate, and beg you to be assured that I am, with great respect & esteem, Your most Obedient Servant

Go: Washington

LS, CtHi; Df, partly in GW's hand, DLC:GW.

1. Presumably GW is referring to Piscataway Creek, which enters the Potomac from Maryland, just south of what is now Fort Washington.

2. Lower Cedar Point in Charles County, Md., is across the Potomac River from Colonial Beach, Va., and about twenty miles south of Port Tobacco, Maryland. John Laidler's ferry near here dated from 1755 and was the most important river crossing of that region of the Potomac.

From Charles Carter

My dear Sir,   Fauquier, Septr 27th 1798

When we set out for the upper Country, Mrs Carter and I indulged the pleasing Thoughts of paying our respects to the good people of Mount Vernon before we return'd to the Place of small Comfort, but Alas, How often are our most sanguine Hopes, Inclinations and Expectations baffled and prove abortive—an unlucky accident which you have heard of, has deprived us of that pleasure, and very nearly taken from me an affectionate Wife—God be praised, the good Woman is now out of danger, and I flatter myself a little more time with proper care will restore her to her usual good state of health.

I need not request of you my dear Sir, to believe me, when I say, the information we recieved of your late Indisposition depress'd our Spirits, and that the Intelligence of your recovery had the contrary effect. Taking this for granted—I desire the favour of you to present me very respectfully to Mrs Washington, and assure her, that I most sincerely congratulate and rejoice with Her upon the happy Occasion—and that it may please Heaven to prolong your Life to a very late period with that strength of Mind and Health of Body you have hitherto enjoyed, is my ardent prayer, and this I beg, not altogether for the sake of your Family—Friends and Connexions, but also for the Good of our Country.[1] Your affectionate humble Servant

Chars Carter

ALS, NjMoNP.

1. GW replied on 25 Oct.: "My dear Sir, Your kind and obliging favor of the 27th Ulto has been received.

"It would have made Mrs Washington and myself very happy to have seen you & Mrs Carter at this place; and in addition to the concern we felt from the disappointment, the cause of it was sincerely regretted. But it is a pleasure to us, to learn from yourself, that you were well, and Mrs Carter in a fair way of having her usual health restored to her. On this happy occasion we sincerely congratulate you, & her.

"I have abundant reason to be thankful for my own recovery. My fever, though not of more than four or five days continuance was severe. It deprived me of 20 lbs. of my weight; which, by this time, is, I believe, nearly restored. We hope your journey to Shirley added nothing to Mrs Carter's indisposition—present the compliments of this family to her in respectful terms. Accept them yourself—and believe me to be always—Your Sincere frd and affecte Hble Servant Go: Washington" (ALS, ViMtV). Nowhere in his surviving diaries does GW record a visit to Mount Vernon from his old friend Charles Carter of Corotoman and Shirley and his second wife, Anne Butler Moore Carter.

From the District of Columbia Commissioners

Sir, Washington, 27th September 1798

We do ourselves the pleasure of enclosing you the number of square feet contained in your two purchases made of the public and Mr Carroll.[1] We received Mr Carroll's answer in writing, on the monday after you left the City, giving his full consent to confirm the Sale of the Lot on the terms proposed, and promising to execute the proper conveyance in the course of the present Week. It may be well to forward a Check to cover the purchase made of him, as his receipt will be requisite to the validity of the Deed⟨.⟩ We enclose a copy of the entry of your purchase made of us.[2]

Mr Blagdin has not yet brought forward his Estimates, but will probably do so in a day or two. If his terms are thought just and reasonable, we will have a proper Contract drawn and forwarded to you for your signature. We have the honor to be, with sentiments of perfect regard and respect, Sir, Yr Mo. Obt Servts

Gusts Scott
William Thornton
Alexr White

LS, DLC:GW.

1. This enclosure reads:

Lot no. 16 square 634	5,357 Sqr. feet
Lot no. 6 purchased from Danl Carroll Esqr. of Duddn	5,355

2. The enclosed extract of the commissioners' minutes, dated 25 Sept., is quoted at length in Alexander White to GW, 8 Sept., n.1.

From Alexander Spotswood

Dear Sir   Fredericksburg Septr 27 1798

Mr Peter favoured me with his Company at Newpost last Tuseday evening; and delivered me your letter of the 24th; with one Inclosed from Mr Anderson to garret; an overseer now in the employ of Mr Fontaine Maury. which letter I forwarded the next day, and this morning had an interview with Garret—he would not determine whether to receive your offer or not until he returned home and Consulted his *wife*—and in the evening, he Says he will return to town & write Mr Anderson—but observed, that should he agree to take your business; you must be at the expence of moving him up—(the distance will be about 60 miles, 120 going and comeing).

This man having no connections in these parts, and having the character of a good overseer—he engaged with me in presence of his present employer—but in a few days he declared of[f]—in Short his coming to you will depend on his wife—and shd She put in her Negative, it is doubtful whether he will write Anderson.

Therefore to keep you from a State of incertitude—I thought it best to write you the Above for fear garret should fail giving Anderson an Answer. Present me Respectfully to Mrs Washington, Miss custis & I am dr Sir Yr Obt Affect. Hble St

A. Spotswood

ALS, ViMtV.

To William Washington

Dear Sir,   Mount Vernon 27 Sep. 1798

Late this afternoon Major Simons presented me with your letter of the 22d of July; and anxious to proceed on his journey, proposes to continue it in the morning early: this allows me but little time to say any thing, when I wished to have said a great deal to you.[1]

I have never yet heard whether you have accepted, or declined, your late appointment. The crisis is important, and if the French persevere in their inequitious and nefarious plans; the friends to the Government & Constitution of this Country however desirous they may be of retirement, will be *obliged* to come forward, and it is better to do it in the first instance, under advantages, than in the hour of necessity, when there is no alternative. This consideration, accompanying my wishes, induce me to hope that I shall see you as a Coadjuter in the Field.

It is to me, a matter of sore regret that the Recruiting service has not commenced, and more astonishing yet, that the Regimental Officers for the Augmented Corps are not appointed.

It has been said (but on what authority I am unable to inform you) that the twelve Regiments, under the Act for augmenting the force of the United States, will be proportioned among them; whereof Virginia, the two Carolinas, Georgia, Tennessee & Kentucky, will be called upon for four; & perhaps the additional Troops of Cavalry. If this plan should be adopted, I presume each of these states will be called upon for a certain part. I do not mean that the *authority* of the State will be required to furnish them— but that, so many Men will be recruited in each, & furnish Officers in proportion thereto.

To you, I need not remark how all important it is, to get well known & well tried Officers in the several grades—or if that cannot be accomplished—to obtain Gentlemen (not from favor or affection, but from real fitness of character⟨⟩) to come forward. On a presumption that the aforementioned plan *may* be adopted, & that no further, or unnecessary delay may take place, let me entreat you, to give me the names of such Gentlemen as you think would fill, with honor & dignity, the several grades of Regimental Officers, in South Carolina—and as far as you are acquainted with them, of North Carolina & Georgia also—annexing the Rank to the name, and in the order (of each grade) you conceive they are entitled to preference—that is to say—supposing four Captains only should be the proportion of South Carolina, and you give eight, number them one, two & so on. the same of the field Officers & Subalterns. And let me hear from you as soon as possible, by Post.[2]

I write, as you will readily perceive, in much haste; but if I am understood, it is sufficient. I pray you to present me in respectful terms to Mrs Washington, and be assured of the friendship and affectionate regard of Dear Sir—Your Obedt Hble Servt

Go: Washington

ALS (letterpress copy), DLC:GW.

William Washington (1752–1810), originally of Stafford County, Va., was GW's cousin. He served as a lieutenant colonel of cavalry in the Revolutionary War before being captured at Eutaw Springs in 1781. After the war he settled in South Carolina to become a prominent and wealthy planter. GW later would call for Washington's assistance in the arrangement of the regiments of the augmented army forming in Georgia, North Carolina, and South Carolina. See GW to William Washington, 28 December.

1. Letter not found. Major James Simons (1761–1815) served briefly under William Washington during the Revolution. He was elected to the South Carolina general assembly in 1785 and served until the following year.

2. William Washington wrote on 19 Oct. and again on 30 October.

To the District of Columbia Commissioners

Gentlemen,   Mount Vernon 28th Sepr 1798

Your favour of yesterday's date is received. and enclosed are checks on the Bank of Alexandria for $428.40 amount of payment for the lot had of Mr D. Carroll, which you will please to deliver when the Conveyance is received; and $178.57 being the third of $535.70 to be paid for lot No. 16 in square 634 purchased from you.[1]

I feel very much obliged by the trouble you have taken in this business; and you will add considerably to the obligation, by examining Mr Blagdins estimate accurately, to prevent any imposition upon me: your knowledge of prices, and perfect acquaintance in matters of this kind, will enable you to form a correct judgment of the componant parts, as well as the aggregate amount of the proposed buildings, whereas my unacquaintedness in the present

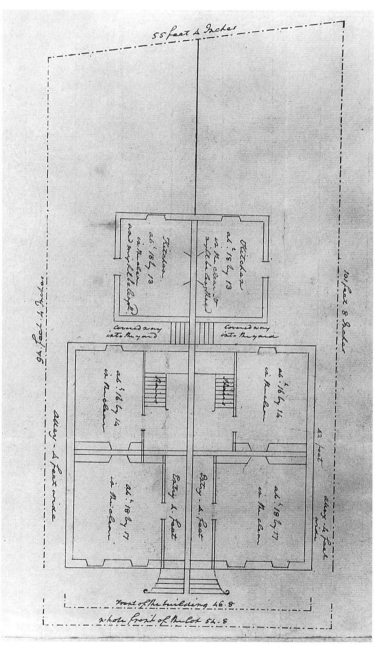

Washington's plan for his Capitol Hill houses, which he enclosed in his letter to Alexander White, 12 Sept. 1798. (Courtesy of Mr. and Mrs. Albert H. Small, Washington, D.C.)

price of materials—Work men's wages—&ca—&ca might subject me (if the Undertaker was so disposed) to great imposition. I am willing to pay the full value—according to the Plan, and will sign any agreement you shall approve; relying infinitely more on your judgment in this business, than on any skill I have in it.[2]

There is a matter I often intended to mention to the Commissioners of the City, but have always forgot to do it, when I was at their Board. Eventually it may be interesting to me, and I shall therefore do it now, as it has again occurred.

When I purchased lots No. 5, 12, 13, and 14, in square 667 (at public sale), it was declared at the time, and I have the Surveyors sketch (without any signature however) shewing it, that they were (that is No. 12, 13, & 14) water lots. There is a street between them and the Eastern branch; and if *any*, not more than a slipe of the bank between the Street and the water. On the strength of this declaration I purchased, & paid pretty smartly for the lots; but in the evidence (received from the former Commissioners) of this purchase, nothing therein contained gives assurance of this fact—and hereafter it may become a disputable point, very much to my injury.[3]

I have troubled you with this statement, accompanied with the Surveyors sketch (to be returned) that you may be enabled to point out the measures necessary to be taken, for my surety, in this case. Indeed, it appears to me that my title to *all* the lots I have purchased from the *Public* is incomplete; having no more than certificates thereof; when, on my part the conditions have been fully complied with. With very great esteem and regard I am—Gentlemen Your Most Obedt & very Hble Servt

Go: Washington

ALS, PHi: Gratz Collection; ALS (letterpress copy), DLC:GW; LB, DLC:GW.

1. For GW's purchase of these lots, see Alexander White to GW, 8 Sept. 1798, n.1.

2. For the next year and more, a considerable portion of GW's correspondence is devoted to matters relating to the erection of his two connected houses just to the north of the new Capitol in the Federal City. The houses were located on the two lots for which he made payments on this day. With District of Columbia commissioner William Thornton acting as adviser and intermediary, GW reached an agreement with the builder George Blagdin on the specifications for the two houses and on the terms for their construction (GW to the District of Columbia Commissioners, 27 Oct. 1798, n.2). During the spring and summer and into the fall Thornton took on the general supervision of the building of the

houses. When on 9 Nov. 1799, only a month before his death, GW "set out [from Mount Vernon] a little after 8 Oclock" and "viewed my building in the Fedl. City," most of the work on the two houses had been done (*Diaries*, 6:375).

3. For GW's purchase in 1793 of the lots in square 667 in the Federal City, see GW to Thomas Law, 7 May 1798, n.2. The commissioners hastened to assure GW on 3 Oct. that he was "clearly entitled to the water Lots agreeably to the plan received from you." GW's "plan" has not been found.

From Henry Lee, Jr.

dear General   G[eorge] town 28th Sepr [1798]

I have at length got to this place & will do myself the pleasure to call at Mt Vernon on my return home.

In the mean time I shd be happy to hear whether you accede to my proposition when last with you of taking good property for the whole debt due to you.

I have houses & lots in the fœderal city: well situated & which to close our business I would part with even at this present dull period, altho the time is fast approaching when property like mine must be in great demand.[1]

Judge Wilsons death places my debt in a worse situation than it was,[2] & it was my faith in that debt that induced me to purchase yr lands.

I make upwards of a thousand b[arre]ls of corn annually in Westm[orelan]d, & would annually supply you with 500 bbls at a fair price should corn suit you. With great respect & affection I have the honor to be yr ob. svt

                                          Henry Lee

ALS, DLC:GW.
 1. See GW's response of 29 September.
 2. Supreme Court associate justice James Wilson died in August.

To Zechariah Lewis

Sir,   Mount Vernon 28th Sepr 1798

The best apology I can make, for suffering your letter of the 11th of July to remain so long unacknowledged, is to offer a plain & simple detail of facts.[1]

Soon after it came to hand, I requested a Gentleman of my

acquaintance in Alexandria, to obtain for me the route & distance from that place to the Natural Bridge. This though promised, from causes unnecessary to enumerate, was not accomplished before I was siezed with a fever, which reduced me low, and left me in such a debilitated state, as to render writing both irksome & improper.

After this, I had to apply through another channel for the information you required & enclosed is the result.[2]

I thank you for sending me Doctr Dwights Sermons,[3] to whom I pray you to present the complimts of—Yr Most Obedt & Hble Servt

                                                Go: Washington

ALS (photocopy), DLC:GW.
    1. Letter not found.
    2. The enclosure has not been found.
    3. GW may be referring to Timothy Dwight's *The Nature, and Danger, of Infidel Philosophy, Exhibited in Two Discourses* . . . (New Haven, 1798), which was in GW's library at his death. In 1797 Lewis, who was a member of the Yale College faculty, sent GW copies of sermons delivered by his father, Isaac Lewis.

To William Russell

Sir,   Mount Vernon 28th Septr 1798
    Your favour of the 8th instt is received, and I thank you for your obliging attention to the articles promised me, when I had the pleasure of seeing you at this place.

    I will direct twenty of my best ewes to be reserved for the Ram you have kindly promised me; which, with the Chaff machine, I shall look for when an opportunity will allow you to send them.

    The cause which has prevented their shipment, is very afflicting to humanity, and must be sorely felt by the City of New York, and other places under the same calamitous circumstances.

    I have sent to the care of Mr Thomas Porter of Alexandria, fifteen bushels of fine forward wheat, in five flour barrels, agreeably to your desire. Having none of my own growth that was pure & unmixed, I purchased this quantity from a neighbour of mine who raises no other kind, & am assured it is genuine.

    I feel very much obliged, Sir, by your present of the Ram, and further kind intentions; for the trouble you have taken to procure

the Chaff machine for me; and not less for your kind wishes—
which I reciprocate with great cordiality—being Sir, Your most
Obedt and very Hble Servant

Go: Washington

ALS, British Library, Add. MSS 44992; ALS (letterpress copy), DLC:GW; LB, DLC:GW.

To Henry Lee, Jr.

Dear Sir,　　　　　　　　　　　Mount Vernon 29th Sepr 1798
　　Your letter of yesterday's date from George Town is received.
　　You know perfectly well what my inducements were to part with
the property you purchased of me, but rather than have any difficulty, or unpleasant disputes respecting the payments, agreeable
to contract, I would take productive property in the Federal City—
in Alexandria—or almost any where—or any thing productive, or
unproductive, at what it would fetch in the market—provided the
title is indisputable—but protest decidedly against receiving any
where their is the smallest pretensions of others.
　　As to the *present* being an unfavourable time to dispose of property in the City, or elsewhere, permit me to observe that it is a
question of very equivocal solution. The rise or fall depends upon
events, which, under present circumstances, few among us are
able to penetrate or foretell the issue. But all this is matter of opinion or speculation, and but little to the purpose.
　　Point out, if you please, the precise property; the precise situation of it; and, if absolutely free from any incumbrance or disputes. This will enable me to determine, at once, if there be a
probability of accomodating matters in the way you propose.[1] It is
necessary I should inform you, that I have tried every expedient
in my power, to obtain payment of Jesse Simms note, but, as yet,
without effect; and that, by looking to my letter of the 8th of Sepr
last year, you will perceive that credit was only to be given when
paid.[2]
　　With respect to Corn, I have partly contracted with my Nephew,
Colo. Wm Washington of Westmoreland, for an annual supply of
500 Barls.
　　I hope nothing will occasion your leaving these parts without my

seeing you. I want much to do it on account of some military concerns, and the sooner it can be made to suit your convenience the more agreeable it would be to me. But for the daily expectation I have been in of this pleasure, I should long since have written to you on this subject. With great esteem & regard I remain Dr Sir Yr obedt & affece Servt

Go: Washington

ALS (letterpress copy), DLC:GW.

1. Lee replied to this letter on 5 Oct., but he did not specify what property he owned in the Federal City or place a price on his lots there. It is likely that he did so on 13 Oct. when Lee spent the night at Mount Vernon, for on 25 Oct. William Thornton wrote GW that Thomas Peter had shown him Lee's estimate of the value of his property in the city. Thornton expressed the belief that Lee had already sold some of the lots listed and that in any case Lee had overpriced them. GW wrote Lee on 4 Nov. refusing to accept any of the lots toward the payment of what Lee owed him for the Dismal Swamp land. For Lee's purchase of the Dismal Swamp land in 1796 and his initial payments, see GW to Lee, 2 April 1797, n.1. For Lee's defense of the value that he had placed on his Federal City lots, see Lee to GW, 28 Feb. 1799.

2. For a discussion of GW's difficulty in collecting on Jesse Simms's bond for $1,000, which Lee had given to GW on 27 Aug. 1797 as partial payment of his Dismal Swamp debt, see Jesse Simms to GW, 8 Jan. 1798, n.1.

From Alexander Hamilton

My dear Sir   New York September 30. 1798

Your obliging favour of the 24th instant has duly come to hand. I see in it a new proof of sentiments towards me which are truly gratifying. But permit me to add my request to the suggestions of your own prudence, that no personal considerations for me may induce more on your part than on mature reflection you may think due to public motives—It is extremely foreign to my wish to create to you the least embarrassment, especially in times like the present when it is more than ever necessary that the interest of the *whole* should be *paramountly* consulted.

I shall strictly comply with the recommendation in the close of your letter; remaining always your very respectful & Affect. Servt

A. Hamilton

ALS, DLC: Hamilton Papers; ADfS, DLC: Hamilton Papers. The letter is docketed by GW.

To James McHenry

Dear Sir,   Mount Vernon 30th Sep. 1798

I have lately received information, which, in my opinion, merits attention. It is that the brawlers against Governmental measures in some of the most discontented parts of this state, have, all of a sudden, become silent; and, it is added, are very desirous of obtaining Commissions in the Army, about to be raised.

This information did not fail to leave an impression upon my mind at the time I received it; but it has acquired strength from a publication I have lately seen in one of the Maryland Gazettes (between the Author of which and my informant, there could have been no interchange of sentiments) to the same effect.[1]

The motives ascribed to them are, that in such a situation they would endeavour to divide, & contaminate the Army, by artful & Seditious discourses; and perhaps at a critical moment, bring on confusion. What weight to give these conjectures you can judge of, as well as I. But, as there will be characters enough of an opposite description, who are ready to receive appointments, circumspection is necessary; for my opinion of the first are, that you could as soon as scrub the blackamore white, as to change the principles of a profest Democrat; and that he will leave nothing unattempted to overturn the Government of this Country.

Finding the resentment of the People at the conduct of France too strong to be resisted, they have, in appearance, adopted their sentiments; and pretend that, notwithstanding the misconduct of Government have brought it upon us, yet, if an Invasion should take place, it will be found that *they* will be among the first to defend it. This is their story at all Elections, and Election meetings, and told in many instances with effect.

Whether there be little, much, or nothing in the information, I shall not take upon me to decide; but it appeared to me to be of sufficient moment to appraise you thereof.[2] With esteem & regd I am—Dear Sir Your Obedt Hble Servt

                                        Go: Washington

ALS, NNGL; ALS (letterpress copy), DLC:GW.

1. Alexander Spotswood communicated this rumor to GW in a letter of 16 Sept. to which GW replied on 24 September. The newspaper item has not been identified.

2. See McHenry's response of 5 October (first letter).

From Landon Carter

Dear Sir   Cleve 1 october 1798

Health is a grand object with man; but it becomes all important when the preservation of it in any one person comprehends all the relations of a People; when like a focus the views of all direct to a single point: Permit me therefore to lay before you some leading principles; some conclusions; and some consequent practice, for the security of health.

I believe it is a fact generally admitted, that all the works of nature are sustained by principles which, beyond a certain point, become destructive—or tecknically speaking, "all things contain within them the seeds of their own dissolution." In pursuance of a conviction of this truth, I sought for that principle in Man: "Dust thou art, and unto [dust] thou shall return" are solemn words pronounced in that last office performed by his weeping friends.

A great modern Philosopher in his nomenclator has arranged five Elements as the constituents of all the variety in nature. one of these I trace to the characterising the matter of Earth—the same is found, by experiment, to form the basis of oils—I therefore suppose it to be the fundamental principle of the animal Œconomy. This principle is also found to be the basis of fixed air, and that compound is denominated an asscid[.] I trace many diseases to an asscid for thier sourze when it is detained in the stomach & is taken up in too great quantities into the system. I conclude then that, by arresting that superabundance while yet in the stomach & before it is taken up I arrest incipient diseases & give it into the hands of the scavenger to be swept thro the bowels properly corrected; so as to be without acrimony to embarrass the way.

To practice upon this rule I compound togeather twenty four of Creme Tarter and Ten of Salt of Tarter and rub them well up in a marble morter. the former is a mild asscid that will resign the alkali to the more sharp asscid on the Stomach—it serves to reconcile the taste of that nauceous Salt, & to Sheath its accridity—and when seperated it serves, itself to blunt acrimony. Out of a quantity in that proportion, I mix into cold water a rising teaspoon full to about an half pint tumbler for a draught—This will give the water, when it is stired up a faint milky cast—if it tastes saltish, it is a sign the powder bears too great a proportion to the water—if it tastes soapy the Crem. Tart. has been sophisticated, and consequently has not contained the intended quantity of that salt to effect the entire neutralisation of the Alkali—The sophistication also renders it disagreable to the taste, when even by an addition that neutralisation is effected; whereas the mixture if genuine, is nearly as tasteless as water—If powered Crem. Tart., when rubbed between the hands and cast off, does not leave a white dust behind it is genuine, not else.

When I have a bad taste in my mouth—an head ache—a tenseness across the stomach just below—an unusual thirst, or a dry burning heat in my Palms—I consider either of them a summons to take a draught of the mixture; & it fails not more or less to remove those uneasy sensations—These tho they are often, in a healthy subject, removed by natural causes, are the beginning of Disease, when some hiden impediment obviates the benevolent exertion: a recurrence to this mixture will not fail to help nature to overcome the impediment, & thereby wave the threatened malady: they go off chiefly by assorient discharges from the bowels—this is the end of them, when my Powder effects relief: If it is taken even in perfect health, like a wholesome water, it is harmless as is the native beverage itself it has no operation of its own, & only acts at all by the agency of the morbid matter which it corrects; while sheathing its acrimony it moves it along in an healthful discharge.

I have used it with unlimited Success with children, and with Adults I have removed in an incipient State Diarhæas Colds & Coughs (nothing breaks a common Cold better) accute pains, in different parts, caused by wind are surely relieved if taken in time.

One case I will take the liberty to exhibit, of a kind which I presume you lately lay ill of I was at a friends house where the lady was ill of an obstinate bilious fever—She was attended by two eminent Physicians—they applied the most forcible cathartics, but the malady gained ground—She burned with thirst, & had no relish for any thing but ice—I pressed my ideas, but was disregarded by one & only not contradicted by the other, Gent. in attendance. I had at the Same time, a Daughter in the house, 6 or 7 years of age; who had a tertian ague—both the Gent. practiced, & made a large use of jesuits Bark; but no change was effected—I requested the politest of the two practitioners to add three grains of the alkaline Salt to each dose of Bark—he expressed a doubt, that it

might not purge; that I undertook to be answerable for, and then
he reluctantly consented: The result was that it did operate—She
only took three portions, and from that time the disorder no more
returned. This no doubt influenced him to make the experiment
in the Lady's case; for when upon mixing a saline draught for her,
his fellow doctor would have him weigh the alkaline salt, he care-
lessly said "he could guess"—He gave such a predominence to the
salt, as to ocassion much grimace and loud complaints of the nau-
seous dose—The immediate effects were that the Patient wished
for small beer, & had a relish for the beverage. The texture of the
viscuous coat, which before had lined her stomack, so as to prevent the approach of the medicines to act was now broken—
amendment commenced and the patient recovered.

I directed my ideas to the case of an aged person of eighty years
and upwards who had had three large inveterate ulcers in the
groin and neighbourhood which the doctors had practised upon
for ten or twelve years; and at last declared incurable when I took
him in hand, his urine had a passage through one of the ulcers
& he had a tumor as large as his fist rising on the outside of his
thigh just opposite—The tumor soon sunk and his water took its
natural course, & now five or six months every ulcer is perfectly
healed—In such inveterate cases an astonishing debility takes
place; owing to the sudden check to an old habit—That I guarded
against with watchful attention—using Laudanum occasionally &
jesuits Bark—for a few days only tho'.

I had a pain in the outside of my left foot, just under the ancle,
so as to make me limp—retrospect brought to mind a very free
use of pepper for several days past—I had, tho, in the night of
each Day taken a draught of my mixture, so that I wondered at the
pain—Reflection put me upon using it early after dinner; but still
confident of its efficascy, I resolved not to abate the use of the
Pepper and the rather substitute the red kind—The pain wore
away very soon, and left the whole sole of that foot and the other
in which there had been no pain, so tender that I could scarce
hobble along.

I will fatigue you with no more cases but after laying before you
a comparative view will bring this long letter to a conclusion.

If a diarrhea is seen to digest into an healthy state of the bowels—If a cold is broken and its effects bounded—If the ague, re-
sisting the usual evacuation followed by the bark yet yields to

this—If a Bilious fever, bidding defiance to eminent Practice, is brought into subjection to it by this—If long standing inveterate ulcers, like a once running stream with its source now directed into another channel are seen to dry away—If incipient gout is seen to cease for want of accumulation to its cause—If all this is seen to be effected by one and the same mean It cannot be a whimsical idea that the source of all must be the same; varying in the effect as the formation or the habit is various in the subjects—If an Alkali is seen to be that mean, an assid is doubtless the cause If the matter of Earth is the basis both of an assid and an[1]

ADf (incomplete), ViU.

1. The remainder of the manuscript is missing, but for an indication of at least some of its contents, see GW's response of 5 October.

To James McHenry

Private
My dear Sir,   Mount Vernon 1st Octr 1798
Your confidential letter of the 19th ulto did not reach Alexandria until the 28th. I thank you for the statement, and lengthy details which it contains. The President may have reasons which will justify the inexecution of the law, for augmenting the force of the United States. With my lights, I can discover none: but, if the force is required at all, I can see very serious evils resulting from the non-appointmt of the Battalion Officers, and consequent delay in the Recruiting Service; for reasons mentioned in a former letter, and unnecessary to repeat in this.

That Mr Wolcott (on whom there may be more calls than he has funds conveniently to answer) is disposed to replenish the Magazines at the expence of the Recruiting Service, I do not much wonder; but if he was more experienced in the *real* difference, not only in point of Service but in point of expence also, between Militia or Raw Rec[rui]ts & discipd Troops, he would feel more for the Officer who was to conduct them and for the resources of the treasury too than he appears to do at present; for I think it is mathematically demonstrable, that ten thousand Militia (to say nothing of the incompetency of them) drawn out for short terms of Service, coming at different times, though required at one time, returning pointedly at the expiration of their term; Consumption of Provisions; waste of the Military Stores; destruction of Camp equipage of every species; and loss of Arms, will cost the public more then fifteen, I believe I might venture to say 20,000 well tutored, & permanent Troops. When Militia are called upon, you have *two sets* to *pay*, & *supply* at the sametime, one set are raising & marching, to supply the place of the other set, who will be going; and both sets of such uncertain dependence, as to baffle all calculation on their strength.

If the Treasury is unable to accomplish both objects, *completely*, let the Magazines be less stored, & the recruiting service progress. Soldiers are not made in a day, but the munitions of War may be contracted for in an hour: and I believe the Enemy will think the raising & training an army, a more serious operation than the replenishing of Magazines—which, at all times, ought to be well stored.

Has Mr Wolcott described the length of the Musket & Bayonet? the Caliber of the first, & shape of the latter? I again repeat, that they ought to be such as to place us on equal ground with the enemy we are to cope with. I am speaking of those he has, and is about to contract for. and I am of opinion a number of rifles ought also to be provided. They might be used to great advantage by skilful hands in a country covered with wood.

You request me to express a *strong* sentiment to Mr *Pickering* respecting clothing for the Army. What has the Secretary of State to do with the cloathing of the Army?

Your letter of the 25th of August to the Superintendant of Military Stores, has produced no effect, as yet; for no return of them is come to my hands.[1]

As no mode is yet adopted by the President, by which the Battalion Officers are to be appointed, and as I think I stand upon very precarious ground, in my relation to him, I am not over zealous in taking *unauthorised* steps, when those that I thought *were authorised*, are not likely to meet with much respect. It will naturally occur to you that to obtain information of proper characters for Officers in the two Carolinas, Georgia, Kentucky & Tennessee, I must have recourse to others. If then the President should resolve upon a mode different from the one you have suggested, I shall be committed, & stand in an awkward predicament. I will however use some preliminary measures to accomplish yr wishes[2] & am sincerely & affectly Yours

Go: Washington

P.S. You have not furnished me with the letter written by you to the President from hence according to my request and your promise; nor with a copy of the Instructn recd from him.[3]

ALS (letterpress copy), DLC:GW.
    1. See McHenry to GW, 16 Nov. (second letter), n.1.
    2. See, for instance, GW to William Washington, 27 September.
    3. See GW to McHenry, 16 Sept., nn.2 and 4. Because the letterpress postscript is largely illegible, it is taken from Fitzpatrick, *Writings of Washington*, 36:479.

To James McHenry

Private and quite confidential
My dear Sir,   Mount Vernon 1st Oct. 1798

You will be at no loss to perceive, from my *private* letter to you of the 16th ulto, extracts from which you sent to the President of the United States; and from my representation to him, dated the 25th following, the rough draught of wch was enclosed in my last,[1] what my determination is, if he perseveres in his Resolution to change the order of the Major Generals, and to disregard the conditions on which I accepted the Commission of Lieutt Genl of the Armies &ca.

Let me then request you, with the frankness & candour of a friend, to give me your opinion *fully*, & *freely* of the measure; to ask if you think I could, with propriety, & due respect for my own character, retain the Commission under such violation, of the terms, on which I accepted it; and what you conceive will be the consequences of my resignation thereof.

If Colo. Pickering, & the Gentlemen who act with you, are minutely acquainted with *all* the circumstances of the case, it would be satisfactory to me, to know their opinions also, with respect to my eventual resignation; *but not as a matter required by me*, but as questions propounded by *yourself*, entirely, & absolutely.

Be so good as to let me know the ground on which *you*, & Colo. Pickering are *certain*, the President is mistaken in his conjectures that the New England States would be disgusted if Hamilton Preceeds Knox, in Rank, and add, if you please whether Pickering's prediliction in favor of the former proceeds from pure conviction of the utility of the measure, or from some personal dislike to the latter. I have some suspicion that he is not a friend to Knox, but cannot suppose that this would have any influence in the case.

I should like to have seen a copy of Mr Wolcott's letter to the President, but as it was not sent, I presume there was some reason for withholding, and do not repeat the request.

I wish to hear from you on the subject of this letter as soon as possible. Burn it, as soon as it is perused, as I will do your answer, that neither the one, nor the other, may appear hereafter.[2] With much truth I am your sincere and Affecte friend

Go: Washington

ALS (letterpress copy), DLC:GW.

1. See GW to McHenry, 26 September.
2. It may be noted that GW retained his letterpress copy.

To Timothy Pickering

Confidential

Dear Sir　　　　　　　　　　Mount Vernon 1st Octr 1798.

This letter will contain very little more than an acknowledgment of the receipts of your letters of the 13th & 18th of last month, which came safe to hand.

The letter written by Mr Wolcott to the President of the United States, and the representation made by me to him, so soon as I received *official* information of the change intended, by him, in the relative Rank of the Major Generals, and of his departure in almost every other instance from what I considered a solemn compact; and the *only* terms on which I would, by an acceptance of the Commission hazard every thing dear & valuable to me, will soon bring matters to a close; so far as it respects myself. But, until the final result of them is known, the less there is said on the subject the better. With great truth & sincerity—I am always Yr Sincere & Obedt Servt

Go: Washington

ALS, MHi: Pickering Papers; ALS (letterpress copy), DLC:GW; copy, in the hand of Pickering's clerk, DLC: Hamilton Papers.

To James Ross

Dear Sir,　　　　　　　　　　Mount Vernon 1st Oct. 1798

You will perceive by the enclosed letters, left open for your perusal, the delinquency of Colo. Shreve, and my determination to enforce payment of the Instalment of his judgment Bond, the 1st of June last.[1]

Whether, as the Bond was deposited in the Bank of Pennsylvania for collection, it rests with me to draw it from thence for the purpose of putting it in Suit—or for them to order it—your better judgment & knowledge of the practice will decide—and you will act accordingly.[2]

My object is to enforce paymt as soon as the usual course of things will admit—1st because I am in real want of the money—and 2d because I believe there is no other certain dependence to obtain it—for Shreve, from first to last has done little else but trifle, both with himself and me. With very sincere esteem and regard I am—Dear Sir Your Most Obedt and Obliged Hble Servant

Go: Washington

ALS (letterpress copy), DLC:GW; LB, DLC:GW.

1. See GW to Israel Shreve, this date.

2. On this day GW wrote to the Bank of Pennsylvania: "Gentlemen, Be pleased to deliver to the Honble James Ross, on his order, the Judgment Bond of Israel Shreve to me—Deposited in the Bank of Pennsylvania for Collection, that the same may be put in suit for recovery of the Instalment due the first of June last. With respect—I am Gentlemen Your Obedt Hble Servant Go: Washington" (letterpress copy, DLC:GW; LB, DLC:GW).

To Israel Shreve

Sir,   Mount Vernon 1st Oct. 1798

I have waited four months to see if, in that time, you would discharge the Instalment of your judgment Bond, due the first of June last. and am determined to wait no longer than the proceedings in a regular course will compel me to do:[1] for which reason I give you notice that by this day's Post I have requested Mr Ross to obtain from the Bank of Pennsylvania (where it was deposited for collection) your judgmt Bond, & put it in suit without further delay.

I think myself extremely ill used by your conduct in this business. You know that it was in order to raise money I sold the land. You have sold a part at nearly the double of what you was to have given me; and yet I have been trifled with by you more than by any person I have had to deal with.

My own want of money, to fulfil engagements, is such, that I inform you beforehand, that any application for further indulgence will be unavailing, and need not be attempted. And further, that henceforward, if the Instalments are not paid at the times they become due, the bond will be inforced without any questions being asked. I am—Sir Your Hble Servant

Go: Washington

ALS, CSmH; ALS (letterpress copy), DLC:GW; LB, DLC:GW.

    1. Shreve wrote GW on 14 May 1798 explaining that it was unlikely that he would be able to obtain the money for the payment due on the tract of land, called Washington's Bottom, which Shreve had bought from GW in 1795. Following GW's instructions of 1 Oct., James Ross wrote GW on 26 Oct. that he would proceed with the legal action against Shreve. Shreve wrote GW on 29 Oct. and again on 21 Dec. begging for more time, promising, if left free, never to "rest untill the money is paid." In his reply of 10 Jan. 1799, GW continued to complain about Shreve's treatment of him but ended by only saying that he would "expect the next payment due on the Instalment Bond, when it becomes due (the first of June next)." For the terms of Shreve's purchase of the Pennsylvania tract, see Timothy Pickering to GW, 21 April 1797, n.1. Shreve, in failing health, was unable to make the payment in June 1799 (see GW to James Ross, 26 June 1799, and Ross to GW, 24 July 1799).

From Joel Barlow

Sir,   Paris 2 Octr 1798

On hearing of your late nomination as commander in chief of the American Armies I rejoice at it, not because I believe the war which that nomination contemplates is yet inevitable and that it will furnish an occasion for a farther display of your military talents, but because it may enable you to exert your influence to a greater effect in preventing the war. By becoming more the centre of information than you could be in your retirement you will be better able to judge of the dispositions of both countries, and to offer such counsels to your own government as may tend to remove the obstacles that still oppose themselves to a reconciliation.

Were you now president of the United States I should not address you this letter; because, not knowing my inclination for the tranqu[i]llity of a retired life, you might think that I was seeking a place, or had some farther object in view than the simple one of promoting peace between the two republics. But I hope under present circumstances that you will believe my motive to be pure & unmixed, and that the object of my letter is only to call your attention to the true state of facts.

Perhaps few men, who cannot pretend to have been in the secrets of either government, are in a better situation than myself to judge of the motives of both; to assign the true causes & trace out the progress of their unhappy misunderstanding; or to appreciate their present dispositions, pretentions & wishes. I am certain there is none who labors more sincerely for the restoration of harmony upon terms honorable to the United States, and advantageous to the cause of liberty.

I will not in this place go over the history of past transactions. It would be of little use. The object is to seize the malady in its present state, and try to arrest its progress. The dispute at this moment may be characterised simply & literally a *misunderstanding*. I cannot persuade myself to give it a harsher name as it applies to either government. It is clear that neither of them has an interest in going to war with the other; and I am equally convinced that neither of them has the inclination; that is, I believe the balance of inclination as well as of interest, on both sides, is in favor of peace. But each government, though sensible of this truth with respect to itself, is ignorant of it with respect to the other. Each believes the other determined on war, and ascribes all its conduct to a deep rooted hostility. The least they can do therefore under this impression is to prepare for an event which they both believe inevitable, while they both wish to avoid it.

But by what fatality is it that a calamity so dreadful must be *rendered* inevitable, because it is *thought* so? Both governments have tongues, & both have ears. why will they not speak? why will they not listen? The causes that have hitherto prevented them are not difficult to assign. I could easily explain them, as I believe, to the satisfaction of all parties; and without throwing so much blame on either government as each of them at present ascribes to the other. But I will avoid speaking of any past provocations on either side. The point that I wish to establish in your mind is that the French Directory is at present sincerely desirous of restoring harmony between this country & the United States, on terms honorable and advantageous to both parties. I wish to convince you of this, & through you the American Government, because that government, being desirous of the same thing, would not fail to take such steps as would lead immediately to the object.

In offering you my proofs of the present disposition on this side you will permit me to observe that some of them are from their nature incapable of being detailed, and others improper to be trusted to the casualties of a letter. But I will mention a few that are ostensible, and, so far as they go, undeniable. *First*, the Directory has declared that it will recieve & treat with any minister from America who shall appear to be sent with a sincere intention of treating and terminating existing difficulties. I have no doubt but this was the intention when the last Envoys were sent; but from some unfortunate circumstances the Directory did not believe it. *Second*, as a preliminary, it has declared that in the negotiation there shall be no question of loans of money, or apologies for offensive speeches pronounced by the Executive on either side. *Third*, all commissions given to privateers in the West Indies are recalled; and when new commissions are issued the owners & commanders are to be restricted under bonds to the legal objects of capture. *Fourth*, An Embargo, that was laid on the American ships within the Republic in consequence of a report that a war had been begun on the part of the United States, was taken off as soon as it was ascertained that such war had not been begun. And a new declaration was at the same time sent to America of the wishes of France to treat.

These facts will doubtless come to your knowledge through other channels before you recieve this letter. But there are other facts which in my mind are equally clear, though to you they will be destitute of corroborating circumstances; and must rest on my own information and opinion: 1st—that this government contemplates a just indemnity for spoliations on American commerce, to be ascertained by commissioners in a manner similar to the one prescribed in our treaty with England. 2nd—that the legislation will soon be changed here with respect to neutrals, and that all flags will be put on the footing of the law of nations. 3rd—that a public agent would have been named and sent to Philadelphia soon after Mr Gerry's departure, were it not for apprehensions that he would not have been recieved. There was a doubt whether the American Government would not have already taken such measures of hostility as to be unwilling to listen to terms of accomodation; and the Directory did not choose to risk the chance of seeing its offers refused. 4th—that the Directory considers these declarations & transactions as a sufficient overture on its part, that it has retreated to an open ground which is quite unsuspicious; that a refusal on the part of the American government to meet on this ground will be followed by immediate war; and that it will be a war of the most terrible & vindictive kind.

This, Sir, is my view of the present state of facts. Should it make that impression on your mind which I desire for the sake of humanity that it may, you will judge whether it does not comport with the independence of the United States & the dignity of their government to send another minister to form new treaties with the French republic. In a war there is clearly nothing to be *gained* by us, not even honour. Honour indeed may be *saved* by War, and so it may by negotiation. But the calamities inseparable from a war of this kind and under present circumstances would be incalculable. I do not say that the Unites States, or any portion of them, would be conquered; but they would sacrifice great numbers of their best citizens, burthen themselves with four times their present debt, overturn the purest system of morals and lose the fairest opportunity that ever a nation had of rising to greatness & happiness on the basis of liberty.

Were I writing to a young general, whose name was still to be created, I might deem it useless to ask him to stifle in its birth a war on which he had founded his hopes of future honours. But you, Sir, having already earned & acquired all that can render a man great & happy, can surely have no object of Ambition but to render your country so. To engage your influence in favor of a new attempt of negotiation[1] I thought it only necessary to convince you that such an attempt would be well recieved here, & probably attended with success. I can do no more than assure you that this is my sincere opinion; and that my information is drawn from unsuspected sources.

I am not accustomed to interpose my advice in the administration of any country; and should not have done it now did I not believe it my duty as a citizen of my own and a friend to all others. I see two great nations rushing on each others bayonnets, without any cause of contention but a misunderstanding. I shudder at the prospect, and wish to throw myself between the vans, and suspend the onset till a word of explanation can pass.

I hope my letter will have thrown some light upon the subject; but if it shall not, I know you will excuse the attempt; for you know my zeal is honest.[2] I have the honour to be Sir, with great respect your most obt & most hume Sert

Joel Barlow

ALS, MHi-A; ALS (duplicate), DLC:GW; copy, DLC:GW. GW docketed the duplicate ALS. Tobias Lear certified on 1 Feb. 1799 that the copy was a true one.

1. The duplicate that Barlow sent GW, which is a generally faithful copy, has here the added words: "before you draw your sword."

2. After receiving this letter from Barlow on 31 Jan. 1799, GW the next day sent it on to President Adams. For reference to Barlow's long stay in Europe, see Timothy Pickering to GW, 5 April 1797 (first letter), n.2.

From James McHenry

Private

My dear General,   Trenton [N.J.] 2 Octbr 1798

I received your confidential letter dated the 26th of Septr ulto last saturday evening. I now return the copy of your letter to the President which I expect will get to him seasonably, and produce a happy effect upon the question it particularly refers to. I had a letter from him dated the 26, this morning, but no notice of the subject of either Mr Wolcotts letter, or mine of the 21st.[1] The latter however may not have reached him. My expectation is, that the affair will terminate happily.

As it may be necessary to begin our inlistments as soon as possible to the Southward it will forward the business provided you can send me as good a list as you have been able to form of persons the best qualified for officers for the four regiments proposed to be officered and raised in that quarter.[2]

I am greatly at a loss for a commandant for the 2 Corps of Artillerists and Engineers. You know the talents & acquirements necessary for a Lt Colonel and perhaps can help me to one or two fit characters.[3]

I have sent the advertisement to the news-papers respecting clothing for the additional regiments and companies of cavalry. But I have not been able to do any thing relative to contracts for their subsistence. The means are always presented as an obstacle.

Young Mr Pinckney (Secry to the Paris Commission) is just arrived at New York.[4] Mr Gerry [is] in England into which his apprehensions drove him to avoid being captured by an English vessel of war which he took for a French privateer. He expressed himself to Mr Pinckney on his arrival in England as if he had every thing to dread from the *hatred* of the French Directory, a circumstance which Mr Pinckney relates as if he thought Mr Gerry had felt an unnecessary alarm. Mr Pinckney was at Burdoux waiting for a passage to this Country which the embargo had obstructed.[5]

The letters from Mr King are no later then the 5th of Augt. The Emperor of Germany & King of Naples, he informs have certainly entered into a defensive alliance, to make a common cause in case either is attacked by France, and if France attacks Naples, on account of supplying the British Fleet, a *casus federis*.[6]

Our conduct seems to have inspired Europe with fresh hopes and fresh courage, and of course raised every where the American character. I am my dear General Your most affectionat⟨ly⟩ & sincerely

James McHenry

ALS, DLC:GW; ADf, MdAA; copy, DLC: Hamilton Papers.

1. McHenry discussed his letter to Adams of 21 Sept. in his letter to GW of the same date. Adams's brief letter to McHenry of 26 Sept. is in MHi-A.

2. In his response of 15 Oct. GW explained how he proposed to draw up lists of prospective officers from the southern states. He enclosed a sketch of what each of those states would have to supply in the way of officers and men to form the six regiments of infantry and six troops of horse which the southern states were to provide (Enclosure I, 15 October).

3. See GW's suggestions in his letter to McHenry of 15 October.

4. McHenry is referring to Henry Middleton Rutledge, Charles Cotesworth Pinckney's nephew and Edward Rutledge's son, who had served as Pinckney's secretary in France.

5. For an account of Elbridge Gerry's activities in France, see Timothy Pickering's letter to GW of 3 October.

6. Rufus King's letter to Timothy Pickering of 5 Aug. is printed in King, *Life and Correspondence of King*, 2 : 382–84.

From the District of Columbia Commissioners

Sir, Washington 3d October 1798

We had the honor of your favor of the 28th ulto enclosing two Checks on the Bank of Alexandria; the one for D. Carroll for $428⁴⁰⁄₁₀₀ the other for the Commissioners $178⁵⁷⁄₁₀₀, and have directed the proper conveyances to be prepared for your purchases of the public; the deed from Mr Carroll was executed this day.[1] Mr Blagdin delivered in his estimate yesterday amounting to $12,982²⁹⁄₁₀₀. To determine on the merits of this estimate will require some investigation & information from sundry mechanics which will take some time. No time shall be lost in making every necessary enquiry, and as soon as possible the result shall be forwarded.[2]

Upon examining the sales book no doubt is left of your being clearly entitled to the water Lots agreeably to the plan received from you. We are, with sentiments of the highest respect Yr most Obt Servts

Gusts Scott
William Thornton
Alexr White

ALS, CSmH.

1. There is in MiDbGr a document dated 3 Oct. 1798 and signed by the three commissioners certifying that on 23 June 1794 GW purchased "Lot numbered One, in Square numbered twenty one, in the City of Washington for the sum of two hundred pounds, Maryland currency . . . and the principal and interest of the purchase-money for said Lot being paid," GW was "entitled to the same Lot, in fee-simple." The deed from Daniel Carroll of Duddington to GW, 3 Oct. 1798, is quoted in Alexander White to GW, 8 Sept., n.1.

2. For references to the commissioners' negotiations with George Blagdin, see GW to the District of Columbia Commissioners, 28 Sept., n.2.

From Timothy Pickering

Sir,   Trenton [N.J.] Oct. 3. 1798

I have to-day received some letters from Mr King dated in London July 28 August 1st & 5th. By them it appears there is more than ever a prospect of a new coalition against France: but a *fact*, and a very important one, stated by Mr King, has chiefly induced me to write. It is this. That Austria & Naples have entered into a defensive alliance for their mutual protection against France; and particularly stipulated, that if France shall attack Naples, for supplying provisions to the British ships of war (which the Neapolitan Government has engaged to do) it shall be deemed a case in which the treaty of alliance is to operate, and Austria is then to send her forces to defend the Neapolitan Dominions. This will most probably produce a war, for which Austria is preparing.

Britain, he says, remains firm; and confident in her resources, no man talks of peace. The newspapers have intimated that a change of ministry was about to take place: Mr King says it is not true; and that no administration has stood firmer in the favor of the King and the confidence of the people, than the present administration of Great Britain. The rebellion in Ireland, he says is crushed: a general amnesty is soon to be published: with the exception of a few persons who are to go into exile.

An embargo is laid on all our ships in the ports of France: but Mr King learns, that except ten or a dozen at Bourdeaux, we have hardly any vessels there. General Pinckney was at Bourdeaux, embarrassed by the embargo: but expected to get a passage to America in the ship in which Consul Dupont & Volney with a cargo of French people went to France. She was a flag of truce, and it is presumed she will not be detained.[1]

This morning I received a letter dated yesterday at New-York, from Mr Henry Rutledge, who was secretary to General Pinckney. He (Mr Rutledge) arrived in the Factor, Capt. Kemp. He informs me that while he lay at Portsmouth, wind-bound, Mr Gerry arrived in the United States brig Sophia from Havre, from whence he sailed the 8th of August, and reached Portsmouth the 9th. It is a curious tale.

The British having for some time blocked up the port of Havre, examined of course every vessel coming from thence, that they could speak with. The Commandant at the Islands of Marcou (near the port of Havre) of which the English are in possession, seeing the Sophia, sent an open boat with a lieutenant and a few men to speak her, & see what she was. Mr Gerry took the alarm on the approach of the boat, & insisted upon Captain Geddes (master of the Sophia) avoiding her. As it was rather calm, they were obliged to have recourse to their sweeps; and after tugging all day at the oars, were pursued fairly across the channel, & took refuge in Portsmouth harbour, whither also came the pursuers, an hour or two after them. Mr Gerry assured Mr Rutledge that the motive of his flight was the fear that the boat might have been dispatched after him by order of the French Government, for the purpose of bringing him back, & of committing him to the Temple, or of sending him a prisoner to the West Indies: adding, "that after his conduct towards the French Government, he was sensible he had every thing to fear from their enemity!" This is amusing enough. So far as we are acquainted with Mr Gerry's conduct in France, it could not possibly excite any other sensation in the French Government but contempt. It is possible, however, that since Mr Gerry discovered the spirit roused in America (and in the Paris Papers of July 13th Mr King says the *measures* of our Government were faithfully given) he may have been less abject, less tame, & have answered Talleyrand with a semblance of resentment, to rescue himself from the contempt which he saw waiting for him in his own country.[2] I am most respectfully sir, Yr obt servant

Timothy Pickering

ALS, PPRF.

1. The three letters from Rufus King to Pickering are printed in King, *Life and Correspondence of King*, 2:372–74, 379–80, 382–84.

2. Henry M. Rutledge's letter to Pickering, dated 2 Oct., is in MHi: Pickering Papers.

To William Augustine Washington

My dear Sir,   Mount Vernon 3d Octr 1798

Your letter of the 27th of July has remained unacknowledged 'till now, that I embrace the opportunity afforded by General Lee's return, to do it.[1]

To a person not in the habit of sending regularly to the Post Office, nearest to them, it is almost useless to write by the Mail; and with very few exceptions, addressing letters by private hands, is almost as bad; very few people paying much attention to them; which, with the shifting of hands, rubbing in the Pocket, and sometimes idle curiosity to know the contents, are great lets to a safe conveyance, in that way.

With respect to the proposed contract for Corn, as my primary object is to be *certain* of getting it, I will agree to divide the freight from your landing to mine (at this place) equally with you; although it would make the Corn come all that higher to me; as neither land, or water transportation, would be more to my Mill (where it will be chiefly wanted) than it would be to the Warehouses, or Wharves in Alexandria. March being a windy month; often cold & disagreeable; about the middle of April would be better, and I would agree to receive it at that time. If with these alterations, from the proposals contained in my letter of the 26th of June last, you incline to enter into a contract upon the terms therein mentioned, for five hundred Barrels of Corn, annually, I am ready to close the contract; to be binding for, and during our lives.

Your answer to this point would be agreeable, as Genl Lee is desirous of entering into a contract with me for the same quantity of Corn (500 Barls); and, on a/c of the payments, it would be very convenient for me to make it; but from the uncertainty of its fulfilment, on his part, I feel no disposition to enter into one with him.[2]

I thank you for the old document⟨s⟩[3] you sent me, respecting the family of our Ancestors. but I am possessed of Papers which prove beyond a doubt, that of the two brothers who Emigrated to this Country in the year 1657, during the troubles of that day, that John Washington, from whom we are descended, was the eldest. The Pedigree from him, I have, and I believe very correct; but the descendents from Lawrence, in a regular course, I have not been able to trace. All those of our name, in and about Chotanck, are from the latter. John, was the Grandfather of my father and uncle, and Great grand father to Warner and me. He left two Sons, Lawrence & John; the former, who was the Eldest, was the father of my father, uncle, & aunt Willis. Mrs Hayward must have been a daughter of the *first* Lawrence, & thence became the cousen of the second Lawrence, & John.[4] We all unite in best wishes for you & family—and I am your sincere and Affectionate Uncle

Go: Washington

ALS (photocopy), ViMtV; ALS (letterpress copy), DLC:GW; LB, DLC:GW.

1. GW enclosed this letter in his letter to William Augustine Washington of 5 October.

2. William Augustine Washington's reply has not been found, but GW's letter to him of 14 Feb. 1799 indicates that his nephew had agreed to the revised terms.

3. The word is at the end of the line and the "s" does not show on the ALS photocopy, but the letter-book copy reads "documents."

4. For correspondence at this time and information regarding the Washington family genealogy, see W. A. Washington to GW, 23 Mar. 1798, n.2, and 24 July 1798. "Aunt Willis" was Mildred Washington Lewis Gregory Willis (1696–c.1745). Her third husband was Col. Henry Willis (c.1691–1740) of Fredericksburg. It was from his sister Mildred Willis that GW's father, Augustine Washington, acquired the Mount Vernon tract.

To the District of Columbia Commissioners

Gentlemen   Mount Vernon 4th Oct. 1798.

I had the honor to receive your letter of the 3d instt, last Night.

Mr Blagdens estimate of the cost of the houses I had proposed to build, far exceeds any aggregate Sum I had contemplated; or think I could command; unless more punctuality was to be found in the fulfilment of Contracts than is, I believe, experienced by any one. Eight, or at most $10,000, was the extent of my calculation. The house Mr Law is about to build (not much if any less than my two) is undertaken for less than $6,000 as he informed me. This information, and the report that Materials & workmens wages were low—disposed me to build houses of better appearance than is necessary perhaps for the primary object which induced the measure.

But I will suspend any final decision until I see Mr Blagdens estimate in detail, with your observations thereupon; and what part of the work I can execute with my own Tradesmen, thereby reducing the advances. I shall only add, that with a high sense of the trouble you have had in this business, and with very great esteem & regard I am Gentlemen Your Most Obedt and obliged Hble Servant

Go: Washington

ALS (letterpress copy), DLC:GW; LB, DLC:GW.

To William Herbert

Dear Sir,   Mount Vernon 4th Oct. 1798.

A day or two ago, I received the enclosed letter—Will you be so good as to enable me to answer it.[1]

Observing to you, not long since, that the want of money prevented my doing something (I have forgot now what) you said, if I understood you rightly, that I might be accomodated at the Bank of Alexandria.

I think it not unlikely that in the course of next spring, or summer, if I undertake a measure which is in contemplation, that I shall have occasion for a larger Sum than I see a prospect of receiving from what is due to me. Let me ask then (if I was not mistaken in what you said) what sum you think I could obtain? On what terms? for what time? and what security wd be required?[2] I am Dear Sir Yr Obedt Hble Servt

Go: Washington

ALS (letterpress copy), DLC:GW; LB, DLC:GW.

1. GW enclosed the letter from Andrew E. Belknap of 20 Sept., which is printed below in a note to GW to Belknap, 8 October.

2. See the reply of 5 Oct. from Herbert, president of the Alexandria bank. See also GW to Herbert, 8 Oct., n.1.

To Landon Carter

Dear Sir, Mount Vernon 5th Oct. 1798.

Your favour of the 1st instt has been received, and if it had been convenient, I should have been glad of your company as you travelled to Annapolis.[1] As you propose however to send in your Servant, and I am generally on horse back between breakfast & dinner, that he may not be delayed, or disappointed, you will receive, enclosed, one letter for the Govr of Maryland (an old acquaintance of mine)—and another for Mr McDowall President of the College.[2] Which, I hope may answer your purposes. They will be left, under this cover, for whomsoever you may send, in case I should be out.

I thank you for the trouble you have taken in delivering your thoughts on the means of preserving health. Having, through life, been blessed with a competent share of it, without using preventatives against sickness, and as little medicine as possible when sick; I can have no inducement now to change my practice. Against the effect of time, and age, no remedy has ever yet been discovered; and like the rest of my fellow mortals, I must (if life is prolonged) submit, & be reconciled, to a gradual decline. With esteem & regard I am—Dear Sir Your Most Obedt Hble Servt

Go: Washington

Please to put wafers in the letters before delivery.

ALS, in private hands. Carter wrote on the cover: "Recieved 9th Novr 1798 from G. Washington." Carter may have intended to write 9 October.

1. The portion of Carter's letter referring to his proposed trip to Annapolis is missing, but see his letter to GW of 8 September.

2. GW's letter to Gov. John Henry, Jr. (c.1750–1798), has not been found, but his letter to John McDowell of this date reads: "Sir: This letter will be presented to you by Landon Carter Esqr. a Gentleman of this State, who is disposed to fix his sons under your care and protection, at St John's College in Annapolis. As Mr Carter will accompany the boys, and arrange matters with you, I have only to add that with esteem & regard I am—Sir Your Obedt Hble Servt Go: Washington" (typescript, ViU).

From William Herbert

Dear Sir—   Alexandria 5th October 1798
  Your favor of yesterday Inclosing a letter from mr Be[l]knap I received this Morning, you may Instruct that Gentleman to Direct the Books he mentions, to my Care. I will distribute them Among the Subscribers here, & receive the money for them, if so ordered By him. it will be necessary that a List of the Subscribers Should Accompany them, with such Instructions as mr Belknap may think Necessary.
  The Loan of Money from the Bank, Which I once mentioned to you, is Attainable. the Amount I Can not precisely Ascertain, but am Inclined to think, it may be Extended from Six to ten thousand Dollars. the mode of Obtaining it, is, To Offer your Note payable in Sixty Days after date, for the Sum or Sums that you may Want, With one Endorser here—This Note or Notes, you must renew at the Expiration of every Sixty Days, as long as you may Want the Money, or untill you find it Convenient to pay of the Debt. If Agreeable to you, I will Indorse your Notes, if You have no other Person in View for that purpose. It may be proper to Inform you, that by the Charter of the Bank, no longer Credit than Sixty days Can be given. Consequently When a longer Credit is required, a renewal of the Note, becomes Indispensable—The reason of requiring an Indorser here, is, that Where the Drawer lives at a Distance, the Indorser must be in Town, so that the runner of the Bank may be able to give Notice of the time of payment three Days before it falls due, to one of the parties, & in Case of non payment, that one of them may be Within reach of the Notary publick, to protect the Note—I return you mr Belknap's Letter & am Very respectfully—Dear Sir—your most obedt Hble Servt
                                        Wm Herbert

ALS, DLC:GW. Herbert's commas and periods are for the most part indistinguishable.

From Henry Lee

dear sir   Washington. ocr 5th [1798]
  Mr Custis presented me with yr letr last night.[1]
  Be assured I shall offer you no property not clear in title unless

I may be imposed on, to prevent which am I here daily engaged in exploring the truth.[2]

I have a tract of land near gunston recd from W. Steptoe at valuation for money lent to him some years past. this I propose to offer among other property all of which will be submitted to you soon: about monday next.[3]

No consideration can induce me to pass Mt Vernon & I shall be most happy in contributing at any time & in any way my endeavors to facilitate your execution of the arduous dutys which at this menacing period, yr love of country has compelled you to undertake, & for which all good men feel towards You encreased respect veneration & gratitude. I remain dear General ever yr affec: frend & ob. st

Henry Lee

ALS, DLC:GW. On the cover Lee wrote "favd by Mr Custis."

1. The letter to Lee from GW that George Washington Parke Custis delivered was probably that of 29 September.

2. See GW to Lee, 29 September.

3. For the location of William Steptoe's land on Pohick Creek which adjoined that of William Fitzhugh of Marmion (1725–1791) as well as George Mason's Gunston Hall land downriver from Mount Vernon, see Mason's lengthy disquisition on the land titles of Fitzhugh and Steptoe in his letter to Fitzhugh of 23 Feb. 1787 (Rutland, *Mason Papers*, 3:868–74).

From James McHenry

My dear General   War Department 5th Octbr 1798

I had the honour to receive last night your letter dated the 30th of Sepr Ulto.

I have reason to beleive that the information it contains is well founded. It would be a real and might produce the most extensive & lasting bad consequences, were the army to be composed of men who have heretofore opposed the government & its measures, and beleived in French professions and infallibility. I have a number of applications from and in favour of such characters, and shall use all the means in my power to have those only appointed in whom their generals & the country can place the greatest confidence. With sincere respect and attachment I have the honour to be Your Ob. & hble St

James McHenry

ALS, DLC:GW; ALS, DLC: James McHenry Papers.

From James McHenry

Confidential.

Trenton [N.J.] 5th [October] 1798

I have received my dear Generals two letters dated the first instant, last night.

You will have seen by the newspapers that I have sent an advertisement inviting proposals for clothing for the new regiments and cavalry; but I have not as yet, been able to accomplish a like measure to supply them with subsistence. It is not however too late, as contracts of this kind can be soon formed. When I mentioned my wish that it might be proper for you to express a strong sentiment to Mr Pickering on the subject of the apparent delay in procuring the necessary cloathing, it was to avoid giving room to Mr Wolcott to think I had been dissatisfied with him; and expecting the same benefit from it by reaction, as if it had been directly addressed to himself.

I shall send you in a few days, the instructions which regulate the size of our muskets & bayonets, and by which those under Mr Wolcotts contracts must be made. I have taken a good deal of trouble upon this point, and hope you will be pleased with them. The French Standard as well for the musket as bayonet is strictly adhered to.

I can no otherwise account for the delay of the superintendant in not sending you a return of our military stores, than by his want of clerks and assistants all of whom have deserted. I shall repeat the order.[1]

If you can take preliminary measures to ascertain the fittest characters for the 4 regiments proposed to be raised in the Southern district, without committing yourself, I should think it adviseable, and wish to see the result as soon as possible that we may be prepared to commence recruiting the moment it will be permitted.

I shall the first hour I can spare copy the letter written by me to the President from Mount Vernon and his instructions to me and transmit them.[2] Want of leisure only has heretofore prevented this being done. Your ever faithful and affectionate

James McHenry

ALS, DLC:GW. McHenry mistakenly dated the letter 5 Aug., instead of 5 October.

1. See McHenry to GW, 16 Nov. (second letter), n.1.
2. See GW to McHenry, 16 Sept., nn.2 and 4.

To William Augustine Washington

My dear Sir   Mount Vernon 5th Octr 1798

The enclosed letter was written, as you will perceive, to go by General Lee; who I know is at George Town, and promised to call here on his way down. But as *his ways* are not like the ways of *other men*, and Jerry has called here on his return from Corbin Washington's, I embrace *his*, as the most speedy & certain conveyance of the two.[1]

All those who have lots in the Federal City, contiguous to the Capitol, are much pressed by the Friends of the permanent Government thereat, to build thereon, for the accomodation of the members; as a *certain* mean of bringing Congress there at the period designated in the Law.

I have been induced to buy a lot in the vicinity of the Capitol for this purpose, although I had, before, as many in the City as I wanted. I mention this circumstance for your consideration, as it is of importance to insure the fixture of Congress there. I am always & sincerely Yr Affecte Uncle

Go: Washington

ALS, PPRF. GW wrote on the cover: "By Jerry."

1. The "enclosed letter" from GW to William Augustine Washington is dated 3 October. Jerry probably was one of William Augustine Washington's slaves. Corbin Washington and his wife Hannah Lee Washington had been living since 1797 at Selby, a few miles northeast of Fairfax Courthouse.

Address from the Virginia Militia

Bedford County, State of Virginia [6 October 1798]

At a full meeting of the Officers of the 10th & 91st Regiments of the Virginia Militia, convened at Bedford Court-House on 6th day of October 1798 for the purpose of being trained &c. it was unanimously agreed that Colo. Thomas Leftwich, Colo. John Trigg, Majr David Saunders, Majr Thomas Hubbard, Majr Samuel Handcock, Majr William Burton, Capt. Joel Leftwich & Capt. Isaac Okey be appointed a Committee to prepare an address to our beloved fellow Citizen George Washington on his acceptance of the late appointment of Lieutenant General & Commander in Chief of the American forces, & expressive of the high sense they entertain, of his abilities to discharge the duties of that important office.

The Committee having convened it was agreed that Thomas Leftwich be appointed Chairman & William Leftwich Junr Secretary, & having prepared the following address which was unanimously agreed to, It was Ordered that a Copy thereof be forthwith transmitted to his Excellency George Washington.

To George Washington Lieutenant General & Commander in Chief of the American forces

Sir

The Officers of the 10th & 91st Regiments of the Virginia Militia, recognise with heartfelt pleasure your acceptance of the Commission of Lieutenant General & Commander in Chief of the american forces & while we deprecate the cause which has disturbed your Calm repose we behold with wonder, the unparelleled example, of a person who had retired from power when in full & legitimate possession of it! (which shews at once in a confirmed view the superiority of your virtues) thus Coming forward & giving additional proof, & energy to that firm & vigilent zeal for the public liberty & happiness, those exemplary virtues & ⟨exacted⟩ talents which have given unrivalled lustre & utility to the whole tenor of your life! A number of us having been eye witnesses to that heroism which has so conspicuously marked your Conduct in leading the american Armies thro the bloody contest of the late revolutionary war! we should be unfaithful to the duties of Our Station as Officers, & regardless of the Conviction of Our minds, if we did not declare the warm emotions of respect & gratitude, which services precious as yours have been, excite in every breast; we trust therefore, that your acceptance of the Commission above mentioned, will operate to strengthen sentiments favorable to the union & Safety of these states, to banish local prejudices & Suspicions, cherish love & concord, check the destructive contests of party spirit, & finally to unite in One Common Cause all its Citizens in maintaining its liberty and independence, the foundations of which have been so auspiciously laid under your Control! & in defending of which, be assured Sir that Our best exertions shall never be witheld.

To this permit us to add our fervent supplications to Heaven, that you may long live to enjoy those blessings whch you have been so instrumental in procuring to your Country, and in that repose which you have always sacrificed in obedience to the will of the nation. Sign'd, by Order of the Committee[1]

> Thomas Leftwich Chm.
> William Leftwich Jr Secry

D, DLC:GW.

1. The Leftwiches were a prominent Bedford County family. Col. Thomas Leftwich (1740–1816) served as a captain of militia in the Revolutionary War and later became colonel of the 10th Regiment of Virginia militia. His brother Joel (1760–1846), an ensign during the Revolution, served in the Virginia legislature from 1792 to 1793 and rose to the rank of brigadier general in the state militia during the War of 1812. The Rev. William Leftwich, Jr. (1768–1848), was a Baptist minister and nephew of Thomas and Joel.

GW responded on 24 Oct.: "Gentlemen, While I thank you for your kind and very flattering Address, and the pleasure which I received from your approbation of my acceptance of the Commission which may once more bring me into public life, I am sure you will do justice to the motives which have operated to draw me from that peaceful retirement, which, I fondly hoped, would never again have been interrupted.

"When injuries and Insults have been heaped upon us, and when the Sovereignty and Independence of our Country are threatned, it is, in my opinion, no longer in the option of a good Citizen to withold his Services from the Public. Let his situation be what it may, he forfeits all claim to the rights of one, if, in such a critical moment, he should not use every means in his power to aid in repelling the unprovoked and indignant aggression.

"Upon this ground have I accepted my Commission; and upon this ground I trust that every true American will be prepared to defend his Country against foreign encroachments; and to perpetuate the blessings which he enjoys under his own Government.

"That there may be no occasion to gird on the Sword, none more ardently prays than I do; and no one, with more truth could add, that, if unfortunately, in defence of our rights we shall be compelled to unsheath it ⟨I⟩ hope, after the object is attained, would return it to its scabbard with more heart-felt satisfaction. But to avert the evil, or to meet it like men, it is necessary under the present aspect of our Affairs to hold it in our hands, and be united in one band. Your prayers, and kind wishes in my behalf, I reciprocate with great Cordiality. Go: Washington" (letterpress copy, DLC:GW).

From Rawleigh Colston

Sir,   Winchester Oct. 6th 1798

Inclosed you have a letter I lately received from Mr Thomas Marshall junr of Kentucky, who wrote me at the same time, that there was some small balance due from you to his father Col. Marshall, which he wished to be paid into my hands: If you will be pleased to inform me the amount, I will when agreeable to you, draw for it in favour of my Correspondent in Alexandria⟨.⟩[1] With my best wishes, for a long continuance of your health I am, with the highest respect, Sir, your mo. Obt St

Rawleigh Colston

ALS, ViMtV.

1. The letter from Thomas Marshall, Jr., is dated 4 August. See also GW to Colston, 21 Oct., and GW to Marshall, 22 October.

To Andrew E. Belknap

Sir,   Mount Vernon 8th Oct. 1798.

Your letter of the 20th Ult. came duly to hand.[1] William Herbert Esqr. of Alexandria will receive, distribute, & collect the money agreeably to the subscription I sent you; but it will be necessary to accompany the Books with the original Paper, or a copy thereof for his information with respect to the subscribers; & Instructions.

You will please to recollect that I am in possession already of the *first* volume of the American Biography written by your deceased & worthy father. and I will just add that, if to my name is annexed more than *one* Copy, it was done with a view to encourage the work *in continuation*; more therefore would be useless to me. And if the surplus could be disposed of where they are, it would be more agreeable to me. but do as you please in this respect. I am—Sir Your Very Hble Servt

Go: Washington

ALS, PPRF; ALS (letterpress copy), DLC:GW; LB, DLC:GW.

1. Belknap's letter of 20 Sept. from Boston reads: "The second volume of American Biography written by my father (Jeremy Belknap) is now published and ready to deliver to subscribers. As I have no acquaintance at Alexandria, I have to request of you to inform me to whose care I shall send the Books which were subscribed for on the paper which you obligingly returned some time since" (DLC:GW).

To William Herbert

Dear Sir   Mount Vernon 8th Oct. 1798

I thank you for the information contained in your letter of the 5th instant & will avail myself of your kind offer, if circumstances shd render it expedient for me to have recourse to the Bank of

Alexandria. Either of the sums mentioned therein, is more than I shall want; and if I could receive what I ought to do, I shall have no occasion for any from that source.[1]

I will inform young Mr Belknap of your obliging offer—and with very great esteem & regard I am—Dear Sir Yr obedt Hble Servt

Go: Washington

ALS (letterpress copy), DLC:GW; LB, DLC:GW.

1. GW asked Herbert on 4 Oct. about the terms of a loan from Herbert's bank in the expectation that he would at some point require a loan to complete the construction of the two houses that he intended to build in Washington. As it happened, GW did not have to resort to borrowing money from the bank in Alexandria until June 1799 (see GW to Herbert, 25 June 1799).

To Samuel Hodgdon

Sir,   Mount Vernon 8th Octr 1798

The Paper mentioned in your letter of the 23d of August I have recd. I wish there had been more of the Patent copying sort, as what you have sent will soon be expended; and I may find it difficult to obtain a supply here. Of the letter Paper, I shall find no want in the stores of Alexandria. If you had accompanied the Paper with Wax and Wafers, they would have been convenient & acceptable. With esteem I am—Sir Your Obedt Hble Servt

Go: Washington

ALS (letterpress copy), DLC:GW.

From John Adams

Sir   Quincy [Mass.] October 9th 1798

I received, yesterday the Letter you did me the Honor to write me on the 25th of September.

You request to be informed, whether my determination to reverse the order of the three Major Generals, is final. and whether I mean to appoint another Adjutant General without your Concurrence. I presume, that before this Day you have received Information, from the Secretary at War, that I some time ago Signed the three Commissions and dated them on the Same day, in hopes Similar to yours that an amicable Adjustment or Acquiescence might take place among the Gentlemen themselves.[1] But, if these hopes should be disappointed, and Controversies should arise, they will of course be submitted to you as Commander in Chief, and if after all any one should be so obstinate as to appeal to me from the Judgment of the Commander in Chief, I was determined to confirm that Judgment. Because, whatever Construction may be put upon the Resolutions of the ancient Congress which have been applied to this Case, and whether they are at all applicable to it or not, there is no doubt to be made, that by the present Constitution of the United States, the President has Authority to determine the Rank of officers.

I have been for some time prepared in my own Mind to nominate Mr Dayton to be Adjutant General, in Case of the Refusal of Mr North. Several others have occurred and been Suggested to me, but none who in point of science or Litterature, political and military Merit or Energy of Character, appear to be equal to him. I have no exclusive attachment to him or any other. If you have any other in contemplation, I pray you to mention him to the Secretary at War who may fill up his Commission immediately, in Case Mr North declines.[2]

I hope your own Health and that [of] Mrs Washington are perfect. Mine is very indifferent and Mrs Adams's extreamly low— confined to the Bed of Sickness for two Months her Destiny is Still very precarious, and mine in consequence of it. With great Respect I have the Honor to be, Sir your most obedient and most humble servant

John Adams

ALS, DLC:GW; LB, MHi-A; copy, in GW's hand, privately owned; copy, in the hand of a clerk, DLC: Hamilton Papers.

1. It was not until 16 Oct. that James McHenry wrote GW that on 30 Sept. President Adams had sent him the commissions of the three major generals, "signed and dated on the same day."

2. For references to the dispute regarding Jonathan Dayton and William North, see James McHenry to GW, 19 Sept., and notes 4 and 8 of that document.

To Benjamin Stoddert

Sir   Mount Vernon 9th Oct. 1798
    Captn John Spotswood (Son of General Spotswood of this State) will have the honor of presenting this letter to you.

He means to offer his Services in the Naval line. He has been long accustomed to a Sea faring life—is a good Navigator—and for many years has been Master & Commander of Vessels. He is sober. His wishes can be best expressed by himself—& you will be the best judge of their propriety.[1] With great esteem & regard I am Sir Your Most Obedt Hble Ser.

Go: Washington

ALS (letterpress copy), DLC:GW.

1. For GW's dealings with John Augustine Spotswood, see Alexander Spotswood to GW, 16 Sept. 1798, n.6. In 1799 GW recommended another son of Alexander Spotswood for a commission in the navy (see GW to Stoddert, 10 July 1799).

From Bartholomew Dandridge

Dear sir,   London 10 October 1798.

Since I had the pleasure to write to you in august informing you of my intention to leave Holland & to return to America, some circumstances have occur'd which induced me to take another course.[1] My ill health was the ground of my wish to quit Holland & an opportunity to remove to a dryer & I hope more healthy climate, & to retain at the same time the advantages which I enjoy'd in other respects, having presented itself I have thought proper to avail my-self of it. Mr King, our Minister here whom you know well, had long been without a Secretary, & an American friend of mine who was at the Hague on his way to London advised me to apply for the vacancy—I authorised him to do it for me—he did so, and in-formed me that it wd be quite agreeable to Mr King to have me with him if Mr Murray consented. I had previously inform'd Mr M. of my intention to quit him, as I wrote you, & he had written to Mr McHenry's Nephew to come to him. As Mr K. was in immediate want Mr M. was so good as to agree to my going directly, taking Majr Mountflorence who was at the Hague & who was with Genl Pinckney at Paris to supply my place *provisionally*. I arrived here on the 6 inst: & have been kindly recd by Mr King. I conceived it incumbent on me to give you this account wch I hope will not be disagreeable to you, & at the same time Sir to offer my services to you while I am here in any way you shall be pleased to require them. I pray you to present my affecte respects to my Aunt & to assure yourself of my unalter'd esteem & attachment.

B. Dandridge

P.S. Just as I was concludg the above *Lord* Fairfax was announced to Mr K.—& to my great surprize when his *Lordship* was ushered in, who shd it be but your old friend Bryan Fairfax. I have had the pleasure to learn from him that you & your family enjoy'd excellent health when he left you. I shall call on him & Know more particularly about you.

ALS, PPRF.

1. Dandridge wrote to GW on 20 August.

From Samuel Knox

Sir   Fredericktown [Md.] 10th of Octr 1798

Being About to publish, by subscription an Essay on the best Method of Introducing an Uniform System of Education adapted to the United States, I Beg leave to solicit the favour of your permission to prefix to it an Introductory address to you.

Though I own this Request is dictated by a share of vanity in presuming to be ambitious of so high a recommendatory sanction to my Essay; yet I truly declare that, what has chiefly prompted me thereto arises from a desire to express, on a Subject of that Nature, How much I Consider the Cause of Education indebted to your patronage through the whole of your publick Character.

The Essay I am about to publish, obtain'd the premium offer'd by the Philosophical Society of Philadelphia, on that subject, together with one written by a Mr Smith of that place. The Society passed a Resolution to publish them; but were disappointed by the Printer who had Undertaken that Business.[1]

On being inform'd of this by their Secretary, And that the publication would be, on this Account, long retarded, by the advice of some friends I was induc'd to publish it, by subscription, in this State—from the view of it's, probably, having some effect in turning the attention of our State-Legislature to that Subject. From this view I have Received the Manuscript from the Secretary of the Phil[adelph]ia Philosophical Society; And shall proceed to publish [as] soon as I Can ascertain whether I am to Have the Honour of dedicating or addressing it to you.[2]

Two or three weeks since I was at Alexandria, designing to have personally waited on you; And if necessary to have given you some view of the Essay—Doctor Steuart near that place who has long known me, promised doing me the favour of introducing me to you; But learning that the State of your Health, at that time, forbade any such trouble, I flatter'd myself that this mode of application might be equally as proper—especially, as I have had the pleasure of seeing it announc'd to the Publick that your Health is again perfectly restor'd.

I Have Spent more than twenty years of my Life in the Education of youth. A considerable part of that time I Resided at Bladensburgh in this State—and remember having once had the Honour of being Introduc'd to you by Coll Fitzgerald of Alexandria—at a publick Examination of the youth in that Academy. Since that time I Study'd four years at one of the most celebrated Universities in Britain—and recd a Master of Art's Degree, from the view of being Useful to Myself; this Country in particular; and Society in general—in the line of my profession as a Teacher of Youth—and a Minister of the Gospel. On my return to this Country I was offer'd the Charge of the Alexandria-Academy by it's Visitors or Trustees with a Salary of 200 pounds Currency per Annum. But having a family to Support, I did not Consider their terms sufficiently liberal; or promising me a sufficient Compensation for the preparatory expence I Had been at in qualifying Myself for the Business.[3]

I take the Liberty of Mentioning these circumstances merely from the view of informing you that in presuming to Solicit the Sanction of your Name to my Publication; and in venturing to lay My thoughts before an enlighten'd Publick on so important a Subject, It has not been without long experience in, as well as mature attention to the most improved Methods of publick Education.

Joining in the general tribute of sincere Congratulation; and thanks to Divine Providence for the restoration of your Health, I am, Sir, your Most devoted Obedt Hble Servt

Saml Knox

ALS, DLC:GW.

Samuel Knox (1756–1832), a Scot who received an M.A. degree from the University of Glasgow in 1792, was a Presbyterian minister and at this time was principal of an academy in Frederick, Maryland. He became well known for his *Essay on the Best System of Liberal Education, Adapted to the Genius of the Government of the United States* (Baltimore, 1799), a copy of which was in GW's library at Mount Vernon at the time of his death.

1. At the meeting of the American Philosophical Society in Philadelphia on 15

Dec. 1797, essays on education submitted for the society's prize were read aloud and two were judged worthy of publication. The members voted to divide the prize between the authors of the two papers, and "the President pro tem then opened the sealed letters—Revd Sam Knox of Bladensburgh, Md., was the author of the first, and Sam[uel] H. Smith of Phila. author of the Second" ("Early Proceedings of the American Philosophical Society, 1744–1838," in *Proceedings of the American Philosophical Society*, 22 [July 1885], pt. 3, p. 265). The minutes for the meeting of 23 Nov. 1798 include this entry: "Mr. Williams reported that the printer had declined to fulfill his contract to print Mr. Knox's paper on Education, which had been returned to Mr. Knox, who would publish it himself" (ibid., 274).

2. GW replied from Mount Vernon on 14 Oct.: "Revd Sir, Your favour of the 10th instant has been duly received, and I feel grateful for the honor of your proposed Dedication of an 'Uniform System of Education, adapted to the United States' to me.

"Had I not declined similar honors, in all cases where previous applications have been made, I certainly should, with much pleasure, have yielded to one on so important a subject as you have written. But this being the case, I am compelled for the sake of consistency to decline accepting the compliment of yours.

"I sincerely wish success to your undertaking and shall, very chearfully, become a Subscriber to the Work. With respect I am—Revd Sir Your Most Obedt Hble Servt Go: Washington" (letterpress copy, DLC:GW; LB, DLC:GW).

3. After his stay in Scotland, Knox returned to the United States in 1795 and secured a pastorate in Bladensburg, Maryland.

Memorandum of Agreement with James Welch

[11 October 1798]

Mr James Welch having signified to me, that he has it is in his power to dispose of part of a tract of Ninety Nine thousand nine hundred and ninety five acres of land lying on Elk River in the County of Randolph, conveyed to me in Trust, and proposing to subject other Lands of equal or greater value in lieu thereof, in like trust, and intimating further that it will be an accomodation to him, and a benefit to me in his payments to make the exchange.

I do therefore hereby certifie, that upon the ascertainment of this fact, that is, that the substituted property is of equal value, & free from all disputes & incumbrances, I am willing to receive it in lieu of such part of the aforementioned tract of 99,995 Acrs. as he shall dispose of, and that I will release my claim accordingly, to the same, upon receiving a proper conveyance of the substituted property[1]—Given under my hand this 11th day of Octr 1798.

Go: Washington

ADfS, DLC:GW.

1. For James Welch's negotiations with GW in November and December 1797 leading to Welch's acquiring GW's Kanawha lands, see Welch to GW, 29 Nov. 1797, n.1, and references. When on 10 Dec. 1797 GW spelled out for his attorney James Keith the terms of sale, he made no mention of Welch's conveyance to him, in trust, of land on the Elk. Keith, however, may have included this in the indenture that GW and Welch signed on 16 Dec. 1797. Welch spent the night of 11 Oct. 1798 at Mount Vernon (*Diaries*, 6:319). In the correspondence between the two men in 1799, in which GW seeks without success to secure payment from Welch, the sale of the land on the Elk again comes up (see GW to Welch, 15 Feb., 7 April, 26 May 1799, and Welch to GW, 10 Mar., 25 April, 16 May 1799).

From the Charles Town Academy Trustees

Sir   Charles Town October 13th 1798

The Trustees of the Charles Town Academy, beg leave to state to you the real situation of the school under their Gurdeanship; hoping that an institution calculated, & designed to dissemenate useful knowlege may meet with some encouragement from You— They have under many discouraging circumstances, and after encountering many difficulties been enabled to complete a two story brick House in this Town, which from the aid of a few individuals is entierly paid for.

The attention and abilities of the Teachers heretofore employed, have they believe deservedly obtained a considerable degree of reputation to the School.

At the late examination (the first monday in this month) the students to the number of thirty acquited themselves much to the credit of the Teachers, and to the entier satisfaction of the Trustees.

But, sir, as the Salary of the Teachers is altogether dependant on the funds arising from the Tuition of the students; the Trustees fear, that the advantages which the community at large, and this neighbourhood in particular, will derive from so useful an institution, can not be perpetuated without some permanent funds for its support—To this end, Sir, is their application to you—and they are induced to it from several consideration; but espetially from the hope, that if they obtain the Patronage of a name so deservedly esteemed by every American, that it will have a happy influence in procuring assistance from others of their fellow citizens—This will be handed to you by Messrs Geo. Washington &

Geo. Hite two of the members of our board who will at the same time put into your hands a copy of the bye Laws for the organization & Government of the Academy, by which means you will be the better informed, of the Plan contemplated (after Mature deliberation) by the Trustees.[1] We are sir in behalf of the board of Trustees of the Charles Tow[n] academy with every sentiment of respect & Esteem your Most obedient & Most Humble Servants

George Washington Chai[rma]n

Chrisr Collins Secy

L, DLC:GW.

GW's nephew George Steptoe Washington (c.1773–1808) was living outside Charles Town at Harewood with his wife, Lucy Payne Washington. Christopher Collins was a Baptist preacher in Charles Town.

1. The letter was sent under cover of a letter of the same day from George Steptoe Washington and George Hite: "The inclosed letter we should have done ourselves the Honour of delivering with our own hands, was it not for the particular situation of our domestick concerns; and being some what apprehensive least the calls of our country might require your absence from Mount Vernon; in which case the inte[n]tion of the Trustees would be altogether frustrated. It is our intention nevertheless to do ourselves the Honour of waiting upon you in person, and to make such further communication as we are charged with by the Board of Trustees" (DLC:GW). In 1795 twelve men were elected trustees of an academy to be built in Charles Town: Philip Pendleton, Thomas Griggs, Thomas Rutherford, Sr., Gabriel Nourse, Christopher Collins, George Steptoe Washington, George Hite, Ferdinando Fairfax, George North, Alexander White, and the Rev. William Hill. Two thousand dollars having been raised, the trustees in 1795 began the construction, under the supervision of George Hite and William Hill, of a building for the school. The Charles Town Academy was incorporated on 3 Feb. 1797.

From Timothy Pickering

Sir,   Trenton [N.J.] Oct. 13 1798

I seize the first conveyance to inform you that General Pinckney is out of France. He embarked with his family, about the middle of August, in the ship Hope, Capt. Hendrick Hendrickson, for New-York, where we may daily expect to hear of his arrival. The letter giving me this information is from a Monsieur Hory, dated at Bourdeaux the 27th of August; it came to hand last evening from Chester (Pennsylvania) where it arrived in the ship Franklin.[1]

Mr Fenwick inclosed me a letter from Mr Skipwith, dated at Paris the 21st of August, in which Skipwith says—"I have received to-day an official copy of the arret of the Directory taking off the embargo laid on our vessels. This arret is not yet published, but I hope it will be soon, in every part of France, and of course put to execution." Fenwick writes on the 28th of August from Bordeaux, saying "This arret has not yet officially reached this port, but is hourly expected: tho' some apprehensions are entertained that if the late accounts from Philadelphia, by the flag vessel the Liberty, that sailed about the 18th of July, and arrived here a few days past, should reach Paris before the execution of the arret raising the embargo, it may be delayed." But I have a private letter from a reputable merchant at Bordeaux, dated the 27th of August, which says—"The news brought by the Liberty has made no great sensation." [2]

I have a Paris paper dated the 24th of August, in which is a paragraph from Philadelphia dated July 24th. This paragraph mentions the acts of Congress for suspending all intercourse between the U. States & the French Dominions—for taking French cruizers on our coast & retaking their prizes—for a provisional army—for a direct tax on lands—and for expelling foreigners. [3]

In the same paper I find a paragraph of which the following is a translation.

"Paris August 23 1798. The Wife of la-Fayette has been some days in Paris. As she went away in virtue of regular passports, and the express permission of the Government, she comes back to restore order in her estates, impaired during her long detention in the Dungeons of the Emperor."

The private letter above mentioned says—"The French Government wishes to keep peace with America. But a war with the emperor seems to be inevitable." The correspondence between Talleyrand and Mr Gerry discovers a solicitude on the part of the former to avoid a rupture: the French Government, doubtless, is not yet ready to attack us. [4]

The Boston papers are beginning to puff Mr Gerry: but take into view the whole series, of his conduct in France, and he must, in the eyes of every man of sense, sink into contempt.

You will probably have seen my letter of the 29th ult. to P[eter] Johnston, returning the address to the President from the Freeholders of Prince Edward County; in that letter I disclosed a fact communicated to me by General Marshall, which I was glad to authenticate by my signature (for published anonymously it would have been denied by some, and doubted by others) and in which you will see an evidence of Talleyrand's unblushing impudence, and of Gerry's timidity & meanness in consenting to give up the names of X & Y when they have dined with him at Talleyrands table, & after dinner renewed their money propositions![5] But there is another fact which I take from his own letter to me dated in Nantasket Road the 1st instant, detailing his correspondence with Talleyrand. When Talleyrand sent him his letter of June 1 asking the names of the persons designated by X Y & Z. Gerry desired to know of the bearer why application was again made to him for the names of the intriguers, when they could be otherwise ascertained. The Bearer answered, that he believed, by the exertions of the Bureau & of the officers of the police of the city, the names were discovered; *and he mentioned them to Mr Gerry*: but he added, that matters were become serious; that the Directory expected something from him, in confirmation of this discovery; *and that this was the use which would be made of his letters.* Yet Gerry thinks to shield himself from the charge of violating the faith of the Envoys pledged to X & Y "that in no event should their names be made public"—by "guarding against the publication *on his authority!*" Pitiful subterfuge! added to unexampled meanness, in stooping to comply, in any form, with the insulting demand![6] I have the honour to be, with great respect, sir, your most obt servant,

Timothy Pickering

ALS, PPRF; ALS (letterpress copy), MHi: Pickering Papers.

1. Daniel Huger (later Charles Lucas Pinckney) Horry, Charles Cotesworth Pinckney's nephew, had been in France since "the commencement of the revolution" (GW to Charles Cotesworth Pinckney, 24 June 1797, n.1). A copy of the letter from Horry of 27 Aug. is in MHi-A, enclosed in a letter from Pickering to John Adams of 13 October.

2. A French decree of 9 July 1798 had placed an embargo on American ships in French ports; this was repealed by another decree on 16 August. Copies of the letters from Fulwar Skipwith of 21 Aug. 1798 and Joseph Fenwick of 28 Aug. are in MHi-A, enclosed in a letter from Pickering to Adams of 13 Oct. 1798. The "reputable merchant" is Theodore Peters, whose letter is in MHi: Pickering Papers.

3. These are "An Act to suspend the commercial intercourse between the United States and France, and the dependencies thereof" (1 *Stat.* 565–66 [13 June 1798]), "An Act further to protect the Commerce of the United States" (1 *Stat.* 578–80 [9 July 1798]), "An Act authorizing the President of the United States to raise a Provisional Army" (1 *Stat.* 558–61 [28 May 1798]), "An Act to lay and collect a direct tax within the United States" (1 *Stat.* 597–604 [14 July

1798]), and either "An Act concerning Aliens" (1 *Stat.* 570–72 [25 June 1798]) or "An Act respecting Alien Enemies" (1 *Stat.* 577–78 [6 July 1798]).

4. For the correspondence between Elbridge Gerry and Talleyrand, see *ASP, Foreign Relations*, 2:209–22.

5. The address from the freeholders of Prince Edward County to John Adams of 21 Aug. took the president severely to task for his French policy and depicted the congressional war resolutions as part of a conspiracy against the rights of the people. Pickering refused to submit the address to Adams and instead wrote his own scathing reply on 29 September. See *Life of Pickering*, 3:471–79.

6. Gerry's letter to Pickering of 1 Oct. is printed in *ASP, Foreign Relations*, 2:204–8.

Letter not found: from Mildred Thornton Washington, 13 Oct. 1798. On 18 Oct. GW wrote Mildred Washington: "Your favour of the 13th instt came duly to hand."

Letter not found: from the District of Columbia Commissioners, 15 Oct. 1798. On 17 Oct. GW acknowledged the receipt of the commissioners' "favour of the 15th."

To James McHenry

Dear Sir   Mount Vernon 15th Octr 1798

Your letter of the 2d, and three of the 5th instant, came duly to hand.[1] Those of the latter date, were received late in the evening preceeding my visit to the Federal City, where I was detained several days on business; and is the cause of their remaining unacknowledged so long.[2]

In the former, you ask if I am acquainted with characters, who have talents and acquirements to fit them for the command of the Corps of Artillerists and Engineers? I am so far from the possession of such knowledge, that I should be unwilling to hazard a recommendation of any, to these important Offices. Mr Edward Rutledge of Charleston So. Carolina commands the Artillery Corps of that State, and is a man of Spirit and abilities. He is, besides, the particular friend of General Pinckney; but I have no idea (if he was agreeable to the President) that the Rank of Lieut. Colonel Commandant would induce him to come forward. Major Rivardi (now in the Service of the U. States) is, I am told, a Scientific character, & a man of experience. He is a Swiss, and was sometime in the Service of Russia. How he has conducted himself in ours, your opportunities, better than any information of mine, will enable you to judge. He is gentlemanly in his appearance, & by those who know him better than I do, said to be a man of abilities & information.[3]

With respect to the Officers for the Regiments, which (by the plan you submitted to the President) are to be raised in the Southern division; I have made, and shall continue to make, such enquiries for suitable ones, as I can do without committing myself, if it should not be approved; and in *this State* I might be able, I presume, with the aids I could derive, to make a tolerable good Selection for the proportion, or quota of the four Regiments it would have to furnish. But this is not to be done in the Southern, and Western States without relying upon others: and in whom can more confidence be placed than in the General Officers therein, who are to experience the good—or the evil—which will result from proper, or improper selections? My opinion therefore is, that after the quota of men, required from each State is ascertained, that the least tardy, & most efficient mode would be, to send a list of the applicants from each to the General Officers, or Officer, (where there are any) residing there in, and therefrom; or from his or their own knowledge of other characters; and such information as can be obtain'd; make a selection of Officers of the different grades; proportioned thereto; and to know whether they will, or will not serve in the grades alloted. This to be final; that the recruiting Service may commence without *further delay*. But if the President chuses to have a check upon this measure, let such arrangements be forwarded without delay to the War Office for sanction, or alteration, at his pleasure; and returned for the purpose abovementioned; for it is of the highest importance that the Augmented force should be raised, & in training as soon as possible.

Generals Pinckney and Washington would, I am confident, be careful in their selection of Officers for the Troops to be raised in South Carolina & Georgia; and from the character of General Davie, I should hope he would not be less attentive to those to be taken from No. Carolina:[4] How this might be in the State of Tennessee, I cannot say; and with respect to Kentucky, I am more at a loss to express any opinion.

Enclosed is a sketch of the quotas which the States in the Southern division would have to furnish of the four Regiments of Infantry, & six Troops of horse according to the Census, & state of the present Representation.[5] If upon due consideration it should be approved, it might go into immediate execution; either by an immediate order from the War Office, or mediately through the Commander in Chief, as shall be deemed best. In the former case, I conceive it ought to be accompanied with Instructions to the Generals, or persons to whom the order issues, to give, in the selection of fit characters, a preference first, to Officers of the Revolutionary army who are in the prime of life; who have distinguished themselves by their bravery, attention, & gentlemanly deportment; & who have not forfeited their pretensions to either of these qualifications since—2dly if such are not to be found; next, to young Gentleman of good families, liberal educations, and high sense of honour; and 3d in neither case to any who are known enemies to their own government: for they will as certainly attempt to create disturbances in the Military, as they have done in the Civil Administration of their Country. With great esteem & regard I am—Dear Sir Your Most Obedt Servt

Go: Washington

P.S. In treating on the Subject of Regimental Officers, for the Augmentation—Colo. Willm Smith of New York again occurs. I know not on what precise ground the nomination of him was rejected by the Senate, and therefore to *advise* bringing him forward again might be improper—nor should I incline to do it, if there was just cause to impeach either his integrity, or his attachment to the measures of Government. But I have always viewed Colo. Smith in the light of an Officer possessing Military talents, and conceive, if he would accept of it, that the command of one of the Regiments about to be raised in the middle district of the United States could not be better bestowed.[6]

G. W——n

ALS, LNHT: George and Katherine Davis Collection; ALS (letterpress copy), DLC:GW.

1. Only two letters from McHenry dated 5 Oct. have been found.

2. GW wrote in his diary: "10 and eleventh absent—in the Federal City—Weather warm & dry the whole time" (*Diaries*, 6:319).

3. For more on Rivardi, see GW to Alexander Hamilton, 25 Feb. 1799 (first letter), n.2.

4. See GW's letter to William Washington of 27 September.

5. See Enclosure I.

6. See James McHenry to GW, 19 Sept., and n.7 of that document.

Enclosure
Troop Quotas

Mount Vernon 15th Octr 1798

By the Act "To augment the Army of the United States, & for other purposes." Twelve Regiments of Infantry, and six Troops of Light Dragoons, are to be added to the present force—By the Establishment of them, the first will consist of 7680 Rank & File, and the 2d of 354. If four Regiments of the former, and all the latter, are to be raised in the States South of the Potomack, the quota of each State, agreeably to the Population, to the present Representation, and to a medium between the two, will be as follow.

viz.

	Population			Representn			Medium		
States	Infantry	Cavalry	Total	Infantry	Cavalry	Total	Infantry	Cavalry	Total
Virginia	1296	180	1476	1216	167	1383	1256	174	1430
No. Carolina	500	69	569	640	88	728	570	79	649
So. Carolina	432	60	492	384	55	439	408	57	465
Georgia	143	20	163	128	17	145	135	18	253
Kentucky	127	16	143	128	16	144	128	16	144
Tennessee	62	8	70	64	8	72	63	8	71

The remoteness of Kentucky and Tennessee from the Seaboard, where it is presumed the theatre of War will be; is opposed to the raising of Dragoons in either of those States. And to avoid broken Companies of Infantry, or Troops of Dragoons in any other State, the following plan of arrangement of both Officers & Privates, conformably to the preceeding calculation & principle (as nearly as the case will admit) is suggested for consideration.

	Infantry							
States	Lieut. Colos. Command.	Majors	Captains	Lieutents	Ensigns	Sergeants	Musick	Rank & File
Virginia	2	4	20	20	20	30	40	1200
No. Carolina	1	2	9	9	9	36	18	576
So. Carolina	1	1	6	6	6	24	12	384
Georgia	—	1	2	2	2	8	4	128
Kentucky	—	—	2	2	2	8	4	128
Tennessee	—	—	1	1	1	4	2	64
	4	8	40	40	40	160	80	2560

	Dragoons							
[States]	Lieut. Colls Comman-dts	Majors	Cap-tains	Lieu-tents	Ensigns	Ser-geants	Musick	Rank & File
[Virginia]	—	1	3	6	3	12	3	177
[No. Carolina]	—	—	2	4	2	8	2	118
[So. Carolina]	—	—	1	2	1	4	1	59
[Georgia]	—	—	—	—	—	—	—	—
[Kentucky]	—	—	—	—	—	—	—	—
[Tennessee]	—	—	—	—	—	—	—	—
	—	1	6	12	6	24	6	354

The appointment of Adjutants, Quarter Masters, Paymasters, Surgeons and Surgeons Mates; Sergeant Majors, Quarter Master Sergeants, and Senior Musicians, does not press; and of necessity must be postponed where Regiments are composed of Troops from different States until they are abt to unite.

The Corporals, Saddlers, and Farriers are included in the above Rank and file.

The Lieutenant Colonel Commandant is not assigned to any State; because it is not known from whence the most eligable character can be obtained. Another Major of Dragoons is also wanting.

If Major Talmadge would accept the command of this Corps, I know of none who is preferable. A Captn Watts of this State—an Officer of celebrity in the Revolutionary War, is very highly recommended by General Lee. as is a Captn Armstrong (now of Georgia) by the same, but what the conduct of these Gentlemen have been latterly, and what their politics now are he knows not. Perhaps the oldest Captain of Dragoons, now in Service, or both of them, may be Meritorious Officers; and entitled to consideration.[1]

Go: Washington

ADS, LNHT: George and Katherine Davis Collection; ADf, DLC:GW; ADS (letter-press copy), DLC:GW.

1. John Watts (1752–1830) of Bedford County served as captain of dragoons during the Revolutionary War and was wounded in 1781 at Eutaw Springs. He appears on the list of Candidates for Army Appointments from Virginia, November 1798, printed below, and served as a lieutenant colonel of the dragoons of the U.S. Army from 8 Jan. 1799; see also GW to James McHenry, 5 May

1799 (second letter), n.3. James Armstrong, who in 1799 received his appointment as a major of infantry, served as a captain of dragoons during the Revolutionary War (see Anthony Wayne to GW, 20 Mar. 1790).

To Timothy Pickering

Dear Sir,   Mount Vernon 15th Octr 1798

The information contained in your letter of the 3d instant was highly grateful to me. Such communications are not only satisfactory to me, but are really useful; for while I hold myself in readiness to obey the call of my Country, it is expedient that I should have more authentic information than News Paper inconsistencies, of the approaching, or receding storm; that I may regulate my private concerns accordingly. So far then as you can give this, with propriety, would be received with thankfulness; and if under the seal of confidence, will be locked up in my own breast.

It is pleasing to hear, that we had so few ships in France when the Directory thereof were pleased to lay an Embargo thereon. I wish, on many accounts, that General Pinckney was as safely landed in his own Country as I hear Mr Gerry is, after his *terrible fright*. I hope, so soon as he is relieved from the Panic with which he was struck, and wch must have continued whilst he remained on the watry element, he will come forward in stronger language than his last letter to Mr Talleyrand contains, and with such explanations as his own character requires, & his Country has a right to demd.

We have nothing new in this quarter; an excessive drought, which still prevails, has been hurtful to our crops; and presses sorely upon the winter grain & grass seeds which have been sown this autumn. Maryland, instead of acquiring strength in her Federal representation, by the last Election, has lost ground.[1] What will be the result of the Elections in this state (in March next) is more I believe than any one can foretell at present. No stone is left unturned that can affect the federal Interest by the Democrats. With great esteem & regard I am—Dr Sir—Yr Obedt Hble Ser.

Go: Washington

ALS, MHi: Pickering Papers; ALS (letterpress copy), DLC:GW; copy, in the hand of Pickering's clerk, DLC: Hamilton Papers.

1. In the October elections the Republicans gained two seats in the U.S. House of Representatives.

From Timothy Pickering

Sir,   Trenton [N.J.] Oct. 15 1798

This morning I saw a New-York paper announcing the arrival of General Pinckney, & that on account of the prevailing fever, he had landed at Paulus Hook: So I expect in two or three days to have the happiness to see him.

The inclosed letter I received yesterday morning, with others by the mail from New-York.[1] I have the honor to be with great respect sir your most obt servt

Timothy Pickering

ALS, DLC:GW.

   1. The enclosed letter has not been found.

From James McHenry

Dear Sir   War Department 16 Octbr 1798

The President of the United States on the 30th of Sepr Ulto inclosed to me commissions for the three Major Generals of the army, signed and dated on the same day.[1]

When I considered the communications which may be expected from this department, at the time of presenting his commission to each of the generals, I found myself embarrassed respecting the course which he meant I should pursue on the occasion. It was my earnest wish to avoid the renewal of a subject, that had already been attended with too many unpleasant circumstances by returning the question upon him for more precise instructions. After therefore considerable deliberation, and as the most respectful course to him, I at last was induced to transmit the commissions to Generals Hamilton & Knox, and to inform them, that I considered the order of nomination and approval by the Senate as determining their relative rank.

I have also, my dear Sir, written to Generals Hamilton & Knox, calling them into service, and soliciting their presence, as soon as possible, and in all events by the 10th of November proximo. I suggested also to the President that it would be desireable I should be authorised to require your attendance, and that his own presence would be important and give facility to all measures relative to this meeting.[2]

My object in convening these officers is to derive from the knowledge they may have of the several characters, who have applied for military appointments, and others disposed to enter into the army, effectual and necessary aid in the selection and application of the most suitable to the different grades, and to prepare in conjunction with them, a list for the Presidents final determination; and also to avail myself of their knowledge and experience in digesting a report to be submitted for his approbation—relative—1st To the measures necessary to be pursued to give efficacy and ensure success to the recruiting service. 2 To the distribution of the military force of the United States. 3d To the most certain, regular and œconomical mode of provisioning the recruits and the troops in the field. 4 The quantity and kind of artillery, military stores and other articles necessary to be procured, in addition to what we already have in our magazines and arsenals, and the proper places for occasional or permanent deposits of the same.[3] With the most sincere respect and esteem I have the honour to be Dr Sir your most hble st

                                                    James McHenry

ALS, DLC:GW; ALS, DLC: James McHenry Papers.

1. John Adams's covering note to the commissions, dated 30 Sept., is in DLC: McHenry Papers.

2. McHenry's letter to Alexander Hamilton of 15 Oct. is printed in Syrett, *Hamilton Papers*, 22:199. McHenry's letter to Adams, dated 15 Oct., is in MHi-A. The letter from McHenry to Knox has not been found.

3. See McHenry's second letter of this date.

From James McHenry

(Confidential)
my dear Sir.   Trenton [N.J] 16 Octbr 1798

You will see by the inclosed the step I have taken, and the information and aid which I expect to derive from the Major Generals in case it is approved, and also the desire I have to draw you for a short time to Philadelphia.[1] I know not how all this is to end, and feel perfectly tired of the uncertainty in which so many important measures are kept fettered and involved.

I hope you will approve of the exposition I have given of my views, and the propriety of my fortifying or correcting my own opinions by those of the Generals. I have informed Hamilton of the points upon which I shall look for his assestance that he may come prepared.

I am extremely anxious to know the result of your letter to the President. Yours ever & affectionately

James McHenry

ALS, DLC:GW. McHenry sent a similarly worded letter to Hamilton on the same day, including possibly the same enclosures.

1. Among the enclosures probably were McHenry's letters to John Adams and to Alexander Hamilton of 15 Oct., as well as a letter written to Henry Knox around the same date. See McHenry's first letter of this date and GW's second letter to McHenry of 21 October.

Letter not found: from William Thornton, 16 Oct. 1798. On 18 Oct. GW wrote Thornton: "I regret, not having received your letter of the 16th until last night."

To the District of Columbia Commissioners

Gentlemen   Mount Vernon 17th Oct. 1798

Your favour of the 15th, enclosing Mr Blagdens statement, relative to my proposed buildings, did not reach my hands until last night.[1]

He has not accompanied this Statement with Specific prices; nor has it altered my opinion of the unreasonableness of the former estimates of some of its parts. But being desirous of closing the matter with Mr Blagden some way, or other, I make him the following offer—viz.—To take the Painting, Glazing and Iron mongery to myself; and allow him besides, Ten thousand five hundred Dollars in full of Commission and every other charge for completing the buildings agreeably to the Specification which he handed to me, and is now in his possession.

If he will agree to this proposal, the contract may be immediately drawn; and he may proceed in all the preparatory measures as soon as he pleases—Money shall be furnished for the purpose. and if it would be convenient & advantageous to him, to have the *whole* of the Scantling and Plank provided by a Bill of the same, & he would furnish me therewith, I would immediately order it from the Eastern Shore of Maryland.[2]

On the other hand, if he will not agree to it, I must have recourse to some other mode to accomplish my object. The final answer of Mr Blagden must be received without delay; as the opportunity of providing materials on good terms may be missed. With great esteem and regard I am Gentlemen Your Most Obedt Servt

Go: Washington

ALS (letterpress copy), DLC:GW; LB, DLC:GW.

1. Neither the letter nor George Blagdin's "statement" has been found.

2. For references to the commissioners' negotiations with Blagdin on GW's behalf, see GW to the District of Columbia Commissioners, 28 Sept., n.2; for the agreement GW reached with Blagdin, see GW to District of Columbia Commissioners, 27 Oct. 1798, n.3.

Letter not found: from Thomas Law, 17 Oct. 1798. On 24 Oct. GW wrote Law: "Your letter of the 17th instant was handed to me."

From George Blagdin

Sir   Commissrs Office [Washington] Octr 18th 1798

The Commissioners handed me your letter of the 17th this morning,[1] in which you propose providing Glass—Painting & Ironmongery yourself—and allow for the residue 10,500 d. which sum I think too little. having revis'd the Estimate with the greatest care—The lowest terms that I cou'd possably engauge on is 11,000 dollors, for which sum I will undertake to do the work in a compleate & workmanlike manner.[2] I am Sir Your Obedt humbe Servt

Geo. Blagdin

ALS, ViMtV.

1. The commissioners wrote GW on this day: "We are favored with yours of the 17th and have conversed with Blagdin on the subject, who writes you, we presume, his ultimate determination" (DGW).

2. Blagdin went to Mount Vernon on 26 Oct., where he and GW agreed on specifications and terms. For the terms, see GW to District of Columbia Commissioners, 27 Oct., n.3.

From Richard Bland Lee

Sir   Alexandria Octr 18th 1798

Genl Lee having intimated to me that you had informed him that my name stood on a list of candidates, in your possession for military appointments, it seems incumbent on me to explain to you the manner & motives of my application.

When the prospect of a war with France seemed inevitable and the government judged it expedient to make provisional arrangements to meet such an event I was impressed with the opinion that it was the duty of every citizen, who valued the Liberty, the safety & honor of his country to contribute all means in his power to their defence. Having frequent occasion to introduce by letter to the Secretary of War, men of merit who were desirous of entering into the army, at this alarming period, I took the liberty of mentioning to him my disposition to devote myself to any duties, to which the Government might judge me adequate & might please to call me; at the same time stating to him that I could not boast of much military experience, having only while at College marched on a few short tours; and received a commission about eleven or twelve years ago of (oldest) major in one of the Regiments of the Militia of Loudoun. But subsequent arrangements of the Militia by the State and a call to a seat in the first house of Representatives joined to the prospect of a long peace, diverted me from any further pursuit of a Military nature. A time however of extreme difficulty having arrived, when order, morals, & property were brought into jeopardy I thought, as I still think, that every Citizen ought to contribute to the community an aid proportionate to his abilities and the interest he held in it.

Permit me here to repeat what I stated to the Governt that I did not wish to stand in the way of any person of experience & fitness in other respects, and should feel no chagrin in being passed by for such characters. I beg it also to be understood that I have no great solicitude for an appointment, unless events may render indispensible the raising of the provisional army. What rank may be judged proper it is not my province to state, but will I make no doubt be fixed by a just regard to my age my education and other circumstances well known to the Government.[1]

Permit me to pray your excuse for this letter and to add that I remain with sentiments of highest veneration & esteem, Sir, your most obt Sert

Richard Bland Lee

ALS, DLC:GW.

Richard Bland Lee (1761–1827) of Loudoun County, a younger brother of Henry Lee and an ardent Federalist, was a member of Congress from 1789 to 1795.

1. GW replied on 27 Oct.: "Dear Sir, Your favor of the 18th Inst. has been duly received. Your application for an appointment in the Provisional Army (if one should be necessary) required no explanation. The application, and the manner in which it was made, do honor to you as a Citizen & Patriot; and affords a pleasing specimen of what may be expected from the lovers of order, good Government and the rights of their Country, if either should be invaded. I can assure you that, to see your name on the list of Candidates, afforded me pleasure; and the sentiments with which it was accompanied, were praiseworthy. With great esteem & regard I am—Dear Sir Your Obedient Hble Servt Go: Washington" (ALS, ICHi; letterpress copy, DLC:GW; LB, DLC:GW).

From James McHenry

private
My dear General   Trenton [N.J.] 18 Octbr 1798.
    The inclosed is copy of a letter from General Pinckney received yesterday morning. I immediately answered it, a copy of which is also inclosed.[1] Yours ever and affectionately

James McHenry

ALS, DLC:GW.
    1. The enclosed letters, both of which are in DLC:GW, are Charles Cotesworth Pinckney's to McHenry of 14 Oct. and McHenry's to Pinckney of 17 October. In his letter to McHenry, Pinckney indicates his acceptance of the commission as major general and requests an appointment for his secretary Henry M. Rutledge. McHenry's congratulatory reply enclosed Pinckney's commission as major general.

To Timothy Pickering

Dear Sir,   Mount Vernon 18th Octr 1798.
    The contents of your letter of the 13th instant, which I received last night, gave me much pleasure; and it has been increased since, by the annunciation (in the Gazettes) of General Pinckneys safe arrival at New York. I hope he will not play the second part of the *difficulty* created by General Knox.
    The extracts of letters from our Consuls, & other characters in France to you, are satisfactory, and useful to me. My opinion always has been (however necessary to be in a state of preparation) that no formidable Invasion is to be apprehended from France while Great Britain and that Country are at War—not from any favourable disposition the latter has towards us, but from actual

inability to transport Troops, & the Munitions of War, while their Ports are blockaded. That they would willingly and perhaps necessarily, employ their Forces in such an Enterprise, in case of Peace, I have little doubt, unless adverse fortune in their foreign relations; a Revolution at home; or a wonderful change of sentiment in the governing powers of their Country, should take place.

If any thing in the conduct of their agents could excite astonishment, it would be Talleyrands effrontery, duplicity, and supposed Diplomatic skill, in his management of matters with Mr Gerry: but as his object, to those who are not determined to be blind, may be read as they run, it is unnecessary to comment upon it: and with respect to Mr Gerry—I observed in my last, that his own character, & public satisfaction, require better evidence than his letter to the Minister of foreign relations, to prove the propriety of his conduct, during his Envoyship.

I fear, from the Paragraph which you have extracted from a Paris Paper of the 23d of August, relative to Madam la Fayette, that the General & his Son are on their Passage to this Country. I had a letter from him dated late in May, wherein he says, that her health was too much impaired to attempt a Sea voyage at *that* time & therefore that she and the female part of his family would go to France, while he, and Son, would visit the United States; whither he expected to arrive in the Month of September. On Public, and his own private account, I hoped this would not have happend while matters were in the train they are at present; but as one part of the information appears to have been accomplished, the other may be expected.

I have read your letter of the 29th Ult. to P. Johnston, on the subject of the Prince Edward Address to the President: and with pleasure. It ought to flash conviction of the impropriety of that address, on all minds that are open to it; but it is not easier to change the principles of the *leaders* of such measures, than it would be to wash a blackamore white. Truth & information is not their object. To blind, and irritate the People against the Government (to affect a change in it) is their sole aim. With much truth & sincere regard I am—Dear Sir Your Obedt & Affecte Servt

Go: Washington

ALS (letterpress copy), DLC:GW. The two lines at the bottom of the first two pages are traced over with pencil. This does not appear to have been done by GW but by someone else at the time the letterpress copy was made.

To Charles Cotesworth Pinckney

My dear Sir   Mount Vernon 18th Octor 1798

The Gazettes have announced your safe arrival at New York. On which happy event I most sincerely congratulate you, Mrs Pinckney and family. We were under no small apprehensions on your account. Although nothing is said respecting it, we hope Miss Pinckney's health is perfectly restored.

As it is not probable that you will travel by Water to Charleston, it is unnecessary, I trust to add, that we should be exceedingly glad to see you at this place on your route by Land; and that you wd make it one of your halting places.[1]

Mrs Washington & Miss Custis unite in every good wish—& in respectful Compliments, to Mrs, Miss Pinckney, & yourself, with My dear Sir Your Most Obedient and Affecte Hble Servan⟨t⟩

Go: Washington

ALS (letterpress copy), DLC:GW.

1. Pinckney and his wife and daughter spent Christmas at Mount Vernon (*Diaries*, 6:327–28).

To William Thornton

Dear Sir,   Mount Vernon 18th Oct. 1798

I regret, not having received your letter of the 16th until last night.[1] Had it reached me before I wrote to the Commissioners yesterday morning by Mr Thos Peter, I should have inclined more (although my wish is to have no trouble with the buildings) towards engaging Mr Blagden's undertaking the Masonry, agreeably to his estimate; doing as much of the wood work *myself*, as my people are competent to, and employing others to do the remainder of it; the Painting, Plastering &ca; and to the offer that was made to Mr Blagden for compleating the *whole*; and furnishing every thing as therein expressed (except Painting, Glazing & Iron mongery): and if he boggles at that offer, I must proceed in this manner, to the Execution of the work; and would be glad to have a contract entered into with him accordingly.[2]

If this mode is adopted, I shall expect from Mr Blagden, & without delay, a compleat Bill of Scantling and Plank; enumerating the quantity & quality; and the length, breadth and thickness of both Scantg & Plank, to suit the different parts of the buildings, that I may take measures for obtaining them in the manner you have suggested. The length, width and thickness of the flooring plank ought to be specified; & whether Sap & knots are to be excluded. In short great particularity & exactness should be observed in making out the Bill, that every thing proper & useful may be had without superfluity or waste. It would be expected of him too, to give the mouldings, & dimensions of such parts of the work as would be prepared by my own people at *this place.*

It would be quite agreeable to me, that the foundation of the buildings should be laid this Autumn, if the weather will permit. At any rate, I conceive *all* the *foundation* Stone & Sand should be carried to the Site. Sure I am, the Carting will be infinitely better before, than after Winter, and workmen I should think easier obtained. The materials must be good whether used in spring or autumn.

The length of your letter, my good Sir, required no apology. It was kind—and I thank you for the details—as I shall do on similar future occasions. For the haste in which this letter is written I ought to ask your forgiveness. Mr Law is waiting[3]—& you know he does not wait patiently for any thing not even for dinner—If you can get at my meaning, my object will be answered. Complimts to Mrs Thornton from this family—and with very great esteem—I am—Dear Sir Yr obedt & obliged

Go: Washington

ALS, DLC: Thornton Papers; ALS (letterpress copy), DLC:GW; LB, DLC:GW.

1. Letter not found. This letter to Thornton of 18 Oct. signals GW's shift from his dependence upon the District of Columbia commissioners, Alexander White, Gustavus Scott, and William Thornton, as a body, to a reliance on Thornton as an individual to deal with the builder Blagdin. On 28 Oct., after he had made his contract with Blagdin, GW accepted an offer Thornton made to act as his go-between with Blagdin.

2. See the agreement reached between GW and Blagdin, GW to District of Columbia Commissioners, 27 Oct., n.3.

3. Thomas Law "came to dinner & staid the Night" on 17 Oct. and "went away after breakfast" the next day (*Diaries*, 6:320).

To Mildred Thornton Washington

Dear Madam,   Mount Vernon 18th Octr 1798.

Your favour of the 13th instt came duly to hand.[1] The contents gave me great pain, on two accounts; first, to find the situation of my brothers affairs in so deplorable a State; and next, that it is so little in my power to afford you effectual relief.

My situation, is very little understood by most people. Whatever may be my property, the income of it, is inadequate to my expences: not from any wish or desire I have to live extravagantly, but from *unavoidable* necessity proceeding from the public walks of life in which I have been, and the acquaintances made thereby, which fill my house continually with company. Were it not for frequent and large sales of Lands which I have made, it would not have been in my power to have supported the expence without running deeply in debt.

I mention these things with no other view than to shew you that, it is not in my power to do for you as much as you might expect. I will, however, provide a thousand dollars in the Bank of Alexandria, to be applied to the removal of the *immediate* distress with which you expect to be assailed; but the mode of applying it, to render it effectual, must be attended with circumspection and caution otherwise it would be useless to you, and the money absolutely thrown away by me. The most eligable one, as far as my view of circumstances, from your Statement of my brother's situation extends, is, to suffer an Execution to be levied upon such *slaves*, and other property, as are absolutely necessary to supply your present wants; and be sold for ready money. These slaves & other things to be bought in on my account, and to remain with you, as my Property. The same things after a fair and open transaction of this kind, will not be liable to future executions; whereas, to apply the *money* in discharge of Execution, the latter may be levied thereon again ⟨& again⟩ as long as there is a debt owing from the Estate; and no relief, unless I could be continually advancing money (which I am not able to do) to redeem them.

I will be answerable for purchases made in this manner, to the amount of a thousand dollars, but am unable to advance more, and this indeed will be drawn from the use to which it was actually appropriated.

You will observe, I have mentioned the sale to be for ready money: the reason is, *you* will get more property by that means than if sold on credit; with respect to *myself*, it can make no difference, as I have no advantage in view, & cannot go beyond the Sum I have mentioned. If Mr Hammond will purchase for you to the above amount, and see that the articles are properly secured against future executions, I will pay the draughts by a check on the Bank of Alexandria upon that evidence of it, being produced to me.[2]

With respect to the conduct of your Son Samuel I shall say nothing, because I know little concerning it. But if he applied the thousand dollars he had from me, or any part of it, towards the building of a house instead of paying his father's debts, it was not only imprudent, but a breach of his engagement to me, for it was for the latter purpose *only*, and *expressly* that I lent him the money.[3]

I am very sorry to hear of the losses you have sustained in your Negros and Crops, and more so for your own bad health, and the unhappy situation of my brother. At all times, and under all circumstances, it would give me sincere pleasure to render you all the Services & kindnesses in the power of Dear Madam Your Most Affecte

Go: Washington

P.S. As I write in haste you must excuse this scrawl.

ALS (letterpress copy), ViMtV.

    1. Letter not found.

    2. Thomas Hammond was married to Mildred Washington Hammond, daughter of Charles and Mildred Thornton Washington.

    3. Young Samuel Washington wrote GW on 7 Nov. to explain his actions and to apologize for those of his mother. For GW's earlier loan to his nephew, see Samuel Washington to GW, 29 July 1797, and note 1 of that document.

From Bushrod Washington

My dear uncle   Richmond October 19th 1798

Upon my return to this place I met with a Commission from the President of the United States appointing me one of the Judges of the supreme Court. This appointment I have accepted, and was induced thereto by the strongest motives.

I was very unwilling to abandon a profession, to which I was much attached, and to the study of which I had devoted the greatest part of my life. A situation which permits me to pursue it, and to improve the knowledge which I have acquired in this science, without endangering my sight (already considerably injured) could not fail to be agreable to me.

Independent of this consideration, I could not upon a small

piece of poor land in Westmoreland have paid debts which I owe, & supported my family.

Knowing the wish you had, that I should be a Candidate for Congress, I have felt much uneasiness lest my acceptance of this appointment should be disagreable to you. The desire of attempting to serve my country in that line had also created in myself an anxiety for success in the election, altho' I foresaw the extreme inconvenience which would result from it, in my private affairs; I was however willing to make the sacrifice. I trust that this candid statement of my situation will be an apology with you for having relinquished my first intention, and I flatter myself that my services will not be less useful to my Country in the office which I now hold, than they would have been in the legislative counsels.

I am Just preparing to go upon the southern Circuit, & shall if possible leave this place tomorrow.

From the best information which I could collect, there is very little doubt, but that a fœderal man will be sent from our district: whether Genl Lee, or Mr Landon Carter will offer is not certainly ascertained, but I believe it will be the latter.[1]

Mrs W. Joins me in love to my aunt & yourself, and believe me to be most sincerely My dear Uncle Your affect. Nephew

B. Washington

ALS, DLC:GW.

1. It was Henry Lee, Jr., not Landon Carter, who would seek the seat in the U.S. House of Representatives held by Walter Jones (1745–1815) of Northumberland County in Virginia's Northern Neck. Shortly before the election in April 1799, Bushrod Washington expressed his uncertainty about the outcome, reporting that "Indisposition has obstructed Genl Lee's exertions very much to his injury," and that "deepr rooted impressions were made against him by the most scandalous and unfounded aspersions upon his private character" (Bushrod Washington to GW, 10 April 1799). On 26 April, two days after the election, Bushrod informed GW that "Genl Lee is elected by a majority of 32 votes" and expressed the opinion that "had the election been postponed a week longer . . . he would have divided even Doctr Jones's County. He had not time completely to do away the illfounded & unceasing calumies which were dayly propogated against him."

From James Washington

Sir,   Berlin 19th Octr 1798

The Government of the U.S. of America have given a brilliant example that it knew well how to unite the true interest and welfare of the State with the happiness & prosperity of its Citizens; insomuch that those who are at the greatest distance cannot but admire a government founded on so excellent a basis. I do not stop here, I dare carry my views further and declare how happy I should be to count myself a subject of that Government, and to obtain the appointment of an Officer in the Army which has the advantage of your Excellency at the head of it.

The name which I bear, and the honor which I have of being a Relation to your Excellency leads me to hope that you will grant me your valuable protection. I am a Native of the Hague in Holland, where there are still some relations of the name. We are a branch which quitted England to establish themselves in Holland. It would be only abusing the precious time of your Excellency to enter at this moment into a detail of the family; I shall therefore content myself with only adding, that I beleive I have in my power authentic proofs to shew that I am related to the greatest man of the age.[1]

I served before the Revolution of 1795 as an Ensign in a Regiment of Infantry in the service of their High Mightiness the States General of the United Provinces. I made the unfortunate Campaign of 1794 when I was 20 years old. During 3 years that I have been in Germany I have applied myself to the study of those Sciences which were most suitable to the career I had commenced, and which I should never have abandoned, had I not been reduced to the alternative of a dismission or perjury towards my lawful Souvereign and thereby have become a wretch in the service of a bad cause. I have made the tour of Saxony and come to Berlin, where I have formed an acquaintance with Mr Adams, who has had the goodness to take charge of this letter to co[n]vey it to your Excellency.[2] In speaking of Mr Adams, permit me to add, that in case you should judge it necessary to have more information concerning me, I flatter myself that the Hereditary Prince of Orange and many other persons of distinction to whom I have the honor of being known, would give satisfaction.

Should I be so happy as to have my proposal approved, and your Excellency should be disposed to favour me with a place in the Army under your Command, I would go next Spring to America to wait the Orders of your Excellency—and to make a disposition favorable to those circumstances, I shall go to the Hague where some affairs require my presence.

I ask pardon of your Excellency for having intruded upon you so long. Should you be pleased to grant the favor I have solicited, my gratitude & acknowledgements will be expressed in the highest degree, and it will be putting it in my power to prove at all times the profound Respect with which I have the Honor to be Your Excellency's most obedient & most Humble sevt[3]

James Washington

Translation, DLC:GW; ALS (in French), DLC:GW.

1. What family relationship, if any, there was between GW and James Washington of Holland has not been determined.

2. See John Quincy Adams to GW, 29 Oct. 1798.

3. See GW's reply of 20 Jan. 1799.

From William Washington

[19 October 1798]

Your letter of September the 27th I received, a few days ago by Major Simons. In conformity with your request I have enclosed a list which consists of such persons who I have reason to believe are desirous of obtaining commissions in the Army . . . [1]

I had indulged the pleasing hope that I had made a final retreat into the peaceful shades of retirement, but at this momentous crisis I shall not hesitate when I shall have my appointment officially announced (at present I know nothing of it, except what appears in the public prints,) to obey the summons of my country, especially when I know that the army is to be commanded by a chief for whom I have had the highest respect and veneration.

Please to make a tender of my best respects to Mrs. Washington. With the greatest respect and esteem, your very obedient servant.

L, printed in Parke-Bernet Galleries, Inc., 30–31 Oct. 1950, Cat. #1190, p. 281, item 1167; L, printed in *Memoirs of the Long Island Historical Society* (Brooklyn, N.Y., 1867–89), 4:xxii-xxiii. The first paragraph, which does not appear in the *Memoirs*, is taken from the Parke-Bernet catalog: the last two are taken from the Long Island Historical Society *Memoirs*. The catalog quotes the second paragraph only in part and omits the third.

1. See GW to William Washington, 27 September. The enclosed list has not been found.

From James McHenry

My dear General.   Trenton [N.J.] 20th Octbr 1798

I received a letter this morning from General Hamilton which I inclose.[1] You will be pleased to return it, as well as the annexed poetry, the production of Mr Horry sent for the perusal of Miss Custis.[2] Yours ever & affectionately

James McHenry

ALS, DLC:GW; ADfS, MiU-C: McHenry Papers.

1. This probably was one of the three letters that Alexander Hamilton wrote McHenry on 19 October. In one of these Hamilton expresses his satisfaction at being ranked first among the three major generals and agrees to meet in Philadelphia in early November (Syrett, *Hamilton Papers*, 22:202–3). In another, from which Timothy Pickering quotes in his letter to GW of this date, Hamilton reports that Charles Cotesworth Pinckney had accepted the ranking of the major generals (ibid., 201–2).

2. Horry was a brother of Nelly Custis's friend Harriott Pinckney Horry Rutledge. The poetry has not been identified.

From Timothy Pickering

Sir,   Trenton [N.J.] Octr 20. 1798.

Recollecting your anxiety that General Pinckney might [not] feel satisfied with the military arrangements of General officers proposed by you, I seize the first moment to relieve you from it. This morning Mr McHenry has received from Genl Hamilton a letter dated yesterday, in which is the following passage:[1] After mentioning the arrival of General Pinckney, Genl Hamilton says—

"You will learn with pleasure that he sent me a message by young Rutledge purporting his entire satisfaction with the military arrangement, and readiness to serve under my command. Communicate this to our friends Pickering & Wolcott, as I am not well enough to write them by this post."

I think, in a former letter, I expressed myself confidently, that General Pinckney's good sense and patriotism, joined with his great respect for you, would ensure his satisfaction with your arrangement.[2]

I have had the honor to receive your letter of the 15th acknowledging the receipt of mine of the 3d instant. Contrary to my usual practice, I find I omitted taking a copy of it: but I recollect it communicated political information, and that my motive at the time was your present important official station, which rendered proper such a communication; as well as to gratify that interest which you could not as a citizen fail to take in the great concerns of your country. I could venture to assure you of my continued attention on this head, if I had competent aid in my office in writing letters on business foreign & domestic, aid which I ought to have, & for which I must ask at the ensuing sessions. I have indeed an excellent chief clerk, vastly more capable tha[n] Mr Taylor for writing letters; but he has so much business as Chief Clerk, that I need another for the particular purpose of maintaining common correspondencies, either directly by himself, or in preparing draughts for my signature.[3]

I have also thought that a direct correspondence between the department of state and the governors of the several states would be very useful, and the idea met the President's approbation. It would be useful by the information I should communicate, and it would gratify and conciliate those whose cordial cooperation is so important, and whose influential situations enable them to command extensively great respect & attention to their opinions.[4]

The correspondence between Talleyrand & Gerry concerning X. Y. & Z. you will recollect offended the "delicacy" of the latter gentleman, who avowed himself by the name of Hautval; and addressed to Talleyrand a letter declaring that "his delicacy could not but be severely hurt to see himself, under the appellation of Z. performing a part in the company with certain intriguers, whose object doubtless was to derive advantage from the credulity of the American envoys, and to make them their dupes." The quality of this gentleman's *delicacy* you will see in the following extract of a letter from Mr King, which I received this morning. "Colonel Trumbull, who was at Paris soon after the arrival there of the Commissioners, has more than once informed me, that Hauteval told him, that both the *douceur* and the loan were indispensable, and urged him to employ his influence with the American Commissioners to offer the bribe as well as the loan." The Corruption of these scoundrels is unbounded. In the publication of the dispatches from our Envoys, altho' not enjoined secrecy in respect to Mr Hauteval, yet as the envoys mentioned him with respectful language, I voluntarily substituted Z. for his proper name.[5] I am with great respect, sir, your most obt servant,

Timothy Pickering

ALS, PPRF; ALS (letterpress copy), MHi: Pickering Papers; copy, in the hand of Pickering's clerk, NN: Timothy Pickering Miscellaneous.

1. The letter from Hamilton to James McHenry, dated 19 Oct., is printed in Syrett, *Hamilton Papers*, 22:201–2.

2. See Pickering to GW, 1 Sept. (second letter).

3. For the clerk George Taylor, Jr., see Pickering to GW, 27 Jan. 1798, and note 2 of that document.

4. See GW's reaction to this proposal in his reply of 26 October.

5. The first quotation is from a letter from Lucien Hauteval to Talleyrand, 1 June 1798, printed in *ASP, Foreign Relations*, 2:226–27. The letter from Rufus King (dated 20 June according to a letter from Pickering to Adams of 20 Oct., in MHi-A) has not been found. Lucien Hauteval, the Z of XYZ, was a Swiss who had formerly been consul at Boston, where he got to know John Trumbull, Elbridge Gerry, and John Quincy Adams. Trumbull was visiting Paris in October 1797 and witnessed Talleyrand's attempts to pressure the American commissioners into offering a loan and a bribe in return for French goodwill (see Trumbull, *Autobiography*, 220–22).

To the South Carolina Society of the Cincinnati

Gentlemen,   Mount Vernon 20th Octr 1798.

I have been honored with your favor of the 30th of August communicating the resolve of the Cincinati of the state of South Carolina respe[c]ting the propriety of altering the Ribband to which the badge of the Society was directed by the constitution to be appendant, as indicative of the union, between the United States and France, and have transmitted it to the Secretary General, to be laid before the Society at the next general meeting of its Delegates.[1] With very great Esteem & regard I have the honour to be Gentlemen Your most Obedt Hble Servt

Go: Washington

LB, DLC:GW; copy, MHi: Society of the Cincinnati Papers.

1. The letter of the South Carolina Society of the Cincinnati, dated 30 Aug. at Charleston, reads: "At a late meeting of the Cincinnati of this State convened for the purpose of addressing the President of the United States on the critical Situation of this Country, It was resolved that a Committee be appointed to write to the General society requesting that they would at their next meeting take into consideration the propriety of altering the Ribband to which the Badge of the society was directed by the Constitution to be appendant as indicative of the

Union between the United states and France. It was thought that such a distinction was no longer applicable to the relative Situations of the two Countries and that it became incumbent on us at such a moment to renounce every military Badge or appearance of Connection with a nation whose civil and political Union by Treaty had been declared by the Legislative authority of our Country to be void and no longer binding on Us. We do therefore in obedience to the above-mentioned resolve communicate to you the wish of our state Society and request you will lay the same before the General society at their next meeting for the consideration of the members thereof. We are with Esteem and Respect Sir Your Most Obedient Servants John F[aucheraud] Grimké Lt Colo. Arty Thomas Pinckney Major Infy Adam Gilchrist Captn Infy" (DLC:GW).

On 23 Oct. GW wrote Henry Knox: "My dear Sir The enclosed, although of old date, is just come to hand. and believing you are still the Secretary Generl of the Society of the Cincinnati, I transmit it to you; to be laid before the next General meeting of its Delegates; as there is no probability that I shall be at it myself.

"Since my letter to you of the 21st I have received one from the Secretary of War, informing me of General Pinckney's arrival, and acceptance of his Appointment in the army of the United States; and his request that the Majors General of the Augmented force would be at Trenton, or Philadelphia by the 10th of next month; expressing at the sametime, an earnest wish that I would be present. Inconvenient as it will be to me, and perhaps hazardous, I will make exertion to be there at that time—and I need not add, that it would give me pleasure to find you among them; as many important points will come before them. I am always Yrs Go: Washington" (letterpress copy, DLC:GW).

To John Adams

Sir,   Mount Vernon 21st October 1798

The letter with which you were pleased to honor me—dated the 9th instant—was received by the last Mail; and demands my particular acknowledgments.

It was with sincere concern I received the account of Mrs Adams's low state of health, and your consequent indisposition. If my fervent wishes would restore her, and you, to perfect health, this object would soon be accomplished: and in these wishes, Mrs Washington unites with, great cordiality.

In her behalf, and for myself, I thank you for your kind wishes respecting us. She is as well as usual, and I am quite recovered of the fever with which I was afflicted sometime ago; and nearly so of the debility in which it left me.

If the Office of Adjutant General had been vacant by the nonacceptance of Mr North, no one could have filled it more agreeably to my wishes than either of the Gentlemen suggested by me in the arrangement made with the Secretary of War—of course General Dayton would have been an acceptable appointment. It appears however, by a letter I have lately received from the War Office, that Mr North has not declined the honor you did him.[1] With great consideration & respect I have the honor to be Sir Your Most Obedient & Most Hble Servant

Go: Washington

ALS, MHi-A; ALS (letterpress copy), DLC:GW.
   1. See James McHenry to GW, 19 Sept., and notes 4 and 8 of that document.

To Rawleigh Colston

Sir   Mount Vernon 21st Octr 1798.
   It is not more than three or four days since your letter enclosing one from Mr Thomas Marshall, has been received.[1]
   That Gentleman is, as I myself also am in doubt whether more than one draug[h]t has not been made upon me by Colo. Marshall, for the taxes which he has been so kind as to pay for my land in Kentucky. But as the voluminous papers which I brought from Philadelphia are not yet finally adjusted, and I am not, in consequence, able to ascertain this fact by an easy reference to them; I shall pay to your order, on demand, the full balance as stated by Mr T. Marshall—viz. £17.7.3: leaving the Sum of £8.17.3 to be discounted hereafter, if, upon the assortment of my Papers it shall appear (as I think it will) that it has been paid to some one, authorised by Colo. Marshall to receive it.[2] I am—Sir Your Most Obedt Hble Servant

Go: Washington

ALS (letterpress copy), DLC:GW; LB, DLC:GW.
   1. Colston's letter is dated 6 October.
   2. See Thomas Marshall, Jr., to GW, 4 Aug., and GW to Marshall, 22 October.

To Alexander Hamilton

My dear Sir,   Mount Vernon 21 Octr 1798.
   The last mail to Alexandria brought me a letter from the President of the United States,[1] in which I am informed that he had

signed, and given the Commissions to yourself, Generals Pinckney & Knox, the same date; in hopes that an amicable adjustment, or acquiescence might take place among you. But, if these hopes should be disappointed, and controversies should arise, they will of course be submitted to me, as Commander in Chief, and if after all, any one should be so obstinate as to appeal to him from the judgment of the Commander in chief, he was determined to confirm that judgment.

General Knox is fully acquainted with my sentiments on this subject; and I hope no fresh difficulties will arise with General Pinckney. Let me entreat you therefore to give, without delay, your *full* aid to the Secy of War. At present I will only add that I am always, & Affectly yours

Go: Washington

ALS, DLC: Hamilton Papers; ALS (letterpress copy), DLC:GW.
　　1. This is the letter from Adams to GW of 9 October.

To Henry Knox

My dear Sir,　　　　　　　　　Mount Vernon 21st Octor 1798.
　　Several causes have concurred, to retard the acknowledgment of the receipt of your favour of the 26th of August.

At the time it came to hand, I was much engaged in matters that could not be well postponed; and before I got through them, I was siezed with a fever which was unremittingly severe for several days, and left me in so debilitated a state as to render writing, and business generally (when it could be avoided) not only irksome, but improper, & was forbidden by my Physicians.

During this state of convalescence, letters which required prompt attention, were pouring in upon me. This state of things; not knowing what the Presidents final decision would be; and not perceiving that I could say more to you on the subject of relative rank than I had done in former letters—unless to dilate on the several points which had before been touched, (and this appeared to me to be unnecessary, as your own ideas would anticipate all I could say) I delayed from day to day to do what I am now in the act of doing—that is writing to you.

I can again, my dear Sir, with much truth & sincerity repeat to you, the declaration made on a former occasion, namely, that if an amicable arrangement of precedence could have been settled between Generals Hamilton, Pinckney, and yourself, previous to the nominations, it wd have been *perfectly* satisfactory to me; but driven as I was, to make it myself, at the time, and in the manner it was transmitted—I was governed by the best view, & best evidence I could obtain of the public sentiment relative thereto. The Senate acted upon it under an impression it was to remain so, and in that light the matter is understood by the Public—and it would be uncandid not to add, that I have found no cause since to believe, I mistook that sentiment. Let me add further, that as an Army was to be raised de novo—fourteen years after the Revolutionary Troops had ceased to exist that I do not see how any Resolution of the ancient Congress can apply at this day, to the Officers of that army. If it does, and the matter is viewed by others as it is by you, will any field officer of that army serve under General Dayton? Would it not deprive the President of the advantage of selection & arrangement? and what difficulties & perplexities would not follow if this idea & conduct should prevail generally? Accompanied with the opinion which you seem to have imbibed, of incidental Rank. Few knowing, & deserving officers of this description would feel very easy under such a decision, or be content with a *feather*, if they conceived that *Rank* meant *nothing* when inserted in their Commissions. On what ground did the Baron de Steuben command a separate Corps in the State of Virginia in the year 1781—and Colo. Hamilton a select one at the Siege of York if Incidental Rank does not give command according to circumstances and discretion of the Commanding General?

But I am running into details which I did not intend. It would (if you could reconcile it to your own feeling) give me sincere pleasure to see you in the augmented Corps—a Major General. We shall have either *no War* or a *severe contest* with France; in either case, if you will allow me to express my opinion, this is the most eligible time for you to come forward. In the first case to assist with your council & aid in making judicious provisions & arrangements to avert it. In the other case, to share in the glory of defending your Country; and by making all secondary considerations yield to that great & primary object, display a mind superior to embarrassing punctilios, at so critical a moment as the present.

After having expressed these sentiments with the frankness of undisguised friendship it is hardly necessary to add that, if you should, finally, decline the appointment of Majr General, that there is no one to whom I would give a more decided preference as an Aid de Camp—the offer of which is highly flattering—honorable—& grateful to my feelings, & for which I entertain a high sense.

But, my dear Genl Knox, (and here again I speak to you in the language of candour, & friendship) examine well your mind on this subject. Do not unite yourself to the ⟨Suit⟩ of a man whom you may consider as the primary cause of what you call a degradation, with unpleasant sensations. This, while it was gnawing upon you, would (if I should come to the knowledge of it) make me unhappy; as my first wish would be that my Military family—and the whole Army—should consider themselves as a band of brothers, willing & ready, to die for each other. I shall add no more than assurances of the sincere friendship & affection with which I am Dear Sir Your ⟨*illegible* friend *illegible*

Go: Washington⟩

ALS (letterpress copy), DLC:GW. Several passages in this letter have been traced over in pencil.

To James McHenry

Private & Confidential
My dear Sir,   Mount Vernon 21st Octr 1798
Enclosed is a copy of the Presidents letter to me, which I request may be, with this letter, burnt as soon as they are read, & no more said respecting the contents than might be proper for him to hear repeated again; Otherwise, a knowledge that the contents of my letters to, and from him, are in possession of others, may induce him to believe, in good earnest, that intriegues are carrying on, in which I am an Actor—than which, nothing is more foreign from my heart.[1]

I return the Press copies which were enclosed to me. But in future, whenever you require my opinion on any points, let them be stated in your letter, or on a paper to remain in my possession; without wch my acts, & proceedings, will appear incomplete & misterious.[2]

Do you mean to furnish me with a copy of the letter you wrote to the President from hence, & of his Instructions to you, or not?[3] Long, long since I informed you that it would be extremely useful to me (if I was to have any hand in selecting the Officers for the four Regiments & Cavalry, proposed to be raised in the Southern division of the Union) to be furnished with a list of the Captains & Subalterns therein, who served in the Revolutionary Army; but none has ever been sent.[4] This, with the dates of their Commissions might be a means of coming at many valuable Officers, and preventing many disputes hereafter.

Has Mr Wolcott received any answer to his letter to the President? and to what effect.[5] You know that I am always Your sincere friend and Affecte Humble Servt

Go: Washington

P.S. It is sometime since Nelly Custis enclosed you a Postnote, furnished by me to discharge your advance for the Colours—Has it ever been received?[6]

ALS, LNHT: George and Katherine Davis Collection; ALS (letterpress copy), DLC:GW; copy in the hand of McHenry's clerk, DLC: Hamilton Papers.

1. Not only did McHenry fail to destroy GW's letter as requested, he had his clerk make a copy of it for Alexander Hamilton.

2. The identity of the letterpress copies to which GW refers here is unclear. As GW's second letter of this date appears to indicate, McHenry's second letter to GW of 16 Oct. and its enclosures did not arrive at Mount Vernon until later in the day.

3. See GW to McHenry, 16 Sept., nn.2 and 4.

4. See GW to McHenry, 3 September. In his letter to McHenry of 13 Nov., GW acknowledged possession of "a list of the Genl & Field Officers who served in the Revolutionary War, and of the Captains and subalterns from the States so. of the Potomac." McHenry had enclosed the latter list in his letter to GW of 30 October. These two lists were likely combined to form a List of Officers [of all ranks, from Virginia, North Carolina, South Carolina and Georgia] of the late War who continued to the end thereof or were deranged by Acts of Congress, which is in DLC: GW, filed at the end of 1798.

5. GW later in the day received McHenry's letter of 16 Oct. informing him of the president's having sent the commissions for the three major generals. See GW to McHenry, 21 Oct. (second letter). On 26 Oct. McHenry noted that Adams had not responded to Wolcott's letter.

6. For details regarding Nelly Custis's request that McHenry have a standard crafted for a company of volunteer dragoons, see McHenry to GW, 13 Aug., and note 3 of that document. See also McHenry's letter to GW to 26 Oct. and note 2 of that document.

To James McHenry

Dear Sir,   Mount Vernon 21st Octr 1798

Your letter of the 16th instt came by the last Mail. The enclosures are well calculated to effect their objects. But the explicit declaration contained in the one to General Knox, added to his knowledge of my sentiments on the subject of relative Rank, leaves little hope, in my mind, that he will obey your summons, and render his aid in the manner required of him.[1]

I hope no difficulty will occur with General Pinckney; and if he cannot be prevailed on to remain at the Seat of Government until the 10th of November, (the ulterior day allowed for the assembling of the Major Generals) that you will avail yourself of all his information relatively to the characters best qualified to Officer the Corps allotted to the States of South Carolina & Georgia; and as far as his knowledge extends, of those of No. Carolina and Tennessee also.

I have said in the beginning of this letter, that the enclosures were well calculated to effect there objects. but I must except that part of them which relates to the Officering the New Corps in the Southern and Western States, as greatly inferior to the one I suggested in my last letter to you, dated the 15th instant: first, because it involves more delay; and 2dly, because the chance of obtaining *good* Officers is not equal.[2]

If the President of the United States, or the Secretary of War had a personal, & intimate knowledge of the characters of the applicants, the mode suggested by me would be indelicate & improper; but at such a distance, & in cases where information *must* govern, from whom (as I observed in my former letter) can it be so much relied on, as from those whose interest—honor—and reputation is pledged for its accuracy?

The applications are made, *chiefly*, through members of Congress. These, often times to get *rid* of them; oftener still perhaps, for local & Electioneering purposes, and to please & gratify their party, more than from any real merit in the applicant, are handed in, backed by sollicitude to succeed, in order to strengthen their interests. Possibly, no injustice might be done, if I was to proceed a step further, and give it as an opinion, that most of the candidates brought forward by the opposition members, possess sentiments similar to their own, and might poison the army by dis-siminating them, if they were appointed. If, however, the plan suggested by you is to be adopted, indeed in any case, you will no doubt see the propriety of obtaining all the information you can from Majr General Pinckney—and if he accepts his appointment, and cannot be prevailed on to remain with you until the other Majr Generals assemble, to request him to call on Brigr General Davie on his route to Charleston, and after a full, & free conversation with him on fit characters to Officer the quota of Troops from the State of No. Carolina (and Tennessee if he can aid in it) to inform you of the result, *without delay*.

I hardly think it will be in my power to attend at Trenton or Philadelphia at the time allotted to the Majr Generals. 1st because I am yet in a Convalescent State (although perfectly recovered of the fever) so far at least as to avoid exposture, and consequent Colds; 2dly, My Secretary (Mr Lear) has had a severe fever, and is now very low; and sevl others of my family much indisposed: and 3dly & principally, because I see no definitive ground to proceed upon, if I should go, from any thing that has hitherto appeared. Nor is it probable you will have received the Presidents Instructions, and Genl Knox's answer in time to serve me with notice of the results, by the 10th of November. I mean for me to get there; on, or about that day.

If General Pinckney could be prevailed on to remain with you, & there was a moral certainty of meeting Generals Hamilton and Knox, I would, maugre the inconveniences, and hazard I might run, attempt to join them, for the valuable purpose of projecting a Plan in *concert* with you, and them; which might be ineffectually accomplished at a partial meeting. I shall, therefore, stand prepared, as well as the situation of things will admit, and wait your *full* communications on these several points—and govern myself accordingly. With great esteem & regard, I am—Dear Sir—Yr Most Obedt Servt

Go: Washington

ALS, LNHT: George and Katherine Davis Collection; ALS (letterpress copy), DLC:GW.

1. For the enclosures, see McHenry to GW, 16 Oct. (second letter), and note 1 of that document. Knox declined the appointment in a letter to McHenry of 23 October. See McHenry to GW, 30 Oct., n.2.

2. See the enclosure to GW's letter to McHenry of 15 October.

To Edward Carrington

Dear Sir,   Mount Vernon 22d Octr 1798

To what cause, or causes, the delay in appointing Officers under the "Act, to augment the Army of the United States, and for other purposes" is to be ascribed, I am unable to say. I fear the spirit that was enkindled at the time of its Passing, has not a little evaporated.

No decisive plan has yet been formed for this purpose, that has come to my knowledge; but the Secretary of War having intimated to me the probability, that four of the twelve Regiments, and the Six Troops of Dragoons would be apportioned to the States south of Maryland; including Kentucky & Tennessee; and requesting me, to furnish him, with the names of suitable characters for the different grades of Officers for these Corps; transmitting at the same time a list of the Applicants, & of the Field Officers of the Revolutionary Army who had served to the end of the War, I am willing to render him all the aid in my power, but am unable to do it efficiently, without the assistance of others—more intimately acquainted with the late Southern Army than I was.[1]

I take the liberty therefore, in a private, & confidential way, to request you, General Marshall & Colo. Heth (in all of whom I can confide) to meet together, as soon as you can, with any sort of convenience, and note such characters in the different grades as you conceive best qualified, and would do most honor to their country, in an *active* & *spirited* war, if such we are to be engaged in, as Officers.

To enable you to do this; and with a view to remind you of the old field Officers, as well as the present applicants, I send you, 1st a list of the former; 2dly a list of the latter, their places of residence, Rank *applied* for, and by whom recommended—and 3dly Pursuing the principle of the Secretary—an apportionment of these four Regiments and Six Troops of Dragoons among the Southern & Western States; by a medium between the Representation, and population of each. These Papers to be returned with the selected list.[2]

You will perceive that this request relates more immediately to Virginia, but if there are any prominant characters in either of the others, for either grade of Officers, it would be obliging, to mention them also.

You will perceive further, that by the apportionment, a precise number of Officers, of the different grades, are required; but in your Selection, I had rather you should *exceed*, than fall *short*; and that I may understand the estimation in which they are held, let them be placed numerically.

In making your selection of *Company* Officers, some attention (as well for the benefit of Recruiting, as other considerations) should be had to a distribution of them through the State. And where Old Officers of celebrity, fit for the different grades can be obtained; who are in the prime of life, habituated to no bad courses, & are known to be well affected, they ought to be preferred. Next to these, young Gentlemen (not youths) of good educations & characters; and as far as it can be ascertained beforehand, possessing a high sense of honor, and love of Country should be brought forward—but in neither case a professed, or known enemy to Government, should be selected; for the same principles which lead them to oppose the Civil administration of their Country wd operate equally against the Military, and Caballing & Parties, would soon be the result.

You will please to consider this letter, its enclosures & all I have said on the subject, as communicated in confidence. and for particular reasons it is wished, that I may receive the result of your meeting and consultation soon—at any rate before the first or 2d of next month.[3] With very great esteem & regard I am—Dear Sir Yr Most Obedt Servant

Go: Washington

P.S. If circumstances should prevent a meeting of all—the opinion of two, or yourself alone, is desired in the time mentioned.

ALS, PWacD; ALS (letterpress copy), DLC:GW.

1. McHenry made the request in a letter to GW of 2 Oct. and again in his second letter to GW of 5 October. See also GW's reply and enclosure to McHenry of 15 October.

2. Three undated lists of applicants for commissions from North Carolina, South Carolina, and Tennessee are in DLC:GW at the end of December 1798. They would appear to correspond to those GW sent to Carrington, as they include name of applicant, residence, rank sought, and by whom recommended. The list of field officers has not been found, but see GW to McHenry, 21 Oct. (first letter), n.4. The third enclosure from GW to Carrington was likely a copy of the enclosure to GW's letter to James McHenry of 15 October.

3. No response to this letter has been found. Carrington's comments, along with those of William Heth and John Marshall, appear next to the names of many

of the candidates in the list of Candidates for Army Appointments from Virginia, November 1798, printed below. For Carrington's involvement in the formation of the Provisional Army of 1799, see James McHenry to GW, 2 May 1799, n.1.

To the District of Columbia Commissioners

Gentlemen.   Mount Vernon 22 Octr 1798
   Your favor of the 18th instt,[1] enclosing a letter from Mr Blagdin of the same date, came duly to hand; and although I am perfectly satisfied that by doing the Carpenters & Joiners work with my own People, by a correct Bill of the materials required, & obtained from a reputable Mill on the Eastern Shore to suit the buildings, that I could save a thousand dollars under that head alone—yet, to avoid trouble to myself—to avoid disputes between workmen, having no controul over, but acting independently of each other; to avoid sending Negro Carpenters to the City, and having them to provide for there, and above all, taking into consideration what may, eventually, happen next year, and my employment in consequence—I have resolved to agree to Mr Blagdin's terms: that is, to give him Eleven thousand dollars to build the two houses, according to the plan agreed on, and agreeably to the specification which has been presented to me; and must be produced & referred to, as the criterion by which the work is to be judged. I, taking upon myself the execution of the Painting & Glasing; and furnishing the Iron Mongery, agreeably to the Bill which he exhibited; the quantity of nails not to over-run the specification—that is, by allowing him the amount of *that* item, he is entitled to no further call upon me for an increase.
   I have never entered into a contract of this sort, and of course little skilled in drawing one; for which reason, it would be an act of kindness if you would cause efficient articles to be drawn under your Inspection & correction: the cost of wch I am willing to pay—Whatever is customary on the part of the *Employer*, I am willing to comply with; nothing occurs to me as necessary, at present, except defraying the cost; and this I am ready to do by depositing the means in the Bank of Columbia, to be drawn for by a Gentleman in the City, upon Mr Blagdin's producing Bills of cost, of the materials for carrying on the Work, and the amount of Workmens wages, every Month, fortnight, or week, as shall be stipulated.
   On the part of the *Employed* I presume there are many essentials,

requiring him to be bound to the performance of—And is it not necessary, & usual that these should be secured by Bondsmen?

But I will add no more on a Subject with which you are much better acquainted than I am. I shall be punctual in the fulfillment of my part of the agreement, and only wish to have the counter part equally well observed. For I find, including the price of the Lots and enclosing them, with the cost of the buildings, in the manner I am proceeding, the Rent I shall be able to obtain, will scarcely give me common interest for the money that will be expended. But having put my hand to the work I must not now look back.[2] With very great esteem & regard I am—Gentlemen Your Most Obedient and Obliged Hble Servant

Go: Washington

ALS (letterpress copy), DLC:GW; LB, DLC:GW.

1. The text of the commissioners' letter is printed in note 1, George Blagdin to GW, 18 October.

2. For the agreement with Blagdin, see GW to District of Columbia Commissioners, 27 Oct., n.3.

To Thomas Marshall, Jr.

Sir,   Mount Vernon 22d Oct. 1798

Your favor of the 4th of August came safe to my hands under cover from Mr Colston—whom I have authorised to draw upon me for the full balance as stated in the a/c transmitted by you.

It dwells however upon my mind (but not perfectly) that the first item therein—viz.—£8.17.3 has been paid to some person who appeared authorised to receive it; but as My voluminous Papers (brought from Philadelphia) are not yet all opened and assorted, I am not able to ascertain this fact, or speak with the least decision on the subject, and there fore have, as beforementioned, desired Mr Colston to draw upon me, in favor of his correspondent in Alexa., for the whole amount.[1]

If, hereafter, it should be recollected by Colo. Marshall, or appear by any receipt I shall find, that the above Sum of £8.17.3 has been paid, it can be allowed in the next account.

I feel much obliged by your kindness in paying the Taxes of my land upon rough Creek, for the years 1796 and 1797; and for the services you have rendered me in entering them at the Auditors Office for future taxes, agreeably to your late Act of Assembly, relative to non-residents. and you would add to the obligation by continuing to pay the dues thereon as they arise, & drawing upon me for the amt.

But previous to this, let me request the favour of you to enquire of Mr Short (if you should see him) whether he has done any thing in this matter, or not; for not having heard for a long time in what Situation, or jeopardy the Land might be, Genl Spotswood who had business to transact with that Gentleman, and he understood it was threatened, was requested to ask him to examine, and do what was needful to rescue it, if really in danger, from the threatned evil—which he kindly promised to do.[2] My best wishes & respects are offered to Colo. Marshall. I am Sir—Your Most Obedt Hble Ser.

Go: Washington

ALS (letterpress copy), DLC:GW; LB, DLC:GW.

1. See Marshall to GW, 4 Aug., Rawleigh Colston to GW, 6 Oct., and GW to Colston, 21 October.

2. See GW to Peyton Short, 16 July 1798, and the references in the notes to that document. See also Short to GW, 1 Nov. 1798.

To James McHenry

Dear Sir   Mount Vernon 23d Octr 1798.

It gave me very sincere pleasure to find by your letter of the 17th[1]—recd last night—that Genl Pinckney accepts his appointment in the Army of the Unite[d] States.

If it would not be too inconvenient for him to remain at the Seat of Government until the 10th of next month (the ulterior day, allotted for the assembling of the Majors General at Trenton or Philadelphia) and you would advise me thereof, *immediately*, I would make every exertion in my power to meet them at that time.

For a variety of reasons, which will readily occur, the sooner such a meeting could take place the better; and perhaps no time, season, or circumstances, would be more convenient than the one proposed; nor more eligable for the purpose of concerting a Plan, upon general hypothesis; and rectifying, as far as possible, the evils which have proceeded from delay in Recrui[tin]g. With great esteem and regard I am—Dr Sir—Your Most Obt Serv⟨t⟩

Go: Washington

ALS (photocopy), sold by Paul C. Richards, catalog no. 206, 8 April 1986; ALS (letterpress copy), DLC:GW.

1. McHenry's letter is dated 18, not 17, October.

From Thomas Pinckney

My dear Sir   Charleston [S.C.] 23d October 1798

The fear of missing my Brother upon the road after an absence of between six and seven years has impelled me to take the liberty of sending the inclosed letter under cover to you.[1] As I know of no place where propriety and affection will unite so powerfully in inducing him to stop as at Mount Vernon, I have little doubt of his receiving this letter in safety.

The election of representatives in Congress for this State has lately taken place; we have as yet received the returns of only five out of our six election districts: of these we know four have chosen men who have no predilection for any foreign Country—Mr Huger of George town is in the place of Mr Benton—Genl Sumpter is the only member, of whose re-election we have heard, who opposed the measures adopted by Congress at their last meeting.[2]

Mrs Pinckney begs to unite her kindest wishes and most sincere respects for Mrs Washington and yourself with those of Dear Sir Your affecte & most obedt Servant

Thomas Pinckney

ALS, DLC:GW.

1. Thomas Pinckney (1750–1828) returned from his various diplomatic missions in Europe in September 1796 after more than three years abroad; his brother Charles Cotesworth Pinckney had sailed for Europe in late September 1796 to replace James Monroe as U.S. minister to France and had just returned to the United States.

2. The South Carolina elections were held on 8 October. Thomas Pinckney was reelected, without opposition, to the U.S. House of Representatives from South Carolina's Charleston district. Benjamin Huger (1768–1823) served as U.S. representative from South Carolina's Cheraw district from 1799 to 1805, as a Federalist. His Republican opponent, Lemuel Benton (1754–1818), had been representing the district since 1793. Thomas Sumter (1734–1822) defeated Richard Winn (1750–1818) to gain reelection to his seat in Congress from South Carolina's Camden district. Sumter and Winn, both Republicans and natives of Virginia, between them represented the Camden district in Congress from 1784 to 1813. Robert Goodloe Harper and John Rutledge, Jr. (1766–1819), both Federalists, were reelected; William Smith (1751–1837), a

Republican representing the Spartanburg district, was defeated by Abraham Nott (1768–1830), a Federalist from Connecticut who had arrived in South Carolina in 1789.

To William Richardson Davie

Sir,   Mount Vernon 24th Octr 1798

I am not informed of the cause, or causes which have impeded the appointment of the Regimental Officers agreeably to the Act "To augment the Army of the United States, and for other purposes." The want of which has, of course (unpropitiously it is to be feared) retarded the Recruiting Service; nor do I know that any plan is yet adopted to effect either of these purposes.

But the Secretary of War having suggested to me, that it was probable four of the twelve Regiments of Infantry, and the six Troops of Light Dragoons would be raised in the states south of the Potomac, including Kentucky and Tennessee, and requesting me to give him assistance in selecting proper Characters for Officers in the different grades therefor, I know of no expedient so likely to give it efficiency as to call upon the General Officers in each State, lately nominated by the President, for their aid. The presumption being, that the Reputation of the Army, in which they may have to act a conspicuous part, and their own honor and responsibility will put them above local attachments, and self-interested views, and, consequently, produce more circumspection in the selection of fit and proper Characters for Officers, than is likely to be obtained by any other means.

It is on this ground I have taken the liberty to address you, and hope for an excuse.

Pursuing the principle, by which the Secretary of War seems to have been governed, about a Regiment of Infantry and a Troop of Dragoons would fall to the lot of No. Carolina and Tennessee; say, nine Companies of the first and the Company of Dragoons to the former, and a Company of Infantry to the latter.

To assist you as much as is in my power, in the accomplishment of this work, I enclose you a list of all the field Officers of the No. Carolina line, who served to the close of the Revolutionary war— and a list of the present Applicants for Commissions; designating their places of residence, the Rank they solicit, and by whom recommended or brought forward.[1]

My Opinion is, that in making a selection of the *field* Officers, an entire range of the State should be taken; but in the Company Officers, regard should be had to distribution; as well for the purpose of facilitating the Recruiting Service, as for other considerations: and, where Officers of *celebrity* in the Revolutionary Army can be obtained; who are yet in the prime of life, habituated to no bad courses—and well disposed, that a preference ought to be given to them. Next to these, gentlemen of Character, liberal Education, and, as far as the fact can be ascertained from inexperience, men who will face danger in any shape it can appear; for if we have a land war, it will be sharp and severe. I must beg leave to add, that all violent opposers of the Government, and French Partisans should be avoided; or they will disseminate the poison of their principles in the Army, and split, what ought to be a band of brothers, into Parties.

As this Application is hypothetical, (no decided plan being formed) you will please to consider *it*, and the contents of this letter, in *all its parts*, as given in confidence. The papers you will be so good as to return, with the selection of Officers for the Troops I have mentioned, for the States of North Carolina and Tennessee; and, for a very particular reason, the sooner it could be done and sent to me, the more agreeable it would be.[2]

It might not be amiss to set down the names of more Officers, of each Grade, than are really wanting for the Regiment and Troop; but that I may know the estimation in which they stand, you will be pleased to place those of each grade numerically. With very great Esteem, I am, Sir, Your most Obedt Hble Servt

Go: Washington

LS, NcU: William L. Saunders Collection; ADfS, DLC:GW.

William Richardson Davie (1756–1820), born in England of Scottish parents, was brought to South Carolina at the age of eight. He graduated from the College of New Jersey (Princeton) in 1776 and became a noted partisan leader in the Carolinas during the Revolution. He studied law and became a political leader in North Carolina, serving in 1787 as a delegate to the Federal Convention. He was elected governor of the state in 1798, and in 1799 John Adams chose him as one of the three ministers plenipotentiary to negotiate a settlement with France.

1. A Copy of the List sent to Genl Davie of Persons in North Carolina, Applying for Commissions in the Army now to be raised, or in the Provisional Army, undated, is in DLC:GW, filed at the end of December 1798. The list of Revolutionary War field officers has not been found, but see GW to James McHenry (first letter), 21 Oct., n.4.

2. Davie replied on 14 November.

From John Lambert

Much Respect'd Sir

Pittsgrove Salem County West Jersey
October 24. 1798

it Gives me much Pleasure to inform you of the very great Improvement we have found by being Careful to Cultivate the Large Sort of Clover. the Summer before this we had About 80 Acres of the Small Red Clover—being a dry Sumer we Could not mow 3 bushels of Seed[.] this Summer being a like dry but haveing about 70 Acres of the Large Sort of red Clover we have mawn we hope 60 bushels of Seed on the like poor worn out Lands. you know the Common run of our lands are worn out but if we Can grow a Quantity of feed or hay the land may be improveed I have Shewn the 2 distinct Sorts growing Close by Each other and it has Convin[c]ed Gentlemen to their Surprise the Very Great difference. As you love improvement I thought you would not think this A trifling Affair.

I intend to keep Some of this Sort of red Clover att Mr John Coopers in ray Streett No. 152 att 16 Dollars a bushel my Neighbours buy it Very redyly att that Price. I hope you will overlook all my Imperfections and believe that no one more Sincerely Respect You than Your Obedient Servant

John Lambert

ALS, DLC:GW. The letter was docketed by Tobias Lear as having been received at "W. City 3d novr" and answered on 20 November. The response has not been found.

In a letter from Philadelphia, dated 11 Nov. 1792, to his Mount Vernon farm manager Anthony Whitting, GW identified John Lambert as "an English farmer from the county of Essex, in England lately arrived in this country to settle, and who appears to be a very sensible and judicious man, and a person of property." Lambert had at that time given GW oats and cabbage seed and a pamphlet with directions for making a plow. GW thought him to be about sixty years old and reported he "has travelled a good deal about this country."

To Thomas Law

Dear Sir,   Mount Vernon 24th Octr 1798.

Your letter of the 17th instant was handed to me by Mr Lear, and I should have sent you the enclosed check on the Bank of Alexandria for two hundred and fifty dollars sooner, had we not expected you at this place on friday or Saturday last, according to promise—and been looking for you every day since.[1]

All I ask is, that you would have me secured in the loan of this sum, for the purpose of erecting a Hotel for Mr Tunnicliff, in the same manner you do the $750 lent on your own A/c.[2]

The family here unite in love and best wishes for Mrs Law, Eliza and yourself; and I am, with great esteem & regard—Dear Sir Your Most Obedt Hble Servt

Go: Washington

ALS (letterpress copy), DLC:GW; LB, DLC:GW.

1. No letter of 17 Oct. from Law has been found. See GW to William Thornton, 18 Oct., n.3.

2. On 21 May 1799 William Tunnicliff, who had been operating the Eastern Branch Hotel on Pennsylvania Avenue between 8th and 9th streets, S.E., announced the opening of his Washington City Hotel near the Capitol, on A Street just off 1st Street, N.E. (W. B. Bryan, "Hotels of Washington Prior to 1814" *Columbia Hist. Soc. Recs.*, 7:79, 84–85). GW has on 24 Oct. 1798 an entry of $250 in Ledger C, 49, for "my subscription for 5 Shares towards building a hotel in the City of Washington pd to Mr Law who promises to see them secured." See also the entry in GW's Day Book for this date.

From Isaiah and Alexander Thomas

Sir,   Walpole, N.H. Oct. 24 1798

As a specimen of literary and miscellaneous "folio of four pages," printed weekly in this place, we send you the paper which accompanies these. Do us the honour to accept of the numbers as they are published. We have a laudable ambition of numbering so worthy a Man among our readers.[1] With profound respect, We are Sir, Your obedt & humble servts

Ish & Alexr Thomas

LS, DLC:GW. Docketed by Tobias Lear: "Answd Novr 20 98."

Isaiah Thomas (1749–1831) was a leading American printer of his day and founder of the American Antiquarian Society in Worcester, Mass., where he lived. From 1798 to 1809 he published the *Farmer's Weekly Museum* with Alexander Thomas (d. 1809) in Walpole, New Hampshire.

1. GW responded from Philadelphia on 20 Nov.: "Gentln I have recd your polite letter of the 24th Ulto requesting my acceptance, as they may be published, of the number of your literary & miscellaneous paper.

"I cannot, consistently with a rule I have prescribed to myself, accept your paper as a present, but, as I wish to promote, as much as is in my power, these publications which may be useful & beneficial to our Count[r]y, I beg you to consider me as a subscriber to your ⟨paper⟩, which you will be pleased to send me accordingly, directed to Mt Vernon, and be pleased to let me know the terms of subscription, and to whom I shall make paymt. I am Gentl. Yr mo. obdt st G. Washington" (retained copy, ViMtV).

To Bushrod Washington

My dear Sir,   Mount Vernon 24th Octr 1798.

Your letter of the 19th instant came duly to hand. I think you were perfectly right in accepting the appointment of Associate Judge—Not only for the reasons you have mentioned, but on every other account.

I only regret that Judge Wilson had it not in his power to have postponed his exit (which I am persuaded he was not indisposed to do) to a later period.[1] The Elections in New Jersey are not favourable, & in Pennsylvania—so far as we have heard—are bad. What *these*, and *such like* will produce, is left for wiser heads than mine to foretell. I auger very ill of them.[2]

I wish your Circuit may be pleasant and honorable to you, and that you may return safe to your family & friends. The Season is propitious for a Southern tour and I hope your attention to the duties of your present Office will give satisfaction. Of *some* of the Judges who have gone that Circuit their has been heavy Complaints—I am Yr sincere friend & affecte Uncle

Go: Washington

ALS, ViMtV.

1. There were rumors that the financially ruined justice of the Supreme Court had committed suicide, but James Wilson, after suffering a stroke, died on 21 Aug. 1798 in Edenton, North Carolina. GW wrote "exist" for "exit."

2. In the elections held in New Jersey in October self-declared Republicans replaced two of the five Federalists who had made up the New Jersey delegation to the U.S. House of Representatives. The election in Pennsylvania was also held this month; the result was an increase in Republicans by one, so that there were now eight instead of seven men identifiable as Republican and five instead of six as Federalists.

From the District of Columbia Commissioners

Sir,   Washington 25th October 1798

We received your Letter of 22d Inst., and in consequence, have caused the Draft of an agreement to be made, such as appeared to us to correspond with your ideas, but lest any alterations might be wished, we advised Mr Blagdin to wait on you with it, and to take with him the Plans, specifications &c., so that if you have stamped paper, the duty on which will be seventy five cents per sheet, the writings may be copied and executed at Mount Vernon; but if not, (as is probably the case) they may be written and executed here, after Mr Blagdin's Return.[1] We are, with sentiments of great respect, Sir, Yr Mo: Obt Servts

William Thornton
Alexr White

LS, DLC:GW.

1. George Blagdin took the "Draft of an agreement" between GW and himself to Mount Vernon on 26 October. See GW to the District of Columbia Commissioners, 27 Oct., and notes.

From William Thornton

Dear Sir   City of Washington Octr 25th 1798.

Some Days before the Board had the honor of your last Communication[1] I had applied to Mr Blagdin to make out all the various Estimates expressed in your Favour to me of the 18th Instt, and I meant to obtain a Specimen of the different mouldings; thinking your People could work better by them, than by Drawings. What I requested was only in proviso; for I thought it might finally be a matter of hesitation, whether it would be better to submit to a higher charge than your People would render necessary, or encounter the Difficulties arising from the procuring of Timber & Scantling, sending it up as required &c: for although it would have been a pleasure to me to have endeavoured as much as laid in my power to relieve you from a portion of the Trouble, yet you would still have had some cares that might be inconvenient; and, upon the whole, as your People will not remain unusefully employed, it will perhaps give you greater Satisfaction in the end, to form a Contract in the mode you have proposed. Mr White and I have formed a Contract, with which Mr Blagdin will wait on you.[2]

Mr T: Peter shewed me an Estimate of General Lee's Property in this City. It is extravagant if he possesses the Lots; but I believe he is not the Proprietor, for I think he sold some of them to Presley Thornton, who re-sold them to John Tayloe of Mount Airy. I cannot ascertain the Fact till I see some of the Parties, and I have not yet had an opportunity; but it would be a matter of little Consequence, as you could not think of allowing such a price.[3]

There may, in the price of your Houses, be a little reduction made in the end Walls; for, as the Board allowed me the Lot adjoining yours (it being awarded to me by Messrs Young & Law for the Premium which I had not demanded from motives of Delicacy, but which I was entitled to for my plans of the Capitol) [4] and I am willing to prepare for a House or Houses on a similar plan, the Chimnies may be run up at the same time, & I will allow you half the Price of that Wall, besides entitling you to build on the Line of Separation, which will give you seven Inches more space in your House; and, with your permission, I will write a few Lines to Amariah Frost, a Magistrate in New England, who purchased on the other side of you, and make the same proposal to him, by which you will gain seven Inches more on the other side, and save half the Expense of the wall, provided he agree to the plan, of which I will send him a Copy. It is not customary to demand the moiety 'till the Parties build, which might be a consideration if the immediate additional Expenditure were great, but it is very inconsiderable, and more than repaid by the increase of space, if reimbursement were never demandable; but we shall be bound to repay it, and I hope sooner than present appearances warrant. Indeed if I had not suffered by some late heavy losses; not in Speculations, but matters of Confidence, to the amount of between four & five thousand Dollars, I should have been enabled to carry up a House now—I hope, however, to assist in making a respectable Row of Houses.[5]

I do not recollect to have heard you mention a Well; nor has Mr Blagdin spoken of one, although it would save him much trouble and expense, and perhaps may be necessary. This however you will consider: in the mean time I shall not notice it to him.

I think five feet areas very narrow: They are damp, and keep the Kitchens so, by excluding the Sun and air; tending thereby to render them unwholesome: Six, seven, or eight Feet, would be better I think; but the Regulations do not at present allow of such extent. In the grand Houses in London they are very wide. Mr Law says as wide as twelve feet. I have seen them, and think he has mistaken; but eight, or perhaps *seven* would do; so that allowing a Foot for the Copeing, the Pavement would be twelve feet in the Clear. Houses that have the Kitchens behind do not require such wide

front areas—but as your Houses will be inaccessible behind, &
large Casks must be gotten into the Cellars it will be worthy of
consideration. I am dear Sir with the greatest respect your affectionate Friend &c.

William Thornton

ALS, CtY: Miscellaneous Collection—Annie Burr Jennings.

1. GW wrote to the District of Columbia Commissioners on 22 October.

2. See GW to the District of Columbia Commissioners, 27 Oct., and to Thornton, 28 October.

3. For the reason that GW took an interest in Henry Lee's property in the
Federal City, see Lee to GW, 28 September.

4. On 21 Sept. 1798 Thornton petitioned the other two District of Columbia
commissioners, Alexander White and Gustavus Scott, for "a lot in the City of
Washington, and five hundred dollars," the reward promised for the acceptance
of his design for the U.S. Capitol. As the lot was supposed "to be designated by
impartial judges," Thornton chose Thomas Law and the two commissioners appointed Notley Young. The lot awarded to Thornton was no. 15 in square 634,
adjacent to GW's lot no. 16 (Harris, *Thornton Papers*, 1:472–73).

5. Amariah Frost (d. 1819) lived in Milford, Massachusetts. For further discussion of the common walls, see GW to Thornton, 28 Oct., and Thornton to GW,
30 October.

To James McHenry

My dear Sir, Mount Vernon 26th Octr 1798.

The enclosures transmitted in your letter of the 20th instant are
retd.[1]

I derived great pleasure from General Pinkneys declaration to
General Hamilton; and wish you to inform him, that I feel happy
in the thought of having him as a Coadjutor, if our disputes with
France are to be decided by the Sword.

Let me hear from you as soon as possible on the subject of my
last letters to you—dated the 21st and 23d Instant—and be assured of the sincere esteem and regard of Your affectionate

Go: Washington

ALS (letterpress copy), DLC:GW.

1. See McHenry to GW, 20 Oct., nn.1 and 2.

From James McHenry

(private & confidential)

My dear General   26 Octbr 1798

I received last night your letter of the 21st, and also your private and confidential one of the same date. I find the President is extremely guarded in his expressions; but I perceive, at the same time, that he will not refuse himself to any of your recommendations.

I have you will see by my letter of the 16th of Octbr given you the foundation for your answer of the 21st.

Inclosed are copies of the Presidents instructions to me and the letter I wrote to him from Mount Vernon relative to your appointment.[1]

I have long since given orders & often renewed them, to have a copy made out for you, of the Captains & subalterns who served in the revolutionary army. It has not been completed owing to the immense press of business on the office.

The President has neither acknowledged nor answered Mr Wolcotts letter. I suppose he does not intend any direct notice of it.

I reced one hundred dollars in a letter from Miss Custis which discharged my advance for the colours. I mentioned to Nelly the obstructions that prevented the procuring of tassels &c.[2]

Gen. Pinckney is still at N. Ark and has made no answer as yet to my letter with his commission. I cannot however suppose, that he will offer any objections to the rank of the Major Generals after the Message he sent to Hamilton.[3]

Has Hodgdon sent you the return of our military store &c.[4] Yours ever & affectionately

James McHenry

ALS, DLC:GW; ADfS, DLC: James McHenry Papers; copy, in the hand of a clerk, DLC: Hamilton Papers.

1. See GW to McHenry, 16 Sept., nn.2 and 4.

2. The Day Book for 24 Sept. records a payment of $100 "sent the Secy of War James McHenry Esqr. to pay for two Standards provided by him at the req. of Mrs Washington & Miss Custis." See GW to James McHenry (first letter), 21 Oct., n.6.

3. Pinckney wrote to McHenry on 31 Oct. accepting the commission. See McHenry to GW, 1 Nov., n.1.

4. See McHenry to GW, 16 Nov. (second letter).

To Timothy Pickering

Dear Sir   Mount Vernon 26th Oct. 1798.

I have been duly favored with your letters of the 15th & 20th Instant; and received great satisfaction from the communications in both.

That General Pinckney not only accepts his appointment in the army of the United States, but accompanies the acceptance with declar[at]ions so open & candid, as those made to General Hamilton, affords me sincere pleasure. It augers well of the aid that may be expected from his Services.

I should suppose that a Correspondence between the Department of State, & the Governors of Individual States, would be attended with salutary consequences, whilst no evil that I can perceive, would flow from it. By such communications as would be proper to make to them, the well disposed part would be possessed of useful information, and those of a contrary description would, in many cases, be bereft of a plea which they often make—the want of it. To enable you to do this, and to execute with ease the other important duties of your Office, you ought, certainly, to be allowed all the Aid that is necessary.

If Mr Gerry has it in his power to dispel the cloud that hovers over him, I wish, on account of his Country; for his own sake; and as the only attonement he can make to his Colleagues for his seperate transactions, & secret conduct with the French Minister, that he would come forward with an open, and manly representation of all the circumstances that occurred, and governed in that business. Though nothing can excuse his *secret* negociations—a measure of this sort is the only One I can see, that can irradicate unfavorable Suspicions. I fear however, that *vanity*, which may have led him into the mistake, and consciousness of being *duped* by the *Diplomatic Skill* of our good, & magnanimous Allies are too powerful for a weak mind to overcome. With very great esteem & regard I am—Dear Sir Your Most Obedt Hble Servt

Go: Washington

ALS, MHi: Pickering Papers; ALS (letterpress copy), DLC:GW.

From James Ross

Dear Sir   Pittsburgh 26 Octr 1798

On my return from Kentuckey two days ago, I found your letter of the first instant respecting the money due from Colo. Shreve. My Absence from home when your letter reached this place has occasioned a delay of a few days, but I have put the business into such a shape, without the bond, that your Money will I think be in the hands of the Sheriff, or paid to me upon the fourth Monday of December, which is the first day of the next Court in Fayette County. Our County Courts are held quarterly, and the Sheriff is Supposed to execute his duty very well if he brings in the money upon the return of the writ: It is indeed almost impossible to prevail with any officer to proceed more expeditiously than in this their Usual course. Your letter to Colo. Shreve, together with one from myself were forwarded to him yesterday so that he is fully apprised of the approaching call from the Sheriff. Having still in my possession a Memorandum of the agreement between you and Colo. Shreve, I shall not want the Bond, and it will of course lie in the Bank untill called for by you, as your order has not been forwarded to the directors. When the money is paid over to me by the Sheriff, credit can be entered upon it for the Sum paid when I am in the city next Winter.[1]

I am surprised at the inattention and want of punctuality which has so uniformly marked the conduct of Colo. Shreve and am well persuaded that it is vain to trust hereafter in any thing Short of legal compulsion should he fail in payment upon the day mentioned in his Bond. With the highest respect I have the honour to be Sir Your most obedient & most Humble Servant

                                                        James Ross

ALS, DLC:GW.

1. See GW to Israel Shreve, 1 Oct., and note 1 to that document.

To the District of Columbia Commissioners

Gentlemen,   Mount Vernon Octr 27 1798

When Mr Blagden came here yesterday with your favor of the 25 inst., and the plans, specifications &c. of my houses, I was out on my usual ride about my farms, and when I returned home I found Company, which prevented my answering your letter by him.[1]

The sketch of an agreement enclosed in your letter comports fully with my ideas. I have made one or two triffling alterations in it in consequence of some conversation with Mr Blagden, and I now take the liberty to enclose two Copies of the Agreement, and an additional Copy of the specifications.[2] The agreements are drawn on unstamped paper; but I presume it may be stamped in George Town. If it cannot be done there, Doctr Thornton will be so good as to have new agreements drawn for me on stamped paper.[3]

I pray you, Gentlemen, to accept my best thanks for the trouble you have had in this business, which I assure you I should not have given, had I not been induced to build these houses more with a view to promote the necessary improvements in the City, than from any expectation of p[r]ivate emolument from them. With great respect & esteem I am Gentln Yr most Obedt Servt

Df, in Tobias Lear's hand, DLC:GW; LB, DLC:GW. The letter-book copy is an accurate copy of Lear's draft.

1. For GW's "Company" on 26 Oct., see GW to William Thornton, 28 October.

2. The specifications for the construction of the two houses agreed to by GW and George Blagdin at this time are in DLC:GW. The lengthy document reads:

"Specification of Carpenters & Joiners work for two Houses intended to be built for Genel Washington viz.—as follows—All the Joists in the floors to be of good Pine, likewise all the other Timbers, Such as Purlins, Rafters, Ceiling Joists, Quarter Partitions Bond Timber, Plating &c. And to the following Scantling.

Viz.	Inches	Inches			[Inches]		
Joists	11	3		Quarter Partitions	5		3
Purlins	8	7		Stooths in the Roof	3		3
Rafters	3	by	3	Roof plate	6	by	4
Lintels	9	3		Bond Timber	9		3
Ceiling Joists	5	3		Cross Ties	4		3

All the Joists, Rafters, Ceiling Joists, Stooths, Quarter Partitions, &c. to be laid not more than 13 Inches apart. All the fire places to have framed Timbers in the floors for Brick Arches. The two Passage Walls to have 4 Bond Timbers, in each, one under every floor, with Cross Ties to the same. The Roof to have 2 Purlins on each Side, and to be framed with Rafters, Ceiling Joists, and Stooth as Pr Section.

The Roof to have 6 Dormer Windows on the Brick side, with Pitched Roofs, and Sliding sashes each window to contain 9 panes of Glass, 8 by 10 Inches. The front side of the Roof to have 2 sky lights to slide, each sky light to Contain 9 panes of Glass 8 by 10 Inches, all well bedded in putty.

Floors

All the Principal floors and Chamber floors to be laid with good 1¼ Inch yellow Pine Plank, laid to a regular gauge, not exceeding 7 Inches Wide, groved and tongued and secret nailed. All the Garret floors to be laid with good 1¼ Pine Plank, groved and tongued and nailed through the front. All the Passage floors to be the same as the Rooms. All the floors in the Rooms & Passages in the Roof to be well laid with good Inch Pine Plank, groved tongued and nailed through the front: all the above Plank to be good sound stuff free from sap and shakes.

Doors

The 4 basement outer Doors to be 4 Panneled with Batten frames moulded on one side and Inch back, to be hung with good hooks and bands and each door to have a good 12 Inch Iron rim lock with Bolt and Knops. The frames to be made of good proper Scantling, with plain linings and single mouldings to the same, and a Tramson light to each frame to contain 4 panes of Glass not less than 10 Inches high. The 2 front doors to be 6 panneled and framed of 2 Inch plank moulded on both sides with framed—Jambs and Circular soffeits to match the doors, and double faced archatraves to the same. The 2 back doors on the principal floor to be 6 Panneled moulded on one side, with plain Jambs and single mouldings to the same; The 2 frames to the same to have each a transom light to contain 4 panes of Glass not less than 12 Inches high.

The 5 Inner Doors on the same floor to be 6 panneled framed of 1½ Inch plank moulded on both sides with framed Jambs and soffeits and double faced Archatraves to the same.

Chamber, 5 Doors to be 6 panneled and moulded on both sides framing 1½ Inch thick framed Jambs and soffeits and double faced archatraves to the same.

The Garrets, 9 Doors, 6 panneled and square on both sides, framed 1¼ Inch plank; Plain Jambs & soffeits and single faced archatraves to the same.

The Rooms in the Roof; 6 Doors 4 pannel'd and Square, on both Sides with plain Jambs, soffeits and Single mouldings to the same—N.B. one framed Jamb with soffeit and archatraves to the same in the Chamber Study; And one D[itt]o in the Garret Story—with plain Jambs and single archatraves, but no Doors to the above. The 2 middle rooms in the Garret Story, and 2 passage Rooms in the roof, to have a transom light over each door, to contain 4 panes of Glass in each 10 Inches high.

Sashes

The principal and chamber Stories to have 20 ovolo sashes with beaded and bosed frames, with 12 panes in each sash. the size of the Glass 12 by 18 Inches.

The Garret Story to have 12 sashes of the same kind with 6 panes in each, Glass—12 by 18 Inches.

The basement Story in front to have 4 sashes each to contain 12 Panes Glass, 12 by 12 Inches. back Sashes in the same Story to have 12 Panes in each, Glass 10 by 12 Inches—all the above Sashes to be 3 panes wide and the frames boxed to hang double—except the front basement one, to hang single & all of the same mouldings.

Shutters and Linings

The 8 sashes on the Principal floor to have folded framed ovolo shutters, to hang in two heights with Square backs, with back linings framed to match. The Pannels flat and 4 in height—The shutters framed 1½ Inch Plank with framed, dado backs and elbows recessed to the ground and double faced archatraves to the same. All the sashes in the Chamber Story to have plain linings, and double faces Archatraves to the same, and those in the front to be recessed to the floor, with plain Dado & Sides to the Same, the archatraves in the Chamber back rooms to stand on the surface.

The 12 Garret, Sashes to have plain linings, with single faced Archatraves, to Stand on the Surface.

The 8 basement sashes to have Plain linings and single mouldings to the same. and the 4 sashes on the back side to have single folded 1½ Inch framed Shutters hung Out side with Cocked Hinges.

Stairs

The two houses to have a good Stair case in each, continued up to the rooms in the roof consisting of 61 Steps in each Stairs, the steps to be 12 inches wide with returned nosings, and plain cut brackets, Poplar rails with Ramps and curved knees, Square newels, diminished and Square banisters, mitred caps and half handrail worked to match, returned rails and banisters on the landings, soffiets plastered. The 2 first flights to have moulded framing to enclose the basement stair heads with a good 6 panneled door to the same in each. The basement Story to have 2 flights of good strong plain Stairs, with 15 Steps in each 12 Inches wide with plain newels, Rails and bannisters to the same. The 2 back doors of basement Story to have 2 flights of good strong stairs, with Capt rails and square Bannisters, and continued platform for both doors, the rises to be not more than 7 Inches and the steps 12 inches wide.

Surbases & Plinths

All the lower Rooms and Chambers together with their passages, to have a good surbase round the same composed of different numbers to girt not less than 5 Inches, with good bold Torus Plinths of a proper height.

All the rooms in the Garret Story and their passages to have good Surbase and Plinths round the same but of a plainer kind. All the rooms in the roof and their passages together with the 2 basement back rooms and passages to have a good plain Chairrail and skirting round the same.

Archatraves

All the archatraves in low rooms and chambers to be double faced, on not less than 6½ Inch ground.

All the archatraves in the Garret Story to be single faced on a 6 Inch ground. all the Doors inside to have 2 archatraves to each; and all the sashes one, except the basement sashes, which are to have single mouldings only—likewise all the doors in the Basement and those in the rooms—in the Roof to have Single mouldings two to each door. All the single mouldings to be not less than ⅝ Inch deep.

In one of the Houses is to be a movable partition in one frame, to move up and be received in the Boxed double stoothing partition in the Chamber made for that purpose. The frame to be 2 inches thick when finished both sides canvased Glued and painted, to match the room.

The Surbases and Plinths, on each side to be painted, in distemper to match the real ones, The frames to have good pullies, lines, Irons, and proper apparatus to raise the same.

Cornices

The 8 fire places on the principal floor, and the Chambers to have each one a good neat Dental Cornice with Frizes and archatraves mouldings to the same to stand on Blocks. The 4 fire places in the Garrets to have a neat plain Cornice composed of Different members with Frizes & archatrave mouldings to the same. The front of the 2 Houses to have a good handsome square modillion cornice, the modillion capped with a bracket continued moulding and Square Cut, the top of the Cornice to have a channel not less than 6 Inches wide lined with lead to receive the Eave and carry off the water.

The 2 passages to have 2 arches in each one in the low room passage and one in the Chamber with circular archatraves Plain Pillasters with Imposts; Bases and Plinths to the same; the archatrave double faced.

Iron Monger & Smith Work

The out Doors of the Basement to be hung with good hooks and bands with a 12 Inch Iron rim lock on each with bolts, The 2 principal and back Doors to be hung with 5 Inch butt Hinges, and each to have a 12 Inch Iron rim lock with bolts and brass knops to the same. All the low room and chamber Doors to have 4½ Inch Hinges and 10 Inch Iron rim locks with Brass Pendents and bolts. All the Doors in the Garret Story, Story in the roof and Inner Doors in the basement to have 3½ Inch Hinges and 9 Inch locks, Iron rim & Brass Pendents.

All the sashes to be hung with brass 1¾ Inch pullies in Iron frames 4 in each sash frame.

All the sashes to have brass-spring fasteners and well hung with good line and proper cast Iron weights.

The inside shutters to be hung with 2½ inch Butt hinges—to have 4 brass Pendent rings to each pair and to be fastened inside with good pivot Bar fasteners, the out side shutters to the Basement back room windows to be hung with good strong cock Hinges and Iron bolts to the same.

Painting & Glazing

All the windows to be Glazed with Good Glass, well bedded in good putty, the Glass to be of the sizes before mentioned—All the Doors, Sashes, Shutters, linings, frames, Stairs, framing, Archatraves, Surbases, Plinths, Mouldings, Cornices, &c. to be well painted three times in Good Oil Colour.

The two Houses to have a Frontispiece consisting of four columns of proper proportion with Plinth Caps, Bases, and a continued intableture over both Doors, with Grounds, Plinths, Imposts, and circular double faced archatraves, and a good Fan light to each—the whole of which to be well painted, sanded, and Painted to match the stone String course, and its form as pr Elevation.

The eave cornice to be well painted & sanded, the same as the Frontispiece and to have 2 good lead water pipes of 3 Inches diameter to the same, to come near the ground, one at each corner. The Roof to be covered with good 2 feet Cyprus Shingles laid to a 6½ Inch gauge on good Inch sheeting plank of Yellow Pine. The whole of the before mentioned work to be done and finished in a Complete Substantial and Workmanlike manner.

Brick Work Plastering & Stone Cutting
Particularized

The heights of each Story is—Cellar or Basement 8 feet, Principal and chamber Stories 12 feet each, Garret 9 feet clear between floor and ceiling. Cellar

Front and back wall each 2 feet thick faced with good common Bricks and backed with Stone. Two end Walls 20 Inches thick—with good mortar and stone—all the inner or Partition Walls of Stone 18 Inches thick—the area Walls 20 Inches thick, faced with Brick and backed with Stone. The Kitchens (suppos'd backward) to be paved with Brick flatwise also passages and area's—Two flights of the Free stone Steps, into area's, ⟨Trimmer⟩ arches to all fire places. Front wall from top of Basement to top of cornice or Square 2 Bricks thick, faced with best stock Brick Rub'd and gaug'd arches over Windows—Stone Window cills, Strings source facia, and Plinth as pr Elevation, Plinth and facia Cramp'd and leaded. 3 Steps and Platform with astragal nosing to front Doors, length as described in Plan—arch over area to support d[itt]o—of Brick except the ends which are of free stone—Two astragal door cills Back wall of best common Bricks—2 brick thick to top of Chamber floor and from thence 1½ Brick—work'd in flemmish bond—plain neat arches to Doors and Windows—Two end walls 1½ Brick thick chimney brests as pr Plan. All the interior Walls—brick in length thick, except that between passages which is 1½ brick thick—all the mortar to be made of good stone lime—with a proper proportion of good sharp sand—4 free stone Chimney pieces—and Harths—in principal and Chamber stories—All Ceilings in Cellar plastered with 2 Coats of lime and Hair—Walls in Kitchen and Passages 2 Coat work also—Low Rooms, Chambers, & Garrets, all with 3 Coats, and Rooms within of Roof 2 Coat work—Plain handsome plaster Cornice in lower Rooms and passages—coping to area—Wall of free Stone 12 inches broad and 6 Inches thick—to receive ends of bannisters, the whole to be done in a Complete and workmanlike manner. Geo. Blagdin

If the frontispiece is done in Stone add 150 Doll[ar]s" (DLC:GW).

3. The contract, or agreement, between GW and Blagdin was drawn up by William Thornton on 5 November. Thornton witnessed the signature of George Blagdin and of the architect James Hoban (c.1758–1831), at this time superintendent of the Capitol. The document, which was sent to GW and is in DLC:GW, reads: "ARTICLES of Agreement this Day made and concluded between George Washington Esquire, Lieutenant General, and Commander in chief of the Armies of the United States, of the one Part, and George Blagdin of the City of Washington Stone Cutter of the other Part, WITNESSETH, that the said George Blagdin in Consideration of eleven thousand Dollars to be paid to him by the said George Washington in manner hereafter mentioned doth agree to build on Lot No. 16 in Square 634 in the said City two Brick Houses, three Stories high, agreeably to the ground-plan, Elevation, & the Specification of the particular parts of the said Buildings hereto annexed, signed by the said George Blagdin, and considered as part of this agreement, except the painting and Glazing of the said Houses: the Glazing to be done by the said George Washington previous to the plaistering; and the Ironmongery to be furnished by the said George Washington agreeably to the abovementioned Specification thereof, as the same shall be required in the Course of the Building—it being understood that the said George Blagdin shall furnish the Nails necessary without any further Demand on the said George Washington than is stated for that Item, in the Specification aforesaid. One of the said Houses to be finished in a complete and workmanlike manner, on or before the first Day of November, in the year one thousand seven hundred & ninety nine; and the other to be finished in like manner, on or before

the first Day of March in the year one thousand eight hundred. It is further agreed upon by the parties to these Presents that if the said Blagdin should have one of the said Houses finished and compleated before the first Day of November aforesaid, then, and in that Case he shall be allowed as much time for compleating the other after the first Day of March aforesaid as he shall have finished the first previous to the first Day of November aforesaid.

"IN CONSIDERATION whereof the said George Washington doth agree and bind himself his Heirs, Executors & Administrators to pay to the said George Blagdin his Executors Administrators or Assigns the aforesaid Sum of eleven thousand Dollars: that is to say, he will advance Sums sufficient to pay for all materials necessary for carrying on the said Buildings on the delivery of such materials; also Sums sufficient to discharge the amount of all Workman's Wages weekly or monthly, as the said George Blagdin may require the same; and when the said Buildings are compleated he will pay whatever may remain of the eleven Thousand Dollars after having paid for the Materials and workmanship aforesaid. It is also agreed that in addition to the eleven thousand Dollars before mentioned the said George Washington will pay to the said George Blagdin one hundred and fifty Dollars on Condition of his making the Frontispiece of the front Doors of Stone instead of Wood—and that he will also allow him, the said George Blagdin, one hundred Dollars for making a wine vault in the Cellar, as specified in the plan of the basement Story of said Houses, provided it shall be found that said Vault shall cost that Sum.

"For the true and faithful Performance of the above Agreement in all its parts, he the said George Blagdin, and James Hoban of the said City, architect, his Surety, bind themselves, their Heirs, Executors, and administrators jointly and severally to the said George Washington, in the Sum of four thousand Dollars, to be paid to the said George Washington, his Executors, Administrators or assigns, in Case of the failure of the said George Blagdin in performance of his said Agreement." There also are in DLC:GW a rough draft and another copy of this agreement.

From Timothy Pickering

Sir,   Trenton [N.J.] Oct. 27 1798

The inclosed interesting pamphlet is a faithful translation from the original French, transmitted to me by Mr King. As it details *facts* which demonstrate the perfidy and violence of the French Government, I had it translated, and recommended it to the printer in this place; hoping the dissemination of it in America might do good.[1] I think the Government could expend money in no way more usefully. It is astonishing to hear what audacious lies are propagated by the partisans of France: one would imagine the utmost ignorance and credulity to be found in the United States incapable of swallowing them. This morning I heard the following.

Mr William Bell of Philadelphia (an honest merchant who lived just over against you in Philadelphia) lately attended the court at Easton in Pennsylvania.[2] On his way thither, he was told by some of the country people (Germans) that they were displeased very much with the Government, for making the *alliance* and *seditious* bills. By the alliance (when desired to explain) Mr Adams, a son of the President, was to marry a daughter of the King of Great Britain; and General Washington was to hold the United States in trust for that King! And it is for these purposes, said they, that an army is to be raised, and *window* taxes levied!

Altho' I have not before heard any thing so foolish and absurd as this, yet the idea of an *Alliance* between the U. States & Great Britain, we daily see is held up as a scarecrow before the eyes of the people. This reminds me of a curious fact. (I call it a fact because I have it from a man of honour to whom the person *who paid the money* told it). Whilst Adet was here, several members of Congress (some of each House) were actually paid, by his direction, considerable sums, for giving him the earliest information, that you had concluded an alliance with Great Britain! This was not the only object for which French money has been paid to members of Congress. I say this on the same authority: but I am not at present at liberty to name my author.[3]

This morning I had a letter dated yesterday from General Pinckney, acknowledging the receipt of your letter, which I forwarded to him.[4] He hopes to be at Trenton next Monday morning. I am very respectfully Sir, your most obt servt

Timothy Pickering

ALS, DLC:GW; ALS (letterpress copy), MHi: Pickering Papers.

1. The pamphlet, which was later purchased by the Boston Athenæum, is *The Conduct of the Government of France towards the Republic of Geneva* by "a Citizen of Trenton." Pickering wrote to John Adams on this day: "The original French of Chauvets letter to Galatin [dated 24 Oct. 1794], exhibiting the perfidy and violence of France in subverting the Swiss Republic, I recd from Mr King. It appeared to me so important a detail of facts at the present moment, I put it into the hands of a son [* This young gentleman is a candidate for a captaincy in the army.] of Mr Abraham Hunt, whom I found at leisure, to translate. It has been faithfully done. I encouraged the printer here to give it to the public in a pamphlet. To-day I recd some copies, & have the honor to inclose a couple" (MHi-A).

2. In 1791 William Bell was a merchant at 217 High Street in Philadelphia.

3. Pierre Auguste Adet was recalled by the Directory in October 1796 and returned to France six months later. For GW's reaction to rumors of a similar

nature earlier in the year, see GW to McHenry, 27 Mar., and note 2 of that document.

4. GW's letter to Charles Cotesworth Pinckney is dated 18 October. Pinckney's letter to Pickering has not been found.

To William Thornton

Dear Sir.   Mount Vernon 28th Oct. 1798
     When Mr Blagden came here on friday, I was engaged in my usual ride; from which I only returned a little before dinner, and found Mr & Mrs Law, with Govr Crawford & his lady here. These circumstances, and Mr Blagden's return immediately after dinner, allowed me no time to acknowledge the receipt of your obliging favor of the 25th Instant.[1]
     For the information you have been so kind as to give me relatively to General Lee's City property, I thank you; but I had no idea of allowing him more for half lots than whole ones were to be obtained at.
     If you have determined to build a house or houses of similar elevation with those I am contracting for, you shall be extremely welcome to avail yourself of my end wall and to run up your chimneys accordingly, without any allowance being made therefor (which I cannot accept) as the kindnesses I have received from you greatly overpay any little convenience or benefit you can derive from my Wall. If Mr Frost is disposed to build a house *immediately*, or very soon; and will give it an accordant elevation, it would be agreeable to me that he should erect Chimnies at the South end similar to your's on the North end of my buildings. With respect to your *own* accomodation you will please to give Mr Blagden such Instructions when he enters upon the Walls as to suit your views perfectly.[2]
     Whether, as there is water so handy, it be necessary to sink a Well, is a matter that circumstances must regulate. If one should be dug, I would range it with the partition Wall of the buildings, that if ever they are occupied as distinct houses, one Pump with two leavers and pipes may subserve both.[3]
     I am in sentiment with you and Mr Law, that a five feet area is too narrow; but whence the remedy? If the regulations will not allow more, and cannot be altered, it must be indured, or the buildings must recede from the Street which would be exceptionable in another respect.

Although the Commissioners have been obliging, and ready throughout the whole of this business to render me every aid I could wish, and I am persuaded would continue to do it; Yet, as I shall be bound by Contract (with Mr Blagden) to supply his wants, agreeably to the Conditions of it, and this can be accomplished with more ease by an Individual than by the Board; the sitting of which, at times, may be impeded by the absence of some of its members when most inconvenient for his calls; & as you reside in the City, and [are] always there, & have moreover been so obliging as to offer to receive the Bills and pay their amount (when presented by Mr Blagden) I will avail myself of this kindness: and accordingly, send a check upon the Bank of Columbia, which will carry a credit of five hundred dollars (left there) when I was in the City last, to be drawn for by you, for the above purpose, as occasion may require: and at all times on notice being given, the Bank shall be replenished, & subject to your draughts to satisfy the Bills of expend[it]ure, of which you will be so good as to inform Mr Blagden.[4]

Upon conversing more fully with Mr Blagden upon the frontis-piece of the Doors, & considering that to make them of Stone in-stead of Wood, will add durability to the work, I have agreed to allow the difference—viz. $150; that they may be executed with the latter—and as he represented in strong terms, the wishes of Mr Francis that a part of the Cellars should be vaulted, for the benefit of Wine, I have agreed to this also. He thinks the addi-tional cost may amount to $100 dollars more; but having made no estimate thereof it shall be charged at what it really stands him.[5]

Whether he begins, or not, to lay the foundation of the build-ings this Autumn, he ought by all means to have the Stone & sand on the spot to begin early in the Spring. The carting now, is so much better than it will be then, that he must find this an eligable measure. His lime too ought to be secured, and his flooring Plank to be good & procured early—tried up—and seasoned—or the floors will shrink. With very great esteem & regard—I am—Dear Sir in haste Yr Obedt & obliged Hble Servt

Go: Washington

P.S. From the fund put into your hands, by the enclosed Check on the Bank of Columbia, be so good as to pay the expence of Re-cording the Deeds from the Commissioners to me—The cost of the Stamps—and other incidental charges accruing on the Lots and Buildings.[6]

ALS, DLC: Thornton Papers; ALS (letterpress copy), DLC:GW; LB, DLC:GW.

1. James Craufurd, governor of Bermuda from 1794 to 1796, was married to Alice Swift Livingston Craufurd (1751–1816) of New York where the two lived (*Diaries*, 6:321).

2. Much of this letter is written in response to Thornton's letter of 25 October.

3. A well proved to be necessary. When on 25 Aug. 1799 GW gave John Francis a rundown of his expenditures for erecting his Washington houses, GW wrote: "A Well of fine Water at the back doors of both houses—30 odd feet deep—walled, & a Pump therein."

4. For GW's dealings with George Blagdin through Thornton, see GW to the District of Columbia Commissioners, 28 Sept., n.2.

5. For the specifications for the construction of the two houses on North Capitol Street, see GW to the District of Columbia Commissioners, 27 Oct., n.2.

6. GW entered in his Day Book on 27 Oct.: "Drew upon the Bank of Columbia for the $500 deposited there the 10th Instt; and placed them in the hands of Doctr Wm Thornton of the City of Washington; to answer the calls of Mr Geo: Blagden—undertaker of my buildings in that place—to provide him materials for the same—to be accounted for." On 30 Oct. Thornton acknowledged the receipt of GW's check for $500.

From John Quincy Adams

Sir   Berlin 29th october 1798

I have the honor to enclose herewith, a letter from a young Gentleman who bears your name, and who flatters himself with being (though distantly) related to you. He is by birth an Hollander, but of a family originally English, which went over from England, and settled in the United Netherlands, sometime near the beginning of the present century.

At the commencement of the present War, he served in the Dutch troops, and was for some months a prisoner in France; but at the period of the Revolution, which made his country an ally to France, he resigned his Commission and is now desirous, if an opportunity of service should present itself in America, to go there— His superior officers several of whom are here bear honorable testimony to his character and conduct—His rank was that of an Ensign—He expects to spend the Winter here, in the further pursuit of military knowledge—From the favorable account I have had of him, I have not hesitated to comply with his request in transmitting the enclosed letter, and in promising to deliver to him such answer as you may think proper to make to his application.[1]

I am happy, in having this opportunity, to express my warm and cordial participation in the joy, which all true Americans have felt, upon finding again secured to our Country, the benefit of your important services, by your acceptance of the command of her armies. However much to be regretted, is the occasion, which has again summoned you from your beloved retirement, there is every reason to hope, that the spirit of firmness and dignity which your example has so powerfully contributed to inspire, and maintain, will either obviate the necessity of another struggle for our independence, or once more carry us victoriously and gloriously through it.

I received in London, the Letter which you did me the honor to write me, at Mount Vernon on the 25th of June of the last year, and beg leave to offer you my grateful thanks for the favorable sentiments, which you were pleased to express in it relative to myself, and my continuance in that line of public service, to which I had the honor of being introduced by your choice; a circumstance which I shall always cherish, as one of the most flattering and honorable events of my life.

Renewing the most ardent wishes for your health and happiness, I remain with perfect respect, Sir, your very humble and obedient Servant.

LB, MHi-A, John Quincy Adams Letter Books.

1. Adams, who at this time was in Berlin negotiating a treaty with Prussia, sent the letter of James Washington, dated 19 Oct. 1798.

From Alexander Hamilton

Dear Sir   New York Oct. 29 1798

Some ill health in my family, now at an end as I hope, interfered with an earlier acknowlegement of your favour of the 21st instant. The contents cannot but be gratifying to me.

It is my intention, if not prevented by further ill health in my family, to proceed on the first of November to Trenton—My aid to the Secretary to the full extent of what he shall permit me to afford will not be withheld. But every day brings fresh room to apprehend that whatever may be the props the administration of the war department cannot prosper in the present *very well disposed* but *very unqualified* hands. Most respectfully & Affecly I have the honor to remain Dr Sir Yr obliged & obet servant

A. Hamilton

P.S. I had forgotten to say that General Pinckney has given proof of a cordial satisfaction with the Military arrangement.

ALS, DLC:GW; ADfS, DLC: Hamilton Papers.

From Israel Shreve

Dear General,   Washington Bottom 29th Octr 1798

I receiv'd your Exceys Letter dated the 1st of this Instant two days ago accompaned with one from Mr Ross who has Just returned from Kentucky, his absence occationed the Letter not comeing to hand sooner, the uswage your Excellency mentions in your Letter that you have receivd from me, I must Acknowledge and that I have Sold some of the Land at nearly double is true. Just after I Purchased a flow of Cash was Left in this Country by the Militia Army, which gave a Sudden rise to Land, which oppertunity I inbraced But Cannot Git the money As it becomes due which Imbarasses me in my Contract with you, Just as I Receivd your Exceys Letter, I was runing out a peace of Land I had just agreed to Let my Brother Samuel have, who is to pay £800 Cash for, he Lives seven miles from Alexandr[i]a within the Bounds of the Federal City he Says he Can Sell for Cash, & will hand the Installment Due Last June to you and by the time next Installment is due I will Collect if possable from those that Ought to have paid up Last May from whom a sufficient Sum was Due & Much more, from this Bargan with my Brother who is a Punctual man I have enough due in time to pay of all the Judgement Bond and £800 to spair from which I Calculate to raise the Installments as they become Due.[1]

Notwithstanding your Excellencys Letter is in rather Severe terms against me yet I hope your goodness will Cause you to forbear a Little. the Land I hold here my Stock &c. with the Bonds I have is my all, I think I Live a Sober Life useing all the industry I am Capable of to Maintain my famaly who must raise or fall with me, if the rigor of the Law is inforced against me It will be Exceeding Distressing not only to my person But to an Aimable Woman and a famaly of Innocent Children, who Look up to me for every thing they Need, your Excellencys forbearance a Little while will be a Great happiness to my famaly, otherwise we must be involved in Misery, If a Cape[2] is Served upon my Body It will not enable me to pay the Debts. If an Execution is Levied on my property and all

Sold by the Shiriff, for want of Money it would Sell for so trifling a Sum, as would be the most Distressing to me & my famaly who as yet Live in repute as a farmer, I Can Dispose of my property better than the Sheriff Can, if I Can Collect money so as to pay of what is due to your Excellency, without being Distressed I Shall have three or four thousand pounds property Left, your Security is good the Land is greatly improved since I Bargained for it, I hope I am not that Careless trifling man as your Excellency may have a right to think I am, the Exceeding Scarcety of Cash has made me unfortunate, I am altogether in your power I know; and plead for your forbearence, I am in the hands of one of the Greatest Charactors in the World, and one who I hope will be Mercifull if not for my Sake, for the Sake of an Innocent famaly My Brother I fully Expect will pay the Installment due into your own hand Sooner than the Law can raise it.

If Life & health permits I Shall See Mr Ross in a few days & inform him of the Bargain with my Brother and use all my endeavours to put of Entering up the judgement untill further orders from your Excellency, as he has Gave me untill the tenth of next month, to be Harrast with the Law is next to Death to me, ⟨Cash⟩ is unnessary As all can be better done without it than with it. I am your Excellencys Most Obedt Servt

Israel Shreve

ALS, DLC:GW.

1. Shreve wrote on the cover "favoured by Col. Samuel Shreve." In his next letter, dated 21 Dec., Shreve wrote that he had sent his son John to his brother in Virginia after GW left Philadelphia: "My Brother had then not Sold," he wrote, "but promised to See you when you returned home and if possable settle of this Installment," to which GW replied on 10 Jan.: "as to your Brother, I have never seen, nor heard a tittle from him."

2. A *cape magnum* is a judicial writ "to summon the tenant to answer the default" (*Black's Law Dictionary*, 261).

From James McHenry

Dear Sir   War Department 30 Octbr 1798
I had the honour to receive your letter of the 23d Instant.

I received a letter this morning from the President, by which I find, that Mrs Adams' health is so low, and her life so precarious, that it will be impossible for him to leave her till it becomes absolutely necessary for him to meet Congress. I regret extremely this circumstance, as well on account of the cause, as being deprived of his opinions. But that no delay may thence arise to the service, he authorises me, in case the generals and I should judge it necessary, that the officers of battalions should be appointed, before the meeting of Congress, to fill up their commissions out of the blanks I have in my possession.[1]

General Pinckney who is here, for a few days, I expect will give his attendance on the 10th of next month, at which time I also expect General Hamilton.

Inclosed is a copy of a letter from General Knox, declining the appointment of third Major General, so that we cannot count upon his aid or assistance.[2]

Having disclosed to you the object of this conference in my letter dated the 16 inst. I flatter myself it will be in your power to give your attendance on or about the 10th of November next at this City or Philadelphia, as the case may be; and that you will bring with you the letters and recommendations respecting candidates from the Southern district, and all such papers as may be useful, as well as the inclosed list of officers who continued in service to the end of our revolutionary war.[3] With sincere respect & esteem I have the honour to be Dr Sir Your most ob. & hble servt

James McHenry

P.S. 8 o'clock P.M. I have this moment received your letter of the 26 inst. and a little *satirical* note from Miss Custis, which I must correct her some day or other for having written.[4]

ALS, DLC:GW; ALS, MHi-A.

1. Adams's letter, dated 22 Oct., is in DLC: McHenry Papers.

2. The enclosed letter to McHenry from Henry Knox, dated 23 Oct., reads in part: "I have received your letter, enclosing a commission, and giving me to understand, that A. Hamilton is ranked as the first, C.C. Pinckney the second, and myself as the third Major General, and this arrangement is considered as definitive. In so plain a case, it is unnecessary to multiply words. The impossibility of my serving under Officers so much my juniors, must have been known, to those who made the arrangement. The principle that no Officer can consent, to his own degradation, by serving in an inferior station, is well known, and established among military men. The duty which I owe to myself, precludes my placing myself, in such a situation. I therefore definitively decline the appointment of third Major General" (DLC:GW).

3. See GW to McHenry, 21 Oct. (first letter), n.4.

4. Letter not found.

From William Thornton

Dear Sir   City of Washington Octr 30th 1798
    I had yesterday the honor of your very kind Letter, inclosing
a check on the Bank of Columbia, for five hundred Dollars, to
be appropriated to the erection of the Houses you contemplate,
which shall be duly applied.[1] The Deeds will require re-copying on
stampt paper, which I will take care to execute.[2]
    I return my sincere thanks for your goodness in offering me the
Advantage to be derived from carrying up Chimnies for a House
adjoining yours, but I had no Idea of increasing my Obligations
when I mentioned this Subject. I thought it would be a mutual
Benefit, and proposed it accordingly. It is customary in Philadelphia, and elsewhere, to carry up the division Walls in this manner,
half the Ground being given up to the party who commences
building, and the expense of the division Wall equalized, as a matter of course. Any other Mode of proceeding would be injurious
to you; and, I hope you will permit me to decline doing you an
injury when I do myself a Benefit. I am under a continual Obligation to you, which I shall never forget, and all I can ever do in
return will be insufficient to shew my regard, attachment, and
grateful remembrance of your past favour. Accept dear Sir, my
best respects, & sincerest Wishes for your Health and Happiness
                                                    William Thornton

ALS, CSmH.
    1. GW wrote on 28 October.
    2. See GW to the District of Columbia Commissioners, 27 Oct., nn.2 and 3.

From William Washington

Dear Sir   Charleston [S.C.] Octobr 30th 1798
    Since my Letter of the last Post, John Parker of Charleston, the
Son of William, has expressed a desire of entering the Army; He is
a young Man of good Character and I think that he may with pro-
priety be placed on the List of Ensigns.[1] John Green of Augusta in
Georgia has lately been strongly recommended to me, by General
Glascock & Colonel Gordon of that State, as a person well quali-
fied for the Commission of Captain either of Cavalry or Infantry.
I have very little acquaintance with Mr Green but I place ⟨more⟩

confidence in the recommendation of General Glascock & Colonel Gordon.[2]

The friends of Lieutenant George Izard have expressed much uneasiness at seeing Mr Francis Huger of Charleston placed over his head with the Rank of Captain in the new raised Corps of Artillerists notwithstanding Mr Izard has been a Lieutenant for several years and Mr Huger, altho he is rather older & sustains a good Character is believed to be very little acquainted with military Matters, and I am apprehensive that without Mr Izard is promoted that their uneasiness will be increased when the Appointments for the Army about to be raised are made; for as none of the Officers who were in the Army during our revolutionary struggle are willing to enter into the Army with the Rank of Captain I have been under the necessity of selecting such young Men as support good Characters & are willing to enter the Army notwithstanding they have not seen any actual Service. Altho Mr Izard is a very young Man yet I think that his solidity of Judgment military knowledge & other qualifications entitles him to the rank of Major particularly when it is considered that we shall be under the necessity of appointing Persons to the next Grade who are not much older & not to be compared to him in point of military Information; If however an objection should lie against him on account of his youth I would wish to see him placed at the head of the Captains required from this State.[3]

As I understand that no person has been appointed to the Command of the Corps of Artillerists lately raised I think proper to mention to you John Faucheraud Grimkie of Charleston as a person well qualified for that Command. He is placed the third on my List of Commandants of Regiments, but he was not placed the last because he was inferior to either of the other two in point of there qualifications which are proper for an Officer, but because he is not of so robust & hale a constitution as either of the others. He was a Lieutenant Colonel in the Artillery Service last war and always esteemed an excellent Officer.[4] I am Dear Sir with the highest Regard & Respect, Yr Very Obedt Servt

W. Washington

ALS, MoSW.

1. William Parker (d. 1784), a Charleston merchant, may have been John Parker's father.

2. Thomas Glascock (1756–1810) was born in Virginia and served as a lieu-

tenant during the Revolutionary War before becoming a general of Georgia militia and a prominent Georgia Federalist. Ambrose Gordon (1751–1804) was born in New Jersey and served as a lieutenant during the Revolutionary War under William Washington, after whom he named his eldest son. John Green has not been identified.

3. For Francis Huger, see Lafayette to GW, 5 Sept. 1798, n.3. For George Izard, see letters from and to Alice DeLancey Izard, 25 June and 20 July, and from and to Jacob Read, 13 and 19 August.

4. John Faucheraud Grimké (1752–1819) was a member of the South Carolina Society of the Cincinnati who wrote to GW on 30 August. See GW to the South Carolina Society of the Cincinnati, 20 Oct., n.1.

From John Frederick Ramnitz

Spandaw near Berlin 31st October 1798
at 2 oClock in the morning

Sir:

From the enclosed news paper printed at Hamburg, the 26th October 1798, I see under New-York head dated the 25th August 98, with much regret, how many of the Citizens of Philadelphia & New York are hurried to the Grave by the raging Yellow Fever—As my Intention is good, I hope your Excellency will forgive my taking the liberty of sending a Medicine without being called upon for it; more so as this medicine from an observation of thirty Eight years, always has saved Mankind in Sickness which had for foundation great Loss of Blood; and as the present Medicine appears not to have been used yet there, I am still in greater hopes that making use thereof; will prove the desired effect; as after the Experience I have had; it has been the quickest and most sure Medicine to clear the Blood of its sharpness.

I therefore must humbly request your Excellency to have the Medicine which I have sent, used by one of the Physicians there agreable to the Instructions enclosed, among those unfortunate who are already taken with the Yellow-Fever, as also to use it as a preservative among those persons that live in the place where the Yellow Fever is raging.

I further beg your Excellency to rest assured that I am well convinced, that there is with you the most experienced Physicians, as well as best methods used in any sickness; still it cannot be attributed to me a forwardness; if I with disinterested view, wish to give my Advice in a Sickness which appears to have taken daily encrease, I therefore beg your Excellency and the Honorable Physicians there, only to consider me as a person who wishes to contribute his best, to save with good Advice what can be saved.

Your Excellency will oblige; if you will not have the Medicine sent, examined by Physicians there, untill it has been used, to avoid Certain prejudices, which might take place.

Therefore to try this Medicine as speedily as possible, I have sent a small lead box containing this Medicine; With pleasure would I have sent a greater quantity of this Medicine; but my Circumstances do not admit of it to defray the Expences; But should this Medicine prove to have the agreable effect, I will immediately discover upon the order of your Excellency, the whole composition thereof; in case this Medicine is not to be had there I will forward 50 @ 100 w. of it without much delay.

I further assure your Excellency as Father of the good Americans, that the Medicines sent is one of the surest as to its operation and that it is not composed of any thing attended with bad consequences, on the contrary it will better the state of the human Body, all this I declare before God—As your Excellency will see that I have no interested view in this case—I sincerely hope; you will have this medicine tried, and shall with pleasure receive an answer that it had its good effect.

I further flatter myself your Excellency will not let my name be known for to avoid public disturbances and disadvantages.

May it please our Superior that the Medicine I have sent, may not remain without blessings; in which case I hope it may be kindly received & supported by your Excellency—In the meantime I am with the greatest Regard Your Excellency's Most Humble Servt
(signed) Medicine Druggist Ramnitz

P.S. Your Excellency will please to forgive my letter, being written in a hurry and not altogether fluently; if I assure you that only two hours before the Mail was closed this day, that I received the news of this fever rageing there; & in that time had to prepare the Medicine, and to give you my opinion thereupon.

I flatter myself in the meantime that long before receipt of the present, the Almighty God will have cleared the country from this tremenduous sickness in the meantime I cannot check my desire, to hurry to your aid, and to exercize with all in my power to watch for your dear Life, which is so much respected and revered in all quarters of the Globe, as well as that of all your beloved Citizens—To close, I can only say yet, that the medicine sent has the qualities not alone to clear the Body of all bad humors, but also to give the Body new strength, I therefore have no small hope, but that it will check the yellow fever, I further assure your Excellency upon Honor, that in the most obstinate sickness in Children, such as small pox, and by grown people in putrid fevers, this Medicine has always operated with success. My earliest wish is yet, that the Almighty God may soon send us the pleasing information, that your Country is cleared of this Calamity.

(signed) John Frederick Ramnitz [1]

L, DLC:GW.

1. This translation of Ramnitz's letter is followed by lengthy instructions for administering the enclosed medicine, at the end of which is the translation of a "Second letter from J. F. Ramnitz to his Excellency General Washington dated Spandaw near Berlin 2d Novemr 1798." The second letter reads: "As yesterday the Mail was detained at Berlin, so that this letter goes off one day later, I have determined to employ this time for to convince your Excellency still more, and now enclose a Certificate from a Physician here, so that, you may place greater Confidence in the Medicine sent. The Compositor of the enclosed testimony is the Kings-Head Chisurgian Gericke; who has been in different Prussian Expeditions, particularly in the last on the Rhine, & had The Inspections of the different Lazarettos, but is at present Battalion Chisurgian in Regt of General V. Amein in garrisson, A Man who is well known for his talents, who is esteemed by the whole Regiment, who possesses the most honorable Principles, and whose testimony from these reasons, well can be given credit to.

"Exclusive of this I must beg your Excellency to permit me to give a faithfull testimony myself, so that you may (considering the very great distance we live from one another) place better confidence in me. Since 34 Years I have been a Citizen and Druggist here and have by my Peaceable and active behaviour, generally acquired the name of an Honest man, of which your Excellency might be convinced from the Magistrates and those who are in superior stations to myself, but particularly I attribute it to myself a very great honor of having been a faithfull subject of the Immortal Fredrick the Great. In the year, Seventeen Hundred & Sixty four, as he returned from the expedition which lasted Seven years, & was laid up with different diseases, I acted as Druggist to the Royal-Court, the particular Honor was shewn me of preparing the different Medicines; which his Royal Highness took in preference to these of his former Physician." In the enclosed "Certificate" Doctor Gericke testifies that Ramnitz's medicine "when all other Medicines would not produce the desired Effect, has proved to be never wanting of Success."

GW wrote Ramnitz on 20 Mar. 1799 thanking him for his letter and for the medicine. He told him that he had sent both the letter and the medicine to Secretary of State Timothy Pickering. See GW to Pickering, 20 Mar. 1799. GW wrote Pickering on 8 Sept. 1799 to inquire whether "any trial [had] ever been made of the medicine" sent by Ramnitz. Pickering replied from Trenton, N.J., on 29 Sept. 1799: "In a late letter you enquired about the medicine sent from Germany, for the yellow fever. As soon as the papers were translated I ⟨communicated⟩ the same to Dr Rush. The translator was also ⟨a⟩ Philadelphia physician. Last spring I received from Hamburg another parcel of medicine for the same object. In these cases the doses were prescribed but not the composition of the medicine. I conceived therefore that no prudent physician would use either; and so I desired our Consul at Hamburg to inform Dr Bolke, who sent the medicine from thence. this Doctor's composition was sent by me to the board of health in Philadelphia, who sent it to the hospital: and in a letter lately recd—Dr Rush writes me—'as Dr Physick and myself were ignorant of the composition, we did not think proper to use it.'

"The fact is, these German physicians, with pretensions to great benevolence, were merely selfish; and hence concealed the composition of their medicines, that they might, if successful, monopolize the profits. They must have been weak and ignorant also, in supposing that any sensible physician would use their ⟨treatments⟩, while they withheld information of their composition. Dr Bolke, indeed ⟨*illegible*⟩ the modesty to propose to come to the U. States at the *public expence* & to have a *salary* ⟨*illegible*⟩ dated to be paid ⟨him⟩ until ⟨he could⟩ otherwise provide for his family!" (MHi: Pickering Papers).

To James Anderson

Mr Anderson,   Mount Vernon 1st Novr 1798

Circumstances may render it necessary for me to make a journey to the Seat of Government: and letters which I expect every Post day, will determine whether I shall take it or not. If I go, my departure will be sudden, and how long I may be absent from home, is uncertain; I do not expect however, that it can exceed four, or at most five Weeks.

With respect to the Farms and Meadows I shall say but little; for as a rotation of Crops is agreed upon; and the fields designated for the Crops of next year; nothing more is necessary than to pursue *strictly* the means that are to carry them into effect—and to obtain, by every contrivance that can be devised, all the manure that can be *raised* or *made* for the Corn Crops, at the several Farms; For unless these fields are highly manured, the reduction of the quantity of ground for this article, will prove a ruinous measure; because all the Succeeding Crops depend *entirely* upon the improvement these fields receive for Corn. of course, if that crop does not succeed, all the rest must fail.

As the Meadows seem to be progressing in a very good, & proper train, I shall say nothing more, relatively to them, but to desire that you will proceed in the course you are in; and apply them to the uses mentd in the Rotation. The

[page missing]

⟨*mutilated*⟩ useless—and the pipe, & lea⟨*mutilated*⟩ tolerably low; to enab⟨*mutilated*⟩ Negro children, to draw w⟨*mutilated*⟩.

The sooner the field N⟨*mutilated* M⟩uddy hole is laid off for Peach ⟨*mutilated* p⟩lanted thereon the better it will be on ⟨*mutilated*⟩—When this is done, let the fi⟨*mutilated*⟩e rod (if the rows are intend⟨*mutilated*⟩art) from the fence which di⟨*mutilated*⟩ Corn) from it: this will make ⟨*mutilated*⟩ with the other fence leading to the Gum⟨sprg⟩ at right angles; and the short rows will but against the fence which divides No. 4 from No. 5. Great care & pains must be taken in laying the list, & crossing of it true, or the Trees will not be in a range more than one way, if they are that. A two pole rod would be too unwieldy to get his distance with between the rows; but it ought not to be less than one rod in length—and in taking his distance, he should be careful always to go straight—or his rows will be wider or narrower in proportion to his mistakes.

After the Wood at Muddy is all used, let the firing for Mansion house and your ⟨own⟩ be taken from the Wood South of the White Gates, where the thinning commenced last year.

Your enquiries after a distiller shd be diligent, that I may not be put to a nonplus, or sustain any injury from the interruption of the work for want of one after January.

The purchasing of Wheat, & selling of flour, I shall leave to your own judgment and discretion. But as the price of the former (except

[page missing]

The work for the Carpenters, ⟨*mutilated*⟩, and Bricklayers; and the other ⟨*mutilated* s⟩hould have it executed; is contained ⟨*mutilated*⟩perate Sheet of Paper, to be referred ⟨to⟩.[1]

It never was my custom to trust ⟨*mutilated*⟩ the measurement of my Corn by the Overse⟨*mutilated*—⟩I *always*, when I had no Manager, and my Manager *always*, when I had one, ⟨or⟩ some ⟨ot⟩her person, if absent or unwell, saw this service performed; to prevent mistakes, ⟨or⟩ to prevent an over report of the measurement by scantily filling the Barrel; and I request that you would see this done, when a sufficient quantity is shucked & ready for lofting.

And I desire moreover, at the farms where there are two Corn houses, that an estimated quantity of Corn, sufficient to answer all the purposes of the Farm from the first day of Jany next, until the first, or middle of November ensuing, may be deposited in one of these—the doors locked & secured, & never opened until the arrival of the new Overseer.

At some convenient time (but before the wet weather sets in) the Barn at Dogue Run should have the Earth raised around the low, and hollow parts of it; in order that all water that descends from the Roof, & higher grounds, may run freely off; otherwise the moisture will penetrate through the Wall & fill the Cellar with water or damps, which will rot the Sleepers & floor, as it did before.

A pump ought to be put into the Well at Union Farm without delay, otherwise the well will be

[page missing]

⟨*mutilated*⟩ that the Crop is know⟨*mutilated*⟩ proceeded from a sudden ⟨*mutilated*⟩ again—a safe way, especi⟨*mutilated*⟩ money will soon be great, a⟨*mutilated* g⟩iven to obtain a tolerab⟨le *mutilated*⟩ let the sales of the latter ⟨*mutilated*⟩ Water to keep the Stones ⟨*mutilated* y⟩our purchases of Whea⟨t *mutilated*⟩ the Mill ought to ha⟨*mutilated*⟩ her in constant ⟨*mutilated*⟩ quantum of work, and judicious buying and selling, that the nett profit must arise—as Millers wages, &ca &ca are the same whether he grinds little or much. Due attention to flour barrels, or staves should be had, that no interruption should proceed from that cause.

I have just received a letter from a Mr Parkinson of England (who may be expected with his family, and a number of domestic Animals every day) which has surprized me not a little; but as I shall leave with you, his letters to me, and my answer, I need not detail the cause of ⟨*mutilated*⟩ but shall give you my opinion of ⟨*mutilated*⟩ which may be shewn to him, if occasion should require it.[2] I sincerely wish you health and success—and am your real friend and well-wisher

Go: Washington

⟨Mou⟩nt Vernon ⟨*mutilated*⟩ November 1798

P.S. I request you will endeavour to be informed of the arrival of Genl Lee, in Alexandria: Present ⟨this⟩ letter to him. Shew him Mr Bushrod Washington's to me—ask him to execute his Deed to me, as I have done mine to him before sevl Witnesses, that it may be admitted to record.[3]

ALS (letterpress copy), DLC:GW. As indicated in the printed text, alternating pages of the letterpress copy of the manuscript are missing.

1. GW enclosed this plan of work for the carpenters, joiners, and bricklayers:
"Work—for—Carpenters

1st   To do all that is required at the Distillery before they quit it, that there may be no further call for their services at that place.

2d   To cover (with Shingles) the fowl houses at the Mansion, making them tight & secure.

3d   Next, complete the contemplated waste in the Mill Race, that the latter may not by giving way in the manner it does interrupt the work of the Mill, and call so frequently for labourers to repair the breaches.

4th   When these are done—to go to River farm and complete the Stables. the other Sheds, the brick work of which is already done.

5th   After the Sheds abovementioned are completed, then erect others in the manner wh⟨ich⟩ has been concluded on, for the Cattle & Sheep—Beginning with those for the former, West ⟨of⟩ the Barn.

6th   When the Work at River farm commences—let the old Barn be taken down very ⟨*mutilated*⟩fully; and the shingles scantling and Nai⟨ls⟩ to the utmost extent they will go, be used ⟨be⟩fore any *New* materials are provided.

7th   If these several matters should be e⟨xe⟩cuted before any other directions are giv⟨en⟩ the Post & Rail, or Planked fencing abo⟨ut⟩ the Mansion house may be repaired—or any thing else, which shall appear to require their labour more.

Work—for the—Joiner

1st   Finish the Garden Gates which he ⟨is⟩ about—which, so soon as done, have fixed in their places and painted (by Thoms Davis) with white lead.

2d   Make door frames in the Cellar—according to Mrs Washingtons request—and do any Jobs there—or about the house she may require.

3d   Provide another hot bed for the Gardener. If the Sashes—now useless in the Green house, can be applied—it would save time and expence.

4th   Make a gate for the New Wall, in front of the house. exactly like those for the Gardens (rising in the middle) but may be single inst⟨ead⟩ of double, as the latter are.

5th   The Gardener wants Sashes, where ⟨the⟩ East door of the Green house is, in order to admit the Rays and warmth of the morning Sun. If making this the size of the door would answer his purpose, It may be done—but I do n⟨ot⟩ incline to break the Wall above the door frame. If is it done, that entrance must be no l⟨onger⟩ used as a door—for the opening & shutting of which would soon destroy all the glass—nor ⟨any of⟩ the glass to be nearer the floor of the house ⟨than⟩ the windows in front are.

6   The bottle rack may be repaired if it is ⟨ca⟩pable of it. If not a new one must be made.

7   If after doing these things he should wa⟨nt⟩ work, he may be preparg stuff for a Book case according to the directions given him.

Work—for the—Bricklayers

1st   Davis, with those who are now with him, may continue sloping the hill— above the New Wall, in the manner I have directed him until it is time to throw up Earth for Brick making in the Spring—when—

2d   He and Muclas may proceed to that business and turn up enough to make at least Sixty thousand.

3d   Upon reconsideration of the first article, above, I believe it will be best for Davis & Muclus to proceed to digging Brick Earth immediately. For as the care of *all* the Stable horses, as well as the Jacks &ca must devolve upon Peter, he will require assistance: of course, Mike must join him, and as Anthony will, prob-ably ⟨be⟩ required to supply the House with Wood ⟨it⟩ will hardly be necessary to keep Davis ⟨and⟩ Muclus alone, at the slope before th⟨at⟩ until they can be joined by the House g⟨ang⟩—When Davis (who understands the de⟨sign⟩) will be indis-pensably necessary to regu⟨late⟩ the Work."

2. See GW's instructions to Anderson of 3 Nov. regarding Richard Parkinson.

3. GW added the postscript later. GW's letter to Henry Lee is dated 4 Novem-ber. For the disposition of the letter, see note 4 of that document.

From James McHenry

Dr Sir   Trenton [N.J.] 1 Novr 1798

I reced yesterday a letter from Major General Pinckney a copy of which as I knew it would give you pleasure is inclosed.[1] Yours ever & affty

James McHenry

ALS, DLC:GW.

1. Charles Cotesworth Pinckney's letter to McHenry of 31 Oct. from Trenton reads: "Agreably to your desire expressed in your favor of yesterday, I shall en-deavor to be with you either at this place, or Philadelphia, by the tenth of the next month. I am sorry that Genl Knox has declined his appointment. A few hours after the vessel in which I came, had cast anchor in the North River, it was intimated to me, that it had been doubted whether I would accept my appoint-ment, as Genl Hamilton who was of inferior rank to me in the last war, was ranked before me in the new arrangement. I declared then, & I still declare, that it was with the greatest pleasure, I saw his name at the head of the list of the Major Generals, & applauded the discernment which had placed him there. I knew that his talents in war were great, that he had a genius capable of forming an extensive military plan, & a spirit courageous & enterprizing, equal to the execution of it. I therefore without any hesitation immediately sent him word by Major Rutledge, that I rejoiced at his appointment & would with pleasure serve under him. It was not untill about ten days ago, that I was informed by my friend Major Haskell, that Genl Knox was dissatisfied that Genl Hamilton & myself, were placed before him. As I consider'd Genl Knox to be a very valuable Officer, tho' I do not esti-mate his talents in a degree equal to those of Genl Hamilton, I told the Major that rather than the feelings of Genl Knox should be hurt, at my being ranked before him, he might take my place in the arrangement, & I desired him when he wrote to the General, to intimate this to him. Genl Knox's *absolute refusal* to serve because, I am placed before him, would render the same offer from me,

now, improper. I do not therefore renew it. But if the authority which appointed me to the rank of Second Major General in the Army, will review the arrangement, & place Genl Knox before me, I will neither quit the service, nor be dissatisfied" (DLC:GW).

From John C. Ogden

Sir   Novr 1st 1798

In continuation of my determination during life to state to public characters by letters,[1] and the country by publications, the tyranny over the consciences, and infringement upon the laws of religious protection and toleration, I have now the pleasure to inform you, that Judge Patterson, in a late adjudication has decided in favor of the claim of Episcopalians, to the church lands in Vermont.

This is an event unexpected by many, who have observed the obstinate, violent, persevering spirit of sacrilege in all countries. The Robinson party in Vermont, who had a large share in this injustice are offended and hope by the State courts to foil the adjudication of the Federal.

This seizure was the result of fifteen years exertions on the part of President Wheelock of Dartmouth College. He presented petitions in behalf of the college to the legislatures of Vermont and New Hampshire, used all his influence and art in the Country, by prejudicing the youth under his care, flattering the bigotry, & indulging the ambition and avarice of the Clergy and leaders, to gain their aid and influence in the nefarious design. He gave the subject of the propriety of the seizure as a theme for discussion to the class he taught, and then decided himself against the church. This is one among thousands of the daily inventions, through the colleges to defeat our laws, spread prejudices and exalt their party.[2]

In no period and in no part of the christian church has a more malicious, avaricious system of tyranny been invented or persisted in, with greater severity, than in the States of New Hampshire, Massachusetts, Connecticut and Vermont, for thirty years.

It is so long since I read Mr Duche's letter to the Commander in Chief, soon after the beginning of the late war, that I cannot decide upon its merits,[3] but if he had reviewed ecclesiastical history he would have found in the tyranny persisted in, under the political plans of Calvinists in Europe & the States, enough to have warned military men and statesmen, almost in the name of heaven, of the usurpations, which were in store for oppressing all denominations and exalting Calvinists by war and sacrilege.

Wicked design has been followed by malevolent persecution & perseverance, as may be seen, by the public and private statement of facts, which legislative debates judicial procedure and public files illucidate. Whig, Tory, Federal, Anti Federal, Democratic Jacobin and Republican projects have alternately been varied by the Calvinists in the northern states to exalt themselves by public commotions.

I will prove it that to them only we owe the present political confusions and infidelity. The same hatred to the churches of Rome and England, which urged on that opposition, which is proved by the publications before the war, is now existing and practised upon. The members of both houses of Congress are, and have been partakers in this pillage. Mr Senator Langdon, Mr Senator Chipman—Mr Freeman of New Hampshire—many men in the national offices very many in the State employments and hundreds of our staunchest federalists are now at the bottom of the oppressions seeking popularity and promotion, or sharing the profits of the lands among themselves.[4]

During this period, the clergy and other members of the church have been impoverished, abused and insulted. No pity has been exercised towards them. Leading members of the church have been intimidated and negligent⟨.⟩ Insult and Injury have united to destroy the exertions to gain justice and give information.

A hope that the Almighty was about to help Calvinists, awoke them to those prayers, sermons and civil feasts, which have brought us into a share with the present confusions of Europe. Some superior advantage, from possible political confusions, led the Calvinists to hope to secure their present sacrilege and pillage, by the prejudices of party. All denominations love peace, good government and toleration too well to be drawn by rebellion, sedition or violence to plunge themselves and the christian church into trouble, and make her & them tributary to any political party. Whether religion or liberty is the pretext, is immaterial, as long as both, are at this moment abused by the Calvinists to convulse the nation, through the means of pulpits and colleges.

The firmness of our chief magistrates and wisdom of our nation, have fortunately prevented convulsions by war in our homes. Calvinists are in some cases federalists, who six years since wished for a share in the confusions of war and were violent advocates for French, Jacobin & Democratic politics.

Copies of this go by the post to Judge Patterson, and very many of our first magistrates,[5] that the decisions of our courts may not be defeated or the restoration of the church property be neglected. That an end may be put to the sufferings of the clergy and their families, in the States of Vermont and New-Hampshire, and universal liberty of conscience continue to exist in the States. I have the honor to be Your Excellency's devoted servant

John C. Ogden

ALS, DLC:GW.

1. For the series of letters that Ogden wrote to GW about his persecution at the hands of New England Calvinists, see Ogden to GW, 20 Sept. 1798, n.1.

2. Judge William Paterson (1745–1806) at this time was an associate justice of the U.S. Supreme Court. Moses Robinson (1742–1813), one of the founders of the republic of Vermont and one of its first U.S. senators (1791–96), was one of the leaders of the fight against Jay's Treaty in 1795. John Wheelock (1754–1817) was the second president of Dartmouth College. The case Ogden was referring to concerned the seizure in 1794 by the Vermont legislature of lands reserved for the Society for the Propagation of the Gospel and for the Church of England. The case came to trial in the Bennington County court in April 1795 and was transferred to the Circuit Court for the Vermont District in November 1796. In October 1798 it came to the attention of circuit court judge Paterson. Although the details of the case are sketchy, Paterson apparently ruled the seizures to be unconstitutional. See Goebel, *History of the Supreme Court*, 591–92, *Church Review and Ecclesiastical Register*, 4 (1852), 586–87, and the *Philadelphia Aurora*, 9 Nov. 1798.

3. Jacob Duché (1738–1798), at the outbreak of the Revolution rector of the parishes of Christ Church and of St. Peter's in Philadelphia, wrote his famous letter to GW on 8 Oct. 1777 opposing America's fight for independence.

4. John Langdon (1741–1819) was an Antifederalist U.S. senator from New Hampshire. Nathaniel Chipman (1752–1843), a legal scholar, was senator from Vermont from 1798 to 1804. Jonathan Freeman, treasurer of Dartmouth College, was a Federalist congressman from New Hampshire from 1797 to 1801.

5. The copy of this letter sent to William Paterson is labeled "Copy of a letter to Genl Washington dated Novr 1st 1798" and was addressed to "The Honble Mr Patterson or Judge [Robert] Morris Brunswick New Jersey" (NjR: William Paterson Papers).

From Peyton Short

Dear sir,   Woodford County (Kentucky) Novr 1st 1798

Immediately after my arrival in this Country I waited on Coll Marshall to know if he had paid up the full amt of your taxes on the two tracts of Land on Rough Creek mentioned in your letter of the 16th July—Having answered me in the affirmative & informed me that he had drawn on you for the same, I conceived it necessary to make no farther enquiry into that subject.

I had occasion not long since to send a Messenger to the Neighbourhood of Capt. Abm Hite, the Owner of Woodrow's military Survey of 300 acrs. interfering with your two tracts affsd & availed myself of that opportunity to write to him proposing the Purchase thereof in your Behalf—He was not at Home—therefore I recd no ansr but daily expect to hear from him—Shd I be able to effect the contemplated purchase you shall immediately hear from me— Colo. Marshall tells me you have mentioned that subject to him— I will therefore Sir, do nothing final without his ratification.[1]

I shall always be happy, whenever you may conceive it in my power to serve you, that you command Sir, Your most respectful Hble Sert

Peyton Short

ALS, NbO. On the cover: "To be forwarded to the Alexandria Post-office Virga."

1. Alexander Spotswood on 15 Mar. 1799 sent GW a letter from Short saying that Abraham Hite was asking $10 an acre for the 300-acre Wodrow tract adjoining GW's land on Rough Creek in Kentucky. GW promptly declined to buy it (GW to Spotswood, 25 Mar. 1799).

From Charles Cotesworth Pinckney

Trenton [N.J.] Novr 2d 1798

Many thanks, my dear Sr, for your very friendly congratulations on my return to my Country[1]—The apprehensions you mention I have reason to think would have been realized had not our Government followed up the publication of the dispatches by energetic measures. My Daughter's health (thank God) is restored— Mrs Pinckney & myself are both well. I enclose you a copy of a Letter which I wrote to the Secretary at War on being informed that Genl Knox had refused to serve in the army as Third Major General.[2] It gives me great pleasure to find that I shall have the happiness of seeing you here or at Philadelphia about the tenth instant. When I proceed to Charleston should you be at Mount Vernon you may be assured I shall avail myself of your polite invitation. My political sentiments on the present situation of our Controversy with France are contained in my answers to the Princeton & Trenton addresses.³ I will not therefore repeat them. Be so good as to present my most respectful Compliments to Mrs Washington & Miss Custis, in which Mrs Pinckney & my Daughter would with pleasure unite, but they know not of my writing this letter, as I left them at Newark. Be assured I ever am with great sincerity Your devoted & affectionate humble servt

Charles Cotesworth Pinckney

ALS, DLC:GW.

   1. GW's letter to Pinckney is dated 18 October.

   2. Pinckney's letter of 31 Oct. to Secretary of War James McHenry is printed in note 1, McHenry to GW, 1 November.

   3. The address from the inhabitants of Princeton, dated 29 Oct., is printed along with Pinckney's reply in the *Gazette of the United States*, 30 October. The address from the corporation of the city of Trenton, 31 Oct., is printed with Pinckney's reply, ibid., 3 November.

Letter not found: to William Thornton, 2 Nov. 1798. ALS, sold by B. Altman & Co., December 1969. Altman's advertisement indicates that the letter was signed "with very great esteem and regard."

To James Anderson

Mr Anderson,   Mount Vernon 3d Novr 1798

   By the way of Boston, I have just received a letter from Mr Richd Parkinson, dated "Liverpool 28th Augt 1798."

   The contents of this letter have surprised me; and that you may know from whence this surprise has proceeded, I shall lodge in your hands (as I am going from home, and may be absent four or five weeks) Mr Parkinsons first and second letters to me; and my answer to him;¹ (a duplicate, and I think a triplicate of which I forwarded).

   By this correspondence you will perceive that, Mr Parkinson, through the medium of Sir Jno. Sinclair, had seen the Plans of my Mount Vernon Farms, and was acquainted with the terms on which they were to be *let*. These terms I also deposit with you. It appears moreover by his first letter, dated the 28th of Augt 1797, that he intended to be in this Country in the month of March; and by his second letter of the 27th of Septr following, that his arrival *might* be delayed until April or May. It is evident also, from the tenor of these letters, that he knew my farms could not remain uningaged longer than the month of September. Yet, he neither comes; sends an agent to act for him; nor even writes a line, to account for the delay; and to know on what footing his forme[r] proposition stood.

Under these circumstances, I had no more expectation of Mr Parkinson's arrival (especially with such a costly Cargo as he represents) than I had of seeing Sir Jno. Sinclair himself, until his letter of the 28th of August from Liverpool came to hand.

Nor under the circumstances I have detailed, (which will appear correct from the papers I leave) do I know what Mr Parkinsons views now are. He surely could not expect, after having placed the Occupancy of one of my farms on a contingency—that is—his liking it upon an examination thereof; after promising that this examination should take place by the month of May last; after letting me hear nothing more from him for a whole year; and after knowing that I was obliged to make arrangements for the ensuing year by the month of September in the present year, to find a farm ready for his reception in Novr.

If he did not expect this, Mr Parkinson stands in no other relation to me, than he does to any other Gentleman in this Country; and if he did expect it, it may with justice be observed, that, he has done so unwarranted by the information that was given him, and has entered upon the measure precipitately, having made no adequate provision for the heavy expence he is running into. But, as matters are circumstanced, the question *now*, is not what ought to have been, but what can be done to serve him.

With respect to my paying £850 for the freight of the Vessel, it is beside the question altogether, for the best of all reasons— viz.—because I have not the means. And with respect to the animals which are said to be embarked, I would put myself to greater, or less inconvenience in providing for them (upon just & reasonable terms) according to what shall appear to be his intention with respect to my River Farm. If it be to lease It on the terms which have been proposed. If there is a prospect of my being secure in letting it, and a prospect that the bargain will be durable; and lastly, if you can devise any expedient by which the business can be accomplished under existing circumstances, as they respect the coming and the going Overseers; the Negros; Stock; and growing grain; I should be well disposed to lend all the aid in my power towards the temporary accomodation of the animals he has brought over. Except the Stallions, for whom, and more especially for their Keepers (who are generally very troublesome people) I have no conveniency at any of the Farms, and to suffer them to be in the Barns, or Stables with their horses, would be to risk the whole by fire. Nor have I any place at the Mansion house for either horses or men, as the conveniences thereat, are not more than adequate to the permanent, and occasional demands by visitors.

In a word, under the present aspect of things; and without seeing Mr Parkinson or knowing under what auspices he comes, I scarcely know what sentiment to express respecting him; or what is proper to be done in this business; and therefore must leave it to you to form an opinion when you can take a nearer view of the subject, after his arrival, if this shd happen during my absence, and act accordingly. To obtain a good tenant for River Farm, on just terms; with the prospects beforementioned, wd be an inducement to me to go great lengths in a temporary accomodation: but if this is not to be expected from Mr Parkinson, I feel no obligation on my part, to rectify mistakes which I had no hand in causing, & endeavoured to guard against.[2] I remain Your friend and well wisher

Go: Washington

ALS, NIC; ALS (letterpress copy), DLC:GW; LB, DLC:GW. GW docketed the ALS, suggesting that it may have been a retained copy.

1. GW's letter to Richard Parkinson is dated 28 Nov. 1797.

2. For a discussion of GW's correspondence with Parkinson and for Parkinson's visit to the United States, see Parkinson to GW, 28 Aug. 1797, n.3.

Letter not found: to John Greenwood, 3 Nov. 1798. When writing to Greenwood on 5 Nov., GW referred to "my last of the 3d instant."

To William B. Harrison

Sir,   Mount Vernon Novr 4th 1798.

It has often been in my mind to ask, (if your tenements near my Mill are not under leases already) whether you would be inclined to let them to me, for a term of years? for what term? and at what Rent?

I can assure you, most sincerely and candidly, that it is not because I want these tenements, that I make this enquiry; but to
be relieved from Neighbours who are really a nuisance; and who
could not live on the Land but by the practice of unjustifiable
shifts. No care or attention within the compass of my power to use,
can preserve my fields and Meadows from injuries, sustained by
their Hogs, & other Stock. Rails are drawn from the Posts, in order
to let in the latter, and slips made to admit the former, in many
places through my ditches, to the destruction of my grain, & grass.

To guard against damages of this sort, is, I do aver, my *sole* inducement to this enquiry. But it is not to be infered from hence,
that I am disposed to pay a Rent disproportioned to the real value
of the Tenements.

I need not observe to you, Sir, that the land was originally poor;
that it is exhausted beyond measure; that there is no timber on it;
very little firing; and scarcely any Fencing. In short, that without
aid from the adjacent Lands, which the tenants cannot obtain
from the present Proprietors by *fair* means, the tenements cannot
be supported much longer. This is a fair statement, & ought to be
taken into consideration in fixing the Rent.

Under these circumstances, it is scarcely necessary to add, that I
am not inclined to take the Tenements upon a short lease; for the
reasons before mentioned; & because I should be obliged to have
recourse to my own land to supply the deficiencies of yours; and
that in a very short time too, to render the fields of any use. Unless
the term therefore, for which it is granted, is commensurate with
the expence to which I, or mine would be run, It would not answer
my purposes to rent it.[1]

It is not my expectation, or desire to disturb the *present* tenants,
or such as you may have engaged, the ensuing year—My views
extend to the year after, *only*, presuming your arrangements are
made for 1799—Your answer will be agreeable to—Sir—Your
Very Hble Servt

Go: Washington

ALS, MH; ALS (letterpress copy), DLC:GW; LB, DLC:GW.

1. When he did not receive a reply from Harrison, who lived in Loudoun
County, GW on 23 Jan. 1799 wrote his rental agent and nephew, Robert Lewis,
sending him a letterpress copy of this letter for delivery to Harrison. The property
which GW wished to gain control of adjoined his own at Mount Vernon near his
gristmill. Harrison in his reply dated 24 Jan. 1799 assured GW that he would

"purge the Lands of those improper Caractors, aluded to in your Letter provided they Can be pointed out to me." GW on 6 Feb. conceded that he had no proof of misdeeds of any particular one of Harrison's tenants but insisted that his "meadows & grain" were being destroyed by one or another of them and that his stock "(of Hogs & Sheep in particular) are constantly deminishing." He again asked Harrison to set the rent for the tract. When Harrison gave GW his terms in a missing letter of 21 Feb. 1799, GW replied at length on 5 Mar., arguing that the rent Harrison was asking was exorbitant. Harrison responded at equal length on 28 Mar. defending his proposed charges as reasonable. GW renewed his arguments on 10 April 1799 and invited Harrison to Mount Vernon to join with him in surveying the tract and discussing terms further, which on 24 April Harrison agreed to do. On 15 May GW, Harrison, and Thomson Mason, whose land also adjoined Harrison's tract, made the survey. The surviving correspondence between GW and Harrison ends with GW's letter of 16 May 1799 in which GW offers to pay Harrison annually thirty dollars per hundred acres with a lease of fifteen years and an option to buy at eight dollars an acre. In early 1793 Robert Lewis had tried without success to buy for GW Harrison's tract near the mill at Mount Vernon (see GW to Lewis, 23 Dec. 1792, 7 Mar., 29 April, 26 July 1793, and Lewis to GW, 4, 9 Jan., 26 Mar., 17 July, 12 Aug. 1793).

From Benjamin Hawkins

Tellico in the State of Tennessee 4 novr 1798
The bearer of this, Mr Silas Dinsmoor is agent of the Cherokees, and one of those chosen to carry into effect the benevolent plan devised by you, for bettering the condition of the Indians in the southern parts of the United States.[1] He is going on a visit to the Secretary of War, and will pay his respects to you. It is with pleasure I recommend him to you, as a man who has faithfully and ably executed the trust reposed in him; and from whom you will have the satisfaction to learn, that the plan has succeeded notwithstanding the violence with which it has been assailed by the mischief makers in this quarter. The Cherokees are no longer to be called Savages, they are a decent orderly set of people, who possess unbounded confidence in the Justice of our government, and are worthy of its continued attention.

I beg you to assure Mrs Washington of my sincere wishes for a long continuance of her health and happiness to accept of the same for yourself and to believe me very sincerely and respectfully My Dear sir, your obedt humbe Servt

Benjamin Hawkins

ALS, DLC:GW.

1. Silas Dinsmoor (Dinsmore), a graduate of Dartmouth College in 1791, went in 1794 to the Cherokee Nation to live as agent of the United States to keep the peace. Dinsmoor visited Mount Vernon on 24 Dec. "on his way to Philadelphia" (*Diaries*, 6:327).

From Henry Knox

My dear Sir   Boston 4 November 1798

I have received your two favors of the 21st and 23d ultimo. They breathe a spirit of friendship and affection which has ever been ardently reciprocated by me.

The appointment of the *third* Major General having been explicity declined by me I have nothing to add on that subject but one single observation. To wit that you are the only decided personal friend who has advised my acceptance of it.

My offer of serving as your aid, in case of an invasion, arose from the sincere effusion of personal attachment, unmixed with regret or resentment.

But the possibility being suggested by you of my harbouring any secret "*gnawings*" upon the subject of rank, precludes decisively my having the satisfaction proposed of sharing your fate in the field.

I will not detain you one moment longer than to say in the presence of almighty God, that there is not a creature upon the surface of this globe, who was, is, and will remain, more your sincere friend than

                                                            H. Knox

ALS, MH.

To Henry Lee, Jr.

Dear Sir   Mount Vernon 4th Novr 1798

Your letters from Fredericksburg and Stratford, have both been received; and their contents will be attended to when the list of applications come under consideration.[1]

Tomorrow (being requested thereto by the Secretary of War) I shall set off for Trenton. This, of course, will deprive me of the pleasure of seeing you, while you are on the promised visit to this County. It is necessary therefore I shd inform you that, no report (as indeed I expected would be the case) has been made by Mr Jesse Simms relative to Major Harrisons Land, adjoining my mill.[2] And that, to my surprise, when I came to examine the details of your City property, more attentively than it was in my power to do in the hurried manner in wch the list of it was presented, and to make enquiry into the value thereof. I found that instead of lots of the Standard size (as I took it for granted they were) that each of those lying on Pennsylvania Avenue have been split into two parts (having only 25 feet front to them) and for these half lots, that I am asked more than lots equally convenient sell at. To receive payments on such terms, when my object was solely to accomodate you, could hardly be expected.[3]

If you are disposed to part with your land near Harpers Ferry; Your land in Loudoun; any unincumbered property in the City; or, in short, almost any other that can be rendered productive—at a reasonable valuation by disinterested men of good character, I would accept it in payment rather than make difficulties, or be involved in disputes; although you well know that nothing will answer my purposes like the money, of which I am in extreme want, and *must* obtain on disadvantageous terms. But it is not to be expected from hence that I will receive the former at an arbitrary price, which every well informed person knows it cannot command.

The Deeds which passed between you and me in the month of April last, I sent to Mr Bushrod Washington to have recorded; asking him at the sametime if they were not defective in proper recitals? Enclosed, or rather with this letter, Mr Anderson will, when he hears of your being in Alexandria present you with his opinion thereon with a Deed ready drawn, according to my Nephews directions for your signature. The one from me to you, I have acknowledged before Evidences, and request you will do the same by that from you to me.[4] With great esteem & regard I am—Dear Sir Your Obedt & Affecte Servt

Go: Washington

ALS (letterpress copy), DLC:GW; LB, DLC:GW.

1. Lee's letters have not been found.

2. For GW's negotiations with William B. Harrison to rent from him his tract of land adjoining GW's Dogue Run farm at Mount Vernon, see GW to Harrison, 4 Nov., n.1. For the involvement of Lee and Jesse Simms in GW's attempts to procure this land, see Henry Lee, Jr., to GW, 28 Feb. 1799, n.2.

3. For the correspondence regarding Lee's lots in the Federal City, see GW to Lee, 29 Sept., n.1.

4. On Bushrod Washington's advice, GW in April 1798 signed a deed conveying back to Henry Lee the tract of land on Rough Creek in Kentucky which GW had acquired from Lee in 1789, and at the same time he had Lee sign a deed reconveying the land to him. When Bushrod examined the deeds, he found Lee's deed faulty and provided GW with a revised deed for Lee to sign. See Bushrod Washington to GW, 13 Mar. 1798, n.4. For earlier steps taken beginning in 1795 to secure for GW a clear title to this Kentucky land, see Alexander Spotswood to GW, 22 Mar. 1797, n.1.

Before leaving for Philadelphia on 5 Nov. 1798, GW on 1 Nov. instructed his farm manager to deliver this letter to Lee when Lee arrived in Alexandria, as he was expected to do, and also to show Lee a copy of Bushrod Washington's letter of 13 Mar. 1798. The deed enclosed for Lee to sign was a copy of the revised deed reconveying the Rough Creek tract to GW, now dated 5 Nov. 1798. Unable to deliver the letter and its enclosures to General Lee, Anderson apparently forwarded it to him. On 31 Dec., having received no response, GW wrote to Lee from Mount Vernon: "Dear Sir, Presuming you have not received the letter [of 4 Nov.], of which the enclosed is a copy, I trouble you with a duplicate of it. And have sent to Mr Bushrod Washington the Deeds to, and from you, for Execution; and pray you to acknowledge before Evidences *that* from you to me—*Now*, also out of date. With great esteem & regard I am—Dear Sir Yr Obedt & Affecte Servt Go: Washington" (letterpress copy, DLC:GW; LB, DLC:GW).

In a postscript to a letter of 31 Dec. to Bushrod Washington GW said he was enclosing his letter of that date to Lee "open for your perusal" and asked him to forward it and the enclosure to Lee and also to get Lee's deed proved in the General Court. On 28 Feb. 1799 Lee wrote GW: "Last Monday evening Mr b. Washington presented me with yr favor covering a duplicate of yr let. of the 4th novr & accompanying deeds for the land given for Magnolio. The deeds have been executed agreably to desire." The new deed conveying the Rough Creek land in Kentucky back to GW, dated 5 Nov. 1798, was witnessed by Corbin Washington and others and was certified by the Westmoreland County court on 25 June 1799 (ICU). See also Wilson Allen to GW, 29 May 1799.

To James McHenry

Dear Sir,   Mount Vernon Nov. 4th 1798

Your letter of the 30th ultimo, with it's enclosures, has been duly received. And, agreeably to the arrangements made for the meeting of the General Officers on or about the 10th inst., I intend setting out tomorrow for Trenton; but, as I shall have some business in the Federal City which may detain me for a short time, and shall travel with my own Horses, which must necessarily be slower than to go on with Stage Horses, it may be Sunday, the 11th inst., before I reach Trenton, should the meeting be there. I shall, however, make no unnecessary delay until I reach the place of destination.

As, under present circumstances, it is not likely that Lodgings, especially in Trenton, could be had without some previous arrangements, I have to beg the favor of your securing for me the best you can, convenient to your Office, or wherever our business is to be transacted, against my arrival. A lodging Room is all I shall want, particularly for myself; my Secretary, Mr Lear, will be with me, who will also want to be accomodated with a lodging room. There will be four servants and six or seven horses, which may or may not be accommodated at the same place with myself, according to circumstances.[1]

I shall take on with me all the letters & papers in my possession relating to Applications, recommendations for Appointments &c.

P.S. I have never yet recd from the Superintendant, any acct of the quantity of Military Stores belonging to the U.S.[2]

Df, in Tobias Lear's hand, DLC:GW.
   1. See McHenry to GW, 9 Nov., and note 2 of that document.
   2. See McHenry to GW, 16 Nov. (second letter).

To Alexander Spotswood

Dear Sir   Mount Vernon 4th Novr 1798.
   Enclosed herewith are Articles of Agreement drawn by Mr Anderson for your present overseer to sign; similar to those which my Overseer at the Mansion house is under.

He, as well as myself, are desirous to have all these matters fixed, that there may be no demur at a season when it may be too late to provide another.

It is always best to reduce agreements of this sort to writing— and every good Overseer who means to discharge his duty faithfully can have no cause to object.

You will be so good as to return the agreement when signed, or his objections (if any) against signing; directed to me, or in my absence to Mr James Anderson;[1] as I shall set out tomorrow for Trenton on business with the Secretary of War, and the Majr Generals of the Augmented army, and wish him to be placed on sure ground as soon as possible. We all unite in every good wish for you,

Mrs Spotswood and family and I remain with great estm & Regd Dear Sir Your Affecte & Obedt Servt

Go: Washington

ALS, in private hands.

1. In a letter of 24 Nov. to GW Spotswood enclosed the articles of agreement with overseer Roger Farrell, and it is quoted at length in note 1 to that letter.

To John Greenwood

Sir, Mount Vernon 5th Novr 1798

In my last of the 3d instant, I requested you to send what you were about to do for me, to the care of the Secretary of War— James McHenry Esqr.[1]—I repeat this request—and inform you that I shall set out this day, to meet him at Trenton—The sooner therefore I could receive the needful *at that place* the more agreeable would it be to Sir Your Obedt Hble Servant[2]

Go: Washington

ALS, NN: Washington Collection. The cover, advertised in Siegel Auction Galleries catalog, November 1992, item 43, shows that the letter was addressed to "Mr Jno. Greenwood No. 3 Church Street near St Paul's New York."

John Greenwood (1760–1819), a native of Massachusetts, was a dentist in New York.

1. Letter not found.

2. For GW's further correspondence with the dentist John Greenwood regarding his false teeth, see GW to Greenwood, 7 Dec. 1798, and note 1 of that document. GW probably began dealing with Greenwood not long after his arrival in New York to assume the office of president (see GW to Greenwood, 16 Feb. 1791).

From Samuel Hodgdon

Sir, Philadelphia 6th Novr 1798

On the 11th I was honored with your letter of the 8th ultimo. Agreeably to your wishes therein expressed, I send by the way of Alexandria a farther supply of Stationary, answering to the enclosed invoice, which I hope will safely and speedily get to hand.[1]

By direction of the Secretary of War, I am making out for your use, a return of the principal articles on hand, in the Ordnance & Military Stores Department;[2] as soon as finished, it shall be forwarded by the most speedy and certain conveyance: but for the disorder that has again ravaged our City it would have been with you some time ago; I have been left alone in my Office, and could not possibly attend to it sooner. With respectfull consideration I am Sir, Your most Obedient Servant

Samuel Hodgdon

LS, DLC:GW.

1. The enclosed invoice dated at Philadelphia 6 Nov. and signed by Hodgdon reads:

Invoice of Stationary

1	Ream patent copying Paper
1⅛	" Superfine gilt Post ditto
3	Pounds best sealing Wax
1	tin Chest of Wafers
1	small box to contain the above.

On 24 Dec. 1798 Tobias Lear wrote Hodgdon from Mount Vernon: "The Commander in Chief has directed me to apply to you for three or four Blank Books for recording his Military letters. The size as at foot to correspond with other Books of a similar nature—If they are made up in a snug package and forwarded by the Stage they will come safe and you will be so good as to have them sent on as soon as convenient" (DLC:GW). Below his signature Lear specified that the books should be 14½ inches long and 9 inches "broad." He also wrote "4 quire paper good quality."

Hodgdon replied to Lear on 9 Jan. 1799: "With this you will receive the four letter Books, which the Commander in Chief directed you to apply to me for— the size is agreeable to the dimensions at the foot of your letter, and the Paper and binding are of the best kind—I hope they will get safely to hand and be approved of by the General—The Box will secure the Books from injury by transporting⟨.⟩ Be pleased to acknowledge the receipt of them, and at the same time inform me whether the last Stationary forwarded is received, it must have arrived when the General was from home" (DLC:GW). Lear then wrote on 23 Jan.: "Your favor of the 9th inst. came to hand by the ⟨last⟩ mail. The Box containing the four letter Books for the Commander in Chief was received a few days before. The Books give entire satisfaction, and the General returns his thanks for your attention to them. The stationary which you forwarded during the General's absence arrived safe and in good Order" (DLC:GW).

2. See McHenry to GW, 16 Nov. (second letter).

From Anna Young

Respected Sir   Norwich Port [Conn.] Novr 6th 1798

You will no Doubt Think odd that I should presume To Write to You but When I let You know my Situation I hope you will Excuse me I shall Endeavour To State the Matter Intelligible as I am capable of You know Sir that there was a Resolve of Congress that if An Officer Or Soldier Died in the Continental Service their Widow Or Orphan Children Should be Entitled to Seven Years Half pay And My Father Col. John Durkee Died In Service My Mother was His Executor and Went On To Hartford and Settled His accounts There then Employed Capt. Benjn Durkee to go on and Settle His account With the Continent and He Did and Came Back and petitiond the General Assembly of the State of Connecticut and Got a Grant for the Half pay My Mothers Death Happened about this time and Before We Had time to Get them there Came an Order from John Pierce Pay Master General to the Treasurer of Connecticut to Stop The half pay till there was an account Settled that Capt. Benjn Durkee had By Fraud recovered of him the Sum 408 Dol.⟨82⟩ I wrote on to Governor Trumbull then A Member of Congress About It I recieved A Letter from him that if I Administered On My Mothers Estate I might recover But Some People told Me that if I Did that I Should be Liable to pay all the Debts that My Father owed Which Was very Great in Consequence of his being in Co-Partnership and his Partners failing all Came on him and the Debts Being Contracted as long ago as the year 1762 that the principal & Interest was a great Deal more than the half pay & My Brothers Not Wishing to assist me in doing any thing about it it has Lain along till this and my Brothers are since Dead and I the only Heir and under Very Necessitous Circumstances Not able to see a Lawyer and if Should they have Such a faculty of protracting Buisness that I fear they Would get the Whole[.][1] Now Sir if you will be kind enough to Let me know Your Opinion about it if by paying out of it what was Obtained by fraud and as the Administrator on my Mothers Estate has Settled it and Done Nothing about it if I Should apply if you Think that Congress Will not Grant it to Me I am not able to Be att any Expence about it My Husband being a poor Man & A Large Family & he in not a Very good State of Health I have Unbeknown to him Wrote to You as I have been Confused by asking Men of knowledge Here some Saying one Way some another & the Great Esteem My Father always Expressed of Your be so Great a Friend to Justice and thinking that You Could tell Whether Or [not] there Was any Chance for me Induced me to petition you for your opinion if you Should Want any more than my Word who are unbeknow to You I can get it from Govr Trumbull Or Benjn Huntington Esqr.[2] Your Compliance Will [be] Looked upon as a E[s]pecial Favor[3] from her whou wishes You Every Blessing am Sir with the Greatest respect Your Friend

Anna Young

ALS, DLC:GW.

1. John Durkee (1728–1781) of Norwich, Conn., served as lieutenant colonel of the 20th Continental Infantry in 1776 and was colonel of the 1st Connecticut Regiment at the time of his death. For Colonel Durkee's military career, see General Orders, 30 June 1776, n.4. Benjamin Durkee, a sergeant at the Battle of Lexington in April 1775, served as a second lieutenant in several Connecticut regiments between 1776 and his retirement in 1778. Jonathan Trumbull, Jr. (1740–1809), who became governor of Connecticut on the death of Oliver Wolcott, Sr., in December 1797, represented Connecticut in the first three sessions of the U.S. Congress.

2. Benjamin Huntington (1736–1800) of Norwich, a lawyer, was a member of the Connecticut legislature almost continuously from 1771 to 1792. He also served in both the Continental Congress and the first U.S. Congress.

3. Anna Young's letter was forwarded to GW in Philadelphia. Tobias Lear drafted a reply on the day that GW received it, 20 Nov.: "Madam, I have received your letter of the 6th inst. requesting my opinion as to the best mode of application to enable you to receive the half pay, which you say is due to you, on account of your late father Colo. John Durkee.

"I would with pleasure, give you any advice or opinion, in my power, on this subject, was I enabled to do it; but never having had occasion to turn my attention to business of this kind I am ignorant of the mode of settlemt which should be pursued in the case which you state. Governor Trumbull, whom you mention in your letter, is much better qualified than I am to give you advice in this business. Or, any one of the present members of Congress, in your neighbourhood, could with more certainty perhaps than any other person, point out to you the steps which you ought to pursue and I have no doubt would readiely do it. I am Madam Yr mo. ob. st" (Df, in the hand of Tobias Lear, ViMtV).

From James Anderson

Sir   Mount Vernon 7 Novr 1798

Inclosed are the reports of last week[1] I am just now Arranging And fixing the Stock in Winter Quarters, When I shall be able to take a correct Account And send in my next for Your information.

Nothing new since Your departure And every part of the work is carrying on in the Order You direct—The Ditchers are employed in making good the weak places of the Mill Race before they begin to the division fence in the Meadows.[2]

The frost is very intense for this season And the drought continues And at all the Farms we are geting in the Corn and shall embrace this faverable opportunity to have it secured.

There are no Accounts of Parkinson,³ nor any further Advice from Sims who engaged to let me hear of Genll Lee on His Arrival in Town,⁴ And I will pospone the forwarding of the Letter to Major Harrison untill I find what can or will be done in the purchase,⁵ Our Mill can do nothing in the Grinding of Wheat. And I am picking up some small parcels But the price advances at Dumfries 9/ to 9/6 p. Bushel It will be doing me a faver to collect account of the prices of Wheat & flour to the Northward, And the Opinion of the probable demand for flour. Docter Stewart will have his Wheat ready next Week When I will send our own Craft or hire a Schooner according to the State of the Weather. If this Settled frost continues open Crafts will do. And if it changes into thaw I must hire—It is not the exposure to wett that I am affraid of in Thaw but that Gales at this season often do happen When the Weather is changeable. All at this House are Well, And beleive me with the greatest respect to be Sir Your most Obedt Humble Sevt

Jas Anderson

ALS, DLC:GW.

1. Anderson's weekly farm reports for this period are deposited in NjMoNP and have been transcribed for CD-ROM:GW. Presumably Anderson is referring here to his report of 3 November.

2. See GW to Anderson, 1 Nov., n.1.

3. See GW to Anderson, 3 November.

4. See GW to Anderson, 1 Nov., postscript, and note 3.

5. This is GW's letter to William B. Harrison of 4 November.

From Samuel Washington

Dear Uncle   Chas Town November 7th 1798

I received the Other day a Letter directed to me, from you upon opening of it, found the enclosed Letter to be for my Mother which I put safe into her hands finding from the direction it was from you, I after a good deal of persuasion got her to shew it to me, upon Reading it, found that she had wrote to you, a coppy of which she had by her, which I also prevailed with her to shew me. The contents gave me great uneasiness on many accounts particularly as her object for writing appeared in a great measure for my benifit I say it destresses me that you should be caled on for more money by this Family after your goodness in Lending me Three hundred pound which kindness I never shall forget.[1]

My Mother in her Letter has express'd fears on her own Account which I think never can come to pass. For this reason, That when I was Married my Father gave me all his Land & Negroes reserving to him self nothing but his house and Garden and house Servents Leaving him self and my Mother to be supported by me, it then became necessary that all his debts should revert on me Therefore all Bonds or Notes that are against the Estate are in my name, the consequence of which is that all Execusions must be Levied on my property and not on his unless my property be not sufficient, which it will take time to determine As the greater part of the debts are not yet sue'd for[.] There is about Three or Four Hundred pound due Doctr Stuart which he has not yet brought suit on, Also Six hundred pound to Capt. Hammond for my Sisters Fortune which he has my Bond for,[2] the rest are sue'd for, (to say) £550 in the hands of Joseph Biddle of Alexandria and about Three hundred pound in small debts which distresses me more than all the rest, as there will be no way of puting them off, Those are all the debts due from the Estate, except what you were so kind as to Lend me, I should not be the Least affraid of paying all the debts and Leaving enough to support My Fathers Family and my own very well, was it not for the debts coming on me at such destresing time for money, that property that I could spare will not sell at half its Value. for double the property now will not sell for what One half will do the next year, provided we have no war with France, for People that have money will not lay it out in property at this critical time, Could I forbear Selling untill next Fall, I mean then to sell off all my Land and pay every thing that I owe and purchase Land that is Rich if it is only half as much it will be better than this that is so poor.

The Latter part of your Letter has given me more pain and uneasiness than all my present dificulties, for fear you should suspect me of applying the Money you Lent me contrary to your Wish My house I paid for with Bonds I got for my Wifes Fortune, I should not have Built a house at all had I been acquainted with the incumbrance the Estate was under at that time, though I had not a House to put my head in, I am induced to trouble you with this full statement of my Affairs in Order to shew you that it will not be in my Mothers power to accept of the Thousands Dollars you ware so good as to offer her to do with it as you wish'd, and was it Practicable and a thing of that kind done it would compleatly ruin me, for it would give my creditors and Idea that I was more in debt than I was worth and they would all push me at Once and Consequently I would be Obliged to sell property for whatever it would bring, Whereas if they come on gradually I can have a better chance of Selling property. Was it not for about Three hundred pound that will come against me this winter I should do very well, for it will be some time before any more can come out against me, by which time I could be able to Sell some Lotts and Land joining Town on Credit which will Induce people to purchase, After my Makeing a Statement of my affairs to my Mother, as I have now done to you it was her request I would answer your Letter my being best-Acquainted with the Situation of the Estate,[3] And to offer you her Most Sincere thanks for your kindness to her. I Am Dear sir your Affectionate Nephew

Saml Washington

ALS, ViMtV.

1. Mildred Washington's letter to GW has not been found, but see GW to Mildred Thornton Washington, 18 October.

2. Thomas Hammond was married to Samuel's sister Mildred.

3. In his answer to this letter on 31 Jan. 1799, GW informed Samuel that he had not received this letter until 13 January.

To Maryland Masons

Gentlemen & Brothers,   [Baltimore] November 8th 1798

Your obliging and affectionate letter, together with a Copy of the constitutions of Masonary, has been put into my hands by your Grand Master; for which I pray you to accept my best thanks.[1]

So far as I am acquainted with the principles and doctrines of Free Masonary, I conceive it to be founded in benevolence, and to be exercised only for the good of Mankind; I cannot, therefore, upon this ground, withhold my approbation of it.

While I offer my grateful acknowledgements for your congratulations on my late appointment, and for the favorable sentiments you are pleased to express of my conduct, permit me to observe, that, at this important and critical moment, when high and repeated indignities have been offered to the Government of our Country, and when the property of our Citizens is plundered without a prospect of redress, I conceive it to be the *indispensable* duty of every American, let his situation and circumstances in life be what they may, to come forward in support of the Government of his choice, and to give all the aid in his power towards mantaining that Independence which we have so dearly purchased; and, under this impression, I did not hesitate to lay aside all personal considerations and accept my appointment.

I pray you to be assured that I receive with gratitude your kind wishes for my health and happiness, and reciprocate them with sincerity. I am, Gentlemen & Brothers, very respectfully your most Obedt Servt

Go: Washington

LS, MdHi; Df, DLC:GW. Both are in Tobias Lear's hand.

1. GW left Mount Vernon with Tobias Lear for Philadelphia on the morning of 5 November. On 7 Nov. he was met by "the Baltimore horse & escorted in and out by the same." He had breakfast in the town and "viewed a Brigade of Militia" (*Diaries*, 6:322). He also received an address signed by William Belton, grand master of the Maryland Masons, and Peter Little, the general secretary, which reads: "Sir & Brother, The Right Worshipful Grand Lodge of Free Masons for the State of Maryland, wishing to testify the respect in which the whole fraternity in this State, hold the Man who is at once the Ornament of the Society and of his Country; voted a Copy of the Constitutions of Masonry lately printed under it's Authority, to be presented to You. Accept, Sir and Brother from our hands, this small token of veneration of Men, who consider it as the greatest boast of their Society, that a Washington *openly* avows himself a Member of it, and thinks it worthy of his approbation; with it accept also, our warmest congratulations, in the name of the body which we represent, on the re-appointment to that elevated station in which you formerly wrought the Salvation of *your* Country; and on your restoration to the inestimable blessings of health; which that the Almighty disposer of events may continue to You uninterruptedly, is the most earnest Prayer of Your most respectfully affectionate Brethren" (DLC:GW).

From James McHenry

Philad. 9th Novr 1798
My dear General   half past 5 O Clock P.M.

I reced about 2 o'clock P.M. Col. Lear's letter, dated at Wilmington, and a few minutes since, his second letter, dated at Chester.[1]

I have engaged lodgings for you at Mrs Whites, in eighth Street near the corner of Market Street, and stabling for your horses at Dunwoody's which is in its neighbourhood. There has been no fever in the house, and I think under all circumstances, it is the most elegible of any of those that have been suggested or that has occurred to my mind.[2]

The President is still at Quincy[,] Hamilton is here, and General Pinckney may be expected on Monday. I got to town yesterday evening, in tolerable health.

You mention coming in by the middle Ferry. We understand by the middle Ferry the Market Street Ferry. This is the best route for several reasons. It is the widest road and avoids all the late encamptments.

General McPherson intends to bring out a few of the volunteers so as to make your reception, a little military.[3] Will you be good enough to inform me by the messenger who delivers this as near as may be the time which he may calculate upon your arrival at the Ferry. He laments his numbers will not be equal to the occasion and his wishes owing to the late sickness. Yours affectionately

James McHenry

ALS, DLC:GW.

1. Letters not found.

2. GW's lodgings were in a boardinghouse kept by the widow Rosannah White at 9 North Eighth Street. Dunwoody's tavern was on Market Street above Eighth Street.

3. The following account of GW's arrival in Philadelphia appeared in the *Gazette of the United States* (Philadelphia) on 10 Nov.: "This day about eleven o'clock, our beloved General arrived in town. Detachments from the different troops of horse met him on the road, at and from Chester, and escorted him to the city. Captains Wharton, McKean, Dunlap, Morrel, and Singer's companies of cavalry—McPherson's blues, and Captain Hozey's company were drawn up in the centre square, and as he approached he alighted from his carriage, and with his secretary Mr. Lear, passed the line uncovered, to the usual salute of presented arms. He was justly and universally received with presented hearts—never did more joy and confidence appear than his presence inspired. Having got into his carriage again, he was escorted to Mrs. White's, in Eighth street, where a guard from McPherson's blues was immediately mounted, to attend their friend and chief, which we understand, is to be regularly relieved during his continuance in this city. Major General Alexander HAMILTON and the Hon James McHENRY, Secretary at War, also arrived in town this day, and accompanied the Lieutenant General to his lodgings in Eighth street." See also *Diaries*, 6:323. William McPherson (1756–1813) commanded a strongly Federalist battalion of cavalry, infantry, and artillery.

To Alexander Hamilton and
Charles Cotesworth Pinckney

Philadelphia 10th November 1798.

Queries—propounded by the Commander in Chief To Majors Genl Hamilton & Pinckney.

1st Is an Invasion of the United States, by France, to be apprehended whilst that Power continues at War with Great Britain?

2d In case such an Invasion should take place, what part of the United States, in their opinion, is most likely to be first attacked?

3d Is it probable that the French will, in the way of exchange, or by other means, become possessed of the Floridas or Louisiana?

4th In case of such an event, what, probably, will be the consequences, as they relate to the United States? What measures will be best to counteract them? and can those measures be carried into effect *promptly*, by the Commander in chief of the Armies? or, must they be previously submitted to the War Office? This question, it will be perceived, presupposes a force in existence.

5th What can be done to supply our *present* deficiency of Engineers? From whence, and by what means are they to be obtained? Should a *Frenchman* be employed *at any rate*?

6th Would not Riflemen, in place of Light Infantry, be eligable as a componant part of each Regiment? and in that case, would Ferguson's Rifles claim a preference?[1]

7th Under the idea that each grand division of the U: States is to furnish four Regiments of the augmented force; and each State, according to the Census, the population, or medium between the two, is to raise its proportion; how many places in each (its extent being considered) and where, ought to be assigned as rendezvouses during the Recruiting Service? At What place ought the *general* rendezvous in each State to be fixed, during the said period? And at what place, or places in the U: States, ought the augmented force to assemble? If at more than one place, how many, where, and the number at each?

8th Of how many pieces of Ordnance, of what sorts, and of what Calliber, ought the Park of artillery to consist, independently of what is attached to Brigades, or Regiments? And how many ought each of these to have?

9th Would it be advisable (after an adequate force is recruited) to withdraw the Troops wch at present occupy the Posts on our Northern and Western Frontiers, & replace them with new raised Corps?

10th Of how many Ranks do the French form their line of Battle *generally?* Do they make much use of Pikes? And would it be an eligable weapon, with which to arm part of our Soldiery, as that is the Nation with which we expect to contend? Genl Pinckney may, from personal observation, be enabled to solve these two questions.

Queries—relative to smaller matters; but meriting consideration, as an army is now commencing more systematically than formerly; the rules, regulations, and distinctions in which, may give a tone to measures which may prevail hereafter.

1st If the clothing of the Regiments, and the fashion of that clothing; with distinctions between one Regiment and another are not already ordered by the proper authority, and in train of execution, what had they best be?

2d Would not cotton, or (still more so) Flannel be advisable for shirting, and linings for the Soldiery?

3d What had best be the distinctions in dress, in the badges— and other peculiarities, between the Commander in Chief and his Suit, and the Majors General & their Aids? Between the latter, & the Brigadiers & theirs? and betwn these again & the Regimental Officers? Also among the Regimental Officers themselves, Commissioned & non-commissioned? and whether the Staff (not in the line of the Army) of the different Departments—both Commissioned & Warrant Officers, ought not to be designated by their dress, or some appropriate mark, or badge? and in every case, & at all times, in the camp or Field be compelled to wear them, as well for the purpose of denoting the Corps to which they belong, as a mean by which irregularities, rioting, and improper conduct may be discovered with more ease.

4th As there has been many objections to, and remarks made upon, the black Cockade, (being that of Great Britain) might not something be devised by way of annexation thereto, to distinguish it from that of any other Nation? I have seen, and it appeared to have no bad effect, a small Eagle (of Pewter, tin, & in some instances silver) fixed by way of Button in the center of a rose cockade; which was not only very distinguishable, but somewhat characteristic.

The sooner these queries are taken into consideration and opinions given on them more agreeable will it be to [2]

Go: Washington

ADS, DLC: Hamilton Papers; ADS, ScC; ADfS, DLC:GW. Lear enclosed copies
of these queries in the letters he drafted for GW to Hamilton and Pinckney on
12 Nov., in which GW also enclosed copies of McHenry's letter and questions of
10 November.
   1. In December 1776 Patrick Ferguson (1744–1780) patented the first breech-
loading rifle used by the British army.
   2. See GW to Alexander Hamilton, 12 November. The answers to these queries, along with those contained in James McHenry's letter to GW of this date,
were submitted in the report to McHenry of 13 December.

From James McHenry

Sir   War Department 10th Novr 1798
   It appears by a letter from the President, dated Quincy Octbr
22d 1798, that it will not be in his power to be in Philadelphia 'till
near the time fixed upon for the meeting of Congress. In order
however, to prevent any injury to the public service, as it respects
officering the troops, directed to be raised by the late acts of Congress, he has written to me as follows. "If you, and the generals,
judge it necessary to appoint the officers of Battalions, before we
can have opportunity to nominate them to the Senate, you may
fill up the commissions with the blanks you have, or if you have
not enough, send new ones by post." [1]
   I have thought it proper, in pursuance of this authority, to
submit to you, a list of all those persons, who have been recommended for commissions in the army, with their letters of pretensions, and also a list of all the officers of the revolutionary army;
and to request that you will, with the aid of Generals Hamilton and
Pinckney, prepare from these, and any other sources of information, a list of the most deserving and suitable characters, in your
estimation, to fill the different grades to which the authority cited
applies. [2]
   I have also, in conformity with my letter to you, dated the 16th
of August ulto [3] to request, that you would submit, to Generals
Hamilton and Pinckney (General Knox having declined his appointment) the following questions and that you would be pleased
to take the same into mature consideration, and report, to me, the
result of your deliberations.
   1. Will it be expedient and proper, to select the officers, and
raise the men for the 12 Regiments of Infantry, and 6 companies

of Cavalry, from the following districts, in the following proportions, or as nearly so, as circumstances will admit. vz.

1. The officers and men, for 4 regiments of Infantry from within the States of New Hampshire, Massachusetts, Connecticut, Rhode Island, and Vermont.

2. The officers and men, for 4 Regiments of Infantry, from within the States of New York New Jersey, Pennsylvania, Delaware and Maryland.

3. The officers and men, for 4 regiments of Infantry from within the States of Virginia, Kentucky, N. Carolina, Tenessee, South Carolina, and Georgia.

4. The whole, or a principal part of the officers and men of the 6 companies of cavalry, from within the district, where it is most likely they will have to serve.

2. If these questions are determined in the affirmative, then, whether in making the selection of officers, the least exceptionable rule, for determining the numbers to be taken from each State, within the respective divisions aforesaid, will not be, by their relative number of inhabitants, according to the census, wherever the application of this rule, will not introduce the least worthy to the exclusion of more meritorious characters.

According to this rule, the following table will exhibit, pretty nearly, the proportion of officers and men, to be drawn from the respective States for the 12 regiments of Infantry.

	Infantry	Lt Colonels	Majors
New Hampshire	396	1	1
Massachusetts	1326	2	4
Rhode Island	192		
Connecticut	663	1	2
Vermont	239		1
New York	719	1	2
New Jersey	380	1	1
Pennsylvania	917	1	2
Delaware	126		1
Maryland	676	1	2
Virginia	1400	2	4
N. Carolina	630	1	2
S. Carolina	420	1	1
Georgia	140		1
Kentucky	140		
Tenessee	86		

	Capts.	Leuts.	Ensigns
[New Hampshire]	4	4	4
[Massachusetts]	20	20	20
[Rhode Island]	3	3	3
[Connecticut]	10	10	10
[Vermont]	3	3	3
[New York]	10	10	10
[New Jersey]	6	6	6
[Pennsylvania]	13	13	13
[Delaware]	1	1	1
[Maryland]	10	10	10
[Virginia]	20	20	20
[North Carolina]	9	9	9
[South Carolina]	6	6	6
[Georgia]	2	2	2
[Kentucky]	2	2	2
[Tennessee]	1	1	4

3d Whether, in the present state of things, it is expedient and proper, to proceed *immediately* to the appointment of the officers, or to suspend their appointment, until the meeting of Congress.

4. Whether, in the present state of our foreign relations, it is expedient and proper, to proceed immediately after the appointment of the officers to recruit the whole of the 12 regiments of Infantry and six companies of cavalry. If inexpedient to recruit the whole, then, what part thereof will it be proper to recruit, and in which district or districts of the union.

5. Whether, if determined that a part only ought to be forthwith recruited, it will be expedient notwithstanding, to appoint the whole of the officers; and whether it ought to be signified to them, that they are not to be intitled to pay &c. previous to being called into actual service.

6. Will it be expedient and proper, to withdraw any of the troops stationed upon the North Western and Southern frontiers, vz. on the Lakes; between the Lakes and the Rivers Ohio and Mississippi⟨,⟩ and on the Tenessee and Georgia frontier bound⟨ing⟩ on the Indians and the river St Mary's, with a view to reinforce the troops on the sea-board frontier.

7. The stations of the before mentioned troops, and their numbers, will be seen by the annexed return, and letters from Brigadier General Wilkinson.[4] If inexpedient that any of these should be withdrawn, will it be proper to reinforce them with the two

companies, directed by a late act of Congress, to be added to each
of the old regiments of Infantry.

8. What distribution, under the present aspect of affairs, ought
to be made of the troops and recruits, *now* on our sea-board frontier; the description, places of rendezvous, stations and numbers
of which is exhibited in the annexed return.

9. What number of the *troops to be raised*, ought to be stationed
in the respective divisions aforesaid, and in what places.

10. Will it be best for the service and discipline, that the recruits
should be supplied by contracts at the inlisting rendezvouses, as
now practiced; or to allow to each recruit, a fixed sum per diem,
in lieu of his ration, previous to his joining the general rendezvous
or encampment within his division.

11. Ought the army, when in the field, to be supplied with rations, by means of purchasing and issuing commissaries, or by contract, as at present.

12. What quantity and kinds of cannon, Field Artillery, military
stores, and other articles necessary to an operating army, such as
may be raised, will it be proper to procure, in addition to what is
exhibited, as on hand, agreeably to the annexed return, by the
Superintendant of military Stores,[5] and that may be expected to
be procured in consequence of the annexed letter from the Secretary of the Treasury to [   ] dated the [   ].[6]

13. Our greatest deposits of artillery and military stores, are at
Springfield, Massachusetts, and Philadelphia Pennsylvania. We are
besides forming magazines near Harpers Ferry, on the Potomac
Virginia, and at Fayetteville N. Carolina. Ought there to be any
other places established for principal magazines than these four,
and the subordinate deposits mentioned in the aforesaid return.

As it will be proper in the course of your deliberations, to ascertain from the Secretary of the Treasury, whether he can furnish
the monies necessary for the military service, I inclose an estimate
made out some time since, shewing the monies which I thought
would be required, and the periods at which it might be wanted,
for the maintenance of the old and new army; and to provide certain military articles for which appropriations have been made by
late acts of Congress, and for cloathing for the provisional army.[7]

It may also be proper, that you should confer, with the Secretary
of State, on the subject of our foreign relations, as well as the Secretary of the Treasury on the extent and reliance which may be

placed on our resources and finances, to assist you to mature your opinion upon some of the points submitted. I need not add, that the Secretary of State and Secretary of the Treasury, will cheerfully give you every information which you may think it necessary to request. With the greatest respect, I have the honour to be, Sir, your most obt & hble St

James McHenry

ALS, DLC:GW; ADfS, MdAA; ADfS, DLC: James McHenry Papers; copy, in McHenry's hand, CtHi: Oliver Wolcott, Jr., Papers; copy, in Lear's hand, DLC: Hamilton Papers.

1. Adams's letter, which McHenry also describes in his letter to GW of 30 Oct., is in DLC: McHenry Papers.

2. McHenry, as GW pointed out in his reply of 13 Nov., failed to enclose any of these documents. See also McHenry to GW, 14 November.

3. McHenry is referring to his letter to GW of 16 October.

4. McHenry did not enclose these documents in this letter. See McHenry to GW, 14 Nov., nn. 9–10.

5. McHenry did not enclose this return. See McHenry to GW, 16 Nov. (second letter).

6. McHenry's copy in CtHi: Wolcott Papers has Rufus King written in place of the first blank. This was likely the letter from Oliver Wolcott, Jr., to King dated 3 July 1798, a copy of which is in DLC:GW. See McHenry to GW, 19 Sept., and note 18 of that document.

7. McHenry did not enclose this document. See McHenry to GW, 14 Nov., n.14.

To Alexander Hamilton

Sir,   Philadelphia Novr 12th 1798

Herewith you will be furnished with the Copy of a letter from the Secretary of War to me, suggesting many very important matters for consideration, and to be reported on.[1]

It is my desire, that you will bestow serious and close attention on them, and be prepared to offer your opinion on each head, when called upon.

I also propose, for your consideration and opinion, a number of queries which had been noted by me, previous to the receipt of the Secretary's letter (now enclosed). In stating these, I had endeavoured to avoid, and make them additional to, the objects which the Secretary of War, in a letter to me, dated the 16th ultimo, informed me would be subjects for my consideration. I find, however, that several of them, in substance, are contained in his *last* letter. But as they were digested previous thereto, and written, I shall, to save copying, lay them before you as they are, without expunging those parts which now appear in the Secretary's Statement.[2] With very great esteem & regard, I am, Sir, Your most Obedt Servt

Go: Washington

LS, in Tobias Lear's hand, DLC: Hamilton Papers; ADfS, DLC:GW. The endorsement of the draft indicates the letter was sent to Charles Cotesworth Pinckney as well.

　　1. See James McHenry to GW, 10 November.
　　2. See GW to Alexander Hamilton and Charles Cotesworth Pinckney, 10 November.

To James McHenry

Sir　　　　　　　　　　　　　　　　　　[13 November 1798]

I observe by the concluding paragraph of your letter of the 10th instant that you contemplate conferences between the Secretaries of State and of the Treasury and myself, for the purpose of obtaining auxiliary information from their departments—Several of the questions which you state seem indeed to require such information. But on reflection, it has occurred to me as most regular, that you should settle with those officers what it may be reciprocally deemed necessary and proper for them to communicate; to the end that they may themselves bring forward, either through you or directly to me as may be agreed, but without any previous application from me, such communications as the case shall be supposed to require. Wherever, too, I am to report a formal opinion, you will I dare say think with me, that the data upon which it shall be given ought substantially to be deposited with me in writing.[1] Personal conferences besides for more full explanation, may be useful and will be very agreeable to me. Allow me to request your speedy attention to this matter.

I find also, that the documents referred to in your letter of the 10th inst. did not accompany it. As these will be necessary in forming an opinion on several points submitted to me in your letter aforesaid, and which I have communicated to Majr Genls Hamilton & Pinckney, I must beg you to furnish me with them without delay.

The documents referred to are as follow—viz.

"List of persons who have been recommended for Commissions in the Army, with their letters of pretensions."

(N.B. A list of Applicants south of the River Potomac, and the⟨ir⟩ letters, are in my hands. The list & letters from the other parts will be wanting).[2]

"Returns and Letters from Brigadier Genl Wilkinson shewing the stations and number of the Troops on the N. Western & Southern frontier."

"Return shewing the description, places of rendezvous, stations and number of Troops, *now* on our Seaboard frontier."

"Return from the Superintendant of Military Stores, shewing the quantity & kinds of Cannon, Field artillery, Military Stores, and other Articles now on hand belonging to the U.S."

(N.B. This Return shd also exhibit the places at which t⟨hese⟩ are deposited, and the quantity at each place).

To these must be added the estimate which you had made out of the monies which you conceived wd be required for military services, and the times at which the same might be wanted.

I have in my hands a list of the Genl & Field Officers who served in the Revolutionary War, and of the Captains and subalterns from the States so. of the Potomac.[3] You will therefore be pleased to add to the documents a list of the Captains & Subalterns, from the other States, that the whole may be before me.[4] I am Sir with very great regard & esteem yr mo. obt ⟨Svt⟩

Go: Washington

Df, in the hands of Alexander Hamilton and Tobias Lear, DLC:GW. Hamilton on this day forwarded the draft with this note: "General Hamilton presents his respects to the Commander in Chief & sends the sketch of a letter in conformity to what passed this morning" (DLC:GW).

1. See McHenry to GW, 19 November.

2. An undated List of applications for Commisi[o]ns in the Army from Virginia No. Carolina So. Carolina Georgia Kintucky & Tennessee is in DLC:GW, filed at the end of December 1798.

3. See McHenry to GW, 21 Oct., n.4.

4. See McHenry's response of 14 Nov. and GW's request for an additional item on the same date.

Notes on an Interview with
George Logan and Robert Blackwell

Tuesday—13th November 1798

Mr Lear, my Secretary, being from our lodgings on business, one of my Servants came into the room where I was writing, and informed me, that a Gentleman in the Parlour below, desired to see me; his name was sent up. In a few minutes I went down, and found the Revd Doctr Blackwell, & Doctr Logan there. I advanced towards, & gave my hand to the former; the latter did the same towards me, I was backward in giving mine. He possibly supposing from hence, that I did not recollect him, he said his name was Logan. Finally ⟨in a⟩ very cool manner, and with an air of much indiffe[re]nce, I gave him my hand, and asked *Doctr Blackwell to be seated*, the other *took* a seat at the sametime. I addressed *all* my conversation to Doctor Blackwell; the other *all* his to me, to which I only gave negative or affirmative answers, as laconically as I could, except asking how Mrs Logan did. He seemed disposed to be very polite—and while Doctr Blackwell & myself were conversing on the late calamitous fever, offered me an asylum at his house if it should return, or I thought myself in any danger in the City— & two or three Rooms by way of accomodation. I thanked him slightly, observing there wd be no call for it.[1]

About this time, Doctr Blackwell took his leave—we all rose from our Seats and I moved a few paces towards the door of the room, expecting the other would follow, and take his leave also; instead of which, he kept his ground & proceeded to inform me more particularly (for he had mentioned it before) that he had seen Genl ⟨Lafa⟩yette at Hamburgh, and his Lady & daughters (I think in France) and related many things concerning their health &ca. He said something also respecting an Interview he had had with our Minister Mr Murray in Holland; (but as I wished to get quit of him; remained standing; and shewed the utmost inattention to what he was saying) I do not now recollect what the purport of it was; except that, he hurried from thence to Paris. His object being, he said, to get there before the departure of our Commissioners (as he called them).

He observed that, the situation of our Affairs in this Country— and the train they were in, with respect to France—had induced him to make the Voyage; in hope, or expectation or words to that

effect of contributing to their amelioration. This drew my attention more pointedly to what he was saying, and induced me to
remark that, there was something very singular in this. That *he*
who could only be viewed as a private character; unarmed with
proper powers; and presumptively unknown in France; should
suppose he could effect what these gentlemen of the first respectability in our Country specially charged under the authority of the
Government, were unable to do. With this observation he seemed
a little confounded; but recovering, said, that not more than five
person's had any knowledge of his going; that he was furnished by
Mr Jefferson and Mr McKean with certificates of his Citizenship.
That Mr Merlin President of the Directory of France, had discovered the greatest desire that France & America should be on the
best terms.[2] I answered, that *he* was more fortunate than our Envoys, for they could neither be received nor heard by Mr Merlin
or the Directory. That if the Powers of France were serious in their
professions, there was a plain and effectual way by which that object could be accomplish'd—namely—to repeal all the obnoxious
arrets, by which the Commerce & Rights of this Country had been
invaded; put an end to further depredations on both; and make
restitution for the Injuries we had received. A conduct like this
I said would speak more forcibly than words—for that the latter
never made an impression on my mind, when they were contradicted by actions. He said that the Directory was apprehensive that
this Country, viz. the Government of it—or our Envoys, I am not
sure which he mentd or alluded to was not well disposed towards
France. I asked what better evidence could be given in refutation
of this opinion, than its long suffering of the outrageous conduct of that Nation towards the U. States—and dispatching three
Gentlemen of unquestionable worth, with ample powers to reconcile all differences—even at the expence of great sacrafices
on our parts. He replied, they have taken of[f] the embargo and
were making restitution of property—ennumerating one instance
I think. With respect to the embargo, I observed that taking it off
or continuing it on, was a matter of no great importance if, as I
had been informed, our Vessels in French Ports were few: He said
that the attempt at a Coalition of European Powers against France
would come to nothing; that the Directory were undr no appre-
hen[sion]s & that Great Britain would have to contend alone;
Insinuating, as I conceived his object at the time to be, that we

should be involved in a dangerous situation if we persisted in our hostile appearances. To this I finally replied that we were driven to those measures in self defence, and asked him if the Directory looked upon us as worms; not even allowed to turn when tread upon? for it was evident to all the world that we had borne and forborne beyond what even common respect for ourselves required and I hoped the spirit of this Country would never suffer itself to be injured with impunity by any nation under the Sun. To this he sd *he told Citizen Merlin* that if the U.S. were Invaded by France they wd unite to a man to oppose the Invaders.[3]

AD, DLC:GW. GW docketed the memorandum: "Genl Washington's acct of his interview with Dr Blackwell and Dr Logan."

1. On 13 Nov. 1798 Dr. George Logan, who had returned only a few days before from his famous mission to France, and the Rev. Robert Blackwell (1748–1831) arrived separately at Rosannah White's boardinghouse on Eighth Street in Philadelphia, where GW was staying. GW knew both men. During the Federal Convention in 1787, he had visited Logan and his wife, Deborah Norris Logan, at Stenton, their place near Germantown, and the Logans visited the Washingtons at Mount Vernon the next year. Blackwell, rector of St. Peter's in Philadelphia, had been assistant rector at the church during the winter of 1781–82 when GW and his wife often attended services there (C. B. P. Jefferys, "The Provincial and Revolutionary History of St. Peter's Church, Philadelphia, 1753–1783," *Pa. Mag.*, 47:328–56). For Logan's mission to France, see James Lloyd to GW, 18 June 1798, n.5.

2. Philip Antoine Merlin (1754–1838) was forced to resign from the French Directory on 18 June 1799.

3. Logan had already reported to the equally hostile secretary of state, Timothy Pickering, and on 26 Nov. he made his report to the more receptive President John Adams. See Frederick B. Tolles's account of the meetings in *George Logan of Philadelphia* (New York, 1953), 174–80.

Letter not found: from Alexander Spotswood, Jr., 13 Nov. 1798. On 22 Nov. GW referred to Spotswood's "letter of the 13th instt," which on 9 Dec. Spotswood assured GW was a forgery.

From William Richardson Davie

Sir,   [14 November 1798]

I had the pleasure to acknowledge the rect of your Excellencys letter of the 24th of October by the last post, and ⟨stated⟩ the measures I should take to effect its object[1] as early as possible.

On looking over the list of applicants for commissions it appeard to me necessary to inform your Excellency, that these recommendations appear to have been made without any regard to the particular establishment on which the officers were to be placed in the regiments to be raised under the act &c. whether on the establishment or in the provisional Army, the want of attention to this circumstance may probably produce some delay and confusion—I have understood from some of the Gentlemen named in the list that they had no intention of going into service unless the provisional army was raised when they could consider it their duty, to turn out, and have given me an assurance to that effect. The list shall be returned agreeably to your request as soon as I obtain information sufficient to enable me to make the necessary remarks upon it—At present however it may be necessary to mention that I observe a Mr Peter Butts Oram recommended by Mr Grove and Mr Martin as a Captain of Cavalry—If this is the same P. B. O. who resided formerly in New bern and I never heard of any other man of that name these Gentlemen have permited their good nature to be imposed upon in this recommendation he is to my knowledge a very unworthy man and left this State about the year 1789 covered with infamy.[2]

As to the Officers for the company of Dragoons, Mr William Gregory of Camden County near Edenton, the same Gentleman who is recommended by Mr Burges and Mr Blount M[ember] C[ongress] as a Field officer has assured me he will accept of the appointment of Capt. of Dragoons, and Mr McKennie Long of Halifax County son of the late Colo. Long of this place will accept of the lieutenancy they are respectable young men of good connections and well calculated for this service[3]—I could easily procure a proper character here for the appointment of cornet but I thought it was better to recommend some person from the District of Hillsboro as their personal acquaintance in these different districts would enable them to recruit the troop immediately, and I have therefore written to the officers of the Cavalry of that District for that purpose.

I wish sincerely it may not be "unpropitious to the service" that the necessary arrangements have not been made to ensure the raising of these regiments this winter such a business is not the work of a week or a month, and if the country is invaded before there is a respectable force on foot we shall be obliged to resort to disagreeable expidient of making drafts.

ADf, Nc-Ar: William Richardson Davie Papers.

1. Davie wrote above the line "comply with your request" as alternate wording for "effect its object," and made several other such insertions above lines.

2. Peter Butts Oram also appears, seeking a captain's commission, on an undated List of Applicants from Virginia in DLC:GW, filed at the end of December 1798. William Barry Grove (1764–1818) was a member of Congress from Fayetteville, North Carolina. Alexander Martin (1738–1807), of Danbury, N.C., was a member of the U.S. Senate.

3. William Gregory was the eldest son of General Isaac Gregory (c.1737–1800) of Camden County, North Carolina. Dempsey Burges (1751–1800), of Camden County, and Thomas Blount (1759–1812), of Edgecombe County, were members of Congress. Lemuel McKinne Long was a son of Colonel Nicholas Long (c.1726–1797).

To James McHenry

Sir,   Philada Nov. 14th 1798

In order to form an opinion on the query contained in your letter of the 10th instant, whether it will be best to furnish Rations for the Troops by Contracts, or by purchasing and issuing Commissaries, it will be necessary that I should know the prices of Rations, now paid by Contract, at the several places where Troops are sta⟨tione⟩d. You will therefore be pleased to add this to the documents which I yesterday requested you to furnish.[1] With great esteem & regard I am Sir Your most Obedt servt

Go: Washington

LS, sold by Sotheby's, 19 May 1997, sale 6981, item 335; retained copy, DLC:GW.

1. McHenry complied on 16 November. See McHenry's second letter of that date to GW. See also McHenry to GW, this date, n.17.

From James McHenry

Sir,   War department 14th November 1798

I had the honor to receive your Excellencys letter of the 13th instant last night.

Some of the documents which were referred to in my letter of the 10th, I find cannot be completed by my Clerks, in any reasonable time. I shall therefore be obliged to submit the original books and records of the Office containing them, in their place, and request the same may be carefully returned.

You will be furnished in consequence, as soon as the same shall be wanted with, 1. The book containing a list of all the candidates and abridgement of their recommendations. 2. The original letters of recommendation.[1]

I have also thought it proper to add to these, which are now sent, the following confidential original communications from No. 3 to 9 inclusive, relative to the same subject, which I request may be returned viz.

No. 3. A lette⟨r⟩ from General Hamilton dated 21st August with a list of Candidates for Army appointments and his remarks.[2]

No. 4. Three confidential letters from Uriah Tracey dated 30 July—18th of August and 17 of September, with a list of Candidates.[3]

No. 5. A letter from J. Allen relative to disqualified characters.[4]

No. 6. Two letters from General Knox with inclosures dated 26th August and 2d November.[5]

No. 7. A letter from William Hindman dated August 12 and one from William Matthews dated 11 October.[6]

No. 8. Observations &c. on North Carolina candidates by John Steele Comptroller of the Treasury.[7]

No. 9. Two letters from Jacob Read dated 10th October and 26th Septem⟨r⟩.[8]

No. 10. The return of Troops and recruits and return of the Station⟨s⟩ for the same.[9]

No. 11. Letters from Brigadier General Wilkinson dated 6th and 9th of April, July 14 August 10 and September 6th 1798 with two letters from the Governor of Georgia dated 8th of August and 14th of October. These you will also be pleased to return.[10]

No. 12. Copy of a letter from the Secretary of War to Brigadier General Wilkinson dated the 2 August 1798.[11]

No. 13. Copy of a letter to Lt Col. Gaither dated the 23d August 1796.[12]

No. 14. Copy of a letter to the Governor of Georgia dated 25 Sep. 1798.[13]

No. 15. Estimate of the demand of the Secretary of War on the Treasury of the United States.[14]

No. 16. The return by the Superintendant of Military Stores.[15]

No. 17. Copy of a letter to the Secretary of State and Secretary of the Treasury dated the 14th instant on the subject of your letter of the 13th.[16]

Perhaps you would prefer that the selecting of fit characters for appointments should be made at this Office, in which case it will be unnecessary to remove the books and other documents. All the other papers are transmitted.

In conformity with your letter of this date I have added a table shewing the contract prices of rations at the several places where troops are stationed.[17]

The Superintendant of Military Stores I find has not the return quite copied.[18] As soon as finished it shall be transmitted.[19] With the greatest respect I have the honor to be Sir Your obedient servant

James McHenry

LS, DLC:GW; ADfS, MdAA.

1. McHenry indicates later in this letter that he will not send the books and letters of application after all.

2. Alexander Hamilton's letter to James McHenry enclosed lists of candidates for army appointments from New York, New Hampshire, Vermont, New Jersey, and Pennsylvania. The lists are in DLC:GW at the end of December 1798 and are printed with Hamilton's letter in Syrett, *Hamilton Papers*, 22:87–146.

3. Letters not found.

4. Letter not found.

5. Letters not found.

6. Letters not found.

7. Letter not found.

8. Letters not found.

9. These would appear to be Return of Troops at the undermentioned places and Names of places at which recruiting rendezvous have been established. Both are undated and in DLC:GW at the end of December 1798.

10. Letters not found.

11. A copy of this letter is in DLC: Hamilton Papers.

12. A copy of this letter is in DLC: McHenry Papers.

13. Letter not found.

14. This estimate was contained in McHenry's letter to Oliver Wolcott, Jr., of 3 Sept., a copy of which is in DLC:GW. See also McHenry to GW, 19 Sept., and note 19 of that document.

15. See note 18.

16. A copy of this letter is in DLC: McHenry Papers.

17. An undated List of contracts for the year 1798, to which is appended Prices of rations at the different posts, is in DLC:GW at the end of December 1798.

18. See McHenry to GW, 16 Nov. (second letter).

19. On 30 Dec. Tobias Lear wrote McHenry: "By order of the Commander in Chief, I have the honor to return to you the following letters, which were submitted to his inspection in your letter of the 14th of November—(vizt)

No. 4. Three confidential letters from Uriah Tracy, dated July 30th—Augt 18th and Septr 17th, with a list of Candidates.

No. 5. A letter from J[ohn] Allen relative to disqualified Candidates.

No. 6. Two letters from General [Henry] Knox, with enclosures, dated Augt 25th and Novr 2d.

No. 7. A letter from William Hindman dated Augt 12th, and one from William Mathews, dated Octr 11th.

No. 11. Letters from Brigadier General [James] Wilkinson, dated 6th & 9th of April—14th July, 10th Augt—and 6 Sept. 1798; with two letters from the Governor of Georgia [James Jackson] dated the 8th of August and 14th of October.

No. 12. Copy of a letter from the Secretary of War to Brigadier General Wilkinson, dated 2d Augt.

No. 13. Copy of a letter to Lt Colonel [Henry] Gaither, dated the 23d of August 1796.

No. 14—Copy of letter to the Governor of Georgia, dated 25th of Septr 1798.

No. 15—Estimate of the Secretary of War on the Treasury of the United States.

No. 17—Copy of a letter to the Secretaries of State and of the Treasury, on the subject of the Commander in Chief's letter of the 13th of Novr.

No. 3—A letter from General [Alexander] Hamilton, dated the 21st of Augt, with a list of Candidates for Army appointmt with his remarks, was taken by General Hamilton.

No. 8 & 9—A letter from John Steele, Comptroller of the Treasury, with observations on the No. Carolina Candidates—and two letters from Jacob Read, dated 26th Septr and 10th of October, were taken by General [Charles Cotesworth] Pinckney, for his information in selecting Characters for Army Appointmts in the Southern States.

No. 10 & 16 are reserved by the Commander in Chief.

General Pinckney left this place on the 28th inst. with his Lady and Daughter in good health, and with a pleasing prospect of meeting no interruption in their Journey" (DLC: McHenry Papers).

From Andrew Moore and
Samuel Legrand Campbell

Sir,   Lexington Virga Novr 14th 1798

The Trustees of Washington Academy having received your letter dated 17th June[1] have directed us to apply for a conveyance of the shares which you have been pleased to bestow on the Seminary over which they Superintend. Mr James Gold will present you with a *form* such as he may be advised is proper, and will take the necessary steps to have it proved and recorded.[2]

The Trustees wish on every suitable occasion to express their high sense of the favor conferred as well as the respect they entertain for your person and character. With due consideration we are in behalf of the Board Your Mo. Obt & Much obliged Servts

Andrew Moore

S. L. Campbell

LS, DLC:GW.

When Liberty Hall Academy (by 1798 Washington Academy and later Washington College) was incorporated in 1782, Andrew Moore (1752–1821), a native of Rockbridge County, was one of the twenty trustees of the academy named in the instrument of incorporation. He had been a member of the U.S. House of Representatives since 1789, and reportedly he was instrumental in persuading GW in 1796 to donate his one hundred shares in the James River Company to Liberty Hall in Lexington, Va. (Hugh Blair Grigsby, "The Founders of Washington College," *Historical Papers* [Washington and Lee University], 2 [1890], 1–111; see particularly pp. 56–62). Samuel Legrand Campbell (1766–1840), also a native of Rockbridge County, was elected a trustee of Liberty Hall Academy on 23 Oct. 1793 and at this time was acting as rector of the academy. He graduated from Liberty Hall in 1788 and studied at the medical college in Philadelphia before beginning his practice in Lexington ("Sketches of Trustees," ibid., 3 [1892], 85–128; see particularly pp. 93–95).

1. GW's letter of 17 June 1798 is printed in Washington Academy Trustees to GW, 12 April 1798, n.2.

2. GW's assignment to Washington Academy of one hundred shares in the James River Company reads: "THIS INDENTURE made the Seventh day of Decemr in the Year One thousand Seven hundred Ninety eight, Betwixt George Washington Mount Vernon Virginia of the one part & the Rector & Trustees of Washington Academy of the other part Witnesseth, that the said George Washington (in pursuance of an Act of the Legislature of the Commonwealth of Virginia, passed the October session one thousand Seven hundred eighty five, entitled 'an Act to amend an Act for Vesting in George Washington esquire, a certain Interest in the Companies established, for opening & extending the Navigation of Powtomack & James Rivers['] hath given granted assigned & appointed, and by these presence doth give grant assign & appoint, to the Rector & Trustees of Washington Academy (formerly known by Liberty Hall Academy) and to their Successors, one hundred complete shares in the James River Company, which said one hundred shares were vested in the said George Washington by the said Commonwealth, as by reference to the Laws thereof will at large appear. *TO HAVE & TO HOLD* the said one hundred shares with all & singuler their appurtenances, to the said Rector and Trustees and their successors (free from all incumbrences whatever except such requisitions, Conditions, & Contingencies as said shares are or shall be subject to, similer to and in Proportion to the other Shares in said Company and in conformity to their respective rules and regulations) To be used by said Rector & Trustees & their successors forever, for the purposes spacified in an act of said Legislature entitled, 'an act entitled an act for incorporating the Rector & Trustees of Liberty Hall Academy' Passed in the Year One thousand Seven hundred & eighty two. In Witness whereof the said George Washington hath hereunto set his hand & seal the day & Year above written. Done at Philada in the Commonwealth of Pennsylvania. Go: Washington" (Vi).

The deed was "Signed Sealed & delivd in the presence of Wm Hay, George Syme, James Gold, [and] John Davidson," recorded in Henrico County court on 8 Mar. 1799, and approved by the James River Company on 28 June 1799. James Gold who conveyed the deed to GW at Mount Vernon was at this time a merchant in Lexington. For the background to this, see Washington Academy Trustees to GW, 12 April 1798, and notes.

From James McHenry

Sir,   War department, Novr 16 1798
   As the enclosed paper, shewing the component parts, number of Men and pay of the Officers composing the present Army Establishment may save you a reference to the several laws upon the subject, I have thought it proper to have it made out and transmitted.[1] With great respect, I am Sir, Your most obedt Servant,
                                                                James McHenry

LS, DLC:GW.
   1. The enclosure lists the ranks of the "Army of the United States on the present Establishment," including "One Regiment of Light Dragoons," "A Corps of Artillerists and Engineers," "An additional Regiment of Artillerists and Engineers," and "Sixteen Regiments of Infantry." It goes on to enumerate monthly pay, monthly forage money, and daily rations for each rank in the army. The list is in DLC:GW and is transcribed in its entirety for CD-ROM:GW.

From James McHenry

Sir,   War department November 16 1798
   I have the honor to transmit you herewith a return of Ordnance and Military Stores, which has this moment been delivered to me by the Superintendant.[1] I am with the greatest respect Your obedient Servant

                                                                James McHenry

LS, DLC:GW.
   1. The enclosure, entitled Return of Ordnance, and the most important Articles of Military Stores belonging to the United States at the several Posts; as herein stated, was the long-delayed product of an order from McHenry to Samuel Hodgdon of 25 August. See McHenry to GW, 19 Sept., n.17. The 35-page return, signed by Samuel Hodgdon and dated 15 Nov., lists types, quantity, and places of deposit of ordnance. It is transcribed in its entirety for CD-ROM:GW.

From Philip Rootes

Sir   Gloucester County November 16th 1798

I was at Mountvernon Some time ago but was disappointed in seeing you. the caus of my tiakning this liberty is to beg the favour which I waited on you to ask, I will unfold the subject matter to you, my Father John Rootes made the Campaigns of 1757 and 1758 in Colo. William Byrds Regiment and was a Capt. in the said Regiment during the Campaigns—this is Certified by Colo. William Bronaugh, my Father at his death informed his family that he had a wright to some Land for his servises in the War between France and Great Brittan by some Calld the Old Indian War—his Widow and Heirs being reducd to great wand by missfortuns, and knowing the justness of the Claime has petitioned the Legislature of this state to make them some small Compensation for the servuces of the deceased as it appears from the Books of the Land office that no military Warrant has Issued to John Rootes—nor heirs—and as the records and Books whereon his Commission was recorded was desstroyed in the last War—The Heirs of the Said John Rootes will ever esteem it a Singular favour of you Sir— if you knew of any such Offerser in the War above describd you will be so good as to inclose me a few lines by the next post, to the Legislature informeing that Honorable body that there was such a person and what Commistion he had—and in what year or years he performed this Servise,[1] A Certificate from you Sir if you know of any susch person will be one of the most necessary Vouches to support our Claim and the favour will ever be Acknowleged by Your most Obedt and most Humble Sert

                                                        Philip Rootes

N.B. please to direct yours to be left at Gloucest. Court House. P.R.

ALS, ViMtV.

1. GW replied from Mount Vernon on 5 Jan. 1799: "Sir, Your letter of the 1⟨6⟩th of November, was received by me whilst I was in Philadelphia—on public business; and too closely engaged to pay attention to matters of private concern. Being but lately returned to this place, must be my apology for not informing you sooner, that the land after which you enquire, as Son of Captn John Rootes deceased, was purchased of your father by the Honble John Page [of Rosewell, (1743–1808)] (then of the Council of this State) for, and on my Account—and the full Sum—viz.—One hundd p⟨ounds⟩ (to the best of my recollection) paid for ⟨the⟩ same, as can be made appear at any time; and the assignment satisfac-

torily exhibited at the Secretary's Office, on which a warrant issued, & a Patent was granted to Sir Your Most Obedt Servt Go: Washington" (letterpress copy, DLC:GW; LB, DLC:GW). For GW's purchase of Capt. John Rootes's warrants used by GW in the 1780s to buy land on the Little Miami, see John Page to GW, 14 Feb. 1774, and note 1 of that document. For more recent correspondence regarding GW's land on the Little Miami, see GW to Winthrop Sargent, 27 Jan. 1798, and GW to Rufus Putnam, 28 Jan. 1798.

Letter not found: from Elizabeth Willing Powel, 17 Nov. 1798. On 17 Nov. GW wrote Mrs. Powel: "I thank you for the information contained in your note of this date."

To Elizabeth Willing Powel

[Philadelphia]
My dear Madam   Saturday Forenoon Novr 17th 1798
I thank you for the information contained in your note of this date [1]—although I am not, nor have not been, under any apprehension of the desolating Fever.

I am to dine this day at Mr Willings, and if you are disengaged, will have the honor of drinking Tea with you in Third Street, afterwards.[2] I am always Your Most Obedt Obliged and Affecte Servant

Go: Washington

ALS, ViMtV.
1. Letter not found.
2. GW dined on this day with Thomas Willing (1731–1821), whom he had known since 1774. Willing was the former business partner of Robert Morris and the brother of Elizabeth Willing Powel, the widow of GW's old friend Samuel Powel and herself a close friend of the Mount Vernon family. GW does not refer in his diaries to visiting Mrs. Powel at this or any other time while in Philadelphia, but the notes that the two exchanged indicate that he probably did so a number of times (see GW to Elizabeth Willing Powel, 1, 4, 7, 9 Dec., and Mrs. Powel to GW, 3, 7 December).

From James McHenry

Sir,   War Department 19th November 1798.
The enclosures, have been furnished, by the Secretary of the Treasury, in pursuance of the request, contained in my letter to him, of the 14th instant (copy of which you are possessed of) and for the purposes therein mentioned.[1]

You are requested, if you wish for copies, of this view, of the Finances, of the United States, to cause the same to be taken, by a confidential person, and to return the Originals. I am Sir with the greatest respect your most obedient humble servant

James McHenry

LS, DLC: Hamilton Papers.

1. A copy of Wolcott's report on the financial status of the United States, dated 16 Nov., is in DLC:GW. It has been transcribed for CD-ROM:GW. For McHenry's letter to Wolcott of 14 Nov., see McHenry to GW, 14 Nov., n.16.

Letter not found: to John Lambert, 20 Nov. 1798. Lambert's letter to GW of 24 Oct.: "Answd Nov. 20 1798."

From Philip Schuyler

My Dear Sir　　　　　　　　　Albany [N.Y.] November 20th 1798

Amongst the regrets experienced from a series of ill health for some years past, and a partial deprivation of eye sight, it is not the least that Mrs Schuyler & myself were deprived of the pleasure of fulfilling the intention we had formed of paying our respects to you and your Amiable Lady at Mount Vernon, that peaceful retreat from which the nefarious conduct of the Government of France has drawn you, and again obliged you to embark on the busy scene of public life, a second time to save your country.

My Grandson Philip Church will have the honor to deliver this, he has determined on the pursuits of a military life in the Service of his native country, If adhereing to the principles inculcated by his parents, by his uncle Hamilton and myself, he shall render himself worthy of your countenance and Attention, permit me respectfully to solicit it for him.[1]

Mrs Schuyler Joins me in all those affectionate wishes for the health & felicity of you and Your Lady, which flow from the purest sources of the Human Heart. I am My Dear Sir Most unfeignedly and respectfully Your Obedient Servant

Ph: Schuyler

ALS, DLC:GW.

Philip John Schuyler (1733–1804), who in 1775 was one of the four major generals under GW, had resigned from the U.S. Senate in January 1798 because of ill health. He was married to Catherine Van Rensselaer Schuyler. One of their daughters, Elizabeth (1757–1854), was the wife of Alexander Hamilton and another, Angelica (1756–1815), was married to John B. Church (1750–1818). Philip (b. 1778), the son of Angelica and John B. Church, attended Eton for six years and then studied law at the Middle Temple in London. In January 1799 he was made a captain in the 12th Regiment of Infantry in the New Army and became aide-de-camp to his uncle Alexander Hamilton on 12 January.

1. Both of Philip Church's parents also wrote to GW, from New York on 14 November. Angelica Church wrote: "Let me request you to excuse a mother for giving to her son, an opportunity to gratify his admiration and to offer his respectful, Homege to the 'Father of his Country.' May he live Sir to merit your notice and the fondest wishes of his parents will then be realised" (DLC:GW). John B. Church's letter reads: "My Son Philip Church will have the Honor of presenting this Letter to your Excellency, he enters the Army under the Auspices of his Uncle who receives him in his Family; will you permit me to reccommend him to your Protection; I can safely vouch for his Integrity, Honor and Love of Truth, and I flatter myself that should an Opportunity offer under your Excellency's Command, he will conduct himself in a Manner to merit your Approbation and Esteem" (ViMtV).

GW sent to Philip Church on 4 Dec. the letters of that date which he had written in response to those from Philip's grandfather and parents. GW wrote Philip Church: "Sir, I beg leave to commit the enclosed letters to your care. If business, duty or inclination should ever call you into the State of Virginia, I shall be very happy to see you at Mount Vernon—the place of my retreat, being with esteem Sir Your most Obedt Hble Servt Go: Washington" (ALS, NjMoNP). GW's letter to John B. Church reads: "Sir Mr Church, your Son, did me the honor to present your favor of the 14th Ulto. His genteel & handsome appearance makes a favorable impression—and his constituting a part of General Hamilton's Military establishment is strongly indicative of his worth. These circumstances, with your recommendation of him, will ensure him every attention from me, that I can bestow with consistency. I have the honor to be Sir Your most Obedt Hble Servt Go: Washington" (ADfS, DLC:GW). He wrote a similar letter to Angelica Church: "Madam, For the honor I have received, in the very obliging and flattering sentiments transmitted in your letter of the 14th Ult., I pray you to accept all my gratitude and thanks.

"From the genteel, & handsome exterior of Mr Church (your Son) and the favorable report of his merits by Genl Hamilton, you have the most pleasing presages of his future usefulness & consequence; and as far as I can contribute thereto—consistently with my other duties, he may freely command me.

"Mrs Washington, was she here, would thank you herself, as I do in her behalf, for your kind remembrance of her, and family. The good wishes you are pleased to offer on my account, I reciprocate with the most respectful consideration; and have the honor to be Madam Your Most Obedient and Very Humble Servant Go: Washington" (ViU: Angelica Church Collection; ADfS, DLC:GW). GW's response to Philip Schuyler's letter reads: "My dear Sir, I have been honored with your letter of the 20th Ulto and congratulate you, very sincerely, on the favorable change you have lately experienced (as I have been informed) in your health.

"I wish it may be perfectly restored. I persuade myself, that it is unnecessary for me to add that, if health and other circumstances had enabled you & Mrs Schuyler to have visited Mrs Washington & myself at Mount Vernon, that it would have been considered as a most pleasing & flattering evidence of your regard. And the more so, as neither she nor I, ever expected to be more than 25 Miles from that retreat, during the remnant of our lives.

"But, strange to relate, here I am! Busied in scenes far removed, & foreign from any I had contemplated when I quitted the Chair of Government.

"Your Grandson, Mr Church, has all the exterior of a fine young man, and from what I have heard of his Intellects and Principles will do justice to, and reward the precepts he has received from yourself, his Parents and uncle Hamilton. So far then as my attentions to him will go—consistent with my other duties—he may assuredly count upon.

"I pray you to present me (and I am sure Mrs Washington would unite in them if she was here) to Mrs Schuyler in the most respectful terms. and let me pray you to be assured of the sincere esteem, regard & wishes of the most affectionate kind of Dear Sir Your most Obedient and Very Humble Servant Go: Washington" (ALS, CSmH; ADfS, DLC:GW).

Letter not found: from Alexander Addison, 21 Nov. 1798. GW wrote Addison on 6 Dec. 1798 that he had received "your favor of the 21st Ulto."

From Lawrence Lewis

My dear Sir,   Mount Vernon November 21st 1798

My Aunt has communicated to me, that part of your letter to her, wherein you kindly request to be rememberd to me, and at the same time appear to be at a loss to account for my absence at the time of your departure from this[1]—Let me assure you my dear Sir, to me it was a source of infinite regret that, indisposition that morning, was in some measure the cause of an appearance of neglect from me, and which deprived me of an opportunity of expressing my wishes for your safety, which was the sincere wish of my heart—Confind to my room, which is remote from the door which carriages drive up to, I did not hear its approach, therefore was not apprized of your departure untill some time after, nor did I expect you to have set off that morning so soon knowing it was your intention to proceed no farther than the City that day— Indisposition however should not have prevented my doing what was evidently my duty, had I not been led to believe, I should have been apprized of your setting off, by Mr Lear's saying when he left my room he should see me again before his departure, this amidst the hurry of business I suppose he forgot—If these circumstances combined can in any manner exculpate me from my appearance of neglect I shall be happy—and be assured my dear Sir, whenever I am intentionally neglectful, or fail in that respect so much the due of an indulgent Uncle and Aunt, I shall think a forfeiture of your friendship, and a dismission from your House (where tis my happiness to be) a punishment justly my due—I am sensible I possess too great a degree of diffidence, which often renders me awkward, and may be construed into inattention, or want of respect—But if I know my own heart, Sir, it proceeds from no such cause—How cheerfully would I devest my self of it—But time as yet has not been able to affect it, altho aided by my own exertions; but you my dear Sir must already have witnessed this defect of nature in me, and will from your indulgent disposition, make such allowances as it deserves.[2]

The arrival of Richard Parkinson, has I imagine been announced to you ere this, after the tedious passage of eleven weeks—On board Ship there was a number of Horses, of which eight or nine died on the passage tho I believe not all, the property of Parkinson; yet he appears to be a considerable looser—I am told the property is considered by the Capt. (i.e. the Horses Cattle and Hogs[)] as yours; and have actuly been shipt as such—Parkinson in frameing this tale, no doubt had his views of interest, knowing himself unable to pay the freight, and the consequence would be a detention of his property on board untill paid for, he deceitfully determine[d] to land the property under your name, well knowing when the deceit should be discovered, the Ship could only come at the freight, but through the tedious forms of the Law— I may judge too harshly of the man, but am strengthened in my opinion of him, from what Rawlings says who has just returned from bord the Ship, and confirms what I heard, that the property was considered as yours.[3]

The late warm weather created with us some uneasiness lest the fever shoul[d] again break out with violence, and render your situation painful and critical—but am happy to finde by the Gazettes our fears were groundless.

I believe you have been informed of my wish to have some appointment in the Army—young in the art of war, my views are by no means ambitious; to you I submit it, to place me in any situation, that in your judgment shall be best—should I be fortunate enough to obtain an appointment, I can affirm a full determination of doing my duty, for by so doing, only, can a Officer expect to gain respect.[4]

My health is much as it was when you left us, every now and then having a return of the ague, which prevents my gaining flesh or strength tho I am happy to informe you I am nearly restored to the perfect use of my eye. The family joins me in best wishes for your health, and safe returne—I am dear Uncle your affectionate nephew

Lawrence Lewis

ALS, PPRF.

1. Letter not found.

2. See GW's response, 2 December.

3. See GW's instructions to James Anderson regarding Richard Parkinson, 3 November.

4. GW wrote Bartholomew Dandridge on 25 Jan. 1799: "Lawrence Lewis is appointed a Captn in the Corps of light Dragoons; but before he enters the Camp of Mars, he is to engage in that of Venus with Nelly Custis, on the 22d of next month; they having, while I was at Philadelphia, without my having the smallest suspicion that such an affair was in agitation, formed their Contract for this purpose."

To Alexander Spotswood, Jr.

Dr Sir,   Philadelphia 22d Novr 1798

Your letter of the 13th instt enclosing a publication under the signature of Gracchus, on the Alien & Sedition Laws, found me at this place—deeply engaged in business.[1]

You ask my opinion of these Laws, professing to place confidence in my judgment, for the compliment of which I thank you. But to give opinions unsupported by reasons might appear dogmatical, especially, as you have declared that, Gracchus has produced "thorough conviction in your mind of the unconstitutionality, and inexpediency of the acts above mentioned." To go into an explanation on these points I have neither leizure nor inclination; because it would occupy more time than I have to spare.

But I will take the liberty of advising such as are not "thoroughly convinced" and whose minds are yet open to conviction, to read the peices, and hear the arguments which have been adduced in favor of, as well as those against the Constitutionality and expediency of those Laws, before they decide. And consider to what lengths a certain description of men, in our Country, have already driven, and seem resolved further to drive matters; and then ask themselves, if it is not time & expedient to resort to protecting Laws against aliens (for Citizens you certainly know are not affected by that Law) who acknowledge *no allegiance* to this Country, and in many instances are sent among us (as there is the best circumstantial evidence) for the *express purpose* of poisoning the minds of our people; and to sow dissentions among them; in order to alienate *their* affections from the Government of their choice, thereby endeavouring to dissolve the Union; and of course, the fair and happy prospects which were unfolding to our View from the Revolution—But, as I have observed before, I have no time to enter the field of Politicks; and therefore shall only add my best respects to the good family at New Post—and the assurances of being Dr Sir Your Very Hble Servant

Go: Washington

ADfS, NjP: deCoppet Collection; LB, DLC:GW. The differences between the two copies are almost entirely matters of punctuation and capitalization.

1. The letter has not been found; on 9 Dec. young Spotswood declared it to be a forgery, in these terms: "Your favor of the 22nd Ultimo, in answer to one of the 13th of the same, (Which from the signiture you have justly attributed to me) I have received—I now declare on my honor, and as I hope, (when I depart from this world of trouble) to enter the holy mansion of almighty God that the sd Letter, dated the 13th, bearing my signiture, is an infamous forgery, And that I never saw, or read, the publication under the signiture of Gracchus, nor did I ever know, that such a publication was in being, untell I received your favour; It gives me infinite pleasure, when I figure to myself from the import which your Letter bears, of the impropriety of the one receivd, by you, conceived to be an address of mine, that it might be personal regard alone, which could have induced you to condecend an answer—Which has afforded me, an opportunity, of makeing known to you, my sentiments, as being the reverse of that ungenerous Scrip, evidently calculated, to answer some ungenerous purpose, that I cannot divine—politicks which from the provoked circumstances of the present times, I may be induced to pay some attention to, *so far*, As may be necessary to form a just opinion, (are quite foreign to my present happy pursuits) and be assure'd, when I reflect upon the present contamination of principals, which pervades some parts of our southern Country, It endears to me, more, and more, that domestic repose, which you yourself have so justly caress'd; I am well apprised of the happy prospects which were to have been expected from the Resolution, as also the most principal attendant circumstances, and so far as the slight documents I have seen, authorizes me, I am convinced, that nothing but those constitutional principals, as maintained by the firmness, of some of our Worthy Citizens, who aided by public, and private virtue, and who have ever been under the

Just influence, of the support of Government, and cultivation of peace—possessing a determination at the same time not dareingly to be insulted, That has preserved us from being drawn into that Unhappy European conflict, Which we have so unjustly been invited, to participate in, and as yet have so wisely evaded—So far, have I erected a monument in my mind to such discription of Men. The Sedition, and Alien Laws, as being the offspring of necessity and safeguard of our Rights, I do, and ever have approved of, for should any discription of men, be induced to stir up dissentions in our Government, thereby, Alienating the affections of the people, from those rules of Civil Order, as prescribed, by general consent; and as a preservative of our Liberty, The plain principals of justice in my mind, *dictates* that some cure should be found for the disease; the necessity of the present ⟨*Area*⟩, demanding a direct, and immediate one, Which I hope will be found in those Laws—The above are the reflections of a calm, and undisturbed mind, And I trust, so long as my reason remains with me, and opposite oppinions not accompanyed with truth, I shall remain as I am, Leaving you to Judge the motives of that Letter I have in truth denied. . . .

"P.S. I will thank you to fo[r]ward me the forged Letter, with the assistance of my friends I may possib[l]y be able to fix it on the person who wrote it, present my respects to Mrs Washington" (ViMtV).

From Alexander Spotswood

Dear Sir   Newpost November 24 1798

For eight Weeks past, I have been constantly at home, engaged in Building a mill—and not Sending regularly to the post office—occasioned your favour of the 4th laying there Sometime before I got it—and a few days before I received it—I had dismissed Farril, for no other cause, than I found it impossible to Keep away his father and acquaintances from his house.[1]

he is strictly an honest man, neat in his person, fine tempered—and of a Robust constitution—he has signed the Articles; one he keeps—the other is herewith inclosed—for makeing corn and wheat—I never had a better overseer—and I hope his Faults which I apprized you of; will be remedied by the Articles which he has signed.

on my return home, I found all my Honey locust trees cut down to three—one of which did not bear, for what cause I know not; The other two bore well—the pods are all gathered & housed, and so soon as they are Sufficiently dry, I will have them threshed and the Seed forwarded—under these trees may be got from 1000 to 1500 Sets from twelve to 18 Inches in higth—I mention this, in case you think it worth while to Send for them, that you may now prepare your ditch for there reception in March next—which I am told is the Month they are Set in Europe.

I have cut and cured a large Stock of the bottle brush grass—and Sweeter hay I never made—by *handfuls* I have tried several *horses*, who are now fed on fine green fodder, and they all eat it heartily—and Such is my prepossession in favour of this grass, that I am determined to Sow two acrces of rich land this next fall with the Seed—and should it really answer for hay, it will be a great source of convenience to the farmer—as the time for its cuting is about the last of August; when corn & wheat harvest is done with.

I take the liberty of mentioning Mr John Crump, who wishes to enter into the Standing army—he is 21 years of age—has been brought up in the Mercantile line, and I am assured by Mr Green, (the gentleman I mentioned to you in a former letter) that he is a young man, of fine moral character—and has constantly been a Strong goverment man.[2]

Mrs Spotswood & my family desire there best regards to you Mrs Washington Miss custis & Washington as well as dr Sir yr affect. Hble St

A. Spotswood

if there is no impropriety, I could wish with your leave to assure Mr Green of his appointment as a captain that he may have a little Notice to close his mercantile transactions—whenever you see this gentleman—I am Sure he will attract yr Notice.

ALS, CSmH. Spotswood wrote on the cover: "in the generals absence to be opened by Mr [James] Anderson."

1. By the terms of the articles of agreement entered into on 24 Nov. by Roger Farrell with James Anderson acting on behalf of GW, witnessed by Alexander Spotswood, Farrell agreed "to serve the said General Washington in the capacity of an Overseer at the Mansion house of Mountvernon for one Year, from & after the first day of January next And during that term of service He will conduct Himself with the utmost Integrity, Sobriety, Industry, & Zeal in the management of the various things put under His care, never absenting Himself (sundays & Holydays excepted) without the permission of the said General Washington, or His manager attending constantly, with some one, or other part of the Hands put under Him, whenever that it happens they are working in separate places, which hands Are, the Waggoner Carter Horse & Cattle ⟨feeders⟩, Also a few (mostly Women) who will be employed in various Works; And the Ditchers, who will be employed in cuting Ditches & planting of Hedges to raise live fences, Whose work He is to mark off, And to be Accountable for their performing their respective parts thereof. In the Fishing season to attend constantly day & night on the Negroes that will be employed thereat, causing them [to] do their respective dutys

in Hauling for And in curing & Packing of the Fish, And in Harvest attend to the cuting, curing and Stacking of Hay in its season, And with the hands under Him assist in the cuting of Grain on the other Farms as there will be little made on the Farm at Mount Vernon. That in the most Particular maner He will attend to the whole Stock of Horses, Mules, Jeannies, Cows, & Sheep as well as the Stallion & Jacks, measuring to each their Portion of Grain, And attend to their being fed with it, Attend to the Hay allowed them, that they have enough and that there are no Waste, And constantly keep a supply of Fat Mutton, and Lamb & Veals in their seasons for the use of the said General Washingtons Table, always keeping the Mansion House fully supplyed in firewood, And keep in good Order the Whole fence, surrounding the Estate—and those at Mount Vernon House, reporting to the Manager what is wrong in these, or any thing under Him, that steps may be taken to recetify these Errors, And that He will at all times be ready to go by Land, or Water (not exceeding the bounds of the River Potomack) upon the business of the said General Washington when directed thereto by Him, or His Manager, He also agrees to discountenance Company resorting to Him, and returning of Visits to others, His own relatives excepted, And upon His entry to the business an Inventory will be put into His hands, of all the Goods, and Tools which will be committed to His care, For the Which He hereby agrees to give receipt to be accountable for the producing of these Goods, & Tools every three Months, or rendering to the Manager a Satisfactory account where they are, or what has become of them, And every Saturdays evening He is to give in a Written report to the Manager, what way the hands have been employed, And what Work they have performed, the State of the Stock, and what Increase or Decrease if any And Finally that He will attend to and strickly Obey the Orders of the said General Washington or His Manager respecting the above & aforesaid particular⟨ly⟩ any other part of the business in the Which He will be employed ⟨*mutilated*⟩" (PHi: Society Collection). In return GW promised "to pay, or cause to be paid unto the said Roger Farril for one Years service One hundred & Thirty three Dollars Thirty three & one third Cents, And find Him in Board, bed Lodging & washing."

2. See Spotswood to GW, 16 Sept., n.5.

From John Gerard William De Brahm

Respected Friend   26d XI mo. 1798

I feel a deep concern to revere, yea Love Eminent Men, who under the discipline of divine Goodness can be most Virtuously instrumental, what they cannot be in their own exertion for the good of Men, whom God does all the good they hinder him not, a drop of their blood is too precious in his Sight as to aprove of its Spilling, he preserves Men in most tender Love.

finding, that the Seed of the fever like embers under the Ashes conceiles in Some buildings and furnitures.

I under discipline of divine mercy made willing to do all good I can, hurry to Supplye the[e] with a Souvereign preservative, from which (tho by mercy kept from common complaints free) yet in my twelfth climacteric created Such infirmities, which are passd remedy, receive comfort from what I inclose in two Vials.[1] I pray God to preserve and bless thee am Respectfully

J: G: W: de Brahm

ALS, DLC:GW.

The polymath John Gerard William De Brahm (1717–1799) is best known for his work as a military engineer and geographer in colonial Georgia, South Carolina, and East Florida. In 1751 he led a party of German Protestants to Ebenezer in Georgia. He soon thereafter was sought out by the governments of South Carolina and Georgia for his talents as a military engineer, and in 1764 the British government made him the surveyor general of the southern district of North America. During the Revolution he remained loyal to Britain, and in 1777 he went to live in London. After his return to America in 1791, he and his third wife, Mary Drayton Fenwick De Brahm of Charleston, S.C., lived in Philadelphia, and De Brahm, who became a Quaker, devoted his writing to alchemy and mystical philosophy (De Vorsey, *De Brahm's Report*, 7–59).

1. While in England De Brahm wrote Queen Charlotte offering to send her an "admirable salt" for George III's illness (ibid., 56).

From James McHenry

Sir   War Department Novr 29th 1798

The enclosed papers contain the proceedings of two Military Courts, lately held at the city of Trenton, state of New Jersey, pursuant to warrants from the Secretary of War.[1]

The dispersed state of the troops in our western country rendered it difficult to collect a sufficient number of officers at any of the posts to compose a General Court Martial and impossible to do so without injury to the service, it therefore, appeared proper when Captain Lewis was arrested in the city of Philadelphia to issue a warrant for convening a Court at the same place to investigate, try and determine upon the charge exhibited against him. Other inducements to this measure were that the cause of arrest originated at Philadelphia, the party and prosecutor were both on the spot, as it was probable, were also the witnesses to prove any facts that might be denied, and these not military persons: and it was known that officers sufficient to form the court were present, or in the vicinity. A Warrant accordingly issued from the War office on the 24th of July last for constituting a general court Martial consisting of five, the smallest number of Members allowed by the articles of War, to meet at the city of Philadelphia to try and determine upon the charge and specifications thereof, exhibitted against Captain Lewis, as well as such others as might be, in proper times, specified and produced to the court, and such sentence pass on the premises, as by the rules and articles of War shall be authorised.

Agreeably to the Warrant, the court met, and proceeded in the trial. Captain Mitchel however one of the members of the court, became indisposed and afterwards died, which reducing the number of members below five the lowest number allowed to constitute a general court Martial, the court was considered as dissolved.

There being no result from the former trial, the same reasons caused it to be thought proper to issue a second Warrant from the War office on the first day of October last constituting a general court martial, de novo, for the trial of Captain Thomas Lewis, to consist of a full court of thirteen members, if so many could be collected at the city of Trenton, New Jersey, and such sentence pass as may be authorized by the rules and articles of War.

Of this court nine members, including the President, convened at Trenton on the 20th of October ultimo; the other members, from various causes could, or did not attend. The Prisoner challenged one, and in his place Lieutenant Massey who had just arrived from Michilimakinac was substituted.

The court sat from the 20th to the 30th of October inclusive and on the latter day passed sentence of acquittal.

This case is submitted respectfully to you Sir, with a view to obtain the opinion of yourself and also of Major Generals Hamilton and Pinckney whether under all circumstances, the President can consistent with that due subordination which is necessary in all armies, and which the practice of challenging superior officers, for any cause, may have a tendency to interrupt and destroy, give, to the sentence of the court the sanction of his unqualified approval? If the opinion be in the negative, then, whether it would not be attended with beneficial consequences that the Presidential sanction be qualified with a reprimand of Captain Lewis, and a denunciation of the practice of Duelling, particularly of challenging superior officers.

It ought to be stated that Captain Lewis was at the time of the

transaction which occasioned the charge against him, on furlough, and that Major Cushing was also not on actual duty. Also,
that the charge is grounded on, and is in the precise words of the
20th article of the appendix, and not on the 2nd article of the 7th
section of the rules and articles of War relative to challenges.

The other proceedings are those of a court of Inquiry, which
met at the city of Trenton on the 18th of October ulto to examine,
inquire and report ⟨*illegible*⟩ing certain allegations against Edward
Miller Captain in the second regiment of Infantry in the service of
the United States, and continued, by adjournment, to the 26th of
the same month, inclusive.

Captain Miller was, during the revolutionary wars, a meritorious
serjeant, and at its conclusion Serjeant Major of the third Connecticut regiment, and as such, he was entitled to and has drawn
the continental bounty in land. In 1791 he was commissioned as
an Ensign, and has since risen by grades at promotion, to the rank
he now holds. He is understood uniformly, to have conducted
himself as a brave and vigilant officer in the field, and to have been
always ready for any duty however hazardous, and frequently employed on such—to have behaved well in the unfortunate affair
under General St Clair, and also in the successful action with the
Indians under General Wayne. He had been ordered to recruit his
company and when he had nearly completed this service he was
ordered with his men from Middle town, Connecticut, to Philadelphia.

A settlement of his accounts, for the recruiting service, being
necessary, a previous muster of the recruits was directed, when several of the men were mustered out. and the accountant of this
Department by letter to the Secretary of War dated the 3rd of July
last reported alligations of irregularities in the conduct of Captain
Miller, and referred to him to determine whether the bounty paid,
and charged by Captain Miller to recruits, now reported to have
been unfit for service at the time of inlistment, should not be deducted from his account. The settlement of Captain Miller's accounts was suspended, his pay has been withheld from [him], and
the pressure of the necessities of a large family consisting of a wife
and eight or nine children becoming distressing he, by letter to
the Secretary, dated Trenton September the 11th last requested
that a court of inquiry might be ordered, to examine into his
conduct.

A warrant issued from the War Office, on the 16 day of October last, authorizing and especially requiring the court of Inquiry, strictly to examine into the allegations contained in the letter from the accountant, dated the 3rd of July last, and to report a State of all the circumstances, and evidence which should appear to them, together with their opinion thereon. The court have not reported these opinions so fully as was expected. It was expected that they would have examined the conduct of Captain Miller on the principle of Honor, and if, notwithstanding some irregularities, Captain Miller, as an officer, and an associate for themselves, could have been excused on the score of misapprehension, inadvertence, or otherwise; and the public indemnified by a competent retribution, on his part, that they should have so reported.

Your opinion, Sir, with that of the Major Generals is likewise requested, whether, consistent with the regularity, œconomy and strict obedience, to orders and inscriptions, indispensable to the service, Captain Miller can, under all circumstances, be continued in the service, upon his remunerating the public, out of his pay, for the losses sustained by his conduct? Whether it will be more proper to revoke his commission, or to order a general court Martial to decide finally on his case. I have the honor to be with very great respect Sir, your most Obd. Hb. st

James McHenry

LS, DLC:GW; LS (letterpress copy), DLC: James McHenry Papers.

1. A report of 2 July 1798 from McHenry to John Adams regarding this affair is in DLC: McHenry Papers; a page of printed letters between Thomas Lewis and T. H. Cushing is also in the McHenry Papers, filed under July 1798. Charles Cotesworth Pinckney replied on behalf of GW on 14 Dec.: "Dear Sir, I am directed by the Commander in Chief to inform you that he has perused & considered the proceedings of the Court of Enquiry on Capn Miller, and of the Court Martial on Capn Lewis, and is of opinion that a Court Martial should be ordered on the former. with regard to the latter he thinks the Court Martial could not do otherwise than acquit him, he certainly had not behaved in a scandalous & infamous manner unbecoming an Officer & a Gentleman, but the Commander in Chief is also of opinion that there was much reprehensible impropriety in his Conduct; for tho it appears from the Evidence that Major Cushing had not behaved in that open candid manner which should characterize the conduct of an Officer, yet he had done nothing which deserved the term 'villanous interference' or which could justify Capn Lewis in sending the message he did to his superior Officer, & particularly without requiring a previous explanation. Opprobrious language should never be used from one Officer to another, and in services where duelling is connived at, it is with a view to introduce urbanity of behaviour in the intercourse between Officers. The Commander in Chief thinks

that at the same time the sentence of the Court should be approved & confirmed, that the conduct of Capn Lewis deserves animadversion" (DLC:GW).

Candidates for Army Appointments from Virginia

[Philadelphia, November 1798]

EDITORIAL NOTE

George Washington, Alexander Hamilton, and Charles Cotesworth Pinckney spent six weeks in Philadelphia in November and December 1798, formulating their recommendations to the president for raising and incorporating the twelve additional regiments for which Congress had provided in July 1798 in the "Act to augment the Army of the United States, and for other purposes." [1] Although there were many other issues relative to recruiting, equipment, and distribution of the army facing GW and his two major generals, the evaluation and recommendation of candidates for the officer corps from the various states proved perhaps the most time-consuming. Secretary of War James McHenry furnished them with lists of the men who had applied for commissions, along with any letters of recommendation. GW, for his part, brought with him lists of candidates from Virginia, North Carolina, South Carolina, Georgia, Kentucky, and Tennessee, as well as pertinent letters. [2]

In a series of meetings beginning as early as 13 Nov., GW, Hamilton, and Pinckney reviewed these lists and letters of application and recommendation. They made lists of the candidates in each state for the various ranks in the New Army and annotated the lists with comments on the qualifications of the individual candidates. Their lists of candidates in eleven of the states have been published in Syrett, *Hamilton Papers*, 22:89–146, 270–312, 320–39. The list for Virginia, which was not included in the *Hamilton Papers*, is printed here. GW's acquaintance with or knowledge of many of the applicants from Virginia makes it probable that he was the source for many of the remarks on the candidates recorded in the Virginia list.

The list of Virginians recommended for commissions in its original form is nineteen pages long, and it is arranged roughly in columns. The first column lists the names of candidates, usually numbered on the basis of a list of applicants. [3] Notations as to age and county of residence often appear underneath the names. The second column contains short summaries of the letters of recommendation, when they existed, for each candidate. Commentaries by GW and others on the character and potential service of the men often appear in the second column but at times are appended to the first column or placed in a third column. Marginal notations appear frequently throughout the list. Most of the document is in Pinckney's hand, though some entries and many annotations, particularly those relating to the opinions of Edward Carrington and William Heth, were written by Hamilton.

Upon concluding their deliberations on 13 Dec., the generals submitted to McHenry their recommendations for appointment of officers in all of the states except Connecticut, the Carolinas, and Georgia.[4] On the president's instructions, McHenry sent copies of the lists of nominees to other members of the cabinet for their perusal. McHenry deleted from the lists the names of those who did "not deserve to be appointed," as well as the names of others who declined their nominations. McHenry then submitted the revised lists to Adams on 29 Dec., who in turn placed them before the Senate on 31 December.[5] After learning of the Senate's actions on the nominations, McHenry wrote to GW on 22 Jan. enclosing a list of those whom the Senate had rejected. The process of notifying and securing acceptances from nominees for commissions lasted through the spring of 1799, during which time GW and McHenry corresponded about problems that arose. On 21 May McHenry sent GW a final revised list of appointees from Virginia.[6]

1. 1 *Stat.* 604–5.

2. See GW to McHenry, 13 Nov. 1798, n.1.

3. See note 1 to this document.

4. See GW to McHenry, 13 Dec. (first letter), and note; for the selection of officers from the Carolinas and Georgia, see GW's letters of 28 Dec. to William Richardson Davie and to William Washington.

5. See McHenry to GW, 28 Dec., n.3.

6. For correspondence between the two in the first half of 1799 relating to appointments in the New Army, see especially McHenry to GW, 10 and 21 Jan., 31 Mar., 29 April, 21 May and enclosure, and GW to McHenry, 28 Jan., 4 Feb., 25 Mar., 7 April (first letter), 23 April, 5, 13 May, and the notes to these documents.

x A John Cropper +   These old officers order of
x B Jonathan Clark +   merit by Heth &
x C Robert Porterfield +   Carrin[gton]
x D Joseph Swearingen +
x E David Stephenson +
x f John Blackwell +
   g Wm Bentley
   h Otway Bird
John Heth (now in service) Carrington
   thinks him worth considering for
   Majority
1. A. Gibson mentioned for Majority now
   in service distinguished at Fort
   Recovery
2. Laurence Butler Major

Virginia

Lt Colonels

No. 3 William Watkins
Halifax
officer last War

Letter ill written
no recommendation

4. John M. Willis
Fredericksburgh
officer last War
Oldest Major in
Virginia line

unquestionable bravery & great popularity
but a great *Gambler* & weighs *4 or 500* lb.
Good for nothing *C. & H.*

14. James Maxwell
Berkely County
officer last War

Morgan   active officer in the
Militia understands tactics   *Attention*
offers himself for immediate service

22. Thomas Finn

Mr Evans says served in the Artillery during
last War as Captn Lieutt with Coll Carrington to whom he says his worth is well
known. Desirous of joining the service of
his Country against any Nation who wishes
to go to War with us. Of great bravery
Quare politics?

24. Thomas
Mathewes

wishes to be Inspector General—will not
serve under his present rank viz. Brigr
Genl.

26. Thomas Parker[1]
of Frederick
37 Years old
recommended very
strongly
by Genl Marshall
very strong
recommendations
from others.
Expects a regiment

5th on the list of Majors Carrington & Heath.
as good an officer as any of his rank last
War—recommended by Josiah Parker. Genl
Morgan from 80 to 120 speaks very
highly of him—uniformly federal—Genl Lee
says he knows no man who would make a
better Colonel of a regiment—respectable
connections—property—⟨H.⟩ Marshall
recommends him—Walter Jones also—Atty
Genl recommends him for a regiment.

Majors

1. Richard B. Lee
Presly Thornton
Northumberland

provisional army
Native American formerly in British service
but refused to come to America—a man of
great worth & probably well *qualified*

50. Richard Black-
burne
Prince William

now Capt. of Artillery desirous of transfer
to Infantry as Major not otherwise.
B. Washington strongly recom.

15. Nathaniel Henry
Shepherds Town
Berkely officer in
N.Y. line to nearly
end of the War

Swearingen   speaks well
   Ed. O. Williams—highly
   Morgan—served with reputation *last war*
   thinks him *judicious—sober*
   J. Maxwell—strict Disciplinarian pretty
   respectabl.   not worthy

129. Thomas Tinsley
Hanover
Now Col. of Militia

Evans   desires command of Regiment good
   information respectable character & friend
   to Govt

93. James Baytop [2]
Gloucester
officer Last War—
Captn

Evans   man of good information &
   respectability—middle aged—wishes in the
   immediate army but will accept in the
   Provisional. 6th on the list of Majors
   Carrington & Heth

119. Samuel Marsh
of Norfolk
serves for the
Provisional Army

Evans—native of Connecticut bred to law
   Brigade Inspector so far as observation
   goes—decent Gentlemanlike & prudent
   —disciplinarian recommended by Coll Parker
   & officers of Brigade.

⟨*illegible*⟩ Thomas
   Finn
⟨*illegible*⟩ *last War*
20. Samuel Tinsley

Evans—barely mentions
   ⟨other Letter⟩ man of *great bravery*
   see T. Finn on other side
Evans—was a captain of Infantry wishes to be
   Major of Artillery

151. [Benjamin]
   Graves
Norfolk

recommended by Josiah Parker for a Majority
   in *provisional* army—good character—
   Cap⟨tn⟩ of State Troops last War— Quare
   Politics

35. John Baylor Arm-
   stead [3]
Loudoun County

will not accept of an appointment inferior to
   a Majority in Infantry or Captcy in Cavalry
   —on the western expedition was aid to Genl
   Morgan—active, & respectably connected—
   recommended by genl Marshall—R. B. Lee—
   Leven Powell—Captn Parker—wishes to serve
   in the regt which may be given to Thomas
   Parker—Friend to the measures of
   Government—very repectable.

51. Wm Bentley [4]
Powetan
mentioned by Carring-
ton & Heath as 7th in
merit for *Lt Col.*
55. Wm Munroe

recommended strongly by Govr Wood—served 7
   years as Captn in the revolutionary War.
   his regt of Militia well disciplined—a
   friend of order & the Constitution of U.S.
   certainly Major perhaps Colonel
Genl Morgan says he served the whole of the
   War, not with him, but is highly spoken of.

59. Thos Richardson
Hanover

   Nothing
      worse C. & H.

62. John Tayloe — Served as Captn of Calvary in the western
Expedition—large fortune federal, amiable;
very respectable as Major—wishes the Cavalry.

65. Otway Bird — wishes Brigade or regt if consistant with
holding his civil office. Carrington &
Heth 8th in scale of merit

74. Roger West
Fairfax County — Coll Fitzgerald—Mr Ludlow Lee—Man of
Fortune—Father of a Family—Major of
Militia—Coll Sims differed from him in
political sentiments, but recommends him
—Unblemished Character—strong Military
ardour. Wishes to command a regiment *in
the provisional army*—Mr Lee the Atty Genl
says he is in prime of Life & well qualified to command a Regt

Field Officers

125. Wm Campbell
Orange County
4th on the list of
Majors Carrington &
Heth. — wishes to be Lieutt Coll Served 6 years
during the War—recommended by Genl
Stevens. Was on the Western Expedition—
federal—Middle aged—recommended by Genl
Lee as Field Officer.

97. John Stith [5]
Brunswick — Brave active & meritorious Officer—was Captn
last War recommended by Govr Wood—federal
—A field Officer—appointment in
provisional army

117. Hugh Holmes
Winchester — Will not accept lower than a Majority recommended by the Atty Genl for that commis-
sion. opposed to some of the measures of
Government C. & H.

99. Robert Beale [6]
Maddison County
Third on list of
Majors
Carrington & Heth — Served from 1776 to the end of the War—
served as Captn expects Majority recommend-
ed by Genl Morgan, & Genl *Marshall*—not
very strongly.

83. Churchill Jones — recommended by Genl White
84. John Watts [7]
Bedford County — recommended by Genl White—*Heth & Carrington*
well intitled to first rank in Virgina
Quota of cavalry if not in U. States—C. & H.

162. Thomas Buckner — No testimonials.
159. Daniel Broad-
head — Taken Prisoner at fort Washington—served in
Pennsylvania line—Man of honour—intelli-
g⟨ent—⟩active—hopes for a Majority at
least—Does not appear to have served after
his captivity—respectable

85. Larking Smith — recommended by Genl White decided enemy of
the Govermt C. & H.

133. Joseph Forman

Friend to the Government—recommended by Mr Fitzhugh—Quare is he of Virginia?

181. Thomas Hoard
Caroline County
1oth on list captains
Carrington & Heth
backward

recommended by Generals Lee & Spotswood distinguished himself last War—in prime of life—excellent citizen & warmly attached to his Government.

158. Simon Morgan
Fauquier
Captain

adjutant General of Virginia—officer in the last war—cool & intrepid—rallied his regt when a subaltern at German Town—shot through the body bravely fighting at Eutaw recommended by Genl Marshall.

175. Elias Parker
Petersburgh
Lieutenant

served in the artillery & Infantry with fair reputation in the last war—in the Massachusetts line—Certificate from Genl Knox.

Capts.

Presly Thornton
John Stith
2. William K. Blue[8]
Berkly County
Lt of *Western Army*
Resigned

desires a Commission wishes to command a batalion Bu[shro]d Washington—excellent heart and as he is informed was a good officer
D. Holms—from his general character is qualified   Thinks himself intitled to a Majority will accept an *old* Captaincy. *Inquire*

see Lieutenants[9]
13. Daniel Ball
Manchester
Lt last War

D. Holms—desirous of a Commissin
Carrington recommends good officer & good citizen   Marshall—*thinks favourably of him*
5th on the list of Lieutenants Carrington & Heth   *Respectable*

16. George Tate
Berkley
Shepherdstown

Swearingen   J. Maxwell Speaks well—Genl Morgan writes strongly in his favour—3

17. Josiah Thornburgh
Berkeley—do
18. James Maxwell
Berkley
Martinsburgh

Morgan speaks well of him—now capt. of Militia—has instructed himself in tactics Maxwell—well—*well enough*
Col. Maxwell speaks favourably of him   [Not much]

19. Robert Gustin
Bath Berkeley

Morgan Foederalist & man of good character   Not much

21. Samuel J. Winston
Hanover

Capt. or Lieutenancy
    Col. Tinsley recommends & evans supports
    young Gentleman much respected & of good
    principles

23. John Hardiman

Evans barely mentions   officer during last
    War —acted as Major—Mr King says valuable
    Quare.

25. Asa Bacon
of Leesburgh

a Man of science—persecuted for federalism.
    native of Connecticutt—unites science,
    sense integrity spirit & patriotism accord-
    ing to the Letters of Nathan Smith & John
    Allen. In the Connecticut List—Captain.

27. John Stewart [10]
Richmond

wishes a Captaincy of Cavalry—no recommenda-
    tions.   Good for nothing *C. & H.*

29. William Armstead
Prince William

Desires a Captaincy of Cavalry—no vouchers—
    doubt his politics C. & H.

30. Charles Shackle-
ford
Culpepper

a young man pretty well recommended *perhaps
    a Lieutenant.*

32. Robert Gregg
Culpepper

a Captain in the Pennsylvania Line in the
    Revolutionary War. Ten years residence in
    Virginia will serve as Captn in Cavalry or
    Major in Infantry—recommended by Coll
    Jameison & Genl Stevens—worth &
    respectability.

36. John Davidson
Richmond
First on the list of
Capts. Carrington &
Heth qualified for any
promotion.

native of Pennsylvania—recommended by Mr
    Hopkins as one who will be an ornament to
    the army & fine supporter of his Countrys
    rights & a friend to its government—30
    years old—active & strong. respectable.

50. Philip Lightfoot
Culpepper

Lived 10 years with Coll Jameison strict
    honour & may be confided in—Friend to
    Government. recommended by Genl Marshall &
    Posey & Major Day & Coll Stevens & Jameison
    very strong

96. James Duncanson
Culpepper

very respectably as Lt
    Jameison Stephens, Posey

43. Charles Fenton
    Mercer
22 years old
Fredericksburgh

a young Gentleman—recommended by Dr Smith of
    Princeton as a young Gentleman of Talent,
    probity industry, & good Politics—Also by
    Genl Lee—very respectable, Captain or
    Lieutenant

44. John Reynolds
Norfolk formerly
of Connecticut

Stability & good morals—commands a Militia Company—federal—expects further recommendations. *good for nothing C. & H.*

45. Daniel C. Lane
Loudoun County
25 years of age

Thinks he can easily raise a Company Captn of Grenadiers in the Regt—recommended by Mr R. B. Lee & Dr Stewart—active & of sound political sentiments—happy to see such men com.

48. David Shields
Rockbridge County
Dudley Odlin
Alexandria

Mr Holmes recommends him as Captn
Antifoederal
formerly of Exeter in Connecticut—will not do here.

56. Samuel Turner

Nothing strong.

64. Bathurst Jones
Hanover

Doubtful

66. Wm Glassoll

good for nothing *C. & H.* Federal—brave but intemperate—said to be reforming.
exclusively provisional army

68. Robert   Fitzgeral[d]
   Young   Simms
Alexandr.   Craig

Young Gentleman desirous of serving his Country from zeal & activity can raise troops will do honor to his Country wishes to be *Major* or 1st Captn *in the provisional army*

69. George Hite
Berkeley
Lt last War in
dragoons wounded
MGill—Genl Lee
Theo Lee
very strong

till lately violent antifederalist now very different Wm Heath—*very brave* & deserving of a *Troop* or *Company*—noble minded—& of different politics from *Rutherford*.
Holmes—*valuable Citizen* military merit
R. Page—possessed eminently of military qualities
Thurston *excellent officer* and a Gentleman.
⟨M. Guine⟩—his military talents entitle him to a Majority
Ths Parker—*peculiar* merit—respectable *family* Gentleman
Genl Marshall [   ]

73. Archibald
   Randolph[11]
About 26 years old

Strongly recommended by Mr B. Washington—Captn of Cavalry. perhaps Lieutt—was aid to Genl Morgan on the Western Expeditn

76. Lemuel Bent
lived 8 years in
Virginia Alexandria
born in Massachusetts

—Coll Fitzgerald—Mr Ames recommend him—
Captn of Militia.
Perhaps Lieutenant

87. Henry Percy
Alexandria

lived 6 years in Virginia—acquainted with
maneuvring a company—served through
the revolutionary War—federal—Coll Sims
says a valuable officer—Good Captain.

81. Garnett Peyton
Stafford Country

federal—good military genius—*strong* Wishes
Captn in the Cavalry—or 1st Leutt in do or
Captn in Infantry—Courageous, Sober discreet, stout popular generally beloved—
warmly recommended by genl Lee.

86. Richard Hill
good for nothing
C. & H.

Served in Harrisons Artillery—wishes a Capcy
in Artillery—no recommendation among his
Papers.

91. Wm Campbell
son of Coll Arthur
Campbell
Washington

Desires a Captaincy—Member of the Legislature of Virginia—His conduct that of a
gentleman—federal.

98. Booker Pegram
Dinwiddie County

recommended to Govr Wood by persons he can
depend upon—Quare Family Antifœderal his
own politics unknown otherwise worthy of
notice C. & H.

116. John Koontz

not recommended

100. James Ware

recommended as a man of good Character not
been in service—Quare politics?

105. Edmund Taylor

Served in the Western Army—expects Majority
but will serve as Captn recommended by
Genls Morgan & Marshall & Captn Parker

101. Patrick Daug-
herty[12]
Frederick County
12th on the list of
Carrington & Heth

Captn Parker says he is an amiable Character
& could soon raise his men—not been in
service.

126. Francis Fouchee
Northumberland County

wishes not to except any thing inferior to a
Captain. amiable—active mind & stout body
—according to Genl Lee—refers to testimonials not before us said to be in secretary
of Wars office—Inquire.

127. John Dowdall
Winchester

very little said of him.

74. Francis Thornton
Near Fredericksburgh

recommended by Genls Lee, Spotswood & many others warmly for the *Provisional* Army as Captain—Connections very respectable & of ample fortune. federal principles.

180. John Greene

Warmly recommended for Captn by Genl Lee, Spotswood & others—strongly federal—a very fine young fellow.

143. Richard Chinn
Loudohn County

respectable—Captain Thos Parker warmly recommends him. If he can get a Capcy his company will enlist.

145. Jesse Sims

Serjeant last War—Hurt if not made Captn —No.

149. Thomas Wilson
Mecklenburgh
County

wishes Captaincy in *the provisional* army—The Marshall of Virginia recommends him strongly.

153. Laurence Wash-
ington
King George

recommended by Genl Lee Captn perhaps Lieutt in Cavalry.

156. Beverley Robert-
son
King Wm County

federal—sober & esteemed recommended by Genl Young.

159. James Caldwell
28 years old
Ohio County

respectable—federal.

163. Isaac Andrews

no testimonials

164. John Rose
Amherst County

Young Gentleman—good Character & family— recommended by Mr Ludwell Lee Quare politics.

165. Gustavus B.
Wallace

recommended by Brigr *Genl Washington* Educated at Princeton—good character well looking—cannot find any Letters concerning him.

170. Robert King
Hanover

active, intelligent spirited recommended by Genl Marshall.

172. Wm C. Carter
Albemarle
or Amherst

respectable & well recommended—perhaps provisional

173. Laurence Lewis
30 years of age
Frederick County

very respectable—aid to Genl Morgan Captn of Cavalry.

176. Thomas Turner
King George
25 years old

unblemished reputation—ardent patriotism— federal—strict honour—popular strongly recommended—Captn of Cavalry perhaps—if not, wishes majority in Infantry voted with the Democratic assembly last time now sup- ported by Federal party, General C. & H.

182. Martin Tapscott
Stafford

Friend to Government—*good man* recommended as
  Captn by Genl Lee.

Edmund Clark
Spotsylvania

Eleventh on the list of *Carrington & Heth*

168. Robert Gregg
Culpepper
officer last War
Capt.

Colo. Jameison—brave Officer & worthy
  independent Citizen—willi[n]g to take Capt.
  of Caval[r]y or Major of Regt

Lieutenants

5. James James
P. William County

Atty G.—gentleman of good *character* & *behaviour army* or navy　Inquire

6. Gerard Roberts
York Town
probably private
or N. C. officer
officer in West
Expedition

Lee—agrees with Marshall
  Marshall Evans.
  His own letter　*very well.*
  Attenti⟨on⟩ as Ensign

7. William Bouyer
Green Briar

8. John G. Brown*
Augusta

9. Jams Brown
Green Briar

10. Michael Flinn
Green Briar

Alfred Moore
not much
*son of Col
S. Brown

Boyer & Brown well known to him
active young men & doubts not will
be found qualified

Brown recommended by Mr Harper & Genl Black-
  burne
The others knows only from information.

J. ⟨Skiles⟩
Tinsley
good man

*young man of good behaviour
Browne of *respectable* connections
and good character can recruit
good men Qr.　Browne stand
pretty well as Lt or *Ensign*

11. William Potts
Petersburgh

Lt in provisional army will accept ensigncy
  Letter pretty *well*　*No recommendation*
  5th Ensign on list of Carrington & Heth

152. Brewer Goodwin
  Junr
Isle of Wight

respectable connections attached to the
  Government perhaps Lieutenant recommended
  by Josiah Parker.

28. Robert Brook[13]
King Wm County
resident of
Philadelphia

worth & amiable Character Govr Wood recommends him as Lieutt of Cavalry—good understanding, spirit activity & attachment
to his Country recommended by Genl Marshall
Mr Burrell, Mr Griffin very respectable

31. Charles Tutt Culpepper	young Gentleman—an only Son—applies with cons[en]t of his Father respectable connexions—fair reputation recommended by genls Marshall Lee Stevens Posey & Coll Jameison —& Mr Williams. Attached to Government —well recommended—a Lieutenancy in Cavalry or Infantry.
49. Thomas Jameison Culpepper	a first Lieutt in State artillery now— respectable family—recommended by genl Stevens.
33. James Tutt Junr Culpepper	wishes Lieutcy in Cavalry—a young man of respectable connections—tolerably recommended
34. Wm D. Clopton New Kent County	recommended by his Uncle—18 years of age. Badly recommended C. & H.
37. Robert Carrington[14] Richmond	a near relation of Coll Carrington wishes to be appointed Lieutenant of Davidsons Company should he get one. Young active about 25—respectably recommended by Mr Hopkins first on the list of Carrington & Heth 26 years old Mr Carrington thinks he would not wish an appointment but in provisional army. his health dellicate
46. Horatio Gates Whiting Richmond between 20 & 21	respectable connections—promising appearance —perhaps *Ensign* bad politics C. & H.
47. Andrew Moore Lusk Fredericksburgh—at present formerly Lexington	recommended by Genl Posey as Lieutt or Ensign—Nephew to Mr Moore late Member of Congress—perhaps Ensign.
72. Reuben Thornton 19 years old	Son in Law to Genl Posey—Desires Lieutenancy or Cornetcy in the Horse—perhaps Cornet.
Hugh McAllister Rockbridge County	Mr Holmes recommends him for a Lieutenancy—no strong.
Mr A. Smith Mooresfield	Mr Holmes recommends him for Ensign. not strong.
49. Mr John Seayres	His Father fell at German Town—was Colonel — Quare other recommendations—Horrible authority for him C. & H.
52. John C. Williams In Prince William	respectable family—& much esteemd Perhaps Ensign—recommended by Genl Stevens—Mr Jameison & Mr Brent & many others— Quare political sentiments & whether John Williams & John C. Williams are the same person—NO

57. Simon Owens   recommended strongly by Genl Morgan as Lieutt
to Tate.

58. Robert Temple   a young man—recommended by Hopkins active
King Wm   sober discreet & Enterprizing—Friend to
Recommended by *A.New*   the Government.
who is bad authority   recom: by N. Burrell W. F. Gains—Son of an
C. & H.   old officer—very respectable—Lieutenant.

60. Thos Davis   weak
Albemarle

61. John Bacon   weak
New Kent   recommended by John Clopton who is bad
authority C. & H.

63. Wm Knight   [   ]

67. Obadiah Clif-   Tolerably respectable—perhaps Lieutenant.
ford[15]
Alexandria

112. William Brent }   Kinkead speaks well in   Nothing
     general terms   very
     Gl Lee—*youth of merit*   positive

113. Thomas Brent }   [   ]   perhaps Ensigns.

70. Charles J. Love   strong healthy good disposition, good char-
Loudohn County   acter—Mr Charles Lee recommends him as
24 years old   Lieutt—pretty well perhaps   *Lieutenant*

75. Charles Loftland   so-so.
Rockingham County

77. B. Dandridge Arm-   Cold recommendation—prefers civil appoint-
stead   ment—Mr Clopton *recommends* him strongly—
New Kent   *Not much.*

78. Charles Lane   recommended by R. B. Lee—not very strongly.
22 years old
Loudohn County

79. John Thornton   free from vice—desirous to enter the Army.
Fitzhugh
19 years old

80. John Williams   Strong.

82. Alexr Henderson[16]   Sprightly active young man, federal—good
21 years old   Ensign.
Dumfries

88. Thomas Blackburn   Mr Stoddart recommends him—won't do.
21 years old

96. James Duncanson   very respectable as Lieutenant. See Captains
Culpepper

106. Mathew Arbuckle   young—sedate & manly—Inquire.

107. L. ⟨Tremper⟩   offers service—not recommended.

109. Richard Graham Dumfries — recommended by the Atty Genl as Ensign in the ⟨Marine⟩ service.

110. Carter B. Fontaine Prince William — man of family—wishes to serve in the Cavalry as Lieutt. about 21 years of age— respectably recommended—perhaps Cornet.

114. Turner Richardson Richmond — recommended by Govr Wood—will not accept lower than Lieutt—Tolerable. Good for nothing C. & H.

115. Wm Finny — no recommendation Good for nothing *C. & H.*

118. John Campbell Frederick — Father died fighting at Eutaw—respectable for Lieutt.

120. Horatio Stark [17] Frederick — Genl Marshall says he is recommended by respectable persons—but the recommendations do not appear.

102. John Braham Frederick	young man of excellent character & could soon raise his men	recommended by Major
103. Addison Armstead Loudohn County Thomas Opie Northumberland	do [do]	Parker as Lieutenants

104. Frederick Thurston Frederick County — recommended by Majr Parker from Genl Morgan as Ensign—was Serjeant in Western Expedition & in several actions.

121. Calvin Morgan Staunton 25 yrs old } 128. Jesse Dold — recommended by Mr Harper as Ensigns their families federal—sober & honest Morgan's recommendation well supported by many others, & recommending him for Lieutt. Morgan's, very respectable—Dold's, good.

123. Joseph Grigsby 28 yrs old — sober—served as Sheriff & Magistrate Quare politics

124. Charles McAllister 22 years old — sober—Quare politics

128. Jesse Dold — recommended by Mr Andw Moore—David Stevenson & Mr Harper—steady, sober, & respectable connexions—Coll Potterfield speaks handsomely of him—well recommended as Ensign— Brother an Officer killed in Wayne's Expedition of great Character.

130. Charles Winter Smith Martinsburgh Berkley County Referred to — wishes employment as an Engineer, artillerist or Physician to the Army— Draughtsman to Bourgoyne—Teacher to the officers at *Montreal*—Inquire

131. George Washing   Genteel Young Man perhaps Ensign Quare.
-ton Humphries

132. John A. Steward   recommended by John Taylor & Jesse Steward
of Belfast has been   not strong.
Six years in this
Country.
of Alexandria

136. Wm G. Hunter   In Captn Tinsleys Company in Georgia not
                          strong.

John Muse   ⟨navy⟩

138. Tunspall Banks   recommends himself

Francis Thornton   recommended by Genl Lee as Captn for
for Captains   Provisional Army—& Genl Spotswood—well
                              connected & of ample fortune.

⟨1⟩39. John Moore   No testimonials but his own Letter produced.

140. John Strother   nothing about politics or abilities
Culpepper   mentioned.

141. Wm Deane   respectable connections—tolerable perhaps
Bath County   Ensign.
about 22 years old

142. Jesse Ewell Junr   federal—very respectable—Ensign perhaps
about 22   Lieutenant.
Dumfries

Richard Chinn   see Capns

143. John Craine Junr   respectable—perhaps Ensign.
Loudohn County

144. Samuel Casson   Wishes to be Midshipman.
Caroline County

148. John Winterberry   tolerable—perhaps Ensign.
Fairfax

150. John Sanders   Recommended to Genl Lee—who does not know
Prince William   him—Quare

Henry Tapscott   recommended by Genl Lee as well fitted for
                              the business of War—at present a Capt. in
                              the Militia.

157. Benjn Temple   federal, sober & esteemed recommended by Genl
King Wm County   Young.

160. Van Bennett   federal—pretty well for Ensign.
Berkley County

166. George Armstead   respectable connections & character.
Loudohn County

167. Thomas Bagot   served 18 Months in the Army recommended by
Fredericksburgh   Thos Parker.

Thomas Blackburn   Marine.

174. Peter Lamkin	recommended by Captn Blackburne Ensign perhaps.
183. Rowan Stafford	Good Landed Estate—federal—qualities of a Soldier recommended by Genl Lee for Cornett
184. H. L. Seayres Richmond	wishes to be Lieutt of arsenal to be established at Richmond, or some respectable station in the Army—Father fell at Germantown—no Letter but his own.
187. Strother Settle 40	strongly recommended by General Morgan. Searjeant & in last war made Officer & served to end of war as Ensign

D, DLC:GW. Most of the notes refer to a list of Applicants in Virginia (DLC:GW), which was most likely the same one used by GW and the two major generals to determine who was applying for commissions in the Virginia regiments.

1. GW appended this comment to Parker's name in the list of Applicants in Virginia: "very good."

2. GW wrote: "supposed to be a good Officer in the R. War."

3. GW wrote: "respectable Chr."

4. GW wrote: "Good Officer Ry War."

5. GW wrote: "If from Brunswick—good Offr R. War."

6. GW wrote: "Offr R. War."

7. GW wrote: "Old & distinguished Off. of Cavalry."

8. GW wrote: "Well spoken of—in the Western Army—Lieut."

9. "O[badiah] Clifford" is crossed out here. Clifford appears again as entry no. 67 with the lieutenants.

10. GW wrote: "would make a gd Of."

11. GW wrote: "very clever."

12. GW wrote: "good Offr Westn Expn."

13. GW wrote: "If of Kg Wm—good."

14. GW wrote: "respe. yg man."

15. See note 9.

16. GW wrote: "⟨a good⟩ young Man."

17. GW wrote: "Well regd."

To Elizabeth Willing Powel

Saturday—1st December 1798.

General Washington presents his best wishes, and affectionate compliments to Mrs Powell.

If Mrs Powell is not otherwise engaged, G.W. will have the pleasure of breakfasting with her tomorrow, at her usual hour, if named to him.[1]

AL, ViMtV.

1. See GW to Elizabeth Willing Powel, 17 Nov., n.2.

To Lawrence Lewis

Dear Lawrence,   Philadelphia 2d Decr 1798.

Your letter of the 21st Ulto has been duly received. In reply, I have to observe that, the end of my enquiry into the cause of my not seeing you the morning I left Mount Vernon, has been altogether mistaken. It was not from a supposed disrespect on your part, but not being able to recollect whether you were at breakfast, and the apparent slight, if you had been too unwell to leave your room, in coming away without seeing you, that led to it. I never had cause to suspect any want of respect from you, or disinclination to oblige me in all things; and as I came away without seeing you, and supposed it proceeded from your indisposition, I wanted you to understand, that my appointment to be in Alexandria at a certain hour—my anxiety to accomplish it—and the pressure of many things upon me until the moment I stepped into the Carriage was the cause of my not bidding you adieu the Morning I left home.

I wish Parkinson's emigration to this Country may answer his own purposes. It is done without previous arrangement; and when measures *commence* badly, they seldom *end* well. I have nothing to do with him or his property. On the contrary I advised him (in answer to a letter he had written me more than a year ago) to come himself, or send an Agent to see, & report things to him, before he embarked his property, on a precarious result.

Making a selection of Officers for the twelve new Regiments— and arranging them to the different States, is a work of infinite more difficulty than I had any conception of. The applications for Commissions are multitudinous, and the pretensions of each, from former services—particular merits—and other causes—must be individually examined; and a due apportionment allotted to each State. When this will be accomplished I am not yet able to say. I shall think of your own wishes, as expressed in your letter. and if any thing *can* be done which Mr Lear & myself may think agreeable to you, it shall.

I cannot with any certainty say, when I shall be able to leave this City. I think however the business must close this week, after which I shall not stay a moment longer than I can avoid—In order to bring it to an end we set from ten oclock until after three—& from

Seven in the evening until past nine. With much sincerity & truth—I am Your Affecte Uncle

Go: Washington

ALS, PWacD.

From Elizabeth Willing Powel

My dear Sir   Market Street [Philadelphia] Decemr 3d 1798

I have the Pleasure to send the Book of Prints that you were so obliging as to accept from your Friend. I have also taken the liberty to add a few that I admire on a presumption that the Mind capable of tracing with Pleasure the military Progress of the Hero whose Battles they delineate will also have the associate Taste and admire fine representations of the Work of God in the human Form.[1]

As you wish to take Miss Custis a Testimonial of your recollection of her, I really know not of any Thing more appropriate at this Season, than a fashionable Muff & Tippet; and such may be procured for less than Thirty Dollars. a Pattern of Muslin for a Dress such as you would choose to present will I find cost Sixty dols. at least—a Pattern for a half or undress may be bought for 23 dols.; but let me know what will be most agreeable to you and I will purchase it with Pleasure and pack it up in a manner the least inconvenient for you.[2]

I hope you have suffered no inconvenience from your long unpleasant Walk in the Rain on Sunday last. My best wishes ever attend you as I am always Your sincere Affectionate Friend

Eliza. Powel

ALS, DLC:GW.

1. For references to prints in GW's library at the time of his death, see Griffin, *Boston Athenæum Washington Collection*, 561–65.

2. For further correspondence regarding Mrs. Powel's purchase of presents for GW to give to Eleanor Parke Custis, Mrs. Washington, and little Eliza Law, see GW to Elizabeth Willing Powel, 4, 7 Dec., and Mrs. Powel to GW, 7 December.

From Elias Boudinot

Rose Hill [Philadelphia] Decr 4 1798

Mr Boudinot presents his most respectful Compliments to Lieutenant Genl Washington and informs him that the Wine he mentioned to him, is all sold—Mr Boudinot has sent money to Madeira to purchase a few Pipes of the best wines the Island affords—He expects they will be shipped in January for this port, and if they arrive safe, and answer his Expectation, Mr B. will let the General know it, and as Mr B. sent for enough to last him as long as he expects to want any, he will with pleasure spare the General a Pipe, if he shall then choose to take it[1]—Mr B. intended to have waited on General Washington again in Person, but his continued ill state of health forbids it.

AL, DLC:GW.

1. For the extended correspondence about Madeira wine for GW, between GW and Tobias Lear on the one hand and Boudinot and others on the other, see GW to Boudinot, 22 June 1799, and notes 1 and 2 of that document.

To Elizabeth Willing Powel

Eight Street [Philadelphia]
My dear Madam,   Tuesday 4th Decr 1798
Receive, I pray you, my best thanks for the Prints you had the goodness to send me; and my acknowledgments of your kind, and obliging offer to chuse some thing handsome, with which to present Miss Custis. The difference between thirty & Sixty (or more) dollars, is not so much a matter of consideration, as the appropriate thing.[1]

I presume, she is provided with a *Muff*; of a tippet I am not so certain; but a handsome Muslin, or any thing else, that is not the whim of the day, cannot be amiss. The cost of which, when furnished, you will please to announce to me. Is there any thing—not of much cost—I could carry Mrs Washington as a memento that she has not been forgotten, in this City? And let me tresspass upon your goodness to procure the second edition of the present (on my acct) that you intend for Eliza Law.[2] Without which, a contest (regardless of right—no unusual thing)—in which an innocent Baby may become the Victim of strife.

My *present* expectation is, that We shall close the business which brought me here, by Friday—Saturday at farthest; when my journey will commence. But before my departure I shall, most assuredly, have the honor of paying my respects to you. With the greatest respect & Affecte. I am always Yours

Go: Washington

ALS, ViMtV.

1. See Elizabeth Willing Powel to GW, 3 Dec., and note 2 of that document.

2. In his letter to Mrs. Powel of 7 Dec., GW refers to "the Doll" for Eliza Law, and in his Day Book he notes also buying on that day "A Doll for Eleanor Peter" for $2.50.

From James McHenry

Dr Sir   [Philadelphia] 5 Decr 1798

I submit the inclosed letters to you and Major General Hamilton & Majr General Pinckney. The young gentleman who presented them to me and in whose favour they are has requested to have the honour to present them to you.[1] With the greatest respect I have the honour to be Dr Sir your most obt ⟨st⟩

James McHenry

ALS, DLC:GW.

1. The letters have not been identified, but they may be those written in support of Philip Church's application for a commission in the New Army. See Philip Schuyler to GW, 20 Nov. 1798, and the letters printed in note 1 to that document.

To Alexander Addison

Sir   Philadelphia 6th Decr 1798.

Your favor of the 21st Ulto enclosing thoughts on the "Liberty of Speech and of the Press in a charge to the Grand Juries of the County Courts of the fifth circuit of the State of Pennsylvania" has been duly received, and I pray you to accept my thanks for this fresh inst[anc]e of your attention & politeness to me.[1]

I am persuaded I *shall* read it with the same pleasure, & marked approbation that I have done your other productions of a similar nature which have come to my hands—I say *shall* because my occupations since I came to this City have been such as scarcely to afford me time to look into a News-paper. With great esteem & respect I have the honor to be Sir Your Most Hble Servant

Go: Washington

ALS, MWiW; LB, DLC:GW.

1. Letter not found. A copy of *Liberty of Speech, and of the Press* (Washington, Pa., 1798), with "General Washington" inscribed on the cover, was in GW's library at the time of his death (Griffin, *Boston Athenæum Washington Collection*, 3).

To John Greenwood

Sir,   Philadelphia 7th Decr 1798

What you sent me last answer exceedingly well; and I send the first to be altered & made like them, if you can.

Your recollection of these—with the directions and observations contained in my two last letters—the latter especially—supercedes the necessity of being particular in this.[1]

I will however just remark that the great error in those (now returned to you) is, that the upper teeth & bars do not fall back enough thus [sketch] but stand more upright so [sketch (a)] by which means the bar at (a) shoots beyond the gums and not only forces the lip out just under the nose, but by not having its proper place to rest upon frets, & makes that part very sore.[2]

I shall add no more than to request you will be so good as to let me have them as soon as you conveniently can; altered or not altered. Direct for me at this place, or at Mount Vernon, as it is not likely I shall be here more than two or three days longer.

I thank you very much for your obliging attention to my requests—and am Sir With esteem & regard Yr very Hble Servt

Go: Washington

P.S. I am willing & ready to pay what ever you may charge me.

ALS, DLC:GW. The letter is marked on the back by GW: "For Mr Jno. Greenwood and to be opened by him only."

1. GW wrote to Greenwood on 3 and 5 November. The letter of 3 Nov. is missing, but it is doubtful that GW was referring to either of these letters. It is far more likely that he was referring to two more recent (missing) letters. Greenwood's response of 8 Dec. is also missing, to which GW responded on 12 Dec. before leaving Philadelphia on 14 Dec.: "Sir, Your letter of the 8th came safe. And as I am hurrying, in order to leave this City tomorrow, I must be short.

"The principal thing you will have to attend to, in the alteration you are about to make, is to let the upper bar fall back from the lower one thus [sketch]; whether the teeth are quite streight, or inclining a little in thus, [sketch] or a little rounding outwards thus [sketch] is immaterial, for I find it is the bars alone both above and below that gives the lips the pouting and swelling appearance— of consequence, if this can be remedied, all will be well.

"I send you the old bars, which you returned to me with the new set, because you have desired. But they may be destroyed, or any thing else done with them you please, for you will find that I have been obliged to file them away so much above, to remedy the evil I have been complaining of as to render them useless perhaps to receive new teeth. But of this you are better able to judge than I am— If you can fix the teeth (now on the new bars which you have) on the old bars which you will receive with this letter I should prefer it because the latter are easy in the Mouth. and you will perceive moreover that when the edges of the upper and lower teeth are put together that the upper falls back into the mouth, which they ought to do, or it will have the effect of forcing the lip out just under the nose.

"I shall only repeat again, that I feel much obliged by your extreme willingness, and readiness to accomodate me and that I am Sir Your Obedt Servant Go: Washington" (ALS, MBOS). GW notes in his Day Book on 13 Dec. that he "sent Mr Jno. Greenwood—Dentist of New York—for Services—$30." GW corresponded with Greenwood about his teeth shortly before he left Philadelphia in 1797 (GW to Greenwood, 25 Jan. 1797; Greenwood to GW, 20 Feb. 1797).

2. Each of the sketches enclosed in GW's letters to Greenwood of 7 and 12 Dec. is composed of two lines, or bars, one above the other, and set at different angles.

From Elizabeth Willing Powel

My dear Sir   [Philadelphia] Friday Decr 7th 1798

The amount of the Articles purchased you will find to be Seventy Four dols. & a half.[1] I must request the Favour of you to deliver the enclosed Letter to Mrs Law.

My Heart is so sincerely afflicted and my Idea's so confused that I can only express my predominant Wish—that God may take you into his holy keeping and preserve you safe both in Traveling and under all Circumstances, and that you may be happy here and hereafter is the ardent Prayer of Your affectionate afflicted Friend

Eliza. Powell

ALS, DLC:GW.

1. Pasted onto the manuscript is a notation, in Elizabeth Willing Powel's hand, indicating that she paid $65 for a "Piece of Muslin," $2.50 for "A Doll," and $7 for a "Thread Case." On 13 Dec. GW paid $62 for a gold watch and key bought for Washington Custis (Day Book). Other items that he purchased in Philadelphia for his family appear in his list of expenditures, printed in GW to James McHenry, 6 Jan. 1799, n.2.

To Elizabeth Willing Powel

My dear Madam,   Philadelphia 7th Decr 1798

The articles you had the goodness to send me this forenoon (when it was not in my power to acknowledge the receipt of them) came very safe, and I pray you again, to accept my thanks for the trouble I have given you in this business.

Enclosed are Seventy five dollars, which is the nearest my present means will enable me to approach $74 $^{50}\!/_{100}$ the cost of them.

Your letter to Mrs Law shall be safely delivered to her and I will endeavor to do the same by the Doll to Eliza.

For your kind and affectionate wishes, I feel a grateful sensibility, and reciprocate them with all the cordiality you could wish, being My dear Madam Your most Obedt & obliged Hble Servant

Go: Washington

ALS, ViMtV.

Clement Biddle to Tobias Lear

Dr sir   Walnut Street [Philadelphia] Decr 8 [17]98

I have sent a bale wth 5 pieces of Blankets on board the Brig for Alexandria and will endeavor to get the bill of loading in time for this Evening—I am waiting for the picture frame from McEllwee which he has repeatedly promised & dissappointed me.[1] Yr very Ob. st

Clement Biddle

ALS, DLC:GW.

1. Biddle wrote Lear again the next morning: "I have delayd sending the bill of loading until this morning in hopes of geting the picture frame from McEllwee the maker, but he put me Off with promises til Evening & did not get it on board but assures me he will before the vessel Sails tomorrow at Ten OClock—the bill of loading for the other Articles is enclosed also the bill for the Blankets which I purchased by the bale at the lowest Cash price—they are more than you directed but could not get a bale to contain less—I am with great Esteem Dr sir Your mo. obed. St" (DLC:GW).

Biddle's account with GW, dated 5 Feb. 1799 and enclosed in Biddle's letter of that date, indicates that the charge for the blankets was $157.26 and for the picture frames, $16.33. Biddle's receipts from Denman & Co., 13 Dec. 1798, for payment for the blankets, and from John McElwee, 19 Dec. 1798, are in ViMtV.

Letter not found: from John Greenwood, 8 Dec. 1798. On 12 Dec. GW wrote Greenwood: "Your letter of the 8th came safe."

To Elizabeth Willing Powel

My dear Madam   Philadelphia 9th Decr 1798

I feel much obliged by your kind & polite invitation to dine with you to day, but am under the necessity of denying myself that pleasure.

I had, previously to the receipt of your Card, resolved not to dine out of my lodgings while business should detain me in the City: and, in consequence, had declined Invitations from Mr Liston, and the Chevr de Freire.[1] But a more conclusive reason than this, is, that I had requested Generals Hamilton & Pinckney to come prepared this morning, at their usual hour—ten 'Oclock—for the whole day; that a few moments for dinner *only* might interrupt our daily labour, having dispensed with the Sabbath on this occasion. But of this you must not be the Informer. Be the Weather as it may, I must plunge through it when our business is brought to a close. I am always & Most obediently & affectionately Yours

Go: Washington

I was engaged with the within named Gentlemen when your card came or it should have been answered last night.

ALS, NNPM.

1. Cipriano Ribeiro Freire was at this time Portugal's minister resident in the United States.

Letter not found: to John Trumbull, 10 Dec. 1798. On 24 Mar. 1799, Trumbull wrote GW: "I have duly received the Letter which you did me the honour to write on the 10th Decr last."

From James McHenry

Dr Sir　　　　　　　　　　　　War Department 11th Decr 1798

Inclosed is a schedule shewing the price of rations and component parts at certain posts from the first day of October 1798 to the 30 day of Septr 1799—agreeably to Contract.[1] I have the honour to be D. Sir your most ob. st

James McHenry

ADfS, MdAA.

1. See McHenry to GW, 14 Nov., n.17.

To Charles Carroll, Jr.

Sir,　　　　　　　　　　　　Philadelphia 13th Decr 1798.

Mr McHenry—Secretary of War—communicated to me your wish to receive an Appointment in the Corps of Light Dragoons, about to be raised.[1]

Conceiving that the inducement to this application could be no other than a laudable zeal to serve your Country, and a desire to set an example to the young Gentlemen of family & fortune in it, which, undoubtedly would be attended with a happy effect; I informed him, that although it was not my practice to compromit my self beforehand by promises, yet, in this instance I would inform him that it had been, and still was my intention (if circumstances should call me to the field) to offer you a place in my Military family, as an Extra: or Volunteer Aid de Camp; under a presumption that, as you could not contemplate Arms as a *profession*, rank could be no object, and I was sure that the pay of an Officer would be none; and therefore, that he was at liberty to hint this matter to you. In what light you have understood him, I know not, wch is the reason of my giving you the trouble of this explanation.

My established Aids de Camp, for reason which I had the honor of communicating to Mr Carroll (your father) must be men of Military experience (if to be had)—and in the choice of whom, many circumstances ought to combine.[2] It is unnecessary I hope to add, that at all times I should be glad to see you at Mount Vernon,[3] and with best respects to Mr Carroll and the Ladies of your family I am—Sir Your Most Obedt Hble Servant

Go: Washington

ALS, CSmH; ADfS, DLC:GW.

1. James McHenry wrote GW on 26 Nov.: "If I have understood your meaning right with respect to young Mr Carroll, and the inclosed meets your approbation you will oblige me by sealing it and sending it with your own letters to the post office. The death of an unckle of Mrs McHenry's which happened this morning will prevent me from having the pleasure of dining with you to-day at the Presidents" (DLC:GW). A draft of McHenry's letter to young Carroll, dated 26 Nov., is in DLC: McHenry Papers.

2. Charles Carroll of Carrollton wrote to GW on 29 July 1798 about his wish for his son Charles Carroll, Jr. (of Homewood), to become an aide-de-camp to GW. GW responded on 2 Aug. stating his policy to appoint no aides until he should actually take the field as commander in chief of the army. Carroll's letter is printed in note 1 to GW's letter of 2 Aug.; see also Carroll to GW, 9 August.

3. For the visit of Charles Carroll, Jr., to Mount Vernon in March 1798, see GW to George Washington Parke Custis, 15 April 1798, and *Diaries*, 6:288. Charles Carroll, Jr., replied from Annapolis on 23 Dec.: "I have had the honor to receive your Letter of the 13th of this month, and am happy that You have attributed my desire of obtaining an appointment in our Army to a zeal of rendering myself serviceable to my Country. The Letter I received from Mr McHenry,

together with the flattering assurance which You have given me, that I shall be employed in your military Family as Extra or volunteer Aid de Camp, (should circumstances call You to the Field) have ultimately fixed my Determination to decline every military Situation, other than the one You have been pleased to offer me. When I first had the honor of applying to You through the medium of my Father to become your Aid de Camp, I did not for a moment contemplate any pecuniary emolument, being only regardful of the honor I should receive, and the probable good which my Example might produce. Since You have been pleased to consider this last circumstance as one of my inducements for the Application, It is sufficient for me to say, that Your notice of it, will be my best apology for a Declaration, which on any other occasion might not be so proper. For Your friendly Invitation to Mount Vernon, Receive, Sir, my warmest acknowledgements; and be assured, that whenever circumstances will permit me to embrace it, that nothing will afford me greater satisfaction" (DLC:GW).

To James McHenry

Private
Dear Sir,   Philadelphia 13th Decr 1798
    I am really ashamed to offer the letters &ca herewith sent, with so many erazures &ca; but it was not to be avoided, unless I had remained so much longer here, as to have allowed my Secretary time to copy the whole over again; And my impatience to be on my return homewards, on Account of the Season—the Roads—and more especially the passage of the Susquehanna—would not admit of this. With consideration & respect—I am—Dear Sir Your most obedt Servt

                                                    Go: Washington

P.S. Mr. Lear, you are sensible, was engaged with myself & the Genl Officers; of course could not be employed in Transcribing what you will now receive, as the result of our deliberation at the mom[en]t we were engaged in other matters.

ALS, owned (1997) by Mr. Joseph Rubinfine, West Palm Beach, Florida. In DLC:GW there are drafts of three letters dated 13 Dec. 1798 to James McHenry from GW, all in the hand of Alexander Hamilton. All three are printed with notes in Syrett, *Hamilton Papers*, 22:341–66. The first of these enclosed letters is cast in the form of a point-by-point response to the thirteen questions posed by McHenry in his letter to GW of 10 Nov., which in effect set the agenda of the just concluded five-week meeting of GW with major generals Hamilton and Charles Cotesworth Pinckney. The second of these letters attempts to set out the organization of the New Army and deals with such things as ranks, promotions, uniforms, and provisions. As McHenry informed GW on 28 Dec., in making his "report [on 24 Dec.] to the President on the military points, proper for the consideration of Congress," he "freely used" these two letters and had invoked GW's "name." See *ASP, Military Affairs*, 1:124–27, and *Annals of Congress, 1797–99*, 2:2199–2201. See also GW's expression of dissatisfaction that the reports to the secretary of war were not "communicated entire" but in the form of "Extracts" (GW to McHenry, 6 Jan. 1799). The third of these enclosed letters, regarding the allegations against William S. Smith, is printed below, separately, as the second letter of this date.

The draft of the first of these enclosed letters from GW to McHenry dated 13 Dec. from GW reads: "Sir Since my arrival at this place I have been closely engaged, with the aid of Generals Hamilton and Pinckney, in fulfilling the objects of your letter of the 10th of November. The result is now submitted.

"The two first questions you propose, respecting the appointment of the Officers and men of the troops to be raised in virtue of the act of Congress of the 16th of July last among districts and states will naturally be answered together.

"1. As to the apportionment of the Commissioned officers of the Infantry, no particular reason is discovered to exist at the present period for combining the states into districts; but it is conceived to be expedient to adopt as a primary rule the relative representative population of the several States. The practice of the government on other occasions, in the appointment of public officers, has had regard as far as was practicable to the same general principle; as one which by a distribution of honors and emoluments among the citizens of the different states, tends both to justice and to public satisfaction. This principle however must frequently yield to the most proper solution of character among those willing as well as qualified to serve, and sometimes to collateral considerations, which arising out of particular cases do not admit of precise specification. In the application of the rule, in this, as in other instances, qualifications of it must be admitted. The arrangement which will be now offered proceeds on this basis. You will observe that it does not deviate from the table you have presented [in McHenry to GW, 10 Nov. 1798]. It is contained in the Schedule A [not found].

"2. As to the non commissioned officers and privates, it is conceived to be both unnecessary and inexpedient to make any absolute apportionment among the states. It is unnecessary, because, contemplating it as desireable that the men shall be drawn in nearly equal proportions from the respective states, this object, where circumstances are favourable, will be attained by the very natural and proper arrangement of assigning to the officers who shall be appointed recruiting districts within the states of which they are. It is inexpedient, because if it shall happen that the proportion of fit men cannot easily be had in a particular state, there ought to be no obsta[c]le to obtaining them elsewhere.

"3. As to the officers of the dragoons, it does not seem adviseable to confine their selection to any subdivision of the U. States. Though very strong conjectures may be formed as to the quarters in which they would probably be employed, in the case of invasion, there can be nothing certain on this point, if this were even the criterion of a proper arrangement. And it may be presumed that it will conduce most to general satisfaction to exclude considerations of a local aspect. But from the small number of this corps, which is to be raised it would be found too fractional and for that among reasons inconvenient to aim at a proporti[on]al distribution among all the states. It is therefore supposed most adviseable to be governed principally by a reference to the characters who have occurred as candidates; leaving the inequality in the distribution to be remedied in the event of a future augmentation of this description of troops. The proportion at present is in various views inadequate; a circumstance which it may be presumed will of course be attended to should the progress of public danger lead to an extension of military preparation.

"The materials furnished by you with the addition of those derived from other sources are insufficient for a due selection of the officers whom it is proposed to allot to the States of Connecticut North and South Carolina & Georgia. Hence the selection for these states must of necessity be deferred. It is conceived, that the best plan for procuring the requisite information and accelerating a desireable conclusion as to the three last mentioned States, will be to charge Major General Pinckney, who will avail himself of the assistance of Brigadier Generals Davy and Washington, to make the arrangement of those officers provisionally, and subject to the ratification of the President. It will be in their power to ascertain who are best *qualified* among those *willing* to serve; which will at the same time assure a good choice and avoid the disappointment and embarrassment of refusals. As to connecticut, you are aware of the progress which has been made and of the misapprehension which has occasioned an obstacle to a definitive arrangement. You will it is presumed be speedily in possession of the further information necessary, and having it can without difficulty complete the arrangement for this state.

"The 3d 4th & 5th of your questions may likewise be answered to gether.

"The act for augmenting the army is peremptory in its provisions. The bounds of executive discretion as to the for[b]earance to execute such a law might perhaps involve an investigation nice in its own nature and of a kind which it is generally most prudent to avoid. But it may safely be said negatively, for reasons too plain to be doubted, that the voluntary suspension of the execution of a similar law could not be justified but by considerations of decisive urgency.

"The existence of any such considerations is unknown.

"Nothing has been communicated respecting our foreign relations to induce the opinion that there has been any change in the situation of the Country as to external danger which dictates an abandonment of the policy of the law in question. It need not now be examined how far it may be at any time prudent to relinquish measures of security suggested by the experience of accumulated hostility, merely because there are probable symptoms of approaching accommodation: It need not be urged that if such symptoms exist they are to be ascribed to the measures of vigour adopted by the Government; and may be frustrated by a relaxation in those measures affording an argument of weakness or irresolution: For has it not been in substance stated from the highest authority that no decisive indications have been given by France of a disposition to redress our past wrongs and do us future justice, that her decree alleged to be intended to restrain the depredations of French Cruisers on our commerce has not given and from its nature cannot give relief—that the most hostile of the acts by which she has oppressed the commerce of neutrals, that which subjects to capture and condemnation of neutral vessels and cargoes, if any part of the latter be of British production or fabric, not only has not been abrogated but has recently received an indirect confirmation—and that hitherto nothing is discoverable in the conduct of France which ought to change or relax our measures of defence.

"Could it be necessary to enforce by argument so authoritative a declaration as it relates to the immediate object of consideration these among other reflections would at once present themselves.

"Though it may be true that some late occurrences have rendered the prospect of invasion by France, less probable or more remote: Yet duly considering the rapid vicissitudes, at all times, of political and military events; the extraordinary fluctuations which have been peculiarly characteristic of the still subsisting contest in Europe; and the more extraordinary position of most of the principal nations of that quarter of the globe; it can never be wise to vary our measures of security with the continually varying aspect of European affairs. A very obvious policy dictates to us a strenuous endeavour as far as may be practicable, to place our safety out of the reach of the casualties which may befal the contending parties and the powers more immediately within their vortex. The way to effect this is to pursue a steady system—to organise all our resources and put them in a state of preparation for prompt action. Regarding the overthrow of Europe at large as a matter not intirely chimerical—it will be our prudence to cultivate a spirit of self-dependence—and to endeavour by unremitting vigilance and exertion under the blessing of providence to hold the scales of our destiny in our own hands. Standing, as it were, in the midst of falling empires, it should be our aim to assume a station and attitude which will preserve us from being overwhelmed in their ruins.

"It has been very properly the policy of our Government to cultivate peace. But in contemplating the possibility of our being driven to unqualified War, it will be wise to anticipate that frequently the most effectual way to defend is to attack. There may be imagined enterprises of very great moment to the permanent interests of this Country which would certainly require a disciplined force. To raise and prepare such a force will always be a work of considerable time; and it ought to be ready for the conjuncture whenever it shall arrive. Not to be ready then may be to lose an opportunity which it may be difficult afterwards to retrieve.

"While a comprehensive view of external circumstances is believed to recommend perseverance in the precautions which have been taken for the safety of the country—nothing has come to my knowlege in our interior situation which leads to a different conclusion. The principal inquiry in this respect concerns the finances. The exhibition of their state from the Department of the Treasury which you have transmitted, as I understand it, opposes no obstacle; nor have I been apprised that any doubt is entertained by the Officer who presides in that Department of the sufficiency of our pecuniary resources. But on this point I cannot be expected to assume the responsibility of a positive opinion. It is the province of the Secretary of the Treasury to pronounce definitively whether any insuperable impediment arises from this source.

"The sound conclusion, viewing the subject in every light is conceived to be— that no avoidable delay ought to be incurred in appointing the whole of the Officers and raising the whole of the men provided for by the act which has been cited. If immediately entered upon and pursued with the utmost activity, it cannot be relied upon that the troops will be raised and disciplined in less than a year. What may not another year produce? Happy will it be for us if we have so much time for preparation, and ill-judged indeed if we do not make the most of it! The adequateness of the force to be raised in relation to a serious invasion is foreign to the present examination. But it is certain that even a force of this extent, well instructed and well disciplined would in such an event be of great utility and importance. Besides the direct effects of its own exertions, the Militia rallying to it would derive from its example and countenance additional courage and perseverance. It would give a consistency and stability to our first efforts of which they would otherwise be destitute; and would tend powerfully to prevent great though perhaps partial calamities.

"The senate being in session the officers to be appointed must of course be nominated to that body.

"The pay of all who shall be appointed ought immediately to commence. They ought all to be employed without delay in different ways, in the recruiting service; but were it otherwise there ought to be no suspension of their pay. The law annexes it as a matter of right. The attempt to apply a restriction by executive discretion might be dissatisfactory; and justice to the public does not seem to require it, because the acceptance of an office which makes the person liable at pleasure to be called into actual service will commonly from the moment of that acceptance interfere with any previous occupation—on which he may have depended—This observation cannot be applicable to myself because I have taken a peculiar and distinct ground to which it is my contention to adhere.

"on the subject of your sixth question the opinion is that under existing circumstances; it is not adviseable to withdraw any of the troops from the quarters of the Country, which you mention, towards the Atlantic frontier. But the disposition in those quarters probably requires careful revision. It is not impossible that it will be found to admit of alterations favourable both to œconomy and to the military objects to be attained. The local knowlege of General Wilkinson would be so useful in an investigation of this sort, that it is deemed very important to direct him forthwith to repair to Philadelphia. If this be impracticable by land he may it is presumed come by way of New Orleans. It is observed that in his late communications with the Spanish Governor he has taken pains to obviate jealousy of the views of the U. States. This was prudent, and he ought to be encouraged to continue the policy. It will also be useful to employ a judicious Engineer to survey our posts on the Lakes in order that it may be ascertained in the various relations of trade and defence, what beneficial changes if any, can be made. In this examination *Presque-Isle* and the *South Western extremity of Lake Erie* will demand particular attention.

"The reply to your seventh question is that the companies directed to [be] added to the regiments of the old establishment ought as soon as convenient to reinforce the Western army. It is probable that in the progress of events they will be not less useful there than on the sea-board. Their destination in the first instance may be Pittsburgh.

"The following disposition of the Artillery (the subject of your Eighth question) is recommended. The two Regiments by their establishment consist of 28 Companies of these nearly a batalion in point of number, forms part of the western army. A complete batalion there will suffice. Let there be assigned to the fortifications at Boston one company to those at New port two companies, to those at west point one and to those at New York two to those at Mud Island two, to those at Baltimore one to those at Norfolk two to those on Cape Fear River One to those at Charles town two to those at Savannah one to those at the mouth of St Mary one. The remaining two batalions had best be reserved for the army in the field. During the Winter they may retain the stations they now occupy. But as soon as they can conveniently go into tents it will be adviseable to assemble them at some central or nearly central point there to be put in a course of regular instruction, together with successive detachments of the Officers and non commissioned Officers of the sea board garrisons, until their services shall be actually required. The field officers will of course be distributed proportionally, assigning to each the superintendence of a certain number of companies; and, as to those in garrison the posts at which they are stationed.

"The permanent disposition of the troops after they shall have been raised which is understood to be an object of your Ninth Question will probably be influenced by circumstances yet to be unfolded, and will best be referred to future consideration.

"An arrangement for the recruiting service is the point of primary urgency. For this purpose each state should be divided into as many districts as there are companies to be raised in it, and to every company a particular district should be allotted, with one place of rendezvous in it, to which the recruits should be brought as fast as they are engaged: a certain number of these company districts wherever it can be done should be placed under the supervision of a field officer. During the Winter in most of the states it would be inconvenient to assemble in larger corps than companies. Great cities are to be avoided. The collection of troops there may lead to disorders and expose more than elsewhere the morals and principles of the soldiery.

"But though it might now be premature to fix a permanent disposition of the troops, it may be not unuseful to indicate certain stations where they may be assembled provisionally and may probably be suffered to continue while matters remain in their present posture. The stations eligible in this view may be found for two Regiments in the vicinity of Providence River somewhere near Uxbridge for two other Regiments in the vicinity of Brunswick in New Jersey—for two other Regiments in the vicinity of the Potomack near Harpers Ferry, for two other Regiments in the vicinity of Augusta but above the falls of the Savannah. This disposition will unite considerations relative to the discipline & health of the troops and to the œconomical supply of their wants by water. It will also have some military aspects, in the first instance towards the security of Boston & New Port; in the second towards that of New York & Philadelphia in the third and fourth towards that of Baltimore Charleston Savannah and the Southern States generally and in the third particularly towards the reinforcement of the Western army in certain events—But the military motives have only a qualified influence; since it is not doubted that in the prospect of a serious attack upon this country the disposition of the army ought to look emphatically to the Southern Region as that which is by far most likely to be the scene of action.

"As to your Tenth question, the opinion is, that the Government ought itself to provide the rations. The plan of furnishing money to the recruits as a substitute for this is likely to be attended with several inconveniences. It will give them a pretence for absence injurious to discipline and facilitating marauding and desertion. Many of the soldiery will be disposed to lay out too much of their money in ardent spirits and too little in provisions, which besides occasioning them to be ill fed will lead to habits of intemperance.

"The subject of your 11th question is peculiarly important. The two modes have severally their advantages and disadvantages. That of purchases by Agents of the Government is liable to much mismanagement and abuse, sometimes from want of skill but much oftener from infidelity—It is too frequently deficient in œconomy; but it is preferable, as it regards the quality of the articles to be supplied, the satisfaction of the troops, and the certainty of the supply; which last is a point of the utmost consequence to the success of every military operation. The mode by contract is sometimes found more œconomical; but as the calculations of contractors have reference primarily to their own profit, they are apt to endeavour to impose on the troops articles of inferior quality; the troops suspecting this are apt to be dissatisfied even where there is no adequate cause and where defects may admit of reasonable excuse. In the attention to cheapness of price and other savings of expence, it from time to time happens that the supplies are not laid in as early as the service requires, or not in sufficient quantity, or are not conveyed with due asperity to the points where they are wanted. Circumstances like these tend to embarrass and even to defeat the best concerted military plans; which, in this mood, depend for their execution too much upon the combinations of individual avarice—It also occasionally happens that the Public, from the failures of the contractors, is under a necessity of interposing with sudden and extraordinary efforts to obviate the mischief and disappointments of those failures, producing, in addition to other evils, an accumulation of expence which the fortunes of the delinquent contractors, are insufficient to indemnify.

"The union of the two modes will probably be found safest and best. Prudence always requires that magazines shall be formed beforehand at stations relative to the probable or expected scene of action. These magazines may be laid in by contract—and the transportation of the supplies from the magazines and the issuing of them to the army may be the business of the Military Agents, who must likewise be authorised & enabled to provide for the deficiencies of the contractors and for whatever may not be comprehended in the contracts—This plan will, to a great extent, admit the competition of private interest to furnish the supplies at the cheapest rate: by narrowing the sphere of action of the public agents it will proportionally diminish the opportunities of abuse; and it will unite as far as is attainable œconomy with the efficiency of military operations.

"But to obtain the full advantages of this plan, it is essential that there shall be a man attached to the army, of distinguished capacity and integrity to be charged with the superintendence of the department of supplies. To procure such a man, as military honor can form no part of his reward, ample pecuniary compensation must be given; and he must be entrusted with large authority for the appointment of subordinate agents accompanied with a correspondent responsibility. Proceeding on this ground there would be a moral certainty of immense savings to the public in the business of supplies; savings the magnitude of which will easily be understood by any man who can estimate the vast difference in the results of extensive money transactions between a management at once skilful & faithful and that which is either unskilful or unfaithful.

"This suggestion contemplates as a part of the plan that the procuring of supplies of every kind which in our past experience has been divided between two departments, of Quarter Master and Commissary, shall be united under one head. This unity will tend to harmony system and vigour. It will avoid the discordant mixture of civil with military functions. The Quarter Master General in this case, instead of being a purveyor as formerly, will besides the duties purely military of his station, be confined to the province of calling for the requisite supplies and of seeing that they are duely furnished; in which he may be rendered a very useful check upon the purveyor.

"The extent of your twelveth question has been matter of some doubt. But no inconvenience can ensue from the answering it with greater latitude than may have been intended. It is conceived that the strongest consideration of national policy & safety require that we should be as fast as possible provided [with] Arsenals and Magazines of Artillery small arms and the principal articles of military stores and camp equipage equal to such a force as may be deemed sufficient to resist with effect the most serious invasion of the most powerful European nation. This precaution, which prudence would at all times recommend, is peculiarly indicated by the existing crisis of Europe. The nature of the case does not furnish any absolute standard of the requisite force. It must be more or less matter of judgment. The opinion is that the calculation ought to be on the basis of fifty thousand men, forty thousand infantry of the line two thousand riflemen four thousand horse, and four thousand Artillery men. And with regard to such articles as are expended by the use not less than a full years supply ought to be ready. This will allow due time from internal and external sources to continue the supply in proportion to the exigencies which shall occur. The schedule B ["Estimate of Artillery small Arms principal articles of Military stores and Camp Equipage for an army of 50000 men," n.d. (DLC:GW)] contains an estimate of the chief of these articles. It is to be observed that the quantities there exhibited are not additional to the present supply but the totals to be provided. As to cloathing, since we may always on a sudden emergency find a considerable supply in our markets, and the articles are more perishable, the quantity in deposit may be much less than of other articles—but it ought not under present circumstances to be less than a years supply for half the abovementioned force especially of the woolen articles.

"I proceed to the last of your questions, that which respects the stations for magazines. It is conceived that three principal permanent stations will suffice and that these ought to be Springfield and Harpers Ferry which are already chosen, and the vicinity of Rocky Mount on the Wateree in South Carolina. These stations are in a great measure central to three great subdivisions of the United States; they are so interior as to be entirely safe and yet on navigable waters which empty into the Ocean and facilitate a water conveyance to every point on our sea Coast—they are also in well settled and healthy districts of Country. That near Harper's ferry it is well known possesses extraordinary advantages for founderies and other manufactories of iron. It is expected that a canal will ere long effect a good navigation between the Wateree & the Catawba; which whenever it shall happen will render the vicinity of the Rocky Mount extremely convenient to the supply of North Carolina by inland navigation. Pittsburgh west Point in New York, the neighbourhood of Trenton in New Jersey and Fayetteville in North Carolina may properly be selected as places of particular and occasional deposit. Large Cities are as much as possible to be avoided.

"The foregoing comprises it is believed a full answer to the questions you have stated. I shall in another letter offer to your consideration some further matters which have occurred and are deemed to be of importance to our military service. With respect & esteem I have the honor to be Sir Yr very obed. servant" (Df, in Hamilton's hand, DLC:GW).

The second enclosed letter, dated "Philadelphia December 13 1798," reads: "Sir, I shall now present to your view the additional objects alluded to in my letter of this date.

"A proper organization for the Troops of the United States is a principal one. In proportion as the policy of the Country is adverse to extensive military establishments ought to be our care to render the principles of our military system as perfect as possible; endeavouring to turn to the best account such force as we at any time may have on foot, and to provide an eligible standard for the augmentations to which particular emergencies may compel a resort.

"The organization of our military force, will, it is conceived, be much improved by modelling it on the following plan.

"Let a regiment of Infantry, composed as at present of two battalions and each battalion of five companies, consist of these Officers and men viz. One Colonel, two Majors, a first and a second; one Adjutant, one Quarter Master, and one Paymaster; each of whom shall be a Lieutenant, One Surgeon and one Surgeons Mate, Ten Captains, Ten first and Ten second Lieutenants, besides the three Lieutenants above mentioned; Two Cadets with the pay and emoluments of Sergeants, Two Sergeant Majors Two Quarter Master Sergeants Two chief Musicians, first and second, Twenty other musicians, forty sergeants, forty Corporals and nine hundred and twenty privates.

"Let a regiment of Dragoons consist of Ten Troops making five Squadrons, and of these Officers and men viz.— One Colonel, Two Majors a first and second, one adjutant, one Quarter Master and one paymaster, each of whom shall be a Lieutenant, One Surgeon and one Surgeons mate, ten Captains, ten first and ten second Lieutenants, besides the three Lieutenants above mentioned, Five Cadets with the pay and emoluments of Sergeants, Two Sergeant majors Two Quarter Master Sergeants, two chief Musicians first and second, Ten other Musicians, Forty sergeants forty corporals and nine hundred and twenty privates; the privates including to each Troops, one Sadler, one Blacksmith and one Bootmaker.

"Let a regiment of Artillery consist of four battalions, each battalion of four companies and of these Officers and Men viz.— One Colonel, Four Majors, One Adjutant, One Quarter Master and one paymaster, each of whom shall be a Lieutenant, One Surgeon and Two Surgeons mates, Sixteen Captains, sixteen first and sixteen second Lieutenants, besides the three Lieutenants above mentioned, thirty two Cadets, with the pay and emoluments of Sergeants, four Sergeant Majors, four quarter master Sergeants, sixty four Sergeants, sixty four corporals, one

Chief Musician and ten other musicians—eight hundred and ninety six privates, including to each company eight artificers.

"The principal reasons for this organization will be briefly suggested.

"It will be observed that the proportion of men to Officers in the Infantry and Cavalry is considerably greater than by the present establishment.

"This presents, in the first place, the advantage of œconomy. By the proportional decrease of the Officers, savings will result in their pay, subsistence and the transportation of their baggage. The last circumstance by lessening the impediments of an Army is also favorable to the celerity of its movements.

"The command of each Officer will become more respectable. This will be an inducement to respectable men to accept military appointments, and it will be an incentive to exertion among those who shall be engaged, by upholding that justifiable pride, which is a necessary ingredient in the military spirit.

"A Company will then admit of an eligible subdivision into platoons, sections, and demi sections each of a proper front.

"Each battalion will then be of the size judged proper for a maneuvring column in the field, and it is that portion of an army which in the most approved systems of tactics is destined to fulfil this object—A battalion ought neither to be too unweildy for rapid movements nor so small as to multiply too much the subdivisions, and render each incapable either of a vigorous impulse or resistance.

"The proportion of Officers to men ought not to be greater than is adequate to the due management and command of them—A careful examination of this point will satisfy every Judge, that the number now proposed will be equal to both. This conclusion will be assisted by the idea that our fundamental order, in conformity with that of the nations of Europe generally, ought to place our infantry in three ranks; to oppose to an enemy who shall be in the same order an equal mass for attack or defense.

"These remarks explain summarily the chief reasons for the most material of the alterations which are suggested.

"But it is not the intention to recommend a present augmentation of the number of rank and file to the proposed standard. It is only wished that it may be adopted as that of the war establishment. The regiments which have been authorized may continue in this respect upon the footing already prescribed; leaving the actual augmentation to depend on events which may create a necessity for the increase of our force.

"The other alterations recommended have relation rather to systematic propriety than to very important military ends.

"The term Lieutenant Colonel in our present establishment has a relative signification, without any thing in fact to which it relates. It was introduced during our revolutionary war to facilitate exchanges of prisoners as our then enemy united the grade of Colonel with that of General. But the permanent form of our military system ought to be regulated by principle, not by the changeable and arbitrary arrangement of a particular nation. The title of Colonel which has greater respectability is more proper for the Commander of a regiment, because it does not, like the other imply a relation having no existence.

"The term ensign is changed into that of Lieutenant, as well because the latter from usage has additional respectability, offering an inducement to desireable candidates, as because the former, in its origin, signified a standard bearer, and supposed that each company had a distinct standard.

"This in practice has ceased to be the case and for a variety of good reasons a standard of Colours to each battalion of Infantry is deemed sufficient. This standard is intended to be confided to a Cadet, in whom it may be expected to excite emulation and exertion. The multiplication of grades, inconvenient with regard to exchanges, is thus avoided.

"In the cavalry it is proper to allow a standard to each squadron consisting of two Troops, and hence it is proposed to have five Cadets to a regiment.

"The nature of the Artillery service, constantly in detachment, renders it proper to compose a regiment of a greater number of Battalions than the other Corps. This our present establishment has recognized. But there is now a disorderly want of uniformity; one regiment being composed of four battalions the other of three. The same organization ought to be common to all. The diminution of the number of Musicians, while it will save expence, is also warranted by the peculiar nature of the Artillery service. They answer in this Corps few of the purposes which they fulfil in the Infantry.

"The existing laws contemplate, and with good reason, that the aids of General Officers (except of the Commander in Chief) and the Officers in the department of Inspection, shall be taken from the regiments. But they do not provide that when so taken their places in the regiments shall be supplied by others. It is conceived that this ought to be the case. The principles of the establishment suppose, for example, that three Officers to a company of a given number are the just and due proportion. If when an Officer be taken from a company to fill one of the stations alluded to, his place be not filled by another, so that the number of Officers to a company may remain the same, it must follow that the company will be deficient in Officers. It is true, that the number of a company is continually diminishing, but it diminishes in Officers as well as men; and it is not known that the proportion is varied. Practice in every institution ought to conform to principle, or there will result more or less of disorder. An Army is in many respects a machine, of which the displacement of any of the organs, if permitted to continue, injures its symmetry and energy, and leads to disorder and weakness. The increase of the number of rank and file, while it strengthens the reasons for replacing the Officers, who may be removed, will more than compensate in point of economy for the addition of Officers by the substitution. This may be reduced to the test of calculation. But though the place of an Officer in his regiment ought to be supplied upon any such removal, he ought not to lose his station in the regiment but ought to rank and rise as if he had continued to serve in it.

"The provision that Aides de camp and the Officers of Inspection shall be drawn from the line of the Army is not restricted as to grade. There ought to be such a restriction. The Aides of Major Generals ought not to be taken from a rank superior to that of Captain, nor those of the Brigadiers from a rank superior to that of first Lieutenant. The Inspectors ought in like manner to be limitted those of Brigades to the rank of Captain those of Divisions to that of Major. This will guard against the multiplication of the superior Grades by removals to fill such stations.

"The judicious establishment of general rules of promotion, liable to exceptions in favour of extraordinary service or merit, is a point of the greatest consequence. It is conceived, that these rules are the most convenient that can be devised; namely that all Officers shall rise in the regiments to which they respectively belong up to the rank of Major inclusively—that afterwards they shall rise in the line of the Army at large; with the limitation, however, that the Officers of Artillery, Cavalry and Infantry shall be confined to their respective Corps, until they shall attain the rank of Colonel.

"It is very material to the due course of military service, that the several classes of an army shall be distinguished from each other by certain known badges, and that there shall be uniformity in dress and equipment, subject to these distinctions. The dress itself indeed will constitute a part of them. It is of inferior moment what they shall be, provided they are conspicuous, œconomical, and not inconsistent with good appearance, which in an army is far from being a matter of indifference. The following uniforms and badges are recommended, but if any of them are supposed liable to exception, they may be changed at pleasure.

"The Uniform of the Commander in Chief to be a blue Coat with yellow buttons and gold Epaulets each having three silver stars, with linings cape and cuffs of Buff, in winter buff vest & breeches, in summer a white vest and Breeches of nankeen. The coat to be without lappels and embroidered on the cape cuffs and pockets. A white plume in the hat to be a further distinction. The Adjutant general, the aids and secretaries of the Commander in Chief, to be likewise distinguished by a white plume.

"The Uniform of the other General Officers to be a blue coat with yellow buttons gold epaulets lining and facings of buff, the under cloaths the same with those of the Commander in Chief.

"The Major Generals to be distinguished by two silver stars in each epaulet, and except the Inspector General, by a black and white plume, the black below— The Brigadier to be distinguished by one silver star on each epaulet and by a red and white plume, the red below. The aids of all General Officers who are taken from Regiments, and the Officers of inspection, to wear the uniforms of the Regiments from which they are taken. The aids to be severally distinguished by the like plumes, which are worn by the General Officers to whom they are respectively attached.

"The uniform of the aids of the Commander in Chief when not taken from Regiments to be a blue coat with yellow buttons and gold epaulets, buff lining and facings, the same under cloaths with the Commander in Chief.

"The Inspector General, his aids and the Officers of inspection generally, to be distinguished by a blue plume. The Quarter master General and other Military Officers in his department to be distinguished by a Green plume.

"The uniform of the Infantry and Artillery to be a blue Coat with white buttons and red facings, white under Cloaths and cocked hats: the Coats of the Infantry to be lined with white, of the Artillery with red. The uniform of the Cavalry to be a Green Coat with white buttons, lining and facings, white vest and breeches with helmet Caps.

"Each Colonel to be distinguished by two Epaulets, each Major by one epaulet on the right Shoulder and a strap on the left. All the field Officers, except as above, and the regimental Staff, to wear red plumes.

"Captains to be distinguished by an epaulet on the right shoulder, Lieutenants

by one on the left shoulder—Cadets by a strap on the right Shoulder—The epaulets and Straps of the regimental Officers to be of Silver.

"Serjeant Majors and Quarter Master sergeants to be distinguished by two red
worsted epaulets—Sergeants by a like epaulet on the right shoulder—Corporals
by a like epaulet on the left Shoulder. The flank Companies to be distinguished
by red wings on the shoulders.

"The Coats of the Musicians to be of the colours of the facings of the Corps to
which they severally belong. The Chief Musicians to wear two white worsted
epaulets.

"All the civil staff of the Army to wear plain blue Coats with yellow buttons and
white under Cloaths. No gold or silver lace except in the epaulets and straps to
be worn.

"The Commissioned Officers and Cadets to wear Swords.

"All persons belonging to the Army to wear a black Cockade with a small white
Eagle in the Centre. The cockade of the non-commissioned Officers, Musicians
and privates to be of leather with Eagles of tin.

"The Regiments to be distinguished from each other numerically. The number of each Regiment to be expressed on the buttons.

"It cannot fail to happen that Cloathing made at a distance from the Army will
in numerous instances be ill fitted to the persons to whom it is issued. This is an
inconvenience, as it respects appearance comfort and use. It merits consideration whether it may not be remedied by making provision by law for the necessary
alteration at the cost of the Soldiery. As there are always to be found Taylors in
an Army, the alterations may be made there during seasons of inactivity; and
moderate compensations may be established to be deducted out of the pay. The
Taylors, who when so employed will be exempted from military duty, will be satisfied with very small allowances; and the Soldiery will probably prefer this expence to the inconveniencies of wearing cloaths which do not fit them.

"On the subject of cloathing it is remarked with regret that the returns which
have been received exhibit none on hand; though from verbal communications
it is understood that measures are in train for obtaining a present supply. It is
desirable that some more effectual plan than has hitherto been pursued should
be adopted, to procure regular and sufficient supplies on reasonable terms—
While we depend on foreigners, will it not be advisable to import the materials
rather than take the chance of markets? And will it not even be expedient with a
view to œconomy to have the Cloathing made up in the Countries from which it
may be brought? The matter certainly deserves serious attention. Our supply in
the mode hitherto practiced is not only very precarious, but must doubtless be
obtained at a very dear rate.

"Another point no less deserving of particular attention is the composition of
the ration of provisions. It was in the last session augmented [by act of 16 July
1798] beyond all former example. It is not recollected that the ration which was
allowed during the war with Great Britain was found insufficient, by troops once
formed to military habits and acquainted with the best methods of managing
their provisions. The present ration, estimating by price, is understood to be
greater than the Ration in that war by at least forty per Cent. This is evidently a
very important augmentation. Various disadvantages attend it, a great increase of

expence, additional difficulty in furnishing under all circumstances the stipulated allowance, consequently a multiplication of the possible causes of discontent, murmur and perhaps even mutiny—the necessity of a greater number of waggons for transportation, and of course the extension of this always serious source of embarrassment to military operations.

"The quantity of spirituous liquors, which is a component part of the ration, is so large as to endanger, where they might not before exist, habits of intemperance, alike fatal to health and discipline. Experience has repeatedly shewn that many Soldiers will exchange their rum for other articles; which is productive of the double mischief of subjecting those with whom the exchange is made to the loss of what is far more necessary and to all the consequences of brutal intoxication.

"The step having been once taken, a change is delicate; but it is believed to be indispensible, and that the temporary evils of a change can bear no proportion to the permanent and immense evils of a continuance of the error.

"It may not perhaps be advisable to bring back the ration to the standard of the last War, but to modify it in some respects differently, so as not materially to effect the aggregate expence.

"It may consist of eighteen Ounces of bread or flour, one pound and a quarter of fresh beef or one pound of salted beef or three quarters of a pound of salted pork; salt, when fresh meat is issued, at the rate of one quart and Candles at the rate of a pound for every hundred Rations.

"With regard to liquor it may be best to exclude it from being a component part of the Ration, allowing a discretion to commanding Officers to cause it to be issued in quantities not exceeding half a gill per day except on extraordinary occasions.

"Vinegar also ought to be furnished when to be had at the rate of two quarts and Soap at the rate of two pounds per hundred rations, but this ought to depend on circumstances, and ought not to make part of the established Ration.

"There are often difficulties in furnishing articles of this description, and the equivalent in money is frequently rather pernicious than beneficial. Where there is a Contract the promise of such Articles is apt to prove more beneficial to the Contractor than to any other person. He commonly so manages it, that the substitute is not a real equivalent.

"But it need not be observed, that whatever is to be done in this respect must be so conducted as not to infract the conditions on which the troops now in Service were enlisted.

"It is deeply to be lamented, that a very precious period of leisure was not improved towards forming among ourselves Engineers and Artillerists, and that owing to this neglect we are in danger of being overtaken by war without competent characters of these descriptions. To form them suddenly is impossible. Much previous study and experiment are essential. If possible to avoid it a war ought not to find us wholly unprovided. It is conceived to be advisable to endeavor to introduce from abroad, at least one distinguished Engineer and one distinguished Officer of Artillery. They may be sought for preferably in the Austrian and next in the prussian Armies. The Grade of Colonel, with adequate pecuniary compensations, may attract Officers of a rank inferior to that grade in those

Armies, who will be of distinguished ability and merit—But in this, as we know from past experience, nothing is more easy than to be imposed upon—nothing more difficult than to avoid imposition—and that therefore it is requisite to commit the business of procuring such characters to some very judicious hand, under every caution that can put him upon his guard.

"If there shall be occasion for the actual employment of military force, a corps of Riflemen will be for several purposes extremely useful. The eligible proportion of Riflemen to Infantry of the line may be taken at a twentieth. Hence in the apportionment of an Army of fifty thousand Men, in my letter of this date, two thousand Riflemen are included; and in the estimate of Arms to be provided, two thousand Rifles: There is a kind of Rifle commonly called *Fergusons* which will deserve particular attention. It is understood, that it has in different European Armies supplanted the old Rifle, as being more quickly loaded and more easily kept clean. If the shot of it be equally or nearly equally sure, those advantages entitle it to a preference. It is very desirable, that this point and its comparative merit in other respects be ascertained by careful examination & experiments.

"Perhaps generally, but more certainly when the Troops shall serve in southern Climates, flannel Shirts will be most conducive to health. Will it not be adviseable to make provision for retaining a discretion in such cases either to allow a less number of flannel Shirts, equivalent to the present allowance of linnen, or if this cannot be, to furnish the Soldiery with the requisite number, deducting the difference of cost out of their pay?

"The only provision for the appointment of a Quarter Master General is to be found in the Act of the 28th of May, authorizing the president to raise a provisional Army, which limits his rank and emoluments to those of Lieut: Colonel. This provision is conceived to be entirely inadequate. The military duties of the Office are of a nature to render it of the first importance in an Army, demanding great Abilities and a character every way worthy of trust. Accordingly it is the general practice, founded upon very substantial reasons, to confide it to an Officer of high Military rank. The probability is that without a similar arrangement on our part, we shall not be able to command a fit character, and in taking one of inferior pretensions we shall subject the service to disadvantages out of all proportion to any objections which may be supposed to militate against the conferring of such rank. It is feared that an appointment under the existing provision will only create embarrassment, should there be real necessity for military exertions, and that the alternative must be, either to leave the Army destitute of so necessary an organ, or to give it one likely in the progress of things to prove unequal to the task.

"It was much desired for preventing future controversy to fix in the first instance the relative grades of the regimental Officers. That of the field Officers has been rendered impossible, without injustice and the hazard of much dissatisfaction, by the impossibility of completing the arrangement in Connecticut and the three most southern States. But upon close examination many obstacles opposed a definitive establishment of the relative rank, even of the Officers of Companies in the Regiments which have been organized. Numerous circumstances, which ought to influence the decision, are unknown; and without this knowledge, a final arrangement might lead to very aukward and perplexing results. In consideration of this difficulty, no more than a temporary one, liable to future revision, has been adopted: It will be necessary to attend to this in the appointments, and to signify to the persons that they are to obey according to the order of nomination, but that the president reserves to himself the right, *where cogent reasons for it* shall appear, to change the relative rank which that order may seem to recognize. He will judge whether in making the nomination to the Senate a like reserve is necessary.

"I am well aware, that several of the matters suggested in this letter will require legislative provision. If the whole or any of them shall be approved by the Executive, no time ought to be lost in recommending them to the consideration of Congress. As to some of them it is very desirable, that the necessary provision by law should precede the inlistment of the Men—to avoid the obstacle to a change which may result from Contract. With great respect & esteem, I have the honor to be, Sir, Your obedient servant, Go: Washington" (LS, PPRF).

To James McHenry

Sir   Philada Decr 13 1798

You will observe that in the arrangement of the officers alloted to New York there is an alternative of Wm S. Smith or Abijah Hammond[1] for Lt Colonel Commandant. Various considerations demand that the motive of this hesitation should be explained. Had military qualifications alone been consulted the name of Colonel Smith would have stood singly and he would have been deemed a valuable acquisition to the service. Had there ever been no other source of objection than the erroneous political opinions of late attributed to him, his honor and attachment to his country would have been relied upon. But as well myself as the two generals whose aid I have had in the nominations have been afflicted with the information well or ill founded that he stands charged in the opinion of his fellow citizens with very serious instances of private misconduct; instances which affect directly his integrity as a man. The instances alleged are various but there is one which has come forward in a shape which did not permit us to refuse it our attention. It respects an attempt knowingly to pledge property to Major Burrows by way of security, which was before conveyed or mortgaged for its full value to Mr William Constable; without giving notice of the circumstance, and with the aggravation, that Major Burrows had become the Creditor of Col. Smith through friendship to an amount which has proved entirely ruinous to him. While the impossibility of disregarding this information forbade the selection of Col. Smith absolutely, the possibility that it might admit of some fair explanation dissuaded from a conclusion against him.

As it will be in your power to obtain further lights on the subject it has appeared adviseable to leave the matter in the undetermined form in which it is presented and to assign the reason for it. You are at perfect liberty to communicate this letter to the President. Candour is particularly due to him in such a case. It is my wish to give him every proof of frankness, respect and esteem.[2] Lest it should be suspected that Major Burrows has officiously interfered to the prejudice of Col. Smith, it is but justice to him to declare that such a suspicion would be entirely without foundation. With great consideration & regard I have the honor to be Sir Your obedt servt

Df, in the hand of Alexander Hamilton, DLC:GW. There are also two versions of this letter in Timothy Pickering's letter book (MHi: Pickering Papers).

1. In a letter to McHenry of 27 Aug. 1798, Alexander Hamilton had this to say: "Mr. Abijah Hammond who was in one of the N Eng Regiments during the War though not soliciting it would accept a Regiment. I do not know his character as an Officer. But from his present condition in Society, being a man of large fortune & fair character, from his being a man of good understanding & of exertion, I conclude that he would make a respectable Commander of a Regiment" (Syrett, *Hamilton Papers*, 22:165–66). As GW indicates here, Hammond, who at this time was a merchant in New York City, was not recommended for an appointment. By "the arrangement of the officers alloted to New York," GW probably was referring to a document in DLC:GW filed at the end of 1798 and headed Company Arrangement New York, which lists thirty men by rank and residence.

2. For the earlier rejection by the Senate of President Adams's nomination of his son-in-law William S. Smith as adjutant general in the New Army, see McHenry to GW, 18 July 1798. Smith had borrowed money in 1796 from William Ward Burrows of Kenderton, Pa., for his land speculation in upstate New York, and he had pledged as security for the loan property that he had already conveyed to William Constable, a New York land speculator (Alexander Hamilton to Oliver Wolcott, Jr., 2 April 1797, and note 10, in Syrett, *Hamilton Papers*, 21:54–55). For John Adams's refutation of the charges of impropriety on the part of Smith in his dealings with Burrows and Constable, see McHenry to GW, 28 December. McHenry and President Adams decided that Smith's name should be put forward as a lieutenant colonel to command a regiment in the New Army, and the Senate approved his nomination (see McHenry to GW, 5 Jan. 1799).

From James McHenry

Thursday morning [13 December 1798]

The Secy of war has the honour to inform the commander in Chief, that he expects a letter this morning respecting Col. Hall which if received shall be immediately sent to him.[1]

AL, DLC:GW.

1. The letter regarding Josias Carvil Hall (1746–1814) of Havre de Grace, Md., who was given command of the 9th Regiment of Infantry in the New Army on 31 Dec. 1799, has not been found. During the Revolutionary War Hall was colonel of the Fourth Battalion of the Maryland Regulars, and in 1794–95 he was general of the 1st Maryland militia brigade.

To James McHenry

Private
Dear Sir,   Chester [Pa.] 14th Decr 1798.

Having requested that the nomination of Mr Custis might be with held (even if it should meet the Presidents approbation under any circumstances) until I could consult his Grandmother (Mrs Washington) and mother Mrs Stuart; I further pray that no mention of his name for such an Office may be made until the result is known; because, if their consent, being an only son, indeed the only male of his family, cannot be had, it would be better that the arrangement of him should pass *entirely* unnoticed, to prevent the uneasy sensations which might arise from disappointment if the knowledge of it should get to him.

He now stands as Cornet, in the Troop proposed to be Commanded by Lawrence Lewis—who was an Aid de Camp to Genl Morgan—on the Insurgent Expedition in 1794.[1]

Just as I was leaving the City to day, I had an opportunity for the first time, of seeing Captn Saml Henley—who is a Man of a handsome & gentlemanly appearance. Having no evidence respecting him, except from his own letter, while we were arrangeing the Massachusetts line, he was not included in it. Afterwards, a letter from Genl Shepherd recommended him; but at *that time* we did not conceive it of sufficient weight to travel the ground over again. I must acknowledge however, that his external appearance (for I had no conversation with him) made so favourable an impression on me, that (being an old Officer too, and brother to a very worthy man) I should be very glad if his conduct will stand the test of investigation—to see him put as a *Captain*, in place of some Captain in that line, who has not served in the Revolutionary War. The particular one I cannot now name, but it will not be difficult to ascertain.[2] With very great esteem & regard I am—Dear Sir Your Most Obedt Hble Servant

Go: Washington

P.S. I know no character in the New England States (since the declination of Genls Knox and Brooks) that have fairer pretensions to be appointed a Brigadier, or even Majr General, than Genl Cobb. And if Genl Dayton does not accept his appointment—pray press Colo. Howard *strongly* to come forward.[3]

ALS, LNHT: George and Katherine Davis Collection; ADfS, in Tobias Lear's hand, DLC:GW.

1. Tobias Lear let the cat out of the bag and wrote to George Washington Parke Custis about his appointment as a cornet in the troop of horse to be formed by Lawrence Lewis. Custis was delighted, and Martha Washington offered no objections. See GW to David Stuart, 30 Dec. 1798.

2. In the list of candidates for army appointments from Massachusetts recently compiled at their meeting in Philadelphia by GW, Alexander Hamilton, and Charles Cotesworth Pinckney, opposite the name of Samuel Henley is this notation: "Capt last war conductor of Military stores since[.] Inquire" (Syrett, *Hamilton Papers*, 22:334). Hamilton provided Senator Benjamin Goodhue of Massachusetts with a list of army candidates from Massachusetts, and after consulting several Massachusetts congressmen Goodhue sent Hamilton a list of candidates with his recommendations about each (ibid., 315–19). Henley's name was not on Senator Goodhue's list.

3. John Eager Howard of Maryland was one of the men whom GW listed as a possible brigadier general in his Suggestions for Military Appointments, 14 July 1798, printed above.

To James McHenry

Sir,   Susquehanna [Pa.] 16th December 1798

Being detained on the East bank of this River by Northwesterly winds & consequent low tides, I shall devote some of the moments of my detention in writing to you on an important subject.[1]

In a conversation [I] had with you in Philadelphia, you discovered the very just opinion, that for the proper & successful direction of our military affairs, it was essential that it should be as far as possible concentrated in one, or a few principal Officers, with whom alone the head of the War Department should communicate. Any other plan would doubtless contravene the ideas of military propriety, and would involve you in an impracticable detail—producing necessarily confusion and imbecility in the System. You seemed also desirous that I should express to you some ideas of the proper arrangement. Close application to other matters with which you charged me whilst I was in Philadelphia, and my extreme impatience (on account of the season & weather) to leave it, must be my apology for not doing this sooner.

You know the ground, Sir, on which I accepted the command of the Army; and that it is a part of my plan to decline the occupations of the Office unless, and until my presence in the field should be required for actual operations, or other imperious circumstances might require my assistance. Persevering in this plan, I cannot undertake to assume a direct agency, incompatible therewith: and a halfway acting, might be more inconvenient than totally declining it. The other General Officers will, I am persuaded, execute with alacrity any service to which they may be destined. In this assurance, I take the liberty to advise you to adopt the following plan.[2]

Let the charge and direction of our Military affairs in the three most southern States be entrusted to General Pinckney. If indeed it will not derange him too much, to take immediately, a more northerly position—and more convenient for the purpose, let Virginia be added, and his position be in it; leaving So. Carolina and Georgia to the care of Brigadier General Washington, subject to the orders of the former; through whom, all the Military concerns of those States should pass to the War Office. General Hamilton may be charged with Superintending, under your direction, all the Troops and Posts which shall not be confided to General Pinckney; including the Army under General Wilkenson. His proxemity to the Seat of Governmt will render this not inconvenient. The Official letters of the Commander of the Western army may pass open through your hands, to enable you to give immediate orders in cases which may be too urgent to wait for the Agency of General Hamilton.

The Companies to be recruited, according to the plan laid down before me in the States of Kentucky and Tennessee, should be subjected to the direction of Major General Pinckney, because they compose a part of the Regimts which are to be raised in the three Southern States; but the present force in Tennessee must be excluded therefrom, otherwise an interference with the Command of Brigad[ie]r Wilkenson, and the mode of his communication with the Department of War, would follow, and confusion result from it.

It will be useful that the whole of the Recruiting Service should be under one direction, and this properly appertains to the Office of Inspector General. He will of course be authorised to call to his aid the other General Officers.

On this plan there will be two principal Organs, through whom all our Military affairs will be transacted with your Department. This will serve to unite and simplify the objects of your attention and will enable you to devote it principally to the considering & maturing of general Plans and to an effectual Superintendence of their execution on a large Scale. With respect & esteem I have the honor to be Sir Your Most Obedt Hble Servt

Go: Washington

ALS, NNGL; retained copy, DLC:GW; copy, DLC: Hamilton Papers. Tobias Lear noted on the retained copy: "Copy sent to Majr Genl Pinckney Decr 30th 1798."

1. GW, who left Philadelphia "After dinner" on 14 Dec., spent that night in Chester and the next one at Elkton, and from there he "Set out after a very early breakfast; and was detained at Susquehanna from 10 Oclock until the next morning" (*Diaries*, 6:326–27).

2. This essentially was the plan followed in 1799. See McHenry to GW, 30 Mar. 1799.

From Jacob Read

Sir   Philadelphia Wednesday 19th Decembr 1798

I obey the request of the Author of the within *Scheme of a Review* in presenting the inclosed copy for your Excellency's perusal[.] Mr Simons supposed you were still in this City which I believe induced him to make the request, and I shou'd not have deemed the subject of sufficient importance to have troubled you with a Letter had not my own feelings been a good deal gratified in an opportunity of presenting to you[r] View the high state of discipline in which the Militia of Charleston are. for to be able with promptitude & exactness to perform the Evolutions ordered in the scheme both officers & men must be much advanced in the Military science.[1]

I with great pleasure avail myself of the present opportunity of enquiring after your own & Lady's health & of expressing the hope that you arrived at Mount Vernon in perfect health & without accident.

Mrs Read requests you will do her the honour to present her respectful Compliments to Mrs Washington to which I pray you also to add mine. I am with the greatest respect and regard Your most obedt Servt

Jacob Read

ALS, NN: Washington Collection.

1. James Simons's *Scheme of the Review, for the 13 November, 1798, in Pursuance of Orders from Brigadier General Washington* (Philadelphia, 1798) is a single sheet. "*Brigadier General Washington*" is William Washington. Read was in Philadelphia as senator from South Carolina.

From Rawleigh Colston

Sir, December 20th 1798

It is truly painful to me to trouble you again on a subject which I am persuaded has already proved very vexatious and unprofitable—The letter which I had pleasure of receiving from you in July last, I transmitted to General Marshall agreeable to your request, and referred him to the proceedings of the Court of Chancery for the necessary information [1]—I have not yet been favoured with an answer from him, which perhaps he may decline from motives of delicacy in respect to our connection, unless he receives a direct Application from you—My friend Mr Keith who will deliver you this, will shew you the Original Platt and Courses of the late Colo. Mercer's land exhibeted to the purchasers and referred to in their deeds, as certified by you—It appears to me very important to the persons in possession of this property, that the survey should be recorded in the County of Frederick—for this purpose I am told it would be proper for you to reacknowledge it before witnesses, on whose testimony it will be admitted to record [2]—There are several persons in possession of these lotts who are in a similar situation with my self, and anxiously wish to know your final determination—If you conceive it necessary for your safety that an amicable suit in Chancery should be instituted, it will be done in the manner most agreeable to your wishes—I am with the highest respect and veneration Sir, your Mo. Ob⟨t⟩

Rawleigh Colston

ALS, DLC:GW.

1. GW's letter to Colston is dated 16 July, but see especially Colston to GW, 1 June 1798, n.1.

2. No response to this inquiry has been found, but on 21 Jan. 1799 GW signed a statement, witnessed in Alexandria by James Keith, Charles Simms, and one other person, which reads: "I do acknowlege that this is the Platt referred to in the Deeds made for the Lands of George Mercer and the Platt exhibited at the Sale of those Lands" (owned [1996] by University Archives, Stamford, Conn.). The plat is missing.

From Bernard Hubley, Jr.

Dear General   Northumberland [Pa.] Decemr 20th 1798

At this period when the exertions of every Federalist is requisite for the preservation of the United States, I should deem it criminal in me not to offer my services; I do not think it necessary to procure a recommendation in my favour to enter or join the Army, though should you conceive it to be, the Militia Officers of the County, with such other Characters of first respectability, would with pleasure give it, the opinion entertained by them of me, is greater than the station I could at present expect, or would wish to hold, their wish and desire, I am convinced would be that I should be a General Officer, and my own is, to have the command of a Regiment; should there be other Characters applying for this station, Men of superior abilities and attachment to our Country, I should wish them to have the preference; You will I beg excuse me for Writing to you on this subject, for I could not refrain as I was an Officer last War, I Wrote to our beloved President, on the twelfth day of July last, offering my services in such station, I should be allowed to become most serviceable, whenever you were ready to take the Field, or should appear at the Head of our Army. shortly after I became a Resident here, I was Commissioned Lieutenant of the County, after being in this Office nearly Four Years, the Legislature of this State, about Six Years since enacted a new Militia Law, I was then Commissioned the Brigade Inspector,

and which I am at present. I am Dear General with every sentiment of affection and esteem Your Most Obdt & Most Hume Servt

Berd Hubley Jun.

ALS, DLC:GW.

Bernard Hubley, Jr. (1754–1810), who in 1808 had the first volume of his
American Revolution printed in Northumberland, Pa., served in Pennsylvania's
German Battalion during the Revolutionary War from August 1776 until 1 Jan.
1781, when he retired as a captain.

From William Russell

Sir   Middletown [Conn.] 20 December 1798
    I returnd Home a few days ago after more than a month's ab-
sence & assure you I was deeply mortified upon finding that your
Ram and Straw Machine were still here—I very much regret that
different attempts to Send them forwards have been ineffectual
& that three several conveyances for their passage engag'd at Hartford have each of them been violated—As I found our River froze
up. *I fear* they must now remain here for the Winter—In the early
part of Summer if not sooner I trust they will certainly go forwards,
in the interim I beg to acknowledge the honor of your last favor &
of your obliging punctuality in procuring the early wheat of which
I hope to have a good account from my Freind in England.[1]
    With the Sheep & Chaff Engine I propose sending an Imple-
ment which I conceive will prove of real utility upon your Planta-
tion & to the whole Country when Communicated—It is called by
the Inventor a "Ground Borer" from its penetrating the ground
exact in the same manner as a Gimblet or Nail passer bores Timber, and by having thiese "Ground Borers" of the exact Size of the
bottom end of the Posts which are to be set up, it afords the means
not only of making the holes with dispatch but likewise of fixing
them quite firm & steady in the ground, the earth around them
remaining quite solid instead of being loose & disturb'd, as in the
common method by the Pick Axe & Spade as hitherto practis'd—
I am told a Man & a Boy will easily bore 12 holes in an hour where
the Ground is free from Rocks & Stones—I feel the more inclind
to mention this instrement to you at this juncture from an idea
that it may *possibly* be of use to you in Military operations where
chevaux de frize are wanted, and possibly in throwing up intrench-

ments—It was my intention to have communicated this invention as generally & as early as I could, but the bare suspicion that it may in any possible contingency be of use to you in your military operations will induce me to let it remain as it is until the apprehensions of Warr shall cease & be happily dispers'd by the basis of a just & honorable Peace—that this happy æra may speedily approach—that your well earned Laurells may continue blooming with increasing vigor thro. life, and be accompanied with the best of blessing's even until Death is the constant & fervent wish of Sir Yor Sincere & Obedt ⟨*mutilated*⟩

Willm Russell

ALS, ViMtV.

1. For Russell's original offer of a ram and "Straw Machine," or "Chaff Engine," see Russell to GW, 8 Sept.; for reference to the correspondence resulting from the long delay in sending these things, see note 1 of that document. GW replied to Russell on 6 Jan. from Mount Vernon: "Sir, I have been duly favored with your letter of the 20th Ulto—and however desirous I was of receiving the Ram, and the Straw Machine in season, I am well apprised of the difficulties which were opposed to their passage, and must submit to the disappointment, in hopes of obtaining them in time for the next.

"Such a ground borer as you describe, will be of singular use to me, and I shall thank you for sending it with the other articles, and the cost thereof; which shall be paid on demand. Having much Posting & railing to do, when the weather will permit, the sooner I could bring this borer into operation the more useful it would be to me.

"I pray you to accept my best thanks for your kind wishes—and mine that you may see the return of many happy new Years—being Sir Your Most Obedient and Very Hble Servant Go: Washington" (letterpress copy, DLC:GW; LB, DLC:GW).

To William Thornton

Dear Sir,   Mount Vernon Decr 20th 1798

Enclosed is a check on the Bank of Alexandria for five hundred Dollars, to enable Mr Blagden, by your draughts, to proceed in laying in Materials for carrying on my buildings in the Federal City.[1]

I saw a building in Philadelphia of about the same front & elevation that are to be given to my two houses, which pleased me. It consisted also of two houses united, Doors in the centre—a pediment in the roof and dormar window on each side of it in front—skylights in the rear.

If this is not incongruous with rules of architecture, I should be

glad to have my two houses executed in this style. Let me request
the favor of you to know from Mr Blagden what additional cost
will be.[2] I am—Dear Sir Your Most Obedt Hble Servt

Go: Washington

ALS, ViMtV; ADfS, DLC:GW; LB, DLC:GW. GW wrote on the cover: "Favored by
Mr [Thomas] Law Esqr."

1. For GW's "buildings in the Federal City," see GW to the District of Columbia Commissioners, 28 Sept., n.2, and 27 Oct., nn.2 and 3. A Day Book entry
for 20 Dec. reads: "By a Check on the Bank of Alexa. in favor of Doctr Willm
Thornton—to be applied towards the building my Houses in the City of Washington by Mr George Blagden—[$]500."

2. After Thornton expressed a lack of enthusiasm for the "pediment in the
roof," GW at first refused to give it up but apparently did so in the end. See
Thornton to GW, 21 Dec., and GW to Thornton, 30 Dec. 1798. See also note 1
of that document.

From Israel Shreve

Dear Gen: Fayette County 21st Decemr 1798

Although you forbid me Writing any more to you in your Last
Letter to me dated the 1st of Octr Last But my Situation is So
intolerable I cannot forbear[.] my aproaching Punishment is
Greater than any crime I have Committed, the Cruel Change
of times in respect to the Circulating of Cash is the whole cause of
my failure of Punctuality[.] at this time I have as I have Said before
as much money Due to me upon bond & Interest as I Owe to
Mankind in the world and upwards of 600 Acres of Land Left
with a pretty good stock &c.—But after all the Exertions I could
make a Cassa was Served upon me the 11th Inst. Returnable next
week when I must Lie in a poor dirty Misurable Loathsom prison
as a Punishment for not paying money at a time when there is next
to none in Circulation, I have known your Excellency Several
times Repreave Crimanals who had forfited their lives & restore
them again to be Citizens I have a good Wife and Several dear
Little Children Round me who has Committed no fault to merit
So greavious a turn in Life If your Excellency Could Condisend to
pass by this grevious punishment it would be hundreds to my advantage and prehaps not one cent to your Disadvantage you may
Say why dont you fall upon those that owe you the money I answer
I have not Judgment Bonds against them and Could not Recover
of them Soon enough to stop this Suit, I wrote you that my Brother

Samuel who Lives 3½ miles from the federal City would pay you this payment that I am Sued for I Sent my Son John to him Since you have been at Philadelphia[.] my Brother had then not Sold But promised to See you when you returned home and if possable Settle of this Installment with you Some how or other, I have Called the people together who principly owe me the Money who have made Such arangements As I think will ensure the next payments Punctually[.] to add to my misfortune I have been Confined to my room for three weeks by Severe Sickness and am Still Scarcely able to walk across the room, I can Say no more only that I know I must Submit to your pleasure[.] if you release me I will never rest untill the money is paid, and Shall have cause ever to Love and regard your Name, and my Children after me I am not filled with resentment knowing the money is Justly due.[1] I am dear General with Great Respect your Most Obedt Servt

Israel Shreve

ALS, NN: Emmet Collection. The letter was addressed to Washington in Philadelphia and changed to Mount Vernon.

1. GW replied on 10 Jan., saying that he would authorize the sheriff to stay the proceedings against Shreve until 1 April 1799.

From William Thornton

Dear Sir City of Washington Decr 21st 1798.

I had this Moment the honor of your Letter of yesterday's Date, inclosing a Check for five hundred Dollars, on the Bank of Alexandria; wch shall be duly appropriated to the prosecution of your two Houses in the City of Washington.

I will make the necessary Enquiries of Mr Blagdin relative to any Alteration you may be pleased to direct. It is a Desideratum in Architecture to hide as much as possible the Roof—for which reason, in London, there is generally a parapet to hide the Dormant Windows. The Pediment may with propriety be introduced, but I have some Doubts with respect to its adding any beauty. It may however give some additional Convenience. Every thing shall be duly considered, and laid before you. Accept, Dear Sir the highest respect of your affectionate Friend

William Thornton

ALS, owned (1995) by Mr. Albert H. Small, Washington, D.C.

From David Shepherd Garland

Sir   Cabellsburg Virga Amhe[r]st Co[unt]y Decr 24 [17]98

I am informed that there is a quantity of Land lying between the Great Kanhawa and Sandy River in this State which was set a part for the payment of some Officers and Soilders who was on an Expedition Against the Indians about or before Braddocks Campain; which Land still remains undevided. I am some what interested in that claim, but from it's antiquity can meet with no person who can give me any sattisfactory information on that subject. Supposing you are well Acquainted with the circumstances Under which this Land was Granted and by what authority and to whom, I trust you will pardon me for making this inquiry; and be so good as to give me such information (if in your power) as will enable me to prosue the inquirey with success, if this Land was granted by Order of the Govner and Council of this State, them Records are all destroyed, but perhaps there still may remain (within your knowledge) some evidence thereof, if so be pleased to inform me. I am with due respect yr m. O. H. St

David S. Garland

A Letter by post to Cabbelsburg Post Office will meet with a ready Conveyance.[1] D.S.G.

ALS, ViMtV.

David Shepherd Garland (1769–1841), a native of Amherst County and a member of the Virginia bar, was elected to the Virginia house of delegates from his county eighteen times between 1799 and 1835. He was elected to the state senate in 1809 and served in the U.S. House of Representatives in 1810 and 1811.

1. No response to Garland's inquiry has been found. For the grant of 200,000 acres to the participants in the Fort Necessity campaign, under the terms of Robert Dinwiddie's Proclamation of 1754, see GW to Botetourt, 8 Dec. 1769, and notes; Petition to Botetourt, c.15 Dec. 1769, and note 1; GW to Botetourt, 5 Oct. 1770, and notes; and Petition to Governor and Council, 1–6 Nov. 1771, and notes.

Letter not found: from Richard Raynal Keene, 24 Dec. 1798. On 28 Dec. GW wrote Keene that he was returning "the papers contained in your letter of the 24th instant . . . [and] the letter also."

From Alexander Spotswood

Dr Sir   December 24. 1798.

I received a letter last Week from Mr Short, dated Novr 1st—he Says Mr Hites absence from home, has prevented his doing any thing towards the purchase of Andrew Woodrows Survey—but so Soon as hite returns, he will have the bussiness closed to your Satisfaction.

I have also recd a letter from Mr Feild, he acknowledges the Rect of mine, covering Sundry papers to enable him to find out the propriety of the land opposite yours on Rough Creek—But observes, that being but newly come into the green river Country, & Takeing up his Settlement in the woods, will of course be much confind at home; but Says he will do every thing in his power to Comply with your Wishes.[1]

your favr to my Son dated 22d Novr Acknowledgeing the rect of his of the 13th Covering the publication of gracchus was handed me by my Servant—& by me opened through Mistake.[2]

I confess I was much Shagreened, that my Son whose political principals in favr of goverment & its administrations; had always been in unison with mine—should at this late hour—Suffer himself to be transformed into a Jacobin, by the publication of gracchus as insignificant & contemptible as the Author himself—However, my mind was Soon eased; on my Son declaring the letter of the 13. with his Signature to it was a forgery—he tels me he has wrote you, denying the Same to be his, and that he has wrote & given to his Brother a duplicate—for fear the first may have Miscarried.[3]

We have had nothing lately from our assembly—and from the, late movement of a certain Jacobin—I am inclined to believe, his agents has wrote him that the assembly will not be so pliant as they wished & expected.[4]

My family enjoy good health & desires there best regards to you Mrs Washington & Miss Custis as well as dr Sr Yr Affe & ⟨Ob st⟩

A. Spotswood

ALS, NjMoNP.

1. See GW to Spotswood, 11 Feb. 1798, n.5.

2. These are letters to and from Alexander Spotswood, Jr. See GW to Alexander Spotswood, Jr., 22 Nov., n.1.

3. The brother was probably John Augustine Spotswood who visited Mount Vernon on 25 December. See John Augustine Washington to GW, 31 December.

4. For the actions of the Virginia legislature, see John Marshall to GW, 8 Jan. 1799, and note 2 of that document.

To George Washington Motier Lafayette

My dear George,   Mount Vernon 25th Decr 1798

Having written a long letter to General La Fayette I shall write but a short one to you; and it shall relate principally, if not altogether, to domestic concerns.

At the time you left this country you could not, less than I did, believe that in the course of events any occurrence could arise, which would again take me from the walks of Mount Ver[no]n— But the injuries we have received, and are threatned with, have induced me once more (if occasion should require it) to tread the thorny path of public life; and for this purpose I have accepted a Commission to command the Armies of the United States—if, unfortunately, we should be forced into a War.

Your acquaintances Lawrence Lewis is appointed Captain of a Troop of ⟨Light Dragoons; but intends, before he enters the Camp of Mars to engage in that of Venus; Eleanor Custis & he having entered into a contract of Marriage; which, I understand, is to be fulfilled on my birth day (the 22d of Feby)—Washington Custis preferring a Military career to literary pursuits, is appointed Cornet in Lewis's Troop, & Washington Craik a Lieutenancy. Young Carroll of Carrolton, will be a Volunteer Aid of mine, and Mr Lear is my Secretary.

Young gentlemen of the first families, fortunes & expectations in the United States, are offering their Services; but I hope, and most ardently pray, that the Directory of your Country will not, by a perseverance in the insults & injuries which they have heaped on this, make it necessary to resort to Arms to repel an Invasion, or to do ourselves justice. I can undertake to affirm, that necessity *only* will drive us to it, although I am but just returned from a six weeks visit in Philadelphia to make arrangements there for it, eventually.

Mrs & Mr Law & their pet, Eliza, Mr & Mrs Peter & their two children, and Doctr Stuart and family (whom I ought to have mentioned first) are all well; and would, if they knew I was writing to you, request to be remembered to you in the most affectionate terms. I recollect no material change that has taken place in men or things since you left America. Alexandria continues to thrive, and the Public buildings in the federal City go on well: and many private ones are commencing for the accomodation of the members of Congress, & Officers of Government, preparatory to the removal of the Government to that place.

Mrs Washington holds you in constant remembrance, and offers you every good wish, which she prays you to extend to your amiable mother and Sisters⟩ whenever it may be in your Power—Nelly, Washington & Lewis would, I am sure, unite heartily in these, were they at home; but all of them are absent—the first at Hope Park—& the other two beyond the Mountains. When the clouds which at present overcast the Political horizon are dispelled, it would give all your friends great pleasure to see you in your old walks—and to none more than to your Sincere & Affectionate friend

Go: Washington

P.S. If Mr Frestal should be with you, or you should have occasion to write to him, be so good as to present him with the best wishes of this family.

ALS (incomplete), NNPM; ALS (letterpress copy), DLC:GW; LB, DLC:GW. The second and third pages of the ALS are missing; the text for those pages has been taken from the letterpress copy and printed in angle brackets.

To Lafayette

My dear Sir,   Mount Vernon 25th Decr 1798

I am indebted to you for the following letters, dated the 6th of October and 20th of December of the last year, and 26th of April, 20th of May, 20th of August & 5th of September in the present.[1] If more have been written, they have fallen into other hands, or miscarried on their passage.

Convinced as you must be of the fact, it would be a mere waste of time to assure you of the sincere, & heart felt pleasure I derived from finding by the above letters, that you had not only regained your liberty, but was in the enjoyment of better health than could have been expected from your long, & rigorous confinement; and that Madame la Fayette and the young ladies were able to survive it at all. On these desirable events I can add with truth, that amongst your numerous friends none can offer their congratulations with more warmth, or who prays more sincerely for the perfect restoration of your lady's health than I do.

It is equally unnecessary for me, to apologize to you for my long silence;[2] when, by a recurrence to your own letters, you will find my excuse; for by these it will appear, that if you had embarked for this country at the epochs mentioned therein, no letters of mine could have arrived in Europe before your departure from thence; until by your favor of the 20th of August I was informed that your Voyage to America was postponed, for the reasons which were then given; and which conveyed the first idea to my mind that a letter from me, might find you in Europe.

The letter last mentioned, together with that of the 5th of September, found me in Philadelphia; whither I had gone for the purpose of making some Military arrangements with the Secretary of War; and where every moment of my time was so much occupied in that business, as to allow no leisure to attend to any thing else.

I have been thus circumstantial in order to impress you with the true cause of my silence, and to remove from your mind, if a doubt had arisen there, that my friendship for you had undergone no diminution or change; and that no one in the United States would receive you with opener arms, or with more ardent affection than I should, after the differences between this Country & France are adjusted, and harmony between the Nations is again restored. But it would be uncandid, and incompatible with that friendship I have always professed for you to say, (and on your own account) that I wish it before. For you may be assured, my dear Sir, that the scenes you would meet with, and the part you would be stimulated to act in case of an open rupture, or even if matters should remain in statu quo, would be such as to place you in a situation which no address, or human prudence, could free you from embarrassment. In a word, you wd lose the confidence of one party or the other, perhaps both—were you here under these circumstances.

To give you a complete view of the politics, and situation of things in this Country would far exceed the limits of a letter; and to trace effects to their causes, would be a work of time. But the sum of them may be given in a few words, and it amounts to this. That a party exists in the United States, formed by a combination of causes, who oppose the government in all its measures, and are determined (as all their conduct evinces) by clogging its wheels, *indirectly* to change the nature of it, and to subvert the Constitution. To effect this, no means which have a tendency to accomplish their purposes, are left unessayed. The friends of Government, who are anxious to maintain its Neutrality, and to preserve the Country in Peace; and to adopt measures to produce these desirable ends are charged by them, as being Monarchists—Aristocrats—& Infractors of the Constitution; which, according to their interpretation of it, would be a mere cypher; while *they*, arrogated to themselves (until the eyes of the People began to discover how outrageously they had been treated in their Commercial concerns by the directory of France, and that that was a ground on which they could no longer tread) the sole merit of being the Friends of France; when, in fact, they had no more regard for that Nation than for the Grand Turk, farther than their own views were promoted by it, denouncing those who differed from them in opinion; whose principles are purely American; and whose sole view was to observe a strict Neutrality; with acting under British Influence; with being directed by her Councils; nay, with being her Pensioners.

This is but a short sketch of what would require much time to illustrate; and is given with no other view than to shew you what would be your situation *here*, at this crisis, under such circumstances as it unfolds.

You have expressed a wish, worthy the benevolence of your heart, that I would exert all my endeavors to avert the calamatous effects of a rupture between our Countries. Believe me, my dear friend, that no man can deprecate a measure of this sort with more horror than I should—that no one, during the whole of my Administration, laboured more incessantly, & with more sincerity & zeal than I did, to avoid this, and to render every justice—nay favor to France—consistent with the Neutrality which had been proclaimed to the World; Sanctioned by Congress; and approved by the State Legislatures and the People at large in their Town & County meetings. But Neutrality was not the point at which France was aiming; for whilst it was crying Peace—Peace—and pretending that they did not wish us to be embroiled in their quarrel with Great Britain, they were pursuing measures in *this Country* so repugnant to its Sovereignty, and so incompatible with every principle of Neutrality, as *must*, inevitably, have produced a War with the latter. And when they found that the Government *here*, was resolved to adhere steadily to its plan of Neutrality, their next step was to destroy the confidence of the People in, & to seperate them from it; for which purpose their Diplomatic Agents were specially Instructed; and in the attempt were aided by inimical characters among ourselves; not as I observed before because they loved France better than any other Nation, but because it was an instrument to facilitate the destruction of their own Government.

Hence proceeded those charges wch I have already enumerated against the friends to Peace & order. No doubt remains on this side of the Water, that to the representations of, & encouragements given by these people, is to be ascribed, in a great measure, the infractions of our treaty with France; their violation of the Laws of Nations; disregard of justice; and even of sound policy. But herein they have not only deceived France, but were deceived themselves, as the event has proved, for no sooner did the Yeomanry of this Country come to a right understanding of the nature of the dispute, than they rose as one man with a tender of their services—their lives—and their fortunes—to support the government of their choice, and to defend their Country. This has produced a declaration from them (how sincere let others judge) that if the French should attempt to invade this country, that they, themselves, would be amongst the foremost to repel the attack.

You add in another place, that the Executive Directory are disposed to an accomodation of all differences. If they are sincere in this declaration, let them evidence it by actions, for words, unaccompanied therewith, will not be much regarded now. I would pledge myself, that the Government & People of the United States, will meet them heart & hand, at *fair* negociation; having no wish more ardent, than to live in Peace with all the World, provided they are suffered to remain undisturbed in their just rights. of this their patience, forbearance, and repeated solicitations under accumulated injuries & insults, are incontestible proofs—but it is not to be inferred from hence that they will suffer any Nation under the Sun (while they retain a proper sense of Virtue & Independence) to trample upon their rights with impunity; or to direct, or influence the internal concerns of their Country.

It has been the policy of France, and that of the opposition party amongst ourselves, to inculcate a belief that all those who have exerted themselves to keep this Country in Peace, did it from an overweening attachment to Great Britain. But it is a solemn truth, and you may count upon it, that it is void of foundation; and propagated for no other purpose than to excite popular clamour against those whose aim was peace, and whom they wished out of their way.

That there are many amongst us who wish to see this country embroiled on the side of Great Britain—and others who are anxious that we should take part with France against her, admits of no doubt. But it is a fact on which you may entirely, and absolutely rely, that the Governing Powers of the Country, & a very large part of the People, are true Americans in principle; attached to the interests of it; and unwilling, under any circumstances whatsoever, to participate in the Politics, or contests of Europe: Much less since they have found that France, having forsaken the ground she first took, is interfering in the internal concerns of all Nations, Neutral as well as Belligerent, and setting the world in an uproar.

After my Valadictory Address to the People of the United States, you would, no doubt, be somewhat surprised to hear that I had again consented to gird on the Sword. But having struggled eight or nine years against the Invasion of our Rights by one Power, & to establish an Independence of it, I could not remain an unconcerned Spectator of the attempts of another Power to accomplish the same object, though in a different way, with less pretensions— indeed without any at all.

On the Politics of Europe, I shall express no opinion; nor make any enquiry who is right, or who is wrong. I wish well to all Nations, and to all men. My politics are plain & simple. I think every Nation has a right to establish that form of government under which *It* conceives It shall live most happy, provided it infracts no Right, or is not dangerous to others. And that, no governments ought to interfere with the internal concerns of another, except for the security of what is due to themselves.

I sincerely hope that Madame la Fayette will accomplish all her wishes in France, and return safe to you with renovated health. I congratulate you on the Marriage of your eldest daughter, and beg to be presented to them both, & to Virginia, in the most respectful & affectionate terms—to George I have written. In all these things Mrs Washington (as the rest of the family would do, if they were at home) most cordially joins me; as she does in wishing you and them every felicity this life can afford; as some consolation for your long, cruel and painful confinement and sufferings.

I shall now only add what you knew well before, that with the most sincere friendship, & affectionate regard—I am always Yours

[Go: Washington]

P.S. Your old Aid de Camp, and my worthy Nephew, George A: Washington, died about five years ago of a Pulmonory complaint: he left three fine children—a daughter and two sons—the eldest of the boys was called after you.

The letters herewith enclosed, and directed—one to yourself, another to George, and the third to Mr Frestal, have been some time in my possession;[3] and detained to be delivered to you *here*, upon the same principle that prevented me from writing to you at an earlier period. G:W.

AL[S], NNPM; ALS (letterpress copy), Lafayette Papers, La Grange, France, microfilm on deposit at DLC; LB, DLC:GW. The signature has been clipped from the receiver's copy.

1. No letter of 20 Dec. 1797 has been found; but GW probably is referring to the letter that Jared Sparks copied and dated 27 Dec., under which date it is printed above. In his response of 9 May 1799, Lafayette does not indicate that any letters of his were missing.

2. GW had not written Lafayette since 5 Dec. 1797. He never wrote to him again.

3. The author of these letters has not been identified.

From John Sevier

Sir   Knoxville [Tenn.] 25th December 1798

I am in suspense as to the probable, or improbability of being called into the Army, a Station I would prefer to Any other that, of being in arms to defend an injured and Grossly insulted Country. Being Under Such impressions, I hope I shall be Neither thought ambitious or restless as to appointment, filling at present the most honorable, my Countrymen have in their power to confer; Nevertheless, permit me sir, through the Small acquaintance I have had the honor to Cultivate With your Excellency, to solicit Your interest in being brought forward if any Vacancy Should present itself; into the Army of the United States: provided; You should deem me adequate to Such a task.

Should I be so happy as to Merit your patronage, I flatter myself neither you nor My Country, would have any Occasion to regret.[1]

Nothing of moment have transpired in this Quarter. A Military ardor & Spirit Warmly diffuses itself throughout the State of Tennessee, And As Many as six companies of Cavalry have tendered their Services, When ever called upon, Who are composed of such men, as Would in My opinion do honor to any Army in the Universe. I have the honor to be sir With sincere and very Great esteem Your Excellencys Mo. Obedt And Hbl. Servt

John Sevier

ALS, DLC:GW.

1. Sevier was one of only two men who were designated to serve as officers in the Provisional Army which was authorized in 1798. Much to GW's displeasure Sevier was named to become a colonel in the Provisional Army should it be called into being. The authority of the president to call out a Provisional Army lapsed on 31 Dec. 1798 but was renewed by Congress in March 1799 (see James McHenry to GW, 2 May 1799, n.1).

Letter not found: from William Thornton, 25 Dec. 1798. On 30 Dec. GW wrote Thornton: "Your favor of the 25th instant . . . has been duly received."

To William Vans Murray

Dear Sir,   Mount Vernon 26th Decr 1798.

Having some cause to believe that the Vessel was captured, in which went the original of the enclosed copy, I forward a duplicate.[1]

I returned a few days ago from Philadelphia, whither I had been for the purpose of making some Military arrangements with the Secretary of War respecting the Force wch is about to be raised.

It was there I received a Letter from Mr Dandrid[g]e, announcing his intention of returning to America (partly on account of his health)—expressing in lively & grateful terms his sense of your attentions to, & kind treatment of him; adding that as experience had more & more convinced him, that a sedentary life was incompatible with both his health & turn of mind (a sentiment he had often expressed whilst he lived with me) he wished for an appointment in the Army we were about to raise. The application arriving in the nick of time, he stands arranged as Captn of a Company of Infantry in one of the Regiments wh. will be raised in Virginia, and it is necessary he should enter upon the duties thereof as soon as it can be made convenient.[2]

Mr Envoy Logan, who arrived at Philadelphia about the time I did, brings very *flattering* accounts of the Disposition of the French Directory *towards this Country*. He has dined with one—supped with another—and in short has been as familiar with them all (that were in place) as the hand is with its glove: and is not a little employed in propagating this Doctrine in all parts of the U: States by means of the Presses which are at the command of that Party. He says the inclination of France to be upon good terms with the United States is *now* so strong, that it *must* be our own mismanagement, & disinclination to Peace, if matters with that Country are not accomodated upon terms honorable & advantageous to this.[3]

Both houses of Congress were formed before I left Philadelphia, but had not been long enough in Session for an opinion of the result to be prognosticated. Their answers to the Speech would, it seems, have passed unanimously, could Mr Varnum of Massachusetts have retained his Spleen. How far this measure is indicative of a tranquil & energetic Session, remains to be decided by more unequivocal evidence.[4]

The Alien & Sedition Laws, are now the desiderata ⟨in⟩ the Oppos[it]ion. But any thing else would have done; and something there will always be, for them to torture, and to disturb the public mind with their unfounded and ill-favored forebodings.

The family join me in presenting Mrs Murray and yourself with the Complimts of the Season, and in wishing you many happy returns of them. With very sincere esteem & regard—I am—Dear Sir Your Most Obedt & Affecte Humble Servant

Go: Washington

ALS (letterpress copy), DLC:GW; LB, DLC:GW.

1. GW wrote Murray on 10 August.

2. GW is referring to Bartholomew Dandridge's letter of 20 Aug.; he had not yet received Dandridge's letter of 10 Oct., telling of his change of plans.

3. See GW's Notes on an Interview with George Logan and Robert Blackwell, 13 Nov. 1798, printed above.

4. Congress convened on 3 Dec. 1798, and on 8 Dec. John Adams addressed both houses of Congress. A committee of five members of the House of Representatives drafted the House's reply to the president, which on 13 Dec. the House amended and adopted (*Annals of Congress, 1797–99*, 3:2420–40). An Antifederalist, Joseph Bradley Varnum (1751–1821) was a member of the House from Massachusetts.

From David Stuart

Dear Sir,   Hope Park Decr 27th 1798

I expect you have not had an opportunity of seeing the inclosed address—written by Mr Evans on the subject of the alien and sedition bills—It is so excellent in my judgement, that tho' it is borrowed, I cannot refuse taking the liberty of furnishing you with it[1]—It is much to be lamented, it did not appear sooner, as it could not have failed I think of dissipating the fears of many well intentioned but meek persons—I hope even now, it will make many of them abandon their great Champion, whose inconsistency at present is more fully established than has ever yet happened—With the compts of the season, I am Dr Sir Your affecte Servt

                                                            Dd Stuart

ALS, DLC:GW.

1. Thomas Evans's *An Address to the People of Richmond, respecting the Alien & Sedition Laws. By a Citizen of This State* was printed in Richmond in 1798 by Augustine Davis. For GW's copy, or copies, see Griffin, *Boston Athenæum Washington Collection*, 77.

To William Richardson Davie

Sir,   Mount Vernon Decr 28th 1798

Your Letters, on the subject of Candidates and proper characters for military appointments in the State of North Carolina, were received when I was in Philadelphia, where I have lately been, at the request of the Secretary of war, to make arrangements for the organization of the additional Army about to be raised. While on this business, in conjuction with Major Generals Hamilton and Pinckney, it was thought best, from the want of knowledge of proper Characters in the three Southern States, to postpone a selection of Military Officers from them, until General Pinckney should go there, and, upon the spot, with the aid of yourself and Brigadier General Washington, point out such Characters as shall be distinguished for their qualifications, and who would be willing to serve.

Major General Pinckney, who will do me the favor to hand this letter to you, now goes on, charged with the Military arrangements in the Southern States, and will pay particular attention to this business, in which I am persuaded he will receive from you all the information and assistance that it may be in your power to give.[1] With sentiments of Consideration and Esteem, I am, Sir, your most Obedt Servt

Go: Washington

LS, Nc-Ar; Df, DLC:GW. Both copies are in Tobias Lear's hand.

1. On 24 Oct. GW sent Governor Davie a list of the field officers serving in the North Carolina line at the close of the Revolutionary War and a list of the North Carolinians who were now applying for or being recommended for army commissions, with the request that Davie provide him with the names of men suitable to serve as officers in a regiment of infantry and a company of dragoons to be raised in North Carolina and Tennessee. In his letter of 14 Nov. (the only earlier letter found), Davie commented on several of the applicants and pointed out that the "business" of raising regiments such as this was "not the work of a week or a month." Before receiving this letter of 28 Dec., Davie wrote GW on 30 Dec. with a list of recommendations.

From John Greenwood

sir   New York Decembr 28. 1798

I send you inclosed two setts of teeth, one fixed on the Old Barrs in part and the sett you sent me from philadelphia which when I Received was very black Ocationed either by your soaking them in port wine, or by your drinking it. Port wine being sower takes of[f] all the polish and All Acids has a tendency to soften every kind of teeth and bone. Acid is Used in Couloring every kind of Ivory. therefore it is very pernicious to the teeth. I Advice you to Either take them out After dinner and put them in cleain water and put in another scett or Cleain them with a brush and som Chalk scraped fine. it will Absorbe the Acid which Collects from the mouth and preserve them longer—I have found another and better way of useing the sealing wax when holes is eaten in the teeth by acid &c.

first Observe and dry the teeth. then take a peice of Wax and Cut it into As small peices as you think will fill up the hole. then take a large nail or any other peice of Iron and heat it hot into the fier. then put your peice of wax into the hole and melt it by meanes of introduceing the Point of the Nail to it. I have tried it and found it to Consoladate and do better then the other way and if done proper it will resist the saliva. it will be handyer for you to take hold of the Nail with small plyers than with a tongs thus the wax must be very small not bigger than this.[1] if your teeth Grows black take some chalk and a Pine or Ceder stick. it will rub it of. If you whant your teeth more yellower soake them in Broath or pot li:quer but not in tea or Acid. Porter is a Good thing to Coulor them and will not hurt but preserve them but it must not be in the least pricked.

You will find I have Altered the upper teeth you sent me from philadelphia[.] leaveing the enamel on the teeth dont preserve them any longer then if it was of[f]. it onely holds the Color better. but to preserve them they must be very Often Changed and Cleaned for whatever atackes them must be repelled as Often or it will gain Ground and destroy the works—the two setts I repaired is done on a different plan then when they are done when made intirely new for the teeth are screwed on the barrs insted of haveing the barrs Cast red hot on them which is the reason I beleive the[y] destroy or desolve so soone near to the barrs.

Sr After hopeing you will not be Oblidged to be troubled very sune in the same Way I subscribe myselvth Your very humble servant

John Greenwood

Sr the Additional Charge is fiveteen dollars.

P.S. I Exspect next spring to move my family into Connecticut state. if I do, I will rite and let you know and wether I give up my present business or not I will As long As I live do any thing in this way for you or in any other way in my power—If your require it.[2]

ALS, PHi: Society Collection. The dots scattered at random through the manuscript have been ignored except when they appear to be at the end of a sentence.

1. At this point Greenwood drew a small sketch of a pair of pliers holding a nail above two squares (of wax), each about the size of a letter in his script.

2. For GW's earlier correspondence with Greenwood about Greenwood's making and fitting false teeth for him, see GW to Greenwood, 5 Nov. and 7 Dec. 1798. GW wrote Greenwood from Mount Vernon on 6 Jan. 1799: "Sir, Your letter of the 28th Ulto with the parcel that accompanied it, came safe to hand; and I feel obliged by your attention to my requests, and for the directions you have given me.

"Enclosed you have Bank notes for fifteen dollars, which I shall be glad to hear has got safe to your hands. If you should remove to Connecticut, I should be glad to be advised of it; and to what place; as I shall always prefer your Services to that of any other, in the line of your present profession. I am Sir Your very Hble Servant Go: Washington" (ALS, NHi: George and Martha Washington Papers). To this Greenwood responded from New York on 11 Jan. 1799: "Sir Your Letter of the 6th Ult. with the two enclosed Bills, Containing fifeteen dollars came safe to my hands for Which I Return you Thanks. I will Rite and let you know if I Remove, from here and where to—as I meain to perform for you in my present Professional line when I have done with every other person. . . . P.S: I never make any Charge Against you either in a book or Otherways" (IEN-D).

To Richard Raynal Keene

Sir, Mount Vernon 28th Decr 1798.

At all times, when it is in my power to do it with tolerable convenience to myself, I feel pleasure in aiding the deserving and meritorious.

But let me observe at the sametime, that a very mistaken opinion prevails with respect to my means of accomplishing this, in a pecuniary way; for was I to judge of these opinions by the numerous applications which are made to me for money, it must be conjectured by them, that I have resources far—very far indeed—beyond what the fact will warrant.

I can assure you, that I find it no easy matter to keep my expenditures within the limits of my receipts; and that, without travelling out of my own circle, I find more than enough to require all the surplusage of the latter, when I have any to spare.

I return the papers contained in your letter of the 24th instant, agreeably to your request; and as I want no evidence of your request, I send the letter also.[1] I am Sir Your Very Hble Servant

Go: Washington

ALS (letterpress copy), DLC:GW; LB, DLC:GW.
1. The letter, which GW returned to Keene, has not been found.

From James McHenry

Dear Sir. Philad. 28 Decr 1798.

I received two letters from you on your route home respecting my young freind Mr Custis, and one under date of the 16th inst. written at Susquehannah.[1]

Your ideas relative to the distribution of the general officers and their respective duties and commands correspond perfectly with my own. I hope no untoward circumstance will intervene to prevent their being carried into execution, and that I shall in a little while have more leisure to write to you than has been of late in my power.

On the 24 inst. I made my report to the President on the military points, proper for the consideration of Congress. This report will be laid before Congress by Message. I have freely used in it the matter with which you furnished me, and fortified it with your name. I have also added other objects important according to my views, and intitled to attention.[2]

The nominations I expected this morning would have been ready to send to the Senate at furthest on monday. I am, now not clear they will go in so soon. The President directed me to submit copies of the list, to the heads of Departments. Two of these gentlemen have made no report. I find that several, who have been named from the Eastward for certain grades who expected higher will not accept, and that there are a few others on the list who do not deserve to be appointed. I shall propose not to name any persons in the room of those left out, at this moment, to give time to further investigate characters and obtain information.[3]

I shewed your letter relative to Col. Smith to the President— and sent a copy of it to Smith. I shall as soon as it can be spared from this quarter forward you his answer. The pith of it is, that in the agitation of his mind he brought a certain deed with others from Mr Wm Constables house to Col. Troop's office, where the business between him & Majr Burrow was transacted, that the mistake was soon discovered and as soon rectified. That it was impossible he could have intended a deception, the mortgage in question being on record &c.[4]

Upon a deliberate weighing of all circumstances as they may affect the public concerns, it may be expedient his name should be presented to the Senate, Something must be yeilded to obtain harmony, and yet I do not know that this will secure it. If presented I think he will be appointed.

I reced yesterday a letter from Col. Lear of the 24 with sundry papers.[5] Will you request him to examine the old papers and see if any of the confidential letters inclosed to you are yet to be returned.[6] Yours affectionately

James McHenry

ALS, DLC:GW, ADf, MdAA.

1. Only one letter to McHenry about George Washington Parke Custis written while GW was en route to Mount Vernon, that of 14 Dec. from Chester, Pa., has been found.

2. For references to McHenry's report to the president based upon the two long letters from GW of 13 Dec. and to its presentation to Congress, see GW to McHenry, 13 Dec. (first letter), source note. On 31 Dec. Adams sent McHenry's report to Congress with this message: "A report of the Secretary of War, made to me on the twenty-fourth of this month, relative to the Military Establishments, I think it my duty to transmit to Congress, and recommend to their consideration" (*Annals of Congress, 1797–99,* 2:2199. McHenry's report is printed in *ASP: Military Affairs,* 1:124–28).

3. For the lists of men that GW, Alexander Hamilton, and Charles Cotesworth Pinckney were recommending for commissions in the New, or Additional, Army, see the editorial note to the List of Candidates for Army Appointments from Virginia, November 1798, printed above. McHenry gave the lists to Adams on 29 Dec., and he submitted these nominations to the Senate on 31 Dec. (see McHenry to Hamilton, 28 Dec. 1798, n.2, in Syrett, *Hamilton Papers,* 22:397–98). See also McHenry to GW, 21 Jan. 1799, and notes.

4. See GW to McHenry, 13 Dec. (second letter), and note 2 of that document.

5. Tobias Lear's letter of 24 Dec. has not been found.

6. Lear wrote McHenry on 30 Dec. listing the confidential letters that McHenry had sent GW on 14 Nov. and indicating that he was returning most of them. Lear's letter to McHenry is printed in note 19, McHenry to GW, 14 Nov. 1798.

To William Washington

Dear Sir,   Mount Vernon 28th Decr 1798

Your letters of the 19th and 30th of October came duly to hand, and would have received an earlier acknowledgment had I not been absent in a journey to Philadelphia (at the request of the Secretary of War) and but newly returned from that City.

The object of this journey was, among other things, to make a selection of characters from the numerous applicants for Military appointments in the Augmented force, for the new Corps.

In this business, Majors General Hamilton & Pinckney, and myself, were closely occupied near five weeks; but not having all the information we wished relative to the two Carolinas & Georgia; and thinking the arrangement for those States (as was my opinion with respect to the whole) would be better made within them than at the Seat of the Government—this part of the business is left to Genl Pinckney, yourself and Genl Davie of North Carolina, to complete.

The former carries with him all the information we possessed respecting the applications, to aid the execution of it. And as Genl Pinckney is enabled, and doubtless will, inform you of the opinions which operated against the removal of Officers from the present existing Corps, to those which are to be raised, I shall briefly add that, besides its being unusual (except in marked cases) the selection would have opened the door to endless discontents.

I thought, as you did, that nothing could ever have withdrawn me from my long sought retirement; during the remnant of a life which is journeying fast to the mansions of my ancestors. But we are little acquainted with ourselves and still less with the ways of Providence. It gives me pleasure, however, to learn from yourself, that you accept your appointment: the evidence of which you have, no doubt, long since received.

Present every good wish of mine, and the compliments of the Season, to Mrs Washington & your family, and be assured of the sincere esteem & regard of Dear Sir Your most Obedt and Affecte Hble Servant

Go: Washington

ALS (letterpress copy), DLC:GW.

From William Richardson Davie

Sir   Halifax [N.C.] Decr 30, [17]98

Inclosed you will receive a reccommendation for several company officers taken from different parts of the state agreeably to the principle of distribution mentioned in your letter of the 24th of October.[1] This list is not complete, but as it was of importance, that the unremitting business should be going on during the winter, or as early as possible, I thought it my duty to forward the names of those Gentleman of whose character, I was fully satisfied: & whose willingness to serve has been ascertained.[2] The remainder from the other Districts shall be sent on as soon as the necessary information can be procured, which will be in the course of a post or two.[3] As to the field officers, I have not yet procured satisfactory information as to proper characters for the appointment of Majors, but would recommend James Reid of Wilmington as a Lieutenant Colonel. He served through the revolutionary war with considerable reputation & was an old Captain at the close of the war.[4] He is the same gentleman mentioned in the list from the War Office under the number 5.[5] I have the honor to be with great respect Sir your most obt servant

W. R. Davie
Brig. General

ALS, DLC:GW; copy, DLC:GW; Df, Nc-Ar: William R. Davie Papers. The copy is dated 3 December.

1. See Enclosure.

2. GW wrote Davie on 10 Jan. 1799: "Sir, By the last Mail I had the pleasure to receive your favor of the 30th ultimo, with the list of such Company Officers as you have been able to select from the State of North Carolina.

"Before this gets to your hands I presume you will have seen Major General Pinckney, to whose care I committed a letter for you, under date of the 28th of December; which will shew you how far I have been able to proceed, with the aid of Major Generals Hamilton and Pinckney, in the selection of Officers for the twelve additional Regiments. The latter Gentleman will have communicated to you the arrangement which has been formed for selecting suitable Characters from the three Southern States. It is therefore unnecessary for me to enlarge on this subject at present. With great consideration & respect I have the honor to be Sir, Your most obedient servant Go: Washington" (LS, NcU: William L. Saunders Collection).

3. The copy of the letter in DLC:GW includes this additional sentence: "With this you will also receive the list of applicants forwarded with your letter of the 24th of October with the necessary remarks."

4. James Read served as a captain in the Continental line and lieutenant colonel of the North Carolina militia during the Revolutionary War. In February 1790 GW appointed him collector of customs for Wilmington, N.C., and in March 1791 gave him the inspectorship of North Carolina survey no. 1. John Adams removed him from the collectorship in the fall of 1797.

5. See GW to Davie, 24 Oct., n.1.

Enclosure
List of North Carolinians Wanting Army Commissions

[c.30 December 1798]

List of persons in North Carolina applying for Commissions in the Army now to be raised.

Names	Residence	Rank expected
1. Robert Troy	Salisbury	Captain

Remarks &c. Recommended by Maj. Genl Smith, Col. W[illiam] Polk, and Archibald Henderson Esq. He is a young man of liberal education, well calculated for the service, and about 23 years of age.

2. William Dickson Lincoln County Captain

He is the son of Genl [Joseph] Dickson, has had a liberal education, is about 22 years old, and strongly recommended by the most respectable characters in that District.

3. Eli Gaither Iredell County Captain

He is well recommended by several Gentlemen on whose judgment I can rely; and is about 30 years of age, a popular character, and well calculated for the service.

4. Edmund Smithwick Martin County Captain

He is about 30 years of age, a respectable character, well recommended, and a young man I have known several years.

5. William Hall Brunswick County Captain

He is about 40 years of age, well recommended as a man of firmness, honor, good character & connections, and anxious to go into the service.

6. John Williams Surry County Captain

He is the Son of Col. Joseph Williams, he is about 22 years of age, and well recommended as a young man of spirit, liberal education, and popular connections.

7. John Nicholas No. Ampton County Captain

Recommended by Genl [Allen] Jones as a respectable and popular man, who has seen some service in the revolutionary war, and a man of known bravery.

8. James Ryan Edenton Captain

He is the same Gentleman whose name is on the list in the War Office, & well recommended to me for this rank.

1. Geo. Washington Davidson Montgomery County Lieutenant

Son of Col. George Davidson, about 21, strongly recommended by Genl R. Smith and A. Henderson.

2. James Macay Rowan County Lieutenant

Well recommended as a suitable character in every respect, and is about 24 years of age.

3. David Evans Junr Fayetteville Lieutenant

(Remark) Well recommended by the Honble W[illiam] B[arry] Grove, and the most respectable characters in that District.

4. Benjamin Smith Richmond County Lieutenant

Recommended by the same.

5. James Love Duplin County Lieutenant

Recommended by the same.

6. Joseph Alexander Burke County Lieutenant

He is about 22 years of age, strongly recommended by Genl Dickson, Col. Polk, Col. [Alfred] Moore, and Wallace Alexander Esq.

7. Samuel Baron Newbern Lieutenant

Strongly recommended, & well calculated for the service.

1. Daniel Newman   Salisbury   Ensign
Recommended to the Secretary by General [John] Steele, & to me by
William Alexander Esq. & Col. Polk.
2. David T. W. Cook   Charlotte   Ensign
Recommended by Major Genl Smith & Col. Polk.
3. Marcus Sharpe   Iredell County   Ensign
Recommended by the most respectable characters in that District.
4. James Morris   Rutherford County Ensign
Well recommended by the most respectable characters in that District.
5. John Wilkinson   Robeson County   Ensign
Recommended by the Honble W. B. Grove.
6. John Carraway   Wilkes County   Ensign
Well recommended for this appointment.

D, DLC:GW.

To John Marshall

My dear Sir,   Mount Vernon 30th Decr 1798.
 If General Pinckney should have left Richmond, let me request
the favor of you to forward the packet herewith sent, in the manner he may have directed; or, as your own judgment shall dictate,
to ensure its delivery to him in Hallifax, or on the Road thro'
North Carolina.[1]
 The Alien & Sedition Laws having employed many Pens—and
we hear a number of tongues, in the Assembly of this State; the
latter, I understand, to a very pernicious purpose; I send you the
production of Judge Addison on these subjects.[2] Whether any
new lights are cast upon them by his charge, you will be better able
to decide when you have read it. My opinion is, that if this, or
other writings flashed conviction as clear as the Sun in its Mere-
dian brightness, it would produce no effect in the conduct of the
leaders of opposition, who, have points to carry, from which nothing will divert them in the prosecution.
 When you have read the charge give it to Bushrod Washington,
or place it to any other uses you may think proper. I wish success
to your Election, most sincerely; and if it should fail (of which I
hope there is not the least danger) I shall not easily forgive myself
for being urgent with you to take a Poll—I offer you the compliments of the Season, and with much truth remain Dear Sir Your
Most Obedt and Affecte Hble Servant
            Go: Washington

ALS, ViA; ALS (letterpress copy), DLC:GW; LB, DLC:GW.

1. On this day GW wrote Charles Cotesworth Pinckney, who left Mount Vernon on the morning of 28 Dec. after a visit of three days with his wife and daughter Eliza: "My dear Sir, Accompanying this, you will receive Letters for Brigadier Generals Davie & Washington; left open for your perusal; to be sealed before delivery.

"The night after your departure being rainy, & the morning following thawing, makes us anxious to hear of your safe arrival as far as Fredericksburgh. Our best wishes will attend you to the end of your journey, and with sincere & affectionate regard, & regret to part with you & the Ladies, I am—my dear Sir— Your Most Obedt Hble Servt Go: Washington" (ALS, OCHP; letterpress copy, DLC:GW). GW's letter to William Richardson Davie is dated 30 Dec.; that to William Washington, 28 December. On 28 Dec., according to the endorsements on the documents, GW gave or sent Pinckney copies of a list of cavalry officers from the various states for the New Army and a list entitled Estimate of Artillery small Arms principal articles of Military stores and Camp Equipage for an army of 50000 men. On 30 Dec., again according to the endorsements, GW sent Pinckney copies of his letter to McHenry of 16 Dec. and lists entitled Prices of rations at the different posts, Names of places at which recruiting rendezvous have been established, and Return of Troops at the undermentioned places. All of these lists are undated and filed in DLC:GW at the end of December 1798.

2. See GW to Alexander Addison, 6 Dec., n.1.

To David Stuart

Dear Sir,   Mount Vernon 30th Decr 1798

Company, ever since my return home, has prevented my mentioning a matter before, which will be the subject of this letter now.

When the applications for Military appointments come to be examined at Philadelphia, it was pleasing to find among them, so many Gentlemen of family, fortune & high expectations, soliciting Commissions; & not in the high grades.

This, and a thorough conviction that it was a vain attempt to keep Washington Custis to any literary pursuits, either in a public Seminary, or at home under the direction of any one, gave me the first idea of bringing him forward as a Cornet of Horse. To this measure too I was induced by a conviction paramount in my breast, that if real danger threatned the Country, no young man ought to be an idle Spectator of its defense; and that, if a state of preparation would avert the evil of an Invasion, he would be entitled to the merit of proffered service, without encountering the dangers of War: and besides, that it might divert his attention from a Matrimonial pursuit (for a while at least) to which his constitution seems to be too prone.

But, though actuated by these ideas, I intended to proceed no farther in the business than to provide a vacancy in one of the Troops of light Dragoons, & to consult Mrs Stuart & his Grandmother, as to their inclinations respecting his filling it; before any intimation of it should be given to him: But, Mr Lear hearing the matter talked of, and not knowing that this was the ground on which I meant to place the appointment (if the arrangement met the Presidents approbation) wrote to Washington on the subject, in order to know if it would be agreeable to him, or not to receive it.

Under these circumstances (and his appearing highly delighted) concealment—I mean an attempt at it—would have proved nugatory—He stands arranged therefore a Cornet in the Troop to be Commanded by Lawrence Lewis (who I intended as his Mentor)—Lawrence Washington junr (of Chotanck) is the Lieutenant of the Troop. But all this it will be remembered is to be approved—first by the President, & consented to by the Senate to make it a valid act; & therefore, the less it is *publicly* talked of the better.

Mrs Washington does not seem to have the least objection to his acceptance of the Commission; but it rests with Mrs Stuart to express her sentiments thereon, and soon; as I requested the Secretary of War to forward the Commissions for *this* Troop of Light Dragoons, under cover to me.

The only hesitation I had, to induce the caution before mentioned, arose from his being an only Son; indeed the only male of his Great great Grandfathers family; but the same Providence that wd watch over & protect him in domestic walks, can extend the same protection to him in a Camp, or the field of battle, if he should ever be in one. With Compliments to the family, and with the greatest esteem and regard I am—Dear Sir Your Obedt & Affecte Servt

Go: Washington

ALS, ViMtV; ALS (letterpress copy), DLC:GW.

To William Thornton

Dear Sir, Mount Vernon 30th Decr 1798

Your favor of the 25th instant, enclosing Messrs Blagden & Lenthals estimate of the cost of adding a Pediment, and Parapet to the roof of my buildings in the Federal City, has been duly received, but the plan, to which it refers, did not accompany it.[1]

This plan, on other accounts, I ought to be possessed of, and Mr Blagden is under promise to take a copy thereof for his own use, to work by, and to send me the original draught. I pray you to remind him of this promise.

Presuming that it is not necessary for Mr Blagden's convenience that I should, at this moment, decide upon the above estimate; nor whether I shall adopt the measure at all; I shall, if no disavantage will attend the delay, suspend my determination until I can visit the City, & receive some further explanations respecting the consequent alterations which will be occasioned by this Pediment— not at present well understood by me; owing to my entire ignorance of the technical terms in which they are expressed. At which time also, I will make arrangements for giving him further pecuniary aids.

Rules of Architecture are calculated, I presume, to give symmetry, and just proportion to all the Orders, & parts of buildings, in order to please the eye. Small departures from *strict* rules are discoverable only by skilful Architects, or by the eye of criticism; while ninety nine in a hundred—deficient of their knowledge—might be pleased with things not quite orthodox. This, more than probable, would be the case relative to a Pediment in the roof over the *doors* of my houses in the City.

That a Parapet in addition (for the reasons you have assigned) would have a pleasing & useful effect, cannot be doubted. When the roof of a building is to be seen, and when it is designed for Chambers it must be seen, something to relieve the view of a plain and dead Surface, is indispensable: for this reason it was, I thought, and still do think, that Dormars are to be prefered to Sky lights in the front; on the other hand, if the roof is so flat as not to be seen at all, or so low as, in a manner to be hid by a Parapet, I should give a decided preference to Sky lights.

These ideas, as you will readily perceive, proceed from a person who avows his ignorance of Architectural principles, and who has no other guide but his eye, to direct his choice. I never, for a moment, contemplated *two* Pediments, one over the door of each house: my great object, was to give the two the appearance of one. But as I have observed in the former part of this letter, I will suspend coming to any decision until the consequences of the proposed alterations are better understood by me.

The freedom with which you have expressed your sentiments on this occasion, is highly pleasing to me. Sorry indeed should I have been on this, as I shall be on any future occurrence, when your opinion may be asked, if they are not rendered with the utmost frankness and candour.

The compliments of the season are presented to Mrs Thornton, yourself &ca by all parts of this family, and with great esteem & regard I remain—Dear Sir Your most Obedt Hble Servant

Go: Washington

ALS, DLC: Thornton Papers; ALS (letterpress copy), DLC:GW; LB, DLC:GW.

1. Neither Thornton's letter nor the estimate of George Blagdin and his partner, John Lenthall (1762–1808), has been found. Lenthall, like Blagdin, was an English builder. For references to adding a pediment and parapet to GW's houses, see GW to Thornton, 20 Dec., and Thornton to GW, 21 December.

From John Augustine Spotswood

Dr Sir   Newpost the 31d Decmbr 1798

Company, & an Agitation of Mind, When last at Mount Vernon Prevented my takeing, that Respectful leave of you and Mrs Washington That I Wished—Permit me now sir, to Return to you, and Mrs Washington my Sincere thanks, with an Assurance, of holding in grateful Remembrance; your polite, kind, and friendly Attention towards me, From the time I first had the Honor of being Introduced to you—to The Day I last left Mount Vernon.[1] Wishing you Sir, & Mrs Washington A Long Continuance of your present health—I Remain Most Respectfully Yo. Obd. Servt

John A. Spotswood

ALS, DLC:GW.

1. Captain Spotswood called at Mount Vernon on Christmas Day 1798 (*Diaries*, 6:327). Either at that time or, probably, earlier, he presented this statement of his financial situation, which GW docketed "Statement, Captn John Spotswood of his property 1798": "My Capital is £1000[;] A Schooner [£]810[,] A Bond of general lees given me by my father now due, Principal [£]2000[.] As Security for the payment of this Bond my father has a Mortgage on the Land he sold general Lee, My father tels me that general Lee has Assured him in the Most pointed Manner, a payment of 6000$ in August next, & which Sum he tels me I shall have; My father has Been for Some time Collecting for me Meterials for Building a

Schooner of 96 tons, to be Completed by August 1799, And has promised me the farther Sum of £400 towards her Completion, this with £600 of my own will Complete the Vessel, and Leave Me a Capital in Money of £2200—And due on the Bond £200; with these Vessels and my Money I mean to fix Myself in Alexandria in the westindia Line of Business, And By Employing of good men to go in My Vessels—and Proceding with Prudence, Caution, and Economy, do not doubt but I Shall do well—And Ultimately, my father Assures me that Newpost and Nottingham farms Containing 600 Acres of Valluable Land, whereon are good and Convenient Buildings of Every kind—with 400 Acres of a Seperate tract one mile Distance from Nottingham house Makeing in the whole 1000 Acres—Shall at his and My Mothers death be possessed by me or my heirs.

"Should General and Mrs Washington be of Opinion that My Present Situation And future prospect is not Sufficiently Elligible, their Candour and friendship Will tell me So when a farther persuit Will be Declined by John Augustine Spotswood." Spotswood may have presented this when he came to Mount Vernon "in the evening" of 4 Oct. (*Diaries*, 6:318–19); his "Agitation of Mind" when leaving Mount Vernon on 25 Dec. presumably was caused by his learning of Eleanor Parke Custis's recent engagement to marry Lawrence Lewis.

To Bushrod Washington

My dear Sir,   Mount Vernon 31st Decr 1798

It gave me pleasure to hear by Judge Cushing, that you had returned from your Southern Circuit in good health. I presume you will soon have to undertake another journey, w⟨hen I shall hope⟩ to see you.[1]

I was not unmindful of your application in behalf of Captn Blackburne. But when the list of applicants came to be unfolded, it was found that there were so many requests of a similar nature, from Officers of the existing Corps, that it was impossible to comply with them, & difficult to discriminate; for which reasons, it was deemed best to reject them in toto; especially, as in the raising of New Corps, it rarely happens that Officers are drawn from the old, and nothing but length of Service, or very distinguished merit, or powerful interest and influence, gives birth to the measure.[2]

By this conveyance, I have sent to Genl Marshall, Judge Addisons charge to Grand Juries of the County Courts of the fifth Circuit, of the State of Pennsylvania; and requested, after he had read it, to give it to you, or dispose of it in any other manner he might think proper. This charge is on the Liberty of Speech and of the Press, and is a justification of the Sedition & Alien Laws.

But I do not believe that any thing contained in *it*; in Evans's Pamphlet; or in any othe⟨r writing will⟩ produce the least change in the conduct of the leaders of opposition, to the measures of the General Government. They have points to carry, from which no reasoning—no inconsistency of conduct—no absurdity—can divert them. If, however, such writings should produce conviction on the minds of those who have hitherto placd faith in their assertions, it will be a fortunate event for this Country.[3]

Has any thing been done, and what, with my correspondent Mr Langhorn? I have heard, since my return from Philadelphia, that there has been some stir in the matter, but of the result I am ignorant.[4] The family here present the Compliments of the Season to you & Mrs Washington. I remain Your sincere friend & affectionate Uncle

Go: Washington

P.S. Let me pray you to get General Lee's Deed to me—drawn agreeably to your directions—acknowledged before Witnesses; who will prove it in the General Court; and I would thank you for causing this to be done.

My Deed to Lee is also sent, to be dealt with as you and he may deem proper: for ⟨further eluci⟩dation of this subject, I send (in confidence) my letters to Genl Lee open for your perusal; after which please to seal & deliver them. You will perceive by the duplicate in what manner I am likely to be plagued, in obtaining payment for my Dismal Swamp Land—Sold him—but not convey'd.[5] G:W.

ALS, owned (1980) by Mr. and Mrs. Harry Spiro, New York City; ALS (letterpress copy), DLC:GW; LB, DLC:GW. Mutilated words and letters in the ALS are supplied from the letterpress copy and are enclosed in angle brackets.

1. William Cushing (1732–1810) of Massachusetts was the first associate justice appointed to the U.S. Supreme Court in 1789.

2. Bushrod Washington wrote GW on 21 Sept. 1798 about a commission in the army for Capt. Richard Scott Blackburn.

3. See GW to John Marshall, 30 December. Thomas Evans (1755–1815) of Accomack County on Virginia's Eastern Shore had been a Federalist member of the U.S. House of Representatives since 1797. For his *Address*, see David Stuart to GW, 27 Dec., n.1.

4. For a summary of the Langhorne affair, see John Langhorne (Peter Carr) to GW, 25 Sept. 1797, n.1.

5. See GW to Henry Lee, Jr., 4 Nov., and note 4 of that document.

Letter not found: to David Stuart, 3 Jan. 1799. On 4 Jan. GW wrote Stuart and referred to "a letter I wrote to you yesterday."

To Timothy Pickering

Dear Sir,   Mount Vernon 4th Jan. 1799

If you should have conceived, that the letters I have written to you since my retirement from the Chair of Government, worth the room they would take up in your Beaureau; and can readily lay your hands upon one written on the 6th of February in the past year, I would thank you for a copy of the last page thereof.

A Press copy was taken of that letter; and all of it, except the last page, sufficiently legible; but that page is so entirely the reverse, as not to be understood, or made out by the context.[1]

Mrs Washington and Miss Custis unite with me in offering you the compliments of the Season—and in wishing that Mrs Pickering, yourself and family may see the return of many, very many happy New Years. I am always Yr Obedt & Affecte Servt

Go: Washington

ALS, MHi: Wendell Papers.

1. The last page of the letterpress copy is indeed virtually unreadable. GW's clerk was able to decipher only a little of it for the letter-book copy.

Letter not found: from David Stuart, 4 Jan. 1799. On 4 Jan. GW wrote Stuart: "Your letter of this date is just received."

To David Stuart

Dear Sir,   Mount Vernon 4th Jan. 1799

Your letter of this date is just received;[1] and the cause why I did not hear from you by the return of my Carriage, was conjectured, as you will perceive by a letter I wrote to you yesterday (covering one from Mrs Washington to Nelly) and sent to the Post Office in Alexandria for conveyance by the Mail.[2]

I do not, myself believe, that there will be a call of the augmented Troops to the Field of Battle, but, (though that may be an inducement to it) it ought not to be the ground on which Washington Custis is to obtain his Mother's, and Grandmothers consent to enter the Army. For if circumstances should require it, there can be no retreat without forfeiture of honour.[3]

It is not easy to predict the consequences which will result from the spirit which seems to pervade the Legislature of this State—and much indeed is it to be regretted, that at a crisis like the present, such men as Mr Henry—either from a love of ease—domestic enjoyments—or disinclination to oppose himself to a ruinous party—will not step forward. If in *principle* he is opposed to the measures of this Party, and his own apprehensions & Patriotism are not powerful enough to awaken him, I can hardly suppose that the sentiments of an individual would have much weight.[4]

Mr Anderson neglected to avail himself of the last Frost to fill my Ice Ho.—and *now* I think the chances for, & against filling it, are about equal. With great esteem & regard I am—Dear Sir Your Obedt & Affecte H: Serv⟨t⟩

Go: Washington

ALS, MWalJFK.

1. Letter not found.

2. Neither the letter from GW nor the one from Martha Washington has been found.

3. See GW to Stuart, 30 December.

4. Stuart wrote on the cover of GW's letter: "This letter was in answer to one in which I begged the Genl to urge Mr [Patrick] Henry to get into the Assembly." GW did write Henry; Henry did run and was elected but died shortly before he could take his seat in the house of delegates. See GW to Henry, 15 Jan., Henry to GW, 12 Feb., and Archibald Blair to GW, 19 June 1799.

From James McHenry

Philadelphia 5 Jany 1799

Inclosed is a copy of my report which I received this morning from the press. You will perceive, that I have used the matter you furnished me with pretty freely, and added several subjects which I hope will meet your approbation as well as the arrangment and general stile of the report.[1]

I am still extremely busy and can see no end to my labours. Yours affectionately and sincerely

James McHenry

Col. Smiths nomination has been concurred in, but the nominations have not yet come from the Senate.[2]

ALS, DLC:GW; ADfS, DLC: James McHenry Papers.

1. For McHenry's report, see McHenry to GW, 28 Dec. 1798, n.2.

2. See GW to McHenry, 13 Dec. 1798 (second letter), n.2.

To James McHenry

Private

Dear Sir,   Mount Vernon 6th jany 1799

Your favor of the 28th Ulto I have duly received.

I have no wish that any sentiments of mine, handed to you officially, should be withheld from Congress, or the Public. All I should have desired, wou'd have been, that such parts of my Report of the proceedings which occupied the attention of the two Major Generals and myself in Philadelphia, and fit for Legislative consideration, might have been communicated entire; with the reasons in support of the measures. Extracts, without these, does not always convey the sense, or the intention of the Reporter.

It is unnecessary I presume to add, that such other parts of the Report as depend upon Executive decision, ought not to be delayed. Many valuable Officers & Men have already been lost by it; and if the arrangement is not announced soon, more will be so. The Regulations with respect to the Uniforms, and Army distinctions, should be announced at the same time (if approved) in clear and peremptory terms; to guard, in the first place, Officers against unnecessary expence—and in the second place to prevent fantastic decorations at the whim of Corps. I do not recollect whether it is so expressed, but it was the meaning, that all Officers who are not *directed* to be distinguished by feathers, are not to wear any; but if it is not *forbidden* at the time of the annunciation, to those who shall, the practice will still prevail in the lower grades; such is the propensity in favor of it.[1]

That those who applied for higher grades than they have been appointed to shd decline accepting them, was, in many instances, apprehended—but to find among others, who were appointed, unworthy characters, is more surprising; although it is an evidence of the truth of the doctrine I advanced, that there was no dependence (except in a few instances) on the *mode* of obtaining information—for reason wch I detailed at the time.

The Papers you have asked for went off before your letter was received—and safe with you, I hope, 'ere this.

I ought to have taken your advice with respect to drawing three, in place of two months pay. Not keeping the a/c of my expenditures to, from, and at Philadelphia myself—Mr Lear paying them out of the money he received there, on his own account. and not coming to the knowledge of their amount until I got home, I presumed two months Pay &ca would have covered all my expences— but with the purchase of a few articles incidental to my journey, I find that the aggregate, amounts to $1115 55/100 and the pay drawn, to 1039 50/100; without including in the first sum the preparatory expence of equipment, for the journey.[2] one item alone of which, a horse, cost me $300.[3]

This communication is incidental; not by way of application for a further allowance; for I had rather sustain the loss, and the fatiegues of the journey, than it should be thought I was aiming to draw an Iota more from the Public, than my declaration at the acceptance of my Commission would authorize. With very great esteem & regard I am—Dear Sir Your Most Obedt and Affectionate Servt

Go: Washington

ALS, NhD.

1. GW is referring to his second report of 13 Dec. 1798 to McHenry, printed as a note in his first letter to McHenry of that date. Secretary of war McHenry issued on 8 Jan. 1799 "Uniform for the Army of the United States," a copy of which he enclosed in his letter to GW of 10 January. McHenry's regulations for army uniforms replaced those issued in 1787, which in any case had been largely ignored. Out of necessity a hodgepodge of military hats and coats had been issued as were available. It was important to GW that the men of the New Army being formed under his command have not only adequate clothing but also proper uniforms. Furthermore, he was determined that his own uniform be suitable. As he wrote McHenry on 10 Feb. 1799, the uniform to be made for him "being the commencement of a distinguishing dress for the Commander in Chief of the armies of the United States . . . and probably will be a permanent one—my wish . . . is, that it may be correctly executed." The correspondence regarding the correct execution of GW's uniform includes GW's letters to McHenry of 27, 28 Jan., 10 Feb., 7, 30 June, 14 July 1799, to James McAlpin, 27 Jan., 10 Feb., 18 Mar., 12 May, 14 July 1799, from McHenry, 10 Jan., 1, 12 Feb., 21 May, 24, 25, 28 June, 24 Aug. 1799, and from McAlpin, 15 Feb., 24, 27 June 1799.

2. GW wrote in his Day Book on 20 Dec. 1798: "By Sundry expences—and purchases—in a journey to Philadelphia—commencing the 5th of November and ending the 19th Instant—as paid by Mr Lear—exclusive of the Expenditures & purchases made by myself—viz.—

On the Road going	$	62. 8
Doctr [　] Spence—Dentist		18.
Sent to Jno. Greenwood of N. Yk Do		30.
A Gold Seal & repg Chain　$14.		
Engraving—Ditto　3.50		
Cleang my Watch & gold Key　4.		21.50
Inspeck [John Inskeep]. 4 dozn Tumblurs		12.
For Miss Custis Books, Paints & Music		25.25
Peter Gavenstine—Fruit		45.
B.W. Morris—Porter—49 dozn		104.80
[James] McAlpen—Taylors Bill—$1.70 & 38.25		39.95
Mrs Washington Gloves & Muslin		66.16
Holster Caps & Cockades—Servants		3.50
Hopkins Razer Strap		1.75
Saml McLean—Leathr Breechs, Servts		15.25
John Bedford Boots　　　　Do		27.24
John Lambert—1 Bush. Clovr Seed		17.
Sheet Iron—for Chimneys		4.73
A fine Carpet		7.
Washington Custis—a bridle		18.
N. Eyre—a Great Coat for myself		14.
Robt Fielding—Repairg Chariot		18.45
Jno. Dinwiddie—Livery Stable		99.48
Shoeing Horses		6.25
Washing at differt Times		5.87
Mrs White—Board—$172.		
Club— 17.52		189.52
Left with Colo. Biddle to pay for a Bk Case		150.
Paid for Sundry Small art[icle]s. by Mr Lear as will appear by his a/c		72.92
		1074.90
Apples—13 Barls pr Fredk Leoffler		39.65
Total		1115.55"

On 7 Dec. 1798 GW recorded the payment to himself of $1,039.50 for "two months pay, Rations and forage recd from the public by Warrant from the Secretary of War" (Day Book). After receiving this letter McHenry had another month's pay sent to GW (McHenry to GW, 10 Jan., n.1).

3. No record of GW's having paid for a horse just prior to his journey to Philadelphia in November has been found, but he notes in his Day Book on 15 Dec. paying David Rees $200 "for a Naraganset horse—Cream colour."

From John Marshall

Dear Sir,　　　　　　　　　　　　　　　Richmond, Jany 8th '99.

I had the pleasure of receiving your letter of the 30th of Dec'r while Genl Pinckney was at this place and of delivering to him the packet it inclosed. He left us with the ladies of his family on the 4th in health and spirits.

I thank you for the charge of Judge Addison; 'tis certainly well written and I wish that as well as some other publications on the same subject could be more generally read. I believe that no argument can moderate the leaders of the opposition—but it may be possible to make some impression on the mass of the people. For this purpose the charge of Judge Addison seems well calculated. I shall forward it to Mr Washington.

However I may regret the passage of one of the acts complained of, I am firmly persuaded that the tempest has not been raised by them.[1] Its cause lies much deeper and is not easily to be removed. Had they never passed, other measures would have been selected, which would have been attacked with equal violence. The misfortune is that an act operating on the press in any manner, affords to its opposers arguments which so captivate the public ear, which so mislead the public mind that the efforts of reason to correct false impressions will often fail of success.

Two very interesting subjects have during the present session peculiarly engaged the attention of the Legislature. The first was a paper produced by Colo. Taylor of Caroline, and which you must have seen, containing resolutions which take advantage of the i⟨rr⟩itation excited by the alien and sedition laws, to criminate the whole conduct of our administration and charge it with the design of introducing monarchy; the other was a proposition from Mr George Th. Taylor of Prince George expressive of sentiments similar to those which have been declared by other legislatures of the union on our controversy with France, in the place of which was substituted by a majority of twenty nine a counter proposition termed an amendment which was offered by Colo. Nicholas of Albermarle and which seems calculated to evince to France and to the world, that Virginia is very far from harmonizing with the American government or her sister States.

The debates on these subjects were long and animated. In the course of them Sentiments were declared and (in my judgment) views were developed of a very serious and alarming extent. To me it seems that there are men who will hold power by any means rather than not hold it; and who would prefer a dissolution of the union to the continuance of an administration not of their own party. They will risk all the ills which may result from the most dangerous experiments rather than permit that happiness to be enjoyed which is dispensed by other hands than their own. It is more than ever essential to make great exertions at the next election, and I am persuaded that by making we obtain a legislature, if not federal, so divided as to be moderate.[2]

I am by no means certain who will be elected for this district. Whatever the issue of the election may be, I shall neither reproach myself nor those at whose instance I have become a candidate, for the step I have taken⟨.⟩ I feel with increased force the obligation of duty to make sacrifices and exertions for the preservation of American Union and independence, as I am more convinced of the reality of the danger which threatens them. The exertions made against me by particular characters throughout this State and even from other states have an activity and a malignity which no personal considerations would excite. If I fail I shall regret the failure more on account of the evidence it will afford of the prevalence of a temper hostile to our government and indiscriminately so to all who will not join in that hostility, than of the personal mortification which would be sustained.[3] With the most respectful attachment, I remain, Sir, your obedt

J. Marshall

Sparks transcript, MH.

1. In his public letter "To a Freeholder" of 20 Sept. 1798, Marshall wrote: "I am not an advocate for the alien and sedition bills: had I been in congress when they passed, I should . . . have opposed them" (Stinchcombe and Cullen, *Marshall Papers*, 3:503–6). Marshall was opposed particularly to the Sedition Act.

2. James Madison wrote the resolutions opposing the Alien and Sedition Acts, known as the Virginia Resolutions, or Virginia Resolves, which John Taylor (1753–1824) of Caroline County introduced in the Virginia house of delegates on 13 Dec. (*The Virginia Report of 1799–1800, Touching the Alien and Sedition Laws* [Richmond, 1850; reprinted, New York, 1970], 22–23). After a prolonged debate, the resolutions were adopted by the house of delegates with few changes on 21 December. The Virginia senate adopted the resolutions on 24 December. George Keith Taylor, Marshall's brother-in-law and a delegate from Prince George County, delivered his first of two lengthy speeches in defense of the constitutionality of the Alien and Sedition Acts on 14 Dec. and his second on 21 Dec. (ibid., 29–38, 122–43). Wilson Cary Nicholas (1761–1820) was a delegate from Albemarle County who was elected in December 1799 to the U.S. Senate to replace the deceased Henry Tazewell. The text of the resolutions and the debate of the house are printed in the *Va. Report of 1799–1800*.

3. For an account of Marshall's candidacy and election to the Sixth Congress in April 1799, see "Congressional Election Campaign: Editorial Note" in Stinchcombe and Cullen, *Marshall Papers*, 3:494–502. For general references to GW's

correspondence regarding the congressional and assembly elections in Virginia in April 1799, see Marshall to GW, 1 May 1799, n.3.

From Daniel Call

Sir,   Richmond January 10th 1799

When Mr Bushrod Washington was appointed a Judge, he put his business in the court of Chancery and court of Appeals into my hands. In consequence of which I take the liberty of inclosing you the within Copy of the decree of the Court of Chancery in the suit against West and others.[1] I have the honor to be with the highest respect Sir your very huml. servt

Daniel Call

ALS, MB.

Daniel Call (c.1765–1848) of Richmond, compiler of the six-volume *Reports of the Virginia Court of Appeals* (Richmond, 1790–1818), was a member of the state council and a leading member of the Virginia bar.

1. GW docketed Call's letter: "Decree-in-Chancery 22d Sepr 1798 Washington agt Sundries respectg Ths Colvills Estate." The enclosed decree has not been found. For references to the final settlement of the Colvill estate, see especially George Pearson to GW, 12 May 1797, n.1.

From Lawrence Lewis

My dear Uncle   Charles Town Jany 10th 1799

Tis with infinite pleasure I informe you of the daily restoration of my health, and I think I may with certainty say it is perfectly reestablished; this appears from my nearly weighing as much as ever I did in my life.

I reach'd this Country by easy stages, and was fortunate enough to find the Roads equal to my wishes—From appearances the late Frost has not been as severe on this side of the Mountain as in the neighbourhood of Leesburgh, the snow being at least one third deeper there.

Farmers here are quite dishartened and say unless they have plentifull snows they shall make no Wheat, that appearances never were more unfavourable, that the Fly was more numerous this Fall than was ever known in this neighbourhood consequently more destructive—The Farmers seem to apprehend no danger from them in the Spring of the Year, a season which I have always been told they were most injurious—The reason given is, that the Land being strong and fertile the Wheat is rapid in its growth, and gets the better of any bite or injury they can do it—That in the Fall as soon as the Wheat is up, they eat off the leaves close to the ground, and by that means leave the roots entirely exposed to the Frost, which is very apt to perish during the Winter—Tis said in many places where Wheat was sown, and came up extreamly well, in the course of five or six Weeks, not a blade was to be seen it being entirely destroyed by the Fly—From such fields nothing is expected.

I have this day been to see my Uncle Charles and family; was happy to find his health much better, than it had been represented to me on the Rode up, he has been very unwell ever since the Winter commencd, but at present is as well as his mode of living will admit—my Aunt is in good health; and with my Uncle desires to be remember to you and my Aunt.[1]

As I now flatter myself, no objection as to the state of health can be made to my union with Miss Eleanor on the 22nd of Febry (the day first fixt on by us) that my dear uncle's concurrenc[e] will not be wanting as to the time proposed and that he will excuse my appearance one Week sooner at Mount Vernon, than the time which was thought necessary for my journey.

I shall leave this Country about the 23d for Culpeper, where I shall be for several days, and hope to be in Fredericksburg the 4⟨th⟩ of Febuary on my way to Mount Vernon.[2]

Excep my dear Uncle, my constant wishe⟨s⟩ for your health and happiness—and I beg to be affectionately rememberd to my Aunt—Your affectionate Nephew

Lawrence Lewis

ALS, PPRF.

1. GW's brother Charles died in September 1799.

2. Lawrence probably visited his sister Betty Lewis Carter and her husband Charles Carter who lived in Culpeper County. See Robert Lewis to GW, 13 February.

From James McHenry

Dear Sir   War Department 10 Jany 1799

I received this morning your letter of the 6th Inst.

I was very certain you had made a short estimate of your expenses when you thought two months pay would cover them. I have therefore directed the month of October to be added and the amount Dolls. 523 20/100 to be remitted you in the usual manner which I hope you will receive. This I presume will about face your expences.[1]

The letters adviseing the gentlemen whose appointments have been concurred in by the Senate will go to them to-morrow. I only received the list the evening of the day before yesterday. The greatest number of the nominations for the Infantry officers from Virginia have been post-poned by the Senate, 'till the arrival of the Senators from that State. Gibbs was so strongly objected to by the Massachusetts representatives and senators, that his name was not sent in.[2]

One printed copy of the regulations for the uniforms of the army will accompany the notice to each officer of his appointment for his government. Inclosed are copies of the regulations and letter.[3]

The Cavalry officers including those from Virginia have been all concurred in, except Hite, whose name was left out of the nominations. He and his connections who live in a very federal part of the country are stated to be antigovernmental and Jacobins, and that his appointment would excite great disgust.[4] I am Dear Sir Yours most truely & sincerely

James McHenry

ALS, DLC:GW; ADfS, MdAA.

1. Samuel Lewis, Sr., a clerk in the War Department, wrote to GW on this date: "I have been directed by the Secretary of War, to transmit you the enclosed Post Note for five hundred and twenty three dollars, and twenty Cents, being the amount of a Warrant issued on account of your Pay Subsistence and Forage for the month of October 1798. You will be pleased to transmit me your receipt for the same" (CSmH). On 15 Jan. 1799 GW recorded in his Day Book $523.20 "Cash recd on a Warrant from the War Office for pay, subsistence and forage for the Month of October," and on the next day he wrote to Lewis: "Sir, Your favor of the 10th instant, with its contents, came duly to hand—Enclosed is a receipt for the Post note of five hundred & twenty three dollars, and twenty Cents, on a/c of the Warrant issued from the War Office for my use. I am Sir Yr Obedient Hble Servant Go: Washington" (ALS, PHi: Washington MSS).

2. For reference to the lists of men recommended as officers for the New Army by GW and generals Hamilton and Pinckney, which President Adams submitted to the Senate on 31 Dec. 1798, see McHenry to GW, 28 Dec. 1798, n.3. McHenry on 22 Jan. 1799 sent GW the names of twenty-seven men on the generals' lists who had not been offered commissions, among whom was Caleb Gibbs, who had been recommended to command a Massachusetts regiment. For further correspondence regarding the rejection of Gibbs, see GW to McHenry, 25 Mar.

1799, and note 1 of that document, 23 April, and Caleb Gibbs to GW, 21 April 1799, and note 3 of that document. In a letter to Alexander Hamilton of 21 Jan. in which he enclosed the list of men not offered commissions, McHenry gives an explanation for the rejection of each and gives the grounds on which Sen. Benjamin Goodhue and several of the Massachusetts congressmen called for the rejection of Caleb Gibbs (Syrett, *Hamilton Papers*, 22:428–31).

3. A copy of "Uniform for the Army of the United States" dated 9 Jan. 1799 and issued by McHenry was enclosed with this letter. The regulations are the same as those suggested by GW in his second report to McHenry of 13 Dec. 1798, printed as a note in GW to McHenry, 13 Dec. 1798 (first letter).

4. George Hite was the son of Jacob and Frances Beale Hite who along with their younger children were killed in South Carolina by Indians in 1776 when young George was a student at William and Mary. During the Revolutionary War, beginning in September 1780, Hite served as an ensign in the 8th Virginia Regiment, and in 1782 and 1783 he was a lieutenant in the 3d Continental Dragoons. At this time he lived in Charles Town in Virginia and was married to Deborah Rutherford Hite, the daughter of Robert Rutherford (1728–1803), a Republican congressman from Virginia's fifth district from 1793 until he lost his seat in 1797 to Daniel Morgan. GW and the two major generals had recommended that Hite be made a captain in the cavalry. McHenry wrote Hamilton that Hite was rejected as being "anti-governmental and of French principles" (Syrett, *Hamilton Papers*, 22:428–31).

To Israel Shreve

Sir,   Mount Vernon 10th Jany 1799

Your letter of the 21st of last Mo. came to my hands by the last Western Mail: But as to your Brother, I have never seen, nor heard a tittle from him: and to be plain, I never expect to obtain what is due from you, to me, but by a resort to a Court of Justice.

You know full well, because you have often been told it in serious & solemn terms, that the only inducement I had to sell the land on which you live, was necessity; to raise money, to enable me to pay the expences of my public Office; to which the compensation was inadequate; and for which I was obliged to have recourse to other means, to effectuate. I am now obliged to borrow money at the Banks, on notes for Sixty days, renewable at the end thereof for 60 days more & so on; by which I am paying an interest nearly the double of what I shall receive. I appeal to your own judgement therefore to decide, if you think this right; especially, as you sold the greater part of the Land for the double of what you gave me, and had always time to prepare for my demands if proper measures had been pursued to meet them. But there are some people in this world (of which I fear you are one) who, from inattention to engagements, or disinclination to pay debts, but by compulsion, that never are, nor never will be prepared, and when this is the case, endulgences are unavailing.

But I have made similar remarks to these, to you, so often, that it is unnecessary to repeat them in this place; I shall therefore, and for the last time inform you, that if you can give the Sheriff satisfactory assurance of his receiving what was due on your judgment Bond last June (according to the Tenor thereof) on or before the first day of April next—this letter deposited in his hands—shall be his authority for staying the proceedings against you in whatever stage it may be, till then—beyond which I cannot extend the time.

It is not my wish to ruin, or even to distress your family; but knowing the terms on which you bought the Land, and my motives for selling it, you have no right to distress me by withholding the money, & ought to be as unwilling.

I shall not conclude without informing you in explicit language, that I shall expect the next payment due on the Instalment Bond, when it becomes due (the first of June next) without fail; and expect measures will be taken to accomplish it, instead of resorting to fresh excuses for staving it off. I am—Sir Yr Very Hble Servant

Go: Washington

ALS (photocopy), DLC:GW; ALS (letterpress copy), DLC:GW; LB, DLC:GW. The ALS was sold by Sotheby's, Parke-Bernet, 24 Sept. 1980, catalog #4481 M, item 283.

From William Heth

Dear Sir   Petersburg 12th Jany 1799

Persuaded that it will afford you much gratification, to see how our much esteemd friend General Pinckney was received at this place, hitherto considerd, as highly democratic; I hasten to hand you a paper, wch contains an history of our doings.[1]

Our toasts are lengthy to be sure—but, they are what I wishd—*pointed*, & *animated*.[2] I have the honor to be, Dear Sir, with the greatest respect & affection Yr Obt Sert

Will. Heth

ALS, DLC:GW.

1. The enclosed newspaper, presumably printed either in Richmond or Petersburg, has not been found, but a report from Petersburg, dated 11 Jan. 1799, appeared in the *City Gazette* in Charleston, S.C., on 26 January: "It having been understood by mere accident on Friday, by the citizens of this place, that Major-General Pinckney, one of the late envoys extraordinary to the French republic, was on his way from Richmond to this town; the mayor and a considerable number of respectable citizens, determined immediately to give him a public dinner. . . . About eleven o'clock in the afternoon of Saturday, he arrived, and was saluted by a discharge of cannon. . . . The citizens met about half after four o'clock, consisting of upwards of seventy respectable inhabitants of the town." On 14 Jan. Heth also sent the newspaper account of Charles Cotesworth Pinckney's reception in Petersburg to Alexander Hamilton and wrote: "Persuaded that it will give you much pleasure to find how our friend Pinkney was recd at this place hitherto considered as highly Democratic—you have enclosed an *history* of our doings. . . . The toasts you will say, are too long. True—but they are what I wished them to be, *pointed, unequivocal, & animated* . . ." (Syrett, *Hamilton Papers*, 22:413–16).

2. GW replied from Mount Vernon on 20 Jan.: "Dear Sir, Your favor of the 12th Inst. enclosing the account of General Pinckney's reception at Petersburgh, came duly to hand.

"The attentions which were shewn him, were, in my opinion, judiciously bestowed; and must be gratifying to the lovers of merit; to none more than to Dear Sir Your Most Obedient and Affecte Hble Servant Go: Washington" (ALS, NjP: deCoppet Collection).

Letter not found: from Clement Biddle, 13 Jan. 1799. On 20 Jan. GW wrote Biddle: "Your letter of the 13 Inst. has been duly received."

Letter not found: to John Marsden Pintard, 13 Jan. 1799. On 22 June 1799 GW wrote Elias Boudinot that he had "written to Mr Pintard on the 13th of January."

From George Turner

City of Washington, Jan: 14th 1799

Conscious of my very limited pretensions to military acquirements, I cannot, without great diffidence, presume to offer my Services to the Commander in Chief, as one of his Aides: Yet, Sir, if attachment to your person and the Service, and a wish to improve under your auspices in the Field, may be considered as an Earnest towards the attainment of other needful Qualifications, I would beg leave to solicit the honour of that appointment. With sentiments of the highest respect I have the honour to be, Sir, Your very Obedient and Humble Servant

G. Turner

ALS, CSmH.

George Turner, who had recently resigned his judgeship in the western territory, visited Mount Vernon in February 1799 with his friend William Thornton (*Diaries*, 6:333). Turner was born in England and during the Revolution served as a captain in the 1st South Carolina Regiment. GW had frequent dealings with him in the 1780s when Turner was assistant secretary general of the Society of the Cincinnati. GW's reply has not been found. Turner, however, wrote Thornton on 2 June 1799: "Have I entered the list of warriors? you ask . . . I answer, No" (Harris, *Thornton Papers*, 1:497–99).

To Patrick Henry

Confidential

Dear Sir   Mount Vernon 15th Jany 1799

At the threshold of this letter, I ought to make an apology for its contents; but if you will give me credit for my motives, I will contend for no more, however erroneous my sentiments may appear to you.[1]

It would be a waste of time, to attempt to bring to the view of a person of your observation & discernment, the endeavors of a certain party among us, to disquiet the Public mind with unfounded alarms; to arraign every act of the Administration; to set the People at varience with their Government; and to embarrass all its measures. Equally useless would it be, to predict what must be the inevitable consequences of such policy, if it cannot be arrested.

Unfortunately, and extremely do I regret it, the State of Virginia has taken the lead in this opposition. I have said the *State* Because the conduct of its Legislature in the Eyes of the World, will authorise the expression; because it is an incontrovertable fact, that the principle leaders of the opposition dwell in it; and because no doubt is entertained, I believe, that with the help of the Chiefs in other States, all the plans are arranged; and systematically pursued by their followers in other parts of the Union; though in no State except Kentucky (that I have heard of) has Legislative countenance been obtained, beyond Virginia.

It has been said, that the great mass of the Citizens of this State are well affected, notwithstanding, to the General Government, and the Union; and I am willing to believe it—nay do believe it: but how is this to be reconciled with their suffrages at the Elections of Representatives; both to Congress & their State Legislature; who are men opposed to the first, and by the tendency of their measures would destroy the latter? Some among us, have endeavored to account for this inconsistency and though convinced themselves, of its truth, they are unable to convince others; who are unacquainted with the internal polity of the State.

One of the reasons assigned is, that the most respectable, & best qualified characters among us, will not come forward. Easy & happy in their circumstances at home, and believing themselves secure in their liberties & property, will not forsake them, or their occupations, and engage in the turmoil of public business; or expose themselves to the calumnies of their opponents, whose weapons are detraction.

But at such a crisis as this, when every thing dear & valuable to us is assailed; when this Party hang upon the Wheels of Government as a dead weight, opposing every measure that is calculated for defence & self preservation; abetting the nefarious views of another Nation, upon our Rights; prefering, as long as they durst contend openly against the spirit & resentment of the People, the interest of France to the Welfare of their own Country; justifying the first at the expence of the latter: When every Act of their own Government is tortured by constructions they will not bear, into attempts to infringe & trample upon the Constitution with a view to introduce Monarchy; When the most unceasing, & purest exertions were making, to maintain a Neutrality which had been proclaimed by the Executive, approved unequivocally by Congress, by the State Legislatures, nay by the People themselves, in various meetings; and to preserve the Country in Peace, are charged as a measure calculated to favor Great Britain at the expence of France, and all those who had any agency in it, are accused of being under the influence of the former, and her Pensioners; When measures are systematically, and pertenaciously pursued, which must eventually dissolve the Union or produce coertion. I say, when these things have become so obvious, ought characters who are best able to rescue their Country from the pending evil to remain at home? rather, ought they not to come forward, and by their talents and influence, stand in the breach wch such conduct has made on the Peace and happiness of this Country, and oppose the widening of it?

Vain will it be to look for Peace and happiness, or for the security of liberty or property, if Civil discord should ensue; and what else can result from the policy of those among us, who, by all the means in their power, are driving matters to extremity, if they cannot be counteracted effectually? The views of Men can only be known, or guessed at, by their words or actions. Can those of the *Leaders* of Opposition be mistaken then, if judged by this Rule? That they are *followed* by numbers who are unacquainted with their designs, and suspect as little, the tendency of their principles, I am fully persuaded—But, if their conduct is viewed with indifference; if there is activity and misrepresentation on one side, and supiness on the other; their numbers, accumulated by Intrieguing, and discontented foreigners under proscription, who were at war with their own governments, and the greater part of them with *all* Government, their numbers will encrease, & nothing, short of Omniscience, can foretel the consequences.

I come now, my good Sir, to the object of my letter—which is—to express a hope, and an earnest wish, that you wd come forward at the ensuing Elections (if not for Congress, which you may think would take you too long from home) as a candidate for representation, in the General Assembly of this Commonwealth.

There are, I have no doubt, very many sensible men who oppose themselves to the torrent that carries away others, who had rather swim with, than stem it, without an able Pilot to conduct them—but these are neither old in Legislation, nor well known in the Community. Your weight of character and influence in the Ho. of Representatives would be a bulwark against such dangerous Sentiments as are delivered there at present. It would be a rallying point for the timid, and an attraction of the wavering. In a word, I conceive it to be of immense importance at this Crisis that you should be there; and I would fain hope that all minor considerations will be made to yield to the measure.

If I have erroneously supposed that your sentiments on these subjects are in unison with mine; or if I have assumed a liberty which the occasion does not warrant, I must conclude as I began, with praying that my motives may be received as an apology; and that my fear, that the tranquillity of the Union, and of this State in particular, is hastening to an awful crisis, have extorted them from me.[2] With great, and very sincere regard and respect, I am—Dear Sir Your Most Obedt & Very Hble Servt

Go: Washington

ALS, CSmH; ALS (letterpress copy), DLC:GW; LB, DLC:GW; copy, NHi.

1. For the likely genesis of this letter, see GW to David Stuart, 4 Jan., n.4.
2. See Henry's response of 12 February.

Letter not found: from Francis Deakins, 16 Jan. 1799. On 25 Jan. GW wrote Deakins: "Your letter of the 16th instant . . . is received."

To John Quincy Adams

Sir   Mount Vernon 20th Jany 1799

I have been honoured with a letter from you, dated at Berlin the 29th of Octr last; covering one from a namesake of mine, & who, very probably, may be a distant relation; as our families were from the same Country. Mine earlier than his; two brothers migrating during the Commonwealth of England. or rather, during the troubles of Charles the First. Not knowing through what other medium to address him, I take the liberty of sending my answer to his request under cover to you.[1]

You know, my good Sir, that it is not the policy of this Country to employ aliens—where it can well be avoided—either in the Civil or Military walks of life: but, for want of provident care & foresight, they will find themselves (indeed begin now to feel it) under the necessity of resorting to foreign aid for skilful men in the Engineering & artillery Corps. and if my namesake is well instructed in either of these branches of Military science—which bye the by is hardly to be expected from his age—there would be no doubt of his favourable reception—without which I think it would be deceptious to encourage hopes of employment in the Army of the United States: for there is a species of self importance in all foreign Officers, that cannot be gratified without doing injustice to meritorious characters of our own Countrymen—who conceive, & justly, where there is no great preponderency of experience, or merit, that they are entitled to the occupancy of all Offices in the gift their Government.

When I offered my Valedictory Address to the People of the

United States, I little thought that any event would arise in my day, that could withdraw me from the Retreat in wch I expected to pass the remnant of a life (worn down with cares) in ruminating on past scenes, & contemplating the future granduer of this rising Empire—But we know little of ourselves, & much less the designs of Providence. With great, & sincere respect & esteem I am—Dear Sir Your Most Obedient and Very Hble Servant

Go: Washington

ALS, MHi-A; ALS (letterpress copy), DLC:GW. The letter is docketed "18. April recd."

1. See GW's letter to James Washington of this date.

To Clement Biddle

Dear Sir,   Mount Vernon 20th Jany 1799
Your letter of the 13th Inst. has been duly received.[1]

It would oblige me very much if you could procure, and send ⟨me⟩ by the first opportunity which may offer, one bushel of English, or blue grass seeds, *Fresh & good*—without which, or if it be defective, or foul, my purpose—which is to sow a Lawn before my door, would not be answered.

If Blue grass-seeds cannot be obtained, send *white* clover seed, if to be had, of equal quantity as above.

From Mr Parish I expected two Hats, which may come with the Boots and Book case, the last of which it would be pleasing to receive.[2] Mrs Washington unites with me in offering the complimts of the Season to Mrs Biddle Yrself & family. I am—Dr Sir—Yr Most Obedt Servt

Go: Washington

ALS (letterpress copy), DLC:GW; LB, DLC:GW. ALS, sold by Robert Batchelder, 1992, catalog no. 84, item 57.

1. Letter not found.

2. As a sort of postscript to this letter, GW wrote Biddle on 23 Jan.: "Dear Sir, In my last, written to you a few days ago, I intended, but forgot it, to enquire what price flour & Wheat bore in your Market.

"I would thank you for giving these in your next. There used to be the prices current in one of the Gazettes of Philadelphia—which, tho' a very useful thing, seems to be discontinued. Let me pray you therefore, when at any time you may have occasion to write to me, to mention the price of the above articles & whether they are likely to rise or fall.

"As a Farmer, Wheat & Flour constitute my principal concerns—it behoves me therefore to dispose of them upon the best terms. I am—Dear Sir Your Most Obedt Servant Go: Washington" (ALS, PHi: Washington-Biddle Correspondence; letterpress copy, DLC:GW; LB, DLC:GW).

Before receiving Biddle's response of 27 Jan., which has not been found, GW wrote to Biddle on 29 Jan.: "When I wrote to you a few days ago for Blue grass-seed, and if that could not be had, then white clover seed in equal quantity; I expected to have finished a piece of ground sufficiently large to receive it. dispairing of this *now* and keeping seed over the year is not a good practice—I request, if you have not *already* purchased a bushel of the one, or the other, as then mentioned that the quantity may not exceed ⟨25 lb.⟩ of whichever of the kind that is sent. If it be purchased, however, I am ready to receive the whole quantity.

"Conceiving I must now be in your debt, if you will transmit the a/c, I will pay the balance as soon as known. With esteem & regard—I am—Dear Sir Your Very Humble Servant Go: Washington" (letterpress copy, DLC:GW; "25 lb." is taken from letter-book copy, DLC:GW). See also GW's answer of 1 Feb. to Biddle's missing letter of 27 Jan. as well as Biddle's letter of 5 Feb., listing what had been sent to GW and enclosing a copy of his account with GW.

On 1 Jan. Tobias Lear wrote Biddle from Mount Vernon: "The General is very anxious to get the Book Case which was made for him in Philadelphia, as he can make no arrangement of his Books & papers until it arrives; he will therefore be much obliged if you will have it ship'd, without fail on board the first Vessel that offers for this River; and it will be doing a favor, and a security to the glass doors &c. of the Book-Case, if the Captain will consent to landing it at Mount Vernon as he goes up the River. He shall not be delayed a moment longer than is necessary to put it on board the Boat (a large one fit for that purpose is here) and he shall have any assistance in doing it, and a reasonable consideration, if he desires it, will be made him. In this case you perceive it will be necessary to take in the Book Case where it can be readily come at. The Vessel on board which the B[l]ankets &c. were ship'd arrived yesterday in Alexandria. Our River is now open, and at this time there appears no prospect of its being closed again this season" (PPIn). Lear again wrote Biddle, on 15 Jan., asking him to forward a letter to Madeira, perhaps GW's missing letter of 13 Jan. to John Marsden Pintard, and saying "As our navigation is now entirely clear . . . I hope there will soon be an opportunity of forwarding the General's book case, hats & boots from Philadelphia" (*Parke-Bernet, Alexander Biddle Papers catalog*, 1943, pt. 3, item 242). For the sending of the bookcase, costing $152.13, see Biddle to GW, 5 February.

To Bryan Fairfax

Dear Sir,   Mount Vernon 20th Jany 1799
Since your departure from Mount Eagle, I have been favored with three letters from you.

The first, dated in Hampton Road, June the 17th, came speedily to hand—the 2d, begun on the 21st and ended the 23d of August, in London, and the 3d from York of the 7th of September, have also been received ⟨at the⟩ following times—viz.—That from York, a day or two before I commenced a journey for Philadelphia on the 4th of November, and the other from London, a few days after my return from thence, on the 20th of December.

For the details contained in these several letters, I pray you to accept my thanks; and congratulations on your safe arrival in England, although the Passage, on the whole, was not altogether as expeditious and as agreeable as you expected—To this prayer, let me add my best wishes for the perfect restoration of your health—and the accomplishment of such other objects as might have induced you to undertake the Voyage. After which it would give your friends in this Country much pleasure to hail your return.

For your care of the letters I took the liberty of committing to you, my grateful acknowledgments are offered.

When I presented my Valedictory address to the People of the United States, in September 1796, I little thought that any event would occur in my day, that could again withdraw me from the Retirement after which I had been so long panting—but we know little of ourselves, and still less of the ways of Providence. The injurious treatment this Country had received from France, in an open violation of the Treaty between the two Countries, and of the Laws of Nations—The Insults & Indignities with which all our Overtures for an amicable adjustment of the disputes were treated—The encreasing depredations on our Commerce, accompanied with outrage & threats, if we did not comply with their demands, ⟨leaving⟩ no hope of obtaining restitution for the past, or preserving the little that remained, or the Country from Invasion, but by the adoption of vigorous measures for self-defence having come fully to the view of the People, their resentments have been roused, and with one voice as it were, have made a tender of their lives and fortunes to repel any attempts which may be made on the Constitution or Government of their Country. In consequence of which, and to be prepared for the dernier resort, if unhappily we shall be driven to it, Troops are to be raised, and the United States placed in a Posture of defence. Under these circumstances, and it appearing to be the wish of my Countrymen, and the request of the governing Powers that I should take charge of their Armies, I am embarked so far in the business as will appear by my letter to the President of the 13th of July last; which, as it has run through all the News-papers here and Published in many of the Foreign Gazettes, you probably may have seen; and though still at home, where indeed I hope to remain, under a persuation that the French will discover the injustice and absurdity of their conduct, I hold myself in readiness to gird on the Sword, if the immergency shall require it.

Notwithstanding the Spirit of the People is so animated, that party among us which have been uniform in their opposition to all the measures of Government; in short to every act, either of Executive or Legislative authority, which seemed to be calculated to defeat French usurpations, and to lessen the influence of that Nation in our Country, hang upon, & clog its wheels as much as in them lye; and with a rancour & virulence which is scarcely to be conceived!—torturing every act, by unnatural construction, into a design to violate the Constitution, Introduce Monarchy, & to establish an Aristocracy. And what is more to be regretted, the same Spirit seems to have laid hold of the major part of the Legislature of this State, while all the other States in the Union (Kentucky, the child of Virginia, excepted) are coming forward with the most unequivocal evidences of their approbation of the measures which have been adopted by both, for self preservation. In what such a spirit, and such proceedings will issue, is beyond the reach of short sighted man to predict with any degree of certainty. I hope well; because I have always believed, & trusted, that that Providence which has carried us through a long & painful War with one of the most powerful Nations in Europe, will not suffer the discontented among ourselves, to produce more than a temporary interruption to the permanent Peace and happiness of this rising Empire. That they have been the cause of our present disquietudes; and the means of Stimulating (by mis-representing the Sentiments of the mass of Citizens of this Country) the Directory of France to their unwarrantable Acts—not from more real affection to the Nation than others possess, but to facilitate the design of subverting their own government—I have no more doubt than that I am now in the act of writing you this letter.

It was at the request of the Secretary of War, my Journey to Philadelphia was undertaken, to assist in the formation of the Augmented Force and to effect some other Military arrangements; and although your letter from York of the 7th of September came to hand before I set out, & was taken with me to be acknowledged from thence, yet my time, & attention, was so much occupied with the business that carried me there, that I never found leisure to do it.

Lady Huntington as you have been told *was* a correspondent of mine; and did me the honor to claim me as a relation; but in what degree, or by what connexion it came to pass, she did not inform me, nor did I ever trouble her Ladyship with an enquiry.[1] The favourable sentiments which others, you say, have been pleased to express respecting me, cannot but be pleasing to a mind who has always walked on a straight line, & endeavoured as far as human frailties & perhaps strong passions, would enable him, to discharge the relative duties to his Maker & fellow-men, without seeking by any indirect or left handed attempts to acquire popularity.

Our Crops of Wheat & Indian Corn last year (except in places) were extremely short. The drought of the Autumn exceeded any thing that has been recollected, insomuch that the Mills were scarcely able to work before New Years day. and the Fly has again begun its ravages on the Wheat in the Counties above us. This calamity, with the severity of the Drought on the Fall seeding, has given a discouraging aspect to the ensuing Crop of Wintr Grain.

We have the pleasure, frequently, of seeing or hearing from Mrs Fairfax; and on Wednesday last, Mrs Washington & myself took a family dinner at Mount Eagle—and left all the family in good health & Spirits in the afternoon[2]—Miss Custis was, at that time, with her Mother, at Hope Park, or she would have accompanied us on that visit. She is now returned, & unites with Mrs Washington & myself in offering best wishes for your health & safe return. And with very great, & sincere esteem & respect, I remain Dear Sir Your Most Obedient, and Affecte Hble Servant

Go: Washington

P.S. Finding that I could not comprise what I had to say in one sheet of Paper I have rambled on until I have almost filled a second.

ALS (letterpress copy), DLC:GW; LB, DLC:GW.

1. The philanthropist Selena Hastings, the countess of Huntingdon (1707–1791), wrote GW sixteen years before, on 20 Feb. 1783, calling him "a relation in which you certainly stand connected with me—Washington Earl Ferrers being my Father, whose mother was a Washington." See Lady Huntingdon's Scheme for Aiding the American Indians, 20 Dec. 1784, printed above.

2. GW does not record in his diaries his visit to Jane Fairfax.

To John Sinclair

Sir   Mount Vernon 20 Jany 1799

On the 10th of last July I had the honor to write you a pretty long letter on various subjects—and hearing, some considerable time afterwards, that the Ship (Suffolk) by which it had been sent, was Captured by a French Cruiser, from whence none of my letters ever reach[ed] their Address—I did, not long since, transmit a duplicate; which, though unaccompanied with the early Wheat that the above Vessel contained, I hope has met a better fate.[1]

I wish also that the proceedings of the National Board of Agriculture, which you informed me It had the goodness to direct should be neatly bound, and sent to me, may not have fallen into the same rapacious hands, as they have never been received.

It is now sometime since I had the honor to receive your favor of the 6th of June, accompanying "The history of the origin and progress of the Statistical account of Scotland" for which I pray you to accept my best thanks. That letter should not have remained so long unacknowledged had it not been received a few days before I commenced a journey to Philadelphia on business with the Secretary of War, where I was detained near seven weeks, & so closely occupied in the matters which carried me there, as to render all Minor considerations inadmissible.

It is not for me, Sir, to express any opinion with respect to the change in the Presidency of the National Board of Agriculture. I have no doubt but that Lord Somerville is a very meritorious character, and well deserves the honor to which he is Elected. I am also perfectly well satisfied that no one as far as my opportunities have enabled me to judge—could fill that office with more zeal—more honor to himself—and more usefulness to the Public, than Sir John Sinclair; and none who will merit in a higher degree than himself, the thanks he has received—Happy is it then for the Nation, to possess such characters to chuse from.

No one is more deeply impressed than I am, of the importance of National encourage⟨mt⟩ to Agriculture. No one can approve more of such an Institution as you have been the promoter of than myself. Nor no one who wishes more ardently than I do, to see such a measure adopted in the United States. but we must look I fear, to a more tranquil period for the accomplishment of it; Endeavouring in the mean while, to draw all the advantages we can from the labours of others. With great respect, and sincere esteem & regard I have the honor to be, Sir, Your Most Obedient, and Obliged Hble Servant

Go: Washington

ALS (letterpress copy), DLC:GW; LB, DLC:GW.

1. GW's letter of 10 Dec. 1798 covering a copy of his letter to Sinclair of 10 July 1798 has been printed as a note to the letter of 10 July.

To James Washington

Sir,   Mount Vernon (in Virginia) 20th January 1799

Through the goodness of Mr Adams, the American Minister at Berlin, I am indebted for the safe conveyance of your letter dated the 19th of Octr in that City: and through the same medium I have the honour to present this acknowledgement of it.

There can be but little doubt, Sir, of our descending from the same stock, as the branches of it proceeded from the same Country. At what time your ancestors left England is not mentioned. Mine came to America nearly one hundred & fifty years ago.

The regular course of application for Military appointments, is to the President of the United States, through the Secretary of War. But it would be deceptious, not to apprise you before hand, that it does not accord with the policy of this Government to bestow offices—Civil or Military—upon Foreigners to the exclusion of our own Citizens; first, because there is an animated zeal in the latter to serve their country; and secondly, because the former, seldom content with the rank they sustained in the Service of their own Country, look for higher Appointments in this; which, when bestowed, unless there is obvious cause to justify the measure, is pregnant with discontent—and therefore is not often practiced; Except in those branches of the Military Science which relate to Engineering and Gunnery: for in these our Military establishment is defective, and men of known and acknowledged abilities with ample testimonials thereof, would be certainly encouraged.

Deeming it better to give this candid detail, than to raise hopes that might prove falacious, is the best apology I can offer for my plain dealing. At the sametime, be pleased to accept assurances of my being Sir, Your Most Obedt and Very Humble Servant

Go: Washington

ALS, owned (1990) by Mrs. Joseph L. Baldwin, Palo Alto, Calif.; ALS (letterpress copy), DLC:GW.

From James McHenry

Dear Sir.   War Department [Philadelphia] 21 Jany 1799

I send you inclosed some minute information respecting the nominations which you may wish to see.[1] I have at the request of a committee of the Senate furnished them with a bill embracing the new organization for the army, and am preparing another for the provisional army, and a third for the Hospital department. I have required from Genl Hamilton assistance and have received it.[2] Yours ever and affectionately

James McHenry

ALS, DLC:GW; ADfS, MdAA.

1. McHenry wrote GW on 22 Jan.: "I omitted to inclose in my letter of yesterday the annexed schedule upon which the letter is a commentary" (DLC:GW). The enclosed list of the twenty-seven men recommended for commissions in the New Army and not offered commissions (DLC:GW) is printed in Syrett, *Hamilton Papers*, 22:430. The list has also been transcribed for CD-ROM:GW. In his letter to Hamilton of 21 Jan. McHenry explains why all of these men were left off the list of those recommended for commissions (ibid., 428–31).

2. In response to McHenry's requests of 10 and 14 Jan., Alexander Hamilton on 16 Jan. sent McHenry a "Draft of a Bill for a Provisional Army" (Syrett, *Hamilton Papers*, 22:409–11, 421–22). President Adams delayed sending the bill to Congress, and "An Act giving eventual authority to the President of the United States to augment the Army" (1 *Stat.* 725–27) was not enacted until 2 Mar. 1799. Hamilton sent his "draft of a Bill for regulating the *Medical Establishment*" on 21 Jan., on which "An Act to regulate the Medical Establishment" (ibid., 721–23), enacted on 2 Mar., was based. The third bill that Hamilton drafted for McHenry, which Congress enacted on 3 Mar. as "An Act for the better organizing of the Troops of the United States; and for other purposes" (ibid., 749–55), was based on McHenry's report of 24 Dec. 1798 to President Adams, which in turn was based on the recommendations made to McHenry on 13 Dec. by GW, Hamilton, and Charles Cotesworth Pinckney (see GW to McHenry, 13 Dec. 1798 [first letter], and notes; see also Hamilton to McHenry, 14 Jan. 1799, in Syrett, *Hamilton Papers*, 22:416–17).

From Elijah Brainerd

Honored Sir—   Randolph [Vt.] 23 January 1799

With great pleasure & deference do I contemplate your high character—Every true American must esteem & respect you as being raised upon the Kingdom of Providence, the political Father of our country—to fill the very first offices of public trust, with great respectability & the most distinguished usefulness to the ten thousands of our nation—and to fill a page in history, unequalled in lustre among the annals of mankind—which can never fail to communicate the most pleasing instruction to posterity—So much I beg leave to say with modesty, humility & gratitude—And pray dear Sir, permit me to lay before you a very short sketch of my life, which now is & has been for three years past, little else than a tale of woe & sorrow—Wish so to express myself as to be truly inoffensive.

The place of my nativity is a town called Haddons lying on and near the mouth of Connecticut river—From my 17th to my 22d year was chiefly in the service of my country—was taken prisoner twice A.D. 1779 at sea by the British, the first time was sat on shore in Virginia at the mouth of Chesepeak-bay—the second time was carried into New-york, & in November exchanged & sat on shore at Boston—having lost my little all of property.

In April 1780 began my studies for a public education at Dartmouth College—graduated Septemr 1785—was indented into the gospel ministry in Septemr 1786[1] by a public ordination over about 70 or 80 families newly settling this central town in Vermont, called Randolph—in population it has flourished greatly, now there are 278 families & 1600 souls, but its finances are much embarrassed owing to the perplexed state of the proprietorship & its rapid settlement.

Served my people in good harmony and with general success for ten years—On the 3d day of January 1798 resigned my ministerial office among my people in an amiable manner, it being only on account of bodily infirmity—My people has been as kind as is usual in similar cases—They still wish to have me preach to them whenever able—and consequently have given them two or three sermons the late summer, but in great feebleness.

My family consists of a kind Partner whom I married January A.D. 1788 the daughter of Joseph Marsh Esqr. of Hartford in this State, and three daughters & two sons between the age of ten & three years—also an indented lad ⟨of⟩ 14 years of age—all sprightly & active, & in common health, except myself.

The history of my infirmity is truly affecting—In 1794 was taken with very distressing rheumatic pain in the goint of my left hip—It was severe by spells and disenabled me from walking, except by crutches, but not from performing my parochial duties till August A.D. 1796—when an able Surgeon laid my hip open, examined the bone, found it carious & judged my case remediless for some weeks—from that day to this the incisions have constantly discharged matter, distressing pain has attended me in that place every day, except intervals of relief obtained by the use of *opium*—and my situation has been very feeble & inervated, have been able only to ride abroad a little now & then till a few months of late, I have gained more strength & acquired a little more ease—My prospects are more animating, so that probably, within a year, or two I may attain to a comfortable state of health, should nothing more extraordinary befall me—But now I have continual pain except while under the operation of my anodyne & in constant need of dressings for my sores—Doctors I have dismissed & wait on nature & time with patience—The good hand of Providence which laid calamity on me, has given me great resolution and fortitude, so that I continue to this day, an object of sympathy & compassion—cannot adequately describe the scene of sorrow & distress which I have gone thro' for three years past.

Confined from business, continually at expense—resources of support for my family impaired & cut off—benefactors have been kind, but still unavoidable bills of expense have accrued & still remain due—Creditors impatient for their pay—My little farm consisting of about 90 acres, about 35 of which under very indifferent & impaired cultivation—no property to hire labor with, the calls of my family still continue—we study the most prudent œconomy & industry, and admit of nothing superfluous, or ostentatious—nevertheless we are reduced to a state of indigency which is truly distressing and pitiable—it shakes my resolution at times—it draws forth the most fervent supplications for relief—Five hundred dollars would enable us soon to attain to that decent & plain style of living beyond which my heart does not aspire, after my late scene, which has taught me contentment with small things—A less sum from the benevolent hand of charity would awaken every sentiment of gratitude in my breast—& give us relief accordingly.

Pray dear Sir, if agreeable & consistent let your kind hand of benevolence lend us some small relief—perhaps a good word with some other great characters, may dispose them to become kind benefactors & send me a little relief also—No one can hardly conceive what a thankful, obedient & grateful object you would relieve in such a case—how it would rejoice my heart & awaken every sentiment of respect & gratitude—I would be a faithful & responsible steward & endeavor to make such calculations & arrangements as to obtain the approbation & confidence of my benefactors.

Thus I have frankly & with sincerity opened my life & feelings—documents & testimonials of full authenticity are at hand of what ⟨I⟩ have written—at least, hope to obtain your sympathy & if guilty of any indelicacy or error, your forgiveness & patience.[2]

Shall consign this to Mr Payne our Senator now ⟨in⟩ whose seat is only 12 miles from me, & whom I have reason ⟨to⟩ confide in as a good friend.

That the great Parent of all good may ever grant you his heavenly benedictions, prosperity & great felicity is the most fervent prayer of your dutiful, most obedient and humble servant

Elijah Brainerd

ALS, DLC:GW. The letter is docketed "Answd March 2d. 99."

Elijah Brainerd (1757–1828) gave up his pastorate at the Congregational church in Randolph, Vt., on 4 Jan. 1798; in 1810 he was installed as the minister of the Presbyterian church in Pelham; later he took orders in the Episcopal church in Warrenton, N.C.

1. Brainerd mistakenly wrote 1795 and 1796.

2. GW responded on 2 Mar.: "Sir, Your letter of the 23d of January has been received.

"While I sympathize with you in your Calamities, and most sincerely com-⟨miser⟩ate the distresses which you have undergone—I regret that it is not in my power at present to afford you any pecuniary relief; for I can truly say, that I feel myself at times much embarrassed to discharge my engagements and unavoidable expenses; owing to repeated disappointments in receiving monies due to me for property sold (as the income of my estate does at this time hardly meet my current expences) and upon which I confidently relied. Besides these, I have daily calls upon me similar to the one in your letter, from those of my acquaintance or neighbourhood as well as for public institutions. These I conceive it my duty first to releive or aid, as far as is in my power. To extend relief further would be truly grateful to my feelings; but I have not the means of doing it. And to ask a contribution for these purposes from others when I do not contribute myself, does not appear to me to be consistent. I therefore pray you, my good Sir, to be assured that in not complying with your wishes I act from necessity and not from choice.

"Your prayers and good wishes for my health & happiness I receive with gratitude and most sincerely reciprocate them. I am, Sir, Your most Obedt Servt" (Df, ViMtV).

This brought a reply from Brainerd on 3 April: "Your good letter I gratefully received—Your sympathy gives me no small consolation. Altho' numerous & important attentions daily await you, yet pray permit me to write a word more and I will not intrude again. Your reasoning and the information of frequent solicitations similar to mine, of which I was ignorant, perfectly satisfy me—another wish on the subject I have not. Perhaps ere long I may be able to go abroad—serve my country, in some way, honorably and myself profitably. May tranquility and great prosperity never fail you—And may you ever felicitate yourself in the full & glowing confidence of our nation, born in a day. . . . Since writing my first letter, have pretty certainly found the primary cause of my almost unparalleled scene of sorrow and distress. On that day we retreated from New York—September A.D. 1776, the company in which I was a soldier, was obliged to take cover on a small side hill on the bank of east river—A round top of a British ship played on & killed some of the company—A certain ball, perhaps a two pound shot, striking a few rods before me, bounded into the air and fell on my hip, where the seat of my sore & distress has ever been. This accident we conclude of late must be the origin of my present calamity. Therefore think I have a most ⟨just⟩ and reasonable demand on my country, at least in some measure—But the day for solicitation of such a nature is, perhaps, over forever—I relate this only to show what a son of calamity I am—My study is patience & humble resignation under the good hand of almighty *God*" (DLC:GW).

To Lawrence Lewis

Dear Lawrence,   Mount Vernon 23d Jany 1799

Your letter of the 10th Instt, I received in Alexandria on Monday; whither I went to become the Guardian of Nelly—thereby to authorise a license for your Nuptials on the 22d of next Mo. when, I presume, if your health is restored there will be no impediment to your Union.[1]

The letters herewith sent, were received two or three days ago, and until your letter of the above date came to hand, I knew not, with certainty, to what place to direct them. They are put under cover to your Brother of Fredericksburgh, to await your arrival at that place.[2]

I enclose the one to your Lieutenant, Mr Lawrence Washington, for safety and because it may be necessary that you should have a conference with him respecting the plan for Recruiting your Troop, when the order, and the means for doing it, are received.[3]

All however, that you, Washington & Custis have to do, at present, is simply to acknowledge the receipt of the letter from the Secretary of War; to inform him whether you do, or do not accept the appointment; and, in either case, to request him to thank the President for the honor he has conferred on you in making it.[4] Perhaps, as this acknowledgement will not be as prompt as might have been expected from you & Custis (for it was supposed that both of you were to be found at Mount Vernon) it would not be amiss if you were to add, that being on an excursion into the upper Country is the cause of it. All here, as I presume you will learn from a more pleasing pen, are well. I, therefore, shall only add that I am Dear Sir Your sincere friend and affectionate Uncle

Go: Washington

ALS, owned (1998) by Col. Edward Twiss, Church Hanborough, Oxfordshire, England, on deposit ViMtV.

1. GW recorded in his diary on 21 Jan. that he "was chosen Guardian by Miss Eleanor Parke Custis" in Alexandria (*Diaries*, 6:331).

2. The "Brother of Fredericksburgh" is probably Lawrence Lewis's half-brother, John Lewis.

3. Lawrence Washington, Jr. (d. 1809), was the son of Lawrence Washington (1728–c.1809) of Chotank.

4. Lawrence Lewis declined the commission after he and Eleanor Parke Custis decided to marry, and on 16 Feb. he had GW forward his letter to James McHenry informing the secretary of war of his decision.

To Robert Lewis

Dear Sir, Mount Vernon 23d Jan. 1799

It is quite time that you shd determine whether you will take *Young Royal Gift* to cover at your House the ensuing Season—or not; that he may be advertised accordingly.

And for your information it is necessary to add that, he is rather slow in covering; indeed will not cover at all, unless there is a Jenny by, to excite & stimulate him to the Act. He is now in his prime being 7 years old spring coming and about 13½ hands high; Son of Royal Gift, out of one of the Imported Jennies, from Malta. If you take the Jack, and have no female Asses in your neighbourhood, it will be necessary to take one or two from hence; and this perhaps would be the safest and best mode.

Some very careful person should have the care of them on the Road—the contrary of which, occasioned the loss of the old Spanish Jack.[1] Let me here from you on this subject as soon as you can, after this letter gets to hand, that I may know, in time, whether *young Royal Gift* is to be advertised for covering *here*, or *with you*.

It would be a very convenient and acceptable thing, for me to receive my Rents, or even a part of them, at as early a period as you can furnish me with them. On what I supposed at the time, a moral certainty of receiving considerable payments (before Christmas) for Lands I had disposed of, I have entered into a Contract for building two houses in the Federal City (for the accomodation of Congress—the members I mean—) and am obliged by that Contract to make considerable advances of money this Winter, and early in the Spring; which I shall not be enabled to do, under the above disappointments, without having recourse to borrowing from the Bank (at its ruinous interest) unless I can be aided by my Rents, & other resources on which I did not calculate. Let me know what dependence I can place on the first.

How far does Major Harrison, who owns the land near my mill, live from you? The latter end of October, or beginning of November last,[2] I wrote him a letter of which the enclosed is a Press Copy, taken at the time. But never having heard from him since, the presumption is, it never reached his hands, or an acknowledgement of it, at least, would have been made. If you should see Majr Harrison, shew him the Copy, and ask what answer he is disposed to give it.[3]

The family here are all well, and unite in best regards to Mrs Lewis and yourself, with—Dear Sir Your sincere friend and Affectionate Uncle

Go: Washington

ALS, PWacD; ALS (letterpress copy), DLC:GW; LB, DLC:GW.

1. For the report of the death in 1796 of GW's prized jack Royal Gift which in 1793 GW lent to William Washington in South Carolina for breeding purposes, see William Washington to GW, 23 July 1796.

2. GW inserted an asterisk here and wrote in the margin: "dated I perceive the 4th of Novembr."

3. GW's letter to William B. Harrison is dated 4 Nov. 1798. See also Lewis's response of 13 February.

To John Tayloe

Dear Sir,   Mount Vernon 23d Jany 1799

The Gazettes, which I presume you have seen, having announced your appointment as Major in the Regiment of Light-Dragoons, I shall add no more than a wish that it may be acceptable to you; as it is a very honorable one for any Gentleman who has not been in, or seen much Service.[1]

The other Major, now is, and has been in the Dragoon Service several years a Captain; is a man of family; genteel in his person; has given proofs of his gallant behaviour, and was wounded in General Wayne's victory over the combined Indian force in the year 1794.[2] Colo. Watts, you will no doubt have heard, was esteemed one of the best Cavalry Officers we had in the Revolutionary War; and whose merit is particularly well known in this State. In a word, I believe it may be said, that a more respectable Corps of Officers cannot well be, than this, if all the appointments are accepted.

Recollecting the desire expressed by you when I had the pleasure of your Company at this place a year or more ago, of purchasing one of my young Jack Asses when I shd be disposed to part with any—and now having three for that purpose; out of respect to your request, I give you notice thereof.

All three of them, were got by that valuable Jack Ass, Compound (who with another equally valuable, was poisoned, or died in most violent agonies, last winter) who was the descendent of Royal Gift, out of an Imported Jenny from Malta. The oldest of the three, is rising five, about twelve hands high. The other two are rising four—one about twelve hands, the other less. The first, & last mentioned, are descended from an Imported Jenny from Surinam; the other, she is Granddam t⟨o.⟩

I have been thus particular, that you may be the better enabled to decide whether the price I shall ask is such as you would ⟨be⟩ disposed to give. It is Eight hundred pounds of any one, who will take the three. Three hundred for the oldest, because he is *full* old enough to cover in the Spring; three hundred for the largest of the four years old, because he promises, I think, to be the largest & finest of the three, & may cover a few mares the ensuing Spring; and two hundred and fifty for the other, because he is the smallest, and probably will continue to be So.

Ready money would be very convenient to me, as my buildings in the City call for it; but I would sell on such credit as could be agreed on, receiving interest for the amt, until paid.[3] With very great esteem & regd I am—Dear Sir Your Most Obedt Hble Servt

Go: Washington

ALS (letterpress copy), DLC:GW.

1. For Tayloe's decision to defer indefinitely the acceptance of his army commission, see GW to Tayloe, 12 Feb., 5 May 1799, and Tayloe to GW, 10 Feb., 26 Mar., 29 April, 14 June 1799.

2. The "other Major" was Solomon Van Rensselaer (1774–1852) of New York. In addition to acting as adjutant general of New York for most of the period between 1801 and 1821, he was wounded while serving as a lieutenant colonel of New York volunteers during the War of 1812. He served as a Federalist member of Congress from 1819 to 1822.

3. GW does not record in his diary a visit from Tayloe in 1797 or 1798. Tayloe wrote GW on 10 Feb. saying that he was not interested in purchasing a jackass.

From William B. Harrison

Sir   Loudoun County Jany 24th 1799

I have Recevd yours of the 4th of Novr a fue days Since & Embrace the first favourable oppertunity to answer the Same, I am Sorry to hear my tenants Near your Mill has disturbd you a gain (when Mr Robert Lewis Calld on me I promisd him to move them and Set a bout it but found they had a Lease given them by Colo. Russell which did not Expire for three years after[1] at the end of which term hearing no further Complaints I Let them Continue from year to year at five hundred wt of Cropt tobacco & five Barrels of fish Less than I was offerd by John Roberson[2] on the Accot of Some old people that was on the Lands who begd to be let Continue what few days they had to Live thereon and that they had always paid their Rents punctually & had Long been tenants to my father in Law &c. one since is dead the other is in the famely and Cear of her Son I there fore feel Relievd on that Score and you may Rely on it I will take the Necessary Steps to purge the Lands of those improper Caractors aluded to in your Letter provided they Can be pointed out to me I am by som of the neighbours told that John Javens who Lives on the⟨re⟩ is a very honest man if So I woud not wish to diturb him provided I do not Sell the Lands and Continue to Rent them, I assure you it is very distant from me to Extort from you an unreasonable price or Rent but to the Contrary Consider my Self Obligated to Render you evry Service in my power & am with all the Respect a mortal Can frame yours &c.

                                          Wm B. Harrison

ALS, CSmH.

1. Colonel Russell is probably William Russell (1735–1793), formerly of Culpeper County and later of Washington County, who was colonel of the 5th and 13th Virginia regiments during the Revolution. See GW to Robert Lewis, 23 Jan. 1799.

2. For the possible identity of Robertson (Robinson), see Harrison to GW, 28 Mar. 1799, n.3.

From Timothy Pickering

Sir,   Philadelphia Jany 24. 1799.

I have been so much occupied since the receipt of your letter desiring a copy of one you wrote last year, that I have not had time to search for the original: as soon as I can I will do it, & if found, forward a copy.[1]

Your letter of the 15th covering one for Mr Murray & one for Lafayette I will take care of, and forward those two to their destination in a few days, when I shall write to Mr Murray.[2]

I take the liberty of inclosing my late report on French affairs: as soon as a correct copy shall be published in a pamphlet, I will do myself the honor to inclose one, together with Mr Gerry's budget. I learn from Massachusetts that he is doing mischief—as I expected.[3] I am with great respect Sir your most obt servt

Timothy Pickering

ALS, NNMM; William A. Smith Collection, property of Metropolitan Museum of Art, on deposit at New York Public Library.

1. See GW to Pickering, 4 January.

2. GW wrote from Mount Vernon on 15 Jan.: "Dear Sir, You would oblige me by forwarding the enclosed letters to their respective Addresses, by such opportunities as you may think safest & best; and if you should hear of their miscarriage (by Capture of the Vessel) that you would be so good as to inform me thereof. I am—Dear Sir Your Affecte and Obedt Hble Servant Go: Washington" (ALS, Vi). GW wrote to both Lafayette and William Vans Murray on Christmas Day.

3. On 21 Jan. 1799 President John Adams forwarded to the Congress the "Report of the Secretary of State on the transactions relating to the United States and France, since the last communication to Congress on that subject." The report covering the period from the spring to the fall of 1798 concentrates on Talleyrand's efforts "to exculpate" himself "from the charge of corruption" and "to detach Mr. [Elbridge] Gerry from his colleagues, and to inveigle him into a separate negotiation" (*ASP: Foreign Relations*, 2:229–38). On 2 Feb. Pickering wrote GW: "In my report, I had noticed . . . Mr Gerry's conduct, as wrong in principle,

and in many particulars very reprehensible: but these (contrary to my wishes) were omitted. . . . For your own eye, I have inserted in the copy of my report now inclosed, the passages referred to, as I had written them."

To Bartholomew Dandridge

Dear Sir,   Mount Vernon 25th Jany 1799

Your letters of the 11th of May, 16th of July, 20th of August and 10th of October are all before me. The receipt of the two first I have acknowledged; but as my letters wch travel across the Atlantic have not been fortunate in getting to their Address, these may have shared the usual fate. Being of little importance, however, no duplicate was sent, nor copy taken: Nor is it at all material *now*, whether they got to hand or not.[1]

Your letter of the 20th of August found me in Philadelphia, whither I had gone at the request of the Secretary of War, to aid in the formation of the new Corps, about to be raised; and in some other Military arrangements which were necessary, at that time, to be adjusted: and coming in the nick of time, your then wish to engage in a Military carreer was attended to; and you were, accordingly, appointed to the Command of an Infantry Company, in the first Regiment of Virginia, to be Commanded by Colo. Thomas Parker of Frederick; which has been rendered valid by the President and Senate, since.

The business which carried me to Philadelphia, detained me *in that City* from the 10th of Novr until the 14th of Decr, and occasioned an absence from home of near Seven weeks, during which time I was so much occupied as not to be able to give you advice of this occurrence; and soon after my return, your letter of the 10th of October came to hand informing me of your having been received into the family of Mr King, as his Secretary.

You have now, I presume, the option of remaining there, or of accepting the Commission beforementioned. In the choice of which you have your own inclination, & some other considerations to consult. Both are attended with uncertainties, but which most so, is not easy to decide. The augmented Corps, in which you are appointed, are by Law, to exist no longer than the dispute with France shall continue; but how long this will be, will require more wisdom than I possess to foretell; and you know, without information from me, what a bug-bear a standing army (as a few Regiments with us, are called, though liable to be disbanded at any moment, by withholding the appropriation for their support) is, in the eyes of all those who are continually raising Spectres & Hobgoblins to affrighten themselves and alarm the People: and how certain it is that ours (with their consent) will not exist a momt longer than it can be avoided by their endeavors; whether the cause which gave rise to it ceases, or not. Of the prospect before you in the Diplomatic line, you are as competent to judge of it as I am; But, as it is probable the Com⟨missi⟩on will be held for you until your determination is known, no time should be lost in announcing of it to me, or at the War Office.[2]

Lawrence Lewis is appointed a Captn in the Corps of light Dragoons; but before he enters the Camp of Mars, he is to engage in that of Venus with Nelly Custis, on the 22d of next month; they having, while I was at Philadelphia, without my having the smallest suspicion that such an affair was in agitation, formed their Contract for this purpose—Washington Craik is appointed a Lieutenant in the said Corps, & Washington Custis is made Cornet in Lewis's Troop; for it was found impracticable to keep him longer at College with any prospect of advantages; so great was his aversion to study; tho' addicted to no extravagant or vicious habits; but from mere indolence, & a deriliction to exercise the powers of his mind, and those talents with which nature had blessed him. The Army, generally, will be very respectably Officered.

The General Assembly of this State is in Session; and, by the accounts of its proceedings is running into every kind of opposition to the measures of the General government, and into all the extravagant Resolutions which folly can devise; in what they will issue, it is difficult to say.

I am sorry to inform you that your brother John Dandridge is no more. He paid the debt of nature a few days since; after having (as we have been informed) been in bad health for sometime.[3]

Your Aunt, who is as well as usual, and Nelly Custis (Washington is from home) unite with me in every good wish for you; and with thanks for your offer of rendering me any Services in your power, I remain Dr Sir—Your affecte friend & Servt

Go: Washington

Present me respectfully to Mr and Mrs King.

ALS (letterpress copy), NN: Washington Papers.

1. The letters in which GW acknowledged Dandridge's letters of 11 May and 16 July 1798 have not been found.

2. Dandridge wrote to GW on 12 Mar. 1799 declining to accept the army commission.

3. John Dandridge, the son of Martha Washington's brother Bartholomew Dandridge (1737–1785) and of Mary Burbidge Dandridge, was a lawyer and lived in New Kent County.

To Francis Deakins

Dear Sir,   Mount Vernon 25th Jany 1799

Your letter of the 16th instant enclosing one from Mr Hesekiah Veatch of the 1st of December last, with a statement of the A/c against Mr Charles McDavitt is received.[1]

Your directions to, & Mr Veatch's proceedings in consequence thereof, respecting the mode of obtaining the Rent due from McDavitt, were very proper, and are very satisfactory to me. The Bond of the latter may either remain in Mr Veatch's hands, or yours, as you shall judge best—to be acted upon when it becomes due.

I have received also, enclosed in ⟨your⟩ letter, a Hogshead of Tobacco, on account of Rent due to me from Mrs Priscilla Beall, as pr receipt enclosed; and feel very much obliged by your kind attention to my interest in these matters.[2] With very great esteem & regard—I am—Dear Sir Your Most Obedt Hble Servant

Go: Washington

ALS (letterpress copy), DLC:GW; LB, DLC:GW.

1. Neither Deakins's letter to GW nor Hezekiah Veatch's letter to Deakins with its enclosure has been found.

2. The receipt, written below the letter, indicates that the hogshead of tobacco which Priscilla Beale handed over to GW toward the payment of her rent had a net weight of 912 pounds.

Letter not found: from Clement Biddle, 27 Jan. 1799. On 1 Feb. GW wrote Biddle: "Your letter of the 27th Ulto was received last Night."

To James McAlpin

Sir,   Mount Vernon 27th Jany 1799.

The Secretary of War, by Command of the President of the U: States, having announced to the Army the Uniforms which are to be worn by Officers of the different grades, I have to request that you would make mine comformably thereto; & send it on, so as to be here at farthest by the 22d of February.[1]

There being some doubt in my mind respecting the Sort of Cuff & Pocket flap—that is—Whether the first shall simply turn up, or have a slash through it, with a flap the colour of the cloth (blue, with three buttons and holes) also embroidered; and whether the second shall have a cross pocket in the usual form, or slashed (that is inclining downwards)—There being a doubt I say respecting these matters, as also whether the Buff waistcoat is to have a corresponding embroidery down the front, and round the flaps to suit that on the Cuff, Cape and Flaps on the Coat, you will please to receive precise directions from the Secretary of War, & conform thereto, on all these points.

Let your blue cloth be of the best & softest French or Spanish; and the finest you can procure, of a deep colour. And the Buff of the very best sort, fine, & not inclining to yellow or Orange, like what I have been accustomed to wear. The buttons are to be plain, flat, and of the best double gilt.[2]

I presume there are many workers in embroidery in the City of Philadelphia—in that case make choice of the one who is most celebrated & esteemed the best. Those who follow this business will, unquestionably, be possessed of a variety of patterns. Let these be taken to the Secretary of War to chuse from.

The waistcoat should be straight breasted, that is without lapels. and the Cuffs of the Coat neither large, nor tight; observing a just medium between the two.

I again repeat my wish that they may be with me by the 22d of Feby—send your account along with the Clothes, and the Money shall be remitted to you; or payment ordered thereby[3]—Sir Your Very Hble Servant

Go: Washington

ALS (letterpress copy), DLC:GW.

James McAlpin was GW's tailor in Philadelphia. See GW to McAlpin, 7 May 1797. He lived at 3 South Fourth Street.

1. See McHenry to GW, 10 Jan., n.3.

2. During the Revolution infantry soldiers had on their uniforms pewter buttons with regiment numbers or "USA" on them. Infantry officers had fancier ones of tin and bone or wood, with similar markings. Artillery buttons were brass with pictures of a cannon and flag or mortars. By this time, some military buttons had eagles on them (*U.S. Army Insignia and Uniforms*, 26, 27). Yellow buttons as

called for in McHenry's "Uniform of the Army of the United States" (DLC:GW) meant brass, and "white" buttons were pewter or silver.

3. See McAlpin's reply of 15 Feb., printed in note 2 of GW to McAlpin, 10 February. Nelly Custis wished for GW to appear on his birthday and her wedding day in his new "splendidly embroidered uniform," but, according to her brother, "the idea of wearing a costume bedizzened with gold embroidery, had never entered the mind of the chief, he being content with the old Continental blue and buff" (Custis, *Recollections*, 450). GW knew how to make a virtue of necessity.

To James McHenry

Private

My dear Sir,   Mount Vernon 27th Jan: 1799

The enclosed letter for Mr McAlpin (my Tayler in Philadelphia) left open for your perusal, may be delivered, or not, as you shall judge best. and if the former takes place, to be accompanied with your sentiments on the doubtful parts of it.[1]

It is predicated first, on the supposition that the Uniform for the different grades of Officers, is conclusively fixed, & to be established as a standing regulation. and secondly, on the presumption that no attempts will be made *this* Session of Congress, to repeal the Law for augmenting the Army of the United States, or to reduce it below its present establishment. If the first is liable to no change, and there is no indication of an attempt to effect the latter, I would go to the expence of providing a uniform previously to the spur of the occasion; conformably to the regulations ordered by the War Department, agreeably to the Presidents Command. On the other hand, if either of the above things is likely to happen, I shall suspend doing it.

On re-considering the Uniform for the Commander in Chief, it has become a matter of doubt with me—(although, as it respected myself, *personally*, I was against *all* Embroidery)—whether embroidery on the Cape, Cuffs and Pockets of the Coat—and none on the *Buff* waistcoat, would not have a disjointed, and aukward appearance.[2] It is neither required, nor forbidden. Which then, in your judgment, or that of Connoisseurs, if you should converse with any on the subject, would be most eligable in itself, & accordent to what is expected. To *you* I submit the matter. As I also do whether the Coat shall have slash Cuffs (with blue flaps passing through them) and slash pockets, or both to be in the usual manner.[3]

These, apparently, are trifling matters to trouble you with; but, as it is the commencement of a New Scene, it is desirable that the thing should take a right direction. I have therefore, upon the whole and since I began this letter, determined to direct Mr McAlpin to apply to, and follow your directions in making the uniform. I should not prefer a heavy embroidery—or one containing much work. A light & neat one, would, in my opinion be more elegant, and more desirable; as well for the Coat, as for the Waistcoat, if the latter is to receive any. If there are workers in this way in Philadelphia (and the French are most likely to understand it) they will, no doubt, have a variety of Patterns to chuse from & I pray you to examine them.

The Eagle too, having become part of the American Cockade; have any of them been brought into use yet? My idea of the size is, that they ought not to be larger than would cover a quarter of a dollar at most and should be represented (for the Officers) as clothed with their feathers. This any ingenious Silver Smith can execute—and if five were sent to me, I would thank you; and would remit the cost, as soon as known to me.[4]

I must further beg, that proper Stars for the Epaulets (the latter I possess) may be sent to me with the other articles, that I may be equipped in dress *at least*—and if there are any tasty cockades (but not whimsically foolish) in wearg—or any one, who can make them, I should be glad if they were sent with the Eagles fixed thereon—ready to be placed in the hats. Does the Presidt & yourself wear ⟨them⟩?[5]

Excuse this scrawl and trouble, as I wish to set out right; and be assured of the sincere esteem & regard of Dear Sir Your Affecte Hble Servant

Go: Washington

ALS, NhD.

1. See GW to James McAlpin, this date.

2. See GW's second report to McHenry of 13 Dec. 1798, printed as a note in GW's first letter to McHenry of that date, in which he says that the coat of the commander in chief's uniform should be "embroidered on the cape [collar] cuffs and pockets."

3. McHenry replied to these questions on 1 February.

4. Cockades were common additions to military headgear at this time. The army uniform regulations of January 1787 ordered artillery and infantry officers to wear a "round," "black leather" cockade "with points" about "four inches in diameter." Some, however, continued to wear cockades made out of silk or other

fabrics (*U.S. Army Insignia and Uniforms*, 27). GW in his second report of 13 Dec. 1798 to McHenry stipulated that "all persons belonging to the Army" should wear a black cockade with a white eagle in the center, the "cockade of non-commissioned Officers, Musicians and privates to be of leather with Eagles of tin." See also GW to Alexander Hamilton and Charles Pinckney, 10 Nov. 1798.

5. For the sending of the stars, see McHenry to GW, 24 June, n.3. GW's uniform was to have gold epaulets with three silver stars on each, while major generals were to have two stars and brigadiers, one. McHenry answered the question about his and the president's cockades in his letter to GW of 12 February.

From James Lloyd

Sir,   Philadelphia 28 Jany 1799

I take the liberty to forward to you, under cover with this, Mr Gerry's correspondence with M. Talleyrand and the report of the Secretary of State, on the transactions relative to the U. States and France.[1]

I did myself the honor to write you a long letter, in the beginning of last July, in which I gave you, agreeably to your request, the best information I was able to procure, of the disposition of the people of Kentucky and Tenassee. Not having received an answer to that letter I have been apprehensive that it miscarried.[2] I have the honor to be, with the highest respect, Sir, Your Excellency's most Obedt Sert

James Lloyd

ALS, DLC:GW.

1. Timothy Pickering sent his report to GW on 24 January.

2. Lloyd's letter is dated 4 July 1798. For GW's explanation of his failure to acknowledge its receipt, see GW to Lloyd, 11 Feb. 1799.

To James McHenry

Dear Sir,   Mount Vernon January 28th 1799

I have duly received your letters of the 5th 10th & 21st & 22d of this month, with their several enclosures.

It is well known to you that in selecting from the documents laid before us, suitable Characters to fill the respective grades in the twelve additional Regimts the Major Generals and myself spared no pains to find such as appeared, on every account, most likely to render efficient service to their Country and do credit to the appointment. At the same time we were not inattentive to a proper distribution of Officers in the several States from which they were taken, so far as we had materials before us from which such distribution could be made. But it appeared in several instances that there were large districts of States from which there were few or no applications. In such cases we could only make up the quota from the other parts of the State from whence applications were more numerous. We had not a personal knowledge of Characters in the districts before mentioned to enable us to give them their due proportion without applications or recommendations; and even if we had possessed that knowledge, we must, without knowing whether certain persons would serve or not, have hazarded nominations & appointments which might not have been accepted. And the inconveniences & disadvantages attending this you know but too well.

That some persons would decline accepting an appointment in a grade below that for which they had applied, was to be expected. But unless evidence of disqualification, which was not known to the General Officers, should be brought forward, it was expected that their selection, made with the greatest care, uninfluenced by any local or personal considerations, and with an eye only to the public good, would not be set aside on light grounds.

In speaking on this subject I would not be understood as expressing any dissatisfaction on account of the withholding, postponing or rejecting names which were handed in; because I presume there is sufficient ground for such conduct. I would only wish to shew, that having before us all the evidence respecting characters which could at that time be obtained, and examining & comparing with the greatest care the relative qualifications & pretension⟨s⟩ of each, we were less liable to commit an Error than if we had to contend with any personal prejudices, or had the same motives to influence our conduct which others might have from local considerations.[1]

I observe in the appointment of the Cavalry Officers that the name of Laurence Lewis is placed the third among the Captains. In the Schedule handed to you, they stood, Hite 1st Captn & Lewis 2d Captn in the six additional Troops. As Hite's nomination has been withheld, I presume that Lewis comes in of course as the first Captain in these six troops. To this place he seems entitled as much from the service he has seen (which was on the Western

Expedition, where he acted as Aid to General Morgan during that time, and which I beleive is the only service that has been seen by either of the other Captains) as from his proper age and respectable standing in society.

In speaking of the Cavalry I must observe that in specifying their Uniform it was intended that their breeches should be of leather, and consequently buff instead of white. This, I doubt not, will strike you as being most proper on every account; and in that case no time should be lost in correcting the error before the officers shall have provided their Uniform.[2]

Enclosed is a letter I recd last Eveg from Genl Spotswood, by which you will see that the name of Thomas instead of John shd be prefixed to Capt. Green of Spotsylvania. This young Gentln from all accounts promises to be a very valu⟨able⟩ Officer as he has been an useful & meritorious Citizen. You will be pleased to have the alteration made in its regular form.[3] With great consideration & esteem I have the honor to be Dr Sir yr mo. ob. st

G. W——n

Df, in Tobias Lear's hand, DLC:GW.

1. GW is referring to the list of men who were recommended for commissions but for one reason or another were not given them. See McHenry to GW, 21 Jan., n.1.

2. See GW's second report to McHenry of 13 Dec. 1798, printed as a note in GW to McHenry (first letter), 13 December.

3. Alexander Spotswood first wrote to GW about Green on 16 Sept. 1798. His recent letter saying that young Green's name was Thomas, not John, has not been found. See also GW to McHenry, 4 Feb. 1799.

Letter not found: from William Thornton, 28 Jan. 1799. On 30 Jan. GW acknowledged the receipt of Thornton's "favor of the 28th instant."

From Henry Lee, Jr.

dear sir.   Richmond 29th Jany [17]99.

In our late session the views of opposition to govt have been disclosed with more than usual frankness.

That you may possess an accurate copy of the address on the part of the minority I beg leave to forward to you the enclosed.[1]

If the people will generally read the proceedings of the legislature I console myself with the hope that the disposition of Virga will change respecting congressional politics. I have the honor to be most respectfully Sir [your] real friend

H. Lee

ALS, NjMoNP.

1. On 23 Jan. 1799, a little more than a month after adopting James Madison's famous Virginia Resolutions opposing the Alien and Sedition Acts, the Republican majority in the Virginia legislature adopted a second attack on the acts, entitled "Address of the General Assembly to the People of the Commonwealth of Virginia." The Federalists in the Virginia legislature, for their part, drew up and promulgated the minority's defense of the acts and a rejection of the principles of Madison's Virginia Resolutions. Since the nineteenth century historians have identified James Madison as author of "Address of the General Assembly" attacking the Alien and Sedition Acts and John Marshall as author of the address defending the acts. The editors of the new edition of Madison's *Papers* demonstrate that Madison in fact was not the author of the assembly's address, and the editors of the new edition of Marshall's *Papers* argue persuasively that it was not Marshall but Henry Lee who wrote the minority's defense of the Alien and Sedition Acts ("Note on the Virginia Resolutions, 10 January 1799, and the Address of the General Assembly to the People of the Commonwealth of Virginia, 23 January 1799" in Mattern, *Madison Papers*, 17:199–206; "Congressional Election Campaign: Editorial Note," in Stinchcombe and Cullen, *Marshall Papers*, 3:494–502). For an account of the various addresses proposed, adopted, and rejected by the Virginia legislature in December 1798 and January 1799, see Risjord, *Chesapeake Politics*, 538–42.

To William Thornton

Dear Sir   Mount Vernon 30th Jany 1799

Your favor of the 28th instant, enclosing Deeds for my Lots in the Federal City—and Messrs Blagden & Lenthals estimate and drawing of the Windows—dressed in the manner proposed—came to my hands yesterday.[1]

The drawing sent, gives a much handsomer appearance to the Windows than the original design did; and I am more disposed to encounter the difference of expence, than to lessen the exterior show of the building—& therefore consent to the proposed alteration.

At the foot of the estimate sent me (relatively to the Windows) is an application for 152, two inch sash pullies (brass wheels in iron frames) and two groce of ⅞th Inch Screws. Be so good as to direct Mr Blagden to purchase these articles on the best terms, and of such sorts as will suit him. And also to employ a Painter to prime the Sashes & Doors, although I know it will cost me five times what I could do it for myself. The job is too small to send a Person from hence for that purpose only.

As a Pump will, ultimately, be necessary for the Well, it may as well be fixed there *now* as hereafter—remembering in the construction thereof, that it be calculated to serve both houses.

I do not clearly comprehend how it should come to pass, that the Specification of the Work, should be at varience with the Plan of the Buildings. I had always conceived that when a Plan was exhibited & agreed to, that it gave the precise dimensions, and that the only use of the former was to ascertain the cost, and to explain the manner, in which the work was to be executed. Professing myself, however, to be a Novice in these matters, I shall readily conform to whatever you shall think right; and so I will do if any thing else of a similar nature should occur, in prosecuting the Work.[2]

If a change in the Windows, should affect the size of the glass, I ought to be informed of it in time; indeed without delay; that no error may be committed in providing the latter.[3]

Is my Deed for the Lot on which I am building, yet in the City Office, or have I mislaid it? I do not find it among the others. Complimts & best wishes—I am—Dr Sir Your Most Obedt Servant

Go: Washington

ALS, DLC: Thornton Papers; ALS (letterpress copy), DLC:GW; LB, DLC:GW.

1. Neither Thornton's letter nor its enclosures has been found.

2. For the specifications agreed upon for GW's two houses being built by George Blagdin on lot 16, square 634, see GW to the District of Columbia Commissioners, 27 Oct. 1798, n.2.

3. For the extensive correspondence regarding the glass for the windows of the houses, which GW was responsible for providing, see GW to Thornton, 15 Feb., n.1.

To John Sevier

Sir,   Mount Vernon Jany 31st 1799

In acknowledging the receipt of your letter of the 25th of December, I must observe, that as the law for raising a provisional Army was not acted upon during the recess of Congress, I presume, from its tenor, that it becomes void of course. And whether or not a similar law will be passed in the pressent session is very problematical.[1]

I have reason to beleive that the President has already made his selection to fill the Offices which had become vacant in the Additional Army.

I am very happy to hear that a military Ardour prevails in the State over which you preside, and I trust it will be directed to the support of the true interest of our common Country if it should ever be called into Action.[2] With due consideration I have the honor to be Sir, Yr most Obedt Servt

Df, in Tobias Lear's hand, DLC:GW.

1. The act of May 1798 authorizing the president to create a Provisional Army expired at the end of the year without President Adams's having taken any action. In March 1799 Congress again gave the president the authority to form a Provisional Army. On the president's instructions James McHenry in May 1799 ordered that men willing and qualified to serve as officers in such an army be identified and informed of their having been chosen as potential officers. See James McHenry to GW, 2 May 1799, n.1.

2. GW heard from Sevier once again. On 10 April 1799 Sevier wrote from Knoxville: "A Mr Eli Hammonds of our District of Mero, is Very Sanguine to obtain the appointment of Captain in the Army, he is a character that Stands extremely well in that part of the State Wherein he resides, has distinguished himself to be a brave & good officer in the Militia, and Was he Appointed, I think Would in all probability raise a good company in his own Vicinity; he is highly recommended to Me, by respectable Characters, and I beg leave to add, that in my opinion he would be a Serviceable officer, and take the liberty to recommend him to your Notice" (DLC: James McHenry Papers). As was his custom, GW forwarded Sevier's letter to Secretary of War McHenry without comment. The frontiersman Eli Hammonds received no army appointment.

To Samuel Washington

Dear Sir   Mount Vernon 31st Jany 1799

Into what channel you put your letter of the 7th of November— is not for me to say, but this I can add, that it never came to my hands until the 13th Instant; when, if you had put it into any Post-Office, it would have been received at this place in three or four days, and whilst I was in Philadelphia in three or four days more.

It is of little avail, to investigate *now*, what has produced the difficulties and dis⟨tresses⟩ into which your fathers affairs, & your own ⟨have gone;⟩ Things passed, may be regretted, but can never be recalled.

At the time I wrote to your Mother, I had, as I thought, a moral certainty of receiving several thousand dollars for Lands which I had sold, West of the Alligany Mountains; and although I had urgent call for the money myself, I was resolved that those evils which she seemed to apprehend should not come upon her, if a $1000 would prevent it, but so far from receiving sevl thousand as I expected, I have not receivd one, on the acct of Land sold. Yet, notwithstanding this—had she drawn, as she was authorised to do, I would, rather than have been worse than I had promised to be, have borrowed the money at the Bank of Alexandria at the ruinous interest at which it is loaned. But as the application of the money for the uses I intended it, will not answer the end I proposed, and as I have no other means at present to obtain it but from the Banks, my offer of course ceases.

⟨But⟩ if contrary to my expectation (and I own I have none) I should receive payment for my land, whch ought, some to have been made in June last, and other in December, I will let you have from one to three hundred pounds—according to the sum I shall receive myself—but I must add, that from present appearances little dependence can be placed on it, from Your Affecte Uncle

Go: Washington

ALS (letterpress copy), NjMoNP. The copy is a very bad one; the words in angle brackets are taken from the copy in the Toner Transcripts printed in Fitzpatrick, *Writings of Washington*, 37:117–18.

To John Adams

Dear Sir   Mount Vernon 1st Feby 1799
The letter herewith enclosed from Mr Joel Barlow (though the old date) came to my hands only yesterday.[1]

I have conceived it to be my duty to transmit it to you without delay—and without a comment; except that it must have been written with a very good, or a very bad design: which of the two, you can judge better than I. For, from the known abilities of that Gentleman, such a letter could not be the result of ignorance *in him*—nor, from the implications which are to be found in it, has it been written without the *privity* of the French Directory.

It is incumbent on me to add, that, I have not been in the habit of corresponding with Mr Barlow. The letter now forwarded, is the first I ever received *from him*; and *to him*, I have never written one.

If then, you should be of opinion that his is calculated to bring on Negotiation upon open, fair and honorable ground, and merits a reply, and will instruct me as to the tenor of it; I shall, with pleasure and alacrity, obey your Orders; more especially if there is reason to believe that it would become a mean, however small, of restoring Peace and tranquillity to the United States upon just, honorable and dignified terms: which I am persuaded is the ardent desire of all the friends of this rising Empire.[2] With great consideration and respect, I have the honor to be. Dear Sir Your Most Obedient and Very Humble Servant

Go: Washington

ALS, MHi-A; ALS (letterpress copy), DLC:GW.

1. Joel Barlow's letter to GW is dated 2 Oct. 1798.
2. Adams did not respond until 19 Feb., when he informed GW that he had "yesterday determined to nominate Mr [William Vans] Murray to be Minister Plenipotentiary to the French Republic."

To Clement Biddle

Dear Sir,   Mount Vernon 1st Feb. 1799

Your letter of the 27th Ulto was received last Night.[1] As the whole quantity of Blue-grass seed was purchased before my last letter to you got to hand, it may be sent on without diminution.

Let it be accompanied, if to be had fresh and good, with twelve pounds of White clover seed; and the like quantity of Lucern. You will remark how pointed I am with respect to the *goodness* & *quality* of the seeds I buy—the reason is, that no imposition upon a Farmer is felt so sorely as that of foul, & defective seeds; because it deranges a whole system, besides occasioning the loss of a year in his plans.[2]

If Captn Ellwood would heave to when off my house; or send a Boat ashore, which would be more certain, I would send off my Boat wch would bring the Book cases without delay.[3] I am—Dr Sir Yr Obedt

Go: Washington

ALS, PHi: Washington-Biddle Correspondence; ALS (letterpress copy), DLC: GW; LB, DLC:GW.

1. Letter not found.
2. GW wrote to Biddle on 20 Jan. asking him to buy grass seed and on 29 Jan. sent him instructions (printed in a note to GW's letter of 20 Jan.) to buy a smaller amount of seed. Biddle sent the seed on 5 Feb. (Biddle to GW, 5 February).
3. The ice in the river at Philadelphia prevented Biddle from sending the

clover and lucerne grass seed, among other things, until March. See GW to Biddle, 18 Feb., 17 Mar., 21, 28 April, and Biddle to GW, 11 April.

From James McHenry

My dear Sir   Philadelphia 1 Feby 1799
I received last night your letter of the 27th of Jany and this morning sent for Mr McAlpin and gave him your orders.

It appears to me, that the round cuff and the usual pockets will be neater and handsomer than if slashed and also more dignified. I prefer for the same reason a plain waistcoat. I shall however take the advice of General McPhierson on the different points and endeavour to have the embroidery of the neatest pattern and done by an expert hand.[1]

It is not easy to discover what Congress will do with the army. I incline to beleive that no reduction will be made in the establishment, and that it is *possible* there may be some companies added to one or other of the Regiments; I mean either to the cavalry or artillery.[2] I am Dr Sir yours affectionately & sincerely

James McHenry

ALS, DLC:GW.

1. See GW to McHenry, 27 January.

2. McHenry enclosed this note for GW: "Mr Harper may be ticklish. He is undoubtedly a man of talents, with excellent points for an officer and has I know felt hurt at his not being promised a place as aid in your family. If you intended in a certain event to have gratified him, I could wish for various good reasons that you should write me in your next letter something flattering respecting his talents and the prominent and laudable part he has taken in our affairs, directing me that, notwithstanding the reservation which you had thought it adviseable to make on this subject I might mention to him that you wished to have him in your family in case of active operations and would reserve an opening &c. &c. This to be destroyed J. McH" (DLC:GW). Before writing his answer on 25 Feb., which was worded in a way that McHenry could show it to Congressman Robert Goodloe Harper, GW wrote, probably on 10 Feb., this private message to McHenry: "I will, shortly, say something more to you on the subject of Mr H——r's wishes. But I do not know that it will differ from what I have already said on that occasion. That he possesses talents I shall not deny, but there is too much of something else accompanying them, which may not render him the most pleasing character in a family. That, however is not all; Experience, local circumstances, Geographical situations, &ca &ca must all pass in review before I decide. And as I have given the same answers to all who have applied to be Aids under the *legal establishment* (and no other I presume would he accept)—and to some too whose pretensions in *many* respects are *superior* to his—Why should *he*

be more hurt by my circumspect conduct than they? Is it not an evidence that the same or similar causes would produce the same effect, to the disquietude of harmony among the persons about me? I do not reject Mr H———r on the one hand; on the other, I wish to be perfectly disengaged; that I may act from Circumstances as they shall occur. Besides, it is not yet certain that I shall want Aids" (AL, PWacD; letterpress copy, DLC:GW).

For an earlier suggestion to GW that he make Harper an aide and for GW's reaction to the suggestion, see Alexander Hamilton to GW, 29 July–1 Aug. 1798, and GW to Hamilton, 9 Aug. 1798. GW's letter of 25 Feb. to McHenry, marked "Private," reads: "Dear Sir, In a letter lately received from you, you have given me reason to believe that it would not be disagreeable to Mr Harper (in case the exigencies of this Country should call me to the Field) to compose part of my Military Sute, as an Aid de Camp. To have a person therein, of his abilities, would be as pleasing as it might be advantages; but you have been early apprised of my determination to remain perfectly disengaged to any of my *established* Aids, until the period shall have arrived when a choice must be made; in the selection of which, a variety of considerations (unnecessary to enumerate to you) must combine in fixing it.

"It is not only possible, but highly probable also, that in such a Crisis as wou'd require my attendance in the Field, his services in the Legislature might be of infinite more importance than he could ⟨ren⟩der in the Military line⟨;⟩ and it is a ⟨maxim⟩ with me, that in times of imminent danger to a Country, every true Patriot should occupy the Post in which he can render them the most effectually. Having expressed these sentiments, the matter must rest here.

"I have, it is true, given young Carroll of Carrollton, expectation of becoming a Volunteer Aid of mine, if I should be called to the Field. But this will give him neither Rank, nor Pay, in the line of the Army. The latter he stood in no need of, and the former as he could not contemplate a Military life as a profession, would have been of little importance to him.

"I thank you for the Eagles, and wish they had been accompanied with the Stars. When the cost of both are known, I will remit, or direct the amount to be paid to you in Philadelphia. With very great esteem I am—Dear Sir Your Most Obedt Hble Servt Go: Washington" (ALS, PWacD; letterpress copy, DLC:GW). For GW's offer to Charles Carroll, Jr., see GW to Carroll, 13 Dec. 1798; for references to the eagles for GW's uniform, see McHenry to GW, 12 February.

Letter not found: to Thomas Peter, 1 Feb. 1799. On 1 Feb. Peter wrote GW: "Your esteemed favor of this date" arrived.

From Thomas Peter

Dear Sir   George-Town [Md.] 1st[-2] Feby 1799
    Your esteemed favor of this date was handed to me by Charles.[1] My Brother George begs you will accept his sincere thanks for your letter of Recommendation to the Secretary of War, and I feel myself highly indebted to you for your friendship in this business.[2]

It is my opinion your observations are very correct with respect to the removal of the Seat of Government before the appointed time. Since I wrote you[3] there has been a Town meeting in consequence of Letters received from the Secretary of the Navey, the people in G.T. & the City have agreed to take into their own families to Board all the Members 2⟨6/⟩ pr Week & the Gentn that were appointed by the Meeting will report to Mr Stoddert To morrow that they have engaged Houses, conditionally at a very low Rent, and a sufficient number to accomodate the officers of Government &c. &c., but I sincerely wish Mr Stodderts zeal in this business may not be productive of more consequences than he is aware off, & should not be at all surprised if there were political manoeuvering by the Enemies of the City with him. We are all as usual excepting Eleanor who has just got some thing of the Hives, we have given her Wine drops & Bathe'd her and I think she is much easier in her breathing already & hope by the morning she will be restor'd to health again. I am, Dear Sir Yours with regard

Thomas Peter

2nd Feby 99. Eleanor this morning is tolerably well.

Copy (photocopy), ViMtV.

1. Letter not found. GW's coachman Charles often acted as a messenger.

2. GW wrote to James McHenry on 1 Feb.: "Dear Sir, The extract which follows, is from Mr Thomas Peter, who married Patsey Custis.

"'I am applied to by my brother to address and solicit you for an appointment in the Army. He would prefer being in the Cavalry if there are any vacancys, if not, in the Infantry. He appears to be fond of a Soldiers life & from his abilities and disposition, I should suppose he might make a useful man.'

"The young Gentleman in whose behalf this application is made is between 18 & twenty years of age; likely, well grown and of good behaviour. He is the Son of Mr Robert Peter of George Town, whom probably you know, and that all the family of them are warm Federalists. I am Dear Sir Your Most Obedt Hble Servt Go: Washington" (letterpress copy, DLC:GW). He wrote to McHenry again on 24 April: "Dear Sir, This letter and its enclosure, will be presented to you by Mr George Peter, whose wishes I made known to you in a former letter. He is Son to Mr Robert Peter of George Town, and as far as my information goes, is an amiable young man.

"His former application pointed more particularly to the Cavalry, but he is equally willing to receive an appointment in the Infantry. His appearance is much in his favour and as he proposes to wait on you in person I shall only add that I am Dear Sir Your Most Obedt Hble Servt Go: Washington" (letterpress copy, DLC:GW).

3. No letter from Thomas Peter more recent than 10 Sept. has been found.

From Timothy Pickering

Private

Sir,   Philadelphia Feby 2 1799

Your last letters to be forwarded to Europe I expect will proceed next week. The three for England I shall put under cover to Mr King and send them by the British packet which is to sail next Wednesday or Thursday.[1]

I have the honor to inclose copies of the Presidents communications to Congress on the 18th & 21st of January, concerning French affairs.[2] In my report, I had noticed (in as gentle terms as possible) Mr Gerry's conduct, as wrong in principle, and in many particulars very reprehensible: but these (contrary to my wishes) were omitted. There was one omission which I deemed important to retain, as it was the text of my observations on Mr Gerry's strange opinion of the sincerity of Talleyrand in his *talks* of negociation prior to the arrival of the Envoys dispatches in Europe. For your own eye, I have inserted in the copy of my report now inclosed, the passages referred to, as I had written them. It was this absurd but mischievous opinion which suggested to me the necessity of making a report on those communications: I call it mischievous, because many will read and respect that opinion without examining and discovering that it is without foundation. Mr Gerry's whole letter is calculated to apologize for his improper conduct—so improper as to be inexcusable—and of this he is apparently conscious; and hence his laboured but weak attempt to justify it.

The report as it now is, will wound his feelings; but the direct application of my remarks, and of divers other passages omitted, were the smallest censures which I thought his conduct merited. My letter of June 25, prefixed to his papers, he will first see in print—for he left France before it could have arrived.[3] I have the honor to be, with great respect, Sir, your most obt Servt

Timothy Pickering

ALS, PPRF; ALS (letterpress copy), MHi: Pickering Papers.

1. The three letters to England were to Bryan Fairfax, to John Sinclair, both 20 Jan., and to Bartholomew Dandridge, 25 Jan.; the letter to Europe was to John Quincy Adams, 20 Jan., enclosing one to James Washington of the same date.

2. Elbridge Gerry remained in Paris until August 1798, though the other two American envoys, Charles Cotesworth Pinckney and John Marshall, had departed in April. On the day of his arrival back in America, 1 Oct. 1798, Gerry sent to

Secretary of State Pickering a report of his activities in Paris during these months, to which he attached copies of his correspondence with French officials, mainly with Talleyrand. On 18 Jan. 1799 President Adams conveyed to Congress Gerry's report with its supporting documents "relative to our affairs with France." The whole is printed in *Annals of Congress, 1797–99*, 3:3464–531. Three days later, on 21 Jan., Adams laid "before Congress a Report of the Secretary of State, containing his observations on some of the documents" submitted by Gerry and sent to Congress on 18 January (ibid., 3531–58; see also Pickering to GW, 24 Jan., n.3). The copies of the documents that Pickering sent to GW have not been found.

3. When Adams submitted to Congress on 18 Jan. Elbridge Gerry's report of 1 Oct. 1798, he included Pickering's letter to Gerry of 25 June 1798 as the first document for Congress to consider. In his letter to Gerry in France, which Gerry never received, Pickering wrote: "It is presumed that you will consider the instructions of the 23d of March [to the three envoys] . . . as an effectual recall; lest, however, by any possibility, those instructions should not have reached you, and you should still be in France, I am directed by the President to transmit to you this letter, and to inform you that you are to consider it as a positive letter of recall" (ibid., 3464–65).

To James McHenry

Dear Sir,   Mount Vernon Feby 4th 1799

Presly Thornton, who is appointed a Captain in one of the Virginia Regiments, and in the list of Officers handed to you, is placed the first Captain in Colo. Bentley's Regiment, and designated of Northumberland, informs me there has been a mistake in your office with respect to him; as a Relation of his, bearing the same names, & living in Caroline County, is understood by you to be the person intended. At the time of making the selection, and until informed of it by the Captn Thornton intended to be nominated, I did not know there was another of the same name existing. The person in my list is the son of Colo. Presly Thornton late of Northumberland County in Virginia. Since his nomination he has taken up his residence in the City of Washington, and he informs me that he will accept his appointment. The Gentleman whom he says is understood at the War Office to be the person intended, is the son of Colo. Anthony Thornton late of Caroline County. I pray you to have this mistake corrected without delay.[1]

Mr Greene of Spotsylvania who had John instead of Thomas prefixed to his name, called upon me yesterday on his way to Philad. where he was going to have the error rectified, but as I informed him that I had written to you on the subject, and thus his presence was not necessary to identify the person, he gave up his journey. With due consideration & esteem I am Dear Sr Yr mo. Ob. St

Df, in Tobias Lear's hand, DLC:GW.

1. Presly Thornton (d. 1811), son of Col. Anthony Thornton of Caroline County, and Presly Thornton (d. 1807), son of Col. Presly Thornton (1721–1769) of Northumberland County, were both born in 1760. They married sisters, their cousins who were daughters of Col. Francis Thornton (d. 1784) of King George County. Whereas Presly, son of Anthony, was a captain in the Continental army during the Revolution, the Presly Thornton who was made a captain in the 8th Infantry Regiment at this time and became Charles Cotesworth Pinckney's aide-de-camp had spent the war years in England where his loyalist mother took him before the outbreak of war in 1775. Captain Presly Thornton wrote Tobias Lear on 31 Jan.: "From a conversation with my friends Mr [Tristram] Dalton & Mr T. Peter I was induced to believe that the very honorable appointment of my name which I perceived in the Public prints as eldest Captain in the Virginia line of the troops to be raised for the service of the United States was intended for me, by the nomination of Genl Washington & in consequence had determined to accept it—but on writing to a friend in Philadelphia to apply to the War Office for Official information, I have just received his Answer that it is there considered to be my relation Presly Thornton of Virginia, Son of Col. Anthony Thornton decd of Caroline County, who served as I have understood part of the last War in Col. [William] Washington's Corps of Cavalry. I have to intreat the favor of you to present my most grateful Acknowledgements to Genl Washington for the honor confered, if the appointment is intended for me, of which I should be happy to receive the earliest information & to assure him of my entire devotion to the Service of my Country whenever called on" (DLC:GW).

From Clement Biddle

Dear Sir   Philad[elphia] February 5. 1799

I have now to answer to your several favors before me by forwarding the bill of loading of Captain Ellwood for the seven packages Containing the Book Case, a bundle with the shoes from Bedford, another with the hatts from parrish and a small Kag which I had prepared with the Grass seed & therefore thought best to send it, all which the Captain promises to have particular Care of and to land them at Mount Vernon, stowing them so as to be Come at next to the Goods he is to deliver at Norfolk—Your Account with the Bills of parcels is also inclosed[1] and I have sent to Mr Fenno to furnish your Account for payment which I expect every moment.[2]

The price of flour since I wrote you[3] has advanced a little, say from 9½ to 10 Ds. for superfine which is owing to an Expectation that the trade to St Domingo may shortly be opened from the discretionary power vested in the president, on the Other hand it is supposed that it will not take place until the messenger from Toussaint who it is said is returning with our Consul to the Cape shall first have gone out to that Island, but if the trade does open, it will Certainly raise the price of flour throughout the United States.[4] I am very Respectfully Yr mo. Obedt and very hume Servt

Clement Biddle

ALS, PPRF.

1. See GW to Biddle, 20 Jan. (the "several favors" are printed in note 2 of that document), and GW to Biddle, 1 February. The enclosed account shows the cost of the bookcase to be $152.13, $18.80 of which was for packing; the grass seed, $3.33; the two hats, $16; the boots and shoes, $22.00. Biddle's receipts for his payments to John Douglass for the bookcase (15 Dec. 1798), to Catherine Roberts for the grass seed (25 Jan. 1799), and to Isaac Parish for the hats (5 Feb. 1799) are deposited at Mount Vernon. John Bedford was shoemaker for GW in Philadelphia.

2. John W. Fenno had become the publisher of the *Gazette of the United States* on 4 Sept. 1798 upon the death of his father John in Philadelphia's yellow fever epidemic.

3. Biddle's most recent letter, dated 27 Jan. and written in response to GW's letters of 20 and 23 Jan., is missing.

4. On 9 February 1799 John Adams signed the bill passed by Congress authorizing him to resume trade with Saint Domingue (Santo Domingo). General Toussaint L'Ouverture, after forcing the French Directory's commissioner to flee the island in October 1798, sent his personal representative Joseph Bunel to Philadelphia with the American consul at Cap François, Jacob Mayer, to secure much-needed food and supplies for his army. In March 1799 Secretary of State Timothy Pickering sent the new Consul General Edward Stevens to Saint Domingue with a shipload of supplies to negotiate with General Toussaint, and before the end of April the two had reached an agreement whereby two Saint Domingue ports would be open to American and British trade.

To William B. Harrison

Sir,   Mount Vernon 6th Feb. 1799

I have received your letter of the 24th Ulto, and thank you for your kind assurance of suffering no tenant to remain on your land (near my mill) who is a nuisance to me.

But it was from a thorough conviction in my mind that no per-

son, or persons, who meant to get a livelihood by dint of labour—
In short who did not depend more upon slight of hand, and unwarrantable shifts than labour, for a support, who would live on it
in the exhausted state in which it is, that induced me to propose
becoming your tenant, for the whole tract.

To this application of mine, your letter gives no answer, which
is the cause of my giving you the trouble of ⟨A⟩ second Letter; for-
asmuch, if you are inclined to lease the Land to me for a term of
years (and I could not take it on a short one, for the reasons mentioned in my last) I may know on what conditions; and if agreeable, be making my arrangements accordingly for the next year.

You will be able to judge, without any observations of mine,
whether it will not be for your interest, and the advantage of the
Land, that the whole shoud be in the hands of one person who
will pay the rent regularly as it becomes due, with out trouble;
and who, by proper inclosures (the fencing of which I should be
obliged to do with timber from my own land) wd be improving,
instead of rendering it less & less valuable every year, leaving it
totally divested of even firewood, or any thing to support it, in the
manner, and under the circumstances it now is, & is going on. I
say your own good sense will enable you to judge of these matters
as well as I can. All I request is, to be informed, whether you will
lease the land to me, or not; and in the former case, on what
terms; being certain that my enclosures will forever be subject to
depredations while the tenements are in the hands of persons who
cannot support their families by fair and honest labour, without
being in a starving condition great part of the year.

With respect to John Javins I have nothing particular to charge
him with, nor do I know any thing with which to impeach his honesty. Nor am I able to fix by legal proof any things against the others—but certain it is the best fences I can make are no proof
against their hogs &ca; and my meadows & grain are continually
destroyed by their Stocks. And it is not less certain that my Stock
(of Hogs & Sheep in particular) are constantly diminishing and
while one of the ⟨Pools⟩ has no visible way of raising them, sells
more things than any other person of his condition in the County.[1]
In a word, I have lately been told that he keeps a tipling house
which is a receptacle for such articles as Negros can steal from
their Owners. I am Sir—Yr Very Hble Servt

Go: Washington

ALS (letterpress copy), DLC:GW; LB, DLC:GW.

1. "One of the Pools" may have been someone related to the William Poole who for a time in the 1760s was GW's miller and tenant at Mount Vernon. See William Poole to GW, 9 July 1758, source note.

To James McHenry

Dear Sir   Mount Vernon Feby 6th 1799

Enclosed are sundry letters which have come to my hands, requesting Appointments in the Army of the United States.

You will observe that all these letters, excepting one, are from foreigners; and as I presume it is a principle pretty well established, that it would be improper to admit persons of this description into our Army, unless it is a few Characters well skilled as Engineers or Artilleriests, I have sent those to your Office that may go into the proper channel for applications, and not rest in my hands.[1]

The name of John Cooper, the writer of one of the enclosed letters, was not among those handed on to me from your office— You will see what he says on the subject of an appointt and will know whether the recommendations he mentions have been sent to you, and how far he may have a chance for an appointt from any vacancy, if he shd be found deserving.[2] With due consider[atio]n &c. I have the Honor &c.

Go. W.

Df, in Tobias Lear's hand, DLC:GW.

1. On a separate page Tobias Lear lists these letters: "one from Monsr Deseassies—dated Kingston, Jamaica, Sepr 5th 1798 . . . from Francis de Horacke—dated Amsterdam Sepr 6th 1798 . . . from Le Marquis de Vienne—dated Mainbernheyn Sept. 11th 1798 . . . from M. Beaujeau, dated Martinique Septr 15th 1798 . . . from Le Chr de Grimoldi—dated Martinique Octr 15th 1798 . . . from J. Kessler—dated Rotenburg in Hessin Octr 26th 1798[,] All desireing appointments in the Armies of the United States—Also one from John Cooper of Boston to the same effect and one from Major P. C. LEnfant, dated New York Novr 19th 1798." None of the letters has been found.

2. In the list of Massachusetts candidates for army commissions, prepared by GW and the two major generals in December 1798, "John Cooper Boston Lt last war of Artillery" is listed among the captains, and opposite his name is the notation: "says his circumstances are same—unsteady" (DLC:GW; Syrett, *Hamilton Papers*, 22:328).

To Jonathan Trumbull, Jr.

My dear Sir, Mount Vernon 6th Feby 1799

By the Ship Nancy from London, just arrived at Alexandria, I have received four copies of the Prints of the Deaths of Montgomery & Warren (the number of setts I presume I subscribed for)— sent me by your Brother.[1]

It is my wish to make him a remittance agreeably to the terms of the Subscription; but having taken no copy of it, and not being able to recollect what is to pay, must be my apology for troubling you with this letter: presuming that the original Paper or a copy thereof, might have been left with you; and more over, that you may be empowered to receive from the Subscribers in the *United States*, the amount of their subscriptions, in which case, upon receiving the advice, I shall, instead of making the remittance of mine to London, transmit it to you.

Whether any thing was to have been paid in advance—& whether in that case I paid mine—is more than I can decide without a resort (for the latter) to my Papers from Philadelphia, which are *yet* to be unpacked, and arranged.

By a Paper accompanying the Prints of Montgomery & Warren, the other part of the original design is suspended, on account of the peculiarity of the times.

As I shall not write to Mr Trumbull until I hear from you, the Sooner you can make it convenient to give me the information herein required, the more agreeable it will be.

I enquire frequently after you, & with pleasure hear always that you enjoy good health. Mrs Washington who is as well as usual, & Nelly Custis who on my birth day (the 22d instant) will change her name for that of Lewis, a Nephew of mine, and brother to those who lived with me in New York & Philadelphia, unite in best wishes and respectful compliments to Mrs Trumbull & yourself, with My dear Sir Yr Most Obedt & Affecte Servt

Go: Washington

ALS, ViMtV; ALS (letterpress copy), NN: Washington Papers; LB, DLC:GW.

1. See John Trumbull to GW, 6 Mar., 18 Sept. 1798, and note 1 of the latter document. See also Jonathan Trumbull's response of 22 February.

From Timothy Pickering

Sir, Philadelphia February 8. 1799

It will give you additional pleasure to learn that such is the increased and increasing respectability of the U. States among the European powers—that from being viewed with indifference & even contempt, our friendship and commerce are courted.

The Russian minister at London has suggested to Mr King that a Commercial treaty with the U. States would be agreeable to the Emperor Paul; and added, That this would be a favourable time to negociate a commercial treaty with the Ottoman Porte; and that Russia would afford to the U. States all its aid to accomplish it. Lord Grenville has given the like assurance of aid on the part of Great Britain.[1]

In consequence of these overtures, Mr King has just been appointed to negociate *at London* a Commercial treaty with Russia:[2] and Mr Smith has been this day nominated to negociate a commercial treaty with the Porte. The former will create *no expense*; and the latter very little expence, besides the presents customary and indispensable in treating with the Eastern Powers; but which a few voyages of our vessels up the Levant will abundantly compensate. These presents I cannot ascertain. Mr Liston informs me that a new British minister to the Porte gives in presents £3000 sterling among the various officers. *Ours* must be accompanied with *Treaty* presents: but I conclude from the best information attainable here, that the whole will not exceed forty or fifty thousand dollars: & once made, the treaty will last forever: the expence may perhaps not amount to more tha[n] half of one of those sums.[3]

Mr Smith will proceed from Lisbon—and no successor will be appointed to him at that court. The Chevalier de Freire has obtained leave of absence from the U.S.—and will no more return. This circumstance will comport very well with the vacancy we shall make at Lisbon.[4]

Another striking proof of our National importance I must not omit: Mr Pitt has made to Mr King a proposition which implies an opinion, that in certain articles (sugar & coffee in particular) Great Britain & the U. States may regulate the commerce of Europe. The subject had not been fully investigated: facts were sought for. But the idea presented by Mr Pitt, whether it shall ever become a reality or not, demonstrates our commercial and even our political importance.[5] I have the honor to be with great respect Sir, your obt servant

Timothy Pickering

ALS, DLC:GW.

1. Rufus King, U.S. minister in London, wrote Pickering on 10 Nov. 1798 of being approached by the Russian minister about the possibility of the United States negotiating treaties of commerce with Russia and the Ottoman Empire (King, *Life and Correspondence of King*, 2:462–64).

2. In his letter to King of 5 Feb. 1799, Pickering wrote: "P.S. The President has this day nominated you Commissioner Plenipotentiary to negociate a Commercial Treaty with Russia 6th Feby" (ibid., 534–36).

3. William Loughton Smith (c.1758–1812) was a congressman from South Carolina when John Adams chose him to become U.S. minister to Portugal, where he served until 1801. On 21 Feb. Pickering wrote GW that Adams's unexpected nomination of William Vans Murray as ambassador to France "damns" the nomination of Smith and King to negotiate commercial treaties. Both projects were indeed dropped.

4. Cipriano Ribeiro Freire arrived in 1794 as Portugal's ambassador to the United States.

5. King wrote Pickering on 10 and 16 Oct. 1798 about his conversations with Prime Minister William Pitt regarding the sugar and coffee trade (ibid., 443–44, 448–51).

To James McAlpin

Sir,   Mount Vernon 10th Feb. 1799

Having requested in a former letter, that you would make me a uniform suit of Cloaths by such directions as the Secretary of War would give; of such kinds of Cloth as I mentioned to you in that letter; and moreover, that they might be with me by the 22d of the present month; I hope my desire in all these particulars will be complied with.[1]

If Mr Washington, one of the Judges, has not left Philadelphia before you receive this letter, & is certain of doing it, so as to be here (where he means to call on his return) by the time abovementioned, he wd afford a good, & safe opportunity by whom to send them.

Let them be packed in a Port manteau to be made for that, & occasional uses thereafter, of very stiff and thick leather of the following size—viz.—two feet in length and two feet nine inches round—with a flap for the convenience of brushes, blacking &ca—and an iron bar (running through staples) and a good lock, for its security. A workman in that line, will be at no loss in discovering what kind of a Portmanteau it is I want, from what is here said.[2]

Transmit your account of the cost of all the articles required, and the amount shall be remitted to you, by Sir Your Hble Servant

Go: Washington

ALS, ViMtV.

1. See GW to McAlpin, 27 January.

2. McAlpin responded on 15 Feb.: "Your letters of the 27th Jany and 10th Feby were delivered to me by the Secretary at War—And in compliance with the orders contained in the first, I immediately sought out, and met with an embroiderer, whom I believe was fully equal to the task required. Our next object was Gold thread to work with, which I am extremely concerned to state, we have not been able to procure, either in Philadelphia, New York or Baltimore. By the first Ships from Europe, plenty of the Article is expected, but as it cannot Arrive soon enough to compleat your Order in the time Mentioned, I am under the painful Necessity of informing of my ill success. I beg leave to assure you, that no pains have been wanting on my part, in searching after the Materials—there is not a Store, or person in Philadelphia likely to possess them, to whom I have not Applied—that failing, I got my friends to write to New York & Baltimore, but without success. As soon as any Arrives, should you not think it too late, you may rely on my using every exertion and care in executing your orders to the utmost of my Abilities, And I hope to your sattisfaction. I was fortunate in procuring a very excellent piece of French Cloth, And the Coat has been long cut out, in readiness for the embroiderer . . . P.S. I should have wrote before, but the Secry at War told me he would Acquaint you with our ill success" (DLC:GW). On 18 Mar. GW wrote McAlpin again: "Sir, Your letter of the 15th Ulto came duly to hand, and I feel obliged by the pains you were at, to obtain gold thread for the Uniform Suit you were requested to make and forward to me. I am perfectly satisfied that nothing was left unattempted on your part, to comply with my Order.

"This article (gold thread) being expected in the Spring Importations, you will provide what is good, and have the suit compleated (by a skilful workmen) agreeably to former directions, and sent in the manner required in my last letter. I am Sir Your Very Hble Servt Go: Washington" (ALS, ViW: Washington Papers; letterpress copy, NN: Washington Papers).

To James McHenry

My dear Sir,　　　　　　　　　　　Mount Vernon 10th Feby 1799

Your letter of the 1st instant is received. Whatever appearance, or shape, the Uniform intended for me, may take, by your direction, will be entirely agreeable to my taste. It being the commencement of a distinguishing dress for the Commander in Chief of the armies of the United States (whomsoever he may be) and probably will be a permanent one—my wish (although as it respects myself personally I have no choice) is, that it may be correctly executed; for which reason I thought it more eligable, in the *first* instance, that the directions concerning it should proceed from the Department of War, than from myself.

I hope it will be made & sent to me by the time mentioned in my last; accompanied with the Cockades, and Stars for the Epaulets; without the whole of which the Dress will not comport with the order; of course must be incomplete.[1]

If my Nephew Mr Bushrod Washington should not have left Philadelphia before the above articles are ready, and is certain of being here by the 22d instant,[2] it would afford a good and safe opportunity for the conveyance of them to me; but if he has doubts on this head, I would not hazard the receipt of them by him, by that time; as you will perceive by the enclosed letter to Mr McAlpin left open for your perusal; and with an excuse for troubling you with these small matters, at a time when I presume you are pressed by important ones, I am with esteem & regard, and much truth My dear Sir Your Affecte Hble Servant

Go: Washington

ALS, NhD; ALS (letterpress copy), DLC:GW.

1. GW mentioned the time by which he desired his uniform in his letter to McAlpin of this date, but not in any previous letter to McHenry. GW did not receive the stars for his epaulets until June. See McHenry to GW, 24 June, n.3, and GW's response of 30 June.

2. Bushrod Washington, who left Mount Vernon on 25 Jan., did not return until 26 Feb. (*Diaries*, 6:332, 336).

To Timothy Pickering

Dear Sir   Mount Vernon 10th Feby 1799

Your letters of the 24th of the last, and 2d of the present Month, have been duly received; for which, & their enclosures, I thank you.

I am not surprised that some Members of the Ho. of Representatives should dis-relish your Report. It contains remarks, and speaks truths which they are desirous should be unknown to the People. I wish the parts which were left out, had been retained. The crisis, in my opinion, calls loudly for plain dealing; that the Citizens at large may be well informed, and decide, with respect to public measures, upon a thorough knowledge of facts. *Conceal-*

ment, is a species of mis-information; and misrepresentation and false alarms found the ground work of opposition. The plan of wch is, to keep the People as much as possible in ignorance & terror; for it is believed by themselves that a perfect understanding of our *real* situation, in regard to our foreign relations would be a death blow to their consequence and struggles; & for that reason, have always something *on foot* to disquiet the public mind.

I am sorry to hear that Mr Gerry is pursuing a mischevous path. That he was led astray by his own vanity & self importance, and was the dupe of *Diplomatic Skill*, I never had a doubt; but these doubts were accompanied by faint hopes (faint indeed they were) that he possessed candour, fortitude & manliness enough to have come forward with an open declaration that, he had been practised upon, & was deceiv'd—But Mr Gerry's Mind is not enlarged enough for such conduct as this; especially, assailed as I presume it was on his arrival, by those whose labours are unceasing, to inculcate their doctrines of hostility against the proceedings of their own government.

The Session of Congress is drawing fast to a close; what traits it will leave behind of strong, & energetic measures, remains to be seen: Such I hope as will shew that, we are ready at all times to negociate upon fair, & honorable terms, but never to be bullied or duped into them. With very great esteem & regd I am always Yours

Go: Washington

ALS, MHi: Pickering Papers; ALS (letterpress copy), DLC:GW; LB, DLC:GW. Pickering docketed the ALS, "On my report to the President on French affairs & Gerry." See note 1 in "Tobias Lear's Narrative Accounts of the Death of George Washington," 14 Dec. 1799, printed in volume 4 of this series.

From John Tayloe

Dear Sir   Mount Airy 10th Febry 1799
I had left Richmond before your letter of the 23rd Jany reached that place—The delay in answering it has proceded from this circumstance, which I trust you will see has been unavoidable.

The Appointment the President of the U. States has been pleased to confer on me is certainly highly honorable; a more flattering testimonial of his approbation than I expected to receive, or had a right to reckon on—To doubt a moment of the acceptance of the commission must appear unaccountable to my friends in general. I beg however to be permitted to explain the reason which produces the hesitation, in the full hope, that you will favor me with your advice in my present dilemma, for I mean to be determined by your opinion. I have with an infinity of fatigue succeeded in my Election to the State Senate against a man who is a warm partisan, in opposition to Government. If I accept the Commission to which I am appointed—I shall vacate my Seat and the inevitable consequence will be—that my place will be supplied by my last opponent—The question then will be—whether I shall best serve my Country—at this momentous crisis in a Civil, or Military capacity, In either situation I shall endeavour to be usefull—Should you recommend a Non acceptance—I can accord only conditionally, that if the Provisional army should be called for—I may be permitted to take my present rank *at least* in the first Regiment of Cavalry raised—This will give time to my friend & Neighbour Landon Carter Esqr. to fill the seat I shall vacate, the unfortunate situation of whose family at this moment precludes his stepping forth[1]—I beg leave in confidence to remark to you—that my pretensions to a Seat in Congress from this District are well grounded—if at the Election in 1801—I should be legally qualified to represent it—Judge therefore I beseech you what course I can with most honor & propriety take, & wherein I can best serve the essential interests of my Country—I have to beg you will interest yourself in producing the change—should you think it adviseable, should you deem it necessary for me to have a personal communication with the Secretary of War, I will repair to Phi[ladelphi]a as soon as Mrs Tayloes present confinement will permit my leaving home—& will do myself the pleasure of calling at Mount-Vernon[2]—I stand much indebted to you for your polite attention—respecting the Jack—Since I saw you Mr Ogle has given me a very fine one[3]—consequently my wants on that head [are] supplied—Beside this—I am anxious to appropriate every shilling I can raise—towards the improvements I contemplate putting up in the F. City[4]—With best respects to Mrs Washington & Miss Custis—I am with Sentiments of respect Your obliged—& Obedt Servt

John Tayloe

ALS, CSmH.

1. Landon Carter (1757–1820) lived at Sabine Hall, just down the road from Tayloe's home, Mount Airy. He was the grandson of GW's old friend Landon Carter (1710–1778) and son of Robert Wormeley Carter (1734–1797).

2. Tayloe had replaced Joseph Chinn as senator in the Virginia legislature for Lancaster, Richmond, and Northumberland counties on the lower Northern Neck. GW agreed with Tayloe that Tayloe should forego a military career at this juncture, and in April 1799 Tayloe won reelection to the senate and continued in office until Dr. Walter Jones, a Republican, replaced him in 1802. In a second letter of this date Tayloe wrote: "I take the liberty to cover you a copy of my last— to the Secretary of War" (MiU-C: Haskell Collection).

3. Benjamin Ogle (1746–1806) was governor of Maryland from 1798 to 1801.

4. For additional information about Tayloe's house in Washington, the Octagon, see William Thornton to GW, 19 April 1799, n.2.

From William Heath

Sir   Roxbury [Mass.] Febry 11th 1799

In the letter which you did me the honor to write me, some time since, you expressed a wish to be a reader of my memoirs of the American revolutionary war, if they were published,[1] The work being now out of press, I take the liberty to forward a Copy, and pray you to do me the honor of accepting it.[2] When you think proper to give the memoirs a perusal, I intreat you to exercise much candour, and to spread a mantle of friendship over their many imperfections, Brought up a farmer, without academic instruction, classic knowledge is beyond [m]y reach—indeed as an author I am quite a novice—My Journal kept without intermission, was intended for my own review, and the information of my own family and friends, and not for publication to the world, The Journal has been carefully continued, to the present time, now swelled to numerous pages, and will not be omitted while life, and health continue. It is therefore not improvable, from the present aspect of things, that if our lives are continued, and you should be again called into the Field in actual Service, (or Otherwise) I may be again, the narrator of your military Actions, Heaven grant, in such case, that I or some other, may have the felicity of recording, that you were a Second time, the *successful* leader of your fellow Countrymen, in defence and maintenance, of those their invalueable rights, and liberties, Independence and Sovereignty, Constitution and Government, (whoever may be the foe) the enjoyment of which hitherto, was purchased at a vast expence of Blood and treasure, and in which you acted so conspicuous a part[3]—Wishing you every felicity, which can be enjoyed here, and hereafter, and with best respects to your amiable Lady, which I pray you to present— I have the Honor to be with the most inviolable attachment Sir Your most humble Servant

W. Heath

ALS, DLC:GW.
1. See GW to Heath, 20 May 1797.
2. See Heath to GW, 17 April 1797, n.1. A copy of Heath's memoirs was in GW's library at the time of his death (Griffin, *Boston Athenæum Washington Collection*, 99).
3. GW replied on 1 Mar.: "Dear Sir, I have been duly favoured with your letter of the 11th Ulto from Roxbury, accompanying your Memoirs of the American War; which I accept, and daresay beforehand shall read, with pleasure, as soon as the bustle in which we now are engaged at the Wedding of our Granddaughter Miss Custis, is over.

"If in doing it, occasion should be found to make any observations thereon, I shall avail myself of the liberty you allow me, to express my sentiments with the utmost candour and freedom. In the mean while, I pray you to accept my best thanks for the testimony of your friendship and politeness in sending me the work so elegantly bound—Mrs Washington is thankful for your kind remembrance of her. and with great esteem & regard—I am—Dr Sir Your Most Obedt Hble Servt Go: Washington" (NN: Washington Papers).

To James Lloyd

Sir,   Mount Vernon 11⟨th⟩ Feby 1799.
Your favor of the 28th Ulto enclosing Mr Gerry's correspondence with M. Talleyrand, came safe; but not so soon after its date as might have been expected; or an earlier acknowledgment thereof would have been returned. For your kind, and polite attention to me in sending me this curious interchange, with the Secretary of State's Report thereon, I pray you to accept my best thanks.

It is not surprising that, the latter should not prove agreeable to the taste of some Gentlemen in the Ho. of R—p—s. It served to place the views & objects of the Fr: Government in too conspicuous a light to be mistaken; and of course did not accord with their purposes. I wish, however, they were in every man's hand, for I am

persuaded the great mass of our Citizens require only to understand matters rightly, to form right decisions; whilst the business
of some among us seems to be, to pervert, and lead their judg-
ments astray by false alarms, and a misrepresentation of facts.

I recollect well, having received a letter from you sometime in
July last on the Subject of Kentucky politics; but as it was in answer
to my queries, and knowing that you wd have left Philadelphia, or
in other words that the Session of Congress was about to close, and
that an acknowledgment of it was not likely to reach that City 'ere
this would happen, I did not reply to it. This is offered as my apology for not writing to you on that occasion.[1] With esteem and regard I remain Sir, Your Most Obedt Hble Servt

Go: Washington

ALS (letterpress copy), DLC:GW.
  1. See Lloyd to GW, 28 Jan., n.2.

From Patrick Henry

Private
Dear sir   Charlotte [County] feby 12th 1799
  Your Favor of the 15th ulto reached me a few Days since. I sincerely thank you for it, & for the flattering Sentiments you entertain for me—But most highly do I thank & honor you for your
unremitting Care of the public Welfare—Think not Sir that I
mean to flatter when I say that the wise Caution which avoided an
Increase of Connection with the French, in the early Stages of
their Revolution, has rendered to America, Services equally important with those which secured our Independence. How rarely
has it happen'd to be the Lot of one Man to save his Country twice!
  The Salvation I speak of from the French was wrought against
the Will of a great portion, if not a Majority of the people—Candour obliges me to acknowledge that I was amongst the Number
of blind & deluded. And I have to thank Heaven, that our Goverment was guided by a clearer Intellect, & a happyer Foresight than
mine. But notwithstanding the Check given to French men & their
principles, Events have proved, that the Contagion of the latter
has spread far & wide: & whilst they have sapped the Foundations
of our Morality & Religion, have prepared the Minds of Men to
equal Hostility against their own Government. And so far as I un-

derstand those who nickname themselves "Democrats," they are at Variance with those Truths which concern our Happiness in the World to come, alike with our Happiness in this—If an uninterupted Importation of French Principles had happened, our Ruin would have been certain & speedy. And even in the present State of Things, it may be doubted whether a Cure can easily be found for the Mischiefs they have occasioned. God grant it may be effected without coming to Extremity—yes my dear sir, I accord with every Sentiment you express to me—I am ashamed to refuse the little Boon you ask of me, when your Example is before my Eyes—My Children would blush to know, that you & their Father were Co[n]temporarys, & that when you asked him to throw in his Mite for the public Happiness, he refused to do it. In Conformity with these Feelings, I have declared myself a Candidate for this County at the next Election, since the Receipt of your Letter, but enjoying very indifferent Health I cannot leave my Home to make the Declaration efficacious as I could wish—The proceedings of the last Assembly have alarmed many thinking people hereabouts; & altho' there be Cause, for serious Apprehension, I trust the Friends of Order, Justice, & Truth will once more experience the Favor of that God who has so often & so signally bestowed his Blessings upon our Country.

Whilst I am thinking of our public affairs, I cannot but feel an Anxiety for the part our Executive has to act with Relation to the naval Assistance so essential to us in Case of War with France. If peace is obtained by her, especially with Britain, in which we are not included, the consequences will be serious indeed—The present conduct pursued towards us, indicates strongly, these two Ideas. First Hostility to our Goverment; & secondly, a fixed purpose of supporting her Partisans here—For the last, Dr Logan seems to me a strong proof—The first is too evident to need Illustration—If, as is probable, it is meant to reserve us singly for future chastisement, when Leisure may suit the purpose how can this Calamity be avoided but by some suitable Arrangement with Britain? I own I know not. Such a Step however, will add largely to the Stock of Combustibles already in the Hands of the discontented—They are blind to the Duplicity of France, & to the Dangers which grow out of the present State of Suspence & Indecision. The Terms of Britain for her Assistance will be heighten'd by every Event which may shew our Want of it—But when, or how, this very delicate Business is to be brought forward is not possible for me to say.

Forgive me for these Suggestions—They are produced in my Mind by the distant View of public Transactions, which Retirement affords—and for Fear of trespassing on your Patience, I conclude; but not 'til I assure you of that reverential Regard & sincere Attachment—with [which] I ever am Dear sir your affectionate humble Servant

P. Henry

ALS, PHi: Gratz Collection.

From James McHenry

Dear Sir   Philadelphia 12 Febry 1799.

McAlpin called upon me this morning to inform me finally, that after the most diligent inquiry for gold thread, both here and at New York, he has not been able to procure a sufficient quantity to complete the embroidery of the coat; and that of course it will be necessary to suspend making it up until after the arrival of the Spring ships in which the article is expected.

As yet the President's cockade remains without the Eagle. Mine is also without one. I shall give you early notice when the alteration takes place; and shall send you to morrow four eagles of the pattern that has been adopted, which I find corresponds with your ideas. I contemplate the black ribbon in the old form for our cockade with the eagle fixed in the centre to the loop and cockade by small holes in its wings.[1]

I have dispatched to Major Gen. Hamilton his instructions, and hope to be able to complete those for Gen. Pinckney to-day.[2] I shall send you copies. I am Dr Sir always & affectionately yours

James McHenry

ALS, DLC:GW; ADf, MdAA.

1. GW asked McHenry about the president's and McHenry's cockades in his letter of 27 Jan. and thanked him for the eagles on 25 Feb. (see note 2 of McHenry to GW, 1 February).

2. McHenry dated his instructions to Alexander Hamilton 4 Feb., but he only sent them on 8 Feb. (Syrett, *Hamilton Papers*, 22:455–65, 473). A copy of the instructions to Charles Cotesworth Pinckney, dated 11 Feb., is in DLC: McHenry Papers. See also the references to Hamilton's instructions in Hamilton to GW, 15 Feb., and note 1 of that document. On 30 Mar. McHenry sent GW a copy of his instructions to Hamilton.

From John C. Ogden

Sir   Prison in Litch field Con[necticu]t Feby 12th 1799

It is painful to trouble a man whom I have so long revered with these letters—But Oliver Wolcott whom you honored with a place, has cast me into prison for a small sum due honestly to him. The suit is pushed for two causes—One to defeat my hopes and expectations of the place of collector of the customs in New Haven. He wishes to have it given to Eli⟨zur⟩ Goodrich—Brother to the member of Congress who married Mr Wolcott's sister.[1]

A second reason is to revenge upon me for my errand to President Adams, with the petitions of the people of the western district of Vermont in behalf of Colol Lyon.

After Oliver Wolcott joined with the church plunderers in Portsmouth to destroy me—I went into Vermont, *six years ago*—during that period Colol Lyon has been my benefactor—and the general friend to the clergy of every faith. He is a churchman, mason and a man. For all these, he is entitled to my love, & care & good offices, as a clergy man & friend. He is an abused man—If his political opinions differ from others, he must abide the consequence.[2]

President Adams was offended at my interference, and give me a very particular answer—He did not ask me reasons—he judged without hearing and evidence—Misinformation was circulated in Philadelphia concerning Colol Lyon—the church, My Mother in-law,[3] & myself—All these things I strove to place right— The infringements upon religious liberty in New England came into view.

All this has freted Mr Wolcott—But he may do his best. The cell in this place is empty—I could live in it six or ⟨seve⟩n months—It is high ti⟨me⟩ th⟨ey⟩ had a Lyon in Connecticut. ⟨*mutilated*⟩ hierarchy & aristocracy are most oppressive. The press is fettered. Bigotry is exalting its head and forging chains.

These are serious sentiments. They are not expressed in the style, in which I love to write to Genl Washington. At all times & in all places I will revere your person, name and memory. I am Your devoted servant

John C. Ogden

ALS, DLC:GW.

1. For references to Ogden's seeking the post of collector of the customs at New Haven, Conn., and to the letters that he wrote to GW over the years, see Ogden to GW, 20 Sept. 1798, n.1. Chauncey Goodrich (1759–1815), a Federal-

ist member of the U.S. House of Representatives from Connecticut from 1795 to 1801, married Mary Ann Wolcott in 1789. On 4 Mar. 1799 Elizur Goodrich (1761–1849) joined his brother as a member of Congress, and in 1801 John Adams made the younger Goodrich collector of customs at New Haven, but shortly thereafter Thomas Jefferson removed him from office.

2. Matthew Lyon, an indentured servant from Ireland, left Connecticut and in 1773 settled in Vermont where he became both rich and influential. Emerging in the 1790s as a strident Antifederalist, he was elected to Congress in 1797. After withstanding a caning from Roger Griswold (see James McHenry to GW, 1 Feb. 1798, n.2) and the Federalist attempt to expel him, he became the first man to be tried under the Sedition Act. He was convicted in October 1798, fined, and sentenced to jail.

3. Ogden's wife was the daughter of Mary Clap Wooster and of David Wooster, a general in the Continental army who died in 1777. Ogden enclosed a sheet headed "Copy of a letter from Mrs Ogden the daughter of an American general who Sacrificed his life & fortune in the late war." Ogden's copy of the letter reads: "Ask the officers of government if their consciences can rest in quiet, when they are informed, that the widow of an American officer, who has spent his days in serving the public and spilt his blood in the defence of his country, and purchasing those rights and liberties, which they are now enjoying, is in distress—She who is borne down with infirmities, and old age, and lost her husband & property by the ravages of war, together with cruel taxes, now depends mostly upon the charity of her friends, and the attention of two young grand children, and a daughter of one of those heroes, who fell in battle, whom they often boast of as sealing their love for their country, with their blood. Can they rest in quiet, when she whose birth, education, and father's & mothers fortune, gave her a right to expect a better fate is reduced to hard labor for her bread, while many both male and female are pampered up and living at their ease, enjoying every thing which government can bestow, while those who have lost all, and whose merits deserve attention from the public, or at least to have justice done them, are lingering ⟨*mutilated*⟩ life of trouble and poverty."

To John Tayloe

Dear Sir   Mount Vernon 12th Feby 1799

By your Servant, I have this moment (on my return from Alexandria) been favoured with your two letters of the 10th instant.[1]

For the compliment you have been pleased to pay me, in asking my opinion of the eligibility of accepting your late appointment in the Army of the United States, I pray you to accept my thanks.

However desirous I might have been of seeing you engaged in that line, candour requires that I should declare, that under your statement of the circumstances of the case, I am inclined to believe that your Services in the civil line, in the present crisis of our affairs, and the temper in which *this State* in particular, appears to be (if it be fair to form a judgement from the Acts of its Legislature) would be more important. The first is contingent, of course may, or may not be called for, according to our doings in the latter. The second *is in existence*, and requires the active (and I will venture to add) the immediate, & unremitting exertions of the friends of Order & good government; to prevent the evils which it is but too apparent another description of men, among us, are endeavouring to involve the Unites States.

No evil, that I perceive, can result at this stage of the Recruiting Service, from the postponement of a final decision, respecting your appointment to a Majority in the Regiment of light Dragoons; and as you have it in contemplation (as appears by your letter to the Secretary of War) to visit Philadelphia shortly,[2] I will suspend a further expression of my sentiments on this subject until I have the pleasure of seeing you at this place.[3] With best respects to Mrs Tayloe, in which Mrs Washington & Miss Custis unite I am—Dear Sir Your Most Obedt Hble Servant

Go: Washington

ALS (letterpress copy), DLC:GW.

1. For Tayloe's second letter of 10 Feb., see note 2.

2. Tayloe's second letter of 10 Feb. to GW covered his letter to Secretary of War James McHenry.

3. Tayloe spent the night of 17 April at Mount Vernon.

From William Taylor

Dr Sir St⟨*illegible*⟩ Nr Manchester [England] Feby 12th 1799

I have taken the Liberty to send for your Acceptance a small cask of early pottatoes for planting, (if you think them worth notice); they are ship'd on board the Felicity of Alexandria and addres'd to Mr John Potts of that place, by whom myself and Mr Cripps were introduc'd to you on the sixth of May Last.[1] there is two sorts of them Viz. early Dwarf and d[itt]o Champion, both of which are as good of their kind as any we have, the Dwarfs are at the bottom of the Cask. I am dr Sr with sincere Respect and Esteem and thanks for the Civilities I receiv'd at Mount Vernon Yrs

William Taylor

N:B: We generally plant them in March if the Season suits, in dry Light soil dung'd with Horse Litter about 4 inches asunder in the rows and the rows about 6 inches[2] from each other, this for the Dwarfs, the Champions a Little farther asunder, and 3 inches deep.

ALS, DLC:GW. On the cover: "pr the ship Felicity for Alexandria to the care of Mr John Potts."

1. In his diary entry for 6 May 1798, GW wrote: "A Mr. Tayler & a Mr. Crips—introduced by Mr. Potts dined here" (*Diaries*, 6:295). John Potts, Jr. (1760–1809), a merchant in Alexandria, was a fairly frequent visitor to Mount Vernon.

2. Taylor wrote above the line here "2 inches deep."

From William Thornton

Dear Sir   City of Washington 12th Feby 1799

This morning I received the Statement of the Glass requisite for your Buildings, which I take the earliest opportunity of transmitting.[1] Mr Blagdin has not yet called for any part of the thousand Dollars you deposited in the Bank of Alexandria. If your forbearance to others should render any Application for Discounts at Bank necessary, I would advise that you do not take up any until it is immediately wanted, of which I shall never fail to give you due notice, and by this mode you would save the Interest, which being compound, by every two month's renewal of the note, amounts to about 7½ ℔ Centum pr Annum, even without the loss of any Days by Dates &c., which only those accustomed to Bank Transactions find easy: however, the rule is, to date so as to let the sixty Days expire the Day before the renewal at Bank is required, that the Directors may have it before them on the Discount Day; for if it fall the Day *after*, the note will require to be paid, & be renewed the following week; on which Account it is necessary to antedate the notes, one, two or three Days. Excuse me for mentioning these things.[2]

Accept my best wishes for many returns of yesterday's Anniversary.[3] Yours most affectionately & with the highest respect

William Thornton

ALS, CSmH.

1. George Blagdin's estimate, dated 12 Feb. 1796 [1799] and signed by him, reads:

"Window glass necessary for Genl Washington Buildings
130 Pains—10 by 8 Inches for Dormers & Transom's
100　do　12⅝ Square for Basement

340 do   19⅛ by 12⅝ for the three story above Basement and Fan lights
In the above calculation a small allowance hath been made for accidents"
(OTM).
For the correspondence about the glass, see GW to Thornton, 15 Feb., n.1.
2. On 15 Feb. GW informed Thornton that he had not yet had to borrow
money from the bank for Blagdin. He did, however, later borrow from the Bank
of Alexandria (see GW to William Herbert, 25 June 1799).
3. GW was 67 years old on 11 February (old style).

From Robert Lewis

Hond Uncle,   Spring Hill February 13th 1799
Your favor of the 23d ulto came duly to hand *with* an inclosed
copy of a letter to Major Harrison—Its contents and inclosure
shall have their proper attention.

In regard to taking Young Royal Gift the ensuing season to cover
at my Stable, I am still inclined to do it, not only on my own account, (as I am extremely anxious to get into the breed of Mules)
but from a desire to accommodate my neighbours who have frequently expressed a wish to have one of your Jacks in this vicinity.
I do not anticipate so great a profit from this business, as might
have been expected the last year, and year before from the services of Compound; as a Mr Green of Culpeper has procured an
imported Jack from some quarter or other which he has given notice a few days since will stand alternately in his County and Fauquier. I do not apprehend Royal Gift will loose many Mares by this
circumstance, when the people have an opportunity of compare-
ing one with the other, as a decided preference must be given to
him from his superior size, and the Stock from which he sprung.

My Collection in the way of Rents has been rather unsuccessfull
than otherwise—The painfull task of distraining has been resorted to in greater degree than usual on account of the general
failure of the crops of Wheat for the three *last* years past, owing to
the ravages of the Hessian flye, and a fluctuating climate—Indeed, many of the Tenants seem inclined to take advantage of a
clause in the old Leases which says, "Where a failure (in their endeavors for a crop) has taken place by any providential stroke" the
rent shall be remitted—But the lowness of their rents has deter'd
them, I believe. Truly pitiable is the situation of some of those who
have renew'd their Leases at a greater rent than formerly. Added

to this and the calamity above stated; the poverty of the soil below the ridge, owing to bad Husbandry; and a restriction from clearing more than what the old Leases required, (which wou'd enable them to make Tobacco now the staple of the upper Country) are almost unsurmountable obstacles to the payment of such rents. The Tenants in Frederick and Berkley have their complaints likewise, altho' blest with a better soil & lower rents, with a few exceptions. They have generally paid up. I shall (if no accident intervenes to prevent) be at Mt Vernon by the 21st or 22d inst. with all the Money I have[1]—and when I hope to be present at the celebration of the nuptials of my Brother and Miss Custis, which he informs me will take place on the latter day. Mrs Lewis begs me to present her respectful and affectionate regards to you—my Aunt—and family, with Your Much Obliged and dutifull Nephew

Robt Lewis

ALS, ViMtV; ADfS, ViMtV.

1. Both GW's Ledger C, 51, and his Day Book show that he received $500 from Robert Lewis on 25 Feb. 1799 "on acct of his Collection of my Rents." On 17 June GW acknowledged the receipt of $290 from Lewis in further payment of rents (Day Book; ADS, PWacD). GW's landholdings in Berkeley, Frederick, Fauquier, and Loudoun were divided into many parcels which were held by tenants. See List of Tenants, 18 Sept. 1785, and notes (printed above), GW to Battaile Muse, 28 July 1785, n.1, and Muse to GW, 28 Nov. 1785.

From William Thornton

Dear Sir   City of Washington Feby 14th 1799

I have this Morning obtained the Prices of the Boston Glass, which is of a very good quality; and, if, on enquiry, no cheaper can be had, equally good, it may be sent for at any time you will be pleased to direct. I should not have failed to make the necessary Enquiries here, but we have no Importers.[1]

My Colleague Mr Scott has been for several Days indisposed, and incapable of meeting me. I visited him yesterday, and think him better: he will be well I hope in a few Days. Mr White is yet at Winchester.

We are affected by the news of yellow-fever still continuing at Philadelphia, and it is said some Families are removing thence. Mr [William] Craig [Craik] the Member of Congress writes that there is no probability of obtaining any further Supply of Money from Congress. We shall push with Economy the Objects committed to our Care, and I doubt not our making ready in due time. I saw one of the Professors of the College of George Town this Morning, and I think the rooms in the new College amply sufficient for the Congress, if they should be disposed to accept the Accommodations offered by the Inhabitants of George Town.[2] I am, dear Sir, with the greatest respect your affectionate & obedt Friend

William Thornton

Mr Law's Family were expected last night. I delivered Mrs Washington's Message to Mrs Peter the Day we returned. My Family join in best respects to her & Miss Custis. To the latter I have bid an eternal Adieu!

Since I closed this Mr Stoddert has written that there is a majority in the House of Reps. for Congress removg hither the next S.S.[3] & he doubts not it will pass the Senate.

ALS, CSmH.

1. GW chose to procure the glass himself. See GW to Thornton, 15 Feb., n.1.
2. See Thomas Peter to GW, 1 Feb., n.4.
3. The editor of the *Thornton Papers* expands "S.S." to read "sessions" (Harris, *Thornton Papers*, 1:486).

To William Augustine Washington

My dear Sir,   Mount Vernon 14th Feby 1799

Mr H: Washington affords me a very good opportunity to inform you, that if your Crop enables you to supply me with a hundred Barrels[1] of Corn over and above the quantity Contracted for, I shall be willing to take it on the terms I do the Five hundred Barrels; and that I shall be willing to receive a part of the whole at any time you may find it convenient to forward it, as the danger of Frost, & shutting up my Creek, I hope is passed for this Season.

I am sorry I hear of your confinement, and trust if it is not quite at an end, that it cannot be far from it. Mrs Washington unites with me in best wishes for you, and I am—My dear Sir Your Affectionate Uncle

Go: Washington

ALS (photocopy), NN: Washington Collection; ALS (letterpress copy), DLC:GW. The ALS was listed for sale in Joseph Rubinfine's list no. 118, item 25.

1. For the agreement between GW and William Augustine Washington that GW would buy from his nephew 500 barrels of corn each year, see GW to W. A. Washington, 26 June, 3 Oct. 1798, and W. A. Washington to GW, 24 July 1798. On 12 Feb. 1799 "Mr. Hen. Wash. came to dinnr" at Mount Vernon (*Diaries*, 6: 334), probably Henry Washington (1765–1812), son of GW's cousins Lawrence (b. 1749) and Susannah Washington.

From Alexander Hamilton

Sir   New York February 15. 1799

The Secretary at War has communicated to me the following disposition with regard to the superintendence of our Military forces and Posts—All those in the States South of Maryland in Tennessee and Kentucke are placed under the Direction of Major General Pinckney: those every where else under my direction—to which he has added the general care of the Recruiting service.

The commencement of the business of recruiting, however, is still postponed; for the reason, as assigned by the Secretary, that a supply of cloathing is not yet ready.

In conformity with your ideas, I have directed General Wilkinson to repair to the seat of Government, in order to a more full examination of the affairs of the Western scence and to the concerting of ulterior arrangements.[1]

On this, and on every other subject of our military concerns, I shall be happy to receive from time to time such suggestions and instructions as you may be pleased to communicate.

I shall regularly advise you of the progress of things and especially of every material occurrence. With perfect respect I have the honor to be Sir Your very Obed. ser.

A. Hamilton

ALS, DLC:GW; copy, DLC: Hamilton Papers; copy, DLC: Hamilton Papers.

1. On 16 Dec. 1798, shortly after completing his five-week conference with major generals Hamilton and Charles Cotesworth Pinckney, GW wrote Secretary of War James McHenry about dividing the administrative control of the army between Hamilton in the North and Pinckney in the South, and he specified that Hamilton "be charged with Superintending . . . all the Troops and Posts which shall not be confided to General Pinckney; including the Army under General Wilkenson." Brigadier General James Wilkinson had been in command

of the Western Army since 1792. On 4 Feb. 1799 McHenry wrote Hamilton that he was "invested with the entire command of all the troops in Garrison on the Northern Lakes in the North Western Territory, including both Banks of the Ohio, and on the Mississippi" (Syrett, *Hamilton Papers*, 22:455–65). Upon receipt of McHenry's letter, Hamilton wrote Wilkinson on 12 Feb. informing him of these developments and ordering him to repair to Philadelphia with a view to their having "a full discussion of the affairs of the Scene in which you have so long had the direction," in order to form "a more perfect plan for present and eventual arrangements" (ibid., 477–79). Before Wilkinson arrived in Philadelphia in August, Hamilton decided that Wilkinson should be made a major general and secured GW's support for the promotion, but the proposal met with opposition from both McHenry and President Adams (see Hamilton to GW, 15 June, and GW to Hamilton, 25 June 1799).

To Timothy Pickering

Private

Dear Sir   Mount Vernon 15th Feby 1799.

Your favour of the 8th instt conveys very pleasing information, and I feel obliged by the communication.

Although you did not give your letter the stamp of *privacy*, I did not think myself at liberty to mention the purport of it to some good Federal characters who were dining with me at the time I received it, and who would have thought it the best Desert I could have offered.[1]

Hence forward, I will consider your letters to me, in three distinct points of view; and I mention it *now*, that I may commit no error hereafter.

First, such communications as you may conceive proper to make to me, *alone*, and mark *confidential*, shall go no farther; those marked *private*, I may, occasionally, impart their contents to well disposed characters; and those without either, will leave me unrestrained.[2] With very great esteem & regard—I am always—Yr Affecte

Go: Washington

ALS, MHi: Pickering Papers; ALS (letterpress copy), DLC:GW; copy, MHi: Pickering Papers.

1. The only dinner guests at Mount Vernon noted at this time were those of 12 Feb., who included Nicholas Fitzhugh, a brother of Fitzhugh, and Henry Washington (*Diaries*, 6:334).

2. See Pickering's response of 21 February.

To William Thornton

Dear Sir,   Mount Vernon 15th Feby 1799

I have received your letter of the 12th instant, with Mr Blagdens estimate of the Glass required for my Houses in the Federal City, and shall take measures for providing it in time.[1]

Presuming that Mr Blagdin is apprised of there being a check on the Bank of Alexandria, subject to his call, the neglect is his, if he does not do it. He shall not *want* the means necessary to push on my buildings on the one hand, and on the other, I hope his demands will not be *greater* than those wants.

I have not, as yet, had recourse to either Bank for a loan, but have no doubt of this being the case soon; when I shall not forget what you have said respecting the proper mode to obtain it. For your good wishes I thank you, and with Compliments remain, Dr Sir—Your most Obedt Hble Servt

Go: Washington

ALS, PWacD; ALS (letterpress copy), DLC:GW.

1. For George Blagdin's estimate of the amount of glass that would be needed for the windows of the two houses that he was building for GW near the Capitol in the Federal City, see Thornton to GW, 12 Feb., n.1. GW was to discover that to obtain the glass would cause him a good deal of bother. He first tried to secure it in Alexandria, and on 16 Mar. Macleod & Lumsden wrote him from that town: "We have just recd your Note—are sorry we cannot supply your order at present; but have ordered a Large quantity of English Crown Glass, in Sheets as blown at the Manufactory, which we expect early this Spring[.] Should that arrive according to our expectation, we can amply supply you, at the following Prices Viz.

> Sqr. 8 . 10   @ 6½d.   ℔ pane
> 12⅝ . 12⅝ @ 2s.6d. ℔ do
> 19⅛ . 12⅝ @ 3/6   ℔ do

Shd you not be supply'd when our Glass arrives, we will be very glad to serve you at the Above Prices" (ViMtV). On 17 Mar. GW wrote to his old comrade in arms Benjamin Lincoln to secure for him in Boston the 570 panes of glass that Blagdin had indicated would be needed for the houses. Lincoln wrote GW on 3 April that the glass could not be sent for three weeks, on 2 May that the glass was packed, and on 11 May that it was on a schooner bound for Alexandria. The glass had arrived by 4 June in Alexandria from Boston via Baltimore, but a day or two later GW learned that one of the boxes contained the wrong glass, which George Gilpin sent back to Baltimore. In early July GW paid Solomon Cotton & Company $500 for the glass sent from Boston (see Lincoln to GW, 3 April, n.1, GW to Lincoln, 1 July, and notes, GW to William Thornton, 4, 16 June, 2 July, and Thornton to GW, 5, 25 June). Whether the replacement for the wrong box of glass was ever received is not clear: on 1 Dec. 1799 GW thanked William Thornton for securing Boston glass for him.

To James Welch

Sir,   Mount Vernon 15th Feb. 1799
    The first of January is past, and February half gone, without my receiving any money from you; seeing you; or even hearing any thing from you, on this subject.[1]
    I am in real want of it, and depended upon your repeated assurances of punctual payment at the time the first Rent became due. I hope I shall not have occasion to remind you of this matter again. I am—Sir Your Very Hble Servant

                                            Go: Washington

ALS (letterpress copy), DLC:GW.
    1. For Welch's acquisition of GW's Kanawha lands, see Welch to GW, 29 Nov. 1797, n.1. When Welch wrote to GW on 10 Mar. 1799 asking for more time to make his first payment, which was due 1 Jan. 1799, it is not clear whether he had received this letter of 15 Feb. from GW or not. In a letter of 7 April GW gave Welch a severe scolding but agreed to wait a little longer.

From Alexander Hamilton

Private
Dear Sir   New York Feby 16. 1799
    Different reasons have conspired to prevent my writing to you since my return to New York—the multiplicity of my avocations, an imperfect state of health and the want of something material to communicate.
    The Official letter herewith transmitted will inform you of the disposition of our Military Affairs which has been recently adopted by the Department of War. There shall be no want of exertion on my part to promote the branches of the service confided to my care.[1]
    But I more and more discover cause to apprehend that obstacles of a very peculiar kind stand in the way of an efficient and successful management of our military concerns, These it would be unsafe at present to explain.
    It may be useful that I should be able to write to you hereafter some confidential matters relating to our Administration without the mention of names. When this happens I shall designate the President by X, the Secretary of State by V, of the Treasury by I, and of the department of War by C.[2]

Everything in the Northern quarter, as far as I can learn, continues favorab⟨le⟩ to the Government. Very affecty & truly I remain
My dear Sir Your obedt Servt

A. Hamilton

Copy, DLC: Hamilton Papers.

1. The letter "herewith transmitted" is dated 15 February. On 25 Feb. GW
responded to the two letters separately: his response to Hamilton's official letter
of 15 Feb. is in Tobias Lear's hand; the response to the private letter of 16 Feb. is
in GW's own hand.

2. No letter from Hamilton to GW using these symbols has been found.

To James McHenry

Dear Sir,   Mount Vernon 16th Feby 1799
    The enclosed letter from Major Lawrence Lewis requires expla-
nation, and it is the purpose of this letter to give it.
    He had, it seems, been making Overtures of Marriage to Miss
Custis some time previous to the formation of the Augmented
Corps in November last, at Philadelphia; without any *apparent* impression, until she found he was arranged as a Captain in the Regiment of Light Dragoons, and was about to try his fortune in the
Camp of Mars. This brought into activity those affections for him,
which *before* she conceived were the result of friendship *only*. And,
I *believe* the condition of the Marriage is, that he is to relinquish
the field of Mars for the Sports of Venus. His own letter must speak
the rest.[1] This explanation, after what has happened, I thought
was due from Dear Sir—Yr Most Obedt Hble S⟨ervt⟩

Go: Washington

ALS, MGG.

1. Lawrence Lewis's letter to McHenry declining his commission as captain of
dragoons has not been found. See also GW to Lawrence Lewis, 23 Jan. 1799.

To James Anderson

Mr Anderson,   Mount Vernon 17th Feb. 1799
    I am not certain that I perfectly understood (when I was speak-
ing to you on the subject the other day) what parts of the Banks in
Union Farm Meadow, were sowed with Clover; and therefore make
the enquiry now; first, because I am strongly impressed with an

idea that that part which is in Wheat, on the North Side of the Branch from the Barn lane downwards (especially as far as the rough plowed ground) would bring tolerable good Clover. and secondly, because no better time, or finer opportunity can possibly offer than the present Snow, for sowing it, if you have Seed ready, or can get that which is good in Alexandria.

I do not, by any means, expect that alone, it would yield a profitable Crop of Clover; but I am persuaded, mixed with Timothy, it would more than compensate for the cost of the Seed; and therefore, I am willing to encounter the expence; provided it can be sowed immediately, before the Snow dissolves, or is blown off the ground which is to receive it by the Winds.

If you have seed of your own ready, it would be very desirable to sow it to morrow. If not, and good Seed is to be bought in Alexandria I would send up for it in order that it might be sown as soon afterwards as possible.

As the ground is already sown with Timothy, on both banks of the large Meadow, and intended to lye to grass after the grain comes off; the worst that can happen if Clover does not Succeed, is the loss of the Seed. I am Your friend &ca

Go: Washington

P.S. I do not mean by sowing these Banks, to omit sowing any other grounds which were allotted for Clover. The Seeds of which if not to be had of a good quality can always (at this Season) be imported from Philaa.

ALS (photocopy), PU: Armstrong Photostats. ALS, sold by Kende Galleries at Gimbel Brothers (1947).

To Thomas Law

Dear Sir,   Mount Vernon 17th Feby 1799
Knowing that Nelly Custis had announced her intended Marriage to her Sisters; informed them of the day on which it was to be celebrated; and invited their presence at the Ceremony; I have given no particular invitations. But lest Mrs Law and yourself should require something more formal than an Invitation from the Bride Elect, I inform you that[1] Friday next is to make her and Lewis one flesh & one bone; Before which Mrs Washington & myself would be very happy to see you and Mrs Law at this place. Best

wishes attend you both, and little Eliza. I am—Dear Sir Yr Affectionate and Obedt Hble Servant

Go: Washington

ALS, owned (1972) by Mrs. Lyndon Baines Johnson, Austin, Texas.

1. Law marked a cross here and noted below: "The 22 Feby the Generals birthday—67th Year ended."

To Clement Biddle

Dear Sir   Mount Vernon Feby 18th 1799

Your letter and a/c current, with the Bills enclosed, have been duly received;[1] and under cover of this letter I send you One hundred Dollars to be placed to my Credit.

Ellwood has not yet called upon me, nor is he arrived at Alexandria that I have heard of.

I thank you for the information respecting the price of Flour; and shall be obliged by your mentioning of it occasionally; especially if the event you alluded to should cause a rise, or depression according to the issue. I am—Dear Sir Your most Obedt Hble Servt

Go: Washington

P.S. Remember the Lucerne & White Clover Seeds, written for in my last letter.[2]

ALS, PHi: Washington-Biddle Correspondence; ALS (letterpress copy), DLC:GW.

1. Biddle to GW, 5 February.
2. GW to Biddle, 1 February.

From Alexander Hamilton

My Dear Sir   New York Feby 18. 1799

Unwilling to take the liberty to ask you to give yourself any particular trouble on the subject I have written the enclosed letters. I beg you to dispose of them as you suppose will best answer the end in view—that is to obtain a speedy distribution of the State into Districts and sub-districts.[1] With the truest attachment I have the honor to be My Dear Sir Your obedt servant

A. Hamilton

ALS, DLC:GW; copy, signed by Hamilton, DLC: Hamilton Papers; copy, DLC: Hamilton Papers.

1. GW responded from Mount Vernon on 26 Feb. in a letter marked "Private": "My dear Sir I received your letter of the 18th instant yesterday. You refer me to enclosed letters for information on the subject therein mentioned. One letter only came, and that under a Seal to General Lee, which I shall forward, unopened, tomorrow by my Nephew Mr Bushrod Washington, who is a neighbour of his.

"Having written to you yesterday both an Official, and private letter, I have only to add in this, that with sincere esteem and Affectionate regard I am—My dear Sir Always Yours Go: Washington" (ALS, DLC: Hamilton Papers; letterpress copy, DLC:GW). Hamilton had enclosed in his letter to Henry Lee of 18 Feb. a letter to Col. Thomas Parker, in which he provided for "the division of Virginia into four districts and Twenty sub-districts or company rendezvouses, designating a place in each for the head Quarters of the rendezvous" (Hamilton to GW, 27 Mar.; see also note 2 of that document). See Hamilton's letter to Lee in Syrett, *Hamilton Papers*, 22:486–87; see also GW to Hamilton, 10 April 1799.

From John Adams

Dear Sir   Philadelphia Feb. 19. 1799

Although I received the Honor of your Letter of the first of this month in its Season, I determined to postpone my Answer to it, till I had deliberated, on it, and the Letter from Barlow inclosed in it, as well as a multitude of other Letters and Documents official and unofficial, which relate to the Same Subject, and determined what Part to act.

I Yesterday determined to nominate Mr Murray to be Minister Plenipotentiary to the French Republic. This I ventured to do upon the Strength of a Letter from Talleyrand himself giving declarations in the Name of Government that any Minister Plenitentiary from the United states shall be received according to the Condition at the close of my Message to Congress of the 21. of June last. As there may be some Reserves for Chicane, however, Murray is not to remove from his station at the Hague untill he shall have received formal assurances that he shall be received and treated in Character.[1]

Barlows Letter, had I assure you very little Weight in determining me to this measure. I shall make few Observations on it. But in my opinion it is not often that We meet with a Composition which betrays so many and so unequivocal Symptoms of blackness of heart. The Wretch has destroyed his own Character to such a degree, that I think it would be derogatory to yours, to give any answer at all to his Letter. Tom Paine is not a more worthless fellow.

The infamous Threat, which he has debased himself to transmit to his Country, to intimidate you and your Country, that certain Conduct "will be followed by War, and that it will be a War of the most terrible and vindictive Kind" ought to be answered by a Mohawk. If I had an Indian Chief that I could converse with freely I would ask him what answer he would give to such a Gasconade? I fancy He would answer that he would if they began their Cruelties, cutt up every frenchman joint by joint, roast him by a slow fire, pinch of his flesh with hot Pincers &c. &c. &c.—I blush to think that such Ideas should be started in this Age.

Tranquility upon just and honourable terms is undoubtedly the ardent desire of the Friends of this Country: and I wish the babyish and womanly blubbering for Peace may not necessitate the Conclusion of a Treaty that will not be just nor very honourable. I dont intend however that they shall. There is not much sincerity in the Cant about Peace—those who Snivell for it now were hot for War against Britain a few Months ago: and would be now if they Saw a Chance. In Elective Governments Peace or War, are alike embraced by Parties when they think they can employ either for Electioneering Purposes. With great Respect and Regard to you & your good Lady, and Yet Miss Custis, I have the Honor to be, sir, your most obedient servant

John Adams

ALS, PHC: Charles Roberts Autograph Letters Collection; LB, MHi-A.

1. William Vans Murray had been holding conversations for several weeks at The Hague with Louis André Pichon, the secretary of the French legation there. He wrote to President Adams on 7 Oct. enclosing a letter from Talleyrand to Pichon in which the French foreign secretary declared: "whatever Plenipotentiary the government of the United States might send to France to put an end to the existing differences between the two countries, would be undoubtedly received with the respect due to the representative of a free, independent, and powerful nation" (Murray's translation in *Executive Journal*, 1:313–14). Adams forwarded Talleyrand's letter to the U.S. Senate on 18 Feb. 1799 when he nominated Murray, "our Minister Resident at the Hague, to be Minister Plenipotentiary of the United States to the French Republic," with the proviso that Murray would "not go to France without direct and unequivocal assurances, from the French government . . . that he shall be received in character; shall enjoy the privileges attached to his character by the law of nations; and that a Minister of equal rank, title, and powers, shall be appointed to treat with him, to discuss and conclude all controversies between the two Republics by a new treaty" (ibid., 313). The opposition to the appointment of Murray from senators of the president's own party was such that Adams nominated Oliver Ellsworth and Patrick

Henry to serve with Murray as envoys to France (see Pickering to GW, 28 Feb.; see also Pickering to GW, 21 Feb. 1799).

To George Deneale

Sir,   Mount Vernon 19th Feby 1799
    You will please to grant a license for the Marriage of Eleanor Parke Custis with Lawrence Lewis, and this shall be your authority for so doing from—Sir Your Very Hble Servt

Go: Washington

ALS, NNPM; ADf, DLC:GW; LB, in hand of Albin Rawlins, owned (1976) by Miss Penissa Wills and Mr. L. J. Wills, Halesowen, England. GW had Thomas Peter and George Washington Parke Custis witness his application to the Fairfax County court clerk for the wedding license.

Letter not found: from William B. Harrison, 21 Feb. 1799. On 5 Mar. GW wrote Harrison: "Your letter of the 21st of Feby ⟨ha⟩s ⟨bee⟩n received."

From Timothy Pickering

(private)
Sir,   Philadelphia Feby 21. 1799.
    I have been honoured with your letter of the 21st.[1] My letter of the 8th contained nothing that need be concealed from your friends. except when I mark a letter confidential, you will be pleased to make such use of it as you think proper. The subject of the present one is not an exception, as to your *discreet friends*: for I am sure no officer about the President can be willing to share any part of the responsibility of his nomination of Mr Murray to negociate a treaty with the French Republic—it is solely the President's act—and we were all thunderstruck when we heard of it. Confidence in the President is lost—the federal citizens thought the thing incredible: the Jacobins alone are pleased. The *honor* of the country is prostrated in the dust—God grant that its *safety* may not be in jeopardy.[2]
    The nomination is committed to a committee consisting of Sedgwick, Stockton, Read, Bingham and Ross: they will study to find some remedy[3]—or rather alleviation—for the mischief is incapable of a remedy. You will see Porcupine's pointed satire of yes-

terday: I lament the occasion: but the satire is just as it is severe. If any thing could more deeply wound or more thoroughly mortify a man of feeling, it would be the slaver of praise since daily issuing from the filthy press of the Aurora.[4] But news-paper satire and praise are of less moment to an honest man than the opinions of his judicious friends; and I believe the President has been informed, that the measure is condemned—that it is considered as dishonourable and disastrous—by all his real friends and the friends of his country; and this without a single exception.

Of the result in the Senate I will do myself the honor to give you early information. In the mean time I remain with sincere respect sir, your obedt servant

Timothy Pickering

This nomination damns the previous ones which gave you so much pleasure, of Mr King & Mr Smith, to negociate with Russia and the Porte—made under auspices so promising, and so grateful to every American sensible to the honor & interest of his country.[5]

ALS, PPRF; ALS (letterpress copy), MHi: Pickering Papers.

1. Pickering should have written "15th."

2. For the nomination of William Vans Murray as minister to France, see John Adams to GW, 19 Feb., and note 1 of that document.

3. The Senate committee (Theodore Sedgwick of Massachusetts, Richard Stockton of New Jersey, Jacob Read of South Carolina, William Bingham of Pennsylvania, and James Ross of Pennsylvania) met with Adams on Saturday night, 23 Feb., and thereafter decided that Murray's nomination should be rejected. Before the committee made its report, Adams on 25 Feb. nominated Oliver Ellsworth and Patrick Henry to serve with Murray as U.S. envoys to France. See Pickering to GW, 28 February.

4. William Cobbett's *Porcupine's Gazette* (Philadelphia) on 20 Feb. denied sarcastically the "most atrocious falshood" that Adams had appointed a minister plenipoten-

tiary to treat with France and added that "had he taken such a step, it would have been instantaneously followed by the loss of every friend worth his preserving." The *Aurora* (Philadelphia), meanwhile, published articles on 19, 20 and 21 Feb. praising Adams's measure, lauding on 21 Feb. "the prudence manifested in such happy time by the President of the United States."

5. On 6 Feb. John Adams nominated Rufus King, U.S. minister to the Court of St. James, to be a commissioner to negotiate a commercial treaty with Russia. Pickering wrote King on 4 May that his instructions "for negociating a Treaty of Amity and commerce with Russia" would be forwarded as soon as President Adams approved them (Pickering to King, 4 May 1799, in King, *Life and Corre-*

spondence of King, 3 : 12–13; see also Pickering to King, 5 Feb., ibid., 2 : 534–36).
Two days later, on 8 Feb. 1799, Adams nominated William Loughton Smith, minister to Poland, "to be Envoy Extraordinary and Minister Plenipotentiary to the Sublime Ottoman Porte," with authority to negotiate a treaty of amity and commerce with the Ottoman Empire (*Executive Journal*, 1 : 311, 312).

From Ezekiel L. Bascom

⟨G[ree]nf[ield]⟩ Massachusetts. County of Hampshire.
Respected Sir,   February 22d A.D. 1799
Permit one of the sons of Columbia to state his situation, and if consistent to ask your patronage. I have a desire to enter some business under Government, either of a civil or military nature, where, by assiduity and attention, I may obtain a handsome support. To the flowers of language and politeness I do not pretend. I shall write that simplicity of style, in which my Father has instructed me. My situation at present is this; My Father is an industrious plowman, and by his economy, and the blessings of Providence, he has been enabled to give me an education such an one as I could obtain at Dartmouth, the honors of which I received in August last. I have since that time pursued my studies with an eminent Divine. I am now his pupil. By his precepts and examples, and by other acquirements, I endeavour to stand on the square with friends and enemies, to live within the compass of justice, and walk on the level of virtue and truth. My age is twenty-one years, my stature six feet. It is my earnest desire, Worthy Sir, through you, to come into the service of my Country. Be pleased to consider me as a son, on a supposition that what I have said is true. I have written plainly my situation which I wish to change for one more eligible to an ambitious mind. I submit all, Sir, to you, relying on your well known candor and generosity. If it is your pleasure to alter my situation, any recommendations, which may be necessary, may, perhaps, be had from his Honor Moses Gill Esq⟨r.⟩ Lieutenant Governor of this State, from the Reverend John Jackson, Pastor of the church in this town, or from the executive authority of Dartmouth College, in Hanover New Hampshire. Be pleased to excuse my freedom, as nothing but an earnest desire to change my situation could have induced the attempt.[1] I am, Sir, with every sentiment of respect, Your obedient, humble Servent

                                          Ezekiel L. Bascom

ALS, DLC:GW.

Ezekiel Lysander Bascom (1779–1841), son of Moses and Eunice Corse Bascom, graduated from Dartmouth College in 1798 and was ordained pastor of the Congregational church of Phillipston, Mass., in September 1800.

1. Tobias Lear wrote Bascom on 11 March: "I am ordered by His Excellency General Washington to acknowledge the receipt of your letter to him, dated the 22d of feby, and to inform you that the regular course of applications for appointments under the Government of the United States, is to the President, or to the Head of the Department in which an appointment is desired; and to add, that the application should be accompanied with such recommendations as may enable the Executive to form a proper estimate of the fitness of the candidate for the office he may wish, unless where the applicant is personally known to the Executive" (DLC:GW).

From Jonathan Trumbull, Jr.

My Dear Sir   Lebanon [Conn.] 22d Febry 1799

I have recieved with much pleasure, your favor of the 6th inst. and take the earliest opportunity to give you such reply as is in my power.

I have no authority or instruction from my Brother respecting the Monies which remain to be paid for his Prints; nor have I any Copy of his original proposals, I find myself possessed of two Receipts from him for payment of One Half the price of two Copies, which I made to him at the time of subscribing; and I presume that you have similar ones, as that was the case generally with the subscribers, unless indeed in some *few* instances, the *whole* was paid at once; which however I know he was not inclined to take, but chose to leave the last Moiety until the delivery of the Prints— Lest you may not readily find your reciepts I enclose a Copy of one of mine, that you may see their tenor[1]—As to the further payment, if any is due from you, I have reason to believe, that my Brother will not wish any Remittance to be made to him in London; since he expects so soon as he is discharged from his present Commission; to return to his native Country & friends, and is wishing to invest in the U. States, what Money he shall obtain in Europe. It is on my Mind that Mr Trumbull has three Agents in America, for delivery of his Prints & receipts of Money for them— Vizt—Mr Daniel Penfield in New York, for the subscribers in the Northern States, Mr Joseph Anthony in Phila. for the Middle States, and Mr [   ] in Charl[e]ston So. Carolina—Your remittance I suspect may be made to Mr Anthony, who probably has a Copy of the proposals, with a List of the Subscribers, with whom he is to negociate, and who also I presume, is furnished with a Copy of the original Subscriptions & payments.[2]

I am extremely sorry to see the *malign Influence*, which at present reigns over the Counsels of your State. For myself however, I hope & trust, that the consequences will not be so unhappy, or so extensive, as some among us in *our tranquil State*, are apprehensive may be the case. I have been furnished with a Copy of their Resolutions, to be laid before our Legislature. I have replied to Govr Wood, That "Altho deeply regretting, that sentiments such as are expressed in the Resolutions, are adopted by the Legislature of our *Elder Sister*, yet I shall take the first opportunity to comply with his request"—this however, will probably not be in my power 'till May next.[3]

Writing as I do on the 22d Day of Febry, I seize with avidity, the opportunity of felicitating my Country on another pleasing occasion of celebrating your Birth Day; and of expressing to you my sincere & most affectionate Wishes, that you may yet live to enjoy many such returng Anniversaries, in health, happiness & honor. At the same time, I pray you to present from me & Mrs Trumbull, our very respectfull & affectionate Regards to Mrs Washington—also to *Mrs Lewis*, for whose happiness I feel a tender solicitude, and for whom I very sincerely wish the possession of every felicity in her new situation, that her youthfull Imagination presents to her view. You will pardon me Sir! if I add to this Commission, my request that you will be pleased to present to Mrs Stuart, when you have opportunity, my kind remembrance of her, with my Congratulations on her Daughters Connexion, and my best wishes for her own future happiness. I have the pleasure—with unabated Affection & regard—to subcribe myself My Dear Sir Your most Obedient & humle Servant

Jona. Trumbull

ALS, DLC:GW; ADf, ViMtV.

1. The enclosed copy of Jonathan Trumbull's receipt reads: "N. York Received the 17th Day of April 1790—of Jona. Trumbull Esqr. the Sum of Three Guineas—being One Half of the Subscription for two prints, One representing the *Battle of Bunkers Hill,* and the other the *Death of General Montgomery;* which I promise to deliver according to the Proposals published in London, & dated Novemr 10th 1788. Anthony C. Poggi[,] Jno. Trumbull[.] N.B. Every subscription

Receipts to be valid, must be signed by A. C. Poggi—and those in America countersigned by J. Trumbull, as well as the persons appointed by him to recieve them" (DLC:GW). GW later discovered that he had paid half the costs of the prints in 1790 (see GW to Joseph Anthony, 17 Mar. 1799, n.1).

2. GW wrote to Joseph Anthony, probably the silversmith with whom GW had had dealings earlier, on 17 March.

3. For the resolutions of the Virginia legislature referred to here, see John Marshall to GW, 8 Jan. 1799, n.2.

To Jane Dennison Fairfax

Mount Vernon 23d Feb. 1799

General and Mrs Washington present their Compliments to Mrs Fairfax and family and request the favour of their Company at dinner with the newly married couple on Wednesday next.[1]

An answer is requested.

AL, ViHi.

1. According to GW's diary two couples dined at Mount Vernon on Wednesday, 27 Feb., but not Mrs. Fairfax, whose husband, Bryan Fairfax, was in England (*Diaries*, 6:336). The Washingtons entertained on Monday, Tuesday, and Wednesday nights, 25, 26, and 27 Feb.(ibid.). See also GW to Andrew, Catherine, and William Ramsay, this date.

To Andrew, Catherine, and William Ramsay

Mount Vernon 23d Feb. 1799

General & Mrs Washington present their Compliments to Mr Andw Ramsay, Mrs Ramsay and Mr Willm Ramsay and request the favour of their Company to dine on Tuesday next, with the couple Newly Married.

An answer is requested.

AL (photocopy), DLC:GW.

William and Andrew Ramsay were merchants in Alexandria. They were the twin sons of Patrick and Elizabeth Ramsay. Andrew was the husband of Catherine Graham Ramsay (d. 1844), daughter of Richard Graham (d. 1796) and Jane Brent Graham. GW records in his diary that the three of them dined at Mount Vernon on 26 Feb., a snowy day, along with the twin's sister Eliza Ramsay Potts, William Hodgson, and three Lee siblings: Mary Lee Fendall, Edmund Jennings Lee, and Lucy Lee (*Diaries*, 6:336).

From James Anderson

Mount Vernon 25 Feby 1799

Received

	Bu.			Bu. lb.			
1798 Novr	122 by Measure	And by Weight	109	15	p. Bu. 8/2	53
	139 by	do	And by	do	127	25	p. do	56
1799							
Feby 16	177 by	do	And by	do	163	1	p. do 8/6	55
	438				399	41		

from Doctor David Stewart Three hundred & ninety nine Bushels & 41/60 lb. of white wheat, weighing p. measured Bushel as stated in the Margin above, And that there are to be Deducted from the price of each Bushel 2d p. pound for every pound that this wheat does weigh less than 58 lb. p. Bushel.

And that Doctor Stewart shall have the same price paid Him whenever He shall call for the Money, that either Messrs Rickets & Newton, or Mr William Hartshorne does pay on that day for wheat of the like quality, and weight as the above Men[tione]d wheat is, And it is hereby understood that it is the Cash price by which I am to be thus regulated, It is also understood as it was particularly agreed upon, that Doctor Stewart Shall discount whatever is the Customary freight paid for bringing wheat from His Estate near George Town, to the Port of Alex[and]ria as I took away this wheat from His Landing, Witness my hand date as above for His Excellency General Washington.

Jas Anderson

ADS, NN: Emmet Collection.

To Alexander Hamilton

Sir, Mount Vernon, Feby 25th 1799.

I have been duly favoured with your letter of the 15th instant.

When the disposition was contemplated for assigning to Major General Pinckney and to yourself your respective districts of superintendence, I was of Opinion (as you will see by the enclosed copy of a letter which I wrote to the Secretary of War on my way from Philadelphia to this place) [1] that the *whole* of General Wilkinson's Brigade should be considered as under your immediate direction; because, if a part of it which is, or may be stationed within States of Kentuckey and Tennessee, should be under the Superintendence of General Pinckney, and the other part under your's, it might occasion great inconvenience, and perhaps confusion, for General Wilkinson to have to communicate sometimes with one of the Major Generals and sometimes with the other. This, I conceive, will still be the case, if the disposition, which [you] mention to have been communicated by the Secretary of War, should continue. I am therefore yet decidedly of opinion, that the *whole* of General Wilkinson's Brigade should be under your superintendence.

If it be determined to pursue the recruiting business at all, I regret extremely that there should have been so much delay in it; for the favourable season is passing off every day, and when the Spring opens great numbers of those who would readily inlist now, will be then engaged in other avocations, and we shall lose the precious moment.

I shall hope to be regularly advised of every occurence which takes place in your military Arrangemt that you may think essential to communicate. With very great regard, I am Sir, Your most Obedt Servt

Go: Washington

P.S. I enclose herewith Returns of Troops, Stores &c. at Niagara, which have been forwarded to me by Major Rivardi—and shall, in acknowledging the receipt of them, desire that the Returns in future may pass through you to the War Office.[2]

LS, in the hand of Tobias Lear, DLC: Hamilton Papers; Df, in Lear's hand, DLC:GW.

1. See GW to James McHenry, 16 Dec. 1798.

2. John Jacob Ulrich Rivardi, a Swiss engineer who was commissioned in March 1794 a major in the U.S. Artillerists and Engineers Corps, wrote to GW from Niagara, N.Y., on 10 Jan. 1799: "The fear of committing an indiscretion by the trespassing on the time of Your Excellency prevented me hitherto from expressing my happiness at being able to consider myself as imediately under your orders. The Misfortunes of Switzerland have rendered America my adoptive Country & I can not but feel the Most lively gratitude when I recollect that it is To you that I owe a Station which enables me to look with Security although with an aching heart on events which otherwise would have involved my family in

more fatal consequences. The Situation of This Post has been unavoidably influence⟨d⟩ by the Calamity which Suspended the transaction of business in Philadelphia—we are reduced to a number inadequate To The Importance & extent of the Fort: we are in the utmost want of Clothing & of Several other Articles nearly as essential. The greatest harmony reigns between this & the Brittish Garrison with the Commandant of which I am on a footi⟨ng⟩ of intimacy. Should the plans of Niagara, with⟨t⟩ that of the alterations proposed not be Sufficient, I Shall be happy To Send others more detailed, Together with a More particular Statement of the repairs which are indispensable" (DLC:GW). On 2 Mar., GW replied: "Sir, Your letter of the 10th of Jany, enclosing Returns from the Garrison at Niagara for the month of Decr—and since that, Returns from the same place for the Month of January, have been received. These Returns I have forwarded to Major General Hamilton, to whom you will, in future, be pleased to address all your official communications; which must go to him of course as Inspector General of the Armies of the United States.

"I am happy to hear of your welfare and that harmony prevails between our Garrison and the British Posts in its vicinity.

"Mrs Washington joins in compliments & best wishes for Mrs Rivaidi with Sir, Your mo. ob. st" (Df, DLC:GW). And two days later, on 4 Mar., Tobias Lear wrote to Alexander Hamilton on GW's behalf: "By order of the Commander in Chief I have the honor to forward to you sundry Returns from the Garrison at Niagara for the Month of Jany wh. have been transmitted by Major Rivardi, who is directed in future to make all his official communication immediately to you" (DLC:GW).

On 30 Mar. Lear wrote to Rivardi under cover of a letter of the same date to Hamilton. Lear's letter to Hamilton reads: "By order of the Commander in Chief I have the honor to transmit to you a letter from Major Rivardi, the Commandg Officer at Niagara, on the subject of a dispute between him and Captn [James] Bruff—that you may issue such orders thereon as shall appear to you to suit the occasion" (DLC:GW). His letter to Rivardi in part reads: "Your letter of the 21st of feby with its enclosures has been duly received, and I have taken an opportunity of laying it before his Excellency the Commander in Chief, by whose order it is transmitted to the Inspector General that he may take such measures thereon as the circumstances of the case shall require . . . The Commander in Chief directs me to repeat the information contained in his last to you that all official communications be made in future to the Inspector General" (DLC:GW).

Then, on 7 April, Lear wrote Hamilton: "By Order of His Excellency the Commander in Chief, I have the honor to transmit to you the Returns from the Garrison at Niagara for the month of February which have been forwarded by Major Rivardi. Major Rivardi has been repeatedly desired to make all his official communications directly to you, which he will undoubtedly do, as soon as the intimation shall reach him" (DLC: Hamilton Papers).

To Alexander Hamilton

Private

My dear Sir   Mount Vernon 25th Feby 1799.

Your private letter of the 16th instant came duly to hand, & safe: and I wish you at all times, and upon all occasions, to communicate interesting occurences with your opinions thereon (in the manner you have designated) with the utmost unreservedness, to me.

If the augmented force was not intended as an interroram[1] measure, the delay in Recruiting it, is unaccountable; and baffles all conjecture on reasonable grounds. The zeal and enthusiasm which were excited by the Publication of the Dispatches from our Commissioners at Paris (which give birth to the Law authorising the raising of twelve Regiments &ca) are evaporated. It is now no more. and if this dull season, when men are idle from want of employment, and from that cause might be induced to enlist, is suffered to pass away also, we shall, by and by, when the business of Agriculture and other avocations call for the labour of them, set out as a forlorn hope, to execute this business.

Had the formation of the Army followed closely the passage of this Act; and Recruiting Orders had tread on the heels of that; the Men which might have been raised at that time, would in point of numbers have been equal to any in the World;[2] inasmuch as the most reputable yeomanry of the Country were ready to have stepped forward with alacrity.

Now, the measure is not only viewed with indifference, but deemed unnecessary by that class of People; whose attentions being turned to other matters, the Officers who in August & September could, with ease, have Enlisted whole Companies of them, will find it difficult to Recruit any; and if this idle & dissipated Season is spent in inactivity, none but the riff-raff of the Country, & the scape gallowses of the large Cities will be to be had.

Far removed from the Scene, I might ascribe these delays to wrong causes, and therefore will hazard no opinion respecting them; but I have no hesitation in pronouncing that, unless a material change takes place, our Military Theatre affords but a gloomy prospect to those who are to perform the principal parts in the Drama. Sincerely and Affectionately I am always Yours

                                        Go: Washington

ALS, DLC: Hamilton Papers; ALS (letterpress copy), DLC:GW.
    1. *In terrorem* is a legal term usually defined as a warning or a threat.
    2. GW made changes in his letterpress copy, here substituting "who" for "which" and "for their" for "in point of," and in the next paragraph he deleted "dissipated" and inserted "frolicsome."

To James Ewing

Sir   Mount Vernon 26th Feby 1799
    The Columbian Alphabet which you were so polite as to send me, came safe, and for which I pray you to accept my thanks. It is curious, and if it could be introduced, might be useful for the purposes proposed; but it will be a work of time, it is to be feared, before it shall be adopted, generally.[1] I am Sir Your most Obedt Hble Servant

                                        Go: Washington

ALS (letterpress copy), NN: Washington Papers; LB, in hand of Albin Rawlins, owned (1976) by Miss Penissa Wills and Mr. L. J. Wills, Halesowen, England.
    James Ewing (1744–1824), the U.S. commissioner of loans in New Jersey from 1786 to 1789, applied to GW in 1790 and 1791 for office under the new government without success. See Ewing to GW, 15 Jan. 1790, and note.
    1. Ewing gave *The Columbian Alphabet*, his 28-page pamphlet published in Trenton in 1798, this descriptive subtitle: *Being an Attempt to New Model the English Alphabet, in Such Manner as to Mark Every Simple Sound by an Appropriate Character, Thereby Rendering the Spelling and Pronunciation More Determinate and Correct, and the Art of Reading and Writing More Easily Attainable.* When Ewing sent a copy to GW he inscribed the flyleaf: "To George Washington to whose name no titles are any Addition this attempt to call the attention of his Countrymen to a very important improvement in their Language, is respectfully presented by his Very humble Servant THE AUTHOR" (Griffin, *Boston Athenæum Washington Collection*, 77–78).

From Henry Lee, Jr.

dear sir   Stratford [Va.] feby 28th[–3 March 17]99
    Last monday evening Mr C. Washington presented me with yr favor covering a duplicate of yr let. of the 4th Novr & accompanying deeds for the land given for Magnolio. The deeds have been executed agreably to desire.[1] The duplicate is the first letr I recd from you on the subject it concerns, which fact will of course apologize for my silence.
    I passed thro. alexa. early in Decr & should have called at Mt

Vernon, but you was then absent, having gone to Philada to meet the general officers of the army—Mr Simms did make every effort to procure Harrisons lands, as did I afterwards thro. Mr W. B. Page—But neither could move him from a his price 5£ pr acre. Yr offer was as many dollars—To attend longer to that subject or to trouble you with a let. upon it seemed to me equally useless.

I wish he could have been induced to have fallen near yr price, I would have made some sacrifice to have procured the land. For I never was more anxious to satisfy a demand than I am the one you possess[2]—Relying on the promises of Judge Wilson the opinion of my worthy friend Mr Morgan, & afterwards on the honor of Mr Morris to whom I paid 10,000£ in cash for bills on his son interest in Loudon which I was assured would be duely paid, I have been brought into a trying & disagreable scene.

But it is vain to occupy yr time with a narrative of the causes of my unprepared condition—My Berkeley Lands I have offered for sale including the ore bank for 6£ pr acre—a price always deemed fair. The gentleman has engaged to meet me there the first week in may, if I sell I shall be ready to releive yr wants.

A sooner day I shd have appointed but having engaged very indiscreetly in a congressional election I cannot quit the district till after the 24th April.

On my return I will wait on you.

I am sorry you view my city lots in the light you do—I recd them in payment at the prices I offerd them for. My plats which you would have seen had we entered into treaty would have shewn their size, but as the proposal was pr square foot, the size of the lot could not effect the fairness of the contract; as the charge would have been commensurate with the quantity of the square feet sold.

I am very apt to give liberal prices for any thing I buy, & I suppose I may have done so in the city lots as in many other instances.

I calculated greatly on the advancing prosperity of the Country, in this I have been disappointed & shall submit to the suffering it will produce, without a murmur—Pecuniary loss I disregard, but there is another loss which I feel & shall for ever feel. Wishing you every happiness I remain with the highest respect yr friend & ob: sert

Henry Lee

Stratford 3d March 99

From Mr George Lee who owes me money I recd a letr of which the following is an extract since my writing to you.

I take the liberty of presenting the same to you that shd the land answer you, I may accede to Mr Lee's proposal.

11 April Loudon

"Being very anxious to settle all my debts & finding it impossible unless I can sell my land in fairfax near Colchester I now make an offer of it to you—there is 408 acres a good house, ¼ timber, one mile from Colchester & 15 from Alexa. conveniently situated to the river"—this land is rented out, but for what sum the writer does not mention, nor can I inform—tho. this I will ascertain in May—His price is 50/ per acre.[3]

With very high respect & attachmt I remain yr ob: frd & ser.

H.L.[4]

ALS, DLC:GW.

1. The letter of 4 Nov. dealt with the matter of GW's securing new deeds to the Kentucky land on Rough Creek which GW got from Lee in 1789 in exchange for the horse Magnolio.

2. In November 1795 Lee bought GW's Dismal Swamp land for $20,000 to be paid in three annual payments beginning 1 Dec. 1796. In February 1797 Lee gave GW a part of what was due on the first payment (see GW to Lee, 2 April 1797, n.1) and another part of it in August 1797 in the form of Jesse Simms's note for $1,000 which he endorsed and transferred to GW (see Simms to GW, 8 Jan. 1798, n.1). After GW was unable to collect on Simms's note, Lee in the late summer or early fall of 1798, according to GW, suggested that Simms might be able to acquire William B. Harrison's land adjoining Mount Vernon, which GW wished to secure control of, and transfer it to GW in payment of his note (see GW to William B. Harrison, 5 Mar. 1799). In a missing letter, probably dated 11 May, GW apparently inquired about the negotiations that Lee's brother-in-law William Byrd Page (1772–1818) had conducted with Harrison for Lee (see Lee to GW, 12 May), and a few days later Harrison arrived at Mount Vernon to negotiate with GW, which culminated in the offer GW made for Harrison's land in his letter dated 16 May.

3. George Lee (c.1768–1805) of Loudoun County was a son of Thomas Ludwell Lee (1730–1778). See GW's inquiry about George Lee's tract in GW to William Thompson, 18 Mar., and note 2 of that document.

4. Lee wrote below his initials: "Lands bringing 4 pr Cent I consider equal to stock at 6 pCent. The first is certain & in our young country must rise—I myself would be satisfied with 3 pr Cent from Lands."

To Jedediah Morse

Revd Sir   Mount Vernon 28th Feby 1799

The letter with which you were pleased to favour me, dated the first instant, accompanying your thanksgiving Sermon came duly to hand.[1]

For the latter I pray you to accept my thanks. I have read it, and the Appendix with pleasure, and wish the latter at least, could meet a more general circulation than it probably will have, for it contains important information, as little known out of a small circle as the dissimenation of it would be useful, if spread through the Community. With great respect I am—Revd Sir Your Most Obedt Servant

Go: Washington

ALS (letterpress copy), NN: Washington Papers; copy, in hand of Albin Rawlins, owned (1976) by Miss Penissa Wills and Mr. L. J. Wills, Halesowen, England; copy, in the hand of Philip Schuyler, NN: Philip Schuyler Papers.

1. Morse wrote GW from Charleston, Mass., on 1 Feb.: "I take the liberty to enclose for your acceptance, a copy of my late Thanksgiving Sermon with an Appendix" (DLC:GW).

From Timothy Pickering

(private)

Sir,   Philadelphia Feby 28. 1799.

I am happy to inform you, that altho' the evil of the original nomination of a minister to treat with France cannot be wholly cured, it has since been palliated, by the nomination of Chief Justice Elsworth, Patrick Henry, and Mr Murray, "to be Envoys Extraordinary & ministers plenipotentiary to the French Republic, with full powers to discuss and settle, by a treaty, all controversies between the United States and France." To this nomination, the President subjoined the following:

"It is not intended that the two former of these gentlemen shall embark for Europe until they shall have received from the Executive Directory, assurances, signified by their Secretary of Foreign Relations, that they shall be received in character, that they shall enjoy all the prerogatives attached to that character by the law of

Nations, and that a Minister or Ministers of equal powers shall be appointed and commissioned to treat with them." [1]

Yesterday the Senate approved the nominations. [2]

A letter of December 15th received from Mr King, gives the like intelligence respecting the shooting of Buonaparte as you will see in the news-papers: Mr King adds—"it is believed in Downing street." The taking of Alexandria is comprehended with the news of the killing of Buonaparte. I have the honor to be, with great respect, sir, your obt servant,

Timothy Pickering

ALS, DLC:GW.

1. Adams's message is dated 25 Feb. 1799 (*ASP: Foreign Relations*, 2:240).

2. On 27 Feb. the Senate approved Oliver Ellsworth's appointment by a vote of 23 to 6, Patrick Henry's, 26 to 3, and William Vans Murray's, 29 to 0 (*Executive Journal*, 1:318–19). After Henry declined the appointment because of failing health, Adams nominated William R. Davie of North Carolina on 1 June 1799 (ibid., 326).

To John Adams

Dear Sir, Mount Vernon March 3d 1799

I have been duly honoured with your favour of the 19th Ulto, mentioning the nomination of Mr Murray to be Minister Plenipotentiary to the French Republic.

With the writer of the letter, which I did myself the honour to enclose in my last to you, I truly observed that I had never held any correspondence; and I only knew him in his public mission from this Country to the Barbary States, the functions of which he discharged at that time with ability & propriety. I have indeed, lately, heard of a letter that has been published, which he wrote to Mr Baldwin, filled with abuse of this Government and its Administration: But I have never met with it in any of the Papers wch I take. [1]

As you have had more opportunities of knowing this man's character than have fallen to me, I have no doubt but you have formed a just estimate of him—and as I had no other desire than to be useful, in transmitting any sentiments you might wish to convey— I shall, impressed with your observations, take no notice of his letter.

I sincerely pray, that in the discharge of these arduous and important duties committed to you, your health may be unimpaired, and that you may long live to enjoy those blessings which must flow to our Country, if we should be so happy as to pass this critical period in an honourable and dignified manner, without being involved in the horrors and calamities of War.

Mrs Washington and Mrs Lewis (late Miss Custis) thank you for your kind remembrance of them, and offer their best respects to you, at the sametime that they unite with me in every good wish for the perfect restoration of health to Mrs Adams. With sentiments of very great respect, I have the honor to be Sir Your Most Obedt & Most Hble Servt

Go: Washington

ALS, MHi-A; ALS (letterpress copy), DLC:GW.

1. Abraham Baldwin (1754–1807) on this day left the House of Representatives, where since 1789 he had been a member from Georgia, to become one of Georgia's U.S. senators the next day. Baldwin was a native of Connecticut, and his friend Joel Barlow was married to his sister Ruth. Barlow had sent his letter to GW of 2 Oct. 1798 under cover of a letter to Baldwin dated 3 Oct. 1798, in which he wrote his brother-in-law: ". . . if you find that neither this [i.e., his letter to GW] nor any other statement of facts is likely to calm the frenzy of him and his associates, but that they continue running wild after a phantom to the ruin of their country, I should think it best to publish it with my name and his . . . and it might be proper to introduce it by publishing the first paragraph of this letter to you" (Todd, *Life and Letters of Barlow*, 162–63). The *Columbia Centinel* (Boston) had printed excerpts of a letter to Baldwin from Barlow dated 1 Mar. 1798 (ibid., 163–74).

To William Booker

Sir,   Mount Vernon 3d Mar. 1799

Mr Anderson has shewn me your letter of the 23d Ultimo, to him, with an estimate of the expence of building horse Mills, differently constructed. For the trouble you have taken in this business, I feel myself very much obliged.

A Mill grinding from 15 to 20 bushls a day, with two horses, would nearly, if not entirely, answer all my purposes; with the occasional aid of the Water Mill, which in the driest Seasons, grinds a little.

For this reason I prefer greatly your last plan—namely—fixing a Mill to one of the threshing machines now erected; if you are perfectly satisfied in your own mind that it will grind according to your estimate—even the smallest quantity—that is 15 bushls a day—and I prefer moreover annexing it to the Machine at Union, as most central to the Farms, & more convenient on other accounts.

Having thus determined, I am now to request, that you will purchase the best pair of Cologn Stones (mentioned in your letter)[1] and, if any thing else can be much better prepared at Richmond than here, to provide & send the whole round by the first conveyance; and be ready to come up yourself to put the whole together, so soon as you shall be advised of their arrival.

Being acquainted with the abilities of my tradesmen in their different lines, you know, of course, what they are capable of executing; and as materials of all sorts (with a little previous notice) can be provided, and in the forwardness you may direct, on the spot, I am persuaded you will run me to no other expence to obtain them from Richmond than shall, in your judgment, be essential. You will please to advise me of the time I may expect you, & them.[2] With esteem—I am Sir—Your Very Hble Servt

Go: Washington

ALS (letterpress copy), NN: Washington Papers.

William Booker built a threshing machine for GW in the summer of 1797. See GW to Booker, 26 June 1797, n.1. After GW reported to Booker in April 1798 that the machine had not lived up to expectations, Booker returned to Mount Vernon in August 1798 to repair it. See GW to Booker, 15 April 1798, and note 2 of that document.

1. Cologne stone is brownstone.

2. In a letter dated 31 Mar., which has not been found, Booker proposed that he come to Mount Vernon in early June to build a horse-powered mill for GW. See GW to Booker, 7 April. Booker delayed his trip to Mount Vernon until 7 July, when he spent several days there building the mill (Booker to GW, 15 May, 6, 24 June; *Diaries*, 6:356; 12 July entry, Day Book).

To Timothy Pickering

Confidential
Dear Sir,   Mount Vernon 3d March 1799
The unexpectedness of the event, communicated in your letter of the 21st Ulto, did, as you may suppose, surprise me not a little.

But far, very far indeed was this surprise short of what I experienced the next day, when by a very intelligent Gentmn (immediately from Philadelphia) [1] I was informed that there had been no *direct* overture from the Government of France to that of the United States, for a Negociation. On the contrary, that Mr Talleyrand was playing the same loose, and round-about game he had attempted the year before with our Envoys, and which, as in that case, might mean any thing, or nothing, as would subserve his purposes best.

Had we approached the ante-chamber of this Gentleman when he opened the door to us, and *there* waited for a formal invitation into the Interior, the Governments would have met upon equal ground; and we might have advanced, or receded, according to circumstances, without commitment. In plainer words, had we said to Mr Talleyrand through the channel of his communication, we still are, as we always have been, ready to settle by fair Negociation, all differences between the two Nations, upon open, just and honourable terms; and it rests with the Directory (after the indignities with which *our* attempts to effect this, have been treated, if they are equally sincere) to come forward in an unequivocal manner, and prove it by their Acts.

Such conduct would have shewn a dignified willingness on our part, to Negociate; and would have tested their sincerity, on the other. Under my present view of the subject, this would have been the course I should have pursued; keeping equally in view the horrors of War, & the dignity of the Government.

But, not being acquainted with all the information, & the motives which induced the measure, I may have taken a wrong impression, & therefore shall say nothing further on the subject, at this time. With sincere esteem & regard I am—Dear Sir Your Most Obedt Servt

Go: Washington

ALS, MHi: Pickering Papers; ALS (letterpress copy), DLC:GW; LB, owned (1976) by Miss Penissa Wills and Mr. L. J. Wills, Halesowen, England.

1. Bushrod Washington arrived at Mount Vernon from Philadelphia on 26 Feb. (*Diaries*, 6:336).

To Alexander Addison

Sir,   Mount Vernon 4th March 1799

Your favour of the 31st of Jany, enclosing your second charge to the Grand Juries of the County Courts of the fifth Circuit of the State of Pennsylvania, at the last Decr Sessions, has been duly received, and for the Enclosure I thank you.[1]

I wish, sincerely, that your good example, in endeavouring to bring the People of these United States more acquainted with the Laws & principles of their Government, was followed. They only require a proper understanding of these, to judge rightly on all great National questions; but unfortunately, infinite more pains is taken to blind them by one discription of men, than there is to open their eyes by the other; which, in my opinion, is the sourse of most of the evils we labour under.

I would pray you, my good Sir, to use your endeavours, that I may be paid the balance of the last Instalment due to me from the Estate of the deceased Colo. Ritchie; & that no failure may happen in complying with *that* which will be due the first of June next ensuing.

I can assure you, most truly, that I am in *real* want of these payments; the most conclusive evidence I can give you of which, is, that I am driven to the necessity of borrowing at the Banks, by renewed notes every Sixty days—which, I am sure you will allow, is a ruinous mode of obtaining money, when I can receive common interest only for that out of which I am kept.[2] With very great esteem—I am Sir Your Most Obedt and Very Humble Servant

                                                  Go: Washington

ALS, NGenoW; ALS (letterpress copy), DLC:GW; LB, owned (1976) by Miss Penissa Wills and Mr. L. J. Wills, Halesowen, England.

1. Addison wrote GW from Washington, Pa., on 31 Jan.: "I have again taken the liberty of inclosing to you a small pamphlet. In doing this it is not and on former occasions it was not my intention to tax your politeness with any acknowledgement such as by your letter of 6th December last you honoured me with. I am sensible that important engagements leave you but little time for purposes of this kind and content myself with a hope that these papers will be received by you as I mean they should as the only testimonials of respect which I have it in my power to offer" (owned [1974] by Mr. Herbert Rubin, New York City).

2. On 6 July 1799 Addison informed GW that he had been a silent partner of Matthew Ritchie in the purchase of GW's Millers Run property in 1796. He also

told GW of his recent efforts to persuade Ritchie's widow and Ritchie's brother to make the payment due from Ritchie's estate.

To James McHenry

Dear Sir,   Mount Vernon March 4th 1799

I have been duly favoured with your letter of the 12th ultimo—and am much obliged by your kind attention to the business which I desired McAlpin to execute for me.

Enclosed is a letter from Mr Alexr A. Peters requesting to be appointed Surgeon or Lieutt in the Army—also one addressed to yourself which came to my hands by the last Mail.[1] I am dear Sir, with due respect & esteem, Your mo. ob. st

Df, in Tobias Lear's hand, DLC:GW; on the reverse is a list of banknotes in an unknown hand.

1. Neither the letter from Alexander Peter, son of Robert and brother of Thomas Peter, nor the other letter to McHenry has been found. By a codicil to his will made shortly before his death, Robert Peter left only twenty pounds to his son Alexander but recommended him to the care of his family, "that he may not suffer for clothes, lodging, or diet" (*Columbia Hist. Soc. Recs.*, 3:217).

To John Moody

Sir,   Mount Vernon March 4th 1799

I have received your letter of the 23d Ulto enclosing one addressed to the Secretary of War, which has been forwarded to that officer according to your desire.[1]

The usual course of applications for Military appointments is to the Secretary of War, who lays the same before the President of the United States, and your application, through that channel, will undoubtedly meet the attention which it may merit. I am Sir, Your most Obedt sevt

G. W——n

Df, in Tobias Lear's hand, DLC:GW. The letter is mistakenly docketed "To Mr Saml Moody."

A John Moody served in several Virginia regiments of the Continental line. Capt. John Moody who died in Hanover County on 3 Oct. 1826 was identified as a veteran of the Revolutionary War (Burgess, *Virginia Soldiers of 1776*, 1:336).

1. John Moody wrote a letter to GW from Richmond on 23 Feb., in which he said: "Inclosed is a Recomendation to the Secretary of Warr in my favour for a

Captains Comision. And I hereby Sollicite an Additional One from you Provided you are in the Habit of Doing So and I flater myself you are always willing to Promote old officers and Soldiers a Majors Comision would be Most agreeable as I am forty two years of age and Rather inclin'd to Corpulence" (DLC:GW).

To William B. Harrison

Sir,   Mount Vernon 5th March 1799.
   Your letter of the 21st Feby ⟨ha⟩s ⟨bee⟩n received.[1]
   I do not know what quantity of Land you hold adjoining me. I have heard it called three, and sometimes 400 acres. But suppose a medium between the two, that is 350 acres, the interest of twelve dollars an acre would make a Rent of more than £75 pr Annum.
   If there is any person, or persons, who can afford to give this, from any thing the land will produce, they must have a different mode of managing it from any I have yet been able to discover: and therefore, though I was willing to have given the full rent, nay more (for the reasons which have been assigned in my former letters) I must relinquish the idea of Renting altogether, unless, after having made the experiment you should be satisfied that no such Rent can ever be obtained; that the present Rents are at their full bearing; and that you must lower your expectations very considerably, or suffer the Land to lye idle. In this case, all I would ask is, that you would give me the offer of it upon the Rent you can actually get from others; for less I should not desire it, and more I would not give.
   If I may be permitted to make the remark, your expectations have been raised upon fallacious ground. The Rents at present are in Tobacco. The Tobacco from an extraordinary coincidence of circumstances, has arisen to a most unheard of price, but I believe there are very few, if any, that expect a continuance of it—especially as the growth of that article seems to be becoming general. Be this however as it may, I expected to have been asked the Rent you now receive, & no more, namely—2000 lbs. of Tobacco. and this, although I should have no expectation of making it out of the Land, I am willing to give upon the other conditions mentioned in your letter of the 21st of Feby; and will pay in Tobacco at the Alexandria Warehouse, or the last price of the article in that Market. And this, I must own, I thought would have proved a sufficient inducement to you to have given me a preference, as your

land would have been in a State of preservation; and your Rent always secure, and receivable without trouble. My Land adjoining (Chapel land as it is called) Rents for no more than ten pounds pr Ann.² —fixed at that in lieu of 1000 lbs. of Tobo; and no one I believe would hesitate to say that it is more than half the value of yours, either in quantity, or quality.

In fixing the Rent you have asked ⟨for⟩ in the letter above, you may have proceeded on another principle—viz.—that the Land is worth twelve dollars an Acre, and therefore the Rent ought to be equivalent to the interest of that sum. Few Landholders I apprehend have been able, or can let land on these terms: yet I shall not deny, if there is any one who would give ⟨this⟩ price for the land, that the interest thereof is equal to a Rent fixed on that principle. But is there a Person to be found who would give twelve dollars an acre for it?

Under particular circumstances, wch I shall relate to you, I signified early last Fall that I would allow ten dollars an acre for the Land; conscious at the sametime, that in its present state, it was not worth any thing like the money; nor did I conceive under other circumstances, that it wd sell for it.

The fact was this—Two or three years ago, I sold Genl Lee a tract of Land, for wch I was to be paid by annual Instalments—with interest: When payment became due he was unprepared to make it; but, in part gave me a note of Mr Jesse Simms for One thousand dollars, payable the January following (1798)—This also went unpaid (& is now in Suit)—But when the General was at Alexandria in August or September last he asked me if I would receive the land you hold near my Mill in payment; and at what price; adding that, Mr Simms could purchase, or, exchange for it:³ I told him, and truly, what, and what only, would be my inducement to ⟨buy⟩—namely—the injuries I sustained by some of the tenants who lived on it, & who I wished were at a greater distance from me in the first place; and in the next place, because it was not my desire to push him if I could any way do without the money he ⟨owed me⟩.

I mention these circumstances because you may have heard something of the matter before; and because, if you are disposed to part with your land at the price I told General Lee I would allow for it, and will receive payment in his hands, I am still willing to become the purchaser ⟨on⟩ those terms. The money, I presume will be perfectly safe in General Lee's hands—and if ⟨he will not⟩ pay it immediately, it ⟨*mutilated*⟩ on ⟨interest⟩ with ⟨you⟩, as it ⟨*mutilated*⟩ if I am not greatly mistaken ⟨*mutilated*⟩, would yield you much more annually than any rent you will ever get for the Land. If you think this proposition—or the other respecting the Renting of it, worth consideration, you will please to Communicate the ⟨*illegible*⟩ of it to—Sir—Yr Most Obedt Servt

Go: Washington

ALS (letterpress copy), PWacD.

1. Letter not found, but the American Art Association (5 Feb. 1928, item 205) offered for sale a two-page docketed letter from Harrison to GW, dated 21 Feb. 1799 from Loudoun County, and printed this excerpt: "I have been honored with the receipt of your letter dated Mount Vernon, the 6th instant. I should have answered your first [letter] as you alluded to in your last, but supposed you only wanted those tenants routed that was a nusance, and thank you for your kindly observations respecting the situation of my lands, and do purposely pass over a futher Comment on that head, as I am sensible you are as well acquainted with the premises as myself if not better and I fear your ideas is too bad of them, I shall not be so fortunate or have the pleasure to rent them to you."

2. GW's Chapel Land was the tract of land that GW bought from Charles West adjoining his mill tract and was the westernmost of his Mount Vernon tracts.

3. See Henry Lee's reference to this in Lee to GW, 28 Feb.–3 Mar. 1799. For Jesse Simms's note, see Simms to GW, 8 Jan. 1798, n.1.

From Charles Cotesworth Pinckney

Dear Sr   Charleston [S.C.] March 8th 1799

Mrs Pinckney, my Daughter Eliza & myself arrived in good health in this City without having met with any accident since we had the pleasure of seeing you, and return Mrs Washington & yourself our best thanks for the kindness we received from you at Mount Vernon.[1]

On Wednesday next I shall set out with Brigr Genl Washington for Georgia to settle the Army arrangements & to reconnoitre the sea coast of Georgia to St Mary's River which divides that state from Florida. I shall then proceed to the posts on the Indian Frontier on the Oconoce River where the Secretary of War informs me some differences & a spirit of insubordination are apparent among the officers. I shall endeavour to settle the differences and introduce order, as I am convinced of the necessity of enforcing a strict discipline in every part of the Army.[2] When I have accomplished this object, I shall return to this City, and as Brigr Genl Washington is desirous of going to Princeton to enter his Son in the College there I have very willingly consented to it, and on his return he will see what Men may have been raised in Virginia, and if the Regiments shall be nearly completed in that State, I shall on his arrival here set out agreeably to your plan for Harper's Ferry to assist in training & disciplining the troops which may be there assembled.[3] On my arrival at that station, I propose taking a Virginian for one of my Aids and will be much obliged to you to point out to me one of the Captains who has the requisite qualifications for that office.[4]

Mrs Pinckney & my Daughter unite with me in best respects to you & Mrs Washington, & request you will remember us to Mr & Miss Custis, Coll Lear & Capn Lewis. I have taken measures to procure some Cran⟨e⟩ Feathers for your plume, & will forward them by Brigr Genl W. Mrs P. encloses to Mrs W. some Melon seeds. I remain with the greatest esteem & regard Your affectionate, obliged & faithful humble ser⟨vant⟩

Charles Cotesworth Pinckney

ALS, DLC:GW.

1. The Pinckneys were at Mount Vernon from 25 to 28 Dec. (*Diaries*, 6:327–28). For further reference to Pinckney's return trip, see William Heth to GW, 12 Jan. 1799, and note 1 of that document.

2. Pinckney reported to GW on 20 April and 4 June 1799 on his tour of inspection of the troops on the southern frontier.

3. While William Washington was en route to Princeton by way of Mount Vernon, his son William (1785–1830) fell ill in North Carolina, and the two did not reach Mount Vernon until 5 or 6 Aug. (*Diaries*, 6:359). In August, long before William Washington had returned to South Carolina, Pinckney, instead of going to Virginia to take command of the troops assembled at Harpers Ferry, left Charleston for Newport, R.I., to seek treatment for his ill wife. As a consequence, GW himself had to assume responsibility for fixing upon winter quarters for the troops in Virginia (see Alexander Hamilton to GW, 23 Sept., GW to Thomas Parker, 28 Sept., and GW to Alexander Hamilton, 29 Sept. 1799, and notes to these documents).

4. GW recommended that Pinckney make Presly Thornton his aide-de-camp. See GW to Pinckney, 31 Mar. (second letter). See also Pinckney to GW, 20 April, n.1.

From James Welch

Sir   Rockingham County Virgna March 10th [17]99
No daut You Expected to have seen me sum time ago; I do ashure you that Sundry disapointments has been the cause that I have not cumplied with my contract I am prapereing as fast as posable to Start 20 Famileyes from this county on to the Kanawa by the time I get thrue that Bisenes I Expect the young Jentelman from Kentuckey that I sent there Last June in order to Sell my Lands for the porpos of Reseing money To pay you; when he arives I hope to have it in my power To make the first payment if you can with convenence in dulge me at this time and not Expose my property To the publeck; I shall deme it as a grate favour; and be more puntule for the future—you will plese write me by post To this place;[1] with due Respect your Hm. St

James Welch

ALS, DLC:GW.
  1. See GW to Welch, 15 Feb., n.1, and 7 April.

From Timothy Pickering

(Confidential)
Sir,   Philadelphia March 11. 1799
I have been honored with your letter of the 3d. The business to which it relates will I believe be put on a footing to produce less mischief than was apprehended—a footing far beyond my hopes.

I have this morning received the two letters inclosed for Mr Lear and J. Dandridge Esqr.[1]

I mention in *confidence*, what I this morning received from Mr King, that General Maitland did enter into a Convention with Genl Touissaint—the stipulations are substantially these. 1. No English troops are to attack the French (or Touissant's part of) Saint Domingo, during the present war. 2. Touissant engages that no Colonial troops shall attack Jamaica during the present war. 3. The English are not to intermeddle in the internal and political arrangements of St Domingo. 4. Touissaint engages not to intermeddle in the internal & political arrangements & government of Jamaica. 5. In consideration of these stipulations, Maitland promised to *persuade* his government (for he had no authority to form this convention) to permit a quantity of provisions to be carried to certain ports of St Domingo (the quantity and ports to be afterwards determined) and the produce of the island to be received in payment & exported—free from all molestation by British cruisers.[2]

The British Government assents to this convention, and a Colo. Grant goes out to St Domingo as the British agent. A prime motive with Maitland in forming the Convention, and with the British Government in approving of it, is stated to be, in order to save the Royalists (of all colours) who had adhered to the British, & ensure to them a quiet residence in the Island. Among them were several thousand black troops, whom the British could not admit into their own islands.

Colo. Grant is to be instructed to insist on another condition— that Touissaint shall put an end to privateering from the ports of St Domingo. This was determined on an intimation from Mr King. I was happy to learn this, because it was the very measure and rule proposed and previously formed as the Condition on which the President would open our commerce to St Domingo. In a word, I am inclined to think the measures and plans of the British in respect to that rich island will perfectly correspond with our own.[3] I am most respectfully, sir, your obt servant

Timothy Pickering.

ALS, DLC:GW; ALS (letterpress copy), MHi: Pickering Papers.

1. GW on 25 Mar. forwarded the letter from Bartholomew Dandridge to his brother Julius Burbidge Dandridge.

2. For earlier references to developments in Saint Domingue, see Clement Biddle to GW, 5 Feb. 1799, and note 4 of that document. Rufus King secured a copy of the convention that Brigadier General Thomas Maitland (c.1759–1824) entered into with Pierre-Dominique Toussaint L'Ouverture on 31 Aug. 1798 and enclosed it in his letter to Pickering of 7 Dec. 1798 (King, *Life and Correspondence of King*, 2:475–77).

3. On 10 Dec. King enclosed to Pickering in the same packet as that of 7 Dec. (see note 2), a copy of his letter of 8 Dec. to Secretary at War Henry Dundas, first Viscount Melville (1742–1811), asking that the Maitland convention with Toussaint "be amended by the addition of an article by which it shall be declared that no Privateer shall be fitted out or permitted to sail from any of the Ports under the dominion of Toussaint to cruise against the Vessels or Trade of the United States, and that no American Prize shall be received or sold in any such Port." He also enclosed Dundas's reply promising that he would direct Lt. Col. James Grant, who was being sent to Saint Domingue to confirm the agreement,

to propose the amendment to the agreement regarding the United States which King desired (ibid., 483–86).

From Bartholomew Dandridge

Duplicate

My dear sir,   London March 12. 1799.

I received your Favor of the 25 January two or three days ago, for which I thank you sincerely. Yours in answer to mine of 11 May & 16 July, I have not yet seen.

I was in hopes that Mr Murray's letters to Mr McHenry & mine to you (for we both wrote) countermanding my request of a Commission in our Army, would have been time enough to have prevented my appointmt, supposing it should have been thought proper to have given me one.[1] I remained in this hope 'till about ten days before the Receipt of your letter, I saw in an American Paper, my appointment announced among others.

I must beg you, Sir, to accept my acknowledgements for your indulgence in still giving me an opportunity of accepting the appt if I should think proper; but the Considerations which you have suggested, coinciding precisely with those which upon reflection had occurred to me, & Mr King whom I candidly consulted on the Subject being of the same opinion, I conclude to *decline* accepting the appointment with which the President & Senate have been pleased to honor me; at the same time Sir assuring you—& them that my feeble services will at no time be withheld whenever the Safety of our Country & Constitution shall require the actual aid & support of the Citizens of the U.S. Presuming this to be sufficient, I take no other mode of making known my Decision in this Case.

Mr K. is extremely kind to me—at the same time that he advised me as a friend to retain my present Employment, he left me perfectly free to stay or go. He is an exceedingly worthy man—fine talents & great firmness—a staunch republican & in no hands could the Honor & Interests of our Country be more safely reposed. My plan in coming to England (as I believe I mentioned to you) was and is when I quit Mr K. to endeavour to make some mercantile arrangement here which will give me permanent employment & livelihood when I get home. My intention is to fix at

Alexa. or the City of Washn. God Knows what changes may happen in the course of twelve or 18 months to frustrate the plans of short-sighted mortals.

Rumour has brought us an accot of the intended marriage of Nelly Custis. I will thank you to present her my sincere wishes for her complete Happiness in the Connubial State. Unless Craik is much more robust than he was when I saw him last, I advise him to lay aside, or rather not to take up his Broadsword. I was utterly at a loss to account for Custis's appointment which I had seen mentioned in a Newspaper, as I supposed he was still at his studies. Your Letter accots for it⟨.⟩ It is much to be lamented that he could not have been induced to employ himself in the manner he ought to have done for a few years longer—he will bitterly regret it when it is too late. remember me kindly to him if you please Sir⟨.⟩ Pray what does Mr Lear do with himself? I have written to him time after time, but never got a scrip from him.

I thank you for the paragraph informing me of the Death of my dear brother; tho' the Intelligence was no less sudden & unthought of, than it is truly & bitterly afflicting to me; for besides being an affectionate brother, there had always subsisted between us the closest friendship. But as it is not for man to arraign the acts or to murmur at the Dispensations of the author of his Being, I endeavour to submit with patient resignation to the Will of the Ruler of the Universe. His loss to his young family must be severely felt, and still more so if possible to my poor mother & her family; and my deepest regret is excited that Providence has not put it in my power to replace that aid & support of which she has been deprived, & which she must so much need. This is the first intelligence (tho' I have repeatedly written) that I have recd of my family since I left america, nor do I know anything further of their situation.

I rejoice that my Aunt continues to enjoy her usual health—I hope she may long continue to do so. Make my affectionate respects & good wishes acceptable to her. I have been ill myself for several weeks & am but just able to write. I am however upon the recovery & hope as the Summer approaches to be entirely restored.

I trust that our Government will surmount & subdue all the Difficulties which it has to contend with from every quarter, & that the noisy turbulence or factious Discontent of some Districts, though certainly to be regretted, will make no Impression on the Stability of the Union. In Europe everything seems to remain in perfect uncertainty, nor can a well grounded conjecture be offered as to what will rise out of the present confusion.

Mr & Mrs K. unite their respects for you & Mrs W. With a grateful sense of your Kind attentions, & my sincere wishes for your health & happiness, I beg you to be assured of my continued esteem & respectful attachment

B. Dandridge

I take the liberty to enclose a Letter for my mother which I pray the favor of you to forwd.

P.S. Knowing that you were in the habit of corresponding with Sir John St C——r, mr K. has several times, in conversation, seemed to express a wish that I should let you Know in what light he is viewed here. Until lately I fancy he was or pretended to be a firm & zealous supporter of Govt when he was appointed to the presidency of the Bd of Ag[ricultur]e—latterly however he made an attempt to gain a higher seat. he proposed to Mr P—— to have him created a *Peer*! & some other thing which I do not at present recollect—however, both his propositions were rejected by mr P.—he immediately tack'd about, became an oppositionist, & has very recently been removed from the Presidency. There is another in this Country not less unworthy your Consideration. I mean Sir Edwd N——m—of this I believe you have had a hint.[2]

ALS, DLC:GW.

1. Dandridge's letter to GW is dated 10 Oct. 1798.

2. "Mr. P——" is William Pitt. For Sir John Sinclair's report of his being replaced as president of the British Board of Agriculture, see Sinclair to GW, 6 June 1798 (second letter). For Sir Edward Newenham's charges that he was being maligned, see Newenham to GW, 30 Oct. 1797, when Newenham wrote: "our Irish *Emigrants* (who, beleive me, have neither Principle or Honor) might have attempted to mis-state my Principles." No response by GW to Newenham's letter has been found, apparently bringing to an end the correspondence between the two men, which began in 1781.

List of Houses at Mount Vernon

Mount Vernon 13 March 1799

List of Houses at Mount Vernon as taken by Mr Dulan (one of the Assessors) the 9th instant on the Premises.[1]

Dwelling House 96 feet by 32, of Wood; 2 Stories high

No. of Windows	No. of Paynes in each	Total
6	18	108
6	12	72
3	12	36
8	15	120
1	62	62
2	16	32
6	18	108
9	12	108
1	10	10
2	18	36
3	12	36

Kitchen	40 by 20		Measured since Mr Dulan took the account
Servants Hall	40	20	
Gardeners house	26	16	
Store house	26	16	
Smoke house	16	16	This building is added to the Assessors Report
Wash house	20	16	
Coach house	20	16	
Stable	84	36	
Salt house	16	16	
Spinning house	38	18	
Negro Quarters			in
Green house	170	18	one
Ice house within Arch	12 by 12		

Go: Washington

ADS, DLC:GW.

1. Mr. Dulan may be Edward Dulin, sheriff of Fairfax County in 1799.

From Alexander Hamilton

Sir   New York March 14. 1799

I have the honor to send you the extract of a letter of the 8th instant (received two days since) from the Secretary of War, together with the Section of the Act to which it relates.[1]

I am entirely of opinion with him, as to the expediency of causing the Pay Master General to reside at the seat of Government— But as the measure is of importance, and especially as the act expressly refers the point to the "Commander in Chief"—I did not think myself at liberty to act without your previous decision.

I request instruction on the point, as soon as shall be convenient, unless you shall think it proper to give yourself the necessary orders to the Pay Master General.[2] With perfect respect & attachment I have the honor to be Sir Your obed. servt

A. Hamilton

ALS, DLC:GW; three copies, DLC: Hamilton Papers. The editors of the *Hamilton Papers* note that a second letter to GW of this date and also a letter of 28 July 1798 from Hamilton to GW are cited in a "List of Letters from General Hamilton to George Washington" in the Columbia University Libraries (Syrett, *Hamilton Papers*, 22:36, 539). Neither of these letters has been found, but Hamilton's letter to GW of 29 July 1798 makes clear that Hamilton had not sent a letter to GW written the day before, or at any time recently, and when GW acknowledges on 25 Mar. 1799 the receipt of Hamilton's letter of 14 Mar., he acknowledges the receipt of only one, not two, letters of that date. The editors of the *Hamilton Papers* also found in the Libraries' "List of Letters from G—— Washington to General Hamilton" citation of five missing letters from GW to Hamilton, dated 14 Sept. and 9 Oct. 1798, 4, 15 Mar. and 11 Aug. 1799. No allusion to any of these letters nor the least hint of their existence has been found anywhere in the correspondence of the two men. Furthermore at this time it was GW's general practice to make letterpress copies of his letters, and whenever a letter of his to one of his regular correspondents such as Hamilton was not acknowledged, he usually referred to the letter by date and inquired whether it had been received.

1. The enclosed extract of a letter from James McHenry to Hamilton of 8 Mar., which is printed in its entirety in Syrett, *Hamilton Papers*, 22:522–24, is McHenry's explanation for his recommendation that the paymaster of the army, Caleb Swan, be ordered to move his office from Cincinnati to Philadelphia. The section of the act "for the better organizing of the Troops of the United States" that Hamilton enclosed directed that this be done (ibid.).

2. See GW to Hamilton, 25 March.

To William Thornton

Dear Sir   Mount Vernon Mar. 14. 1799

As the season for transplanting Trees is passing away, and this business cannot be much longer delayed with propriety, or safety to the Plants, I embrace the going up of Colo. Lear to the City, to send you the scaley bark hiccory trees promised you sometime since. They are from the large Nut grown in Gloucester County, of this State.

I put such of the Spanish Chesnut as I could save last Autumn, in the Earth, to be planted this Spring. If they vegitate & come up, you shall partake. It is best I believe not to disturb them at this time.

Your favour of the 14th Ulto, enclosing the quantity of Glass wanted for my houses in the City, and the Boston prices thereof, came safe; for which I thank you; and shall endeavour to be provided in time.[1] With complimts to Mrs Thornton—I remain with esteem & regard Dear Sir Your Most Obedt Servant

Go: Washington

ALS, DLC: Thornton Papers. The letter was sent "By Colo. Lear."

1. The letter in which Thornton enclosed the estimate for the glass that would be needed for GW's houses being built in Washington was dated 14 February. GW acknowledged its receipt on 15 February. For the acquiring of glass for the houses, see GW to Thornton, 15 Feb., n.1.

From Alexander Spotswood

Dear Sir   Newpost March 15. 1799

Altho, after peruseing the enclosure which came to hand Yesterday, you may determine not to possess A. Woodrows 300 acree Survey on Rough creek—Yet it must be pleaseing to you to Find (if Mr Hite be wright in his calculation) That your lands are of Superior Vallue to what you ever held them—for if Mr Hites Spot be worth 10$ pr Acree—certainly yours must be worth 5$.[1]

Supposeing greens paper to have no circulation yr way have cut out & inclosed you a peice for yr peruseal—and I suppose shoretly the Tales of the Tubs—will come forward.[2] Mrs Spotswood & my family desires there best regards to you & Mrs Washington as well as Dr Sr yr Afft. & obt St

A. Spotswood

ALS, DLC:GW.

1. See Spotswood to GW, 31 Mar. 1797, n.1. See also GW to Spotswood, 25 Mar. 1799.

2. Timothy Green was the publisher of the Fredericksburg *Virginia Herald*. On Tuesday, 12 Mar., the Fredericksburg paper carried an item from the Charleston (S.C.) *Daily Advertiser* of 22 Feb. telling of the arrest and imprisonment of five French citizens (two female, three male), some of whom were mulattoes, who arrived in Charleston on 21 Feb. as passengers in the brig *Minerva* from Hamburg. Secretary of State Timothy Pickering had written to Gov. Edward Rutledge and to Charles Cotesworth Pinckney to inform them that he had learned that these people were French agents and had concealed papers "in two false bottomed tubs." The Charleston paper concluded the story in this way: "The four

[three] men and their [two] female accomplice[s], are now confined at Fort Pinckney, their trunks and baggage are taken to the customhouse, and the important *Tales of the Tubs* are under the examination of Major General Pinckney, to whom they were immediately delivered. The development will come out in season." See GW's comments on the clipping in his letter to Alexander Spotswood of 25 March. As Pinckney soon learned, the mulatto Matthew Solomon and his companions were en route to Saint Domingue to attempt to instigate a revolt against the French government.

To Joseph Anthony

Sir   Mount Vernon March 17th 1799

I have, lately, received from John Trumbull Esqr. (now in London) four setts of the Battle of Bunkers Hill, and death of General Montgomery; for which I subscribed, & am ready to pay; if I knew who was authorised to receive what is due thereupon.

Conceiving it most likely that his brother, Governor Trumbull, was so empowered, I wrote to him on the subject, but received for answer that he was not. He added, however, that he thought it probably you might be so; being of opinion that it was not his brother's wish that the Subscribers should remit the amount of their Subscriptions to him, in London. If the Govr is right in this conjecture, be so good as to inform me, and what I owe on this account; as I have entirely forgot the terms of the Subscription.[1]
I am—Sir Your Very Hble Servant

                                        Go: Washington

ALS, owned (1990) by Mr. Joseph Maddelena, Beverly Hills, Calif.; ALS (letterpress copy), DLC:GW.

1. For the *Battle of Bunker's Hill* and *Attack on Quebec* engravings, see John Trumbull to GW, 18 Sept. 1798, and note 1 of that document; see also GW to Jonathan Trumbull, Jr., 6 Feb. 1799, Trumbull's reply of 22 February, and John Trumbull to GW, 24 Mar. 1799. Joseph Anthony replied from Philadelphia on 26 Mar.: "Yours of the 17 Inst. duly came to hand my being in the Country prevented my returning a immediate Answer.

"Respecting Mr Trumbulls prints, I am Instructed by him to Receive the Subscriptions and remitt the Amount to him in London, the Terms to Subscribers were three Guineas for each print one half to be paid at Subscribing and the other half upon the delivery of the print" (DLC:GW).

GW again wrote Anthony from Mount Vernon on 30 Sept. 1799: "Sir I ought to begin this letter with an apology for having neglected to do, what should have been done long ago—that is—to remit the balance due on my subscription for Mr Trumbulls Prints.

"The truth is—that by waiting awhile for the unpacking of my Papers, to see if any thing would be found elucidative of my payment on this occasion, the thing had escaped me altogether, and occured again by accident.

"I now find that on the 5th of April 1790, I paid to John Trumbull Esqr. twelve guineas, which is entered in my Books as being one half of the Subscription for four copies of two Prints to be published by him. This, I presume, was paid at the time of my Subscribing; and as you observe in your letter of the 26th of March, that the other half of the subscription money was to be paid on delivery of the Prints, I enclose you a check on the Bank of Pennsylvania for twelve guineas more—say fifty six dollars—for which sum, when you shall have received it, I pray you to advise me, specifying in the receipt, the purpose for which it was paid. I am Sir Your Obedt Hble Servant Go: Washington" (letterpress copy, NN: Washington Papers). GW followed this up with a final letter to Anthony from Mount Vernon on 13 Nov. 1799: "Sir, In September last, I enclosed you a Check on the Bank of Pennsylvania for fifty six dollars, to discharge my subscription for Mr John Trumball's Prints; requesting, when the money was paid, that you would be pleased to send me a receipt therefor; expressing the purpose for which it was paid. Having heard nothing from you since, a doubt has arisen in my mind of the letter enclosing the Check, ever having reached you, which is the cause of this enquiry from Sir Your Most Obedt Hble Servt Go: Washington" (ALS, MHi; letterpress copy, NN: Washington Papers).

To George Ball

Sir　　　　　　　　　　　　　　　Mount Vernon 17th March 1799.

It is somewhat singular, that instead of receiving Three hundred and three pounds in April of the last year, as per agreement for the land I sold you (lying in Gloucester County of this State) that I should never have seen, nor heard a tittle from you, respecting this payment, at the time it became due, nor since for near a year.

The first Instalment of the residue will become due the 10th of next month, & I beg you to be assured that I am in real want of the money; and that it was the want of money alone, which had induced me to part with this, and other landed property, which I have always considered as the most secure, and ultimately the most valuable, of any in this Country.[1]

I shall expect to see, or hear from you to good effect, by the day abovementioned.[2] I am—Sir Your Hble Servant

Go: Washington

ALS (letterpress copy), DLC:GW.

1. For the terms of GW's sale to George Ball of land in Gloucester County in 1797, see GW to Ball, 6 Mar. 1797, n.1.

2. GW enclosed his letter to Ball for forwarding under cover of a letter of the same date to John Page, which reads: "Dear Sir, In April, after I had quit the

Walks of Public life (1797), I agreed with one George Ball for the Land I held in Gloucester County; on account of which, he made me a small payment of £200, or thereabouts; was to have paid about three hundred more the April following; and the balle in two annual Instalments thereafter. Since which I have never seen Mr Ball, nor have heard from him on this subject. And what is still more extraordinary, I do not know whether he removed to the Land, or where he now lives; consequently, do not know with certainty at what place to direct to him.

"This, my good Sir, must be my apology for giving you the trouble of the enclosed; in order, if he lives in Gloucester (on the land) that it may be forwarded to him; if not, to be returned to—Dr Sir Yr Most Obedt Hble Servant Go: Washington Best respects to Mrs Page" (ALS [photocopy], sold by Charles Hamilton, 24 Feb. 1977, auction no. 103, item 268; letterpress copy, NN: Washington Papers). John Page (1743–1808) lived at Rosewell in Gloucester County.

Page replied from Rosewell on 5 April: "I received your Letter of the 17th of last Month on the 31st, and on the next day I delivered, to Mr Ball a young Lawyer who I understood for some time past lived with his Father on the Land which he or his Father had purchased of you, the Letter which you inclosed to my Care, telling him, that you had entrusted it to my Care, as you knew not whether he had settled on your Land or not, or where he lived; adding that a speedy answer was necessary" (DLC:GW).

Ball's reply of 6 April has not been found, but on 25 Sept. GW again wrote Ball from Mount Vernon: "Sir, From the tenor of your letter of the 6th of April, in answer to mine of the 17th March, I could not have conceived that I should have been without the money due for the Land I agreed to let you have, at, or near the first of October. And why you should have supposed I did not want money, when you had been told that it was my only inducement for selling the Land, is to me, inconceivable.

"I now, in explicit terms, beg you to be persuaded of three things—1st That nothing but the want of it, induced me to part with the land; because I knew full well from long experience, that the rise in the price of land was more than an equivalent thereof & common interest of money; 2dly that my present call for that article is *great* and *urgent*; and 3rdly that I must no longer be trifled with in the payment of what is due from you to me; for this will compel me to resort to means which cannot fail to be disagreeable to us both. I therefore request that you would inform me in explicit terms, at what time I may expect (without fail) what is due to me by your engagement, that I may arrange matters accordingly. I am Sir Your very Humble Servant Go: Washington" (letterpress copy, NN: Washington Papers).

To Clement Biddle

Dear Sir,   Mount Vernon Mar. 17th 1799

On the 18th Ulto, I remitted you in a letter, One hundred Dollars in Bank Notes of the United States. Having received no acknowledgement of the letter's getting to hand; and being yet without the Lucerne Seed, therein mentioned, (as well as in former letters) I am not entirely free from apprehension of a miscarriage, although I have heard of no accident to the Mail.

As the Season of sowing Lucerne Seed is just at hand, I would beg to have the quantity mentioned in my former letters sent by the mail Stage, rather than encounter delay. In this way I frequently have small parcels sent to me. Be so good as to mention the Phila. prices of Flour; & prospect of its rising or falling. I am— Dear Sir Your Most Obedient Servant

Go: Washington

ALS (letterpress copy), DLC:GW.

To Benjamin Lincoln

My dear Sir,   Mount Vernon Mar: 17th 1799

I have been induced (in convenient as it is to my Finances) to build two houses in the Federal City—near the Capital—to accomodate a person who means to lay himself out for the accomodation of the members of Congress; when that body shall have removed to the permanent Seat of the Government.

For those buildings I shall want Glass, in quantity, quality & size, as per enclosed list; and being informed that it may be had of the best kind, and cheap from the Manufactury of this Article, in or near Boston, I take the liberty of soliciting your aid to procure it (not knowing who has the Direction of the work).

I should be glad to have it sent to me soon, as the buildings will, I expect, be run up this Spring. Let the parcels of glass be accompanied with the account of cost, and the amount shall be immediately paid. If to do this to some person in Alexandria would answer, it would be convenient for me; but if this will not suit the purposes of the Manufactory, I will devise some mode of making a remittance to Boston—otherwise than hazarding Bank Notes in a letter, that distance.[1] With great and sincere esteem and respect, I am, My dear Sir Your Most Obedt & Affece Servt

Go: Washington

ALS, MH; ALS (letterpress copy), DLC:GW.

1. For the shipment of the glass and other correspondence regarding it, see GW to William Thornton, 15 Feb., n.1, and Lincoln to GW, 3 April, n.1. Below his signature GW wrote:

130 Panes—10 by 8 Inches
100 Ditto—12⅝ths Square
340 Ditto—19⅛ by 12⅝ths

To Tobias Lear

Dear Sir,   Mount Vernon March 18th 1799

I recollect no business of sufficient importance to require your return hither, sooner than Doctr Thornton conceives will allow him sufficent time to effect your cure. Were the case however otherwise, far would it be from me, to request this return before so desirable an object is accomplished. I do not therefore wish you to hurry it, on account of my business.[1]

Charles takes a horse up for Washington, which I pray may be sent to Mr Laws—or wherever he is.[2]

Mrs Washington and myself are, as you left us; & join in best wishes for Doctr Thornton's success in your case. With very great esteem, & compliments to enquiring friends, I am Your Affectionate

                              Go: Washington

ALS, CSmH. The letter was sent "By Charles."

1. See William Thornton to GW, this date.

2. The newly wedded couple, Lawrence and Eleanor Custis Lewis, visited her sisters in the Federal City from 5 to 23 Mar.; her brother George Washington Parke Custis seems to have either accompanied them or joined them there (*Diaries*, 6:337, 339).

To William Thompson

Dear Sir,   Mount Vernon 18th Mar: 1799

Colo. Thos[1] Lee (of Loudoun) is possessed, I am informed, of a tract of about 400 acres of Land within a mile of Colchester, which he is disposed to sell.

Let me request the favour of you to describe it to me as accurately as you can from your *own* knowledge, or from the information of others on whose judgment you can rely.

In doing this, say what the kind & quality of the Soil is; Whether level or broken; What the nature of growth is; what proportion is in Wood; How timbered; What tenements are on it; the condition of them; whether much worn & gullied, or in good heart; and whether they are tenants at Will or on leases, & what kind of leases, with the kind of improvements. How watered also.

To this catalogue of enquiries, permit me to ask, what, in your opinion, and the opinion of such as are acquainted with the value,

& prices of Land in that neighbourhood, & situated as it is, it is worth in *Cash*—also on credit, and what credit.

I will offer no apology for giving you the trouble to make these enquiries, but shall thank you for answering them; as I have an object in requesting this kindness from you[2]—With esteem I am Dear Sir Your obedient Hble Servt

Go: Washington

ALS, PWacD; ALS (letterpress copy), NN: Washington Papers.

William Thompson was a merchant in Colchester with whom GW had long been acquainted.

1. GW should have written "George"; see Henry Lee to GW, 28 February.

2. Thompson replied from Colchester on 23 Mar.: "Yours of the 18th Instant I duly received, & in Conformity therwith, have made The Necessary Inqueries respecting the Land Colo. Lee holds near this Place—which you have herewith Enclosed. I think the Description very Accurate as I got the Man who first Leasd it, & Lived on it 10 Years, to Assist me in it, it'⟨s⟩ to be Presumed he ought to know it's Situation &Ca" (DLC:GW).

Thompson enclosed "A description of A Tract of Land Belonging to Colo. [George] Lee near Colchester," which reads: "there are of it, 400 Acrees; much worn & Broken, Some Few Gullies, it is deemed To be kind Land, very easy to be Worked, Produces good Corn, Oats & Rye, & Tolerable Wheat. Tobacco might be made on it, but not without Manure, it is thought there is a Sufficiency of Rail Timber & Fine Wood on it to support it 10 Years. the Dwelling House is 32 by 18 framed but Very much out of Repair indeed it may be said to be in a shattered Condition. the Negro Quarters are allso much out of Repair; the Plaice is well Watered by Springs & a Stream of Water runs through it by the name of Giles Run. it is Under Lease to Doctr [Archibald] Morton for Two Lives, subject to an Annual Rent of 3000 lb. of Crop Tobacco I am told there are Five sub Tennants on it who pay 600 lb. Tobo ℔ Annum, & only have Their Places From Year to Year. was the Land Clear of all Incumbrances it woud be worth 40/ ℔ Acre, but as it stands Circumstanced it Cannot be worth more than 30/ to 35/."

From William Thornton

Dr Sir   City of Washington 18th March 1799

I received your Favour of the 14th Inst. with the present of the three valuable Trees with which you have honored me by Coll Lear—The weather was so bad that he could not send them till the Day before yesterday, so that they were two Days out of the Ground, and there was no mould round them. I know as a Farmer that good mould is very scarce in some places. As soon as I got the Trees I planted them myself with great care, for I value them as

Trees, but a thousand times more as your Gift, and hope to crack[1] of this present many years hence.

I am of your opinion that it is best not to disturb the chesnuts till they have made some progress. Please to accept my thanks for the present already received, and for your kind promise of a participation of the chesnuts.

Colo. Lear complained of one of his Legs very much. I examined & found it in a very bad state, but promised if he would stay with me for a week to attempt to render him some Service. He said he could not stay—you would have occasion for him, but I told him you could have no occasion for a person who was defective in his *understanding*. If it should not be inconvenient to favour him with a furlough he will favour me with his company for a few Days.[2] I am delighted with his attachment and devotion to your service. All your families here are well. I am—dear Sir with my best respects to your Lady your obliged and affectionate friend W.T.

ADfS, DLC: William Thornton Papers.

1. Thornton used "to crack" in its meaning "to boast."
2. See GW to Thornton, 24 March.

To Timothy Pickering

Dear Sir,   Mount Vernon 20th March 1799

I am indepted to you for two letters—28th of the last, and 11th of the present month. For the information given in both—particularly the latter—I feel gratified and obliged. I hope the measure communicated therein will eventuate beneficially for this Country.

I lately received the German letter, herewith forwarded to you;[1] as I do the Box also, which accompanied it—unopened.

The writer, as far as I have been enabled to understand the purport of the letter, seems to have been actuated by very benevolent motives. His desire, that his name may not appear, is an evidence that they were not ostentatious. For these reasons, and because Doctor Ramnitz seems to be under the impression of my being in the Administration of the Government, but above all, from an ardent wish that the Medicine might prove efficatious in that dreadful calamity with which our principal Towns have been visited, I send it, and his letter, to you, to be disposed of in such a manner as in your judgment is most likely to try the experiment which is suggested by the apparently, well meaning Author.

The letter enclosed, is an acknowledgment of the receipt of these things with information of the measure I have taken, consequent thereof[2]—Let me ask you to put it under cover of your own dispatches to Berlin, when you may have occasion to write to our Minister at that Court. With sincere esteem, & Affecte Regard, I am—Dear Sir Your Most Obedt Servt

Go: Washington

ALS, MHi: Pickering Papers; ALS (letterpress copy), DLC:GW.

1. There were in fact translations of two letters, not one, from John Frederick Ramnitz, one dated 31 Oct. 1798 and the other 2 Nov. 1798, with enclosures.

2. See GW's letter to Ramnitz, this date.

To John Frederick Ramnitz

Mount Vernon in Virginia
Sir   20th March 1799

Your letter of the 31st of October last, with a Box of Medicine, which you con⟨sidered⟩ would prove efficatious in the dreadful fever with which our large Sea Port Towns have been visited, got safe to my hands—and conveys a strong, and pleasing evidence of your human and benevolent intention, & wishes to afford relief to the suffering Inhabitants of them.

Having for more than two years been seated in retirement on my paternal Estate—remote from the scenes of public life, & far removed from the calamity which has pressed sorely on Philadelphia and New York, I could do no more than commiserate their situation—unable to point out a remedy for it. If your Medicine, on trial, will afford this, happy indeed will it be for those places and mankind in general, that you have discovered it—and the blessings of thousands would attend you.

Being, as I have observed above, no longer in the walks of Public life, and far removed from Philadelphia, I have sent your letter & medicine to Colo. Pickering (our Secretary of State) who resides in that City, and one in whom I can place entire confidence, to act, as you requested I would, with the latter—concealing your name.[1] I can do no less, however, than to offer you my thanks in behalf of all those who may receive benefit by the application; and to assure you of the sense I entertain of your benevolent intentions in forwarding of the Medicine to Sir Your Most Obedient and Very Humble Servant

Go: Washington

ALS (letterpress copy), DLC:GW. GW docketed the letter, "To Mr J.F. Ramnitz Druggist near Berlin."

1. GW sent this letter under cover of his letter to Timothy Pickering, this date, for forwarding. See also the references in note 1 to the letter to Pickering.

From Clement Biddle

Dr Sir   Philada March 21st 1799

Your favor inclosing the hundred Dollars came duly to hand and I should have acknowledged it[1] but was in daily expectations of the river, which was unseasonably stopd by the ice, opening & to find an opportunity to send the Grass seed which did not Offer until Captain Hand a regular trade⟨r⟩ by whom I had shipped the 12 lb. of white Clover Seed and 12 lbs. of Lucern Grass Seed of which the bill of Loading is inclosed cost 13 Ds. to your Debit.[2] The white Clover seed the seller says can be thoroughly depended on—the Lucern seed is imported & landed within a few days but being imported the seller is not so certain of but tis the latest and none was in town before—I shall attend to forwarding small packages in future by stage but the present were shipped & I expect have sailed & were directed to be left at the Custom house in Alexandria. I am very respectfully Yr mo. obedt & very humle Serv.

Clement Biddle

Flour is superfine 9¼ Ds. Common 8¾ Ds. ℔ bbl., rather dull, but from the numerous Arrivals expected to be in more demand— Wheat according to the Quality 10/ to 12/6 ℔ bushel & the best Virginia wheat would Command 13/—this Information from a principal flour factor.

ALS, DLC:GW.

1. GW to Biddle, 18 February.

2. The bill of lading has not been found. On 28 April GW wrote Biddle that he had "receiv'd the Seeds which you sent me by Captn Hand—after several fruitless enquiries after them." See also GW to Biddle, 21 April.

Letter not found: from Tobias Lear, 24 March 1799. On 26 Mar., GW wrote Lear: "Your letter of the 24th. Inst. . . . was delivered to me last night."

To William Thornton

Dear Sir   Mount Vernon 24th Mar. 1799

I received your letter of the 18th instant a day or two ago, previous to wch, I had desired Colo. Lear to remain in the City as long as he could derive benefit from your friendly prescription to his *Understanding*. It, or more properly *they*, stand so much in need of skilful assistance, that an entire derangement may take place without it.

Enclosed is a letter (put under this cover for surety of its getting to hand) for him. I sent him two others a day or two ago.[1] With esteem & regard—I am—Dr Sir Your Most Obedient Hble Ser.

Go: Washington

ALS, owned (1994) by Mr. Joseph Maddelena, Beverly Hills, California.

1. The enclosed letter to Tobias Lear has not been found, but see GW to Lear, 18 March.

From John Trumbull

72 Welbeck St

Dear Sir   London March 24th 1799.

I have duly received the Letter which you did me the honour to write on the 10th Decr last,[1] with its enclosure of the 25th July, the original of which never came to hand. I beg to offer my thanks for the very obliging and friendly expressions with which you honor me in both. On the 18th of September I again wrote to you by the Nancy, Davidson, bound to Alexandria, and by her sent a small Box directed to you, & containing the Four pairs of Prints for which you was so good as to subscribe so long ago: I hope they have reached you safe.[2]

New Scenes are indeed bursting upon us at every moment of this eventful Period; and I trust, Sir! that you are now destined to act a more important part, in this great Drama, than you have done in the former period of your Life: to save again your Country, and to establish her Security and Greatness upon a Basis broad and firm as is the Continent of which She forms a part. I beg your pardon but I cannot refrain from hazarding to you some political speculations, which I hope you will not think impertinent.

A few Months since, Portugal was threatned with the immediate vengeance of France, preparations were made for the invasion, a passage for Troops was demanded from Spain. & the establishment of the Iberian Republic upon the Ruins of those two Kingdoms seemed inevitable and at hand: but the negotiations with Russia, the Porte, and at Rastadt assumed a more threatning aspect during the Winter, and France accepted a considerable Sum of Mony from the two devoted Nations, as the purchase of another year's existence.

Hostilities are now recommenced on the side of the Alps, with doubtful success; but the Activity of the one party who always attack, and the slow movements, and incorrigible Error of the other in always acting on the defensive, and in Detachments, leave us but too much reason to apprehend a new Series of Disasters.

The publication, by the French, of the secret articles of the Treaty of Campo Formio, scarcely leaves to France any longer the superiority in Perfidy and Baseness; it shews the World that the conduct of the Emperor has been equally flagitious as theirs; and is admirably calculated to encrease the mutual want of confidence among the Allies.

Russia enters the field feebly with 25,000 men. the Porte is nerveless. Prussia smiles at the approaching & increased Calamities of her Rival—And England alone, of all the European powers display any of that Fortitude and Energy which alone can save them: She may survive the ruin of her Continental neighbours; but distracted with mutual Jealousy, depressed by repeated ill success, and these Evils rendered still more dangerous by the want of any great mind capable of suspending their Effects—*they* appear to be devoted to early ruin: and the coming Winter will probably see the French Republic, again Victorious, and more tremendous than ever.

Should the Campaign end in this manner, France will then be at leisure to attend to Spain and Portugal; and so thoroughly are they *prepared* that their fall will be as rapid as those at Sardinia, Naples & Switzerland, and their subversion require little more time than is necessary to the march of an unresisted army: And the Government of the new Republic being organized, Hosts of supernumerary & hungry French and Iberian Jacobins will hasten to secure the rich dependencies of America.

Two years ago the best Politicians of France regarded the possession of Louisiana and the Floridas, as sufficient to hold the

Spanish Colonies in check, "and to influence the Affairs of the United States" but with their unexampled success their ambitious views have extended, and when Spain & Portugal shall have been revolutionized, where will be the difficulty of diffusing the same principles and influence over all the American Possessions of those Powers? Countries where Oppression has long since prepared the Minds of Men for change, where Liberty and Independance are the Objects of all Men's Wishes, and where they who shall first offer those Blessings, will be received with Rapture.

What will be the situation of the United States, when they shall have Fifteen Millions of Jacobins at their Doors, intimately connected with, and disposeable by a Power whom we have exasperated beyond the possibility of forgiveness, by the disclosure of their infamous personal Corruption & base principles of negotiation, as well as by the subsequent Addresses and Answers? Shall we then rely upon our distance from the Danger? or upon the protection of foreign Navies? or will the infant State of our own be sufficient to secure us? I may appear to exaggerate; these Objects may appear too vast to be brought into operation with such rapidity. But what Miracles have we not witnessed within a few Years? and what is there too vast not to be feared from Men whose infinite Industry, Talents Activity and Ambition are allied with principles which give them friends in the Bosom of every Nation, and who are seconded by all the desperadoes, & profligate poor, in every Country?

I certainly do not exaggerate when I say that Europe is rotten to the Heart. and that, in Europe, America has not one friend, on whose support She can rely. (so true is this, that I should apprehend little less danger to my Country, under another form, from the Ruin than from the Successes of the French Republic)—instead then of looking to Europe for safety, or Connexion of any kind, other than with this Nation for a temporary purpose: does it not appear that the true object of American Policy is nearer home? The Emancipation of our Southern neighbors, the establishment, among them, of wise and just Governments, on the Principles of rational Liberty—the diffusion of knowledge, and the cultivation of the Friendship and Affection of those whom Providence has destined to be necessarily & intimately connected with us, either as Friends or Foes: these appear to me to be Objects worthy of all the Attention and all the Energy of great, of honest, of enlightened & benevolent Minds; Objects which if properly pursued will lead our Country with rapidity to a degree of solid power and honest Fame, equally superior to Danger and to Reproach.

It may be said to be imprudent to aid in establishing Empires which may soon become our Rivals or our Enemies. true they *may* become our Enemies, even if we aid to establish them; but if we do not assist them, and the work is left to France, they *must* become so. A Revolution may very soon take place there—the seed is sown, and the fruit will inevitably ripen. if that Revolution be conducted on Jacobin principles, those vast Countries, drenched with the Blood of all that is rich or eminent, or virtuous, will, with all their wealth become irresistible instruments in the hands of France, of spreading Tyranny and Desolation over the remainder of the Earth; and We shall be the first to sink under such an accumulated Weight of Power: but if we have wisdom & Energy to abandon our Defensive System, which has proved fatal to every Nation which has adopted it during the present Contest; and to anticipate the views of the Enemy; We not only deprive him of the immense resources which He even now derives from that source, through the medium of Spanish and Portuguese contributions, but we secure ourselves from the most serious and imminent danger to which we are exposed; We establish the Glory of our Country, with its Security; We add to both an inexhaustible source of future commercial prosperity and maritime Greatness; And We give to Liberty, to real and rational Liberty, a secure and wide asylum, where men unpolluted by the bloody Crimes, the base corruption, & the shameless profligacy of Europe may rest in Peace.

To accomplish this great and splendid object, the renewed confusions of Europe leave us ONE YEAR more. I pray God that We may improve that short period with all our Energies; for I see no other means of securing ourselves from the common Ruin which hangs over the Heads of all civilized Nations.

I hope to have the Happiness of seeing the Evening of your Life more useful and more glorious than its Noon, and of saluting you, my Dear Sir, not merely as the Father of the United States, but of the United Empires of America.

I trust that you will not think I have been forward or officious in thus freely communicating to you my Ideas of the dangers of our common Country, and of the means of averting them—living amidst Scenes of daily and astonishing change, and a near witness to the boundless and succesful Ambition of France, and of the Perfidy, the mutual Jealosies, the Distraction and the Weakness of the rest of Europe: I look with encreasing Anxiety to my Country when I see her pursuing the same *Defensive* System which has lead so many Nations to successive Ruin. This is no time for common Policy or temporizing measures—the Danger is imminent, the Plans of our Enemy are vast as the World; and we must oppose to them Policy equally vast—Activity equally indefatigable & Courage equally ardent—these honestly and earnestly exerted in the Cause of real Liberty and Virtue, will Triumph over all the Arts and Power of Vice.

May Heaven long preserve a life & Health from which human Nature has received so much, and from which She has still so much to hope and to Expect.

I beg you to present my respectful remembrance to Mrs Washington, and to accept the assurances of the encreased Respect gratitude and Veneration of Dear Sir your much obliged & faithful servant & friend

Jno. Trumbull

ALS, DLC:GW; ADfS, ViMtV; LB, DLC: John Trumbull Letter Book.

1. Letter not found.

2. GW wrote Jonathan Trumbull, Jr., John Trumbull's brother, on 6 Feb. 1799 that the prints had "just arrived." See also John Trumbull to GW, 18 Sept. 1798, and note 1 of that document.

From John Churchman

March 25th 1799.

John Churchman presents his respectful compliments to General Washington, & altho almost out of Season, he wishes to make an apology for a certain Transaction which he understood was made known to the General, just before he resigned the important Office of President, a Transaction which might have done J. Churchman some Honor had he acted with caution, but he is afraid it has been construed to the contrary, therefore as his reputation is concerned which is dearer to him than life, he begs Liberty to State the case, & hopes to be pardoned for so doing.

After J. Churchman had got on Ship Board, he received under cover directed to himself, from the American Consul at Bordeaux, a Packet directed to Timothy Pickering Esqr. Secretary of State, Seeing the cover was directed to J. Churchman, he first broke the outside Seal; & without taking time to examine he broke the Seal of the Letter to the Secretary of State before he suspected it was for any other person besides himself, for as he had a short time before received through the hands of the American minister then at Paris, & the Consul at Bordeaux, a Copy of a Diploma from an European Academy of Sciences, he expected this Letter contained the original Diploma, & immediately after he discovered his error, he Sealed up the Letter & delivered it in Person to a Servant at the Door of the Secretary on the evening of the Day on which he Landed. Altho a Stranger to him he would have been very glad to have Spoken to the Secretary at that time, only on account of a tedious Voyage he happened to be scarce of clean Linen. A few days after this, J. Churchman introduced himself to the Secretary of State as the Bearer of his Letter, at which the Secretary said (in such a manner that alarmed him) that he was glad to hear it for the Letter had been opened, at this J. Churchman was at first afraid of being prosecuted, & said he did not open the Letter, neither did he for he only broke the Seal, but soon after on the same day J. Churchman took fresh courage, called on the Secretary of State again, & explained the whole affair to him, & was treated so Politely by him, that J. Churchman was very sorry he had not the resolution to have been so candid at the first interview.[1]

N.B. A copy of the above was shewn to the Secretary of State some time past with a very little Variation.

AL, DLC:GW.

John Churchman (1753–1805), a surveyor and mapmaker, received considerable attention in the late 1780s and early 1790s for his controversial "Scheme for determining the Longitude from a combined observation of the latitude & variation of the magnetic needle" (Churchman to GW, 7 May 1789). See Thomas Ruston to GW, 20 Mar. 1789, introducing Churchman, and Churchman's petition to GW, 7 May 1789, and see the editors' notes in both these documents.

1. On 29 July 1796 Secretary of State Timothy Pickering wrote GW: "About noon to-day Mr John Churchman . . . called at the office. He came last from Bourdeaux, and was the bearer of Mr [James] Monroe's letter of the 2d of May. I told him it had been broken open; & after a few questions, asked him to give me a certificate of the circumstances which attended his receipt of it; and offered him pen, ink & paper to write it; unless he chose to do it at home. He said he would go home, and call himself at five in the afternoon (if that hour was convenient to me) as the matter required some consideration. He called at five accord-

ingly; and then told me (with some emotion) that he thought it best to be candid . . . He had himself broken the seal, tho' by mere accident; and as soon as he discovered his mistake, closed the letter again without reading it." Pickering goes on to recount Churchman's explanation of how this happened and then tells GW that he accepted the explanation. The U.S. consul to whom Churchman referred was Joseph Fenwick. For the removal of Fenwick as consul, see Comments on Monroe's *View of the Conduct of the Executive of the United States*, c. March 1798, printed above.

To Julius Burbidge Dandridge

Dear Sir, Mount Vernon 25 Mar. 1799

The enclosed came undercover to me a few days ago, and not knowing into whose hands better to place it than yours, I forward it to you accordingly.

The doing so, furnishes an opportunity of condoling with you, and the other friends of Mr John Dandridge, on his death; an event I sincerely regretted.

From the Superscription, I know the enclosed letter is from your brother Bartholomew; who, no doubt, has therein, informed of his *present* situation; should I be mistaken however, in this conjecture, he is *now* Secretary to our Minister (Mr King) in London; a Post as honourable, as it may ultimately prove advantageous to him in his passage through life.[1] The family at this place are all well, and offer you there best wishes. With esteem I am Dear Sir Your Obedient & Hble Servant

Go: Washington

ALS (letterpress copy), NN: Washington Papers.

Julius Burbidge Dandridge was a younger brother of John and Bartholomew Dandridge. He died unmarried.

1. See Bartholomew Dandridge to GW, 10 Oct. 1798, 12 Mar. 1799, and GW to Bartholomew Dandridge, 25 Jan. 1799. See also Timothy Pickering to GW, 11 March.

To Alexander Hamilton

Dear Sir Mount Vernon 25th Mar: 1799

Your letter of the 14th instant with its enclosures, came to hand by the last Post.

In the present State of the Army (or more properly the Embryo of one, for I do not perceive from any thing that has come to my knowledge that we are likely to move beyond this) and until the Augmented force shall have been Recruited, Assembled and in the Field, the residence of the Paymaster Genl (I did not know there was one until your letter announced it) will be found most eligable at the Seat of the General Government; and you will please to give such Orders respecting it, as you shall think proper, for I am unwilling to issue any.

Under this Cover, you will find a letter which I have just received from Colo. Hamtramck, with a short acknowledgment of its receipt; which you will be so good as to forward with your dispatches for the Western Army.[1] With very great esteem & regd I am Dr Sir—Yr Most Obedt Servt

Go: Washington

ALS, DLC: Hamilton Papers; ALS (letterpress copy), DLC:GW.

1. Lt. Col. John Francis Hamtramck (d. 1803), commandant of the 1st Regiment of Infantry in the U.S. Army, wrote GW from Fort Wayne on 28 Jan. 1799: "it is impossible for me to Express to you the joy and Satisfaction I received when I first heard of your having once more taken up that sword, which has rendered your name so Dear to American posterity, and your fame so immortal in the annals of the American Revolution. General Wilkinsen having Been a spectator and an Eye Witness to the Decline of my health on the Mississippi, has permitted me to return to Duty in a more Northern Latitude—he has writen to the Secretary of War respecting the Command he wishes me to have—I have also reported my Self to him, but I have t[h]ought proper also to inform you of my return. I would offer you a Detail of the Situation of the troops on the Mississippi, and of the Contemplated fortification for the National Barrier, but as those things have already Been officially Communicated by General Wilkinsen to the War Office, and which have, or will no Doubt be laid Before you I will therefore Conclude . . ." (DLC: Hamilton Papers). GW's letter to Hamtramck of 25 Mar. reads: "Sir Your polite and flattering letter of the 28th of January, dated at Fort Wayne, has just got to my hands. For the favourable sentiments you have been pleased to express for me, I pray you to accept my grateful thanks.

"If any thing besides a duty, which I think every good Citizen owes his Country when its rights are invaded, and every thing dear to it is threatned, could console me for quitting the peaceful scenes on which I had entered with avidity, it would be the meeting again in the Field of Mars of so many of my Compatriots in Arms, with whom I had toiled through more than a Seven years War; and for whose aid & exertions, I was so much indebted. Among this number I certainly shall place Colo. Hamtramck.

"The particular care of all matters, which relate to the Western Army, and Posts in that Region, is Committed to Majr General Hamilton, to whom all Returns, Reports &ca are to be made. With esteem & regard—I am Sir Your most Obedt ⟨*illegible* Go: Washington⟩" (letterpress copy, DLC:GW).

To James McHenry

My dear Sir,   Mount Vernon 25th March 1799

You will not only consider this letter as a *private one*, but as a *friendly one*, from G: W. to J: M. And if the sentiments which you will find in it, are delivered with more freedom and candour than are agreeable, say so; not by implication only, but in explicit language; and I will promise to offend no more by such conduct; but confine myself (if occasion should require it) to an Official Correspondence.

Thus premising, let me, in the name and behalf of the Officers who have been appointed, and of the Army intended to be raised, ask what keeps back the Commissions; and arrests the Recruiting Service?

Be assured that *both*, among the friends of Government, excite astonishment and discontent. Blame is in every Mind, but it is not known where to fix it. Some attach it to the P.—some to the S: of W.—and some, *fertile in invention*, seek for other causes. Many of the appointed Officers have quitd their former occupations, that they might be in perfect readiness to proceed in their Military duties the moment they should receive their Commissions & Recruiting Instructions. Others, who were about to enter into business, and plans of future life, stand suspended. Many are highly disgusted; some talk of giving up the idea of becoming Officers, unable to remain longer in the aukward situation they are involved; and *all* are complaining. Applications are made by numbers to me, to know what the cause of the delay is, what they are to expect, and what they ought to do. What could I say? Am I not kept in as much ignorance as they are themselves? Am I advised of any new appointments? any changes which have taken place? any of the views or designs of Government relatively to the Army? It is not unreasonable to suppose, that if there be reasons of State, operating the policy of these delays, that I was entitled to sufficient confidence to be let into the secret; or, if they proceeded from uncontroulable causes, *I*, still more than the *Public*, ought not to have been left in the field of Conjecture, without a guide to direct me to the knowledge of them. For I shall frankly declare, that I do not, nor ever shall, consider myself in the light of a Mercenary Officer—Nothing short of a high sense of the Amor Patriæ, could have placed me in my present situation; and though

I stand bound, and will obey the call of my Country whenever it is made, agreeably to my letter of acceptance—none will regret the event with more poignancy; none will forsake the walks of retirement with more heartful sorrow; nor none, who wd leave it with more real inconvenience to their private concerns, than I should do. A sixteen years absence from home (with short intervals only) could not fail to derange them considerably; & to require *all the time* I can spare from the usual avocations of life, to bring them into tune again. But this is not all, nor the worst, for being the Executor, the Administrator, & Trustee of, & for other Estates, my greatest anxiety is to leave all these concerns in such a clear, and distinct form, as that no reproach may attach it self to me, when I have taken my departure for the land of Spirits.

I have been thus full, as it relates to myself, in order to shew you, that information in all matters of a Military nature, are necessary for my Government; thereby, having a prospective view of things, I may prepare accordingly; and not, though detached from the Army until the exigency of our Affairs may require my presence with it, appear as a person just dropped from the Clouds, when I take the Command: ignorant of preceeding occurances: nor will it, without doing great violence to the concerns of others— equally with my own—be in my power to "take up my bed & walk" at an unexpected requirement; without great exertions, which it may not be in my power to make, on a sudden call; unless previously hastened (which would be unnecessary) unless I could discover, before hand, the utility of the measure, by the gradual unfolding of the prospects before us.

I shall now, with your permission, make a few observations as they respect the Recruiting Service. Had the Organization of the Augmented Corps, & consequent Instructions for raising it, tread as close on the passage of the Law, as the nature of the case would have permitted, a finer army for the size of it (with the Discipline it might have received) the World had never Seen: but the golden opportunity is passed, & probably will never occur again. The zeal, enthusiasm, and indeed resentments, which warmed the breasts of the American youth, and would have induced the sons of the respectable Yeomanry (in all parts of the United States) to have enlisted as non-commissioned Officers & Privates, is now no more; they are evaporated, & a listlessness has supplied its place. The next, most favourable opportunity namely—the idle, & dreary scenes of winter which bring on dissipation & want, from the cessation of labour, has also passed away! the enlivening prospect of Spring, the calls of the Husbandman, indeed of every avocation, for labourers in the approaching busy season, hath supplanted all thoughts of becoming Soldiers; and *now*, many young Gentlemen who had (conditionally) last Summer & Autumn, engaged their Companies, will find it difficult to enlist a *single man* of those so engaged. The latter Pretending, that having waited a considerable time to see if their services would be wanted in the Field, and no overtures for them made it became necessary for them to seek some other employment.

What is the natural consequence of all this? why, that we must take the Rif raf of the populous Cities; Convicts; & foreigners: or, have Officers without men. But even this is not the worst of it. The Augmented Corps (if I have conceived the matter rightly) must have been intended as a well organized, and well disciplined body of Men, for others (in case of need) to resort to, & take example from. Will this be the case if the enemy should invade this Country? Far from it! What better, in the first instance, are Regiments so composed than Militia? and what prospect have those who Command them, of rendering Service to their Country, or doing honor to themselves in the Field, opposed to Veteran Troops, practiced in Tactics, and unaccustomed to defeat? These, my dear McHenry, are serious considerations to a Man who has nothing to gain, and is putting every thing to a hazard.

When I began this letter, I intended to have stopped *here*; but as I may not again write to you with the freedom I now do, I shall make a few remarks on some other transactions, which have not struck me in the most favourable point of view.

The two Major Generals and myself were called to Philadelphia in November last, and there detained five weeks (very inconveniently to all of us) at an inclement season, in wading through volumes of applications & recommendations to Military Appointments; and I will venture to say that it was executed with as much assiduity, and under as little influence of favor or prejudice, as a work of that sort (from the materials which were laid before us) ever was accomplished: and what has followed? Why any Member of Congress who had a friend to serve, or a prejudice to endulge, could set them at naught. Out of a number, I will select one instance only in proof of this—it is a striking one—the case of Gibbes, I allude to. He was personally known to you, General Hamilton & myself, in his former services. He served through the *whole* Revolutionary war, from the Assembling of the first Troops at Cambridge, to the closing of the Military Drama at the conclusion of Peace without reproach; and in the last Act of it, If I mistake not, was a Major in the selected Corps of light Infantry. He was strongly recommended by Generals Lincoln, Knox, Brooks & Jackson; all on the same theatre with himself and who ought to be perfectly acquainted with his respectability & pretensions: yet the Veto of a Member of Congress (I presume) was *more respected*; & sufficient to set him aside.[1]

Another thing I will remark on, because if the practice is continued, you will find that serious discontents, & evils will result from it.

I find by the Gazettes (I have *no other* information of these matters) that Lieutt Mercer, of the Light Dragoons, is promoted to the Rank of Captn in that Corps. In the arrangement of Officers, where every attention was paid (that personal knowledge or information could reach) to *merit, age, respectability & standing* in the community, he was not even placed (if my memory serves me) high up among the Lieutenants. What then will those Lieutenants who were his *Seniors* in that arrangement, greatly his *Seniors* in age, of at *least* as much *respectability*—*better known*—and of *equal merit* think, of having him placed over *them*? Mercer, compared to some of them, is a boy; and in such an Army as it was our wish to form, it will have an odd appearance to place a young man of 20 or 21 years of age over a Lieutent of 30, in *every other respect his equal*.

I do not mean to derogate from the merits or deserts of this young Gentleman; on the contrary, I wish to see them *properly* rewarded, although his whole family are *bitter* in their enmity to the General Government: nor would I be understood to mean that if a Captain (and so of any other grade) declines his appointment, that, *during the act of formation*, the vacancy is to be filled by the next in Seniority, *necessarily*. So far from this, I maintain, that where a vacancy is occasioned by non-acceptance, that it may, without injustice, be filled by *a new character*, as in the first instance; but it is my opinion at the sametime, that if you have recourse to *promotion* that the arrangement which was made by the Board of General Officers (in all its parts) who had regard to all the Combinations, and qualifications that have been enumerated, in settling the relative rank, is the safest guide you could have resorted to.

It is not my intention to dispute the *Powers* of the President to

make *this*, or *any other* promotion his inclination, or the solicitation of others, may prompt him to; but I will add, without fear of
contradiction by any one acquainted with the usages, & prescrip-
tive rights of armies, that if he wishes to preserve the Peace & harmony of *ours*, rules must be observed; and the feelings of the Officers attended to, in Promotions.

These observations, relatively to the promotion of Lieutenant
Mercer, are not the result of any discontent I have heard expressed on the occasion; for except those who take the Philadelphia Gazettes, but a few of the Officers may be acquainted therewith; and of that few, I have seen none since its annunciation to
the public. It is on general ground they are made, & by judging of
the feelings of others, by what would be my own, in a similar case;
for I do not think it will be a very reconcilable matter, to Gentlemen of more respectable ages, better known in the walks of life,
and much more likely to Recruit men, to have a youth fresh from
College, placed over their heads.[2]

As vacancies have happened in the Cavalry by non-acceptances
&ca, and promotions have begun; may I ask if there would be any
impropriety in letting Mr Custis step from a Cornecy, into the
Rank of Lieutenant? If I mistake not, in the arrangement given in,
he stands the first for promotion—that is—he was made the senior Cornet. The Major Generals were desirous of placing him as
Lieutenant in the first instance; but, his age considered, I thought
it more eligible that he should enter in the lowest grade of Commissioned Officers. If ample fortune—good Education—more
than common abilities—and good dispos[it]ions—free from Vice
of any kind, gives him a title, in the 19th year of his age, his pretensions thereto (though not to the injury of another) are good.
But it is not my desire to ask this as a favor. I never have, nor never
shall, solicit any thing for my self, or connexions. I mean nothing
more than the statement of a fact, in order to bring his situation
to view.

There is one matter more, which I was in doubt whether to mention to you, or not, because it is of a more delicate nature than any
I have touched upon; but finally, friendship have got the better of
my scruples.

It respects yourself *personally*. Whilst I was in Philadelphia—
and after the Members of Congress had begun to Assemble, it
was hinted to me, in pretty *strong terms* by more than one of them,

that the Department of War would not—nay could not—be conducted to advantage (if War should ensue) under your auspices; for instead of attending to the *great* outlines, and *principles* of your Office, & keeping the subordinate Officers of the Department rigidly to their respective duties, *they*, were inattentive, while *you*, were bewildered with trifles.

You will recollect, I dare say, that more than once, I expressed to you my opinion of the expediency of committing the *Details* of the Department to the execution of others; and to bestow your thoughts and attention to the more important Duties of it; which, in the scenes we were contemplating, were alone sufficient to occupy the time, and all the consideration of the Secretary. I went no farther *then*, nor should I have renewed the subject *now*, had not the delay in issuing of the Commissions, and commencing the Recruiting Service, excited general reprobation, and blame, though, as I have observed before, no one knows where, with precision, to fix it—generally however, it is attributed to the want of system, & exertion in the Department of War. To apprise you of this, is my motive for this communication.[3]

I prefaced the sentiments of this letter with a request, that they might be considered as proceeding from a private man to his friend. No one would be struck more forcibly than myself, with the impropriety of such a letter from the Commander in Chief of the Army of the U. States to the Secretary of War. If they are received in good part, the end is obtained. If otherwise, my motives, & the purity of my intentions, is the best apology I can offer for the liberty I have taken. In either case however, be assured of this truth, that with very great esteem and regard, I remain My dear Sir Your most Obedient and Affectionate Hble Servt

Go: Washington

ALS, NhD; ALS (letterpress copy), DLC:GW.

1. In their recommendations to McHenry in December 1798, GW and generals Alexander Hamilton and Charles Cotesworth Pinckney named Caleb Gibbs to command one of the Massachusetts regiments, with the rank of lieutenant colonel. On 21 Jan. McHenry wrote Hamilton that Gibbs was "seriously objected to" on several grounds by Benjamin Goodhue, senator from Massachusetts, and by Harrison Gray Otis, Samuel Sewall, Dwight Foster, and Isaac Parker, members of the U.S. House of Representatives from Massachusetts (Syrett, *Hamilton Papers*, 22:428–31). When Hamilton protested the passing over of Gibbs, McHenry wrote that Gibbs's "character is very low in Boston, that he is looked upon as a triffler, and has no weight whatever in that quarter of the union" (Hamilton to

McHenry, 6 Feb., McHenry to Hamilton, 8 Feb., ibid., 466–68, 472–73). In response to GW's complaint of 25 Mar., McHenry wrote on 31 Mar. that it was not only the influential members of Congress who opposed Gibbs's appointment but Secretary of State Timothy Pickering and Secretary of the Treasury Oliver Wolcott did so as well. When writing to McHenry on 23 April, GW again objected to the recommendation regarding Gibbs's appointment, but when Gibbs wrote on 21 April seeking GW's support in securing a military appointment, GW replied that it would be improper for him "to bring you forward again."

2. On 25 July 1798 GW forwarded a letter from 20-year-old Charles Fenton Mercer inquiring about a commission in the New Army, and on the same day he wrote Mercer that he would "second your wish to enter into the Army of the United States." In the list of nominations that GW forwarded to McHenry in December 1798 young Mercer was listed as a lieutenant of dragoons, but in the list of nominations by Adams that were forwarded to the Senate, Mercer was named a captain (see McHenry to GW, 28 Dec. 1798, n.3). When writing to McHenry on 23 April, GW spelled out in detail why he considered conferring a captain's commission on young Mercer to be a serious blunder. On 29 April McHenry reported that Mercer had turned down the offered commission. See also GW to McHenry, 5 May.

3. From the outset GW and Alexander Hamilton had shared the opinion that McHenry was not up to the task of supervising the raising and organizing of the New Army and that he should seek the aid of Hamilton in these things. See Hamilton to GW, 29 July–1 Aug., and GW to Hamilton, 9 Aug. 1798.

To Alexander Spotswood

Dear Sir,   Mount Vernon 25⟨th⟩ Mar. 1799

I do not know *how* it happened but so *it is*, that a considerable interval always takes place between the date of your letters to me, and my receipt of them; notwithstanding I send regularly to the Post Office every other day, and frequently every day, when I have reason to expect letters on business.

Premising this, I have to add, that your letter of the 15th instant enclosing one from Mr Short (which I return) did not reach me until yesterday.

When you shall have occasion to write to that Gentleman, you would oblige me, by offering him my thanks for the trouble he has been at to ascertain Mr Abrahm Hite's price for Woodrows Survey; and at the sametime he is informed of my declining the purchase, I cannot but feel pleasure in finding that lands on Rough Creek look so high; for as you have justly observed, if Mr Hites land is valued at 10$ pr acre, mine which surrounds it, ought, by analogy, to bear some proportion thereto. When I authorised Mr Short to proceed to the amount of 20/ pr acre, I conceived I had stretched the value to its utmost limits; the result of his negociation will have a tendency to make me enquire a little more minutely into the value of my own: for although I am not able to *give* such prices for Lands in that part of the world, I should have no objection to *receiving* them, if persons can be found who are inclined to become purchasers on similar terms.[1]

I thank you for the Paragraph cut out of Greens Paper, although I had seen it before. What *the tale of the Tubs* has turned out to be, I have not heard; but the manner in which it was concealed, is strongly evinsive that it was intended for the *select only*. Many tales of this kind have been, and will continue to be related whilst we have a Party in this Country who are disposed to give them efficasy. One similar to this (just before I left the Administration of the Government) was concealed in a parcel of Tobo on the Ohio, but unfortunately was not known until it was too late.[2] Yet, the Laws of self perservation against these People are set to view in the most odious light. Except colds, we are all well here—& unite in every good wish for you & Yours, with Your Affece frd.

⟨Go: Washington⟩

ALS (letterpress copy), DLC:GW.

1. GW asked Peyton Short on 16 July 1798 to investigate the possibility of his purchasing the Wodrow tract in Kentucky. See also the references in note 1 to Spotswood's letter of 15 March.

2. See note 2, Spotswood to GW, 15 March.

To Tobias Lear

Dear Sir, MOUNT VERNON 26th. March 1799.

Your letter of the 24th. Inst. enclosing one from Major Rivardi was delivered to me last night.[1]

It gives me pleasure that you are recovering from your lameness, and repeat the wish contained in my last that you would use the means for perfect restoration, and remain as long with Doctr. Thornton as he may conceive advisable.[2]

With respect to the letter from Major Rivardi, it would be proper to send it, by my direction, to Genl. Hamilton that he may issue such orders in consequence thereof as to him shall appear to suit the occasion; informing the Major thereof. Refering him to my former letter for the mode of his communications in future.

Mrs. Washington has had (it is now better) a very bad Cold in other respects the family are as well as usual, & unite with me in good wishes for you & Complts. to Doctr. Thornton's family. I am Yr. Sincere friend & Affecte. Servt.

P.S. If you should happen to see Mr. Blagden, pray ask him when he expects to be in mortar—in other words, when he expects to lay the foundation stone.[3]

Lear, *Letters and Recollections*, 127–28.

1. Neither Lear's letter of 24 Mar. nor that of John Jacob Ulrich Rivardi has been found, but see GW to Rivardi, 2 Mar., printed in GW to Alexander Hamilton, 25 Feb. 1799, n.2.

2. GW wrote to Lear to this effect on 18 March. See also GW to William Thornton, 24 March.

3. For the correspondence relating to the construction of GW's houses in Washington, see especially GW to District of Columbia Commissioners, 28 Sept. 1798, n.2. Thomas Law wrote GW on about 25 April that the cornerstone of his double house was being laid the next day. See also William Thornton's report to GW on George Blagdin's progress, 19 April.

From John Tayloe

Mannsfield [Spotsylvania County]

Dear Sir   26th March 1799

After getting thus far on my way to your house—I have been taken with a fever & a severe indisposition—which obliges me to return home as quickly as possible—I pray you therefore to excuse me for not returning you in person many thanks for your civilities—& marked attention. & assure yourself I will embrace the earliest opportunity in doing so[1]—T'was my intention to have set out for Phi[ladelphi]a ten days ago—but for the enclosed letter—which I enclose for your perusal—In this business I shall not act untill I can have an interview with you[2]—If at your leisure—I could have the pleasure of an acknowledgement of this[3] you will confer an obligation on—Your respectfull & obliged Servt—

John Tayloe

ALS, DLC:GW.

1. Mannsfield was the house of Mann Page, Jr. (c. 1749–1803). Page was married to Mary Tayloe Page (b. 1759), the sister of John Tayloe of Mount Airy in Richmond County who wrote this letter. Mannsfield was near Fredericksburg

in Spotsylvania County. Tayloe visited Mount Vernon 17–18 April 1799 (*Diaries*, 6:342–43).

2. For the possible nature of the "business" to which Tayloe refers, see Tayloe to GW, 10 Feb., and GW's response of 12 February.

3. GW wrote on 31 March.

From Mason Locke Weems

Very honord Sir.   Dumfries March 26 [17]99

I was t'other day in Norfolk where a very particular friend of mine Captn James Tucker a man of merit and money, begd me to ask a favor of you which we both concluded your goodness wd readily grant.

Captn Tucker is a Wealthy Merchant of Norfolk, largely in the importing line. He has lately been applied to for a quantity of Merchandize on *credit* by a Gentleman who calls himself Major James Welch and who says moreover that he is the man who purchasd your excellency's Western lands of which report says you sold so much some time ago.

Captn Tucker wishes to know whether a Major Welch *did* purchase your excellency's lands or a part of them, and whether he met your excellency's expectations in the way of Payment.[1]

If your excellency will condescend to honor me with a line on this subject it will be very gratefully acknowledgd both by Captn Tucker & his and your Excellency's much Obligd

M. L. Weems.

ALS, DLC:GW.

The Rev. Mason Locke Weems (1759–1825) married Frances Ewell in July 1795, and the couple lived in Dumfries near the home of her father, Col. Jesse Ewell. Weems no longer served as a cleric and instead devoted himself to the sale and promotion of books (Weems, *Life of Washington*, xi).

1. See GW's response of 31 March. See also James Welch's description of his business activities, Welch to GW, 25 April.

From Alexander Hamilton

Private
Dr Sir   New York March 27. 1799.

At length we are on the point of commencing the recruiting service in five of the States, Connecticut, New York, New Jersey,

Pensylvania & Delaware. It is hoped, that it will not be long in successively embracing the others, where officers have been appointed. But in our affairs 'till a thing is actually begun, there is no calculating the delay, which may ensue. You have been informed that the recruiting service has been put under my direction, but for many matters of detail I must go to the Secretary for a sanction and it is not always that it is rapidly obtained. Things however are at last getting into such a state that this business may be expected to progress without interruption.

The letter some time since sent you for General Lee was intended to be left open. It respected the division of Virginia into four districts and Twenty sub-districts or company rendezvouses, designating a place in each for the head Quarters of the rendezvous—I have as yet had no acknowledgement of it.[1]

Before General Morgan left Philadelphia, I got him to give me a plan. Inclosed is a copy.[2] If you think a better arrangement can be made, shall I ask the favour of you to have it done⟨.⟩ For I cannot now rely on the success of my resort to General Lee in any reasonable time.[3] Very respectfully & Affecly I have the honor to be Sir Your obed. serv.

A. Hamilton

Will you have the goodness to put the letters herewith in a train to reach their destination with certainty. They are open that you may perceive their object.[4]

ALS, DLC:GW.

    1. See Hamilton to GW, 18 Feb., and note 1 of that document.

    2. The enclosure was a copy of Virginia divided and subdivided into Districts, for recruiting, undated, in DLC: Hamilton Papers.

    3. Hamilton wrote to Henry Lee on 18 Feb. about the recruiting service in Virginia (Syrett, *Hamilton Papers*, 22:486–87).

    4. The letters, directed to Thomas Parker and William C. Bentley, were copies of a "Circular to the Commandants of Regiments." See GW to Hamilton, 10 April, and note 3 of that document, and GW to Daniel Morgan, 10 April.

From William B. Harrison

Dr Sir   March 28th 1799 Leesburgh

This day I met with your Letter of the 4th Instant[1] in the office of this place I do not know precisely the number of Acres I hold

in the track of Land aloded to my Self I did under take to Survey
it once at which time you did me the Honor to ride & Show me
the Beginning Corner & after that you Left us we proceeded to
search for Lines & Corners for two days at last quit witht doing any
thing & have never attempted it Since[.] I Recivd a Letter from a
Mr Beal in 91 informing me of A Survey that was Likely to take
place of Lands that Joind the Chappel Lands Calld for the Corners
running with the Lines &c. and woud Consequently Establish
mine, and that Colo. mason & Mr Chicester woud be present, it
was out of my power to attend, I am told the survey did actually
take place & the Corners were provd to the Satisfacton of the parties present So that I have only to survey agreable thereto to Ascertain my quantity which I mean to do this Spring,[2] as for the Rent
being 2000 lbs. of tobacco, you are misinformd the Rent has been
Ever Since the Old Lease was out 2500 lbs. & Eight pounds Cash
which I have Recivd Commonly about the time it becom due, and
was offerd 3000 lbs. of tobacco by John Robinson and five pounds
of fish two of Shad & three of herings which was to have been
delivd in Alexandria[3] I did not choose to take it for Reasons I
assignd you in a former Letter, & as for asking a Rent that is un
Reasonable from you or taking much Less it is not my Intention
or desire but to the Contrary If either Extream it shall be the
Latter for Reasons assignd in yours of the 4th of Novmbr, I never
have been offrd twelve dollars Cash pr a[c]re for those Lands I was
Offerd twelve & a half by a good man if I woud give three years
Credit for part of the money which part was to have been divided
in three annual payments the Last at the End of the third year I
have also been offerd 2400 pounds on a Mr Welch the gentleman
that offerd it woud not Garrantee the Bonds for Reason he did not
make a practice to do so & I woud not take them with out,[4] I was
also offerd twenty five hundred pounds which was to have been
on a Mr Hambleton who formally Lived in Alexandria 20/ of the
money pr acre was to have been paid down the other part to be on
Long Credit, after the first payment it was proposd that I shoud
make a Title[5] this I Refused & have had several other offers not
worth mentioning, I woud not wish to deal in the way pointed
out in yours to me if I take paper at all it must be yours for no
Other will do, If you incline to Rent my Lands you may have a
Lease During your Life & your La[d]y's on the terms I proposed

in my former Letter to you I mention this Circumstance being diferent, and as what might be thought a high Rent now woud in all probality be in a few *a very few* years Low one and it is to be observd that I might have had a Considerable more Rent from the same set of tenants if I had given them a Lease for any Length of time, they have only held the Same from year to year, I knew nothing of your proffer to Genl Lee & it is more than probable I may have barterd Mr Sims with my Lands as I all ways found him the Night of the market in Alexandria and very punctual as far as we have delt as you have said in a former Letter you must & shoud improve them from your own Lands I am ⟨*mutilated*⟩nd to give you the Refusial not with standing it may be of Great disadvantage to me in parting with or Renting them for I might meet with a man that woud wish to purchase Decisively a way & before I coud give you the Refusial he Could not wait & might Consequently Choose to be off I am with All the Respect A mortal Can frame yours &c.

Wm B. Harrison

N.B. please observe the Refusial is intended to Extend only to Renting & if I discover on further Examining & surveying my Lands that I can or ought to take Less you shall amediately hear from me. Wm B. H.

ALS, DLC:GW.

1. GW's letter is dated 5, not 4, March.

2. GW wrote Harrison on 10 April that he had "never heard of Colo. [George] Mason's and Mr [Richard] Chichester's Survey of the Lands hereabouts"; but he invited Harrison to come to Mount Vernon and survey the tract with the help of Albin Rawlins. Harrison accepted the invitation on 24 April and arrived at Mount Vernon on 14 May. On 15 May GW, Harrison, and Thomson Mason surveyed the tract (*Diaries*, 6:347–48). Mason, who lived just north of River farm at Mount Vernon, was married to Sarah McCarty Chichester Mason, daughter of another neighbor, Richard Chichester, who had died in 1796.

3. John Robinson may be John Robertson who was a tenant on Penelope Manley French's land when GW acquired it in 1786 and added it to his holdings at Mount Vernon. See GW's comments on "Robinson" in his letter to Harrison of 10 April.

4. See GW's comments on James Welch in his reply, 10 April. See also Henry Lee to GW, 28 Feb., and GW to Harrison, 5 March.

5. At least three men named Hamilton were involved in real estate transactions in Alexandria in the 1790s, the brothers James and Robert Hamilton and Theodorus James Hamilton (Munson, *Alexandria Hustings Court Deeds, 1783–97*; ibid., *1797–1801*).

From Samuel Washington

Dear Uncle   Chas Town March 28th 1799

I received your kind Letter by Coll Lear but never had it in my power to Answer it untill know being Oblige to Leave home,[1] you ware kind enough to Mention if you recd the Money you expected that you would Let me have some I am know in the greatest want of it as the Executions that I mention'd to you in my former letter have come out against me to the Amount of Three or four hundred pound which I am affraid will take nearly all my Negroes to pay them, not Only the Loss of my Negroes but I shall Lose the Makeing of a crop which is all the way I have to support two Families. Know My Dear Uncle could you posibly Lend me that sum you will be the means of releasing me from the hands of the Sheriff for ever for if I am Once Clare I will warrant never to owe one Dollar as Long as I Live there is but one Suit besides those Executions against me, and that I shall be able to discharge this fall by the sale of my Land which I am in hopes of doing by that time. I will then return you the whole you are good enough to Lend me, I wished to have paid you a Visit, but my Father has been so Ill and still continues unwell that I am affraid to Leave him could you do any thing for me I shall thank to enclose the check on the Bank to me by the first post, which I can turn it here in to Money for I am affraid I cant keep the Sheriff of much Longer,[2] I remain Dear Uncle you Affecton⟨e⟩ Nephew

                                        Saml Washington

ALS, ViMtV.

   1. GW's letter is dated 31 Jan. 1799.
   2. GW wrote on 2 April that he would let Samuel have one thousand dollars.

From James McHenry

(Private)

Dear Sir   Philadelphia 30 March 1799

I received by yesterdays mail your letter of the 25th inst.

For the present and until I can enjoy a few hours leisure from the most urgent business, I must content myself with a simple acknowledgment of the kindness of intention and friendship it discovers.

Such has been the pressure of business upon the Clerks, that they have only been able to make out a copy of my instructions to General Hamilton dated the 4th of Febry ulto, which is inclosed.[1] From these you will be at no loss to conceive of General Pinckney's, which will be sent to you as soon as they can be got copied.

Troops have marched against the Insurgents, and a further detachment is to march from this City on wednesday next. The people they are to go against are ignorant & mulish.[2] I am Dr Sir most sincerely & affectionately your obt

James McHenry

ALS, DLC:GW.

1. McHenry's instructions to Alexander Hamilton are contained in his letter to Hamilton of 4 Feb., which McHenry enclosed. See Syrett, *Hamilton Papers*, 22: 455–65. Hamilton was to have direct control of all the troops in the Northwest and on the Atlantic seaboard north of Virginia, much as GW had suggested to McHenry on 16 Dec. 1798.

2. McHenry is referring to what has been called Fries's Rebellion in Pennsylvania. John Fries, who had commanded militia companies in the Revolution and in the Whiskey Rebellion, led the opposition in Bucks, Northampton, and Montgomery counties to the collection of new taxes by the United States. On 12 Mar. 1799 John Adams issued a proclamation ordering the army to suppress the resisters, which was promptly accomplished.

Letter not found: from William Booker, 31 Mar. 1799. On 7 April GW wrote Booker: "Your letter of the 31st Ulto has been duly received."

To Tobias Lear

Dear Sir,   MOUNT VERNON 31st. March 1799.

If perchance you should happen to see Mr. Blagden before you leave the City, be so good as to get from him a statement of the preparations for my buildings therein. I do not find by inquiry of Mr. Lewis, that there is much show of this on the ground![1] I advised strongly that the foundation stone and lime, should be laid in last Autumn, when the Roads were good;—had this been done the Work might have commenced (without the hazard of disappointment) with the opening of Spring. Now, bad Roads, & multiplied excuses may be a plea for the backwardness of the Work.

I pray you also to enquire if there be any advice of the arrival of the Ship Hamilton (on board of which I had six Hhds. of Tobo.)

at London.[2] We all unite in best wishes for you—and I am Your Affecte friend

Do not forget my Gardener's Dictionary at Mr. Laws.[3]

Lear, *Letters and Recollections*, 128.
    1. See GW to Lear, 26 Mar., n.3.
    2. For the tobacco that GW sent to London on consignment, see Thomas Peter to GW, 3 Sept. 1798, and the references in note 2 to that document.
    3. GW may be referring to Philip Miller's *Abridgement of the Gardener's Dictionary* (London, 1763), which was listed in the inventory of his library taken after his death.

From James McHenry

My dear Sir.   Philadelphia 31 March 1799
    This is sunday, and I shall employ, a part of it, in returning my acknowledgments for the candor, friendship and sincerity which is evidenced in your letter of the 25th instant.
    In answering to your questions I shall follow your own order.
    You ask in the name and in behalf of the officers who have been appointed, and of the army intended to be raised, what keeps back the commissions and arrests the recruiting service.
    Let me observe in the first place that the officers appointed by the President out of the list which you recommended, were written to on the 10th of January last and requested to signify, whether they accepted or not their appointments. Out of the number then appointed and written to, there are ninety five from whom no answers have been received, twenty one of which number belong to the State of Virginia.[1]
    Considering the number appointed, and that a sufficiency of time has not yet elapsed to receive answers of acceptance or non acceptance from them, it will not be supposed, when this circumstance is called into view and fairly examined, that any officer has a right to complain of neglect, or that his commission has been unnecessarily detained.
    In the second place, you will recollect, that the nominations for the Regiment, whose officers were to be drawn from Connecticut, did not take place 'till the last days of the late session of Congress, and that it is not yet one month since these have been appointed.[2]
    In the third place, the officers who have been notified of their

appointment ought to have understood, that it was not contemplated to settle the question of their relative rank until after the whole appointments for the additional Regiments should be completed. Each of them, has been expresly told, "that until a complete nomination & appointment of the whole number of officers for the troops to be raised, took place, the President had thought it adviseable to reserve the subject of relative rank for future arrangement.["]

Has this event yet happened? Far otherwise. It was only the 16th inst. I received from Major General Pinckney the names furnished him by Governor Davie, of persons for the officers agreed to be drawn from the States of North Carolina, Kentucky & Tenessee. I forwarded these the same day to the President requesting authority to signify to them their being appointed. As for the officers to be taken from South Carolina and Georgia General Pinckney has not yet forwarded their names.[3]

It was intended by you and the General officers, that the last appointed of the new Regiments, were to stand precisely upon the same ground as it respected rank, as those first appointed. Why then should officers, knowing this, wish to anticipate commissions, previous to their relative rank being determ[in]ed?

Further, if the officers are men of sense, they must know, that being in possession of the letter of appointment, their appointment is as complete as if they were commissioned; and that where no exception to their being intitled to pay, 'till called into service, has been expressed in their letter of appointment they will receive from the date of their letter of acceptance, the pay & emoluments of their office.

I hope this exposition will, at least, be satisfactory to you. Perhaps you will recollect, a relative circumstance under one of my predecessors; The officers for the army directed to be raised March the 5th 1792, were not commissioned for twelve months after they had been appointed. I do not know whether this occasioned any uneasiness among the officers, or censures upon the then Secretary of war. If it did not, I have only to lament, that where there is so much less reason for censure, I should be the sufferer.

While on this subject I must intreat you to say to me with your usual candor and friendship, whether you think I should have done right in ordering a partial issue of commissions?

But, what is it arrests the recruiting service.

You know what prevented it from being commenced last year. that it was not until the 15th of October, the relative rank of the Major Generals could be decided, and, that the difficulties and obstructions prescribed by the treasury department disenabled me from making any provision of Cloathing. You know also, that the situation in which two of our large Cities were placed by a pestilential disease, had there been a sufficiency of money at my disposal, would not have permitted of purchasing the necessary cloath for the army, or the making of it up could it have been procured. In addition—the United States cannot at this moment furnish a sufficient quantity of white cloath for vests and overalls for the army to be raised.

What have I done? I have at an early day directed the Purveyor to purchase a sufficiency of cloath for the army of the old and new establishment; and have had at work as many hands as he could obtain to make it up. This mode was preferrd to obtaining the cloathing by Contract, as more expeditious and perhaps more œconomical. the work is going forward with great alacrity, and I am assured that there will be turned into store from henceforward a weekly supply adequate to the calls of the recruiting service however vigorously conducted.

What more have I done? I have as you will see in my instructions to Major Generl Hamilton dated the 4th of Febry, ulto, confided to this officer the sole direction of the recruiting service. I have invited him, "to lose no time in dividing the states from which officers have been lately appointed, into as many districts, as there are companies to be raised in them, and forwarding to the officers to be employed respectively in each district, through the commandant their recruiting instructions, with orders, either to hold himself prepared to enter upon the service, the moment he receives your ulterior directions, or to engage provisionally, as many recruits as are willing to enrol themselves on his list, and who may be promised pay from the day of their being enrolled and sworn, with their bounty upon the officers receiving his final instructions, or (which perhaps is safer) upon their arrival at the general rendezvous."

The existing recruiting instructions to Recruiting officers were referrd to him for revision or such additional articles as he might deem necessary; and he was desired to indicate to me as soon as possible, the several stations where rations must be provided that measures may be taken accordingly.[4]

I received on the 23 of March an arrangement of districts for the States of Connecticut, New York, New Jersey, Pennsylvania and Delaware.[5] I also received from him—

On the 30th inst. or yesterday an arrangement of Virginia into districts.[6]

He has also informed me, that a plan for the two Carolinas & Georgia has been asked of General Pinckney, but that there has not been time to obtain his reply.

I have also received from the General the recruiting instructions revised, and have had them reprinted with some additions and forwarded to him. Inclosed is one of them.

I have also directed two parcels of cloathing nearly equal to a requisition made by him, for the Connecticut and New York recruiting Districts and expect to have a sufficiency for the other Districts ready to answer his calls as they arise.

Could either the General, or the Secretary of war, have done more, or done it sooner, to commence the recruiting service? If you think we could not, let me intreat you, to prevent the operation of any censure, which may be attempted in your presence to be fixed upon either; or which you may have in your power to dissipate.

I shall make but one other reflexion on this subject. I lament as much as you, the oppertunities we have lost, to raise an army of the best men, and that it is too probable we must accept of such men as in general are found to compose the great bulk of every army. When I spoke of the time we had lost, after all my proposals for organising the army had been rejected or procrastinated, what was the reply of the President on the 28th of October 1798. He observed. "As to the recruiting service, I wonder whether there has been any enthusiasm, which would induce men of common sense to inlist for five dollars a month, who could have fifteen when they pleased by sea or for common work at land? There has been no rational plan that I have seen as yet formed for the maintenance of the army. One thing I know, that Regiments are costly articles every where and more so in this Country than in any other under the sun. If this nation sees a great army to maintain without an enemy to fight, there may arise an enthusiasm, that seems to be little foreseen. At present there is no more prospect of seeing a French army here, than there is in heaven."[7]

Recall after reading this, my propositions, respecting the appointment of officers, the arrangement for the recruiting the men &c., to the President which you had approved of, and which was communicated to him by letter on the 4th of August 1798, and make your own reflexions.[8]

I find I have too little time left me to-day, to go fully into some other points in your letter. I must therefore reserve what I have to detail to another opportunity. Let therefore a few words suffice for the present.

It was not one representative alone who opposed the appointment of Gibbs; but every influencial member from Massachusetts in both branches; to which is to be added both Mr Wolcott and Mr Pickering.

Mercer has been pressed upon the President in a manner which could not be resisted.[9]

This is all I have time to say.

You will no doubt perceive, that the situation in which I have been thrown during the last year, by others, who prevented all those measures from being carried into effect, which the public expected would necessarily take place, in conformity to the laws, could not fail to attach to me much censure and excite in the minds of persons, who could not be informed of the facts, that I wanted capacity for the proper conducting of my department. What could I do in such a case? I have submitted, to a censure which those who know all the case, ought to relieve me from, on every fair occasion when it can be done with propriety.

Be assured I shall attend to my little friends promotion the moment I can find a vacant nich above that which he now fills.

Accept once more of my sincere thanks for your letter, and let me intreat you to continue to give me such proofs of your friendship as often as you think they will be useful to apprise me of the public expectations, or any omissions or faults into which I may fall. Sincerely and most affectionately I am my dearest Sir your ob. st

James McHenry

Excuse any thing in this letter which may have proceeded from the haste in which it has been written. It is the first draught, and I have not read over.

ALS, DLC:GW; ALS (letterpress copy), DLC: James McHenry Papers.

1. For the selection and appointment of the officers for the New Army, see McHenry to GW, 28 Dec. 1798, n.3.

2. The Connecticut officers for the New Army were not appointed until 13 Feb. (*Executive Journal*, 1:311–12).

3. For Governor William R. Davie's list of officers, see Davie to GW, 30 Dec. 1798, and its enclosure.

4. See McHenry to Alexander Hamilton, 18 Dec. 1798 and 4 Feb. 1799 (Syrett, *Hamilton Papers*, 22:372–73, 455–65).

5. See Hamilton to McHenry, 16, 19 Mar. 1799, ibid., 549–50, 556–57.

6. See Hamilton to GW, 27 March.

7. Adams's letter is in fact dated 22 Oct. and is in DLC: McHenry Papers.

8. For McHenry's letter to John Adams of 4 Aug. 1798, see McHenry to GW, 8 Aug. 1798, n.1.

9. For the controversy over the military appointments of Caleb Gibbs and Charles Fenton Mercer, see GW to McHenry, 25 Mar. 1799, nn.1 and 2.

To Charles Cotesworth Pinckney

My dear Sir   Mount Vernon 31st Mar: 1799.

When Major Pinckney was here (returning from Philadelphia) he expressed the earnest wish of the Gentlemen of South Carolina to get into the breeding of Mules from good Jacks—I said, but I believe not in a way to be understood, that I should part with some of my young Jacks (three of which he saw) descendents from Royal Gift, out of Imported Jennies.[1]

In a letter which I have written to General Washington I have mentioned this circumstance that if your brother, himself, or any other of their friends are disposed to purchase they may know where, and on what terms they can be supplied with these valuable animals.

I sent him a correct discription of two young Jacks—copy of which, for Major Pinckney's information, I enclose as it is probable my namesake may be on his journey hitherwards before my letter may have reached Charleston.[2] With much esteem I am always Your Affectionate ⟨Servt⟩

Go: Washington

ALS (letterpress copy), DLC:GW.

1. Thomas Pinckney spent the night of 9 Mar. at Mount Vernon (*Diaries*, 6:338).

2. See GW to William Washington, this date, n.2. William Washington arrived at Mount Vernon on 6 Aug. with his only son, William Washington (1785–1830).

To Charles Cotesworth Pinckney

My dear Sir,   Mount Vernon March 31st 1799

Your favour of the 8th instt from Charleston has been duly received, and gave us the pleasure of hearing that you, Mrs & Miss Pinckney, had arrived in good health at that place. The first few days of January excepted, you could not have been more favoured in the Weather than all the remainder of that month, & until the middle of Febry afforded.

Although your Report of the arrangement for South Carolina & Georgia; Your Reconnoitre of the Sea board to St Mary's; & visit of the Posts on the Indian Frontier of the latter State; will be made to the Department of War, I should be glad nevertheless to know the result of them: for although I do not mean to *Act* in the present State of our Military concerns, yet it is my wish, to be regularly informed of the *real* situation of them; that I may not have every thing to learn, if the exigencies of our affairs should require my attendance in the Field. To have been informed of the arrangemts made by you, with General (now Governor) Davie, would have been satisfactory also.[1]

I am disposed to believe (from circumstances which had just got to my knowledge before I left the helm of Government) that the Garrisons on the Frontier of Georgia require a strict Inspection; not only for the purpose of restoring due subordination—but for the correction of other misdemeaners, in the Officers. Your determination therefore to look closely into these matters, and to establish strict Discipline is highly proper, and will certainly be supported. An Army cannot be governed without; for[2] no mistake in him, who commands it, is greater, or more fatal to its existance, and the welfare of its Country, than Lax Discipline. Nor is it the right road to true & permanent popularity. Civility is due to, but obedience is required from, all its members—these accompanied with strict justice, & a proper attention to army rights & Wants, will secure love & respect, while one indulgence begets an application for another, & another, until order is lost in disorder and contempt brings up the Rear.

I shall be very glad to see Brigadr General Washington on his rout to Princeton, but he will find but little to do (in the Military line) in this State. To what cause to attribute the delay, I know not, but the fact is, that not an Officer (that I have heard of) has received his Commission; nor one, who has had any Orders to Recruit.[3] The enthusiasm of last Summer and Autumn, was suffered to evaporate for want of these. The dreary months of Winter, which (for want of employment in that class of men who usually become Soldiers) bring on idleness & dissipation, is now succeeded by the opening of Spring, when labourers are in demand by the husbandmen, and other avocations, and has passed away also. In a word, all is a mistery to me.

I have very little more knowledge of the Captains in the Virginia line, as arranged by us at Philadelphia, than what was derived from the source of information then laid before us. I have no hesitation however, in mentioning the name of a Gentleman (conditionally) to whom under my present view of them, I should give a *decided* preference—It is Presley Thornton. Son of one of the most respectable Gentlemen (now deceased, of the same name) in this State. He is thirty, or thereabouts; amiable in his character; He was a British Officer during our Revolution, but would not fight against his Country & therefore went to Gibralter & was in Garrison there during its Siege by the Spaniards where, it is said, he distinguished himself by his gallant behaviour.

The condition I alluded to, and which I annex to this recommendation, is—that if I shd want him myself, & circumstances in the combinations I should have to make in the choice of my own Aids de Camp, should not be opposed to is, that you may not take it amiss my calling him into my Military sute. I have never given him the most distant hint of such an intention, nor would I have him know that it ever was in contemplation; especially as it is an event that may never happen. Indeed, I mean to be under no engagement to any of my established Aids, until I am about to enter on my Mil[itar]y duties.[4]

Mrs Washington is much obliged to Mrs Pinckney for the Mellon Seeds—as I am to you for your attention to the Plumes; & with Mrs Lewis (that now is) &ca best wishes to you, Mrs Pinckney & family, & to enquirg frds—I am always your sincere & Affecte Servt

Go: Washington

P.S. Mr Lewis & Nelly Custis fulfilled their Matrimonial engagemt on the 22d of February. In consequence, the former, havg relinquished the Camp of Mars for the Sports of Venus, has declined his Mily appointmt.

ALS (photocopy), DLC:GW; ALS (letterpress copy), DLC:GW.

1. Pinckney wrote on 20 April that he could not give GW a "copy of the arrangement for North Carolina" until his return to Charleston, and the arrangement of officers for South Carolina would have to be further delayed. For William R. Davie's list of North Carolina officers, see Davie to GW, 30 Dec. 1798, and its enclosure.

2. In his letterpress copy GW struck out "for" and inserted "and."

3. For William Washington's delay in his trip northward, see Pinckney to GW, 8 Mar., n.3.

4. For Presly Thornton's appointment as Pinckney's aide-de-camp, see Pinckney to GW, 8 Mar. and 20 April, and note 1 of the second document.

To Benjamin Stoddart

Dear Sir,   Mount Vernon 31st March 1799.

This letter will be presented to you by Burwell Bassett Esqr. one of the Senate of this Commonwealth—and a Nephew to Mrs Washington—whom I beg leave to introduce to your civilities.

Mr Bassett will mention to you the wish of another of Mrs Washingtons Nephews—Mr Robert Henley—to obtain a birth as Midshipman in one of our Frigates (if youths of Sixteen are admitted).[1]

I am not, myself, acquainted with this young Gentleman; but on Mr Bassetts report of him, ⟨who is⟩ you may entirely rely. I have the honor to be with esteem & respect Dear Sir Your Obedt Hble Servant

Go: Washington

ALS (letterpress copy), DLC:GW.

1. Robert Henley (1783–1828) was the son of Martha Washington's younger sister Elizabeth Dandridge Aylett Henley and her husband Leonard Henley (d. 1798) of James City County. Henley was made a midshipman on 8 April and served in the U.S. Navy until his death, gaining a measure of fame in September 1814 as the commander of the brig *Eagle* in the battle of Lake Champlain.

To John Tayloe

Dear Sir,   Mount Vernon Mar. 31st 1799

Your favour of the 26th from Mansfield, with its enclosure (which I return) came duly to hand.

I regret your not being able to proceed further than Mansfield, on your journey hither, and still more the cause, which, 'ere this, I hope is entirely removed.

At all times, and upon all occasions, I should be glad to see you under my Roof—and with best respects to Mrs Tayloe, in which Mrs Washington joins I remain with esteem & regard Dear Sir Your Obedt & Very Hble Servt

Go: Washington

ALS (letterpress copy), DLC:GW.

To William Washington

My dear Sir,   Mount Vernon Mar: 31st 1799.

By a letter which I have just received from General Pinckney, I find you may be shortly expected in this State, on your way to Princeton. It is unnecessary I hope for me to say, that whether you come alone or bring Mrs Washington with you, that we shall be very happy to see you at this place.

In the *Military line* I fear you will find but little duty to detain you long in this State⟨,⟩ for strange as it may seem, it is not less true that not a Military Commission has issued yet that has come to my knowledge, nor a single order for Recruiting. The cause of these delays is, to me, incomprehensable.[1]

When Major Pinckney was here (on his return from Congress) he mentioned the great desire the Gentlemen of So. Carolina had of getting into the breed of Mules. I did not, I believe, in such direct terms as for him to understand, intimate that I would sell two or three young Jacks, descended from Royal Gift, which would be of sufficient age to cover next Season, on⟨e of⟩ them indeed might have done so this Spring ⟨with⟩out injury. At the time the Major was ⟨here⟩ I thought I could have parted with *three*, ⟨but⟩ one of my Jacks that *now* Covers, by a ⟨*mutilated*⟩ of which I fear he will never recover, ⟨makes⟩ it necessary for me to retain one of the 3, to ⟨sup⟩ply his place; especially as I lost two (⟨*mutilated*⟩ valuable ones) last y⟨ear *mutilated*⟩nary manner: one of them, Compound, ⟨*mutilated*⟩ money scarcely would have induced me to pa⟨rt with⟩.

Enclosed, is a description of the ⟨*mutilated*⟩ I would sell, their breed, and price; that if Major Pinckney, yourself, or any other of your acquaintance to the Southward, is in ⟨*mutilated*⟩ of such, you may know where, & on what t⟨erms⟩ you can be supplied. It is presumed they ⟨are not far⟩ short of their gr⟨owth⟩ and that they ⟨are⟩ of the most valuable breed in this country ⟨none⟩ can deny.[2]

Mrs Washington unites with me ⟨in⟩ best wishes for you and your Lady—and I am—My dear Sir Your friend & affecte Serv⟨ant⟩

Go: Washington

ALS (letterpress copy), DLC:GW.

1. See GW's second letter of this date to Charles Cotesworth Pinckney, and notes.

2. The enclosed description, dated 31 Mar. 1799, in GW's hand, reads: "Two young Jacks, full brothers, out of an Imported Jenny from Surinam; got by Compound, who was got by Royal Gift (an Imported Jack from Spain) on an Imported Jenney from Malta (full fourteen hands high) & a most valuable Jack.

"These Jacks have never been to Mares. The oldest of them was four last July. Measures three feet eleven inches before, and four feet behind. The other was three years old last August, and measures three feet eight Inches before & three feet ten inches behind.

"They are boney and strong; and it is presumed will grow considerably yet.

"The price of the oldest, is $750 and of the youngest $650. Compound their Sire was remarkable for getting fine Mules.

"Three, four or more Jennies may be had—all from those which I have Imported, & got by Compound, or the Knight of Malta.

Go: Washington."

GW also sent a copy of this description to Thomas Pinckney. See GW to Charles Cotesworth Pinckney, 31 March (first letter). For another description of the jackasses, see GW to John Tayloe, 23 Jan. 1799.

To Mason Locke Weems

Sir,   Mount Vernon 31st March 1799

Your letter of the 26th instt came duly to hand. In answer thereto, I inform you that, my sale to Mr James Welch, of the Lands I hold upon the Great Kanhawa, is conditional only.

He has a Lease of them at a certain annual Rent—which if punctually paid, for Six years, and at the end thereof shall pay one fourth of the sum fixed on as the value of them; and the like sum by Instalments the three following years, and this without any let or hindrance—that then, and in that case only, I am to convey them in Fee simple—not else.

This is the nature of the agreemt between Mr Welch and Sir— Your very Hble Servant

Go: Washington

P.S. It may not be amiss to add that the first years Rent (due in Ja[nuar]y last) is not yet paid.[1]

ALS (letterpress copy), DLC:GW.
    1. See GW to James Welch, 15 February.

From Nicholas Fitzhugh

Dear Sir   Ravensworth April 1 1799
    I send you by the Bearer some Seed of the Hughs's Crab apple which I have lately received from a Gentleman in King George County in whose Care and attention I have the greatest confidence and am therefore satisfied that they may be depended on as being genuine. The fruit of the seedling crab is considerably larger, more juicy & supposed to make as good Cyder & a greater quantity than the grafted fruit—another circumstance which will render it preferable to grafting is that the Tree from the seed is more flourishing & hardy.[1] With respectful Compliments to Mrs Washington, Mr & Mrs Lewis I am Yours with Esteem
                                        N. Fitzhugh

ALS, DLC:GW.
    Nicholas Fitzhugh lived at Ravensworth in Fairfax County with his wife, Sarah Ashton Fitzhugh, the daughter of GW's niece Ann Washington Ashton.
    1. In answer to an inquiry, Thomas Jefferson wrote James Mease on 29 June 1814: "of the history of Hughe's crab apple I can furnish nothing more than that I remember it well upwards of 60. years ago, & that it was then a common apple on James river" (Betts, *Jefferson's Garden Book*, 533). L. H. Bailey identifies the Hughes crabapple as *Malus toringoides*, a white-flowering tree with yellow to reddish fruit, from China (Bailey, *Manual of Cultivated Plants*, 517).

To Samuel Washington

Dear Sir,   Mount Vernon 2d April 1799.
    Your letter of the 28th of last Month came to my hands last night.
    Inconvenient as it is to me (and nothing can be more so, than it is at this time) to part with what little money I have in the Bank of Alexandria; yet, rather than suffer your Negros to be taken in Execution, and sold perhaps at half price, I will answer your draughts to the amount of One thousand dollars, but not one cent beyond;

as that sum will take nearly every farthing I have in the Bank, & is insufficient to meet demands which, every moment, I expect will be made upon myself.

The reason why I chuse to answer your draughts, instead of sending you a check on the Bank; is, because the latter is too hazardous to risk by the Post. A check is always made payable to the bearer, consequently if my letter was to get into improper hands, you might derive no benefit from it, whilst I should lose it altogether; and neither of us be acquainted with the fact until it would be too late to apply a remedy: for the bearer would receive the money without any questions being asked; the check would be a voucher at the Bank that it had been paid; I should be charged therewith; and until a settlement with you, should never know whether you had received it, or not. On the other hand, an order drawn upon me, in favour of any one, that person, or his Assignee, will receive a Check to the amount thereof, on the Bank: and no risk is run, by the draugher, or payer.

Nothing but the desire of preserving you, from what you say would be your ruin, has induced me to advance this money; for I have not only not received the money I wrote you I expected, but am now convinced I shall not do it without going into a Court of justice, to recover it; while taxes (and very heavy ones); unavoidable expences; and buildings which I was importuned (on Public considerations) to erect in the Federal City (and by contract am to advance money to carry on when demanded) will drive me to the necessity (if I can obtain it at all) of borrowing at the ruinous interest it is loaned, at the Bank.

I cannot conclude this letter without remarking, that Building such a house as I am told you have (under such circumstances as you were) was an extremely imprudent act; whether done with the money you borrowed from me, or obtained by other means. Knowing that you had made yourself liable for your fathers Debts, the discharge of them ought to have been your first consideration; or, at any rate, if to build was indispensable, a small house, or house upon such a plan as might have become part of a whole, when compleated, ought to have contented you. What has happened however cannot now be undone, and the object of these remarks is to advise caution.

It would be convenient to me, to draw your Orders at as long a day as you can obtain; but I will pay at sight, rather than you shd suffer. If orders upon me will not be received, or received with reluctance, you must either come down yourself, or send some one in whom you can confide, for the money. At any rate write me, without delay, that I may know what to expect, & be prepared.[1] I am sorry to hear that your father has been so much indisposed; My best wishes & love are offered to all the family, and I am Dear Sir—Your affecte Uncle

Go: Washington

ALS, CSmH; ALS (letterpress copy), NN: Washington Collection.

1. See Samuel Washington's response of 25 April.

From Alexander Hamilton

Private

Dr Sir   New York April 3. 1799

Agreeably to your letter of the 25 of March, which with its inclosures have come duly to hand, I have written to the Pay Master General to repair to the Seat of Government. Your letter to Col. Hamtranck goes by the same opportunity.[1]

The arrangements for beginning to recruit in the States of Connecticut, New York, Jersey, Pensylvania and Delaware, are so mature that it will be very extraordinary, if the business does not actually commence in a Week. Nothing in my power will be omitted to press it forward in the other States. The prospect of success in the middle and Northern States is not bad.[2]

I get nothing very precise about the Insurrection. But every thing continues to wear the character of feebleness, in respect to the measures for suppressing it. And though I hope it will not become very serious, yet it will not be astonishing, if from mismanagement, it should become more troublesome than it need to be.[3] With greatest respect & attachment I remain Dr Sir Your Obed. Sr.

A. Hamilton

ALS, DLC:GW; copy, DLC: Hamilton Papers; copy, DLC: Hamilton Papers.

1. See Hamilton to Caleb Swan, 3 April, in Syrett, *Hamilton Papers*, 23:6–7. GW's letter to John Francis Hamtramck is printed in the note to GW's letter to Hamilton of 25 March.

2. Hamilton gave recruiting instructions to the regimental commanders in the New Army in March. See Hamilton to GW, 27 Mar., and notes.

3. For Fries's Rebellion in Pennsylvania, see James McHenry to GW, 30 Mar., n.2.

From Benjamin Lincoln

Boston [April] 3d 1799

I received yesterday, My Dear General, your favour of the 17th Ulto—I have seen the Manufacturer of Glass and have given to him the different sizes you have written for and the Number of each. He cannot accomodate you, at this moment, with the largest panes of the best kind of Glass he therefore wishes three week in which time he will have the whole ready boxed for Shiping; After I [s]hall embrace the earliest opportunity of forwarding it.

I conversed respecting the place of payment thereon, found that if the money should be paid at Baltimore it would be equal to its being paid here. With the Acct you will have the name of the house there to which it is to be paid.[1] With the greatest esteem I am my dear General your most obedient servant

B. Lincoln

ALS, DLC:GW. The letter was incorrectly dated "May 3d." GW wrote below the docket, "Ought to have been 3d April 1799."

1. Lincoln wrote from Boston on 2 May: "I have the pleasure to inform you my dear General that your glass is packed & ready for Shiping and that I shall take the earliest oppy of forwarding it to you It will be recommended to the care of Mr [Thomas] Porter. My friend Mr Crocker will call pay his respects & deliver this line" (DLC:GW). Lincoln wrote again on 11 May: "I have the pleasure of Shipping on board the Schoner Lucy[,] Daniel Howes Master[,] bound to Alexandria two boxes of Glass for you I have requested our friend Mr [Thomas] Porter to receive it & pay freight As soon as I receive the bill I will forward it" (DLC:GW).

On 4 June, the same day that GW wrote William Thornton that the glass had arrived in Alexandria from Boston, Lincoln wrote to GW: "The Glass maker has this moment mentioned to me that he has discovered a mistake in sending on your Glass that one of your boxes 12⅝ by 12⅝ was left behind and an other box with different glass sent in the place of it, By the Schooner Nancy[,] Frost master[,] you will receive the right box—By the enclosed bill you will know the expence and at the foot of it you will learn the house to which payment is to be made. N.B. The Glass must be set Convex out" (DLC:GW). GW wrote Thornton on 16 June about the mistake in the shipping of the glass and gave him instructions about returning the box containing the wrong glass.

GW's correspondence regarding his payment for the glass is printed in note 1, GW to Lincoln, 1 July.

Letter not found: from Daniel Morgan, 3 April 1799. On 10 April GW wrote Morgan: "I had the pleasure to receive your letter of the 3d instant."[1]

1. The letter to GW was a duplicate of Morgan's letter to Alexander Hamilton, the text of which is printed in GW to Morgan, 10 April, n.1.

Letter not found: from Charles Demoumonier, 5 April 1799. On 6 April Tobias Lear wrote Demoumonier: "General Washington has received your letter to him dated the 5 inst. . . ."

To William Booker

Sir,   Mount Vernon April 7th 1799
Your letter of the 31st Ulto has been duly received.[1]

The first of June will answer my purposes very well, for you to be here; and I shall expect you at that time, or by the 10th accordingly.

It will not, I presume, require much time to erect the Mill, and if done before the Water of my Grist Mill fails, it is all I require. In the meanwhile the Scantling shall be prepared agreeably to your directions.[2] With esteem I am Sir Your Obedt Hble Servant

Go: Washington

ALS (letterpress copy), DLC:GW.
    1. Letter not found.
    2. See GW to Booker, 3 Mar., and notes.

To James McHenry

Private
My dear Sir,   Mount Vernon 7th April 1799
When your letters of the 30th & 31st Ulto were brought here, I was on a Survey of some land I hold in the vicinity of Alexandria; on which, as I was informed, & as the fact proved, considerable trespass had been committed. To complete this business I was employed near three days; and now, company will allow me to do but little more than to acknowledge the receipt of those letters.[1]

Two things, however, I shall not forbear mentioning at this time. The first is, that while I was at Phila. & since, when I heard your conduct arraigned for not having the Augmented Force organized sooner, & for the consequent delay in Recruiting; I did then, & on all other proper occasions, declare that circumstances over which you had no controul, were the causes thereof; & that no blame ought to be attached to you. The other matter is, that if the issuing of Commissions to those who have accepted their Appointments, is to be suspended until you hear from all those who have not acknowledged the receipt of your Circular letter, or some missive (if the Circular is not competent thereto) is not given by which the accepting Officers may know what they have to rely on—be entitled to pay—and be authorized (when they shall be so Instructed) to enter on the Recruiting Service, that it may be months—nay a year—before this will happen.

Those who live in Post Towns—near Post Offices—or who are in the habit of enquiring at these places for letters, would have been enabled to answer your Address to them in time; but a number of others may be uninformed of your letter to them at this hour; especially as many of them may have been sent to wrong Offices, & will only be heard of by the Advertisement of them.

Let me ask then, if there would be any ineligibility in inserting in the Gazettes of the respective States, the names & grades of those belonging thereto, who have returned no answer—requesting a yea—or nay—without further delay; assigning the reason for such a mode of application.

A notification of this kind would reach them through the medium of some friend, even if they did not see the Gazettes themselves; & accomplish in a short time what may be tedious without.[2] I will add no more at present than that I am always Your Affece

Go: Washington

ALS, NhD; ALS (letterpress copy), DLC:GW.

1. GW "Went up to four mile run" on 3 April to survey his land there (*Diaries*, 6:340). For references to GW's tract of land on Four Mile Run, see GW to Ludwell Lee, 26 April, and note 2 of that document.

2. See GW to McHenry, 23 April, and note 4 of that document.

To James McHenry

Sir,   Mount Vernon Apl 7th 1799

Enclosed are two letters of application for Appointments in the Army of the United States—One from Genl Morgan covering a letter from Capt. A. C. Randolph applying for an office in the Cavalry instead of the Infantry where you will find him among the newly appointed Captains. I have little or no personal knowledge of Capt. Randolph; but from the manner in which Genl Morgan speaks of him, and the opportunities he must have had of forming an opinion of him & his qualifications from observation, I have no doubt but his recommendation will have great weight.[1]

The other letter is from Mr Theoderic Lee, a brother to Majr Gen. Henry Lee. With this Gentleman I have had no opportunity of forming any personal knowledge. He lives in Berkley County in this State and has been married about 4 or 5 years. His brother the Atty Genl of the U.S. or some other persons of his acquaintance may be able to give you any information respecting Mr Lee if it shd be desired.[2] I have the honor to be very respectfully Sir Yr Mo. Ob. St

G. W——

Df, in Tobias Lear's hand, DLC:GW.

1. The letter from Daniel Morgan of 3 April that GW forwarded to McHenry is in fact a duplicate, made by Morgan and sent by him to GW, of his letter to Hamilton of that date, which is printed below in note 1 to GW's letter of 10 April to Morgan. Archibald C. Randolph's letter to Morgan, dated 14 Mar. 1799, is in the Hamilton Papers (DLC). Henry Lee wrote to GW on 22 May 1799 saying that Randolph was qualified for a cavalry command, and on 12 June Morgan repeated his recommendation of him.

2. The letter from Theodorick Lee (1766–1849) has not been found. GW had at least met Lee, for he records in his diary a visit by Lee to Mount Vernon in October 1786 (*Diaries*, 5:53). Lee was not among those named as officers in the Virginia regiments of the New Army (see List of Officers for Virginia Regiments in the New Army, c.21 May 1799, enclosed in James McHenry to GW, 21 May 1799).

Letter not found: from William Vans Murray, 7 April 1799. On 26 Oct. 1799 GW wrote Murray that "Within the space of a few days" he had four letters from Murray, including a "duplicate of one of the 7th of April (the original is missing)."

To James Welch

Sir   Mount Vernon April 7th 1799
I have received your letter of the 10th of March from Rockingham County, and although I have no expectation of deriving any

payment from your Kentucky Expedition, yet, I will (inconvenient as it is to me) wait a while longer to know the result of it: desiring you to be persuaded, in the meantime, that you have not got a person *now*, that will be trifled with in your dealings.

It would be uncandid, Mr Welch, not to inform you, that I have heard too much of your character lately, not to expect tale after tale, and relation after relation, of your numerous disappointments, by way of excuses for the non-compliance of your agreement with me: but this I can assure you will not answer your purposes. It is not difficult for a person who has no ground on which to expect a thousand cents, to talk with facility and ease of his expectation of receiving ten times as many dollars—the relation of disappointments of which, according to his account, he conceives is quite sufficient to ward off the payment of his own solemn Contracts, & to satisfy his Credito⟨rs⟩.

I am not unacquainted, Sir, with your repeated declarations of your having purchased my Lands on the Great Kanawa, & endeavouring by that means, and such like impositions, & misrepresentations, to obtain extensive credit where you were not known. Letters, to enquire into the truth of these things, have been written to me on the Subject.[1] Be cautious therefore how you provoke explanation⟨s⟩ that must, inevitably, end in your disgrace and entire loss of character. A character is valuable to all men, and not less so to a Speculator.

I will, before I conclude, assure you in the most unequivocal terms of two things—First, that I am in extreme want of the money which you gave me a solemn promise I should receive the first of January last; and secondly—that however you may have succeeded in imposing upon, and deceiving others, you shall not practice the like game with me, with impunity. To contract new Debts, is not the way to pay old ones. Nor is it a proof that you have any disposition to do it, when you are proposing to buy lands &ca &ca on credit (or partial advances) which can answer no other purpose than that of speculation—or (if you have them) of withholding the means which ought to be applied in the discharge of engagements, & debts, proceeding therefrom, which you are bound by every tie to do.

Consider this letter well; and then write without any deception[2] to Sir, Your Very Hble Servt

Go: Washington

ALS (letterpress copy), DLC:GW.

1. For Parson Weems's inquiry about Welch, see Mason Locke Weems to GW, 26 Mar. 1799.

2. See Welch to GW, 25 April, 16 May 1799.

From Thomas Law

Dear Sir,   Washington April 9th 1799.

I am honoured with your obliging note by Mr Lear,[1] the "Barclay" is arrived at Philadelphia[2] Mr Miller sends by Mr Simpson on the same ships two bags, one countg 30 lb. of grain, and the other 40 lb. of a different kind, together with some 12 or 14 smaller seeds of the cold weather for the purpose of food for mare and horse.[3] There are 175 parcels of different seeds all marked with the scientific names &ca.[4]

We are all occupied in the city by gardening. Eliza desires her most afft. regards & I remain With unfeigned esteem and respect, Your afft. humble servt

                                                            Thos Law

Sprague transcript, DLC:GW.

1. GW's note to Law has not been found, but it could have been dated as late as 7 April when Lear wrote to Alexander Hamilton from Mount Vernon. See GW to Hamilton, 25 Feb. 1799 (first letter), n.2.

2. In an undated letter, assigned the date c.25 April, Law wrote GW that the "George Berkely" had arrived in Philadelphia with "the Boxes." See note 4.

3. Mr. Miller may be the prominent Philadelphia merchant John Miller, Jr. Mr. Simpson has not been identified.

4. It would seem that Law had received and was forwarding to GW the enclosed List of Plants in Box No. 1. For Genl Washington and List of seeds in Box No. 2 For Genl Washington before the two boxes from India (or the East Indies) had themselves arrived at Georgetown from Philadelphia (see note 2). In his letter dated c.25 April, Law indicates that that letter itself along with the two boxes were being conveyed across the Potomac to GW at Mount Vernon in the *George Berkeley*. The list of the botanic names of forty-six plants in box 1 includes ornamental trees, shrubs, herbs, and other plants of all sorts, many semitropical and tropical: such plants as loquat, mango, lichee and betel nuts, crape myrtle, gardenia, French honeysuckle, marjoram, spirea, cactus, and coffee. This list and the list of 175 packets of seeds of different exotic plants are in DLC:GW.

To Alexander Hamilton

Private

My dear Sir,   Mount Vernon 10th April 1799

I have received your letter of the 27th ulto, enclosing a design of dividing the State of Virginia into Divisions, & subdivisions, for the head quarters of the Rendezvouses in each: asking my opinion of the proper distribution of them, for the convenience of the Recruiting Service.

The Grand division of the State, I conceive to be well allotted— and with the following alterations, the sub-division of it may be so likewise: but of the latter, I can speak with no precision, because of the number of New Counties which have been established, the situation of which I know not, and even the names of some were unknown to me before.

The alterations I propose, are as follow—1st to make Hobbs-hole, instead of the Bolling Green, the 8th Rendezvous (refering to the plan you sent me)—because, as you will perceive by the Map of Virginia, Caroline County is the uppermost in *that* subdistrict, and the Bolling Green lyes at the upper corner of the said County. 2d Let Fairfax & Loudoun Counties (which were formerly one) form a subdivision in place of Fairfax & Fauquier, which are seperated by other Counties. Alexandria, or Leesburgh may be the head quarters of that Rendezvous. The first is, (comparatively), large & populous, & on Navigation; the other is 40 miles above Navigation, & a small Village—both are healthy, and well supplied with provisions &ca. 3d Prince William and Fauquier ought to be annexed, instead of Prince William & Loudoun, which join at the extreme corners *only*. Dumfries in Prince William, or Fauquier Court Ho. might be the Rendezvous. The first is on Navigation; the latter 40 miles above, & more central. 4th York Town is more in the centre of the 6th subdivision than Williamsburgh; & 5th Northumberland Court House is too low for the 9th subdivision; either Westmoreland or Richmond Court Houses in point of centrality, would be more eligable.[1]

General Lee's absences from home, canvassing for the ensuing Election of Representatives to Congress, and an indisposition with which he has (as I have lately heard) been siesed, from it, has been, I presume, the cause of your not having received an answer to your letter; for I am certain Mr Bushrod Washington wd have left it at his house as he returned home, agreeably to his promise to me.[2]

Your letters to Colonels Parker and Bently I have forwarded by the Post; the 1st under Cover to General Morgan, to whom Parker is a neighbour; the other to Colo. Carrington who will be able to give it a safe Conveyance from Richmond; to the Post Office in which, it must have proceeded.[3]

Not an Officer in this State (that has come to my knowledge) has yet received his Commission; to the great dissatisfaction of *all*, & relinquishment of many; who would no longer remain in a state of suspence and idleness. With great truth, I remain My dear Sir Your Affecte Hble Servant

Go: Washington

ALS, DLC: Hamilton Papers; ALS (letterpress copy), DLC:GW.

1. For reference to Hamilton's enclosed "design of dividing the State of Virginia into Divisions" for recruiting, see Hamilton to GW, 27 Mar., n.2. Hamilton responded from New York on 17 April: "I have the honor of your letter of the 10th instant and am much obliged by the trouble you have been so good as to take. The alterations you suggest are adopted. . . . P.S. I have written to the Secy of War on the Subject of Comissions" (DLC: Hamilton Papers). Hamilton's letter to Secretary of War James McHenry, 15 April, is calendared in Syrett, *Hamilton Papers*, 23:44.

2. Hamilton enclosed his letter to Henry Lee of 18 Feb. in a letter to GW of that date. See also Hamilton to GW, 27 March. Henry Lee answered on 12 April Hamilton's letter of 18 Feb. (DLC: Hamilton Papers).

3. For the forwarding of Hamilton's letter to Col. Thomas Parker, see GW to Daniel Morgan, 10 April. GW's draft of a letter to Edward Carrington of this date reads: "Dear Sir, The enclosed letter was forwarded to me by the Inspector General of the Armies of the United States, to whose superintendance the recruiting service is committed that it might be put into the best channel for getting to Colo. [William C.] Bentley's hands with safety and dispatch. As I am unacquainted with the Post Office which is most convenient to Colo. Bentley, and know not how to forward it directly to him, I have taken the liberty of putting it under cover to you, requesting you will be so good as to have it transmitted to its address by the most ready & certain conveyance. With very great regard, I am Dear Sir, Your most Obedt Servt" (Df, DLC:GW).

To William B. Harrison

Sir,　　　　　　　　　　　　　　　　Mount Vernon 10th April 1799

Your letter of the 28th of last month has been duly received, and is entitled to my thanks for the details it contains; and for the assurance you have given me ⟨o⟩f a preference in Renting yr Land. But as there is not the smallest probability of my Renting, or buying, while you hold both at the rates which have been mentioned, I by no means desire that you should miss an opportunity of doing either, on my Account.

It is not for me to say, by what means others would be enabled to pay a Rent of more than two hundred dollars pr Annum; for admitting there were only 300 acres in the tract, & rating these at $12 pr acre the interest thereof would come to $216 dollars, & as this is your mode of fixing, and asking a Rent of me—I must decline it. It is not, I say, for me to pronounce what others can do in this way.[1] but I will aver that I could not pay that Rent by any thing I could raise on the land, as I think you would have no hesitation in acknowledging, if you were to examine the situation of it with accuracy. Nor would I be concerned with it at all, unless I could have a lease of it for a certain term of years because, if I am not more mistaken than I believe I am, there is not wood on it to supply fencing & firing three years (if that) and because, therefore, I should have surrounded it with a large & deep ditch—probably with a hedge also—which would cost more money than ought to be laid out upon uncertain contingencies. And moreover, because $216 is ⟨*illegible*⟩ more than 2500 lbs. of Tobacco or 3000 either, can be estimated at; even with the addition of 5 bls of Fish.

Who Jno. Robinson is, I know not, with certainty, but if it is the person I conjecture, I believe it may be said without much impropriety that there is a wide difference between engaging a Rent, and paying it: that, however, is no look out of mine. Nor do I know who the person is that offered you £2400 for the Land, payable in Welch's Bonds, but you may receive it ⟨from⟩ me as a fact, that he had better reason for not warranting those Bonds than he disclosed to you, as I could make you sensible of, if it was necessary & proper, to go into the detail. I *know* Welch, *WELL*—I have good reason to know him—and *believe* if you had been disposed to have laid out Cash, or any thing else of *real* value, for those Bonds, you might have got a *great* bargain if the *sound of a large* nominal price instead of a *small* real one, would have constituted it.[2]

As to Mr Hamilton, you perhaps are as well, if not better acquainted with him than I am, and therefore I shall add nothing concerning this person but will make the same observation on purchasing, as I did on Renting, namely that contracting is one thing—& fulfilling an engagement is another; but, if payment however is well secured, it may be good at last—and as Hudibras says every thing is worth what it will fetch[3]—If you can get the interest of twelve dollars an acre as Rent, or that sum per acre on a Sale of the Land, and the one, or the other *actually* paid, the Land is worth that sum to you. The Tenant, or Purchaser is to consider what the value of it is to him, & the man who means to pay, will do so. You observe that what may be deemed a high Rent *now*, will prove a low one some years hence; in general, the observation is true; but it applies more particularly to New lands, lands in the interior part of the Country, or Lands under particular circumstances—and capable of improvement; But not to old & worn out land, devoid of Timber & Wood, without a prospect of pro⟨duci⟩ng either—and no earthly means of improving it. These fall, or are left for new lands.

I never heard of Colo. Mason's and Mr Chichester's Survey of the Lands hereabouts; but as you talk of getting yours run round this Spring, if you will come & take a bed at my house, I have a Clerk (living with me) who Surveys very well & shall do it for you without cost, the next day. and on account of the putting out of the Leaves of the Trees, the sooner it is done the better. The lines between you & me, I know perfectly—the others no doubt can be found[4]—With esteem I am—Sir—Yr Very Hble Servt

Go: Washington

ALS (letterpress copy), DLC:GW.

1. GW inserted, or traced over, a number of words in pencil. Here, he struck out "do in this way" and wrote in "afford to give."

2. For GW's views on James Welch's character, see his letter to Welch of 7 April 1799.

3. GW had owned a copy of Samuel Butler's *Hudibras* for at least forty years. See *Papers, Colonial Series*, 6:292.

4. See Harrison's response of 24 April; see also Harrison to GW, 28 March.

To James McHenry

Sir,　　　　　　　　　　　　　　　Mount Vernon April 10. 1799

Enclosed is a letter and sundry Certificates which have been handed to me by a Monsr Demoumonier, a French Gentln who is desirious of entering into the service of the United States in the military line.[1]

I forward this letter & these documents to you as I have done all of a similar nature which have come to my hand; but how far it may comport with the line of policy marked out by the Govt of the U.S. to admit a foreigner i[n]to its Service, and particuliarly a Frenchman at this time, you know better than myself. I shall therefore make no observation on the subject. I have the honor to be very respectfuly Sir your mo. ob. st

G. Washington

Df, in Tobias Lear's hand, DLC:GW.

1. On 6 April Tobias Lear wrote Charles Demoumonier: "General Washington has received your letter to him dated the 5 inst. expressing a wish to enter into the American Service, and enclosing sundry certificates &c. to shew the ground on which your pretension is founded. In obedience to the General's commands I have to inform you, that the appointment of Officers in the American Army does not lie with him but with the President of the United States; to whom application should be made, through the Secretary of War. When applications of a similar nature to your's is made to the General, he causes them to be transmitted to the Secretary of War, who will place them in the proper channel to receive the attention they shall merit. If it is your wish that the papers accompanying your letter to General Washington should be forwarded to the Secretary of War, the General will cause it to be done on your signifying the same; otherwise they will be returned to you in a letter lodged in the Post office" (DLC:GW). Neither Demoumonier's letter nor its enclosures have been found. Demoumonier, who has not been identified, replied to Lear from Alexandria on the same day: "Yours of this date has just come to hand and it is my wish that my papers accompanying my Letter may be forwarded by General Washington to the Secretary of War as you mention" (DLC:GW).

To Daniel Morgan

Dear Sir,   Mount Vernon April 10th 1799

I had the pleasure to receive your letter of the 3d instant, covering the Copy of a letter from Captn A.C. Randolph to yourself, expressing a wish to be removed from the Infantry to the Cavalry. These letters I have forwarded to the Secretary of War, who, I have no doubt, will, considering the favourable auspices under which Captn Randolph is introduced, make any arrangement he can, consistent with the good of the service, to promote his wishes.[1]

I take the liberty to enclose to your care a letter from General Hamilton, the Inspector General of the Armies of the United States, to Colo. Thomas Parker. This letter relates to the recruiting service, which is under the direction of the Inspector General, and it is desireable that it should get to Colo. Parkers hands as soon as possible: I have, therefore, put it under cover to you as being the most sure and direct mode of conveyance.[2]

I assure you, my dear Sir, it gave me not a little pleasure to find the account of your death in the new's papers was not founded in fact[3]—and I sincerely pray that many years may elapse before that event takes place, and that in the meantime, you may be restored to the full enjoyment of your health, and to your usefulness in Society, being, with very great regard Your sincere friend & servt

Go: Washington

LS, in Tobias Lear's hand, NN: Myers Collection; copy, in Albin Rawlins's hand, DLC:GW.

1. The letter of 3 April that Morgan wrote to GW has not been found, but in his letter to Alexander Hamilton of that date Morgan appended this postscript: "I have wrote duplicates of the above to the Secretary of War [James McHenry] & Genl Washington." Morgan's letter to Hamilton reads: "I take the liberty to inclose you a letter from Major Archibald C. Randolph on the subject of his appointment in the Army of the United States. Knowing him intimately I can with certainty pronounce that his talents as a Soldier declare him better calculated for the Cavalry than the Infantry, his virtues as a man are such as give him universal estimation among those who know how to appreciate merit, confident that you are ever rendered happy in being the means of forwarding virtue to its wished for ends, I must intreat your assistance in procuring for Major Randolph the appointment expressed in his letter by him to me. Major Randolph has seen considerable service he marched in 1794 against the Insurgents, commanding one of the best Troops of Cavalry in the Virginia line, in which service he continued three months, on the dismission of the Army he was appointed to the command of a Squadron of Cavalry, and attached to the Army I had the honor to command, where he served six months longer. On the disbanding this Army, I promoted him to the rank of Major, and gave him the command of a Battalion for a further six months service, those troops he march'd to Presqe-Ile—in those situations as stated above he conducted himself with so much attention, discipline & vigilance as to gain the hearts and wishes of all those who had the pleasure of his acquaintance. I cannot conclude this letter without declaring to you, that I think him calculated to make a great officer" (DLC: Hamilton Papers). See also GW to McHenry, 7 April (second letter).

2. See Hamilton to GW, 27 March.

3. Morgan left Congress in late February because of illness, and on 18 April 1799 a letter from Morgan appeared in the *Columbian Mirror and Alexandria Advertiser* in which Morgan says his family had despaired of his life, but the erroneous notice of his death to which GW refers has not been found.

From Bushrod Washington

Walnut-farm April 10. [17]99

My dear Uncle   near the Cross roads

The deed from Genl Lee to you has been duly executed, acknowledged and certified, so as to entitle it to be recorded in the General Court. I shall in a few days send it down to the clerk of that Court, to record it in June. I enclose your deed to Lee, that you may have it proved in Fairfax Court this month, and being certified by the Clerk you will immediately enclose it to "Mr ——— Allen clerk of the General Court—Richmond" with a request that he will in June have it admitted to record.[1]

I wish I could speak of the Congressional election in this District with any sort of confidence. The general opinion is, that the majority either way will be very inconsiderable, and this I believe will be the event. Indisposition has obstructed Genl Lee's exertions very much to his injury. The favorable moments were improved by the enemies of the Government, and deep[e]r rooted impressions were made against him by the most scandalous and unfounded aspersions upon his private character. No misrepresentation of the views & conduct of the Government was too monstrous to deter its enemies; but as this would of itself have been ineffectual, it was deemed necessary to assasinate his reputation as much as possible. He is now making great exertions, and is successful in removing many prejudices. There is but a small part of this County affected by Jacobin principles; I have been to every house in that neighbourhood, and endeavoured to expose the many ridiculous and scandalous misrepresentations which had been made of the Government. I hope I was not entirely unsuccessful. Argument in public is carefully avoided by those Men, because they have not truth to support the facts upon which they reason in secret. There is very little doubt, but that this County will send fœderal men to the assembly.[2]

I am informed that Mr Tayloe intends to resign his commission in the army. Under this idea, Mr Thomas Turner has applied to me to mention to you his wishes to get into the Cavalry, supposing that the above resignation will render the exchange of his present office for a Captancy in the Cavalry, not improper. Whether this be the case or not, I cannot say; but as his application originally was for an appointment in this service, and as he considers himself better fitted for this than the infantry, I shall be very happy if he could be gratified. I am intimately acquainted with him, and am persuaded that he will make a valuable officer. He is an ardent and an useful friend of the Government in this part of the Country, and is besides a young man of high honor.[3] Nancy unites with me in love to yourself & my Aunt—Believe me to be most sincerely My dear Uncle your Affect. Nephew & much obliged Sert

B. Washington

Since writing the above I recd by Colo. Ball your Letter and your present of the F⟨ederalist⟩ for which I return you many thanks. B.W.[4]

ALS, ViMtV.

1. In March 1798 Bushrod Washington advised GW to secure from Lee a new deed to the land in Kentucky that Lee had conveyed to GW in 1795, and it took until February 1799 to achieve this. See Bushrod Washington to GW, 13 Mar. 1798, n.4, Alexander Spotswood to GW, 22 Mar. 1797, n.1, and Henry Lee, Jr., to GW, 28 Feb. 1799, n.1. Wilson Allen became clerk of the Virginia General Court in June 1797.

2. Bushrod Washington wrote GW on 26 April to inform him of the election of Light-Horse Harry Lee to Congress and of "two federal men" to represent Westmoreland County in the Virginia House of Delegates.

3. John Tayloe wrote GW on 10 Feb. of his misgivings about accepting the offered commission as major of the Regiment of Light Dragoons because of the likelihood of his being replaced in the state senate by a Republican. GW replied two days later and agreed that Tayloe's "Services in the civil line" were more important than they would be in the military. See also Tayloe to GW, 26 Mar., and note 2 of that document. GW wrote James McHenry on 23 April about Thomas Turner; see also Bushrod Washington to GW, 21 Sept. 1798, n.1.

4. GW's letter to Bushrod Washington has not been found. The most recent known letter from GW to his nephew is dated 31 Dec. 1798, but Bushrod had been at Mount Vernon as recently as 26 February.

From Clement Biddle

Dear Sir   Philad. April 11 1799

I have received $25.82 Interest for 1 April On your funded debt which is to your credit.[1]

Mr Latimer our Collector informed me there were four packages in the Custom house directed for you Which he would deliver

to me as he knew I did your business—Capt. Ellwood being ready
to sail I have put them on board his Vessel and you have the bill of
Loading inclosed.[2] I am with Great respect Dr Sir Your very hu.
Serv.

Clement Biddle

ALS, DLC:GW.

1. On 28 May 1797 GW authorized Biddle to receive the interest on his "certificates at the Treasury," and a year later to the day he authorized Biddle to sell
most of them. On 1 July 1798 GW noted in Ledger C, 19, that Biddle had received $25.82 as interest on "the remaing 6 & 3 prCent Stock."

2. For the likely contents of the "four packages," see GW to Biddle, 21 April.
See also Thomas Law to GW, c.25 April. George Latimer was collector of the
customs at Philadelphia.

From William Hambly

Hond Sir   Falmo[uth, England] April 13th 1799
    I have taken the liberty of sending you a fine old Cheshire
Cheese—consigned to my Friends Messrs Thompson & Veitch of
Alexandria—which I hope will arrive safe and in good Condition. I have requested my Friends to send the Cheese on its arrival
to Mount Vernon—and I hope you will do me the Honour to
accept it—which will afford me much real pleasure. I feel very
much obliged by your Present of Hams—which unfortunately
went into the Hands of Victor Hughes, or some of his Fraternity.[1]
I hope kind Heaven will long preserve your invaluable Life—and
America will ⟨long⟩ enough the Blessings of internal Tranquility—
under the influences of her well established System.
    Permit me to assure you of my High respect for your immacu-
late Character—and that I remain most sincerely Your obt humble Servant

W: Hambly

ALS, DLC:GW.

1. On 17 Feb. 1797 Hambly wrote GW about having sent him through Thompson & Veitch "an old Cheshire Cheese," for which on 28 July 1798 GW thanked
him and told him of sending him in England "half a dozen Hams" cured by
Martha Washington. On 1 Sept. 1799 GW wrote Hambly to thank him for the
cheese sent at this time and to say that he was "making another trial" to "get a
few (Virginia) Hams" to Falmouth. Victor Hugues (Hughes) was the French Directory's special agent in the West Indies.

From James Anderson (of Scotland)

Isleworth, near London, April 15th, 1799. In a very long and repetitious passage Anderson expounds on the military, naval, and commercial advantages to Britain, and disadvantages to France, of France's public policy. He then writes: "To such persons as believe that the stability of States, and the happiness of a people, are to be measured exactly by the amount of their wealth, and the extent of their foreign trade and manufactures, these facts will be deemed of the most soothing nature for Britain; but to me they convey not any such idea. Nations, like individuals, have not their happiness augmented in proportion to the increase of their riches. They generally act with much more propriety when they are in moderate circumstances, than when superabounding in wealth. Power engenders pride, haughtiness, and a most intolerable self-sufficiency; this disgusts those with whom they must have dealings, and encourages rivals. It creates enemies at the same time; enemies, whose ill will is only displayed at the first in secret; but by and by they become open and declared as such. Wars of course follow, and many evils which it would be painful to enumerate. These evils will be, to you, very obvious, and might have been (or rather may be) foreseen by our rulers, whose duty it should have been to counteract their influence. This, I am sorry to say, has not been done. Owing to the greater profits that are to be made in trade or manufactures than in agriculture, at the same time that such persons are more independent of others, and at greater liberty to act as occasion may require, young men of spirit and enterprise naturally prefer the first, and neglect the last. Fiscal regulations might easily be adopted to counteract in some measure this evil; but this has not been attended to. Some late taxes, particularly the salt tax and the income tax, have a direct contrary effect; for they press much more heavily on country gentlemen and farmers, than on those who are engaged in trade and manufactures: bad is thus made worse, and a spirit of turbulence and insubordination is disseminated among the lower orders of society, which must break out on the first check that business, in their particular line, experiences; and this must give rise to a system of coercive government that is only productive of general misery, and individual distress; not to mention the discontents that are the never failing attendants on the occasional recurrence of years of scarcity, which are inevitable where this system of economy is adhered to.

"None of these effects would have been experienced if the less brilliant but more steady operations of agriculture had been duly cherished and encouraged. There would have been no difficulty in finding other sources of productive taxes here, had they been fought for; but it too often happens in financial arrangements, that men overlook the only *certain* means of augmenting the revenue, viz. that of adopting measures to promote the health of the body politic in all its members; and, instead of supplying the goose with plenty of nourishing food to make her with certainty lay abundance of golden eggs for many years to come, in their eagerness to get all the eggs at once, they kill the goose herself, and thus cut off the source of that future supply which would have been certain. Such, Sir, are the reflections which occur to my mind, when I contemplate this important subject: but I interfere not with the department of any one. Of too little importance to have any influence on the political system, I see these things as if I saw them not; and quietly go forward in my retired course of life, without annoying others, or perplexing myself about things that I cannot mend.

"Having in some measure regained my usual state of health, I have, at last, begun the work that I had in contemplation, the first number of which will accompany this; and which (entitled, *Recreations in Agriculture, Natural History, Arts, and Miscellaneous Literature*) I beg you will honour with your acceptance, as a small testimony of the most respectful esteem and warmest attachment on my part. It can lay claim to that honour on no account but one, which is, that, however my judgment may err, it is my sincerest wish that every line in it may be calculated, in one way or other, to promote the welfare or happiness of some human being; and it shall be my uninterrupted study to make it do so. At my time of life (now declining into the vale of years) disengaged as I am from all those worldly pursuits which excite the active energies of most men, things appear under a very different aspect from what they did in the morning of life: feeling not the smallest tincture of ambition, nor the stimulating impulse of the love of gain, I stood in need of some object that could give a little activity to the mind, so as to suffer the thread of life to be spun out till the period of its termination shall arrive, without experiencing in too strong a degree that languid apathy which is the unavoidable attendant upon total inactivity. In casting about for this kind of stimulus to exertion, I could discover none that promised to be either so steady in its effects, or so pleasing in its operation, as that which I have chosen. For as I have come under certain obligations to the public, I cannot consider myself to be at liberty, in case of any fit of indolence, to abandon it; and therefore must go on, unless very powerful reasons shall oppose it. As the mind must thus be steadily directed at all times towards an object that has ever been strongly interesting to me, I hope it will prove an agreeable *recreation* to myself at least; to insure which, I have determined, that while it is continued, not one word shall be admitted into it that does not appear to me to be calculated to answer the purpose above stated. It is, therefore, probable, that the work will assume a tone somewhat different from most publications, the authors of which are in general actuated by considerations that can have scarcely any effect upon me. How far the public may relish a performance conducted in this manner, or whether I shall be able to carry it into effect in the way I propose, remains to be ascertained. In all events my part is taken; nor shall I on that account be subjected to any embarrassment. Should the sale be such as not fully to indemnify the expense of carrying it forward in a *proper* manner, I shall, without hesitation or struggle of any sort, relinquish the work; conceiving that to be the most unequivocal criterion that can be adopted, either that the plan is improper, or the execution deficient; and I shall in this respect be directed by the public.

"The succeeding numbers of this work shall be forwarded to you as soon as an opportunity offers after the publication of each: I am only at a loss to know through what channel they may with most safety be sent. Will you have the goodness to let me know the name of your bookseller in Philadelphia? They might be forwarded to his care.[1]

"It gives me much satisfaction to learn, that the gardener behaves himself properly; for I was anxious on that account. A good servant is, in this country, a rare acquisition. It does not always happen that a good master meets with such; but he has a much better chance for it than others. I hope he will continue to please."[2]

Selections from the Correspondence of George Washington, and James Anderson (Charlestown, Mass., 1800), 20–32. In the introduction to this work, Anderson suggests that GW may not have received this letter, "for the same ship that brought the news to this country of General WASHINGTON's death, also brought intelligence that the parcel which contained that letter had reached Philadelphia" (p.11).

1. Twelve numbers of Anderson's *Recreations in Agriculture, Natural-History, Arts and Miscellaneous Literature*, arranged in two volumes and published in 1799 and 1800, eventually found their way into GW's library (Griffin, *Boston Athenæum Washington Collection*, 10).

2. The gardener at Mount Vernon, William Spence, arrived from Scotland in October 1797. See GW to James Anderson of Scotland, 25 July 1798, n.3.

To Henry Lee, Jr.

Dear Sir,   Mount Vernon 18th April 1799

Your favor of the 28th of Feby came duly to hand. On the subject of which I shall say nothing until I have the pleasure of seeing you in May, as promised.

The intention of this letter is to enquire—as you have frequently offered it—whether you have, at this time, any Corn for Sale.

I want more than my Nephew of Westmoreland can furnish me with, and will allow for what you can spare the same price I am to give him[1]—that is—the Alexandria *Cash* price, at the time of delivery (sharing the freight equally)—or, I will allow fifteen shillings per barrel—the now, as I am informed, marked price, & what Mr Tayloe informs me he has just received for a vessel load he had sent to Baltimore.

Pray write me by *first* post—whether I may expect any from you, or not; how much; and when; Yours always, & sincerely ⟨&⟩ Affectionately

Go: Washington

ALS (letterpress copy), DLC:GW.

1. For GW's arrangement with his nephew William Augustine Washington to have him supply five hundred barrels of corn annually, see especially GW to Washington, 26 June, 3 Oct. 1798, and Washington to GW, 24 July 1798. See also Washington to GW, 2 May 1799. John Tayloe spent the night of 17 April at Mount Vernon (*Diaries*, 6:342–43).

From John Searson

Sir,   City Washington 18th April 1799

'Twas from the Amiable Caracter I had heard of your Excellency, (even in Europe) for Benevolence, and Humanity, that Induc'd my application, when I last arriv'd in Philadelphia in Anno 1796 and presented to your Excellency Poem on Down-Hill, (the Seat of the Earl of Bristol) you then being President of the united States: Since that period, have publish'd in Philada and New York by a Subscription of 1200 Subscribers, Poems on various Occasions, which was well received, and one of which, was forwarded (by desire of your Excellency) by Colonel Biddle to Mount Vernon;[1] And Since that Obtain'd subscriptions for 1000 Copies, at Baltimore, Alexandria, and City of Washington for the Publication of a Book never publish'd here before Call'd *The Art of Contentment* in prose and Verse but at my advanced years, find my Self Inadequat for the Business, the fatigue of travelling for Subscriptions, and returning the Books, being more than I Can well bear.[2] As I am now so near Mount Vernon, I hope in a little time to do my Self the Honor of waiting on your Excellency, so as to Obtain an Adequate Idea of Mount-Vernon, and should I return to

Europe, Publish a Poem on it there.[3] I was about 20 years chiefly in the Business of a Wholesale Mercht in Philadelphia but was unfortunately Subjected to a failure from a series of Noted losses and misfortunes in Trade, And in my youthful days, have been Tutor in one of the most reputable familys in New york, And Master of some of the best English Academys or Schools in this Country as well as Europe, have in London Now, two respectable Relations Who have both Seats in the House of Commons; offer'd obtaining for Me Clerk's place in one of the first East India Stores, But my Wish to visit America before my decease was so great as to Induce my Visiting it, having Spent the greater part of my Life in so fine a Country, but alas! on my return, found my old friends, and Acquaintance, all deceas'd or Mov'd, so that my Case Seem'd that of Humanity. And Governor Jay Could not Consistent with his Sphere of Acting, prefer me to any office without a Superior Interest here: Thus situated I have had no place of Settlement since my Arrival, nor support, but by my little Publications—Perhaps your Excellency from Humane & Benevolent Principles, might think of Some little place of Support in Some Sphere of Life in this Country, suitable to my years and Qualifications. I have to beg your Excellencys pardon for a few thoughts on my reduc'd Situation—I leave this City in a few days for Alexandria. Mrs Law near the Capitol (the other day) took a Book, and was glad to hear her say your Excellency and lady were well. May that omnipotent Ruler of the universe, ever Surround you and yours, with every real and permanent felicity is the sincere Prayer of (may it please your Excellency) Your Ever Devoted And Obedient Servant

John Searson

ALS, DLC:GW.

1. For the poems sent to GW by Searson, see Searson to GW, 2 Aug. 1797, n.2. *Poems on Various Subjects and Different Occasions*, which was in GW's library, was published in Philadelphia in 1797.

2. *The Art of Contentment; with Several Entertaining Pieces of Poetry, Descriptive of the Present Times, in the U. States of America* was printed in Baltimore in 1796.

3. Searson visited Mount Vernon on 15 May and later in the year published a book of poems entitled *Mount Vernon*.

Letter not found: from Jesse Simms, 19 April 1799. On 22 April GW wrote Simms: "I shall give no definitive answer to your letter of the 19th instant."

From William Thornton

Dear Sir   City of Washington April 19th 1799

When Colonel Lear was here he said you were desirous of knowing if Mr Blagdin had laid in all the materials requisite for your Houses, as you thought they would not only be likely to rise, but probably be difficultly obtained properly Seasoned.[1] I called on him, but not meeting with him I went the Day before yesterday to his Partner Mr Lenthall, who informed me that every Contract was made, and every material provided for. The Lumber is not yet delivered, but Mr Littleton Dennis, of the Eastern Shore, Maryland, who regularly supplied us, has been engaged in preparing what they will want, and I think he may be depended on.[2] I visited the workmen the Day before yesterday, & they progress to my Satisfaction. I took the liberty of directing Stone Sills to be laid, instead of wooden ones, to the outer Doors of the Basement, as wood decays very soon, when so much exposed to the damp; but I desired Mr Blagdin would do them with as little expense as possible. If wooden Sills could easily have been renewed I should not have directed them of Stone, but he informed me they could not without much trouble.

Mr J. Tayloe of Virga has contracted to build a House in the City near the President's Square of $13,000 value.[3]

Mr Van Stophorst from Holland, and several respectable Characters from Baltimore, paid me a visit this morning; & mean to do themselves the honor of paying you their respects tomorrow.[4]

Poor Miss Dalton was interr'd yesterday—She died the Day before by a sudden mortification. She rode out two Days before.[5]

All your Friends here are well. I hope Colonel Lear recovers. Accept, dear Sir, my most affectionate good wishes & highest respect.

                                                              William Thornton

ALS, DLC:GW.

1. See GW to Tobias Lear, 31 March.

2. Littleton Dennis of Somerset County, Md., supplied lumber for public building in the Federal City.

3. Thornton designed John Tayloe's town house in Washington, built at the intersection of New York Avenue and 18th Street, N.W., known as the Octagon. The editor of Thornton's papers quotes Tayloe's son as saying that GW "took much interest" in the building of the house (Harris, *Thornton Papers*, 1:584).

4. On 22 April GW wrote in his diary: "Mr. Vanstapherst came to dinner" (*Diaries*, 6:343). For the probable identity of Van Staphorst, see the editors' note, ibid., 343–44. For the guests that GW had "tomorrow," see the diary entry for 20 April.

5. The *Columbian Centinel* (Boston) reported on 1 May the death in Washington of Miss Sally Dalton, probably the daughter of Tristram Dalton.

Index

NOTE: Identifications of persons, places, and things in volumes 1 and 2 of the *Retirement Series* are noted within parentheses.

Adams, Abigail: illness of, 88, 120, 157–58; greetings to, 404
Adams, John, 28, 72, 82, 222, 299, 323, 383; and GW's commission, 4–6, 15; and ranking of major generals, 4–6, 11–13, 14–16, 18–23, 29–30, 34, 37–43, 44–45, 65, 66, 72, 87–88, 103, 105, 121–22, 123, 124–25, 142; and officers for New Army, 14, 15, 16–19, 63, 64, 88, 97, 98, 126, 127, 134, 193, 226, 313, 327, 333, 338, 349, 366–67, 408, 415, 441–42, 453, 454, 457, 477; and officers for Provisional Army, 14, 16–17, 38–39, 42–43; at Quincy, 14, 17, 18, 23, 157–58, 190, 193; and Prince Edward Co. (Va.) Freeholders, 95, 97, 109; and meeting of generals in Philadelphia, 103–4; appoints Bushrod Washington to U.S. Supreme Court, 113; and Timothy Pickering, 118; and William Richardson Davie, 135; and public opinion, 151; and George Logan, 202; and William Stephens Smith, 266, 292; addresses Congress, 287; James McHenry's military report to, 292, 293, 305, 306, 328; and relations with France, 337, 355; and army uniforms, 340–41, 342; uniform of, 343, 372; and organization of Provisional Army, 349; and Joel Barlow's letter to GW, 350–51, 387–88; and trade with Saint Domingue, 358; nominates ministers to France, 363, 387, 388–89, 389–90, 402–3; and John C. Ogden, 373; and Elizur Goodrich, 374; and James Wil-

kinson, 381; criticizes Thomas Paine, 387; Timothy Pickering criticizes, 389–90; and organization of New Army, 438, 456–57; and Fries's Rebellion, 452; *letters from:* to James McHenry, 6, 19, 20–21, 22, 157–58, 193, 456; to GW, 87–88, 387–89; *letters to:* from James McHenry, 5, 19–20, 21–22; from GW, 36–44, 120–21, 350–51, 403–4; from Timothy Pickering, 151; from Bernard Hubley, Jr., 272; from William Vans Murray, 388
Adams, John Quincy: and James Washington of Holland, 115, 154, 327; and Lucien Hauteval, 119; as U.S. minister to Prussia, 155, 428; *letters from:* to GW, 154–55; *letters to:* from GW, 320–21
Addison, Alexander (*see* 2 : 277–78): *Liberty of Speech and of the Press*, 244, 297, 302–3, 309, 407; and Millers Run tract, 407–8; *letters from:* to GW, 214, 407; *letters to:* from GW, 244, 407–8
Adet, Pierre-Auguste: and bribery of Congress, 151
Agriculture: and manures, 2, 164, 375; effect of Quasi-War on property values, 187; Hessian fly, 311–12, 325, 377. *See also* Mount Vernon
crops: oats, 1, 426; winter grain, 102; clover, 136, 384–85; hay, 136; corn, 164, 165, 186, 219, 426; grass, 176; wheat, 219, 273, 311–12, 325, 377, 385, 426; indian corn, 325; tobacco, 378, 409, 426; timothy, 385; rye, 426

Agriculture (*continued*)
  equipment: chaff engine, 56–57,
    273–74; pump, 166; ground
    borer, 273–74; threshing ma-
    chine, 404–5
  livestock: sheep, 56–57, 167, 177,
    220, 273–74, 359; cattle, 167,
    215, 219, 220; horses, 168, 175,
    215, 219, 220, 308, 425, 472;
    jackasses, 168, 220, 333, 334,
    335, 336, 367, 377, 458, 462–
    63; hogs, 176, 177, 215, 359;
    mules, 220, 377, 458, 462
  produce: corn, 2, 55, 57, 76–77,
    218, 379–80, 484–85; flour, 2,
    165, 186, 321–22, 358, 386,
    424, 429; wheat, 2, 4, 56, 165,
    166, 186, 218, 321–22, 326,
    395, 429; whiskey, 2; peaches,
    165; bottle brush grass, 219;
    hay, 220; fish, 336, 449, 475; to-
    bacco, 336, 452–53; potatoes,
    375–76; cider, 464; Hughes
    crab apple, 464
  seed: grass, 1, 102, 357, 358; cab-
    bage, 136; clover, 136, 385;
    oats, 136; honey locust tree,
    218–19; bottle brush grass,
    219; bluegrass, 321, 322, 351–
    52; white clover, 321, 322, 351–
    52, 386, 429; lucerne, 351–52,
    386, 423–24, 429; melon, 412,
    460; Hughes crab apple, 464;
    exotic plants, 472
  weather: drought, 99, 102, 136,
    185–86, 311, 325; frost, 185,
    186, 312; fluctuating, 377;
    snow, 385
Alexander, Joseph: and rank in New
    Army, 296
Alexander, Wallace: and officers for
    New Army, 296
Alexander, William: and officers for
    New Army, 297
Alexandria: GW visits, 241; pros-
    perity of, 280
Alexandria Academy: and Samuel
    Knox, 91
Alien and Sedition Acts: and public
    opinion, 150–51; GW defends,
    216–17; writings in support of,
    244, 288, 297, 302–3, 309; de-

bated, 287, 309–10, 346–47;
    John Marshall's view of, 309–10
Allen, John: and officers for New
    Army, 231; *letters from:* to James
    McHenry, 205, 206
Allen, Wilson: as clerk of Virginia
    General Court, 479, 480
Amein, General V., 163
American Philosophical Society:
    and Samuel Knox, 90, 91–92
Ames, Mr.: and officers for New
    Army, 233
Anderson, James (*see* 1:81): as
    Mount Vernon farm manager,
    1–4, 164–68, 185–86, 305,
    384–85, 395; GW's criticism of,
    1–4; buys wheat, 2; manages
    distillery, 3, 4, 165; acts for GW,
    35, 36, 50, 179, 180, 181, 186;
    and Richard Parkinson, 173–
    75; *letters from:* to GW, 4, 185–
    86, 395; to Mr. Garrett, 35–36,
    50; *letters to:* from GW, 1–4,
    164–68, 173–75, 384–85;
    from William Booker, 404
Anderson, James (of Scotland; *see*
    1:81): *Recreations in Agriculture*,
    483–84; *letters from:* to GW,
    482–84
Anderson, John: leaves Mount Ver-
    non, 3; manages distillery, 3–4
Andrews, Isaac: and rank in New
    Army, 234
Anthony, Joseph (*see* 1:308): and
    John Trumbull's prints, 392–
    93, 421–22; id., 394; *letters from:*
    to GW, 421; *letters to:* from GW,
    421–22
Anthony (slave): carries firewood,
    168
Arbuckle, Matthew: and rank in
    New Army, 237
Armstead, Addison: and rank in
    New Army, 238
Armstead, B. Dandridge: and rank
    in New Army, 237
Armstead, George: and rank in New
    Army, 239
Armstead, John Baylor: and rank in
    New Army, 228, 240
Armstead, William: and rank in New
    Army, 231

Armstrong, James: and rank in New Army, 101; id., 102

Ashton, Ann Washington (*see* 2 : 111), 464

Aurora (Philadelphia; *see* 1 : 300): and U.S. relations with France, 390

Austria: alliance with Naples, 73, 74

Bacon, Asa: and rank in New Army, 231

Bacon, John: and rank in New Army, 237

Bagot, Thomas: and rank in New Army, 239

Baldwin, Abraham: id., 404; *letters to:* from Joel Barlow, 403, 404

Ball, Daniel: and rank in New Army, 230

Ball, George: and debt to GW, 422–23; forwards letter, 480; *letters to:* from GW, 422–23

Baltimore: GW's reception in, 189

Banks, Tunspall: and rank in New Army, 239

Barlow, Joel (*see* 1 : 74): urges reconciliation with France, 68–72, 350–51, 387–88, 403–4; John Adams criticizes, 387–88; GW's opinion of, 403; criticizes GW, 404; *letters from:* to GW, 68–72; to Abraham Baldwin, 403–4

Barlow, Ruth Baldwin, 404

Baron, Samuel: and rank in New Army, 296

Bascom, Eunice Corse, 392

Bascom, Ezekiel L.: seeks appointment, 391–92; id., 392; *letters from:* to GW, 391–92; *letters to:* from Tobias Lear, 392

Bascom, Moses, 392

Bassett, Burwell, Jr. (*see* 1 : 486): recommends Robert Henley, 461

Baytop, James: and rank in New Army, 228, 240

Beal, Mr.: and William B. Harrison's land, 449

Beale, Priscilla: as tenant, 340

Beale, Robert: and rank in New Army, 229, 240

Beaujeau, M.: seeks commission, 360

Bedford, John: and shoes for GW, 308, 357, 358; id., 358

Bedford Court House: militia officers meet at, 83–85

Belknap, Andrew E.: and *American Biography*, 78, 80, 86–87; *letters from:* to GW, 86; *letters to:* from GW, 86

Belknap, Jeremy (*see* 2 : 304): and *American Biography*, 86

Bell, William: id., 151; reports on public opinion, 151

Belton, William: as grand master of the Maryland Masons, 189

Bennett, Van: and rank in New Army, 239

Bent, Lemuel (*see* 2 : 480–81): and rank in New Army, 233

Bentley, William C., 356; and rank in New Army, 226, 228; and Virginia military districts, 474; *letters to:* from Alexander Hamilton, 448

Benton, Lemuel: election bid defeated, 133; id., 133

Berkeley County tract: rent payments for, 378

Betton, Solomon: and overseer for GW, 35; id., 36

Biddle, Clement: acts for GW, 247, 308, 321–22, 351–52, 357–58, 386, 423–24, 429, 480–81; forwards poems, 485; *letters from:* to Tobias Lear, 247; to GW, 316, 340, 357–58, 429, 480–81; *letters to:* from GW, 321–22, 351–52, 386, 423–24; from Tobias Lear, 322

Biddle, Joseph: and Samuel Washington, 187

Biddle, Rebekah Cornell: greetings to, 321

Bingham, William (*see* 1 : 48): and U.S. minister to France, 389, 390

Bird, Otway: and rank in New Army, 226, 229

Blackburn, Richard Scott: and rank in New Army, 31–32, 227, 302; id., 32; and officers for New Army, 240

Blackburn, Thomas: seeks commission, 237, 239

Blackburne, Genl. *See* Blackwell, John

Blackwell, John: and rank in New Army, 226; and officers for New Army, 235

Blackwell, Robert: GW's notes on meeting with, 200–202; id., 202

Blagdin, George: and GW's Capitol Hill houses, 50, 52–54, 73, 77–78, 105–6, 110–11, 130–31, 138–39, 140, 144–50, 152, 153, 154, 274, 275, 276, 299–301, 347–48, 376–77, 382, 446, 452, 487; at Mount Vernon, 152; *letters from:* to GW, 106

Blount, Thomas: and officers for New Army, 203; id., 204

Blue, William K.: and rank in New Army, 230

Bolke, Dr.: sends yellow fever medicine, 164

Bonaparte, Napoleon: rumored assassination of, 403

Booker, William: builds mill for GW, 404–5, 468; builds threshing machine for GW, 405; provides agricultural advice, 405; *letters from:* to James Anderson, 404; to GW, 452; *letters to:* from GW, 404–5, 468

Boudinot, Elias (*see* 1 : 18): and wine for GW, 242–43; illness of, 243; *letters from:* to GW, 242–43

Bouyer, William: and rank in New Army, 235

Braddock, Edward, 277

Braham, John: and rank in New Army, 238

Brahm, John Gerard William De: sends yellow fever medicine to GW, 220–21; id., 221; *letters from:* to GW, 220–21; to Queen Charlotte of Great Britain, 221

Brahm, Mary Drayton Fenwick De: id., 221

Brainerd, Elijah: requests aid from GW, 328–32; id., 331; *letters from:* to GW, 328–32; *letters to:* from GW, 331

Brent, Mr.: and officers for New Army, 236

Brent, Thomas: and rank in New Army, 237

Brent, William: and rank in New Army, 237

Broadhead, Daniel: and rank in New Army, 229

Bronaugh, William (*see* 1 : 79), 210

Brook (Brooke), Robert: and rank in New Army, 235, 240

Brooks, John: and rank in New Army, 6, 268; and officers for New Army, 18, 441

Brooks, Thomas: as joiner, 6–7, 33, 35; conveys letter, 33

Brown, James: and rank in New Army, 235

Brown, John G.: and rank in New Army, 235

Brown, S., 235

Bruff, James: and John Jacob Ulrich Rivardi, 397

Buckner, Thomas: and rank in New Army, 229

Buford, Abraham, 7, 9

Bunel, Joseph: as emissary to U.S., 358

Burges, Dempsey: and officers for New Army, 203; id., 204

Burgoyne, John, 238

Burr, Aaron, 26; and rank in New Army, 6

Burrows, William Ward: and William Stephens Smith, 265–66, 292

Burton, William: address to GW, 83

Burwell, Nathaniel (*see* 1 : 369): and officers for New Army, 235, 237

Butler, Laurence: and rank in New Army, 226

Butler, Samuel: *Hudibras*, 476

Byrd, William, 210

Caldwell, James: and rank in New Army, 234

Call, Daniel: and Colvill estate, 311; id., 311; *letters from:* to GW, 311

Campbell, Arthur, 233

Campbell, John: and rank in New Army, 238

Campbell, Samuel Legrand: as trustee of Washington Academy, 207–8; id., 208; *letters from:* to GW, 207–9

Campbell, William: and rank in New Army, 229, 233

Campo Formio, treaty of, 431

Carr, Peter (*see* 1:375). *See* Langhorne, John

Carraway, John: and rank in New Army, 297

Carrington, Edward (*see* 1:217, 2:302): and rank in New Army, 6, 7; and officers for New Army, 128–30, 226–38; forwards letter, 474; *letters to:* from GW, 128–30, 474

Carrington, Robert: and rank in New Army, 236, 240

Carroll, Charles, Jr.: as aide to GW, 249–50, 279, 353; *letters from:* to GW, 249–50; *letters to:* from GW, 248–50

Carroll, Charles (of Carrollton; *see* 2:116): greetings to, 249; recommends Charles Carroll, Jr., 249, 250

Carroll, Daniel: and Capitol Hill lot, 32–33, 49, 50, 52, 73–74

Carter, Anne Butler Moore (*see* 1:494): illness of, 48, 49; greetings to, 49

Carter, Betty Lewis (*see* 1:218): Lawrence Lewis visits, 312

Carter, Charles (of Culpeper County; *see* 1:218): Lawrence Lewis visits, 312

Carter, Charles (of Shirley; *see* 1:145): cancels visit to Mount Vernon, 48–49; *letters from:* to GW, 48–49; *letters to:* from GW, 49

Carter, Landon (1710–1778): id., 368

Carter, Landon (1757–1820; *see* 1:32): views on medicine, 60–63; forwards letters, 79; and Virginia elections of 1799, 114; and John Tayloe, 367; id., 368;

letters from: to GW, 60–63; *letters to:* from GW, 79

Carter, Robert Charles (*see* 2:591): education of, 79

Carter, Robert W.: education of, 79

Carter, Robert Wormeley (1734–1797): id., 368

Carter, St. Leger Landon: education of, 79

Carter, William C.: seeks army commission, 234

Casson, Samuel: seeks navy commission, 239

Chapel Land (Mount Vernon), 410, 411; id., 411; boundaries of, 449

Charles (slave): as messenger, 353, 354; and horse for George Washington Parke Custis, 425

Charles I (of England), 320

Charles Town Academy: description of, 93–94; seeks GW's patronage, 93–94

Charles Town Academy Trustees: *letters from:* to GW, 93–94

Charlotte, queen of Great Britain: *letters to:* from John Gerard William De Brahm, 221

Chauvet, David: *letters from:* to Albert Gallatin, 150–51

Cherokee (Indians): relations with U.S., 177–78

Chichester, Richard: and William B. Harrison's land, 449, 450, 476; id., 450

Chinn, Joseph, 368

Chinn, Richard: and rank in New Army, 234, 239

Chipman, Nathaniel: as member of Congress, 170; id., 171

Church, Angelica Schuyler: id., 213; recommends Philip Church for New Army, 213; *letters from:* to GW, 213; *letters to:* from GW, 213

Church, John B.: id., 213; recommends Philip Church for New Army, 213; *letters from:* to GW, 213; *letters to:* from GW, 213

Church, Philip: as Alexander Hamilton's clerk, 43; and rank in New

Church, Philip (*continued*)
Army, 212–14; GW's opinion
of, 213, 214; id., 213; *letters
from:* to Alexander Hamilton,
244; to Charles Cotesworth
Pinckney, 244; *letters to:* from
GW, 213
Churchman, John: and Timothy
Pickering, 434–36; id., 435;
letters from: to GW, 434–36
Cincinnati, South Carolina Society
of: and relations with France,
119–20; *letters from:* to GW,
119–20; *letters to:* from GW,
119–20
Clark, Edmund: and rank in New
Army, 235
Clark, Jonathan: and rank in New
Army, 226
Clifford, Obadiah: and rank in New
Army, 237, 240
Clopton, John (*see* 2:531): and offi-
cers for New Army, 237
Clopton, William D.: and rank in
New Army, 236
Cobb, David (*see* 2:577): and rank
in New Army, 6, 19, 268
Cobbett, William (*see* 1:25): as edi-
tor of *Porcupine's Gazette*, 390
Collins, Christopher: as trustee of
Charles Town Academy, 94;
id., 94
Colston, Rawleigh (*see* 2:309):
and GW's Rough Creek tract,
85–86, 121, 131; and George
Mercer's land, 271–72; *letters
from:* to GW, 85–86, 271–72;
letters to: from GW, 121
Colvill, Thomas: estate of, 311
Compound (jackass), 463; death
of, 335
Congress: and Washington navy
yard, 10, 11; and ranking of
major generals, 12, 38, 40–41,
123; resolve of 24 November
1778, 12; resolve of 4 January
1776, 12; and officers for New
Army, 15, 19, 126–27, 158,
193, 226, 292, 299, 305, 313–
14, 338, 415, 440–41, 443–44,
453; and organization of Provisional Army, 16, 26, 328, 348,
349; accommodation of in Federal City, 32–33, 83, 280, 354,
378–79, 424; and relations
with France, 95, 96–97, 337–
38, 355, 365, 388, 403; Bushrod Washington rejects candidacy for, 114; bribery of, 151;
and Episcopal church lands in
Vermont, 170; and military
pensions, 184; and organization of New Army, 195–96,
225, 328, 342, 352; and supplies for New Army, 196; John
Adams addresses, 287; and
James McHenry's military report to John Adams, 292–93;
and organization of Hospital
Department, 328; and criticism
of James McHenry, 442–43
Constable, William: and William
Stephens Smith, 265, 266, 292;
id., 266
Cook, David T. W.: and rank in New
Army, 297
Cooper, John, 136; and rank in New
Army, 360
Craig, Mr.: and officers for New
Army, 232
Craik, George Washington: and
rank in New Army, 279, 339,
416
Craik, William (*see* 2:138): and ac-
commodation of Congress in
Federal City, 378–79
Craine, John, Jr.: and rank in New
Army, 239
Craufurd, Alice Swift Livingston: at
Mount Vernon, 152; id., 154
Craufurd, James: at Mount Vernon,
152; id., 154
Cripps, Mr.: at Mount Vernon, 375,
376
Crocker, Mr.: conveys letter, 467
Cropper, John: and rank in New
Army, 226
Crump, John: rank in New Army,
219
Cushing, T. H.: and court-martial of
Thomas Lewis, 223, 224
Cushing, William: and Bushrod
Washington, 302; id., 303
Custis, Eleanor (Nelly) Parke: greet-

ings to, 9, 34, 173, 219, 278, 367, 379, 388, 393, 412, 464; greetings from, 110, 304, 325, 339, 361, 375, 404, 460; receives poetry from Daniel Huger Horry, 117; military colors for, 125, 142; betrothed to Lawrence Lewis, 216, 279, 302, 312, 332, 333, 339, 361, 384; GW's gifts for, 242, 243, 308; at Hope Park, 280, 325; GW made guardian of, 332, 333; and GW's uniform, 342; marriage to Lawrence Lewis, 369, 378, 385–86, 393–94, 416, 460; marriage license for, 389; in Federal City, 425; *letters from:* to James McHenry, 158; *letters to:* from Martha Washington, 304

Custis, George Washington Parke (*see* 1:49), 291; greetings to, 9, 219, 412; conveys letter, 80; GW's gift for, 246; and rank in New Army, 267, 268, 279, 298, 304–5, 332–33, 339, 416, 442; away from Mount Vernon, 280, 339; bridle for, 308; and GW's uniform, 342; in Federal City, 425; horse for, 425; *letters to:* from Tobias Lear, 268, 299

Dalton, Sally: death of, 487, 488
Dalton, Tristram (*see* 2:438), 488; and Presly Thornton, 357
Dandridge, Bartholomew, Jr. (*see* 1: 23–24): as secretary to Rufus King, 89, 415, 436; and rank in New Army, 286–87, 338–39; declines commission, 415; illness of, 416; *letters from:* to GW, 89–90, 415–17; to Julius Burbidge Dandridge, 413, 414, 436; to Mary Burbidge Dandridge, 417; *letters to:* from GW, 338–40
Dandridge, Bartholomew (1737–1785): id., 340
Dandridge, John: death of, 339, 416, 436; id., 340
Dandridge, Julius Burbidge: id., 436; *letters to:* from Bartholo-

mew Dandridge, 413, 414, 436; from GW, 436
Dandridge, Mary Burbidge (*see* 1: 496), 340; and death of John Dandridge, 416; *letters to:* from Bartholomew Dandridge, 417
Dartmouth College, 329, 391, 392
Daugherty, Patrick: and rank in New Army, 233, 240
Davidson, Captain (shipmaster), 13, 430
Davidson, George, 296
Davidson, George Washington: and rank in New Army, 296
Davidson, John: witnesses deed, 208; and rank in New Army, 231, 236
Davie, William Richardson, 298; and officers for New Army, 98, 127, 134–35, 202–4, 252, 288–89, 293, 294–97, 454, 459; id., 135; nominated envoy to France, 403; *letters from:* to GW, 202–4, 294–97; *letters to:* from GW, 134–35, 288–89
Davis, Augustine (*see* 1:368): prints address, 288
Davis, Thomas (of Albemarle County): and rank in New Army, 237
Davis, Thomas (Tom; slave): as painter, 167; landscaping and brickmaking at Mount Vernon, 167, 168
Day, Benjamin: and officers for New Army, 231
Dayton, Jonathan, 123; and rank in New Army, 6, 15, 16–17, 41, 88, 121, 268; id., 26
Deakins, Francis (*see* 2:24): as GW's land agent in Montgomery County, 340; *letters from:* to GW, 320; *letters to:* from GW, 340
Deane, William: and rank in New Army, 239
Dearborne, Henry: and rank in New Army, 19; id., 27
Demoumonier, Charles: and rank in New Army, 476–77; *letters from:* to GW, 468; to Tobias Lear, 477; *letters to:* from Tobias Lear, 477

Deneale, George (*see* 2:243): and marriage license for Nelly Custis, 389; *letters to:* from GW, 389

Denman & Co. (firm): and blankets for GW, 247

Dennis, Littleton: and GW's Capitol Hill houses, 487; id., 487

Deseassies, Mr.: seeks commission, 360

Dickson, Joseph, 296

Dickson, William: and rank in New Army, 296

Dinsmoor, Silas: as agent of Cherokee Indians, 177, 178; visits Mount Vernon, 177, 178; id., 178

Dinwiddie, Jonathan: GW's payment to, 308

Dinwiddie, Robert: Proclamation of 1754, 277

Dismal Swamp tract: payments for, 55, 57, 58, 80–81, 179, 303, 400–401, 410–11

District of Columbia Commissioners: *letters from:* to GW, 49–50, 73–74, 97, 106, 138–39; *letters to:* from GW, 52–55, 77–78, 105–6, 130–31, 144–50. *See also* Scott, Gustavus; Thornton, William; White, Alexander

Dogue Run farm: meadow at, 1–2; rented to Lawrence Lewis, 4; barn at, 166

Dold, Jesse: and rank in New Army, 238

Douglass, John: and bookcase for GW, 358

Dowdall, John: and rank in New Army, 233

Duché, Jacob: letter to GW of 8 October 1777, 169; id., 171

Dueling: court-martial for, 221–23, 224–25; GW's opinion of, 224–25

Dulin, Edward: and houses at Mount Vernon, 417–18; id., 418

Duncanson, James: and rank in New Army, 231, 237

Dundas, Henry, first Viscount Melville: id., 414; *letters from:* to Rufus King, 414–15; *letters to:* from Rufus King, 414

Dunlap, John: as member of William McPherson's cavalry, 190

Dunwoody's (Philadelphia tavern): stabling of GW's horses at, 190

Du Pont, Victor-Marie: as consul, 75

Durkee, Benjamin: and pension for John Durkee, 184, 185; id., 185

Durkee, John: military pension for, 184, 185; id., 185

Dwight, Timothy: greetings to, 56; *The Nature, and Danger, of Infidel Philosophy, Exhibited in Two Discourses . . .* , 56

Easton, Pa.: court at, 151

Ellsworth, Oliver (*see* 1:9): as envoy to France, 388, 390, 402–3

Ellwood, John, Jr. (shipmaster), 351, 357, 386, 481

Evans, David, Jr.: and rank in New Army, 296

Evans, Thomas: and officers for New Army, 227, 228, 231, 235; *An Address to the People of Richmond, respecting the Alien & Sedition Laws*, 288, 303; id., 303

Ewell, Frances, 447

Ewell, Jesse, 447

Ewell, Jesse, Jr.: and rank in New Army, 239

Ewing, James: *Columbian Alphabet*, 399; id., 399; *letters to:* from GW, 399

Eyre, N.: GW's payment to, 308

Factor (ship), 75

Fairfax, Bryan (*see* 1:46): meets Rufus King, 90; arrival of in England, 323, 394; *letters to:* from GW, 322–25

Fairfax, Ferdinando: as trustee of Charles Town Academy, 94

Fairfax, Jane Dennison (Donaldson; *see* 2:267), 325; dinner invitation to, 394; *letters to:* from GW, 394

Farrell, Roger: as overseer, 6, 35, 181, 182; Alexander Spotswood's opinion of, 218; dismissed by Alexander Spotswood, 218; contract with GW, 219–20

Fauquier County tract: rent payments for, 378

Fayetteville, N.C.: magazine at, 196

Federal City: Marine Hospital in, 10, 47; navy yard for, 10–11, 45–48; accommodation of Congress in, 32–33, 83, 280, 354, 378–79, 424; GW's lots in, 32–33, 49, 50, 52, 54, 73–74, 83; defense of, 46–47; GW's houses in, 52–55, 73–74, 77–78, 105–6, 110–11, 130–31, 138–39, 140–41, 144–50, 152–54, 159, 274–75, 276, 299–301, 334, 335, 347–48, 376–77, 382, 420, 424, 446, 452, 465, 467, 487; Henry Lee's property in, 55, 57, 58, 139–40, 152, 179, 400; Thomas Law's house in, 78; GW visits, 97, 99; opening of Washington City Hotel, 136–37; Amariah Frost's property in, 140, 152; design of U.S. Capitol, 140, 141; William Thornton's property in, 140, 141, 152, 159; construction of buildings in, 280; John Tayloe's house in, 367, 487

Felicity (ship), 375

Fendall, Mary Lee: at Mount Vernon, 394

Fenno, John: death of, 358

Fenno, John W.: *Gazette of the United States*, 357, 358; id., 358

Fenwick, Joseph (*see* 2:217): as U.S. consul at Bordeaux, 434–35, 436; *letters from:* to Timothy Pickering, 94–95

Ferdinand I (of Naples): and alliance with Austria, 73

Ferguson, Patrick: rifles of, 191, 193; id., 193

Ferrers, Washington Shirley, 2d earl, 325

Fielding, Robert: GW's payment to, 308

Fields, Benjamin (*see* 2:88): and Wodrow tract, 278; *letters from:* to Alexander Spotswood, 278

Finn, Thomas: and rank in New Army, 227, 228

Finny, William: and rank in New Army, 238

Fitzgerald, John: and Samuel Knox, 91; and officers for New Army, 229, 232–33

Fitzhugh, John Thornton: and rank in New Army, 237

Fitzhugh, Nicholas (*see* 2:145): and officers for New Army, 230; at Mount Vernon, 381; id., 464; and seeds for GW, 464; *letters from:* to GW, 464

Fitzhugh, Sarah Ashton (*see* 2:145): id., 464

Fitzhugh, William (of Marmion): id., 81

Flinn, Michael: and rank in New Army, 235

Fontaine, Carter B.: and rank in New Army, 238

Forman, Joseph: and rank in New Army, 230

Foster, Dwight: and Caleb Gibbs, 443

Fouchee, Francis: and rank in New Army, 233

Four Mile Run tract: depredations on, 468, 469

France: policy of, 69–71, 74–75, 94–95, 96, 102, 108–9, 150–51, 201–2, 252–53, 282–83, 337, 406, 430–32, 482; military strategy and tactics of, 191, 192; agents of in U.S., 420–21, 445

Francis, John: and GW's Capitol Hill houses, 153, 154

Francis II (of Austria): and alliance with Naples, 73; and Treaty of Campo Formio, 431

Franklin (ship), 94

Frederick County tract: rent payments for, 378

Frederick the Great (of Prussia): and John Frederick Ramnitz's medicine, 163

Freeman, Jonathan: as member of Congress, 170; id., 171

Freemasons, Society of: and Maryland Masons, 188–89

Freire, Cipriano Ribeiro: GW declines invitation from, 248; id., 248, 363; leaves U.S., 362
French, Penelope Manley: GW acquires land from, 450
Frestel, Felix (*see* 1:206), 285; greetings to, 280
Fries, John: id., 452
Fries's Rebellion, 466; id., 452
Frost, Amariah: Federal City property of, 140, 152; and GW's Capitol Hill houses, 140; id., 141
Frost, Captain (shipmaster), 467

Gains, William Fleming: and officers for New Army, 237
Gaither, Eli: and rank in New Army, 296
Gaither, Henry: *letters to:* from James McHenry, 205, 207
Gallatin, Albert: *letters to:* from David Chauvet, 150, 151
Garland, David Shepherd: id., 277; seeks information from GW, 277; *letters from:* to GW, 277
Garrett, Mr.: as overseer, 35, 36, 50; *letters to:* from James Anderson, 35–36, 50
Gates, Horatio: and rank in New Army, 6
Gavenstine, Peter: GW's payment to, 308
Geddes, Captain (shipmaster), 75
George Berkeley (ship), 472
George III (of Great Britain), 74; and American public opinion, 151; illness of, 221
Georgetown College: accommodation of Congress at, 378
Gericke, Dr.: endorses yellow fever medicine, 163
Gerry, Elbridge, 70; arrives in England, 72–73, 75–76, 102; and relations with France, 95, 96, 102, 109, 118, 119, 143, 337–38, 344, 355, 369; GW's opinion of, 102, 109, 143, 366; budget of, 337; Timothy Pickering's criticism of, 337–38, 355; *letters from:* to Timothy Pickering, 96;

letters to: from Timothy Pickering, 356
Gibbs, Caleb (*see* 1:10): and rank in New Army, 313–14, 440–41, 443–44, 457
Gibson, A.: and rank in New Army, 226
Gill, Moses: and Ezekiel L. Bascom, 391
Gilman, Nicholas: and rank in New Army, 19; id., 27
Gilpin, George (*see* 1:125): and glass for GW, 382
Glascock, Thomas: and officers for New Army, 159–60; id., 160–61
Glassol, William: and rank in New Army, 232
Gloucester County tract: payments for, 422–23
Gold, James: and GW's gift to Washington Academy, 207, 208–9; id., 208–9
Goodhue, Benjamin (*see* 1:330): and officers for New Army, 268; and Caleb Gibbs, 314, 443
Goodrich, Chauncey, 373; id., 373–74
Goodrich, Elizur: as collector of customs, 373, 374; id., 374
Goodwin, Brewer, Jr.: and rank in New Army, 235
Gordon, Ambrose: and officers for New Army, 159–60; id., 161
Gracchus (pseud.): and Alien and Sedition Acts, 216–17, 278
Graham, Jane Brent, 394
Graham, Richard: and rank in New Army, 238; id., 394
Grant, James: as British agent to Saint Domingue, 414–15
Graves, Benjamin: seeks army commission, 228
Great Britain: policy of, 74–75, 482; and American public opinion, 151; U.S. relations with, 362, 363; relations with Saint Domingue, 413–14
Green, Mr. (of Culpeper): imports jackass, 377
Green, John (of Culpeper), 8; id., 9

Green, John (of Georgia): and rank in New Army, 159–60

Green, Thomas (John Greene): and rank in New Army, 8, 219, 234, 346; id., 9; and officers for New Army, 219; visits Mount Vernon, 356–57

Green, Timothy: as editor of *Virginia Herald*, 420, 445

Greenwood, John: id., 182; and teeth for GW, 182, 245–46, 289–91; plans move to Connecticut, 290; GW's payment to, 308; *letters from:* to GW, 247, 289–91; *letters to:* from GW, 175, 182, 245–46, 290–91

Gregg, Robert: and rank in New Army, 231, 235

Gregory, Isaac: id., 204

Gregory, William: and rank in New Army, 203; id., 204

Grenville, William Wyndham Grenville, Baron, 362

Griffin, Mr.: and officers for New Army, 235

Griggs, Thomas: as trustee of Charles Town Academy, 94

Grigsby, Joseph: and rank in New Army, 238

Grimké, John Faucheraud: and rank in New Army, 160; id., 161

Grimoldi, Chevalier de: seeks commission, 360

Griswold, Roger: and Matthew Lyon, 374

Grove, William Barry: and officers for New Army, 203, 296–97; id., 204

Guine, M.: and officers for New Army, 232

Gunston Hall, 81

Gustin, Robert: and rank in New Army, 230

Hall, Josias Carvil: id., 267; and rank in New Army, 267

Hall, William (of Massachusetts), 27; and rank in New Army, 19

Hall, William (of North Carolina): and rank in New Army, 296

Hambly, William: sends cheese to GW, 481; *letters from:* to GW, 481

Hamilton, Mr.: and William B. Harrison's land, 449, 475

Hamilton, Alexander, 43, 141, 222, 372; and ranking of major generals, 5, 6, 11, 12, 14, 15–16, 18–23, 34, 38, 40–42, 44–45, 58, 65, 103, 121–22, 123, 158, 168–69; and meeting of generals in Philadelphia, 103–4, 104–5, 117, 127, 155, 158, 225–26, 248, 250, 251, 288; accepts commission as major general, 117; at Yorktown, 123; criticizes James McHenry, 155, 444; illness in family of, 155; arrives in Philadelphia, 190; and organization of New Army, 191–93, 197–98, 198–99, 383, 447–48, 455–56, 466; and officers for New Army, 193, 225–26, 268, 293, 295, 313–14; and Philip Church, 212, 213, 214; military command of, 269, 270, 380–81, 395–96, 437, 452, 455; drafts military bills, 328; at New York, 380, 383; and James Wilkinson, 381; coding of letters to GW, 383, 384; and Virginia military districts, 386–87, 448, 473–74; and military returns, 397; and paymaster general, 418–19, 436–37, 466; and Caleb Gibbs, 440–41, 443–44; and John Jacob Ulrich Rivardi, 445–46; *letters from:* to GW, 58, 155–56, 380–81, 383–84, 386–87, 418–19, 447–48, 466–67, 474; to James McHenry, 117, 205–6, 266, 443–44, 456; to James Wilkinson, 381; to Henry Lee, Jr., 387, 448; to Thomas Parker, 387, 448, 474, 477–78; to William C. Bentley, 448; *letters to:* from GW, 34, 121–22, 191–93, 197–98, 387, 395–97, 398–99, 436–37, 473–74; from James McHenry, 103, 314, 381, 418, 419, 443–44, 455; from Charles Cotesworth Pinck-

Hamilton, Alexander (*continued*)
ney, 142, 143, 168; from Philip
Church, 244; from William
Heth, 316; from Tobias Lear,
397; from Daniel Morgan, 478
Hamilton, Elizabeth Schuyler: id.,
213
Hamilton, James, 450
Hamilton, Robert, 450
Hamilton, Theodorus James, 450
Hamilton (ship), 452–53
Hammond, Abijah: and rank in New
Army, 265, 266; id., 266
Hammond, Eli: and rank in New
Army, 349
Hammond, Mildred Thornton
Washington, 187, 188; id., 113
Hammond, Thomas: acts for Mil-
dred Thornton Washington,
112–13; Samuel Washington's
debt to, 187; id., 188
Hamtramck, John Francis, 466;
command of, 437; id., 437; *let-
ters from:* to GW, 437; *letters to:*
from GW, 437
Hand, Captain (shipmaster): and
seeds for GW, 429
Hand, Edward (*see* 2:414): and rank
in New Army, 6
Handcock, Samuel: address to GW,
83
Hardiman, John: and rank in New
Army, 231
Harper, Robert Goodloe (*see* 1:246,
2:33): elected to Congress,
133; and officers for New Army,
235, 238; GW's opinion of,
352–53; seeks position as GW's
aide, 352–53
Harper's Ferry: arsenal at, 24, 196,
257–58
Harrison, Charles, 233
Harrison, William B., 377; GW seeks
to acquire land of, 175–77,
179, 186, 334, 336, 358–60,
400, 401, 409–11, 448–50,
474–76; at Mount Vernon,
450; *letters from:* to GW, 336–
37, 389, 411, 448–50; *letters to:*
from GW, 175–77, 358–60,
409–11, 474–76

Hartshorne, William (*see* 1:153):
buys wheat, 395
Haskell, E.: and Charles Cotesworth
Pinckney, 168
Hauteval, Lucien: as "Z," 118–19;
id., 119; *letters from:* to Talley-
rand, 118, 119
Hawkins, Benjamin (*see* 1:179): and
Cherokee Indians, 177–78; *let-
ters from:* to GW, 177–78
Hay, William: witnesses deed, 208
Hayward, Martha Washington (*see* 2:
452), 77
Heath, William (*see* 1:104): Revolu-
tionary War memoirs of, 368–
69; *letters from:* to GW, 368–69;
letters to: from GW, 369
Henderson, Alexander: and rank in
New Army, 237, 240
Henderson, Archibald: and officers
for New Army, 295, 296
Hendrickson, Hendrick (shipmas-
ter), 94
Henley, Elizabeth Dandridge Aylett,
461
Henley, Leonard: id., 461
Henley, Robert: id., 461; seeks place
in navy, 461
Henley, Samuel: and rank in New
Army, 267–68
Henry, John, Jr.: id., 79; *letters to:*
from GW, 79
Henry, Nathaniel: and rank in New
Army, 228
Henry, Patrick: death of, 305; and
Virginia politics, 305; GW urges
to run for office, 317–20; views
on relations with France, 370–
71; agrees to run for office,
371; illness of, 371; views on relations with Great Britain, 371–
72; nominated envoy to France,
388–89, 390, 402–3; *letters
from:* to GW, 370–72; *letters to:*
from GW, 317–20
Herbert, William (*see* 1:131, 2:26):
acts for Andrew Belknap, 78,
80, 86, 87; and loan to GW,
78–79, 80, 86–87; *letters from:*
to GW, 80; *letters to:* from GW,
78–79, 86–87

Heth, John: and rank in New Army, 226

Heth, William (*see* 2:406): and rank in New Army, 7; and officers for New Army, 128–29, 226–38; *letters from:* to GW, 315–16; to Alexander Hamilton, 316; *letters to:* from GW, 316

Hill, Richard: and rank in New Army, 233

Hill, William: as trustee of Charles Town Academy, 94

Hindman, William: *letters from:* to James McHenry, 205, 207

Hite, Abraham: and the Wodrow tract, 172, 278, 420, 444

Hite, Deborah Rutherford: id., 314

Hite, Frances Beale: killed by Indians, 314

Hite, George: as trustee of Charles Town Academy, 94; and rank in New Army, 232, 313–14, 345; id., 314; *letters from:* to GW, 94

Hite, Jacob: killed by Indians, 314

Hoban, James: and GW's Capitol Hill houses, 149, 150; id., 149

Hodgdon, Samuel (*see* 2:22): and military stores, 23–24, 27, 64, 82, 142, 181, 182–83, 196, 199, 205, 206, 209; sends paper to GW, 87, 182, 183; sends blank books to GW, 183; *letters from:* to GW, 182–83; to Tobias Lear, 183; *letters to:* from James McHenry, 27; from GW, 87; from Tobias Lear, 183

Hodgson, William (*see* 1:423): at Mount Vernon, 394

Holmes, David: and officers for New Army, 230, 232, 236

Holmes, Hugh: and rank in New Army, 229

Hope (ship), 94

Hope Park (house): Nelly Custis and Martha Washington visit, 280, 325

Hopkins, Mr.: GW's payment to, 308

Hopkins, John (*see* 2:69): and officers for New Army, 231, 236, 237

Horacke, Francis de: seeks commission, 360

Hord, Thomas: and rank in New Army, 7–8, 230

Horry, Charles Lucas Pinckney. *See* Horry, Daniel Huger

Horry, Daniel Huger (Charles Lucas Pinckney; *see* 1:208, 2:246): id., 96, 117; sends poetry to Nelly Custis, 117; *letters from:* to Timothy Pickering, 94

Hospital Department: organization of, 328

Howard, John Eager (*see* 1:91): and rank in New Army, 268

Howes, Daniel (shipmaster), 467

Hozey, Isaac: as member of William McPherson's cavalry, 190

Hubbard, Thomas: address to GW, 83

Hubley, Bernard, Jr.: and rank in New Army, 272–73; id., 273; *letters from:* to John Adams, 272; to GW, 272–73

Huger, Benjamin: elected to Congress, 133; id., 133

Huger, Francis (*see* 2:588): and rank in New Army, 160

Hugues, Victor: as French agent in West Indies, 481

Humphries, George Washington: and rank in New Army, 239

Hunt, Abraham, 151

Hunter, William G.: and rank in New Army, 239

Huntingdon, Selena Hastings, countess of: correspondence with GW, 325; id., 325

Huntington, Benjamin: and pension for John Durkee, 184; id., 185

Indians: conditions among, 177

Inskeep, John: GW's payment to, 308

Ireland: rebellion in, 75

Izard, George (*see* 1:367–68): and rank in New Army, 160

Jackson, Henry (*see* 2:577): and officers for New Army, 441

Jackson, James (*see* 2:300): *letters from:* to James McHenry, 205, 207; *letters to:* from James McHenry, 205, 207

Jackson, John: and Ezekiel L. Bascom, 391

Jameison, Mr.: and officers for New Army, 236

Jameison, Thomas: and rank in New Army, 236

James, James: and rank in New Army, 235

Jameson, John: and officers for New Army, 231, 235, 236

James River Company: GW donates shares to Washington Academy, 208–9

Javens, (Javins) John: as tenant, 336, 359

Jay, John: and John Searson, 486; *letters to:* from John C. Ogden, 29

Jay Treaty, 70; and Moses Robinson, 171

Jefferson, Thomas, 28; and George Logan, 201; and Elizur Goodrich, 374; and Hughes crab apple, 464; *letters from:* to James Mease, 464

Jerry (slave): conveys letter, 83

Johnston, Peter: and Prince Edward Co. (Va.) Freeholders, 95, 109; *letters to:* from Timothy Pickering, 95–96, 109

Jones, Allen: and officers for New Army, 296

Jones, Bathurst: and rank in New Army, 232

Jones, Churchill: and rank in New Army, 229

Jones, Walter (*see* 2:564): id., 114; and officers for New Army, 227; elected to Virginia senate, 368

Kanawha tracts: lease of, 92–93; payments for, 383, 413, 447, 463–64, 470–72

Keene, Richard Raynal: seeks loan from GW, 291; *letters from:* to GW, 277; *letters to:* from GW, 291

Keith, James (*see* 1:361): and GW's Kanawha tracts, 93; and George Mercer's land, 271–72

Kemp, Captain (shipmaster), 75

Kessler, J.: seeks commission, 360

King, Mr.: and officers for New Army, 231

King, May Alsop: greetings to, 339; greetings from, 417

King, Robert: and rank in New Army, 234

King, Rufus (*see* 1:123), 24, 355; reports on events in Europe, 73, 74–75, 403; and Bartholomew Dandridge, 89, 338, 415, 436; meets Bryan Fairfax, 90; and XYZ affair, 118; and Chauvet-Gallatin letter, 150, 151; greetings to, 339; and U.S. relations with Europe, 362, 363; nominated U.S. commissioner to Russia, 390; and U.S. relations with Saint Domingue, 414–15; greetings from, 417; *letters from:* to Timothy Pickering, 73, 74–76, 118, 403, 413–14; to Henry Dundas, 414; *letters to:* from Oliver Wolcott, Jr., 24, 196, 197; from Timothy Pickering, 390; from Henry Dundas, 414–15

Kinkead, Mr.: and officers for New Army, 237

Knight, William: and rank in New Army, 237

Knight of Malta (jackass), 463

Knox, Henry, 17; and ranking of major generals, 5, 6, 11–12, 14, 15–16, 18–23, 30, 38, 41, 42, 44–45, 65, 103, 108, 122–24, 126, 127, 168–69; and officers for New Army, 18, 230, 441; and meeting of generals in Philadelphia, 103–4, 120, 127; as secretary general of the Society of the Cincinnati, 119, 120; declines commission as major general, 158, 172, 178, 193, 268; as secretary of war, 454; *letters from:* to James McHenry, 158, 205, 207; to GW, 178; *letters to:* from James McHenry, 103; from GW, 120, 122–24

Knox, Samuel: *An Essay on the Best System of Liberal Education . . .* , 90–92; seeks to dedicate volume to GW, 90–92; id., 91; *letters from:* to GW, 90–92; *letters to:* from GW, 92

Koontz, John: and rank in New Army, 233

Lafayette, Anastasie-Louise-Pauline: greetings to, 284

Lafayette, George Washington Motier (*see* 1:206), 284, 285; and his father, 109; *letters to:* from GW, 279–80

Lafayette, Marie-Adrienne-Françoise de Noailles, marquise de, 200; in Paris, 95, 109; greetings to, 280, 284

Lafayette, Marie-Joseph-Paul-Yves-Roch-Gilbert, 279, 337; proposed visit of to America, 109, 281; in Hamburg, 200; *letters from:* to GW, 109; *letters to:* from GW, 280–85

Lafayette, Virginie: greetings to, 284

Laidler, John: and his ferry on Potomac River, 47, 48

Lambert, John: agricultural advice of, 136; id., 136; GW's payment to, 308; *letters from:* to GW, 136; *letters to:* from GW, 212

Lamkin, Peter: and rank in New Army, 240

Lands of GW: Federal City lots, 32–33, 49, 50, 52, 54, 55, 73–74, 83. *See also individual entries*

Berkeley County tract: tenants on, 377–78

Dismal Swamp tract: payments for, 55, 57, 58, 80–81, 179, 303, 400–401, 410

Fauquier County tract: tenants on, 377–78

Four Mile Run tract: depredations on, 468, 469

Frederick County tract: tenants on, 377–78

Gloucester County tract: payments for, 422–23

Kanawha tracts: agreement with James Welch for, 92–93; payments for, 383, 413, 447, 463–64, 470–72

Little Miami tracts: title to, 210–11

Loudoun County tract: tenants on, 377–78

Millers Run tract: payments for, 407–8

Montgomery County tract: tenants on, 340

Ohio River tracts: terms for sale requested, 44

Rough Creek tract: taxes on, 85–86, 121, 131–32, 166, 171–72; deeds to, 179, 180, 303, 399, 401, 479, 480; and the Wodrow tract, 278; value of, 420, 444–45

Washington's Bottom tract: payments for, 66–68, 144, 156–57, 275–76, 314–15

Lane, Charles: and rank in New Army, 237

Lane, Daniel C.: and rank in New Army, 232

Langdon, John: as member of Congress, 170; id., 171

Langhorne, John (Peter Carr): letter to GW, 303

Latimer, George: as collector of customs at Philadelphia, 480–81

Latour-Maubourg, Marie-Charles-César de Fay, comte de (*see* 1:384): greetings to, 284

Law, Eliza (*see* 1:259), 279; greetings to, 137, 386; GW's gift for, 243, 246–47

Law, Eliza Parke Custis (*see* 1:34), 279; greetings to, 137, 386; at Mount Vernon, 152; wedding invitation to, 385–86; greetings from, 472; and John Searson, 486; *letters to:* from Elizabeth Willing Powel, 246–47

Law, Thomas (*see* 1:34), 279, 425, 453; and GW's Federal City lots, 32–33; builds house in Federal City, 78; at Mount Vernon, 111, 152; and William Tunnicliff's hotel, 136–37; and William

Law, Thomas (*continued*)
Thornton's Federal City property, 140, 141; and GW's Capitol Hill houses, 152, 446; conveys letter, 275; visits Federal
City, 379; wedding invitation to,
385–86; and seeds for GW,
472; *letters from:* to GW, 32–33,
106, 472; *letters to:* from GW,
136–37, 385–86
Lear, Tobias (*see* 1:25), 72, 136,
241, 360, 384, 413; acknowledges letter, 29; illness of, 127,
425, 427, 430, 445, 487; conveys letter, 136, 451, 472; accompanies GW to Philadelphia,
181, 189, 190, 200; and blank
books for GW, 183; drafts letter
for GW, 185; and Lawrence
Lewis, 214; as GW's secretary,
250, 279, 292; and George
Washington Parke Custis, 268,
299; and GW's expenses in
Philadelphia, 307–8; greetings to, 412; and Bartholomew
Dandridge, 416; visits Federal
City, 419; and trees for William
Thornton, 426; acts for GW,
452–53; *letters from:* to Samuel
Hodgdon, 183; to James Mc-
Henry, 189, 206–7; to George
Washington Parke Custis, 268,
299; to Clement Biddle, 322; to
Ezekiel L. Bascom, 392; to
Alexander Hamilton, 397; to
John Jacob Ulrich Rivardi, 397;
to GW, 429; to Charles Demou-
monier, 477; *letters to:* from
Samuel Hodgdon, 183; from
Clement Biddle, 247; from
Presly Thornton, 357; from
GW, 425, 445–46, 452–53;
from Charles Demoumonier,
477
Lee, Charles (*see* 1:126): and Rich-
ard Scott Blackburn, 31; and of-
ficers for New Army, 225, 227,
229, 237, 238; as U.S. attorney
general, 470
Lee, Edmund Jennings (*see* 2:226):
at Mount Vernon, 394
Lee, George: and Henry Lee, Jr.,

401; id., 401; and his Colchester land, 425–26; *letters from:* to
Henry Lee, Jr., 401
Lee, Henry, Jr. (1:43), 17, 186, 470;
and rank in New Army, 6; and
debt to GW, 55, 57, 58, 80–81,
179, 303, 400, 401, 410–11,
450; Federal City property of,
55, 57, 58, 139–40, 152, 179,
400; offers corn, 55, 57, 76–77;
and Jesse Simms's note, 57, 58,
179; and officers for New Army,
57–58, 101, 227, 229, 230,
231, 232, 233, 234, 235, 236,
237, 239, 240; conveys letter,
76; Pohick Creek land of, 81; at
Georgetown, 83; and Richard
Bland Lee, 106, 107; runs for
office, 114, 400, 473–74, 479,
480; and GW's Rough Creek
tract, 166, 179, 180, 303, 399,
401, 479, 480; buys land from
Alexander Spotswood, 301; and
Virginia Resolutions, 346–47;
and William B. Harrison's land,
400; and organization of New
Army, 448; illness of, 473–74;
GW seeks corn from, 484–85;
letters from: to GW, 55, 346–47,
399–401; *letters to:* from GW,
57–58, 178–80, 484–85; from
Alexander Hamilton,
387, 448; from George Lee,
401
Lee, Lucy: at Mount Vernon, 394
Lee, Ludlow. *See* Lee, Ludwell
Lee, Ludwell (*see* 1:136): and officers for New Army, 229, 234;
id., 401
Lee, Richard Bland: seeks commission, 106–8, 227; id., 107; and
officers for New Army, 228,
232, 237; *letters from:* to GW,
106–8; *letters to:* from GW, 108
Lee, Theodorick: and officers for
New Army, 232; id., 470; at
Mount Vernon, 470; and rank
in New Army, 470
Leftwich, Joel: address to GW, 83;
id., 85
Leftwich, Thomas: address to GW,
83–85; id., 85

Leftwich, William, Jr.: address to GW, 84–85; id., 85
Leigh, Marmaduke: seeks to buy GW's Ohio land, 44; *letters from:* to GW, 44
L'Enfant, Pierre-Charles: seeks commission, 360
Lenthall, John: and GW's Capitol Hill houses, 299, 301, 347, 487; id., 301
Leoffler, Frederick: GW's payment to, 308
Lewis, Eleanor (Nelly) Parke Custis. *See* Custis, Eleanor (Nelly) Parke
Lewis, Isaac (*see* 1:260): sermons of, 56
Lewis, John, 332; id., 333
Lewis, Judith Carter Browne: greetings to, 334; greetings from, 378
Lewis, Lawrence (*see* 1:270): rents land from GW, 4; apologizes to GW, 214–15; at Mount Vernon, 214–15; and rank in New Army, 215–16, 234, 267, 268, 279, 299, 332–33, 339, 345–46; betrothed to Nelly Custis, 216, 279, 302, 312, 332, 333, 339, 361, 384, 389; illness of, 216; at Charles Town, 280, 311–12; declines commission, 333, 384; marriage to Nelly Custis, 378, 385–86, 394, 460; greetings to, 412, 464; in Federal City, 425; and GW's Capitol Hill houses, 452; *letters from:* to GW, 214–16, 311–12; to James McHenry, 384; *letters to:* from GW, 241–42, 332–33
Lewis, Robert: conveys letter, 176; acts for GW, 177; as GW's rental agent, 334, 377–78; and William B. Harrison's land, 336; *letters from:* to GW, 377–78; *letters to:* from GW, 333–34
Lewis, Samuel, Sr.: *letters from:* to GW, 313; *letters to:* from GW, 313
Lewis, Thomas: trial of, 221–23, 224–25
Lewis, Zechariah (*see* 1:224): sends

books to GW, 56; *letters to:* from GW, 55–56
Liberty (ship), 95
Liberty Hall Academy. *See* Washington Academy
Lightfoot, Philip: and rank in New Army, 231
Lincoln, Benjamin: and rank in New Army, 6; and glass for GW, 382, 424, 467; and officers for New Army, 441; *letters from:* to GW, 467; *letters to:* from GW, 424
Liston, Robert (*see* 1:468): GW declines invitation from, 248; provides advice, 362
Little, Peter: as general secretary of Maryland Masons, 189
Little Miami tracts: GW's title to, 210–11
Lloyd, James (*see* 2:241): forwards letter, 344; *letters from:* to GW, 344; *letters to:* from GW, 369–70
Loftland, Charles: and rank in New Army, 237
Logan, Deborah Norris, 200; id., 202
Logan, George (*see* 2:343): GW's notes on meeting with, 200–202; mission to France of, 200–202, 287; id., 202; at Mount Vernon, 202
London (England): architecture of, 140, 276
Long, Lemuel McKinne: and rank in New Army, 203; id., 204
Long, Nicholas, 203; id., 204
Loudoun County tract: rent payments for, 378
L'Ouverture, Toussaint: and relations with U.S., 358; and relations with Great Britain, 413–14
Love, Charles J.: and rank in New Army, 237
Love, James: and rank in New Army, 296
Lovell, Captain (shipmaster), 13
Lower Cedar Point, Md.: id., 48
Lucy (ship), 467
Lusk, Andrew Moore: and rank in New Army, 236

Lyon, Matthew (*see* 2:66–67): and John C. Ogden, 373; id., 374

McAllister, Hugh: and rank in New Army, 236
McAlpin, James: GW's payment to, 308; and uniform for GW, 340–42, 343, 352, 363–64, 365, 372, 408; id., 341; *letters from:* to GW, 364; *letters to:* from GW, 340–42, 363–64
McCallister, Charles: and rank in New Army, 238
Macay, James: and rank in New Army, 296
McDavitt, Charles: as tenant, 340
McDowell, John (*see* 2:119): as president of St. John's College, 79; *letters to:* from GW, 79
McElwee, John: and picture frame for GW, 247
McHenry, James (*see* 1:47), 31, 87, 88, 122, 177, 233, 383; and ranking of major generals, 4–6, 11, 12, 14–16, 18–23, 29–30, 34, 37–38, 39, 43, 44–45, 65–66, 103, 124–25; and officers for New Army, 15, 16–19, 97–99, 125, 128, 134, 142, 158, 193, 194–95, 225–26, 292, 299, 313, 314, 327, 328, 332–33, 349, 353, 354, 360, 408, 469–70, 474, 476–77, 478; and organization of New Army, 18–19, 104, 126–27, 128, 134, 193–97, 197–98, 198–99, 204–7, 209, 291–92, 380, 395–96, 411, 448, 468–69; and military supplies, 24–25; criticizes militia, 25; and GW's commission, 37, 38; and sedition in New Army, 59, 81; and clothing for New Army, 82; and meeting of generals in Philadelphia, 103–4, 104–5, 178, 181–82, 286, 288, 293, 324, 326, 338; and Richard Bland Lee, 107; and Nelly Custis, 125; and colors for Nelly Custis, 142; criticism of, 155, 442–43; and teeth for

GW, 182; arrives in Philadelphia, 190; reports on military courts, 221–25; forwards letters, 244; and Charles Carroll, Jr., 248, 249–50; GW's reports to, 250–65; and William Stephens Smith, 266; and civil-military relations, 268–69; military report to John Adams, 292, 293, 305–6, 328; and military uniforms, 306, 307, 313–14, 340–42, 342–44; and GW's military pay, 312–13; uniform of, 343, 372; and officers for Provisional Army, 349; and uniform for GW, 352, 363, 364–65, 372, 408; conveys letters, 364; and James Wilkinson, 381; and paymaster general, 418, 419; and recruiting, 438; response to GW's criticism, 457; *letters from:* to John Adams, 5, 19–20, 21–22; to GW, 14–27, 29–30, 72–73, 81, 82, 103–4, 104–5, 108, 117, 142, 157–58, 168–69, 189–90, 193–97, 204–7, 209, 211–12, 221–25, 244, 248, 249, 267, 291–93, 305–6, 312–14, 328, 352–53, 372, 451–52, 453–58; to Samuel Hodgdon, 27; to Alexander Hamilton, 103, 314, 381, 418–19, 443–44, 455; to Henry Knox, 103; to Charles Cotesworth Pinckney, 108; to Henry Gaither, 205, 207; to James Jackson, 205, 207; to James Wilkinson, 205, 207; to Oliver Wolcott, Jr., 205, 207; to Timothy Pickering, 205, 207; *letters to:* from GW, 4–6, 44–45, 59, 63–65, 65–66, 97–99, 124–27, 132–33, 141, 180–81, 198–99, 204, 250–65, 265–68, 268–70, 306–8, 342–44, 344–46, 352–53, 354, 356–57, 360, 364–65, 384, 408, 438–44, 468–69, 469–70, 476–77; from John Adams, 6, 19, 20–22, 157–58, 193, 456; from Charles Cotesworth Pinckney, 108, 168–69, 172, 224–25;

from Alexander Hamilton, 117, 205–6, 266, 443–44, 456; from Henry Knox, 158, 205, 207; from Nelly Custis, 158; from Tobias Lear, 189, 206–7; from Jacob Read, 205, 207; from James Jackson, 205, 207; from James Wilkinson, 205, 207, 437; from John Allen, 205, 206; from John Steele, 205, 207; from Uriah Tracy, 205, 206; from William Hindman, 205, 207; from William Matthews, 205, 207; from John Tayloe, 368, 375; from Lawrence Lewis, 384; from William Vans Murray, 415

McHenry, John, Jr.: as secretary, 89

McHenry, Margaret Allison Caldwell, 249

McKean, Joseph B.: as member of William McPherson's cavalry, 190

McKean, Thomas (*see* 2:376): and George Logan, 201

McLean, Samuel: GW's payment to, 308

Macleod & Lumsden (firm): and glass for GW, 382; *letters from:* to GW, 382

McPherson, William: and GW's reception in Philadelphia, 190; id., 190; advice on uniforms, 352

Madison, James: and Virginia Resolutions, 310, 347

Magill, Charles: and officers for New Army, 232

Magnolio (horse): traded to Henry Lee, 180, 399, 401

Maitland, Thomas: and convention with Saint Domingue, 413–14; id., 414

Mannsfield (house): id., 446–47; John Tayloe at, 461–62

Mansion House farm: overseer at, 35, 181, 219–20; firewood for, 165, 220; fencing at, 167; fowl houses at, 167; provisions for horses and visitors at, 175

Marsh, Joseph, 329

Marsh, Samuel: seeks army commission, 228

Marshall, John: runs for office, 32, 297, 310; and XYZ affair, 95; and officers for New Army, 128, 129, 227–36, 238; and George Mercer's land, 271; GW sends pamphlet to, 297, 302–3, 309; view of Alien and Sedition Acts, 309–10; and Virginia Resolutions, 347; as envoy to France, 355; *letters from:* to GW, 308–11; *letters to:* from GW, 297–98

Marshall, Thomas (*see* 1:204): and GW's Rough Creek tract, 85–86, 121, 131, 171–72; greetings to, 132

Marshall, Thomas, Jr.: and GW's Rough Creek tract, 85–86, 121, 131–32; *letters to:* from GW, 131–32

Martin, Alexander (*see* 2:72): and officers for New Army, 203; id., 204

Maryland elections of 1798: id., 102

Maryland Masons: address from: to GW, 189; *letters to:* from GW, 188–89

Maryland Point: id., 11

Mason, George, 81; and William B. Harrison's land, 449, 450, 476

Mason, Sarah McCarty Chichester (*see* 2:145): id., 450

Mason, Thomson (*see* 2:145): and William B. Harrison's land, 177, 450; id., 450

Massey, Lieutenant: on court-martial, 222

Matthews, Thomas: and rank in New Army, 227

Matthews, William: *letters from:* to James McHenry, 205, 207

Maury, Fontaine: and overseer for GW, 35, 50; id., 36

Maxwell, James: and rank in New Army, 227, 230; and officers for New Army, 228, 230

Mayer, Jacob: as American consul at Cap François, 358

Mease, James: *letters to:* from Thomas Jefferson, 464

Medicine: Landon Carter's views on, 60–63; for yellow fever, 161–64, 220–21, 427–29; opium, 330

Mercer, Charles Fenton (*see* 2:456): and rank in New Army, 231, 441–42, 444, 457

Mercer, George: land of, 271–72

Mercer, James (*see* 2:456), 36

Mercer, Lucinda: id., 36

Merlin, Philip-Antoine: and George Logan, 201, 202; id., 202

Mike (slave): cares for livestock, 168

Miller, Edward: court of inquiry regarding, 223–24

Miller, John, Jr.: id., 472; and seeds for GW, 472

Miller, Philip: *Abridgement of the Gardener's Dictionary*, 453

Millers Run tract: payments for, 407–8

Minerva (ship), 420

Mitchel, Captain: death of, 222

Monroe, James: *letters from:* to Timothy Pickering, 434–36

Montflorence, James G.: as secretary, 89

Montgomery County (Md.) tract: tenants of, 340

Moody, John: id., 408; and rank in New Army, 408–9; *letters from:* to GW, 408–9; *letters to:* from GW, 408–9

Moore, Alfred: and officers for New Army, 235, 296

Moore, Andrew: as trustee of Washington Academy, 207–8; id., 208; and officers for New Army, 236, 238; *letters from:* to GW, 207–9

Moore, John: and rank in New Army, 239

Morgan, Calvin: and rank in New Army, 238

Morgan, Daniel (*see* 1:440), 234, 238, 267, 346; and rank in New Army, 6; and officers for New Army, 227, 228, 229, 232, 233, 237–38, 240, 469–70, 477, 478; elected to Congress, 314; and Virginia military districts, 448; forwards letter, 474, 477; false account of his death, 478; *letters from:* to GW, 468; to Alexander Hamilton, 478; *letters to:* from GW, 477–78

Morgan, Simon: and rank in New Army, 230

Morrell (Morrel), John: as member of William McPherson's cavalry, 190

Morris, B. W.: GW's payment to, 308

Morris, James: and rank in New Army, 297

Morris, Robert, 171; and Thomas Willing, 211; and Henry Lee, Jr., 400

Morse, Jedediah (*see* 1:177): Thanksgiving sermon of, 402; *letters from:* to GW, 402; *letters to:* from GW, 402

Morton, Archibald: and wheat for Mount Vernon, 2, 4; as tenant, 426

Mount Airy (house), 368

Mount Eagle (house): GW visits, 325

Mount Vernon: duties of farm manager at, 1–3, 165, 220; profits of farms at, 2–3; joiner for, 6–7, 33, 35; peach trees at, 165; tenants for, 166, 173–75, 186, 215, 241; depredations on, 176–77; ice house at, 305; lawn at, 321, 322; landing at, 322, 351; Chapel Land of, 410, 411, 449; list of houses at, 417–18; gardener for, 484. *See also* Agriculture; Slaves

distillery: profits of, 2; operation of, 3, 4; distiller for sought, 165; carpentry at, 167

fishery, 2; duties of slaves at, 219–20

mill, 2, 4, 175, 176, 334, 336, 358, 410; corn for, 76–77; wheat for, 166; carpentry at, 167; idle, 186; construction of, 404–5, 468

overseers of, 2–3, 6, 9, 33, 35, 36, 50, 181, 218–20; duties of, 219–20

supplies for: wheat, 2, 186; corn, 57, 76–77; manure, 164; firewood, 165, 168, 220; barrels, 166; bricks, 167–68; meat, 220; blankets, 247, 322; picture frame, 247; bookcase, 321, 322, 351, 357, 358; brownstone, 405; trees, 419–20. *See also* Dogue Run farm; Mansion House farm; Muddy Hole farm; River farm; Union farm

Muclas (slave): as brickmaker, 168

Muddy Hole farm: firewood from, 165; peach trees at, 165

Muhlenberg, John Peter Gabriel: and rank in New Army, 6

Munroe, William: and rank in New Army, 228

Murray, Charlotte Hughins (*see* 1: 78): greetings to, 287

Murray, William Vans (*see* 1 : 78), 337; and Bartholomew Dandridge, 89; and George Logan, 200; as minister to France, 351, 363, 387, 389–90, 402–3, 405–6; *letters from:* to John Adams, 388; to James McHenry, 415; to GW, 470; *letters to:* from GW, 286–87

Muse, John: seeks navy commission, 239

Nancy (ship), 13, 361, 430, 467

Naples: alliance with Austria, 73, 74

Navy: applications for positions in, 9–10, 89, 239, 461; Washington navy yard, 10–11, 45–48; and conflict with France, 95–96

New, A.: and officers for New Army, 237

New Army: ranking of major generals, 4–5, 11–13, 14, 15–16, 19–23, 29–30, 34, 37–43, 44–45, 58, 65–66, 72, 87–88, 103, 108, 117, 120, 121–22, 122–24, 126, 142, 158, 168–69, 172, 178; officers for, 6, 7–8, 9, 14, 15, 16–19, 26, 31–32, 33–34, 35, 42–43, 51–52, 63, 64, 72, 73, 82, 87–88, 97–99, 100–102, 104, 114–16, 120–21, 126–27, 128–30, 134–35, 142, 154–55, 158, 159–61, 193–95, 199, 202–7, 209, 212–14, 215–16, 219, 225–40, 241, 244, 248–52, 258–61, 264–68, 272–73, 286–87, 288–89, 291–93, 293–97, 298–99, 302, 304–5, 306, 313–14, 316–17, 320, 327, 328, 332–33, 334–35, 336, 338–39, 344–46, 352–53, 353–54, 356–57, 360, 366–67, 374–75, 408–9, 415, 416, 440–42, 443–44, 453–54, 457, 460, 461, 469–70, 474, 476–80; sedition in, 8–9, 35, 59, 81, 129, 135; organization of, 18, 26, 100–102, 191, 193–97, 250–65, 328, 411, 418–19, 436–44, 447–48, 452, 455–58, 459–61, 466, 468–69; military aids and secretary for GW, 19, 23; ordnance for, 23–24, 27, 63–64, 82, 104, 182–83, 191, 192, 193, 196, 199, 205, 206, 209, 257–58, 264, 298; clothing for, 24, 64, 72, 82, 192, 262, 264, 380, 455, 456; funding of, 24, 25, 196, 199, 205, 207, 211–12, 253–54, 455; and strategy, 24–25, 40, 43, 191; meeting of generals concerning, 103–4, 104–5, 120, 126, 127, 132, 155, 158, 172, 178, 180–81, 182, 225–40, 241–42, 250–65; deployment of, 104, 191–92, 195–96, 199, 254–55, 298, 380–81, 396–97, 411–12, 437, 459; rations for, 104, 196, 204, 206, 248, 255–57, 262–63, 298; engineers for, 191; uniforms for, 261–62, 306, 307, 313, 314, 340–44, 346, 352, 353, 363–65, 372, 408, 412, 460; commands of major generals, 268–70, 380–81, 395–96, 452

Newenham, Edward (*see* 1 : 291): criticism of, 417

New Jersey elections of 1798: id., 138

Newman, Daniel: and rank in New Army, 297

New York City: yellow fever epidemic in, 56, 103, 161, 428

Niagara: garrison at, 396, 397

Nicholas, John (*see* 1:477): and rank in New Army, 296

Nicholas, Wilson Cary: and Alien and Sedition Acts, 309, 310; id., 310

Norfolk, Va.: unhealthy air at, 31

North, George: as trustee of Charles Town Academy, 94

North, William (*see* 2:510): as adjutant general, 17, 19, 39, 88, 120–21; id., 27

Nott, Abraham: elected to Congress, 134; id., 134

Nourse, Gabriel: as trustee of Charles Town Academy, 94

Odlin, Dudley: and rank in New Army, 232

Ogden, John Cosens: id., 29; *letters from:* to GW, 27–29, 169–71, 373–74; to John Jay, 29

Ogden, Mary Clap Wooster, 374

Ogle, Benjamin: gives jackass to John Tayloe, 367; id., 368

Ohio River tracts: query regarding, 44

Okey, Isaac: address to GW, 83

Olney, Jeremiah: and rank in New Army, 19

Opie, Thomas: and rank in New Army, 238

Oram, Peter Butts: and rank in New Army, 203, 204

Otis, Harrison Gray: and Caleb Gibbs, 443

Ottoman Empire: U.S. relations with, 362, 363, 390, 391

Owens, Simon: and rank in New Army, 237

Page, John: acts for GW, 210; id., 210, 423; and GW's Gloucester County tract, 422–23; *letters from:* to GW, 423; *letters to:* from GW, 422–23

Page, Mann, Jr.: id., 446

Page, Margaret Lowther: greetings to, 423

Page, Mary Tayloe: id., 446

Page, Robert: and officers for New Army, 232

Page, William Byrd: and William B. Harrison's land, 400–401; id., 401

Paine, Elijah, 331

Paine, Thomas, 387

Parish, Isaac: and hats for GW, 321, 358

Parker, Elias: and rank in New Army, 230

Parker, Isaac: and Caleb Gibbs, 443

Parker, John: and rank in New Army, 159, 160

Parker, Josiah: and officers for New Army, 227, 228, 235

Parker, Thomas (*see* 2:480): and rank in New Army, 227, 228, 240, 338; and officers for New Army, 232, 233, 234, 238, 239; and Virginia military districts, 474; *letters to:* from Alexander Hamilton, 387, 448, 477–78

Parker, William, 159; id., 160

Parkinson, Richard (*see* 1:324), 186; leaves for Mount Vernon, 166; GW's instructions to James Anderson regarding, 173–75; arrives in U.S., 215, 241; Lawrence Lewis's opinion of, 215; *letters from:* to GW, 173

Parks, Andrew: forwards letter, 6; id., 9; at Mount Vernon, 9

Parks, Harriot Washington: id., 9

Paterson, William: and Episcopal church lands in Vermont, 169, 171; id., 171

Paul I (of Russia): and relations with U.S., 362

Peck, William: and rank in New Army, 19

Pegram, Booker: and rank in New Army, 233

Pendleton, Philip: as trustee of Charles Town Academy, 94

Penfield, Daniel: as John Trumbull's agent, 392

Pennsylvania, Bank of: and judgment bond of Israel Shreve, 67–68; *letters to:* from GW, 67. *See also* Ross, James

Pennsylvania elections of 1798: id.,
138
Pennsylvania Germans: and Alien
and Sedition Acts, 151
Percy, Henry: and rank in New
Army, 233
Peter, Alexander: id., 408; and rank
in New Army, 408
Peter, Columbia Washington, 279
Peter, George: and rank in New
Army, 353, 354
Peter, Martha Eliza Eleanor (*see* 1 :
186), 279; GW's gift for, 244;
illness of, 354
Peter, Martha Parke Custis (*see* 1 :
34), 279, 354; *letters to:* from
Martha Washington, 379
Peter, Robert, 354, 408
Peter, Thomas, 279, 408; conveys
letter, 50, 110; and Henry Lee's
Federal City property, 58, 139;
and Presly Thornton, 357; *let-*
ters from: to GW, 353–54; *letters*
to: from GW, 353
Peter (slave): cares for livestock, 168
Peters, Theodore: id., 96; *letters from:*
to Timothy Pickering, 95
Peyton, Garnett: and rank in New
Army, 233
Philadelphia: architecture of, 159,
274; yellow fever epidemic in,
161, 182–83, 190, 200, 211,
215, 358, 378, 397, 428; lodgings for GW in, 189–90; GW's
reception in, 190; arsenal at,
196; court-martial in, 221–22;
GW's expenses in, 307–8
Physick, Philip Syng: and yellow fever medicine, 164
Pichon, Louis-André: and William
Vans Murray, 388; *letters to:*
from Talleyrand, 388
Pickering, Rebecca White: greetings
to, 304
Pickering, Timothy (*see* 1 : 35), 22,
117, 383; and ranking of major
generals, 11–13, 30, 65; and
John Sevier, 16; and officers for
New Army, 16–17; and clothing
for New Army, 24, 64, 82; and
Prince Edward Co. (Va.) Free-

holders, 95, 97, 109; reports on
events in France, 95–97; plan
for political communications,
118, 143; *The Conduct of the*
Government of France towards the
Republic of Geneva, 150–51;
publishes Chauvet-Gallatin letter, 150–51; and yellow fever
medicine, 163–64; and organization of New Army, 196, 198;
and George Logan, 202; GW
seeks letter from, 304; forwards
letters, 337, 355; criticizes Elbridge Gerry, 337–38, 355; report on relations with France,
337–38, 344, 355, 369; and
relations with Saint Domingue,
358; designation of letters to
GW, 381, 389; criticizes John
Adams, 389–90; and U.S. envoys to France, 402–3; and
John Churchman, 434–36; and
Caleb Gibbs, 444, 457; *letters*
from: to GW, 11–13, 74–76,
94–97, 103, 117–19, 150–52,
163–64, 337–38, 355–56,
362–63, 389–91, 402–3, 413–
15, 435–36; to Peter Johnston,
95–96, 109; to John Adams,
151; to Elbridge Gerry, 356; to
Rufus King, 390; to Charles
Cotesworth Pinckney, 420; to
Edward Rutledge, 420; *letters to:*
from GW, 66, 102, 108–9, 143,
304, 337, 365–66, 381, 405–6,
427–28; from Rufus King, 73,
74–76, 118, 403, 413–14; from
Daniel Huger Horry, 94; from
Joseph Fenwick, 94–95; from
Fulwar Skipwith, 94–95; from
Theodore Peters, 95; from Elbridge Gerry, 96; from Charles
Cotesworth Pinckney, 151;
from Benjamin Rush, 164;
from James McHenry, 205, 207;
from James Monroe, 434–36
Pierce, John: and pension for John
Durkee, 184
Pinckney, Charles Cotesworth (*see* 1 :
42), 73, 89, 96, 102, 222, 372;
and ranking of major generals,

Pinckney, Charles Cotesworth
(*continued*)
6, 11, 12, 14, 15–16, 18–23,
38, 42, 122, 123, 126, 142, 158,
168–69; at Bordeaux, 73, 75;
leaves France, 94; and Edward
Rutledge, 97; and officers for
New Army, 98, 126, 127, 193,
207, 225–26, 252, 288–89,
293–94, 295, 313, 443, 454,
459, 461; arrives in U.S., 103,
108, 110, 120, 133, 172; accepts commission as major general, 108, 117, 120, 132, 141,
143, 156, 168–69; at Mount
Vernon, 110; and meeting of
generals in Philadelphia, 127,
132, 158, 168, 172, 225–26,
248, 250–51, 288; at Newark,
142; at Trenton, 151, 158;
opinion of Alexander Hamilton, 168; opinion of Henry
Knox, 168–69; views on relations with France, 172–73; arrives in Philadelphia, 190; and
organization of New Army,
191–93, 198–99, 411–12, 456,
459–61; leaves Philadelphia,
207; military command of,
269–70, 380, 395–96, 452; his
journey south, 297, 298; at
Richmond, 308–9; reception
of in Petersburg, 315–16; as envoy to France, 355; and Presly
Thornton, 357; arrives in
Charleston, 411; and reputed
French agents in U.S., 420–21;
letters from: to James McHenry,
108, 168–69, 172, 224–25; to
Alexander Hamilton, 142, 143,
168; to Timothy Pickering, 151;
to GW, 172–73, 411–12; to inhabitants of Princeton and
Trenton, 173; *letters to:* from
James McHenry, 108; from GW,
110, 191–93, 298, 458, 459–
61; from Thomas Pinckney,
133; from Philip Church,
244; from Timothy Pickering,
420
Pinckney, Eliza, 207, 298, 411, 459;
greetings to, 110; illness of,

110, 172; at Newark, 173; greetings from, 412
Pinckney, Frances Motte Middleton:
greetings from, 133
Pinckney, Mary Stead, 172, 207,
298, 411, 459; greetings to,
110, 460; at Newark, 173; greetings from, 412; illness of, 412;
and seeds for Martha Washington, 412, 460
Pinckney, Thomas (*see* 1:158, 2:
256): and Charles Cotesworth
Pinckney, 133; id., 133; and
South Carolina elections of
1798, 133; and GW's jackasses,
458, 462–63; at Mount Ver-
non, 458; *letters from:* to Charles
Cotesworth Pinckney, 133; to
GW, 133–34
Pintard, John Marsden: *letters to:*
from GW, 316
Piscataway Creek: id., 48
Pitt, William: and U.S. commerce
with Great Britain, 362–63;
and John Sinclair, 417
Poggi, Anthony C.: signs receipt,
393–94
Polk, William: and officers for New
Army, 295, 296, 297
Poole, William: id., 360
Porcupine's Gazette: and U.S. minister
to France, 389–90
Porter, Thomas: as Alexandria mer-
chant, 56; and glass for GW,
467
Porterfield, Robert: and rank in
New Army, 226; and officers for
New Army, 238
Posey, Thomas (*see* 1:350): and offi-
cers for New Army, 231, 236
Potomac River: navigation of, 10,
46–48; resources of, 46–47
Potts, Eliza Ramsay: at Mount Ver-
non, 394
Potts, John, Jr.: and potatoes for
GW, 375; id., 376
Potts, William: and rank in New
Army, 235
Powel, Elizabeth Willing (*see* 1:12):
GW meets, 211, 240, 243; pur-
chases gifts, 242, 243, 246, 247;
farewell to GW, 246; GW's fare-

well to, 247; GW declines invitation from, 247–48; *letters from:* to GW, 211, 242, 246; to Eliza Parke Custis Law, 246–47; *letters to:* from GW, 211, 240, 243–44, 246–48
Powel, Samuel (*see* 1:12), 211
Powell, Leven: and officers for New Army, 228
Price, Uvedale (*see* 2:166): volumes on the picturesque, 14
Prince Edward Co. (Va.) Freeholders: address to John Adams, 95, 97, 109
Princeton, N.J.: address of inhabitants to Charles Cotesworth Pinckney, 173
Provisional Army: officers for, 14, 16–17, 38–39, 42–43, 106–8, 203, 227, 228, 229, 232, 234, 235, 236, 239, 285–86, 349, 367; organization of, 26, 95, 96, 107, 108, 286, 328, 348–49; clothing for, 196

Ramnitz, John Frederick: and yellow fever medicine, 161–64, 427–29; *letters from:* to GW, 161–64; *letters to:* from GW, 428–29
Ramsay, Andrew: dinner invitation to, 394; id., 394; *letters to:* from GW, 394
Ramsay, Catherine Graham: dinner invitation to, 394; id., 394; *letters to:* from GW, 394
Ramsay, Elizabeth, 394
Ramsay, Patrick, 394
Ramsay, William (*see* 1:55): dinner invitation to, 394; id., 394; *letters to:* from GW, 394
Randolph, Archibald C.: and rank in New Army, 232, 470, 477–78
Rawlins, Albin (*see* 1:437–38): and GW's letter books, 366
Rawlins, George: and Richard Parkinson, 215
Read, Catherine Van Horne: greetings from, 271
Read, Jacob (*see* 2:525): forwards broadside, 270–71; and U.S. minister to France, 389–90; *letters from:* to James McHenry, 205, 207; to GW, 270–71
Read, James: and rank in New Army, 294–95; id., 295
Rees, David: GW buys horse from, 308
Reynolds, John: and rank in New Army, 232
Rhodes, Richard: as overseer, 6, 9, 33, 35, 36
Richards, Mr.: and joiner for Mount Vernon, 6–7, 9
Richardson, Thomas: and rank in New Army, 229
Richardson, Turner: and rank in New Army, 238
Rickets & Newton (firm): buys wheat, 395
Ritchie, Matthew (*see* 1:127): and Millers Run tract, 407–8
Rivardi, Mrs.: greetings to, 397
Rivardi, John Jacob Ulrich: and rank in New Army, 97–98; id., 396; and military returns, 396–97; *letters from:* to GW, 396–97, 445–46; *letters to:* from GW, 397; from Tobias Lear, 397
River farm, 450; barn at, 167; stables and sheds at, 167; and Richard Parkinson, 174, 175; tenant for sought, 175
Roberts, Catherine: and grass seed for GW, 358
Roberts, Gerard: and rank in New Army, 235
Robertson, Beverly: and rank in New Army, 234
Robertson (Robinson), John: and William B. Harrison's land, 336, 449–50, 475; id., 450
Robinson, Moses: and Episcopal church lands in Vermont, 169, 171; id., 171
Rocky Mount, S.C.: arsenal at, 257–58
Rootes, John: and Little Miami tracts, 210–11
Rootes, Philip: at Mount Vernon, 210; seeks certificate from GW, 210; *letters from:* to GW, 210–11
Rose, John: and rank in New Army, 234

Ross, James: and Israel Shreve, 66–67, 68; and GW's Pennsylvania lands, 144, 156, 157; and U.S. minister to France, 389–90; *letters from:* to GW, 144; *letters to:* from GW, 66–67

Rough Creek tract: taxes on, 85–86, 121, 131–32, 171–72; deeds to, 166, 179, 180, 303, 399, 401, 479, 480; ownership of land adjoining, 278; value of, 420, 444–45

Rowan, Mr.: and rank in New Army, 240

Royal Gift (jackass), 333, 335, 458, 462, 463

Rush, Benjamin: and yellow fever medicine, 164; *letters from:* to Timothy Pickering, 164

Russell, William (*see* 2:594): and farm equipment for Mount Vernon, 56–57, 273–74; and sheep for GW, 56–57, 273–74; and William B. Harrison's land, 336; id., 337; *letters from:* to GW, 273–74; *letters to:* from GW, 56–57, 274

Russia: U.S. relations with, 362, 363, 390–91

Rutherford, Robert (*see* 1:440), 232; id., 314

Rutherford, Thomas, Sr.: as trustee of Charles Town Academy, 94

Rutledge, Edward (*see* 2:442), 73; and rank in New Army, 97; *letters to:* from Timothy Pickering, 420

Rutledge, Harriott Pinckney Horry: id., 117

Rutledge, Henry Middleton: arrives in New York, 72, 75; id., 73; conveys letter, 117, 168

Rutledge, John, Jr.: elected to Congress, 133; id., 133

Ryan, James: and rank in New Army, 296

Sabine Hall (house), 368

St. Clair, Arthur, 223

Saint Domingue: British relations with, 413–14; U.S. relations with, 414–15; attempt to instigate revolt in, 421

St. John's College (Annapolis, Md.), 79

St. Peter's Church (Philadelphia): GW attends, 202

Sanders, John: and rank in New Army, 239

Saunders, David: address to GW, 83

Schuyler, Catherine Van Rensselaer: greetings from, 212; id., 212; greetings to, 214

Schuyler, Philip: id., 212; illness of, 212, 213–14; recommends Philip Church for New Army, 212; *letters from:* to GW, 212–14; *letters to:* from GW, 213–14

Scott, Gustavus (*see* 1:42, 2:9): as D.C. commissioner, 111; illness of, 378. *See also* District of Columbia Commissioners

Searson, John (*see* 1:284): *The Art of Contentment*, 485–86; at Mount Vernon, 486; seeks position, 486; *letters from:* to GW, 485–86

Seayres, H. L.: and rank in New Army, 240

Seayres, John: and rank in New Army, 236

Sedgwick, Theodore (*see* 2:157): and U.S. minister to France, 389, 390

Selby (house), 83

Settle, Strother: and rank in New Army, 240

Sevier, John: and rank in Provisional Army, 16, 285–86, 348–49; id., 26; GW criticizes, 38–39; and officers for New Army, 349; *letters from:* to GW, 285–86, 349; *letters to:* from GW, 348–49

Sewall, Samuel: and Caleb Gibbs, 443

Shackleford, Charles: and rank in New Army, 231

Sharpe, Marcus: and rank in New Army, 297

Shepherd, William: and officers for New Army, 267

Sherburne, Henry: and rank in New Army, 19

Shields, David: and rank in New Army, 232

Short, Peyton (*see* 2:88): and GW's Rough Creek tract, 132, 171–72; and Wodrow tract, 278, 444–45; *letters from:* to GW, 171–72; to Alexander Spotswood, 278

Shreve, Israel (*see* 1:106): and debt to GW, 66–67, 67–68, 144, 156–57, 275–76, 314–15; illness of, 276; *letters from:* to GW, 156–57, 275–76; *letters to:* from GW, 67–68, 314–15

Shreve, John: and Washington's Bottom tract payments, 157, 276

Shreve, Samuel: and Washington's Bottom tract payments, 156–57, 275–76, 314

Simms, Charles (*see* 2:51): and officers for New Army, 229, 232, 233; witnesses statement, 272

Simms, Jesse (*see* 2:7), 186; Henry Lee's note on, 57, 58, 179, 401, 410; and rank in New Army, 234; and William B. Harrison's land, 400, 401, 450; *letters from:* to GW, 486

Simons, James: conveys letter, 51, 116; id., 52; *Scheme of the Review,* 270–71

Simpson, Mr.: and seeds for GW, 472

Sinclair, John (*see* 1:14): and Richard Parkinson, 173, 174; GW praises, 326; *Statistical Account of Scotland,* 326; criticism of, 417; *letters to:* from GW, 326–27

Singer, Abraham: as member of William McPherson's cavalry, 190

Skiles, J.: and officers for New Army, 235

Skipwith, Fulwar: reports on events in France, 94–95; *letters from:* to Timothy Pickering, 94–95

Slaves: arming of, 40; as messengers, 83, 353, 354; sale of, 112, 451, 464; losses among, 113; as carpenters, 130; children drawing water, 165; as brickmakers,

167, 168; as painters, 167; care for livestock, 168; carry firewood, 168; as fishermen, 219–20; allegations of theft against, 359; dwellings of, 418, 426

Smith, A.: and rank in New Army, 236

Smith, Benjamin: and rank in New Army, 296

Smith, Charles Winter: and rank in New Army, 238

Smith, Larking: and rank in New Army, 229

Smith, Nathan: and officers for New Army, 231

Smith, R.: and officers for New Army, 295, 296, 297

Smith, Samuel H.: essay on education, 90, 92

Smith, Samuel Stanhope (*see* 1:154): and officers for New Army, 231

Smith, William: election bid defeated, 133–34; id., 133–34

Smith, William Loughton (*see* 2:33): and relations with Ottoman Empire, 362, 391; id., 363

Smith, William Stephens: and rank in New Army, 6, 14, 15–17, 99, 265–66, 305; Senate's rejection of nomination of, 16–17; GW's opinion of, 26, 99; financial affairs of, 265–66, 292

Smithwick, Edmund: and rank in New Army, 296

Solomon, Matthew: and Saint Domingue, 421

Solomon Cotton & Co. (firm): and glass for GW, 382

Somerville, John Southey, Lord: and British Board of Agriculture, 326

Sophia (ship), 75

South Carolina elections of 1798: id., 133–34

Spain: policy of, 254

Spence, Dr.: as Philadelphia dentist, 308

Spence, William: as gardener at Mount Vernon, 484

Spotswood, Alexander (*see* 1:43), 89; seeks overseer and joiner for GW, 6–7, 33, 35, 36, 50, 181, 182; and officers for New Army, 7–9, 33–34, 219, 230, 234, 239, 346; and sedition in New Army, 8–9, 59; and GW's Rough Creek tract, 132; and the Wodrow tract, 172; and Alien and Sedition Acts, 278; and John Augustine Spotswood, 301–2; *letters from:* to GW, 6–10, 33–34, 50, 218–20, 278–79, 420–21; *letters to:* from GW, 35–36, 181–82, 444–45; from Benjamin Fields, 278; from Peyton Short, 278

Spotswood, Alexander, Jr.: and Alien and Sedition Acts, 216–18, 278; letter of forged, 216–18; *letters from:* to GW, 202, 217–18; *letters to:* from GW, 216–18

Spotswood, Elizabeth Washington (*see* 1:43), 302; greetings from, 9, 219, 420; greetings to, 181–82

Spotswood, John Augustine (*see* 1:326): arrives in Baltimore, 9, 36; at Mount Vernon, 9; seeks place in navy, 9–10, 88–89; carries letter, 278; leaves Mount Vernon, 301; finances of, 301–2; *letters from:* to GW, 301–2

Springfield, Mass.: arsenal at, 24, 196, 257

Stark, Horatio: and rank in New Army, 238, 240

Steele, John: and officers for New Army, 297; *letters from:* to James McHenry, 205, 207

Stenton (house): id., 202

Stephenson, David: and rank in New Army, 226

Steptoe, William: transfers land to Henry Lee, 81

Steuart, Charles (*see* 2:520): and Samuel Knox, 90–91

Steuben, Friedrich Wilhelm Augustus, Baron von, 123

Stevens, Ebenezer: and officers for New Army, 231

Stevens, Edward: and officers for New Army, 229, 231, 236; as consul to Saint Domnigue, 358

Stevenson, David: and officers for New Army, 238

Steward, Jesse: and officers for New Army, 239

Steward, John A.: and rank in New Army, 239

Stewart, John: and rank in New Army, 231, 240

Stith, John: and rank in New Army, 33–34, 229, 230; id., 34

Stockton, Richard (*see* 2:157): and U.S. minister to France, 389, 390

Stoddert, Benjamin, 22; and John Augustine Spotswood, 9, 88–89; and Washington navy yard, 10–11, 45–48; id., 11; and officers for New Army, 237; and Federal City, 354, 379; application to, 461; *letters from:* to GW, 10–11; *letters to:* from GW, 45–48, 88–89, 461

Strother, John: and rank in New Army, 239

Stuart, David, 279; sells wheat, 186, 395; Samuel Washington's debt to, 187; and officers for New Army, 232; opinion of Alien and Sedition Acts, 288; *letters from:* to GW, 288, 304; *letters to:* from GW, 298–99, 304–5

Stuart, Eleanor Calvert Custis: and George Washington Parke Custis, 267, 299, 304–5; greetings to, 393

Suffolk (ship), 13, 326

Sumter, Thomas: elected to Congress, 133; id., 133

Supreme Court: Bushrod Washington appointed to, 113–14, 138, 311; and Episcopal church lands in Vermont, 169, 171

Susquehanna River: passage of, 250

Swan, Caleb: as paymaster general, 418–19, 436–37, 466

Swearingen, Joseph: and rank in New Army, 226; and officers for New Army, 228, 230

Switzerland: French policy toward, 151

Syme, George: witnesses deed, 208

Talleyrand: and French relations with U.S., 76, 95, 96, 102, 109, 118–19, 143, 337, 344, 355, 369, 387, 388, 406; *letters from:* to Louis-André Pichon, 388; *letters to:* from Lucien Hauteval, 118–19

Tallmadge, Benjamin (*see* 2:442): and rank in New Army, 19, 101

Tapscott, Henry: and rank in New Army, 239

Tapscott, Martin: and rank in New Army, 235

Tarleton, Banastre, 7, 9

Tate, George: and rank in New Army, 230, 237

Tayloe, Ann Ogle (*see* 2:442), 367; greetings to, 375, 462

Tayloe, John (*see* 2:438): and Henry Lee's Federal City property, 139; and rank in New Army, 229, 334–35, 366–67, 374–75, 479, 480; elected to Virginia Senate, 367, 368; illness of, 446; at Mount Vernon, 447, 485; at Mannsfield, 461–62; house of in Federal City, 487; *letters from:* to GW, 366–68, 446–47; to James McHenry, 368, 375; *letters to:* from GW, 334–36, 374–75, 461–62

Taylor, Edmund: and rank in New Army, 233

Taylor, George, Jr. (*see* 1:329, 2:52): as Timothy Pickering's clerk, 118

Taylor, George Keith: and Alien and Sedition Acts, 309, 310; id., 310

Taylor, John: and officers for New Army, 239; and Alien and Sedition Acts, 309, 310; id., 310

Taylor, William: at Mount Vernon, 375, 376; sends potatoes to GW, 375–76; *letters from:* to GW, 375–76

Tazewell, Henry (*see* 1:244): death of, 310

Temple, Benjamin: and rank in New Army, 239

Temple, Robert: and rank in New Army, 237

Tenants, 175–77, 449–50; rent payments by, 334, 340, 377–78; depredations by, 336, 358, 359, 410; leases of, 425

Thomas, Alexander: id., 137; as editor of *Farmer's Weekly Museum*, 137–38; *letters from:* to GW, 137–38; *letters to:* from GW, 137–38

Thomas, Isaiah: id., 137; as editor of *Farmer's Weekly Museum*, 137–38; *letters from:* to GW, 137–38; *letters to:* from GW, 137–38

Thompson, William: and George Lee's land, 425–26; id., 426; *letters from:* to GW, 426; *letters to:* from GW, 425–26

Thompson & Veitch (firm): and cheese for GW, 481

Thornburgh, Josiah: and rank in New Army, 230

Thornton, Anna Marie Brodeau: greetings to, 111, 301, 420

Thornton, Anthony, 356, 357

Thornton, Francis (b. 1760): seeks army commission, 8, 9, 234, 239; id., 9

Thornton, Francis (d. 1784): id., 357

Thornton, Francis (died c.1795), 8

Thornton, Presly (1721–1769), 356, 460; id., 357

Thornton, Presly (1760–1807): and Henry Lee's Federal City property, 139; and rank in New Army, 227, 230, 356–57, 460; id., 357; *letters from:* to Tobias Lear, 357

Thornton, Presly (1760–1811), 356; id., 357

Thornton, Reuben: and rank in New Army, 236

Thornton, William (*see* 1:386): and
GW's Capitol Hill houses, 54,
110–11, 139–41, 145, 149,
152–54, 159, 274–75, 276,
299–301, 347–48, 376–77,
378, 382, 420, 467, 487; and
Henry Lee's Federal City property, 58; designs U.S. Capitol,
140, 141; property of in Federal City, 140, 141, 152; visits
Mount Vernon, 317; GW sends
trees to, 419–20, 426–27; and
Tobias Lear, 425, 427, 430,
445; greetings to, 446; designs
John Tayloe's house, 487; *letters
from:* to GW, 105, 139–41, 159,
276, 286, 346, 376–77, 378–
79, 426–27, 487–88; *letters to:*
from GW, 110–11, 152–54,
173, 274–75, 299–301, 347–
48, 382, 419–20, 430; from
George Turner, 317. *See also*
District of Columbia Com-
missioners
Thurston, Mr.: and officers for New
Army, 232
Thurston, Frederick: and rank in
New Army, 238
Tinsley, Samuel, 239; and rank in
New Army, 228
Tinsley, Thomas: and rank in New
Army, 228; and officers for New
Army, 231, 235
Tobacco notes: as rent payments,
340, 409–10, 426
Tracy, Uriah (*see* 2:33): *letters from:*
to James McHenry, 205–6
Tremper, L.: and rank in New Army,
237
Trenton, N.J.: address of inhabitants
to Charles Cotesworth Pinck-
ney, 173; lodgings for prospec-
tive meeting in, 180–81; mili-
tary courts at, 221–23, 224–25
Trescott, Lemuel: and rank in New
Army, 19
Trigg, John: address to GW, 83
Troup, Robert: and William Ste-
phens Smith, 292
Troy, Robert: and rank in New
Army, 295

Trumbull, Eunice Backus: greetings
to, 361; greetings from, 393
Trumbull, John (*see* 1:122): Revolutionary prints of, 13–14, 361,
392–94, 421–22, 430; and XYZ
affair, 118, 119; in London,
392, 421; view of U.S. diplo-
macy, 430–34; *letters from:* to
GW, 13–14, 430–34; *letters to:*
from GW, 248
Trumbull, Jonathan, Jr.: and pension for John Durkee, 184; id.,
185; and John Trumbull's
prints, 361, 392–94, 421; and
Virginia Resolutions, 393; *letters
from:* to GW, 392–94; to James
Wood, 393; *letters to:* from GW,
361
Tucker, James: and James Welch,
447
Tunnicliff, William: id., 137; opens
hotel in Federal City, 137
Turner, George: seeks commission
as aide, 316–17; id., 317; visits
Mount Vernon, 317; *letters from:*
to GW, 316–17; to William
Thornton, 317
Turner, Samuel: and rank in New
Army, 232
Turner, Thomas: and rank in New
Army, 31, 32, 234, 479–80; id.,
32
Tutt, Charles: and rank in New
Army, 236
Tutt, James, Jr.: and rank in New
Army, 236

Union Farm: meadow at, 1–2, 384–
85; well at, 166; threshing machine at, 405

Van Rensselaer, Solomon: and rank
in New Army, 335; id., 336
Van Staphorst, Mr.: at Mount Vernon, 487, 488
Varnum, Joseph Bradley: conduct of
in Congress, 287; id., 287
Veatch, Hezekiah: as rent collector,
340

Vermont: seizure of Episcopal church lands in, 169, 171

Vienne, marquis de: seeks commission, 360

Virginia: militia officers' meeting, 83–85; list of officer candidates from, 225–40; military districts of, 386–87, 448, 456, 473, 474, 477–78

Virginia elections of 1799, 32, 102, 114

Virginia militia: address from: to GW, 83–85; address to: from GW, 85

Virginia Resolutions: debated, 309–10, 346–47

Volney, Constantin-François Chasseboeuf, comte de (*see* 1 : 267): as consul, 75

Wadsworth, Elijah: and rank in New Army, 19; id., 27

Wallace, Gustavus B.: and rank in New Army, 234

Ware, James: and rank in New Army, 233

Washington, Anna Maria (*see* 1 : 187), 285

Washington, Augustine (1694–1743), 77

Washington, Bushrod (*see* 1 : 272), 473–74; and officers for New Army, 31–32, 227, 230, 232; appointed to U.S. Supreme Court, 113–14, 138, 311; land in Westmoreland Co. (Va.), 114; leaves Richmond, 114; opinion of Henry Lee, Jr., 114; rejects candidacy for Congress, 114; and Virginia elections of 1799, 114, 479, 480; and GW's Rough Creek tract, 166, 179, 180, 303, 479, 480; and Alexander Addison's pamphlet, 297, 309; and uniform for GW, 363, 365; conveys letter, 387; at Mount Vernon, 406; *letters from:* to GW, 31–32, 113–14, 479–80; *letters to:* from GW, 138, 302–3

Washington, Charles, 9; estate of, 111–12, 113, 187, 188, 349, 465; greetings from, 312; illness of, 312, 451, 466

Washington, Charles Augustine, 285

Washington, Corbin (*see* 1 : 410): at Selby, 83; witnesses deed, 180; conveys letter, 399

Washington, D.C. *See* Federal City

Washington, Dorothea Thornton: fortune of, 187

Washington, George: plans for work at Mount Vernon, 1–3, 164–68; criticizes James Anderson, 1–4; commission as commander in chief, 4–5, 5–6, 37–38, 43; and John Trumbull's prints, 13–14, 361, 392–93, 393–94, 421–22, 430; military aids and secretary for, 19, 23; seeks overseer, 35–36, 218; criticizes John Adams, 36–44; illness of, 48–49, 56, 120, 122, 127; contracts for corn, 57, 76–77; considers resigning his commission, 65–66; seeks to enforce payment from Israel Shreve, 66–68, 144; criticizes Israel Shreve, 67–68, 314–15; urged to reconcile with France, 68–72; daily habits of, 76, 79, 144–45, 152, 200, 211, 220, 241–42, 248; borrows money, 78–79, 80, 86–87, 314, 377, 382, 407; introduces Landon Carter, 79; subscribes to *American Biography*, 86; seeks paper, 87, 182; introduces John Spotswood, 88–89; dedication of essay to, 90–91; declines dedication, 92; subscribes to essay on education, 92; patronage of sought, 93–94; visits Federal City, 97, 99, 180; recommends officers for New Army, 97–98, 99, 101, 240, 267–68, 440–41, 460; congratulates Charles Cotesworth Pinckney, 110; and loan to Samuel Washington, 111–13, 186–88, 349–50, 464–66; and meeting of gener-

Washington, George (*continued*)
    als in Philadelphia, 120, 126,
        127, 132, 164, 178, 180–81,
        182, 210, 214, 225–40, 241–
        42, 243, 244, 247–48, 250–65,
        281, 286, 288, 293, 324–25,
        326, 338, 440; urges Henry
        Knox to accept appointment,
        122–24; loan for Washington
        City Hotel, 136–37; subscribes
        to *Farmer's Weekly Museum*, 137–
        38; commends Bushrod Wash-
        ington, 138; public opinion of,
        151; and yellow fever medicine,
        161–64, 427–29; and William
        B. Harrison's land, 175–77,
        334, 336, 358–60, 400, 409–
        11, 448–50, 474–76; and Indi-
        ans, 177–78; and his teeth,
        182, 245–46, 289–91, 308;
        leaves Mount Vernon, 182,
        214, 241; seeks letter books,
        183; and military pensions,
        185; reception of in Balti-
        more, 189; lodgings in Phila-
        delphia, 189–90; reception of
        in Philadelphia, 190; queries of
        concerning New Army, 191–93,
        197–98; interview with George
        Logan and Robert Blackwell,
        200–202; returns to Mount
        Vernon, 210; meets Elizabeth
        Willing Powel, 211; invitations
        from, 240, 385–86, 394; seeks
        wine, 242–43; leaves Philadel-
        phia, 243, 245, 250, 268, 270;
        forwards letters, 246, 247, 408,
        436, 474; invitations to, 247–
        48; appoints aide, 248–50; and
        commission for George Wash-
        ington Parke Custis, 267; as
        trustee of George Mercer's Vir-
        ginia land, 271–72; discourages
        Lafayette from visiting U.S.,
        281; applications to for loan,
        291, 328–32, 451; sends pa-
        pers to Charles Cotesworth
        Pinckney, 297, 298, 308–9;
        seeks letter, 304; military pay
        of, 307, 308, 312–13; expenses
        of in Philadelphia, 307–8;
        clothing for, 308, 321–22, 357,
        358; as trustee of Colvill estate,
        311; urges Patrick Henry to run
        for office, 317–20; and his pa-
        pers, 322, 421–22; and count-
        ess of Huntingdon, 325; praises
        John Sinclair, 326; becomes
        guardian of Nelly Custis, 332–
        33; seeks to sell jackasses, 333,
        334, 335, 458, 462–63; uni-
        form of, 340–44, 352, 353,
        363–65, 372, 408, 412, 460;
        and marriage of Nelly Custis,
        342, 384, 385–86, 389, 394;
        advises John Tayloe to decline
        commission, 374–75; seeks
        corn, 379–80, 484–85; desig-
        nation of letters from Timothy
        Pickering, 381, 389; encoding
        of letters from Alexander Ham-
        ilton, 383, 384; applications to
        for office, 391–92, 486; criti-
        cism of, 404; and Wodrow tract,
        420, 444–45; inquires concern-
        ing George Lee's land, 425–26;
        criticizes James McHenry, 442–
        43, 444; and Philip Miller's *Gar-
        dener's Dictionary*, 453; intro-
        duces Burwell Bassett, 461;
        criticizes James Welch, 470–71;
        praises Daniel Morgan, 478;
        treasury certificates of, 480–81;
        and John Tayloe's Federal City
        house, 487
Capitol Hill houses of, 50, 52–55,
        73–74, 77–78, 87, 105–6,
        110–11, 130–31, 138–41,
        152–54, 159, 274–75, 276,
        299–301, 334, 335, 347–48,
        376–77, 378, 382, 420, 424,
        446, 452, 465, 467, 487; specifi-
        cations for, 144–50
gifts from: to Washington Acad-
        emy, 207–8; to Nelly Custis,
        242, 243, 246, 308; dolls, 243,
        244, 246, 247; to Martha
        Washington, 243, 246, 308; to
        George Washington Parke Cus-
        tis, 246, 308; trees, 419, 426–
        27; to Bushrod Washington,
        480; ham, 481
gifts to: books, 13, 14, 56; ram,
        56, 273–74; seed, 136, 472; *Far-*

mer's Weekly Museum, 137–38;
medicine, 220–21; prints, 242,
243; pamphlets, 244, 270–71,
288, 399, 402, 407, 483–84;
William Heath's memoirs, 368–
69; potatoes, 375–76; crab
apple seeds, 464; cheese, 481;
poetry, 485–86
lands of: Federal City lots, 32–
33, 49, 50, 52, 54, 55, 73, 74,
83; Ohio River tracts, 44; Dismal Swamp tract, 55, 57, 58,
80–81, 179, 303, 400–401,
410; Washington's Bottom tract,
66–68, 144, 156–57, 275–76,
314–15; Rough Creek tract,
85–86, 121, 131–32, 166, 171–
72, 179, 180, 278, 303, 399,
401, 420, 444–45, 479, 480;
Kanawha tracts, 92–93, 383,
413, 447, 463–64, 470–72;
Little Miami tracts, 210–11;
Montgomery County tract, 340;
Berkeley County tract, 377–78;
Fauquier County tract, 377–78;
Frederick County tract, 377–
78; Loudoun County tract,
377–78; Millers Run tract, 407–
8; Gloucester County tract,
422–23; Four Mile Run tract,
468–69
opinions of: William Stephens
Smith, 26, 99, 265–66; John Sevier, 38–39; Alexander Hamilton, 41–42; Henry Knox, 42;
Henry Lee, Jr., 83; John Spots-
wood, 89; Edward Rutledge, 97;
John Jacob Rivardi, 97–98; El-
bridge Gerry, 102, 109, 143,
366; Thomas Law, 111; Charles
Cotesworth Pinckney, 143;
Richard Parkinson, 173–75,
241; George Logan, 200–202,
287; Philip Church, 213–14;
Samuel Henley, 267–68; John
Greenwood, 290–91; George
Washington Parke Custis, 298–
99, 442; Patrick Henry, 305;
Solomon Van Rensselaer, 335;
Joel Barlow, 350–51, 403; Rob-
ert Goodloe Harper, 352–53;
Caleb Gibbs, 440–41; Charles

Fenton Mercer, 441–42; Presly
Thornton (d. 1807), 460; James
Welch, 475
views on: role of farm manager,
1–3; keeping accounts, 2; his
expenses, 2–3, 112, 131, 291,
314, 331, 334, 349–50, 465;
ranking of major generals, 4–5,
34, 37–38, 40–42, 44–45, 65–
66, 108, 121–22, 122–24, 126;
sedition in New Army, 35, 59,
129, 135; role of adjutant general, 39; strategy, 40, 43, 191;
state of recruiting, 43,
51, 63, 64, 126–27, 128, 132,
134, 253–54, 255, 396, 398,
438–40, 459–60, 462; Washington navy yard, 45–48; resources of Potomac River,
46, 47; defense of Potomac
River, 46–47; qualifications for
officers, 51, 99, 129, 135, 213–
14; Antifederalists, 59, 102,
109, 281–82, 297, 317–20,
324; his want of money, 67, 78,
112, 383, 407, 422, 423, 464–
65, 470–71; writing letters, 76;
Washington family genealogy,
77; health, 79; accommodation
of Congress in Federal City,
83; duties of citizens, 85, 188–
89; likelihood of conflict with
France, 108–9, 304, 436–37;
his papers, 121; New Jersey
and Pennsylvania elections of
1798, 138; Freemasonry, 188;
consulting with cabinet, 198; relations with France, 201–2,
252–53, 279, 282–84, 323,
324, 350–51, 365–66, 369–70,
406; yellow fever, 211; Alien
and Sedition Acts, 216–17,
287, 297, 302–3, 445; dueling,
224; conduct of officers, 224–
25; qualifications of aides, 249;
organization of New Army,
250–65; rifles, 264; commands
of major generals, 268–70,
395–96; rights of nations, 284;
rules of architecture, 300; Virginia politics, 305, 317–20,
338–39; foreign officers, 320,

Washington, George (*continued*)
327, 360; his personal conduct,
325; promotion of agriculture,
326–27; the Columbian alphabet, 399; French army, 440;
military discipline, 459; value of
character, 471; Virginia military
districts, 473; value of things,
476. *See also* Agriculture; Lands
of GW; Mount Vernon; New
Army; Tenants
Washington, George Augustine
(c.1758–1793): death of, 285
Washington, George Fayette, 285
Washington, George Steptoe (*see* 1 :
317): as trustee of Charles
Town Academy, 93–94; id., 94;
letters from: to GW, 94
Washington, Hannah Lee: at Selby,
83
Washington, Henry: conveys letter,
379; id., 380; at Mount Vernon,
381
Washington, James (of Holland):
seeks commission, 114–16,
154, 320, 327; *letters from:* to
GW, 114–16; *letters to:* from
GW, 327–28
Washington, Jane Riley Elliott, 462;
greetings to, 52, 294, 463
Washington, John (brother of Law-
rence; 1659–1697), 77
Washington, John (GW's uncle;
1692–1746; *see* 2 : 153, 155),
77
Washington, John (immigrant;
1632–1677; *see* 2 : 153), 77
Washington, Julia Ann (Nancy)
Blackburn (*see* 1 : 273): greetings to, 303; greetings from,
480
Washington, Lawrence (1659–
1697), 77
Washington, Lawrence (1749–
c.1774): id., 380
Washington, Lawrence, Jr. (c.1760–
1809): and officers for New
Army, 34; and rank in New
Army, 234, 299; and recruiting,
332; id., 333
Washington, Lawrence (immigrant;
1635–1677; *see* 2 : 153), 77

Washington, Lawrence (of Chotank;
1728–c.1809; *see* 2 : 155): id.,
333
Washington, Lucy Payne, 94
Washington, Martha, 49, 88, 202,
302, 340, 385, 449, 486; greetings to, 9, 14, 34, 49, 116, 133,
173, 177, 212, 218–19, 271,
278, 301, 312, 367, 369, 378,
379, 388, 393, 412, 416–17,
420, 427, 434, 464, 480; greetings from, 110, 213–14, 280,
284, 304, 321, 325, 339, 361,
375, 379, 394, 404, 425, 446,
462, 463; and Abigail Adams,
120; and military colors, 142;
and work for the joiner, 167;
and Lawrence Lewis, 214; GW's
gift for, 243, 308; and George
Washington Parke Custis, 267,
268, 299, 304–5; at Mount
Eagle and Hope Park, 325;
melon seeds for, 412, 460; illness of, 446; and Burwell Bassett, 461; cures hams, 481; *letters from:* to Nelly Custis, 304; to
Martha Parke Custis Peter, 379;
letters to: from GW, 214
Washington, Mildred Thornton (*see*
1 : 331), 9; and loan from GW,
111–13, 186–88, 349–50;
greetings from, 312; *letters from:*
to GW, 97; *letters to:* from GW,
111–13
Washington, Samuel (*see* 1 : 242):
and loan from GW, 113, 186–
88, 349–50, 451, 464–66; *letters from:* to GW, 186–88, 451;
letters to: from GW, 349–50,
464–66
Washington, Susannah, 380
Washington, Warner (1722–1790;
see 2 : 153), 77
Washington, William (1752–1810),
298, 357; and rank in New
Army, 51, 116; and officers
for New Army, 51–52, 98,
116, 159–61, 234, 252, 288,
293–94; id., 52; military command of, 269; and organization
of New Army, 411–12; and
feathers for GW, 412; at Mount

Vernon, 458; travels to Princeton, 459, 462; *letters from:* to GW, 116, 159–61; *letters to:* from GW, 51–52, 293–94, 462–63

Washington, William (1785–1830): id., 412, 458; at Princeton, 412; at Mount Vernon, 458

Washington, William Augustine (*see* 1:410): corn contract with GW, 57, 76–77, 379–80, 485; illness of, 379; *letters to:* from GW, 76–77, 83, 379–80

Washington Academy: GW's gift to, 207–9; id., 208

Washington's Bottom tract: payments for, 66–68, 144, 156–57, 275–76, 314–15

Watkins, William: and rank in New Army, 227

Watts, John: id., 101; and rank in New Army, 101, 229, 240, 335

Wayne, Anthony, 223, 238

Weems, Mason Locke: id., 447; and James Welch, 447, 463–64; *letters from:* to GW, 447; *letters to:* from GW, 463–64

Welch, James: memorandum of agreement with, 92–93; and debt to GW, 383, 413, 463–64, 470–72; query concerning, 447; and William B. Harrison's land, 449; GW criticizes, 470–71, 475; *letters from:* to GW, 413; *letters to:* from GW, 383, 470–72

West, Benjamin: and books for GW, 13, 14

West, Roger (*see* 2:402): seeks army commission, 229

West, Thomas: and Colvill estate, 311

Wharton, Robert: as member of William McPherson's cavalry, 190

Wheelock, John: as president of Dartmouth College, 169, 171; and Episcopal church lands in Vermont, 169, 171; id., 171

White, Alexander (*see* 2:9): and GW's Federal City lots, 33; as trustee of Charles Town Academy, 94; as D.C. commissioner,

111; and GW's Capitol Hill houses, 139, 141; at Winchester, 378. *See also* District of Columbia Commissioners

White, Anthony Walton (*see* 1:344): nominated for Provisional Army, 16; id., 26; and officers for New Army, 229

White, Rosannah, 202; and GW's accommodations in Philadelphia, 189–90; id., 190; GW's payment to, 308

Whiting, Horatio Gates: and rank in New Army, 236

Whitting, Anthony: *letters to:* from GW, 136

Wilkinson, James (*see* 1:534): and deployment of New Army, 195, 199, 254; negotiations with Spanish, 254; military command of, 269–70, 380–81, 396; rank of, 381; and John Francis Hamtramck, 437; *letters from:* to James McHenry, 205, 207, 437; *letters to:* from James McHenry, 205, 207; from Alexander Hamilton, 381

Wilkinson, John: and rank in New Army, 297

William V (of Orange and Nassau): and James Washington of Holland, 115

Williams, Mr.: and Samuel Knox, 92; and officers for New Army, 236

Williams, Edward O.: and officers for New Army, 228

Williams, John, 236; and rank in New Army, 237

Williams, John (of North Carolina): and rank in New Army, 296

Williams, John C.: and rank in New Army, 236

Williams, Joseph, 296

Willing, Thomas: GW dines with, 211; id., 211

Willis, Henry: id., 77

Willis, John M. (*see* 2:615): and rank in New Army, 227

Willis, Mildred Washington Lewis Gregory (1696–c.1745): id., 77

Wilson, James (*see* 1 : 320): death of, 55, 138; id., 55; and Henry Lee, Jr., 400

Wilson, Thomas: and rank in New Army, 234

Winn, Richard: election bid defeated, 133; id., 133

Winston, Samuel J.: and rank in New Army, 231

Winterberry, John: and rank in New Army, 239

Wodrow (Woodrow), Andrew: his tract, 278, 420

Wodrow tract: GW seeks to purchase, 172, 278, 420, 444–45

Wolcott, Mary Ann, 374

Wolcott, Oliver, Jr. (*see* 1 : 105), 17, 22, 117, 383; and ranking of major generals, 6; and memorial to John Adams, 11, 12–13, 22–23, 30, 66, 72, 125, 142; and arms for New Army, 24, 63–64, 82; and John C. Ogden, 29, 373; and supplies for New Army, 196–97, 198; reports on financial status of U.S., 211–12; and funding for New Army, 253; and Caleb Gibbs, 444, 457; *letters from:* to Rufus King, 24, 196–97; *letters to:* from James McHenry, 205, 207

Wolcott, Oliver, Sr.: death of, 185

Wood, James (*see* 1 : 317): as Virginia governor, 31; and officers for New Army, 228–29, 233, 235, 238; *letters to:* from Jonathan Trumbull, Jr., 393

Wooster, David, 374

Wooster, Mary Clap: distresses of, 373, 374; id., 374

XYZ affair: correspondence regarding, 95–96, 102, 118–19

Yellow fever epidemic: in New York City, 56, 103, 161, 428; in Philadelphia, 161, 182–83, 190, 200, 211, 215, 358, 378, 397, 428; medicine for, 220–21, 427–29; effect on military organization, 455

Young, Anna: petitions GW, 183–85; *letters from:* to GW, 183–85; *letters to:* from GW, 185

Young, Henry: and officers for New Army, 234, 239

Young, Notley (*see* 1 : 531): and William Thornton's Federal City property, 140–41

Young, Robert (*see* 2 : 442): and rank in New Army, 232

Young Royal Gift (jackass): as stud, 333, 377